Fundamentals of Curriculum Development

REVISED EDITION

Fundamentals of Curriculum Development

REVISED EDITION

B. OTHANEL SMITH

WILLIAM O. STANLEY

J. HARLAN SHORES

University of Illinois

Harcourt, Brace & World, Inc.

New York / Chicago / San Francisco / Atlanta

Preface to the Revised Edition

IN THE FIRST EDITION of this book we presented a descriptive and critical analysis of the fundamental principles upon which various theories of curriculum development have been constructed. Then, by reference to actual programs and practices, we indicated several patterns of curriculum development and planning in order that some of these basic theoretical principles might be seen in practical application. Our essential intent in this new edition remains the same. However, we hope that certain revisions, rearrangements, and additions to the text will improve on the original and make the book useful to an increasing number of students and curriculum workers.

Theories of curriculum development have changed little since the book first appeared, but a considerable number of new programs have emerged and new materials have been developed during this time. Wherever these new programs and materials seem to illustrate better the principles and patterns of curriculum development, we have added them, sometimes substituting them for older materials. In this way the outlook on curriculum practices has been brought up to date.

Many instructors who have used the book have given us suggestions for improving its form and content. At least a score of students have also offered valuable criticisms. To all these people the authors are grateful. Two people read the book in its entirety with the purpose of suggesting ways to make the book more useful both to students and to instructors. To Dr. Arthur E. Hamalainen, Plandome Road School,

Manhasset, New York, and Dr. Donald H. Hughes, State Teachers College, Cortland, New York, we are especially indebted. While we were unable to follow all the valuable suggestions given us by these experienced critics, many of the improvements to be found in the present edition are direct reflections of their helpful comments.

In any relatively new field of study, such as that of curriculum development, where the terminology has not yet been stabilized, vagueness and ambiguity of terms present an inevitable obstacle to clear expression. A special effort has been made to clarify the exposition throughout the text—especially at points where particular difficulties came to our attention.

The order of chapters has been changed so that the student will meet concrete examples of materials and curriculum techniques early in the text. The more complex discussion of underlying issues, involving intricate theoretical considerations now appears in the latter part of the book. We made this shift in the belief that the beginning student will be better able to deal with these theoretical issues after he has become familiar with actual programs and practices of curriculum planning. The more advanced student may wish to turn at the outset to the theoretical treatment in order to gain a more fundamental understanding of the psychological and philosophical issues involved in curriculum development.

Finally, it should be noted that, in the interest of brevity, we deleted the treatment of certain topics. These we felt to be merely peripheral rather than central to the main tasks of curriculum planning and development and hence peripheral also to the basic theme of the book.

Chapter 15 contains substantial quotations from *Guides to Curriculum Building—Junior High School Level*. This material, issued by G. E. Watson, State Superintendent, is used with permission from the Wisconsin Co-operative Educational Planning Program, Room 147 North, State Capitol, Madison 2, Wisconsin.

B. OTHANEL SMITH

WILLIAM O. STANLEY

J. HARLAN SHORES

Preface to the First Edition

THE TASK of curriculum development has at least four significant aspects: first, the determination of educational directions; second, the choice of principles and procedures for selecting and ordering the potential experiences comprising the instructional program; third, the selection of a pattern of curriculum organization; and, fourth, the determination of principles and procedures by which changes in the curriculum can be made, evaluated, and sustained. Each of these four aspects represents an important factor that must be taken into account at some point in any effective program of curriculum development. They need not, however, be considered in the order in which they have been listed. On the contrary, the order of consideration should vary with the nature of the task, the character of the school-community situation, and the interests and habits of the personnel involved.

This book has been written with all these points definitely in mind. The parts of the treatment, with the exception of Part Two, correspond roughly to the four fundamental aspects of curriculum development. Part Two, dealing as it does with the basic issues underlying all curriculum planning, has necessarily been concerned with all four of these phases. The order in which the parts are taken up may be varied to suit the needs of a particular class.

A brief explanation of certain features of the book may be helpful to the reader. It is assumed that no one can think effectively about the directions of modern education—to say nothing of its content and methods—without some acquaintance with psychological and sociological theories and facts. Most students of education have some knowledge of educational psychology, since it is a standard course in almost every professional curriculum for teachers. For this reason psychological principles and facts have been introduced at points where they are relevant rather than in special chapters devoted to the psychological aspects of curriculum development.

Sociological facts and theories, however, may not be as familiar to members of the profession or to teachers in training, since courses dealing with the social aspects of education are not offered as frequently, nor required as often, as courses in educational psychology. Accordingly, the sociological materials have been treated on their own account in Part One and then introduced again later where they are relevant to the problems under discussion. When a thorough acquaintance with the social aspects of education can be taken for granted, this part of the book can be omitted.

Underlying the significant aspects of curriculum development are certain issues that require clarification, especially for those professional workers whose duties make it necessary that they be thoroughly grounded in curriculum theories. Hence an extensive discussion of curriculum theories has been included as Part Two. The student will find that an exploration of these basic issues will enable him to deal more effectively with curriculum controversies that arise in both school and community. It is perhaps not too much to say that the success of many attacks on educational advancement is due in part to the fact that the profession often does not know the theory of its program well enough to explain and to defend the program before the public. The beginning student in curriculum development may find that the treatment of these issues can best be taken up after the less theoretical parts of the text have been mastered.

Throughout the book the authors have, of course, referred to practices of both current and historical interests, but they have tried wherever possible to keep these subordinate to the discussion of principles and procedures by which curriculum problems can be attacked. This seems to be more desirable than dwelling at length on descriptions of specific curriculum programs either past or present. Although emphasis has been placed upon concepts and procedures rather than on detailed discussion of curriculum practices, the concepts and procedures have been extensively illustrated by reference to actual curriculum programs and practices. This has been done throughout the book in order to bring principles and procedures into intimate contact with the realities of the school situation.

The authors are indebted to many persons, only a few of whom can be mentioned in the space available. Professor William H. Burton, of Harvard University, read the entire manuscript and made many suggestions, which helped to improve the text in almost every chapter. Professor Kenneth D. Benne and Dean Willard B. Spalding, both of the University of Illinois, read the manuscript in part. Dean Spalding's criticisms were especially helpful in Part One, and Professor Benne's, in Part Five. Professor Donald M. Sharpe, Indiana State Teachers College, Terre Haute, gave substantial assistance at points where administrative approaches and procedures were treated. It is needless to add that none of these persons is in any way responsible for whatever errors and weaknesses this book may exhibit.

The authors wish also to acknowledge the extensive editorial work done by Mrs. Helen Schultz. Without her painstaking work many parts of the text would have been less clear. We are also indebted to Mr. George Guy and Mrs. Lois Bohon for checking the references.

B. OTHANEL SMITH

WILLIAM O. STANLEY

J. HARLAN SHORES

Contents

PART TWO

Principles and Procedures of Curriculum Development

Contents

PART THREE

Patterns of Curriculum Organization

PART FOUR

Human Relations in Curriculum Development

Contents

PART FIVE

Theoretical Curriculum Issues

SOCIAL DIAGNOSIS

Part One | # FOR CURRICULUM
DEVELOPMENT

IN THE BROAD SENSE *of the word, education refers to the entire social process by which individuals acquire the ways, beliefs, and standards of society. Schooling is a specialized aspect of this social process. And any school program will find its bearings only in relation to this wider context of human development.*

The school, like other institutions, is shaped by the larger fabric of ways, beliefs, and ideas held and cherished by the people of a society at a particular time. On the other hand, what goes on in the school also affects the social system. It has been said that an unknown society can be described completely from knowledge of its educational system. Whether this is true or not, it is certain that a social system is significantly mirrored in its educational program. Since the strands of the social fabric are inextricably woven into the school, the educational program can be understood adequately only as it is perceived in its manifold connections with the total social pattern.

The relations between school and society are important enough in a period of relatively little social change. In a time of profound social change, the relationship is even more important because society then is not all of one piece. Old and new social elements are to be found side by side—and frequently in competition with one another for survival. In such a period the school tends to reflect the older elements of society. The teaching profession needs to be on guard at such a time against making the school a repository of outworn ideas, ideals, and skills. It then becomes the task of the teaching profession to keep the schools up-to-date, and, when possible, to shape the educational program in such a way as to influence the form and direction of social development.

If the schools are to be on the side of the constructive influences in a period of social transformation, the teaching profession must be aware of the significant facts derived from social diagnoses made by outstanding scholars in the fields of psychology and the social sciences. The profession must know what changes are occurring in such aspects of society as the economic system, the value system, home and community life, and occupational activities. It must also understand the tasks these changes set for the school.

Since society in the United States is now in a period of profound change, Part One of this book attempts to present the social realities that should be considered in a program of curriculum development and to indicate what these realities mean for education. There is considerable evidence to support the thesis that the nature of current social change requires reconstruction of the purposes, content, and methods of general education beyond anything yet attempted. The question of whether this degree of educational change is required or not is a matter for the reader to decide for himself. But that facts concerning crucial aspects of society should be taken into account in curriculum work is no longer a matter of debate. Persons who have given serious attention to the problems of curriculum development now agree that curriculum principles and procedures should be grounded in social reality.

Chapter 1

Culture and the Curriculum

T H E   P E O P L E of every society are confronted by the problem of inducting the immature members into their culture, that is, into the ways of the group. The individual at birth is a cultural barbarian, in that he has none of the habits, ideas, attitudes, and skills characterizing the adult members of society. These are acquired as he grows into full-fledged societal membership. In primitive societies the individual acquires these learnings informally from association with adults in their daily activities. A boy learns the traditions of the group through its folk tales, festivals, and rituals. He learns to hunt, to till the soil, or to shape the tribal tools with his hands by sharing in these activities with his elders. Long before these things have been acquired, however, his conduct and modes of thinking will have been influenced by the family patterns. In literate societies instruction in group ways becomes partly a specialized function. An institution—the school charged with the responsibility for teaching certain things—is created. A sequence of potential experiences is set up in the school for the purpose of disciplining children and youth in group ways of thinking and acting. This set of experiences is referred to as the *curriculum*.

The curriculum is always, in every society, a reflection of what the people think, feel, believe, and do. To understand the structure and function of the curriculum, it is necessary to understand what is meant

3

by culture, what the essential elements of a culture are, and how these are organized and interrelated. The principal theme of this chapter is the concept of culture and the universal relationship that obtains between the curriculum and the culture of a society. The discussion will make little reference to the culture of the United States and its meaning for curriculum building, since that topic has been reserved for treatment in the chapters that immediately follow.

1. *The Meaning of Culture*

A culture is the fabric of ideas, ideals, beliefs, skills, tools, aesthetic objects, methods of thinking, customs, and institutions into which each member of society is born. The way individuals make a living, the games they play, the stories they tell, the heroes they worship, the music they play, the way they care for their children, their family organization, their modes of transportation and communication—all of these and countless other items too numerous to mention (or, for that matter, for any single individual to know about) comprise the culture of a people. The culture is that part of his environment which man himself has made.

The term *culture* is to be distinguished from the concept of *society*. A society is a group of organized individuals who think of themselves as a distinct group. A society is not a mere aggregate of individuals, for in such a collection the individuals do not recognize themselves as members of a distinct social unit. To be a society a collection of persons must have something in common—a set of loyalties and sentiments, an *esprit de corps*—which induces the individual under certain circumstances to subordinate or even to sacrifice himself for the good of the group. Since these common elements are part of culture, it follows that without a culture there could be no society, and without a society there could be no culture. Yet the two are not identical. A society is composed of people. A culture consists of the things the people have learned to do, to believe, to value, to enjoy, and so on in the course of their history.

Thus, culture will vary from society to society and within the same society over a given period of time. For it is obvious that what people do, believe, value, and the like, varies from one society to another and within a given society if a long enough time span is allowed.

Moreover, what a particular individual believes and does and how he reacts to various stimuli depend upon the culture in which he grows up. If an occidental child were transplanted at birth to an oriental culture, he would grow up to assume the ways of behavior peculiar to that culture. He would become as oriental in his views, attitudes, skills, and habits of conduct as any individual whose ancestors were oriental from time immemorial. In like manner, an oriental child growing up in the culture of the western world would build ways of behaving and adjusting like those of the other members of western society. Perhaps it is not too much to say that the basic personality structure of the individual is shaped by the culture into which he is born and grows to maturity.

2. *The Structure of a Culture*

A culture may be analyzed in a number of ways, depending upon the purpose for which the analysis is made. For the purpose of understanding and reconstructing the curriculum, the analysis suggested by Ralph Linton in *The Study of Man* seems to be the most promising. With slight modifications it will be followed here.

The elements of a culture—that is, the things the people know, believe, do, and so on—may be put into three categories. First, there are those elements that are universally distributed among the adult population. Individuals throughout the society may, for example, eat the same foods, wear the same style of clothes, use the same language, greet one another in the same way, require the same obedience and respect from their children. They may possess the same religious notions, cherish the same political and economic ideas, and accept the same rules of polite conduct. All such things as are generally accepted by the members of the society are called *universals*. It should be understood, however, that universals are such only for a particular society. Since the character of culture varies from society to society, it is possible that a universal element in one society would not appear at all in another.

Second, some elements of a culture are found among only a portion of the adult population. In every society there are some things that only a part of the people know about or can do. These are called *specialties*. They consist principally of vocational callings demanding technical knowledges and skills. There is some division of labor in every society. The women know how to do certain things that are not known by the men. The men are skilled in activities outside the sphere of women. Then there are finer divisions of labor. Men in some localities may make their living by tilling the soil, those of another locality by herding cattle. There are also those who tend the sick and appease the spirits. In industrial societies, especially those permeated by science and technology, division of labor is so advanced that the specialties contain a relatively large portion of the cultural elements.

In addition to specialties of an occupational nature, there are those that belong to groups of individuals who occupy various social positions. For example, in a society having a recognizable social elite, individuals of this privileged class will have points of view and ways of believing peculiar to themselves. In like manner the lower social strata will have ways of thinking and believing not found in the upper classes.

Although the specialties are not shared directly and intimately by all individuals, in a relatively simple society most of them are understood in a general way by everyone. An individual may not know how to prepare food, but he will know whether or not it has been properly done. He may not have the skill and knowledge possessed by the physician, but he will understand the function of the physician in society and the importance of health. He will also know in a general way how a physician is supposed to behave and whether or not his practice departs significantly from what is generally expected. In a highly industrialized society, however, the meaning of specialties tends to be blurred in the public mind and restricted to those persons immediately engaged in them. Indeed, labor becomes so highly specialized and its products so complex and technical that not even the laborers themselves fully understand either the processes or the outcomes of production. As a result, in American society in recent years stress has been placed upon educating for wise choices among commercial objects.

Third, there are certain cultural elements that belong among neither the universals nor the specialties. These elements, like the specialties, are not generally distributed among the members of society. But unlike the specialties, they are not shared even by all the members of any of the various occupational groups, or, for that matter, by all the members of any socially recognized group within the society. These elements consist of ways of thinking and doing that depart from commonly accepted ideas or practices. For example, a new way of making soap may be accepted only by a few individuals here and there. A new way of teaching, a new way of preparing foods, or a new way of doing any one of a thousand other things may be accepted by only a few persons. These cultural elements are called *alternatives*. They embrace all the ways of obtaining results which depart from generally accepted techniques and procedures. In other words, the alternatives represent those elements of the culture about which the individual can exercise choice.

Alternatives may enter a culture by way of invention within the society or by diffusion from another culture. Cultures that are more or less unchanging over a period of years will, as a rule, have relatively few alternatives. The alternatives constitute the growing edge of the culture. As new ways of doing things emerge and come to be accepted, they are absorbed by either the universals or the specialties.

The Cultural Core as the Fundamental Rules of Life

The foregoing cultural elements may be combined so as to divide a culture into two aspects. The first is a group of elements that are more or less persistent and unchanging, consisting of mutually compatible, though not always logically consistent, universals and specialties. It tends on the whole to be stable, for it consists of those elements that have been tried out and accepted. Additions and deletions are, therefore, apt to meet with resistance. The second group, surrounding these central elements, consists of the unintegrated and frequently inconsistent alternatives, which are candidates for admission to the central body of cultural content.

Linton uses the term core to designate the central body of universals and specialties. The term will be used in the present discussion, however, to refer to the heart of this persistent aspect of the culture. It will refer to the fundamental rules, knowledges, and skills by which the people live, by which they carry on and rationalize their conduct, and upon which they build their expectations and hopes. These are the elements from which the society draws its stability and vitality. They underlie all social institutions and constitute the bases of moral and social judgment.

The general pattern and the spirit of a culture are shaped by its core. The kind of political and economic habits and institutions a people have, the extent to which they compete with one another or work cooperatively together, the things they strive for, and the way they control those who deviate from accepted patterns of conduct are all determined in some measure by these vital cultural elements. Moreover, the individual largely gains his personal stability and emotional security from the cultural core, for there he finds his deepest sentiments and his most cherished objects of allegiance and faith.

3. *Cultural Roots of the Curriculum*

If an observer looks at the curriculum of the school in any society, he will find, either stated or implied, a set of educational objectives, a body of subject matter, a list of exercises or activities to be performed, and a way of determining whether or not the objectives have been reached by the students. He will find also some kind of control which the teacher is required to exercise over the learners. These things comprising the curriculum are always, in every society, derived from the culture. The objectives stressed will be those that reflect the controlling ideas and sentiments contained in the universals. The subject matter will tend to be that which is believed to embrace the most significant ideas and most generally used knowledges and skills. The way in which the learners are controlled will reflect the prevailing methods of social control of the society at large. As the instrument of society for the education of the young, the curriculum will reflect the ideals, knowledges, and skills that are believed to be significant, or that are related to the common activities of the members of society. The curriculum is, therefore, interwoven with the social fabric that sustains it.

In every society a distinction is made between the curriculum of common education and that of special education. Common education will be based upon the universal elements of the culture and such aspects of the specialties as are of general concern. Special education will be based largely upon the dominant specialties of the culture. It will be designed to train the individual for a particular social or vocational position.

Common Education Based upon Cultural Universals

Common education is concerned with the problem of maintaining the society as a closely knit and well-integrated unit. It is only natural, therefore, that the rules and knowledges by which the people as a whole regulate their conduct and anticipate the behavior of one another should be its principal content. Not all the universals, however, will be contained in the common curriculum. It will ordinarily not incorporate such superficial elements as the method of greeting friends or the way to tie shoes. As a rule, these things are left to the individual to acquire informally and often unconsciously through participation in the common life of the people. Instead, the curriculum will tend to emphasize the more fundamental universals, or cultural core, such as the values, sentiments, knowledges, and skills that provide society with stability and vitality and individuals with the motivations and deep-lying controls of conduct.

The heart of the universals, as already pointed out, is the standards and knowledges by which the people decide what is right and wrong, good and evil, beautiful and ugly, true and false, appropriate and inappropriate in all sorts of activities—political, economic, aesthetic, educational, or what not. These standards constitute the moral content of the society. Next to them in importance are the knowledges and skills that have to do with the control and improvement of the common activities of the people such as their political and economic behavior. Together these constitute the subject matter of common education.

Special Education Related to the Specialties of the Culture

Returning now to special education, it is to be remembered that the specialties of a culture are usually those ways of thinking and acting associated either with vocational groups or social classes, or both.

Hence special education may follow the interests of either one or both of these special groups. In societies having a recognized social elite, it will be found that instruments of education will be set aside for training the immature members of the elite group in the special points of view and patterns of conduct of these privileged adults. The presence of *exclusive* private or finishing schools is evidence of the existence of an elite class having particular outlooks, polite manners, and behavioral patterns which it wishes to maintain. Indeed, the existence of such classes has led in some nations to the creation of dual educational systems—one for the folk and another for the upper classes. For this reason higher forms of education, including secondary as well as higher schools, have tended historically to be designed for the privileged few. Even in the more democratically inclined countries, where a single educational ladder has been adopted, the curriculum of the upper rungs reflects a privileged origin.

Education for vocational purposes is always correlated with the needs of persons of particular socio-economic level. Hence it is sometimes difficult to distinguish from that form of special education designed to equip the individual to occupy a particular position in society. The sons of upper-class families in western nations who go to private schools, or to publicly supported schools specially designed for them, in order to pursue the so-called "cultural" subjects—not to mention programs leading to "higher" professions—are thereby being trained for upper-class vocations. This type of training usually is just as vocational for them as the study of how to read blueprints would be for a prospective plumber, because the so-called "cultural" courses prepare them for domestic governmental positions, for foreign diplomatic service, or for positions in industrial bureaucracies. In any case, the display of relatively useless knowledge, information, and skills, marking their possessor as a member of the leisure class, will be of inestimable value, for it gains admission to the polite circles of other countries as well as his own.

The point of this discussion is not that all vocational education is class education. Only in societies where certain vocations are associated with particular social classes will this tend to be true. Social systems that emphasize an open-door policy for all occupations—making it possible for every individual irrespective of race, creed, or social background to acquire the knowledges and skills he is capable and desirous of obtaining—will reduce the chances that some occupations will be monopolized by privileged classes. In these societies vocational education will be least associated with class education.

Class Education Sometimes Confused with Common Education

Not only is there a tendency for class education to be confused with vocational training, but also with common education. When a society passes from a class to a classless system (or to one in which classes exist only in a loose sense), the educational ideals and programs designed in the earlier phase for the education of the upper classes tend to persist in the later phase, under the guise of general or common education. It is for this reason that the curriculum of the American high schools, as well as that of American colleges, has been so slow to adjust to the demands of mass education. Thorstein Veblen, about fifty years ago, made it clear that remnants of the leisure class educational program persisted in schools and colleges.[1] These remnants may still be detected today.

Moreover, the colleges tend on the whole to continue to provide vocational programs under the banner of liberal education. A former president of Harvard University—James B. Conant—has aptly phrased this point.

By and large, the general education which our conventional four-year liberal arts colleges provide in one form or another is given as a background for two vocations—the learned professions and the managerial positions in business. This type of education, however much it may be improved (and it will be improved greatly in the coming years, I feel sure), cannot be considered apart from the vocations for which it prepares. In short, it has no over-all general validity for it cannot be considered apart from the clientele for which it has been developed over the years.[2]

1 Thorstein Veblen, *The Theory of the Leisure Class.*
2 James Bryant Conant, "Public Education and the Structure of American Society," *Teachers College Record,* Vol. 47, No. 3 (December, 1945), pp. 164–165. By permission.

NOTE: Except where acknowledgment is made for a direct quotation, footnotes do not contain full publication data. Complete information on all books and articles cited may be found in the Bibliography.

It is disturbing that in the United States, where the prevailing social creed denies the desirability of social classes, there should be social groups trying to reinstate and bolster up outworn systems of class education in the name of general or liberal education. Few things have encumbered thinking about the development of a more adequate program of common education in the United States, as well as in other countries, so much as adherence to educational ideas brought over from the class system of past cultural phases.

4. *Cultural Change and the Curriculum*

The discussion in the preceding section has developed the relation existing between a stable, well-integrated, and relatively static culture, on the one hand, and the curriculum that emerges within it, on the other. What happens to the curriculum when the culture is changing is just as important. (In modern society, it may be more important.) Since the curriculum is interwoven with the whole cultural fabric, it follows that as the culture undergoes serious modifications the curriculum will become an object of concern, especially among the more sensitive members of the teaching profession and of the society at large. The adequacy of the old curriculum for the new cultural circumstances will be searchingly questioned and changes in the curriculum proposed.

In societies experiencing little cultural change, the culture will be largely taken on unconsciously by the individual—although the school, where it exists, will emphasize certain elements of the culture by making them explicit through verbalization. On the other hand, in societies where fundamental associations are breaking down under the impact of new social forces, fewer standards of conduct and elements of knowledge will be picked up informally, and these will tend to be inconsistent and conflicting. The problem of maintaining a stable, integrated culture in such a society will, therefore, be quite different from the problem in a static social system. The demands made upon the school with regard to this problem will be correspondingly more taxing, and failure to meet them will be more fraught with social disaster.

Cultural Change Related to Increase of Alternatives

Before proceeding further with the discussion of the curriculum problems that arise in a changing society, it will be well to take a brief look at the nature of cultural change. A culture not only consists of elements, but these elements are so interrelated and mutually adjusted that they form a configuration, or cultural pattern. When alternative elements appear in a culture, they tend to disturb the cultural pattern. They come into competition with elements comprising the universals and specialties, and their general acceptance requires a modification of the relationships among various aspects of the culture. When the number of alternatives is low as compared with the universals, the culture will have a high degree of stability. As alternatives increase relative to the universals, social change is increased; and the need for reintegration becomes more and more imperative if the culture is not to disintegrate.

Alternatives that emerge from time to time, or are borrowed from other cultures, have varying capacities for cultural disruption. Some alternatives, such as new types of ornaments, new techniques of decorating, or new kinds of wearing apparel, will have little effect upon the cultural pattern. The introduction of the wrist watch, for example, had no influence upon the basic structure of American society. Other innovations, such as changes in ways of making a living or the development of new sources of energy, will seriously upset a culture and necessitate far-reaching readjustments. This is true because one of the basic aspects of the life of a people is the manner in which it secures the necessities of existence. The superstructure of society is erected in large part upon the way people exploit the material world in the search for food, clothing, and shelter. Any change in the methods of such exploitation will, therefore, shake the whole cultural fabric and require large-scale social reconstruction.

The Tanala: An Illustration of Cultural Change

Later chapters will show how the culture of the United States has been shaken to its foundation by innovations that have been wiping out the traditional modes of material production. This topic requires an extended analysis and would be too complex for an illustrative case at the present juncture of the discussion. An illustration will be drawn instead from the simpler culture of the Tanala, a hill tribe of western Madagascar. The cultural changes here described illustrate how property relations, family structure, community life, political arrangements, and even methods of warfare were reconstructed by the introduction of a new way of growing rice. The picture is suggestive of how American culture is being reshaped by science and technology.[3]

The Tanala are a hill tribe of western Madagascar. . . . Prior to about 200 years ago the economic basis of their life was the cultivation of dry rice by the cutting and burning method. Under the local conditions this method gave a good crop the first year and a moderately good one from the same land five to ten years later. After this the land had to be abandoned until it had once more produced a fairly heavy growth of jungle, twenty to twenty-five years as a minimum. Since the newly cleared land produced the best crops, the usual native method was to utilize all the original jungle which could be profitably exploited with the village as a center, then move the village to a new locality and begin the process again. Under these conditions there was no opportunity for individual ownership of land to develop. The village as a whole held a territory within which it moved from site to site, and forest products such as game taken from this territory belonged to the man who obtained them. Joint families owned the crops growing on jungle land which they had cleared, but the division of land for this use was made as equitable as possible. According to one account, the village elders staked out equal frontages of land to be cleared and assigned one of these to each joint family. The family members, working in a group, then cleared back from the line as far as they thought necessary to provide for their needs. If a family had had bad luck with its crops one year, it would be given an advantage the next. As a result, no marked inequalities in wealth between the joint families ever developed. As there was no market for any surplus, there was no attempt to cultivate more land than was actually needed, and the product was divided by the joint family's head, each household receiving according to its needs.

The cultivation of wet rice appeared first among the clans on the eastern edge of the Tanala territory, having been borrowed from the Betsileo. It began as a simple adjunct to dry rice, the new crop being planted in naturally wet places in the bottoms of the valleys. From the first this work seems to have been done by households rather than joint families, the task

[3] Ralph Linton, *The Study of Man* (New York: Appleton-Century-Crofts, Inc.; copyright 1936), pp 348–353. By permission.

being too small to necessitate the co-operation of the whole group. Later came small systems of terraces, also borrowed, but by the time this improvement was accepted the pattern of household cultivation of the new crop had become thoroughly established, so that joint families, as such, rarely built terrace systems or shared the produce.

Even before the introduction of wet rice the Tanala had well-developed patterns of personal property, and these, in combination with the idea of family rights to land during the brief period in which it bore a crop, opened the door to individual ownership of land and the exclusive right of a household to the rice patch it cultivated. Since rice terraces were actually growing crops throughout most of the year and had to be kept in repair even between seasons, the land which they occupied never really went out of use and therefore never reverted to the village to be reassigned. Only a limited amount of land could be utilized for this purpose, due to soil, height of water available for irrigation, and other natural factors. Hence those households which had not had the energy and foresight to take up rice land at first soon found themselves permanently excluded. Insensibly there grew up within what had formerly been a classless society a class of landholders, and with this went a weakening of the joint family organization. Loyalty to this unit had been maintained largely by the economic interdependence of its members and their constant need for co-operation. But a household could tend its fields of irrigated rice unaided, and its head felt a not unnatural reluctance to share the produce with persons who had contributed nothing toward it.

The rise of individual land tenure did not affect the expropriated very seriously at first, since they could continue with the older method of exploiting village land not available for irrigation. However, land within easy reach of the village would be increasingly exhausted, and the landless households had to go farther and farther afield to find jungle. Often their fields were so far away that they could not possibly go and return in the same day, so they developed the custom of building combined granaries and sleeping quarters there. These distant fields also became increasingly household rather than joint family enterprises. Perhaps the breakdown of the joint family patterns of co-operation had already progressed too far when the system was instituted, or the joint family may have been unwilling to risk any large number of men so far from home. This camping-out was dangerous, since a hostile war party could cut off a small group with ease.

One of the greatest stresses within the culture arose in connection with the periodic moving of the village. This was a deep-rooted custom, but now the villages were split into the landless, who needed to move, and the landowners, who had a capital investment in the locality and were unwilling to move. A further breakdown of the joint family system resulted. Under the old conditions villages not infrequently split and formed new units, but such splits were always along joint family lines. At most, a man who stood at the head of three or four households within the lineage would secede with his group and found a distinct lineage in the new village. Now when villages split it was the expropriated who moved, so that the immigrant group formed a cross section of the original lineages. In the new locality the same process went on again until the land which had formed the range of the original mobile village was dotted with descendant villages, each held in place by the irrigated fields about it.

The combination of increasingly settled life and breakdown of the joint family into its component households had still further results. The mobile villages had been socially self-contained, endogamous units. The settled villages were much less so. The joint family retained its religious importance, based on the worship of a common ancestor, after it had lost much of its functional importance and even after its component households had been scattered. Family members from different villages would still be called together on some ceremonial occasions, and this going and coming helped to break down the old patterns of village isolation. Intermarriages became increasingly common, especially among the clans of the Menabe division whose pattern of cross-cousin marriage often made such matings necessary. Thus the original pattern of independent village groups was increasingly transformed into a tribal one.

The new conditions also had important repercussions on the patterns of native warfare. The mobile villages had always fortified themselves with a simple ditch and stockade, but there was little point in expending a vast amount of labor on a site which would presently be abandoned. An enemy war party, using surprise, had a fair opportunity of taking such a village, seizing a rich booty of cattle and personable young women, and driving the group out of its territory, which could then be added to the enemy's own range. In fact this was a normal procedure whenever a village felt itself crowded. Now that permanent residence in a village was assured, the villagers could set themselves seriously to the work of fortification, and by the time the Europeans arrived some of the eastern villages, which had gotten wet rice first and hence been settled longest, had made themselves impregnable to anything short of artillery. I was told of one village which was protected by three concentric ditches each twenty feet wide and of

the same depth, straight-sided and with hedges of prickly pear planted between. The Tanala probably copied this form of defense from the Betsileo,
although they had not adopted it while they still followed the mobile pattern. The new conditions made what was already a well-known foreign
trait desirable, and it was accepted accordingly.

Since the natives had no siege machinery, these great fortifications reduced war to a stalemate. It was impossible for an attacking party to
take a village except by treachery, and the large, determined war parties of
the earlier period degenerated more and more into small groups of raiders
who aimed to cut off stragglers. This tendency was increased by an increase
in the value of slaves. The presence of Arab, European, and Imerina slave
traders, who gave guns in exchange, had something to do with this, but
their activities were never carried on on a large scale. In part, at least, this
increased importance of slaves was correlated with the new crop. Under
the old system slaves were of little economic value, while now they could
be put to work in the rice fields. With the rise of slavery there came an
increasing need for techniques of ransom and other relations involving
captive slaves, and these were gradually developed. In particular, a technique arose for regularizing the relations between a slave woman and her
master, her family paying half her market value and thus promoting her to
the status of a legal wife. In this way still further bonds were established
between villages, even when these belonged to different clans, and the whole
tribe was drawn more and more together.

The last step in this drama of change came less than a century ago. In
the early mobile period Tanala organization was highly democratic. The
head of one of the lineages in a village acted as a magistrate and executive,
but there was no formal investiture of any sort and he had no real power.
Outside the village there was no recognized authority of any sort. The
settled tribes to the east, on the other hand, had had kings for some centuries and were in the process of developing a sort of feudal system which
cut across the old clan-locality lines and strengthened the central authority.
About 1840 one of the Tanala clans established domination over several
of the other northern clans, declared itself royal, and announced that the
hereditary head of its senior lineage was now King of the Tanala Menabe.
Incidentally, the control of this king always remained rather weak and he
never really controlled any of the groups who were still mobile. Over the
settled clans he was able to exercise some real authority, but the kingdom
came to an end before adequate machinery for government could be developed or borrowed. This first king introduced two new elements of cul-

ture, both taken from the Betsileo. He built himself an individual tomb, thus breaking a long-established Tanala custom, and after his death the Tanala accepted the belief that the souls of their kings passed into snakes.

The changes in Tanala culture due to the introduction of wet rice farming may be summarized as follows: (1) personal property increased in importance, (2) new techniques of farming were introduced, (3) a new pattern of community life arose, (4) exogamous marriages increased, (5) importance of family ties decreased, (6) slaves became valuable, (7) the political unit changed from the joint family to the kingdom, (8) emphasis upon personal goals and personal success increased, (9) competition in the struggle for existence was accentuated, (10) new types of conflicts were engendered by the accentuated competition in the struggle for existence.

This illustration makes clear how a single basic alternative, once it is accepted, has consequences that spread throughout the entire cultural system, making it necessary to readjust cultural elements on a wide scale or else suffer cultural decay and possibly cultural dissolution. It also helps us to understand what is meant by cultural integration. When innovations occur in a culture, they become candidates for acceptance; and, when they are accepted, changes in other elements must be made so that a new balance of cultural factors results. This mutual adjustment of factors is what is meant by integration. Cultural integration can be thought of as an end product—a pattern of relationships already achieved. It can also be thought of as a process of adjustment, as something going on in one aspect or another of a culture as new cultural elements arise and compete with others for acceptance.

There can also be various degrees of integration, depending upon the extent of the adjustment of factors at different times in the history of a culture. When the number of alternatives is low relative to the universals of a culture, a high degree of integration obtains. When the alternatives increase, relative to the universals, more rapidly than they can be assimilated, the culture inclines toward disintegration. This phase is distinctly noticeable in the Tanala culture as the impact of wet rice farming begins to break up the family pattern and to uproot people from the communal community. If this trend continues until the rules by which the people live are largely wiped out, and if no other loyalties arise to take their place, the culture disintegrates altogether. In the

career of mankind many cultures have arisen, have flourished vigorously, and yet have perished because they failed to build a new cultural
synthesis when the alternatives became numerous.

In a period of cultural disruption the anxieties of individuals are increased in number and intensity. "A society," as Wirth has reminded us,
"is possible in the last analysis because the individuals in it carry
around in their heads some sort of picture of that society." [4] When the
universals of a culture begin to change significantly, especially if the
change reaches down to the fundamental rules of conduct, the picture
of society becomes blurred, and individuals find themselves unable to
carry on normal activities in a rational way. They are led by the old
rules to expect other persons to behave in certain ways. But if these
rules are no longer valid, other persons will not conform to these expectations. As this occurs on a wider and wider scale, the individual
becomes bewildered; his sense of common reality vanishes, and with it
goes his sense of personal stability and security. It is interesting to find
that in his psychological interpretation of the changes in Tanala culture
Kardiner points to the rise of personal anxieties growing out of the
changes in the individual's relation to productive property. Kardiner
says:

> The significance of property (already quite pronounced in Tanala cul-
> ture) is augmented until it becomes the sole means of enhancing the ego.
> The pursuit of property becomes the most important element in the security
> system of the individual. . . . There was an influx of new needs for the
> individual. New needs as well as new anxieties were added to the individ-
> ual's problem of adjustment. New needs were created in that the individual
> required different qualities to get along in this new society, and new anxie-
> ties in that he was susceptible to new dangers, dangers of poverty and
> degradation.[5]

Curriculum Problems Arising from Cultural Change

Turning to the curriculum, certain problems are always prominent
in a period of cultural upset and reintegration. If the Tanala had had

---

[4] Karl Mannheim, *Ideology and Utopia* (New York: Harcourt, Brace & Co.; 1936),
p. xxv.
[5] From *Readings in Social Psychology,* edited by Theodore M. Newcomb and Eugene L. Hartley. Copyright 1947 by Henry Holt and Company, Inc., pp. 51–52.

schools, the teaching profession would have been confronted by serious educational problems growing out of changes incident to the introduction of wet rice farming. As property changed from communal to personal ownership and control, as the old pattern of family life began to disintegrate and the new pattern based on household ownership emerged, as the community became divided between those who owned land and those who did not, the teaching profession would have become uncertain as to what objectives should be sought through the educational system. The educational journals of Tanala would have carried article after article on the need for clarifying the objectives of education. In faculty and committee meetings teachers would have disagreed upon what the schools should attempt to achieve. Some writers would have extolled the old virtues and ways of life. Others would have frowned upon the old ways, extolling the new ideals and the advantages to be gained from the new method of production and the way of life it entailed.

Teachers would not have known whether they should emphasize the sacredness of communal property, in keeping with the tradition of the tribe, or the virtues of private ownership and control, which the wet rice farmers were defending. They would not have known whether the old joint family pattern of co-operation should be bolstered by giving it increased attention in the curriculum, or whether the household family-enterprise unit should be stressed instead. They would not have known whether to emphasize the old community life with its periodic moving of the village, or to support the scattering of the villagers dictated by the demands of wet rice farming and the consequent stripping of ownership from the less enterprising of the population. They would not have known whether to stress the old informal mode of living together or the emerging tendency toward a tribal kingdom. They would have been uncertain about these things because there was no consensus among the people with respect to them. The old concensus, upon which the traditional educational program was based, would have been so much in doubt that the mandate of the teaching profession would not have been clear.

Of course, the teaching profession might have contented itself by appealing to such abstractions as the development of a good citizen or the teaching of the fundamentals. But these would have been as much in question as anything else. Who would have been a good citizen in Tanala? To what traditions, ideals, beliefs, and patterns of conduct would he have been loyal? Would he have had the point of view and motivations of the wet rice farmer or the dry rice farmer? What would have been the fundamentals? Of course, the native tongue and perhaps the modes of calculation might have been included. Beyond these what would have been basic in the behavior of the people? What attitudes? What beliefs and loyalties?

The purpose here is not to paint a hopeless picture of the curriculum problems of the Tanala. There were, of course, some elements of the old culture that remained and could have been used as bases for judging the purposes and program of the school—some measure of family loyalty, allegiance to the tribe itself, and doubtless a great number of ideals which this account of cultural change among the Tanala does not contain. The import of the discussion is, first, that a period of cultural transformation will upset the curriculum and require that it be reconstructed with respect to purpose, content, method of instruction, and means of evaluation; and, second, that the teaching profession will experience a period of uncertainty as to the kind of educational program to build.

The primary educational task arises from the fact that in a period of transformation the common orientation of the people is disturbed. They are confused as to what to believe, what to strive for, what to defend. Consequently, they are often in conflict one with another. Depending upon the degree of disintegration, the capacity of the people to think, feel, and act as a unit is reduced. They continue to live together, but communication among them breaks down; for as the community of ideas and habits dissolves, individuals no longer respond alike to the same situation. When this condition exists, the school must design a curriculum that will help to expand the common orientation in which each individual shares. The school curriculum alone cannot resolve the difficulty, but it can make a major contribution in this direction.

The task of curriculum building will be principally that of constructing the curriculum so that cultural elements, both new and old, will be mutually adjusted and a new cultural synthesis achieved. The task is to build a curriculum that will achieve a set of consistent ideas and values in which all members of society can share. A desirable curriculum is one that reflects a consistent cultural point of view and attempts to achieve a mutual adjustment of cultural elements in terms of a common orientation. An undesirable curriculum, on the other hand, is one that accentuates the maladjustment of cultural elements by stressing those traditional ideals, knowledges, sentiments, and skills no longer relevant to social realities.

The rise of science and technology has done far more to American culture—and, for that matter, to most of the cultures of the world—than did the introduction of wet rice farming to the Tanala culture. American culture is in a period of reconstruction because science and technology have revamped the means by which men exploit their environment. The consequences of these new means have been felt in every aspect of the culture—the family, the community, agriculture, industry, business, politics, religion, education, and morality.

It will be the purpose of the remaining chapters of this part of the book to set forth some of the more significant cultural changes caused by science and technology, and to indicate some of the more important curriculum problems thereby raised.

▶ *Following Up*
This Chapter

1. Make a list of some of the things you believe, and try to determine how you came to accept them. Try to determine which of these beliefs are universals, which are specialties, and which are alternatives.

2. Make a list of cultural alternatives, and try to find out where they came from and whether or not they have significant social consequences. Which of them seem to have important meanings for the school curriculum?

3. What would you consider some of the desirable characteristics of a good educational program in a period of cultural change? What would be some of the pressing curriculum problems in such a period?

4. Select one or more recent courses of study or curriculum manuals from your library, and try to determine some of the universals they emphasize. Also, try to determine what specialities and alternatives, if any, they include.

5. In what way, if at all, do the courses of study you have selected contribute either to cultural integration or disintegration?

▶ Suggested Reading

1. Margaret Mead's *Coming of Age in Samoa* and *Growing Up in New Guinea* (published together under the title *From the South Seas*) are among the finest interpretations of the interdependence of education and cultural systems. Her *And Keep Your Powder Dry* is an equally good interpretation of culture in the United States.

2. You will find interesting descriptions of different cultures in Ruth Benedict's *Patterns of Culture;* Margaret Mead's *Co-operation and Competition among Primitive People;* and Clyde Kluckhohn's *Mirror for Man.* Good discussions of the structure and dynamics of cultural systems are found in Ralph Linton's *The Study of Man;* Melville Herskovits' *Man and His Work;* and Bronislaw Malinowski's *A Scientific Theory of Culture.*

3. Cultural interpretation of personality is treated in Ralph Linton's *Cultural Background of Personality.* For psychological interpretations of the effects of cultural factors on human development, see Abram Kardiner's *The Individual and His Society* and his *Psychological Frontiers of Society.* See also *Personality in Nature, Society, and Culture,* edited by Clyde Kluckhohn and Henry A. Murray.

4. *The Saber-Tooth Curriculum,* by Harold Benjamin, is one of the best and most delightful descriptions of the relation between cultural change and curriculum theory and practice.

NOTE: The Bibliography, page 651, lists alphabetically by author all books referred to in these reading lists, in the body of the text, and in the footnotes to the text. For publication data, refer to the Bibliography.

Chapter 2

Community Changes and Problems of Curriculum Development

FOR TWO CENTURIES the people of America were rooted in self-sufficient, isolated communities characterized by neighborliness and intimacy of association. To be sure, there were petty differences in each community and even distrust among some of its members; but the people were immersed in the same point of view and saw eye-to-eye as to aspirations, standards of right and wrong, and ways of doing things.

During the last seventy-five years, however, this way of life has been rapidly disappearing, so that American society is no longer characterized by the old-fashioned community but by urban communities and huge metropolitan areas. With this transformation of the pattern of American society, as in the case of the Tanalas, has come the necessity for readjusting many basic elements of the old cultural pattern. This change has been brought about by the advancement of science and technology. If these twin forces have unlocked fabulous resources, conquered space, and made poverty unnecessary, they have also created new problems of cultural adjustment, which must be solved if men are to enjoy the fruits of these achievements.

1. *Science and Technology Influence Culture*

If scientific and technological advancement had resulted only in mechanical conveniences and physical comforts, there would have been no tendency today to look upon it as a mixed blessing. But, as with the introduction of wet rice farming by the Tanalas, the progress of science and technology has been attended by far-reaching cultural changes, which have created grave social problems. It is necessary only to point to the more obvious problems of maintaining home and family stability, economic and industrial order, and world peace to convince the most skeptical of the impact of invention and mass production on the life of the people. Out of these changing circumstances emerge the principal educational problems with which the teaching profession is now concerned.

It is perhaps not too much to say that every significant curriculum problem of today is rooted in one way or another in the general problem of cultural reintegration created by the increasing advancement of science and technology. These forces are uprooting the people of American society in the same way as wet rice farming uprooted the Tanalas. If there be a difference in the two cultures at this point, it is to be found in the greater rapidity and complexity of changes in modern culture and the accelerated rate at which cultural alternatives continue to appear as scientific knowledge and techniques accumulate.

For a simple illustration of how society is affected by science and technology, turn back to the invention, a little over a hundred years ago, of the steam locomotive and the establishment of the first railway lines. The iron horse provided a faster mode of transportation than the stagecoach; in addition, its freight and passenger capacity was considerably greater. Moreover, behind railway development was the growth of factories for the manufacture of locomotives, passenger coaches, freight cars, and other railway equipment. Thus new industries requiring new knowledges and skills sprang up as the railway system emerged and expanded. Also, new types of occupations multiplied both in the factories and in the operation of the railway system. In addition, the old stagecoach business was gradually eliminated by the expanding railroads, resulting in the disappearance of hundreds of jobs in the stagecoach industry.[1]

These changes are some of the direct consequences of the invention of the steam locomotive. In addition, there were less obvious changes occurring as a result of the same invention. As the railroads spread out across the country like a huge web, new regions and communities were brought within the range of ready accessibility. New communities by the hundreds sprang up along these main channels of communication, laying the groundwork for the urban movement to come later. This web of steel connecting one point of the country with another expanded the markets for the goods of industry and the produce of the farm. It now became possible for an industry to distribute its products to the four corners of the nation. Thus was established the beginning of the mass market, which was an indispensable condition for the development of mass production and the huge industrial and corporate units essential to it. Mass production, in turn, required not only huge industrial plants but also concentration of manpower in urban centers to carry on the work of collective enterprise. It may seem a far cry from the invention of the steam locomotive to the megalopolitan world of today. Yet, while no one would attribute the whole of urbanization to this one invention, there is nevertheless a tenuous but unbroken line from the iron horse to the Empire State Building.

It is plain that one of the ways in which invention affects social life is by creating new jobs and wiping out others. Another is by conquering geographic distance, so that people of the nation and of the whole world are brought into a closer relationship. Still another is by creating the conditions leading to the concentration of people into huge centers of population, uprooting man from the soil and breaking the face-to-face ties so characteristic of village life.

Increased Specialization of Labor and Social Interdependence

Science and technology have another impact upon society. It is seldom recognized, and yet its importance for curriculum development is equal to, if not greater than, those just noted. The power and efficiency of science and technology rest upon the principle of division of labor.

---

[1] For an excellent discussion of the influence of science as expressed through inventions, see Report of the President's Research Committee on Social Trends, *Recent Social Trends in the United States,* Vol. 1, pp. 122–166.

This principle is manifest in the fact that scientific discovery is accelerated by isolating special features of nature for intensive investigation. Like politics, which has followed the principle of divide and conquer, science has followed the principle of isolate and conquer. Isolation lends itself to minute divisions of labor, so that today there are not just physicists, but physicists who are experts in electricity, in mechanics, in nuclear physics, and in a host of other areas unknown to the general public.

The spirit of specialization has crept into industry and into practically all the professions. The factory system progressed on the wheels of specialized knowledge, skills, and activities, which were co-ordinated by engineers and business bureaucrats to produce a single product. The stereotype of the factory worker making a small part of a single product, which he never sees as a whole nor helps to plan, is so well known as to need no elaboration.

The same condition prevails in the professions, though perhaps in a lesser degree. The general medical practitioner is being replaced by the specialist, particularly in the cities. In the legal profession there are criminal lawyers, civil lawyers, corporation lawyers, and so on. Even the teaching profession is exhibiting to an alarming degree the segmentation and narrowness that often accompany a highly developed division of labor. The administrator is often highly specialized, knowing little or nothing about the art of teaching but a great deal about the duties and responsibilities of his office. Teachers, in turn, are highly specialized, in mathematics, science, English, history, and so on, with little knowledge about the total operation of the school. In this regard they are like factory workers, with the administrators corresponding to the managers of industry.

Moreover, the whole educational program is divided, the curriculum being broken into highly specialized bodies of information. Thus the student goes through the educational program by being exposed to this fragment of knowledge here and that one there until he accumulates the units required for graduation. In the whole process no one has been in a position to see him as a person, as a socio-psychological creature. He has always been viewed as a student of mathematics, of English, or what not, on the basis of which view he is judged by the school to be either a success or a failure.

The reverse side of the picture is that division of labor breeds interdependence. If a product is to be made by a large number of individuals, each of whom is responsible for only a small element of the total, the product cannot be manufactured if any individual fails to fulfill his responsibility. As a result, the labor of multitudes of individuals in almost every great enterprise, research project, or professional undertaking must be meshed in a comprehensive pattern. The organization and the management of any of these undertakings resemble the structure and the operation of a great army more than those of the village enterprise of a century ago.

2. Changes in Community Life

The community life of the eighteenth and nineteenth centuries is beautifully expressed in its idealized form in the following passage from the pen of William Henry Hudson.

Each (house) had its center of human life with life of bird and beast, and the centers were in touch with one another, connected like a row of children linked together by their hands; all together forming one organism, instinct with one life, moved by one mind, like a many-colored serpent lying at rest, extended at full length upon the ground.

I imagined the case of a cottager at one end of the village occupied in chopping up a tough piece of wood or stump and accidentally letting fall his heavy sharp axe onto his foot, inflicting a grievous wound. The tidings of the accident would fly from mouth to mouth to the other extremity of the village, a mile distant; not only would every individual quickly know of it, but have at the same time a vivid mental image of his fellow villager at the moment of his misadventure, the sharp glittering axe falling onto his foot, the red blood flowing from the wound; and he would at the same time feel the wound in his own foot and the shock to his system.

In like manner all thoughts and feelings would pass freely from one to another, although not necessarily communicated by speech; and all would be participants in virtue of that sympathy and solidarity uniting the members of a small isolated community. No one would be capable of a thought or emotion which would seem strange to the others. The temper, the mood, the outlook, of the individual and the village, would be the same.[2]

2 William Henry Hudson, *A Traveller in Little Things* (New York: E. P. Dutton & Co.; 1921), pp. 110–112. By permission

Although few, if any, communities ever corresponded exactly to this picture of intimacy and personal sympathy, it is nevertheless true that the early American community was a closely knit unit based upon face-to-face relations, affection, and friendship.

The Individual in the Small Community of the Nineteenth Century

It would be ridiculous to assume that the small, isolated communities of a century ago were populated by angels. Nothing could be further from the truth. They were constituted of men and women afflicted with the ignorance, prejudices, and narrow points of view that prevailed in the old-fashioned village. But whatever their shortcomings—and there were many—and whatever their differences, these people were basically in agreement as to the meaning of life and the rights and responsibilities of the individual.

The individual shaped his conduct, and indeed his whole life-plan, by the demands of local opinion and sentiment. His ideas of right and wrong, good and bad, correct and incorrect were induced by the customs and traditions of the community. In short, his whole personality was nourished by the soil of interpersonal relations and shaped to the pattern of community life.

As recently as the latter part of the nineteenth century American society was still largely a collection of these local units of intimate association, in which industry was chiefly agricultural and production was carried on mainly by hand tools. Today all of this has been changed. Whatever might have been the merits of the old-fashioned community, it is rapidly declining as a force in American society; and there is no likelihood, short of the destruction of modern civilization, that this form of social existence will be restored.

The Individual in the Urbanized Society of Today

When the nation was first established there were only two cities with a population of over 25,000. It was not until 1820 that the nation could claim a city of 100,000. In 1890 approximately 35 per cent of the nation's population lived in urban centers of 2,500 and over. By 1930 urban concentration had increased to the point that about 56 per cent of the people lived in communities of 2,500 or more. The growth in urban population slowed down between 1930 and 1940, so that the urban population in 1940 had climbed to only 56.5 per cent. In 1940, 28.8 per cent of the people lived in cities of 100,000 or more population.[3] But after 1940 the trend toward urbanization was resumed. By 1950, 63 per cent of the total population lived in urban communities, 29.4 per cent in cities of 100,000 or more.[4] Indeed, in 1950, 84.5 million people (56 per cent of the total population) lived in 168 metropolitan areas—cities of 50,000 or more together with their suburban districts. Of this total only 1.4 million lived in areas with less than 100,000 people, while 44.4 million lived in areas of a million or more. Equally significant, more than four-fifths of the total population gain of the nation between 1940 and 1950 occurred in these 168 metropolitan areas.[5]

Modern cities arose in response to the new industrial and business activities created by scientific inventions. Their rise and growth are closely associated with the industrial revolution. The introduction of power-driven machinery brought the factory system into operation. This system, in turn, called for division of labor and the concentration of multitudes of workers in industrial areas. As techniques and methods of agricultural production improved, requiring the use of more and more mechanical equipment from the factories, fewer farm workers were required to produce the food needed by the urban population. As a result, the farm population were encouraged to migrate to industrial regions where they could find employment and the supposed advantages of city life. Urban areas have thus become the workshop of the country as well as the home of the majority of the people.

The foregoing facts indicate that the old-fashioned community with its patterns of intimate personal association has now been displaced, to a great degree, by large towns and cities with their impersonal modes of life. Except for a comparatively small number of communities, especially those in remote regions where the railways and highways have not penetrated, the molding and integrating influence of the old-fash-

---

[3] National Resources Committee, Supplementary Report of the Urbanism Committee, *Urban Government,* Vol. 1, p. 6. J. Frederic Dewhurst and Associates, *America's Needs and Resources,* p. 40.

[4] J. Frederic Dewhurst and Associates, *America's Needs and Resources: A New Survey,* p. 952.

[5] *Ibid.,* pp. 72–73.

ioned community has largely disappeared. In its place have emerged the bewildering complexities of large communities and cities and the specialized influence of organized groups, so prevalent in the structure of American society today.

In urban centers the incidence of crime, suicide, and mental breakdown tends to involve a larger proportion of the population than it does in rural areas. But these social and personal disorders are not attributable to the mere size of urban communities. On the whole, current sociological theory tends to explain these disorders in terms of the disorganization of life in urban communities. With the growth of urbanism has come a breakdown of primary group relationships. Social consensus, one of the primary sources of personal stability, has deteriorated to the point where the individual is more or less socially isolated. The controlling influence of face-to-face relationships in small intimate group life has all but disappeared. Under these conditions the individual shares less and less in a community of feeling and tradition and in common beliefs and interests. The patterns of custom and tradition are no longer present; or, if they persist, they are too obscure to afford a clear path of conduct. Hence the individual tends to become a law unto himself, except for his occupational life, and to exercise narrow, selfish judgment under the influence of unbridled impulse.

With the growth of urbanism the life of the individual becomes less and less shaped by the total community and more and more molded by his occupation and other specialized activities. If the daily routine of an individual were surveyed, it would be found that from morning till night he is involved in the joint activities of some commercial or industrial enterprise, or of a hospital, school, relief association, political association, or the like. In each of these enterprises or associations would be found a set of by-laws, either written or understood, a set of techniques or skills, and a pattern or routine for regulating and carrying on the activities of those who are thus associated. His daily experiences in such a scheme leave their mark upon the individual. They build a narrow vocational outlook, which enhances the vocational efficiency of the individual but at the same time robs him of the breadth of character and insight required by the interdependence of his specialized world.

Moreover, the personnel of each enterprise or association would be found to be organized into some sort of working relationship. There would be division of labor with individuals ordered into some kind of hierarchy. There would be privileges and responsibilities associated with each position in the hierarchy. Each individual's picture of society would thus be shaped not only by his occupation but also by his particular position in the institutional pattern. Thus it is that the interests and points of view of the workers of an industry or business are, as a rule, considerably different from those of the officers, managers, and supervisors. This difference is seen in the fact that laborers and managers of industry, or the teachers and administrators of a school system, do not always see eye-to-eye on important issues regarding the way their respective activities are to be managed. After allowing for conspicuous exceptions, divisions of public opinion often run not only along occupational lines—as when we speak of the farm bloc and the oil bloc —but also along the lines of relationships to institutional structure— as when we speak of industrial interests as against those of labor, even though industrial leaders and laborers are both in the same industry.

People have been brought closer and closer together, geographically and mechanically, by the conquest of space and the creation of mechanical interdependence through minute division of labor. At the same time, however, specialization has divided people with respect to their mental outlooks—their moral ideas, knowledges, skills, tastes. What an individual believes is right and wrong, good and bad, correct and incorrect, goes back to his experience, his experience to his activity, and his activity to his specialized labor. Hence each individual carries around in his head a specialized picture of society, representing but a fragment of the total social pattern.

No one has expressed more powerfully the influence of occupations upon men than Thomas Wolfe in the following account of the social insight of George Webber.[6]

As George observed the signs that betrayed what Bendien was beyond any mistaking, he felt confirmed in an opinion that had been growing on him of late. He had begun to see that the true races of mankind are not at all what we are told in youth that they are. They are not defined either by

[6] Thomas Wolfe, *You Can't Go Home Again* (New York: Harper & Brothers. Copyright 1940 by Maxwell Perkins, as Executor), pp. 553–555.

national frontiers or by the characteristics assigned to them by the subtle investigations of anthropologists. More and more George was coming to believe that the real divisions of humanity cut across these barriers and arise out of differences in the very souls of men.

George had first had his attention called to the phenomenon by an observation of H. L. Mencken. In his extraordinary work on the American language, Mencken gave an example of the American sporting writers' jargon —"Babe Smacks Forty-second with Bases Loaded"—and pointed out that such a headline would be as completely meaningless to an Oxford don as the dialect of some newly discovered tribe of Eskimos. True enough; but what shocked George to attention when he read it was that Mencken drew the wrong inference from his fact. The headline would be meaningless to the Oxford don, not because it was written in the American language, but because the Oxford don had no knowledge of baseball. The same headline might be just as meaningless to a Harvard professor, and for the same reason.

It seemed to George that the Oxford don and the Harvard professor had far more kinship with each other—a far greater understanding of each other's ways of thinking, feeling, and living—than either would have with millions of people of his own nationality. This observation led George to realize that academic life has created its own race of men who are set apart from the rest of humanity by the affinity of their souls. This academic race, it seemed to him, had innumerable peculiar characteristics of its own, among them the fact that, like the sporting gentry, they had invented their own private languages for communication with one another. The internationalism of science was another characteristic: there is no such thing as English chemistry or American physics or (Stalin to the contrary notwithstanding) Russian biology, but only chemistry, physics, and biology. So, too, it follows that one tells a good deal more about a man when one says he is a chemist than when one says he is an Englishman.

In the same way, Babe Ruth would probably feel more closely akin to the English professional cricketer, Jack Hobbs, than to a professor of Greek at Princeton. This would be true also among prize fighters. George thought of that whole world that is so complete within itself—the fighters, the trainers, the managers, the promoters, the touts, the pimps, the gamblers, the grafters, the hangers-on, the newspaper "experts" in New York, London, Paris, Berlin, Rome, and Buenos Aires. These men were not really Americans, Englishmen, Frenchmen, Germans, Italians, and Argentines. They were simply citizens of the world of prize-fighting, more at home with one another than with other men of their respective nations.

While this picture may be somewhat overdrawn, it is certainly true that kinship among members of the same occupational group is one of the chief forces now molding the character of men in modern society.

Social Action Influenced by Special-Interest Groups

Social action is now attained, for the most part, through the play of powerful groups organized around specialized occupational interests. Nowadays an individual is a member of one or more organizations such as a labor union, chamber of commerce, manufacturer's association, farm bureau, farmer's union, business or professional organization, and so on *ad infinitum*. If he wants to attain some social, economic, or political objective, he works through these organizations. Seldom does he depend chiefly upon the sentiment of a local community to bring about the action he desires. To put the same thought in another way, the industrial, trade, professional, and wage-earning interests are usually more important in bringing about social action than are local community interests.

Yet these occupational interests per se have no representation in the government of the community, state, or nation. Partly because of this fact and partly because of the absence of a common social faith strong enough to keep them in harmonious working relationships, these groups, especially those of business, labor, and agriculture, are constantly in conflict and in a struggle for power and special privilege. The elected representatives of the people are thus harassed by powerful pressure groups. The issue of special interests versus the general welfare becomes a matter of grave concern.

One measure of the influence of these groups is the size of some of the more important ones in business, agriculture, and labor. The business community carries on its public activities chiefly through three large associations. The first of these is a loosely bound number of "trade associations." A trade association is a voluntary organization of enterprises engaged in the same kind of business or industry. For example, such an association may consist of individuals or corporations engaged in the fishing industry or in wholesale trade. In 1938 there were approximately 1,500 of these associations operating at the national and regional levels. In addition, there were about 6,500 local or state associations. These organizations primarily serve to assist in the development of uniform policies within a variety of industries, to distribute information among their members, to mold public opinion favorably to business and to exercise pressure upon the government at points where social and economic policies are being shaped.[7]

Another of these huge business organizations is the United States Chamber of Commerce. With its headquarters located in Washington, as in the case of many other organizations, it claims to represent the interest of business in general. Through its affiliated units located throughout the nation in almost every important city and state, as well as through its national office, this organization wields great influence in business, government, and the formation of public opinion. In 1938, it had about 1,100 affiliated chambers and more than 9,000 individual and firm memberships. Its annual income from membership alone has been estimated to be over $1,000,000. Writing in 1941, D. C. Blaisdell depicted its power in American life in the following passage:

From its national headquarters across Lafayette Square from the White House emanate the opinions constituting the voice of the nation's business. The desire of the Senator to know the thoughts of business would now be fully satisfied. Not only Congress, but also the President and his Cabinet, bureau chiefs, and heads of the independent agencies, are thus informed of collective business opinion. Federated in the chamber are fifteen hundred commercial organizations and trade associations, including as members more than seven thousand of the most important corporations, firms, and individuals of the country. Representing such a constituency, and having under its direction in Washington a competent staff experienced in all phases of business activity, the chamber is indeed in a strategic position to dispense its product—"service to American business." [8]

The National Association of Manufacturers represents industrial corporations, but it also speaks for business in general. In 1949 it included approximately 16,000 individual and firm members. Through the National Industrial Council, which comprises trade associations and local

[7] For an extended report on the number, function, and activities of these associations, see Temporary National Economic Committee, *Trade Association Survey. Investigation of Concentration of Economic Power.* Monograph No. 18.

[8] Temporary National Economic Committee. *Economic Power and Political Pressure. Investigation of Concentration of Economic Power.* Monograph No. 26. (Washington, D.C.: U. S. Government Printing Office, 1941), p. 26.

units in various states and cities, it is believed that the National Association of Manufacturers reaches at least 30,000 corporations. Its annual revenue is estimated to be over $1,000,000. The activities of this association have been varied, concerned for the most part with crucial aspects of American life. It has attempted to influence the social and economic point of view of the school through the publications of the association and through investigations of textbooks with respect to the character of their social and political content.[9] Its lobbying activities in the nation's capital were the object of congressional investigation as early as 1913. As a rule, it has stood for high tariffs, low taxes, and a balanced federal budget. Its opposition to the activities of labor unions has been long and persistent.

Turning to agriculture, the interests of farmers are represented by three large associations—the Grange, the Farmers Union, and the Farm Bureau Federation. The Grange, organized in 1867, today claims a membership of about 870,000. In its early years it worked for state regulation of railroads and helped to create the Interstate Commerce Commission. It has continued to exercise leadership and influence at the local level, but in recent years has played a decreasing role in national affairs. The Farmers Union is a relatively new organization, born in the depression years and now consisting of about 100,000 members. It has been concerned with such purposes as the improvement of the welfare of the sharecropper and the perpetuation of the Farm Security Administration, which provided federal assistance to the low-income farmer. It is not unfriendly to organized labor and on occasions has cooperated with it. From the standpoint of political pressure the Farm Bureau Federation is the most powerful of all the farm organizations. It claims a membership of almost 1,600,000 and chiefly represents the large farming interests and the more well-to-do farmer.

The role of labor as a power group is perhaps much better known to the general public than that of any other group in American society. This is because the actions of labor are more broadly circulated by the news-covering agencies than are those of any other group. The principal labor organization is the American Federation of Labor. In addition, there are several independent unions, such as the Railroad Broth-

---

[9] Temporary National Economic Committee, *Economic Power and Political Pressures*, p. 20.

erhoods, International Association of Machinists, and the National Federation of Telephone Workers. The Congress of Industrial Organizations was organized in 1935, by a group within the American Federation of Labor, to represent the unskilled and semi-skilled workers of mass-production industries such as steel, rubber, and automobiles. The actions of the Committee for Industrial Organization, as the group called themselves, were not acceptable to the leadership of the American Federation of Labor, and the following year all C.I.O. unions were expelled from the American Federation of Labor. Thus the labor movement was split. But in 1955 the American Federation of Labor and the Congress of Industrial Organization merged. In that year there were approximately 17,500,000 trade union members in the United States. About 2,500,000 of these were in independent unions, and the remainder were in unions affiliated with the new A.F.L.–C.I.O.

These big organizations of workers influence their members through local unions, which hold periodic meetings where not only immediate problems of labor but also broad economic and social issues are sometimes explored. The American Federation of Labor alone claims some 35,000 local unions. Furthermore, the membership is influenced through labor newspapers, pamphlets, comic books, and film strips, all of which deal with crucial social issues and labor problems, policies, and programs. In addition, unions, like business and agricultural organizations, exercise pressure upon government officials, especially at points where the interests of labor are at stake.

To these few large interest groups could be added scores of others, such as the American Medical Association, the National Education Association, the American Bar Association, and the American Bankers Association. Each of these has its own special interest to promote. It should be recognized, however, that the officers of these organizations, with perhaps few exceptions, believe themselves to be serving the interest of the public as they promote the aims of their particular organization. This is true because they tend to identify their group interests with the good of the country as a whole. When teachers, for example, exercise pressure through their organizations to secure more financial support for the schools, they do so on the theory that this action will build better schools and that better schools are for the good of the people. In a similar way the laborer, banker, farmer, industrialist, or professional man often believes that the efforts of his organization are in the interest of the general welfare. That this belief is frequently false does not invalidate the good intentions of any of these men. It only indicates the degree to which the common life of the people, as expressed in common ends and opinions, has been fragmented under the impact of the tremendous social forces of the modern world.

3. *Social Stratification of Communities*

Next to the effect of the general cultural pattern upon the individual, perhaps the most important influence upon him is the concrete social position he occupies in the community. The behavior of the child as well as that of the adult is shaped in large measure by the fact that those with whom they are associated most intimately belong to a particular social class.

The term *social class,* as used here, refers to different levels of social stratification as determined by the way members of a community rank one another. It has no reference to class consciousness nor to meanings associated with the expression "class struggle." Sometimes individuals recognize that they belong to the "upper crust," or to the "substantial people," or to the "under dogs"; but such awareness is not essential to the meaning of "social class," as used here. Furthermore, social class is to be distinguished from social caste. A caste emerges when a class system becomes so rigid that movement of individuals from one class to another is practically impossible. If a group of individuals becomes aware of itself as having a common descent and other characteristics which it believes to be superior to other classes, the group tends to set itself apart and to deny members of other social classes the privilege of joining it. When the boundaries surrounding such a social group become impenetrable, a caste emerges. The separation of Negroes and Whites in American society illustrates a caste system. Within each of these castes, however, there are different social strata corresponding to social classes.

With few exceptions members of American society have never subscribed to a class system. Many of them came to the New World to escape the class system under which they had lived. Moreover, the conditions of economic equality which prevail on the frontiers were conducive to a general feeling of social equality. Although such equality was an ideal seldom attained completely in any community, it was more nearly a reality among frontier people than later generations sometimes suppose. It is not surprising to find one impartial observer after another during the last century testifying to the relatively minor amount, if not complete absence, of class distinctions in American society. Writing in 1840 of life in a New England township, de Tocqueville observed:

> Every individual is always supposed to be as well informed, as virtuous, and as strong as any of his fellow citizens. He obeys society, not because he is inferior to those who conduct it or because he is less capable than any other of governing himself, but because he acknowledges the utility of an association with his fellowmen and he knows that no such association can exist without a regulating force. He is a subject in all that concerns the duties of citizens to each other; he is free, and responsible to God alone, for all that concerns himself.[10]

Almost a half century later, Lord James Bryce could still write that, "In the United States, public opinion is the opinion of the whole nation, with little distinction of social classes." [11] Perhaps the ideal of a society without social distinctions and the degree of its attainment in America has not been better stated than in the following passage from James Truslow Adams:

> The American dream that has lured tens of millions of all nations to our shores in the past century has not been a dream of merely material plenty, though that has doubtless counted heavily. It has been much more than that. It has been a dream of being able to grow to fullest development as man and woman, unhampered by the barriers which had slowly been erected in older civilizations, unrepressed by social orders which had developed for the benefit of classes rather than for the simple human being of any and every class. And that dream has been realized more fully in actual life here than anywhere else, though very imperfectly even among ourselves.[12]

[10] Alexis de Tocqueville, *Democracy in America* (New York: Alfred A. Knopf; 1945), Vol. I, p. 64.
[11] James Bryce, *The American Commonwealth* (New York: The Macmillan Co.; 1893), Vol. II, pp. 272–273.
[12] James Truslow Adams, *The Epic of America* (Boston: Little, Brown & Co. and The Atlantic Monthly Press; 1931), p. 405. By permission.

A long tradition of social equality based upon a value system which outlaws social classes makes it difficult for the average American to accept the fact of social classes in his society. He is prone to deny their existence, especially in his own community. When faced by questions about the existence of social classes in Middletown, "Business people," according to Robert and Helen Lynd, "seemed uneasy in the face of such a question, and one got a distinct impression that they do not like to think of 'classes' and feel happier in ignoring the possibility of their existence." [13]

Evidence of a Class System

But despite testimony to the contrary, social classes have long existed to some extent in American society. This fact has been substantiated by outstanding historians. They have found evidence of social classes in colonial times, in the constitutional convention, and in the political conflicts of the first half of the nineteenth century.[14] In addition, sociological investigations during the last two decades have confirmed the existence of a class structure in American society. If the existence of such a structure has not been established beyond reasonable doubt, at least the accumulation of evidence has now reached the point that the burden of proof falls upon him who doubts the presence of social classes.

Sociologists and anthropologists who have studied social classes in the United States have not based their investigations upon a rigidly defined concept of class at the outset. Instead they have approached the question empirically, preferring to let the extent and character of social stratification emerge from the facts disclosed by inquiry. In most of the studies, social classes were determined by the way in which members of a community classified one another in conversation with a research worker who had first established rapport in the community. In a number of reports of these investigations, the classes are designated by the terms *upper, middle,* and *lower.* Each of these classes is sometimes further divided into two sub-strata: upper upper, lower upper, upper middle, lower middle, upper lower, and lower lower. People do not ordinarily use these terms, however, in indicating their own rank nor that

[13] Robert S. Lynd and Helen Lynd, *Middletown in Transition* (New York: Harcourt, Brace & Co.; 1937), p. 444. By permission.
[14] Charles A. Beard, and Mary R. Beard, *The Rise of American Civilization.* Arthur M. Schlesinger, Jr., *The Age of Jackson.*

of others. The term *middle class* evokes more favorable social attitudes and, hence, is more often used in ordinary parlance. In interviews, however, a person is more apt to speak of another individual or family in such words as "our kind of folks," "people like us," "po'whites," "we poor folks," "society folks," and the like, depending upon his own position in the social scale.

The way the people of a community think about the various classes in their locality is illustrated in the following quotation from a study of the caste and class system of a southern community:

As one becomes acquainted with the white people of Old City, he soon realizes that they are continually classifying themselves and others. There are "Negroes" and "Whites"—the caste groups—a relatively simple dichotomy. There are also "leading families," "the four hundred," "the society crowd," "plain people," "nice, respectable people," "good people, but nobody," "po'whites," "red necks," etc.,—all terms used to refer to different groups within the white caste. Not only do the whites frequently refer to these subdivisions within their own caste group, but they do so in such a manner as to indicate that they think in terms of a social hierarchy with some people at the "top," some at the "bottom," with some people "equal" to themselves, and others "above" or "below" them. There are recurrent expressions such as "He isn't our social equal," "She isn't our kind," "They are just nobody," "Those folk are the way-high-ups," "They're nothing but white trash," "Oh, they're plain people like us." These expressions refer not only to individuals but also to groups, so that one may speak of superordinate and subordinate groups within the white society. And, most important of all, people tend to act in conformity with these conceptions of their "place" and the social position of others in the society.[15]

These attitudes toward one another and the group to which each belongs appear to hold good whether the community is located in New England, the Middle West, the South, or any other part of the nation. The social distinctions reported by these sociological studies are therefore those which prevail in the communities themselves. The term *class,* as used in these investigations, refers to a group of people—upper, middle, or lower class—who have been classified by members of the community as belonging to a superior or inferior social position, according to whatever factors were operating in the minds of the community members at the time.

[15] From *Readings in Social Psychology,* edited by Theodore M. Newcomb and Eugene L. Hartley. Copyright 1947 by Henry Holt and Company, Inc., pp. 467–468.

The investigation reported in *Deep South* confirmed the existence of a definite class structure in a southern community.[16] This structure exhibited six strata beginning with the upper upper class and ending with the lower lower class. All classes, except the lower ones, were in agreement as to what the various classes were. The lower classes tended to lump the upper middle and the upper upper and lower upper classes together into one group referred to as "society" or "the folks with money." In other words, their perception of classes is not as finely developed as that of the classes above them. Class feeling toward other strata, however, differs from class to class. In general, the stratum just above a particular class is resented by the class. The people of the lower lower class feel that they are "just as good as anybody," while the upper lower class in their view consists of "snobs trying to push up." The upper lower class feels that the people of the lower middle class are "people who are up because they have a little money." The lower middle class thinks that the upper middle stratum is composed of "people who think they are somebody." And so it goes, although the resentment is reduced toward the upper end of the social scale. The lower upper group, for example, only reluctantly expresses antagonism toward the class above it.

The more extensive study by Warner and Lunt supplies additional evidence of a class system.[17] This study made an intensive investigation of "Yankee City," a New England town, with respect to the existence of classes and their relation to all the various aspects of the individual's life—his schooling, economic status, choice of reading materials, movies, recreation, geographic location in the community, and so on. This investigation also ascertained six different social strata ranging from the lower lower to the upper upper class.

The class system is not limited to those sections of the country that have been settled the longest or that were least affected by the equalitarian influences of the frontier conditions. This is clearly demonstrated in *Plainville, U.S.A.*, a study of the class structure in a mid-west community. From this study it is clearly evident that a system of social groups ranked in order of superiority-inferiority exists in this small Missouri village. Yet the people of Plainville tend to deny the existence of

[16] Allison Davis, Burleigh Gardner, and Mary R. Gardner, *Deep South*.
[17] W. Lloyd Warner and Paul S. Lunt, *The Social Life of a Modern Community*.

social classes in their community. "They are aware that class distinctions exist 'outside,' " especially in cities. About Plainville they often
say with some pride, "This is *one* place where ever' body is equal. You
don't find no classes here." [18] Despite these protests and denials, the
citizens of Plainville do carry around in their heads a classification of
persons into various social strata. There are, for example, the prairie
people who are for the most part the "better" people and are composed
of a small "upper crust" and a large group of "honest, hard-working
people." The hill people, on the other hand, consist of the "good lower
class people" and a few at the very bottom "who live like animals."
There are, of course, other factors besides the mere location in which a
person lives that enter into the determination of the social class to
which one belongs. Among these are wealth, family history, manners,
and the methods of farming—whether a man uses technological developments or follows old practices.

In this connection it is interesting to note that awareness of social
class is found in school children. [19] They become conscious of class distinctions between the fourth and sixth grades. In these grades children
pick out, with considerable accuracy, those boys and girls who "do not
have much money." They base their judgment upon the clothes of their
classmates and what they bring to school. But they do not choose their
friends by reference to class status. Between grades six and eight children come to distinguish more sharply between middle-class and work-
ing-class children. And they begin to choose friends largely from among
members of their own class groups.

Effects of Social Stratification

If social stratification represented merely a convenient way of grouping people in a community, it would be of little significance in curriculum development. Unfortunately such stratification has far-reaching
social consequences as well as effects upon the personality of individuals. The fact that a class system is inconsistent with the democratic
ideal of equality is so obvious as to need no elaboration. Of course, under favorable circumstances, a democratic society can get along with

[18] James West, *Plainville, U.S.A.* (New York: Columbia University Press; 1945).
[19] Celia Burns Stendler, *Children of Brasstown.* See also Hollingshead, *Elmtown's
Youth.*

social classes as long as there is a large measure of mobility from class to class. But this admission does not remove the fact that social class and democratic ideals are logically incompatible. Nor does it obviate the fact that, in periods of social confusion, the existence of strong class barriers may prove to be a millstone around the neck of a democratic people.

The character of an individual, including such elements as his beliefs, ideals, ways of thinking, and social outlook, is shaped by many different forces. Some of the more important of these forces are those associated with the social position the individual occupies in the community. His social position determines in large measure who his associates and friends will be, the kind of job he will hold, where he will live in the community, the kind of family into which he will marry, and other important aspects of his life too numerous to mention. Each of these has deep influence upon the individual's beliefs, aspirations, loyalties, and the way he perceives the social events that occur about him.

Moreover, the class into which a child is born determines how he will be reared.[20] Middle-class children are more closely controlled in all their activities than are lower-class children. They have less time to use as they please than the children of the lower class. Since the middle class believes in individual initiative and in the sanctity of property, this class teaches its children to respect property and to be on the watch for opportunities to gain social recognition and financial advantages. The middle class also emphasizes respect for law and order, bodily cleanliness, and success in school. In contrast, the lower class makes fewer demands upon its children. Its children are permitted a larger measure of independence than are middle-class children. They can stay out later at night, go to the movies alone earlier, and work for a wage much earlier than children of the middle class. Much less emphasis is placed upon respect for property and for law and order. Nor does the lower class stimulate its children to such high ambitions as does the middle class.

It seems clear from the foregoing observations that each social class tends to create personality patterns peculiar to itself. In addition to the

[20] Newcomb and Hartley, *Readings in Social Psychology,* pp. 494–501. Allison Davis, and Robert J. Havighurst, *Father of the Man.* W. Lloyd Warner; Robert J. Havighurst; and Martin B. Loeb, *Who Shall Be Educated?*

basic elements of the general pattern of culture, each individual takes on comparable elements of the special pattern of culture characterizing his social class. He tends to see the world from the standpoint of his class—to think those things are real that are honored by those who are in the same social stratum as himself, to judge himself and others by standards accepted by his peers, and to identify himself with those "causes" with which his social class is identified. He accepts and does those things, not because he recognizes them as belonging to the perspective of his social class—for he is usually unaware of their class identification—but rather because he believes these things are both right and important for all persons. Only when a group becomes *class conscious* does it think and plan deliberately in terms of class interests. To sum up the matter, each social class generates a particular social outlook imbibed by every individual born into it.

The presence of social classes is an indication of a measure of social disunity. For if each class has a social orientation of its own, the community will suffer a division of perspectives to the degree that it is marked by class divisions. Then, as members of the various classes become aware of the outlooks and expectations of persons in other social strata, they tend to become confused and uncertain of their own basic beliefs and loyalties. While there is still a measure of unity in American communities, it is important to remember that the erosion of this unity will increase with the growth in class consciousness and in the rigidity of the boundaries between classes. "From shirt sleeves to shirt sleeves in three generations" has long been an American slogan. While this slogan does not deny the existence of social levels, it at least implies that they should not be based upon the fortunes of birth.

4. *Changes in Family Life*

The same forces that have brought about a decline in the local community and its role in the development of individuals have also brought about a decline in the influence of the family as a social unit. Historically the family is based principally upon the requirements of reproduction and the care of the young. While these are constant functions of the family—that is, they are found in the families of all cultures—

the pattern of family life is always shaped by the total cultural pattern. The place of the woman in the family, the way the children are treated, and a hundred other characteristics of family life in a particular time and place go back to the spirit, ideals, and behavior patterns of the culture. For example, in a society characterized by stern social discipline, it is to be expected that the family will exercise rigorous, if not harsh, control over its members. Because of the dependence of the family upon cultural circumstances, it is to be expected that as society is modified the family will sooner or later come in for its share of changes.

In nontechnological societies, and even yet in the rural sections of the United States, the family is both a producing and a consuming unit. The home, the work, and even much of the social life are centered in one place. This is clearly illustrated in the family life of the pre-technological period. Manufacturing was carried on largely in the household, where a master and a journeyman and one or two apprentices constituted the workers. In some instances, as in the case of a nail manufacturer, soap boiler, potter, or small master weaver, the producer would own a small farm and divide his time between the soil and the industry. Under this domestic system the family was a self-contained unit, in that it produced most, if not all, of what was needed for its own use in addition to producing for the market.

Even more important from a social and educational standpoint is the fact that the members of the family were intimately associated. The occupational activities of the father were understood and appreciated by the entire family. The activities of the mother were likewise recognized and valued. Moreover, many activities and responsibilities were shared by the children, so that some of the most basic elements of character were implanted by associations in this primary social unit. Each family built common ideals, sentiments, and patterns of behavior into its members; for each one shared in common economic and social activities. These ideals and sentiments were in turn reinforced by the community life of the village or small town. With slight modifications this condition is still found in the rural sections of the nation. To be sure, the radio, automobile, telephone, and other mechanical conveniences have had their impact on the rural family. Nevertheless, the basic attitudes and points of view shaped by the direct relation of the family to the means of production are still present, even if somewhat eroded.

Family Functions Have Been Reduced

Beginning first in the cotton goods industry, groups of workers or "mill hands" were collected around factories which merged with or gave rise to urban centers. The laborer was taken out of the home and located in great manufacturing establishments. This movement from the home to the factory came quickly, almost within the span of the forty years from 1760 to 1800. As long as the great bulk of the population still lived on the farm, as was the case in the United States until about the turn of the nineteenth century, the family was still largely untouched by the disturbances accompanying this shift of the laborer from the home to the factory. With the growth of great cities which drew their sustenance from mechanized industry and commerce, large numbers of families began to feel tensions and conflicts. Today over 63 per cent of the population lives in urban territory, and it is reasonable to suppose that more than half of the families of the nation are subject to the disrupting influence of technological developments and their principal concomitants—collectivization and urbanization.

The urban family presents a very different picture from the rural household. Here the work is no longer done in common. The family loses its producing function and becomes mostly, if not entirely, a consuming unit. The work of the father is done away from home, and that of the mother—unless, as is increasingly the case, she is also employed outside the home—is confined largely to keeping the house and preparing meals. The children have few, if any, responsibilities except for assisting the mother in her work. With modern food packing, domestic conveniences, and laborsaving devices this responsibility is reduced in many families almost to the vanishing point.

Loss of the Family's Capacity to Build a Common Social Perspective

The activities of the family are thus specialized and divested of their common meaning.[21] The father leaves home early in the morning to work in an office or factory, or in some other type of occupation. He returns in the evening, often tired and irritated from the troubles of the

[21] For an excellent discussion of this point, see Robert Cooley Angell, *Integration of American Society*, pp. 135–149.

day's work. The members of the family, especially the children, know little or nothing about his occupational life. It is not unusual for children to have no understanding of the occupational activities of their father until they are well into the adolescent period, or even much older. The reality of his job is found in the money that enables the family to survive. The children, relieved of home chores and finding little opportunity in crowded city blocks for leisure activities, seek outlets in playgrounds, clubs, amusement parks, skating rinks, moving pictures, dance halls, and street loafing. In some instances the mother is gainfully employed and hence away from home during a large part of the day. In 1900 there were 7,200,000 women gainfully employed, including 6 per cent of the total number of married women. By 1953 this figure had increased to 19,000,000 women, with 25 per cent of the married women of the nation gainfully employed.[22]

About the only time when the whole family has an opportunity to get together as a group and to exchange the experiences of the day is at the evening meal. This gathering, however, is often marred by the disappointments and irritations brought over from the activities of the day or by the pressure of activities anticipated for the evening by either the children or the parents. The integration of the family, already strained to the limit by the forces of urban life, thus tends to be neglected—the father going his way, the mother going her way, and the children pursuing diverse courses. The family ties are weakened and the molding influence of the family upon the young tends to decline.

Since each member of the urban family is related differently to the means by which the family maintains its existence, the differentiation of interests among the members increases. Their activities become more diverse; hence their experiences and points of view become more and more heterogeneous. In contrast to the rural family, the city family is apt to have fewer and fewer common values, common experiences, and common points of view, so that its chief cementing force tends to be economic pressure and a few social sanctions. Thus the capacity of the family to build a common outlook in the members of society has been considerably reduced.

Another result of these changes in the pattern of family life is the

[22] J. Frederic Dewhurst and Associates, *America's Needs and Resources: A New Survey*, pp. 244, 726.

almost complete isolation of children from the world of adults. Perhaps no other people in recorded history has forced its children and youth to live in a culture of their own making so completely as have the people of modern industrial nations. The rise of youth organizations is mute testimony to the fact that the immature members of society have been sealed off in a world of their own. The emergence of the factory destroyed the apprenticeship system and, by robbing the work of children of its educational value, converted their occupational activities into child labor. The further divesting of the home of opportunities for responsible work experience has served to drive children and youth almost completely into child or adolescent cultures. Consequently their experiences are robbed of the content so necessary for effective participation of youth in the primary task of this century—the task of cultural reintegration.

5. Changes in Occupations and Employment

Prior to the rise and development of modern industry and the factory system, men were for the most part self-employed. This kind of employment rapidly declined during the nineteenth century; and, except for small businesses, professional workers, and farmers, most gainfully occupied people today are employed by others. They are wage earners who depend upon a regular cash income for their livelihood. Sudden and sweeping changes in industry and commerce may thus have direct and far-reaching effects upon the life-plans of the worker.

Technological Developments and Shifting of Workers

Technical changes may influence employment in several ways. They may bring about a permanent reduction of the number of workers required in certain occupations and increases in others. They may also produce temporary displacement of workers. The first of these is illustrated in the changes that have occurred in the number of workers in agriculture since 1870. In that year over half of the gainfully employed persons of the country were in this occupational group. The improvement of farm machinery and the opening up of new opportunities in the cities have jointly brought about a consistent decline in the per cent of workers employed in agriculture. By 1890 the per cent engaged in this occupation had declined from 50.3 to 42.4 of those gainfully employed. By 1910 there were only 31.4 per cent so engaged, and by 1930 this number was further reduced to 21.5 per cent.[23] During the 1930's there was a slight increase in the per cent of farm workers due to widespread unemployment in the cities and to low-cost housing and food on the farms. After 1940, however, the trend was again reversed; in 1950 only 11.9 per cent of the labor force was engaged in agriculture.[24]

Moreover, in the seventy years from 1870 to 1940, over one-fourth of the active labor force of the country shifted from the production of physical goods, including agriculture, mining, manufacturing, and construction, to other activities such as transportation, trade, and clerical work. In 1870 approximately 75 per cent of the active labor force of the country was engaged in the production of physical goods. By 1950 only 46 per cent of the workers were so occupied.[25] This sweeping reduction of the number of workers in agriculture, mining, and industry has been accompanied by increased production of physical goods due to scientific and technological developments. At the same time markets have expanded and the general level of consumption has increased, leading to increased job opportunities in wholesale and retail trades and in transportation and communication services to handle the distribution of goods. These new jobs in turn have required sharp increases in clerical and selling occupations. In 1870, trade, transportation, and clerical occupations engaged 10.8 per cent of those gainfully employed. By 1950 these same occupations were engaging over 34 per cent of those gainfully occupied. From these facts it is clear that, although technological achievements may and frequently do result in unemployment, they create jobs as well as take them away. Occupations and even entire industries have been eliminated by engineering achievements, but these same achievements have frequently created new jobs in services, trades, industries, and so on.

[23] J. Frederic Dewhurst and Associates, *America's Needs and Resources: A New Survey*, p. 732.
[24] *Ibid.*, p. 732.
[25] *Ibid.*, p. 733.

Technological Developments Displace Workers

The displacement of workers is one of the tragic results of technological developments. By better management and more efficient machines, technological innovations may displace workers directly, or they may displace them indirectly in ways too numerous to mention here. For an example of direct displacement, the development of a higher quality of steel for machine tools made it possible to operate machines at a higher speed and reduced the amount of sharpening ordinarily required. The result was a reduction of the labor needs of the industries using these tools.[26]

A displaced worker does not easily find re-employment. If he is fortunate, he may find a job in the occupation for which he is trained and at a wage equal to that of his former job. The fortunate individual is, unhappily, the exception. The more likely outcome is weeks and months of job-hunting and finally employment at a lower wage and in a less promising position.

It is difficult to secure accurate data regarding the causes of unemployment. Many factors are operating, and it is difficult to separate the displacements due to technological developments and increased efficiency of management from those due to other causes. For whatever cause the worker is displaced, he seldom finds it easy to secure re-employment. A study of rubber workers in 1930 in New Haven and Hartford showed that of 1,190 individuals the average loss of time due to displacement was 4.3 months. Only 19 per cent were able to find work that paid as well as their former jobs. Another investigation showed that in the prosperous years from 1919 to 1926 the average loss of time of 370 displaced men's-clothing cutters in Chicago was 5.6 months. Thirty per cent of those re-employed secured work at increased wages, while approximately half were re-employed at reduced incomes.[27] Other studies further substantiate the difficulties the displaced worker encounters in his search for re-employment.

[26] For a review of the research on the effects of these displacements, see National Resources Committee, *Technological Trends and National Policy,* Report of the Subcommittee on Technology, pp. 79–81.

[27] *Ibid.,* pp. 83–84.

Flexibility of Skills Required in the Modern Industrial System

With dislocation of workers due to sweeping industrial changes, or with displacements due to technological innovations in specific industries or establishments, the significance for the worker is apt to be the same in many instances—namely, "skill obsolescence." The rise and fall of industries and occupations places upon the worker a tremendous burden of uncertainty, readjustment, and re-education. When an industry is completely eliminated, when a new process of making a product is employed, or when engineering achievements replace old machines, the worker who is thereby displaced is called upon to develop new skills if he is to find employment. Moreover, the introduction of laborsaving devices such as calculating machines, dictaphones, bookkeeping machines, and the like, requires new skills and techniques among office workers. In the modern industrial system the worker is called upon to maintain a higher degree of flexibility in the skills by which he earns a living than in any other period of recorded history.

6. What These Changes Mean for Curriculum Development

The dissolution of the old-fashioned community, the decline in influence of the family unit, the reduced influence of face-to-face relationships, the rise of huge social organizations, and the increasing instability of occupations and employment are some of the more important consequences of the scientific and technological revolution. What do these changes mean for curriculum development?

Need for a New Common Sense

In a period of gradual change the common sense of the people is sufficient to deal with the problems that arise. In simple community life, problems involve face-to-face relations and can be handled in terms of the common experience of the group and the mature judgment of the older members of the community. But the cultural changes described above have rendered the old common sense inadequate for the resolution of issues that now divide the people. This common sense is still quite satisfactory for dealing with relations among neighbors. Yet it is wholly unsatisfactory for dealing with relations between individuals and huge social organizations such as corporate enterprises and those of businessmen, laborers, farmers, and professional people. If a person attempts to deal with these giant social units on the basis of the same attitudes and ideas that guide him in more intimate associations, he is soon disillusioned. The social organization operates on the basis of uniform policies shaped largely in terms of what is convenient and desirable from the standpoint of the organization, and not in terms of what is desirable in the life of the small community. These policies, being applicable to all persons alike, disregard individual needs and interests. Moreover, the individual has little or nothing to do with shaping them. To him they represent rigid structures limiting his choices and actions. In dealing with these structures his old common sense does not work — yet he has no new common sense to which to appeal.

It is plain, then, that one of the imperatives of the current phase of cultural development is a new common sense, one that is adequate for a period in which most relationships among people will be those impersonal and remote associations growing out of the interdependent character of society. The new common sense must be broad enough to include rules and ideas for governing relationships between men and organizations, between organizations themselves, and between man and man. What is needed is a set of attitudes and ideas by which to tell what is right and wrong, desirable and undesirable, with respect to the policies and actions of large social groups that have supplanted the old-fashioned community and its simple life of sympathy and intimacy. It is the obligation of those who are responsible for curriculum building to provide opportunities for children, young people, and adults to engage in the common task of rebuilding ideas and attitudes so as to make them valid for the purpose of social judgment and action in a period dominated by a complex web of impersonal social relations.

Need for Realistic Social Understanding

It is equally necessary to the development and maintenance of social sanity for the individual to understand what is happening in the world around him. Only if the individual is aware of what is happening to community life, including the family and occupations, will he be able to deal with the social problems that will certainly confront him. Too many people are now unable to make an accurate social diagnosis of the circumstances in which they find themselves. As a result, they tend to become victims of the realities they are up against, instead of masters of them.

There is nothing mysterious about the social forces now impinging upon men. But the failure of the schools to provide the opportunity for people to face the basic issues of this age and to explore them in the light of accurate facts and dependable values results in individual and group behavior that has little reference to social realities. The things that sometimes occur in the career of the individual—loss of a job, the dissolution of his family, and the like—appear to him to be the result of some mysterious hidden force, or the wicked actions of politicians or some other scapegoat.

Need for Methods and Techniques of Resolving Social Conflicts

With the growth of urbanism, specialization of labor, and organized group interests, society has become more and more divided into conflicting camps. Social issues have not only increased in number but also in depth and severity. With various sides of these issues supported by powerful organized groups, social struggles become more and more threatening to the entire society. The old community was blessed with a common frame of reference, which afforded a measure of certainty and objectivity and supplied the people with a sense of mutual respect and confidence. In sharp contrast, current society presents a spectacle of warring interests and contrasting creeds and points of view. Each party has its own purposes and plans, which it strives to achieve without regard to the points of view and interests of the contending factions. Under these conditions communication tends to break down, and agreement by deliberation and understanding becomes more difficult.

These increasing conflicts growing out of variations of perspectives indicate the importance of stressing effective methods of resolving social issues. In a society devoted to the resolution of differences among men by appeal to reason and fact, rather than by sheer force, it is extremely important that emphasis be placed upon the development of effective group deliberation and action. More opportunity for group thinking and planning is thus an imperative in education today. Such thinking and planning must be directed to the resolution of issues about which the society itself is divided. Only if these issues are given primary attention in the educational program can experience be provided in the kind of thinking this age of conflict demands. Youth and adults alike must learn to think effectively in situations in which they themselves are personally involved. For the issues now dividing the people are those that exhibit large degrees of personal involvement. The curriculum must recognize this fact if it is to be adequate to the social tasks of today.

Need to Eliminate Class Bias from the Curriculum

The disclosure of social strata in community life requires that the teaching profession become aware of its own class bias and the degree to which the educational program has been influenced by class values. The teaching profession has been recruited largely from the lower part of the middle class. Moreover, it seems safe to assume that the professional training of teachers has not been such as to awaken them to the values and perspectives of the various social strata. Partly as a result of this defect in professional training, and partly as a result of the fact that the schools have been oriented historically to the middle and upper classes, the curriculum of the school today is largely designed, even in the more advanced programs, to emphasize middle-class values and modes of conduct. For example, the extracurricular program of most schools, by its very nature, practically rules out individuals of the lower social strata.[28] Moreover, the fact that those who drop out of school come largely from the lower social classes indicates that the holding power of the school is weakest among the lower classes and strongest among the middle and upper classes.[29]

It should not be assumed from what has just been said that the curriculum worker should attempt to make a wholesale repudiation of middle-class values and to replace them indiscriminately with lower-

---

[28] Harold C. Hand, *Principal Findings of the 1947–1948 Basic Studies of the Illinois Secondary School Curriculum Program.*

[29] *Ibid.* See also H. M. Bell, *Youth Tell Their Story;* R. E. Eckert and T. O. Marshall, *When Youth Leave School,* p. 72.

class values. Rather, the need is for careful consideration of the values of all social classes, with a view to discovering those that are most nearly in line with the requirements of the social and psychological realities of modern society and that lead to thorough democratization of every aspect of American life. This approach should be taken with a sympathetic recognition of the biases of the school program, the teaching profession, and the various social classes. It should also include clear understanding of the democratic value system, especially the ideal of equality in its relations to the total system. If this approach is followed—including the qualifications just mentioned—it may be possible to build a curriculum for all the children of all the people that will strengthen and extend democracy in both theory and practice.

In addition, the curriculum must be planned to include a breadth of experience and to develop as high a degree of flexibility as possible. For the average adult must recognize, and adjust himself, not only to a wide variety of circumstances, but also to a world of shifting occupations and employment opportunities.

▶ *Following Up*
  This Chapter

1. Make a study of some community with which you are familiar, indicating the changes in it recognized by individuals who have lived there for most of their lives. Try to find out whether or not the school has recognized these changes in its instructional program.

2. Compare and contrast the old-fashioned rural family with a modern urban family. Which will have the greatest educative effect on its members? Is the difference one of amount or of kind? Both? What does your answer mean for curriculum change?

3. It is sometimes said that in modern industrial society the individual is "lost." In what sense, if at all, is this true? What meaning does your answer to this question have for curriculum development?

4. Make a list of adjustments that you believe the schools have made in recognition of changes in home, community, and occupational life.

5. "There is greater need now than ever for the school to emphasize the development of effective group *deliberation and action*." Do you agree with this statement? Why?

▶ Suggested
Reading

1. One of the most stimulating studies of fundamental changes in American culture is Robert Cooley Angell's *Integration of American Society*. An equally good analysis of American society, although somewhat older, is John Dewey's *The Public and Its Problems*. In the same class are Karl Mannheim's *Diagnosis of Our Time* and his *Man and Society in an Age of Reconstruction*. A more readable book is *Our Changing Civilization: How Science and Technology are Reconstructing Modern Life*, by J. H. Randall, Jr. William O. Stanley's *Education and Social Integration* explores the significance of many of the changes indicated in this chapter. See also Harold Rugg's *Foundations for American Education*, especially Part Three.

2. For studies of changes in urban communities, classic references are still Robert and Helen Lynd's *Middletown* and their *Middletown in Transition*. More recent descriptions are to be found in W. L. Warner's "Yankee City" series, especially Vol. I, Warner and Lunt, *The Social Life of a Modern Community*. In sharp contrast to the studies by the Lynds, the "Yankee City" series emphasizes the existence of a class structure in America. Intensive studies of rural society are reported under the general title, *Culture of a Contemporary Rural Community*, Rural Life Studies, Nos. 1–6.

3. From the standpoint of the relation of the curriculum to social change, the following are especially valuable: Harold Rugg's edited volume "Democracy and the Curriculum," *Third Yearbook* of the John Dewey Society; *Developing a Curriculum for Modern Living*, by Florence B. Stratemeyer, Hamden L. Forkner, Margaret G. McKim, and others; and Theodore Brameld's *Design for America*, a report of an educational experiment using the future as a frame of reference.

4. A storehouse of facts about social change in the United States is, of course, the report of Mr. Hoover's Research Committee on Recent Social Trends, *Recent Social Trends in the United States* (1933). A more recent volume, along somewhat different lines, is *America's Needs and Resources*, by J. Frederic Dewhurst and Associates. See also *The School in the American Social Order*, by N. Edwards and H. G. Richey, Chapters 11 and 15; *Education and American Civilization*, by George S. Counts; *Social Foundations of Education*, by Harold Rugg and William Withers; and *Social Foundations of Education*, by William O. Stanley and others.

Chapter 3

The Value Crisis
and the Curriculum

THE PERVASIVE EFFECTS of science and technology on
the family, on the community, on occupational life, and on the economic system have been described, together with the problems these
effects have created in the realm of curriculum development. These
effects in themselves would produce severe drains on the capacity of a
people to readjust their habits of conduct. But the impact of science and
technology does not end with these alterations. The acids generated
by these twin elements have trickled down into the American system
of values, dissolving fundamental ideals and leaving the entire system
in a state of confusion. The core of universal values, which supplies
the culture with its vitality and stability, has become smaller and
smaller relative to the alternative and the specialized elements. People
are no longer certain about such significant components of their culture as how to rear children, what ends the economic system should
serve, who should control the means of production, how much control
government should exercise over the activities of individuals and groups,
what should be left to local initiative, and what should be the limits
on sovereignty of nations.

The breakdown in the system of values is reflected in uncertainty
about the purposes of formal education and in controversies about the
content and the methods of education. Persistent demands are heard for
more discipline in the fundamental processes, more stress on the intel-

lectual virtues, more attention to vocational training, more time for religious and moral instruction, more emphasis upon the scientific method of thinking, more stress upon social discipline, and more attention to the cultivation of the powers of self-expression and self-control.

These contrasting claims frequently leave the teacher in a state of confusion as to what direction he should follow. They underscore the need for commonly accepted standards by which to choose among them. Few things are as important in curriculum development—and, indeed, in society generally—as a body of universal values on the basis of which important decisions can be made with the confidence that they will be favorably received. Therefore, the questions to be explored in this chapter are as follows: What is our value system? What changes have occurred in it? What has been retained of the system? How can it be improved and used in curriculum building?

1. *The Meaning of a Value System*

Values are frequently believed to be intangible and difficult to define; whereas facts are thought to be concrete and easily grasped. This is the result of habitual modes of thinking, however, and not of any inherent obscurity of values or easy accessibility of facts. To define what is meant by fact—to indicate all the conditions any statement must meet before it can be said to assert a fact—has proved over the centuries to be no easy task. If the meaning of value is less clear, the reason is probably lack of attention rather than inherent difficulties. Only a few aspects of the conception of value can be set forth here, but these should be sufficient to clarify its meaning for present purposes.

What Are Values?

People express two kinds of beliefs. One has reference to what a given set of circumstances actually *is*, or *was*; the other, to what it *ought* to be or *ought* to have been. The first of these is usually referred to as facts; the second, as valuations, judgments, opinions. In their valuations people express their beliefs both as to what the facts are and their sense of what is right, honest, fair, desirable, most worth while— that is, their values. Their values are frequently expressed as maxims,

such as "honesty is the best policy" and "treat thy neighbor as thyself."
In short, the values of people are the rules of conduct by which they
shape their behavior and from which they derive their hopes.

People do not render opinions, however, purely on the basis of the
rules. In order to apply a rule, something must be known or believed
about the situation. Thus in football it must be known or believed that
the player was off-side, that he was unnecessarily rough, and the like,
in order to justify the application of a rule. This means that the referee
will offer certain beliefs about what the actual situation was in justify-
ing his decision when it is questioned. Statements that refer to what an
actual situation is, or was, are usually called factual statements, even
though they may not be true. A person can say, for example, that there
are ghosts in his home, or that he has been to the moon, or that he can
change his height to suit his convenience, but such statements would
not be true. Factual statements, whether true or false, are used to indicate what is believed to be reality. If they are true, we have an accurate picture of the situation. If they are false, our view of the situation is erroneous.

On the other hand, statements such as the rules of conduct in a
society are propositions about what ought to be or ought to have been.
In their judgments and opinions, people always express both what they
believe the situation to be and their understanding of the rules. Men
generally wish to be rational in their opinions and evaluations of events
and persons. Consequently, their judgments usually conform to their
perception of both the rules and the facts. But it does not follow that
these judgments are always dependable. Today people are often mis-
informed both about the true state of affairs and about the meaning
of the rules. Indeed, they are frequently uncertain about what rules
they should accept.

The Meaning and Functions of a Value System

A value system is an interdependent, mutually adjusted, and consistent set of rules. This, of course, is an ideal notion of such a system.
As far as we now know, no rules of conduct of any actual culture have
ever conformed exactly to this ideal. All cultures harbor some rules
that are incompatible with others. Rules, as noted in the first chapter,
constitute the elements of the cultural core. But the core of a culture

always contains some principles that cannot be squared with others believed to be equally valid. For an example approaching an ideal value system, it is necessary to turn to a smaller social unit than a cultural system. A game fulfills that purpose.

A game is based on a miniature value system. Football, for example, is played in accordance with a set of regulations that are internally consistent and binding on all players alike. These rules do not describe how the game is actually played at a given moment, for the players may break the rules. They do prescribe, however, how the game *should* be played. On the basis of the rules the behavior of each player can be evaluated. It is possible to say what his behavior *ought* to be or *ought* to have been. A player who departs from the rules is subject to reprimand, and the team he represents, to specified penalties. The rules also set forth the purpose of the game in the definition of what it means to win. The ideals of each player with respect to the game are those formulated within the framework of the commonly accepted regulations by which the game is played. What a player strives to do, what he considers success to be, what he conceives to be good and bad, and what he expects of other players are all embraced in the rules of the game. In short, the football "morality" of each player is determined by the extent to which his behavior conforms to the "mores" of the game as expressed in its rules.

From this illustration the following functions of a value system can be derived:

1. It supplies the individual with a sense of purpose and direction.
2. It gives the group a common orientation and supplies the basis of individual action and of unified, collective action.
3. It serves as the basis for judging the behavior of individuals.
4. It enables the individual to know what to expect of others as well as how to conduct himself.
5. It fixes the sense of right and wrong, fair and foul, desirable and undesirable, moral and immoral.

The value system serves these functions, however, only to the degree that its rules are mutually adjusted and compatible. If new rules are introduced that are in direct contrast to the old ones, and conflicting behavior is thereby evoked, the individual may feel that the game can no longer be played without confusion and conflict.

The Value System in an Advanced Society

The illustration of the game is obviously an oversimplification, deliberately chosen to sharpen the concept of a value system. Societies are more complex than games. A society is more comparable to an alliance of games, all of which are being played simultaneously, with what is being done in one game influencing in more or less degree what is going on in all the others. There are, for example, the game of family, the business and industrial game, the agricultural game, the games of teaching and of other professions, and the game of politics. Each of these games is played in accordance with generally understood rules.

In the business and industrial game, it is believed, for example, that business can run itself and that interference by government is undesirable; that progress comes through competition; and that every man must look out for his own interest if he is to succeed. Such rules enable the individual to anticipate the behavior of others in the same game. If he is a businessman, he knows how other businessmen will react in various situations. He believes that if he plays the game well he will be successful in business. On the assumption that the rules will be followed by others and that they will not be significantly changed, the business-man can build his life-plan with reasonable assurance that it will be realized and, if it is not, that he can blame no one save himself.

Family life is no less carried on by rules. There are rules governing the relations between children and parents, brother and sister, brother and brother, husband and wife. Children know what things they may do and what things are forbidden. They know that they may not stay out late in the evening without the consent of their parents, that they may not stay out of school except by the permission of their father and mother, and that they may not refuse to obey their parents. The husband and wife, no less than the children, are bound by conventions. By the rules of married life, sex activities of both husband and wife are restricted. By the same rules, the husband is burdened with the responsibility of making a living, and the wife with the task of making a home. In addition, there are rules that apply to all members of the family alike. Each one, for example, may be expected to share in the blessing at mealtime.

Some rules are generally shared by the people—not because the people engage in particular activities to which they apply, as in the case of

family life and the use of the highways, but because they are so pervasive that they permeate almost all activities in one way or another.
There is, for instance, a general notion of discipline, which means an
inclination to follow the rules whatever the game may be, to make behavior conform to what is expected of a person in his position in the
scheme of things, whether it be in school, family, industry, or any
other phase of life. There is the principle of freedom—which, in the
United States, has had a number of interpretations but has principally
meant the absence of government restraint, especially in business affairs.
There is the general principle of equality—which, again, has been
variously interpreted as meaning equality before the law, equality of
opportunity, equality at the polls, and the like. There is the principle
that the work of the individual is primarily for monetary rewards and
that the criterion of achievement is material gain.

Such rules as these, generally speaking, are the deep-lying norms of
the society and are so much a part of each individual that he is seldom
aware of their existence. When verbalized, they tend to be so general
that they are usually considered abstract, lacking any specific reference. But despite this fact, these general rules are the cement of the
social structure, supplying a binding force for the integration of all the
institutions of society. In terms of the analysis of culture set forth in
the first chapter, these rules are the elements of the cultural core and
are frequently referred to as *values*. In American society, they are
chiefly represented by the democratic creed.

Just as in football, where the expectations and aspirations of the
players and the evaluation of each one's behavior are all shaped more
or less automatically by the rules of the game, so it is in the larger
game of society. By the rules that govern activities in specialized
spheres as well as by those that permeate the whole social fabric, members of society shape their public conduct and judge themselves and
their fellow men. A good citizen is generally believed to be one who
abides by the rules of the society, especially those rules the violation
of which is most readily observable as well as most emotionally disturbing to the members of society. By these rules, the conduct of any
individual is judged to be right, good, fair, just, moral, desirable—or the
opposite. Accordingly, the individual knows what is expected of him;
by the same token he knows what to expect of others in particular
situations or relationships. No less important is the fact that the rules

provide a common context of sentiment, emotion, and thought which supplies the basis of unified public action.

It would be a mistake to suppose that people deliberately mold their conduct by a set of rules. Just as in football, where the players are unconscious of the rules until a disagreement involving them arises, so it is in society. Social rules are not written down, as are those of football, nor are they clearly formulated in the minds of those who live by them. But they are commonly understood. They function, for the most part, at the level of unconscious habit. Ordinarily they are taken for granted, so much are they embedded in the daily behavior of the people.

2. The Plight of the American System of Values

American culture is a mosaic of pieces borrowed from all the phases, social classes, and occupational interests of Western history. Many ideas of what is valuable, desirable, and right have come down from ancient Greece, Rome, and the Middle Ages; others are the creation of the last five hundred years; and still others are of more recent origin. Some of these ideas are the expressions of the hopes and aspirations of the masses in their struggle for freedoms and equalities. Many of them are the rationalizations of ruling classes who, from time to time, have stamped their symbols on the cultural fabric. It is not surprising, therefore, that the principles by which the members of American society live are afflicted with a large measure of contradiction and ambiguity.

Contradictory Rules in the American Value System

A list of all the rules of American society, together with their qualifications and contradictory propositions, would constitute an encyclopedia of American morals. Fortunately, such a compilation is unnecessary for the present purpose. The brief list drawn by Lynd from his study of "Middletown" will serve to make clear what some of the rules are and how they are qualified by contrasting ideas.

1. The United States is the best and greatest nation on earth and will always remain so.

2. Individualism, "the survival of the fittest," is the law of nature and the secret of America's greatness; and restrictions on individual freedom are un-American and kill initiative.

But: No man should live for himself alone; for people ought to be loyal and stand together and work for common purposes.

3. The thing that distinguishes man from the beasts is the fact that he is rational; and therefore man can be trusted, if let alone, to guide his conduct wisely.

But: Some people are brighter than others; and, as every practical politician and businessman knows, you can't afford simply to sit back and wait for people to make up their minds.

4. Democracy, as discovered and perfected by the American people, is the ultimate form of living together. All men are created free and equal, and the United States has made this fact a living reality.

But: You would never get anywhere, of course, if you constantly left things to popular vote. No business could be run that way, and of course no businessman would tolerate it.

5. Everyone should try to be successful.

But: The kind of person you are is more important than how successful you are.

6. The family is our basic institution and the sacred core of our national life.

But: Business is our most important institution, and, since national welfare depends upon it, other institutions must conform to its needs.

7. Religion and "the finer things of life" are our ultimate values and the things all of us are really working for.

But: A man owes it to himself and to his family to make as much money as he can.

8. Life would not be tolerable if we did not believe in progress and know that things are getting better. We should, therefore, welcome new things.

But: The old, tried fundamentals are best; and it is a mistake for busybodies to try to change things too fast or to upset the fundamentals.

9. Hard work and thrift are signs of character and the way to get ahead.

But: No shrewd person tries to get ahead nowadays by just working hard, and nobody gets rich nowadays by pinching nickels. It is important to know the right people. If you want to make money, you have to look and act like money. Anyway, you only live once.

10. Honesty is the best policy.

But: Business is business, and a businessman would be a fool if he didn't cover his hand.

11. America is a land of unlimited opportunity, and people get pretty much what's coming to them here in this country.

But: Of course, not everybody can be boss, and factories can't give jobs if there aren't jobs to give.

12. Capital and labor are partners.

But: It is a bad policy to pay higher wages than you have to. If people don't like to work for you for what you offer them, they can go elsewhere.

13. Education is a fine thing.

But: It is the practical men who get things done.

14. Science is a fine thing in its place, and our future depends upon it.

But: Science has no right to interfere with such things as business and our other fundamental institutions. The thing to do is to *use* science, but not let it upset things.

15. Children are a blessing.

But: You should not have more children than you can afford.

16. Women are the finest of God's creatures.

But: Women aren't very practical and are usually inferior to men in reasoning power and general ability.

17. Patriotism and public service are fine things.

But: Of course, a man has to look out for himself.

18. Our Judicial system insures justice to every man, rich or poor.

But: A man is a fool not to hire the best lawyer he can afford.

19. Poverty is deplorable and should be abolished.

But: There never has been enough to go around, and the Bible tells us that "The poor you have always with you."

20. No man deserves to have what he hasn't worked for. It demoralizes him to do so.

But: You can't let people starve.[1]

The members of each pair of statements do not enjoy equal acceptance among the people. The weight given to each will vary with circumstances and from one social class or group to another.

[1] Robert S. Lynd, *Knowledge for What?* (Princeton: Princeton University Press; 1939), pp. 60–62. By permission. For a more extended list of these principles, see *Middletown in Transition,* by Robert S. and Helen Lynd (New York: Harcourt, Brace & Co.; 1937), Chapter XII.

Contradictory Rules in the Game of Life

From these contrasting rules it would appear that the members of American society do not know definitely what they should do, nor what is expected of them. Surely no game could be played by rules so contradictory and ambivalent as these. And yet American society goes along with a considerable degree of order. How is this so? This is possible because the society is compartmentalized and because men are capable of carrying contradictions around in their heads, acting first on one principle and then on its opposite without the slightest awareness of the inconsistency.

Attention has already been called to the fact that society is composed, as it were, of a number of games—the business game, the family game, the political game, and so on. Rules used in one of these games may be in contradiction to those used in another. A given rule may be used when an individual is involved in a business transaction. Its exact opposite may be employed immediately after by the same individual in dealing with a member of his family. Thus a great number of the contradictory rules never appear as such to the individual, since the compartmentalization of life does not allow the rules to be used in juxtaposition.

Contradictions are found no less in the case of those more general rules that apply to several or all compartments than in the case of those specialized rules that belong to specialized groups and activities. For example, the principles of equality and freedom are presumed to be universals, in that they are supposed to be applied to all instances of social relations regardless of creed, race, or social position of individuals. But they are so ambiguous in the public mind that one meaning can be applied in one domain of society and the opposite interpretation in another. One interpretation of freedom may concern human beings in general, as when it is said that restrictions on business are un-American. In another interpretation, freedom is limited so that it does not apply to some people. Thus, in some places, it is believed that women should not be in the banking business, or that Negroes should not be entitled to the same employment opportunities as white people. Such contrasting interpretations are usually kept in separate compartments of the individual's mind, so that he is unaware of their inconsistency, or else he pays little attention to it as long as the vast majority of the people erect the same mental bulkheads.

Social Effects of Confusions in the Value System

Contrasting interpretations of the rules and compartmentalization of society and personality inevitably lead to undesirable consequences. First, it is clear that such a loosely knit, ambiguous, and inconsistent set of values can be used to justify discrimination against individual's and even against collections of people on the basis of such things as race, religion, poverty, and social position. A person who subscribes to the notion of equal educational opportunity at the level of general abstraction may find himself in conflict with this principle when he sees that it involves not only free schools but also free books, materials, and even meals. The individual in question may then justify his refusal to go along with this interpretation of equal opportunity by appealing to another principle—that since people do not appreciate the things they do not earn, free meals, books, and the like should not be supplied at public expense. Thus discrimination against those whose poverty prevents them from attending school, or from learning if they do attend, is justified in his mind.

Second, the effect on the social structure is undesirable. The commonly understood rules of society constitute the basic elements of the frame of reference in terms of which different individuals are able to see the world alike, to accept the same criterion of truth, honesty, rightness, and human decency. Without this common apperceptive mass of cultural regulations, the social structure begins to weaken and to produce a state of social insanity marked by crime, suicide, personal delinquency, and other forms of disorder.

As long as the rules of various compartments of society do not come into serious conflict, and as long as contrasting interpretations of more general principles are kept in their respective spheres, the individual may not experience serious insecurity or confusion. The society will tend to be orderly, and social conduct more or less rational. But when the principles involved in the various social "games" begin to change and new rules emerge and compete with the old ones for survival, social confusion and disorder increase. When the central core of universal rules, however loosely interpreted, begins to suffer the same sort of changes and competition or becomes overlaid with conflict, social maladjustments are compounded. These changes, as was implied in the preceding chapters, are now taking place in American society, with consequent moral confusion and social disorder.

As compartmentalized rules and special interpretations increase, the common core of values is relatively reduced in size. As will presently be seen, this is one of the trends in the American value system. This reduction of the core means that it will become increasingly difficult to achieve consensus on significant social issues, for there will be less and less common ground on which all the people can stand while they reach agreements on the points in question. The various parties to the issues, seeing the social realities from their particular standpoints, will seek courses of action which lead to consequences of special benefit to themselves or to their group. The common good will become less and less significant as a cohesive force and as a criterion by which to judge the actions of individuals, public officials, and social organizations. Organized interests tend to multiply and to increase their pressure for special privileges, while the whole social structure shows a tendency to move in the direction of disintegration.

Third, the effects upon personality are no less distressing. When the rules of a given aspect of society, such as business or politics, begin to change, so that new and old rules are found side by side, the effects on an individual are direct and immediate. He is then apt to find himself confused and uncertain as to what is the right or the desirable course of action. It is as though a football team were trying to play by contradictory regulations. This is, of course, precisely what has happened in most areas of society. The rules of family life, for example, are changing. It is now considered quite proper for a wife to have an independent career if she desires it. But the old rule that the place of woman is in the home still lingers in the minds and emotions of many people. Even when they obey the new rule, they are haunted by the residue of prior sentiments and tendencies. Likewise, the rules of almost every aspect of American culture are undergoing modifications, new ones being added and old ones dropped or reconstructed. This results in widespread insecurity and maladjustment.

Since the individual justifies his conduct by the complex of rules under which he lives and by his beliefs as to the realities of the situations he is called upon to face, he will feel morally vindicated, convinced of his rightness, and personally secure when the rules are relatively stable from generation to generation. Righteous indignation—as frequently expressed in the past generations but decreasingly found in the present one—was possible not only because the individual believed in the principles that had been violated but also because all persons who counted in his life were loyal to the same rules. When men are skeptical of the principles by which they live, their indignation becomes arbitrary in their own views as well as in the eyes of those toward whom their wrath is directed.

What these conflicts, uncertainties, and confusions do to personal structure is suggested by Karen Horney's social interpretation of neurotic personality:

When we remember that in every neurosis there are contradictory tendencies which the neurotic is unable to reconcile, the question arises as to whether there are not likewise certain definite contradictions in our culture, which underlie the typical neurotic conflicts. . . .

The first contradiction to be mentioned is that between competition and success on the one hand, and brotherly love and humility on the other. On the one hand everything is done to spur us toward success, which means that we must be not only assertive but aggressive, able to push others out of the way. On the other hand, we are deeply imbued with Christian ideals, which declare that it is selfish to want anything for ourselves, that we should be humble, turn the other cheek, be yielding. For this contradiction there are only two solutions within the normal range: to take one of these strivings seriously and discard the other; to take both seriously with the result that the individual is seriously inhibited in both directions.

The second contradiction is that between the stimulation of our needs and our factual frustrations in satisfying them. For economic reasons, needs are constantly being stimulated in our culture by such means as advertisements, "conspicuous consumption," the ideal of "keeping up with the Joneses." For the great majority, however, the actual fulfillment of these needs is closely restricted. The psychic consequence for the individual is a constant discrepancy between his desires and their fulfillment.

Another contradiction exists between the alleged freedom of the individual and all his factual limitations. The individual is told by a society that he is free, independent, can decide his life according to his own free will: "the great game of life" is open to him, and he can get what he wants if he is efficient and energetic. In actual fact, for the majority of people, all these possibilities are limited. What has been said facetiously of the impossibility of choosing one's parents can well be extended to life in general—choosing and succeeding in an occupation, choosing ways of recreation, choosing a mate. The result for the individual is a wavering between a feeling of boundless power in determining his own fate and a feeling of entire helplessness.

These contradictions embedded in our culture are precisely the conflicts which the neurotic struggles to reconcile. . . .[2]

3. Sociological Factors Disturbing the Value System

The processes of cultural inheritance have laid down deposits in American culture from the great epochs of history. These deposits give rise to conflicting rules of conduct and contrasting personal and social orientations. While these deposits are not easy for a society to assimilate, they do not constitute an insuperable obstacle to social integration. Indeed, almost all societies are required by the accidents of history, by the course of social evolution and inheritance, to assimilate principles of conduct and points of view that are not wholly compatible with their value systems. By such readjustments societies are enriched with new perspectives and new possibilities of cultural improvement.

Readjustments due to these forces have, in fact, been going on in Western society since before the decline of ancient Greece. Their presence in American culture is only the result of the natural course of events during the past twenty centuries. In the present discussion attention is called to the inheritance of contrasting cultural elements, not because it is something unusual, but because the problem of assimilation—which has been going on in America for the past three hundred years—has now become overlaid with and complicated by disturbing sociological conditions. As a result, at the very time when the American people are involved in building a consistent life perspective, they are thrust into new social circumstances which invalidate many of the very principles that are in the process of assimilation.

[2] Karen Horney, *The Neurotic Personality of Our Time* (New York: W. W. Norton; 1937), pp. 287–289. By permission.

Decline of Community Life and the Breakdown of the Value System

The first of these disturbing sociological conditions is the change from the intimate, face-to-face relationships of the neighborhood and small community to the impersonal, abstract relationships of the urban community and the national and global network of interdependencies. Before the age of machines the artisan ordinarily owned his tools and worked for himself as a producer. Then, ownership, production, and control were vested in a single person or household. Life was comparatively simple. An individual was concerned with his own affairs or with the affairs of those with whom he was so intimate that their concerns were often considered his own. Purposes were simple, and the means of their achievement were, as a rule, within the community itself. Science and technology have largely dissolved the simple community, and with it has gone the feeling of intimacy and the face-to-face relationships that sustain the attitudes of neighborliness, mutual help, and brotherhood.

The warm human relationships between individuals of the old-fashioned community have been replaced by complex chains of social actions and reactions, a network of bewildering social processes. For example, only in a few instances is the product of an individual's labor now used directly to satisfy his own needs or those of his friends and neighbors. Instead, it is sold on an impersonal market which extends far beyond the personal knowledge of the worker. With few exceptions each individual pursues a narrow activity for which he receives money to purchase, from the impersonal market, materials and services to satisfy his wants. And the activity in which he engages has subtle and remote connections of which he is ignorant and which, if he were informed of them, would appear as abstract and impersonal as the structure of atoms.

Everyone is caught up in a vast system of invisible social connections. This is but to say that science and technology, while breeding interdependence on a wide scale, have at the same time divorced the individual from the direct perception of the consequences of his activities. The effects of the policies of laborers upon farmers, the policies of farmers upon laborers, and the policies of bankers and industrialists upon both laborers and farmers are not readily discernible. If seen at all, they are recognized only in an impersonal manner. With the loss of the controlling influence of the direct perception of the effects of one's actions have gone also many of the common rules of conduct which grew up in response to the intimate associations of the old-fashioned community. Under these new circumstances, the individual does not know what the old commandment, "love thy neighbor," means; he does not always know what it means to be honest or whether a given act is brotherly.

While science and technology have multiplied energy, mechanized industry, and increased knowledge, they have also uprooted habitual modes of action and all but destroyed the old rules of conduct. Each individual, as has already been pointed out, now works in a narrow channel of specialized activities and is insensitive to the vast social drama in which, unwittingly, he daily plays a part. Outside of these activities he feels lost. Old ideas and virtues are abstractions. Revered phrases recall to mind duties and responsibilities, but he no longer knows where to take hold in order to execute them. He feels himself swept along by forces which somehow lie beyond his control and which he does not understand. As a result, in the broad field of social policy one course of action is apt to look as good as another, as long as his specialized activities and beliefs are not perceptually involved. His sense of social direction is weakened or destroyed, and social and intellectual confusion is the natural outcome.

In the control of their conduct men must learn to search for remote connections. This is not an easy task, for men have been habituated, by centuries of simple community life, to think in terms of immediate and direct consequences. To deal with matters of policy in modern society requires not only the foreseeing of immediate consequences, but also the habit of searching for hidden and delayed consequences. The achievement of a more inclusive form of social integration depends in large measure upon the translation of the simple community virtues into more comprehensive rules of conduct—rules so comprehensive that their application requires a thoughtful search for the connections between one's policies and plans and those of men remote in space and time. Karl Mannheim has summed up the matter:

. . . "Love your neighbor" should not be taken literally but should be translated according to the conditions of a great society. This consists in

setting up institutions embodying some abstract principle which corresponds to the primary virtue of sympathy and brotherliness. The equal
political rights of citizens in a democracy are abstract equivalents of the
concrete primary virtues of sympathy and brotherliness.

In this case it is the method of translation which makes the value system
function once more. But only social workers could tell us how often people
fail in life because they never have been taught how to translate the virtues in which they have been trained in their homes into the conditions of
society at large. To educate for family life and neighborhood functions is
different from educating for national and world citizenship. Our whole
educational tradition and value system is still adapted to the needs of a
parochial world, and yet we wonder that people fail when they are expected
to act on a broader plane.[3]

The Impact of Communication, Transportation, and Social Mobility

A second social factor that has helped to upset the value system is the
growth of communication and transportation, and the fact of social
mobility. As long as persons remain in their respective social spheres,
not knowing what people of other social strata think or by what rules
they rationalize their conduct, their own principles are unchallenged.
But when individuals move from one social stratum to another—as is
the case in modern democracies—or when they come into contact with
the ideals and points of view of various cultures and social groups by
communication and transportation, their own ideas of what is right and
wrong, good and bad, desirable and undesirable then come into conflict
with the ideas and points of view of other social groups and cultural
systems. Under these circumstances people are required to evaluate
their rules of conduct and, if need be, to make adjustments in these
elements of their culture in order to secure a more compatible set of
rules. If they fail to do this, they are apt to become confused and uncertain as to what to accept, or else they become intolerant of anything
that challenges their values.

An illustration of this problem is clearly seen when an individual
who has grown to maturity in the ways of a small country town moves
into a large city. He immediately learns that many of his ideas of
proper social relations are no longer adequate. His old principles are

[3] Karl Mannheim, *Diagnosis of Our Time* (London: Kegan Paul, Trench, Trubner
& Co.; 1943), p. 18. By permission of Routledge and Kegan Paul, Ltd.

no longer valid. Either he recognizes this and readjusts his ways of thinking, or else he finds himself involved in all sorts of personal and social conflicts. If this illustration is extended into the thousands of intergroup relationships of modern society and the countless contacts of great cultural systems of the world, it is plain that intermixing of value systems is inevitable and extensive.

Such diffusion has of course always gone on to some degree in almost every phase of history. But usually the processes of diffusion have been so slow that the assimilation and adjustment of cultural elements could be taken care of by the long process of unconscious readjustment. Nowadays, however, the interpenetration of groups and cultures goes on at such a rapid pace that readjustments are left to unconscious processes only at the risk of grave consequences for both society and the individual.

At a time of deep concern about fundamental beliefs, it is little less than tragic that the most effective method of thinking—namely, the scientific method—suffers from a long tradition that it cannot be successfully applied to questions of evaluation. This tradition is nowhere more clearly exhibited than in the social sciences, where scientific efforts have usually led to disregard of the value elements, which are the very factors at issue. With proper adaptations the scientific method, broadly conceived, probably can be made to include matters of basic belief and choice. What stands in the way is the long habituation, on the part of both social scientists and the people, to the theory that choice-making in the realm of values must be left to the unconscious processes of automatic adjustment.

In former periods—when cultural changes were so gradual that only by looking back over a long span of history could men detect the slow dissolution and transformation of their institutions, customs, and rules of conduct—neglect of the processes of choice-making was understandable. But now events occur with such rapidity that an individual may witness, within the scope of a few years, changes in rules of behavior and points of view that have endured for centuries. Individuals now directly experience degrees of social change which men of other times could experience only vicariously through the study of history. Under these conditions, men must learn to deal rationally with problems of choice to build new and more adequate standards of valuation.

4. The Core of the American System of Values

Although the American value system has been rapidly eroding under the swirling forces of social change, it still contains a central core of commonly accepted working principles. An impartial Scandinavian scholar, after a thorough study of American culture, summed the matter up in the following way:

> Still there is evidently a strong unity in this nation and a basic homogeneity and stability in its valuations. Americans of all national origins, classes, regions, creeds, and colors have something in common: a social *ethos*, a political creed. It is difficult to avoid the judgment that this "American Creed" is the cement in the structure of this great and disparate nation.[4]

The Democratic Tradition

This creed—the American democratic tradition—is not easily defined. It has been variously stated at different times and by different writers. But its basic principles are expressed in the following passage:

> Before we demonstrate why it is a top-level priority of the American public . . . school to teach youth to understand and to appreciate the democratic way of life as the citizens of our Republic conceive it, let us make clear what we are talking about by pointing out what the principal components of American democracy are. These are ideals—ideals of conduct derived from beliefs held by the generality of our people. Like all ideals, they are seldom if ever fully achieved, but this in no way denies their validity as objects of desire. Here, as inferred from the works of scholars who have made a study of American social thought, are what our key democratic ideals are seen to be when the great documents which we Americans revere, the court decisions which we honor, the laws by which we govern ourselves, the institutions which we support, the attributes which we admire in our fellow citizens, and the folkways we practice are competently analyzed:
>
> 1. We hold that all human beings are of supreme and equal moral worth, that human life and well-being are to be valued above all material things,

[4] Gunnar Myrdal, *An American Dilemma* (New York: Harper & Brothers; 1944), Vol. 1, p. 3. By permission.

and that the dignity and worth of each person should be equally respected at all times and in all ways. Hence we assert:

a. That all valuations, all tests of the desirability of all policies and institutional arrangements, should principally be made in terms of what each does or promises to do to promote human welfare and that the well-being of each person should count equally in all such valuations.

b. That the good life, however conceived, should be made equally available to all persons through equality of educational opportunity, equality at the ballot box, and equality before the law.

2. We believe that human beings should be the architects of their own destiny, that they have the capacity to govern themselves wisely, and that the distribution of this capacity does not follow the contours of caste, class, family, ecclesiastical, or property lines. Hence, we repudiate all doctrines of rule by hereditary or divine right and reject all forms of totalitarianism, dictatorship, and tyranny. To the contrary, we assert:

a. That the people are sovereign and that governments derive their just powers from the consent of the governed, that human beings are the masters rather than the instruments of the state.

b. That government *for* the people can be assured only if there is government *by* the people.

3. We have faith in human intelligence. We believe that by taking thought man can build a better world. Consequently, we assert that human well-being can best be advanced only if there is an unrestricted play of free intelligence upon all problems and difficulties. Hence,

a. The guarantees given in our Constitution to freedom of thought, belief, speech, assembly, and press—freedoms which are not to be abrogated or curtailed by any person, majority, or (except in time of dire emergency) even by the government itself; in the Constitution it is stipulated that Congress shall make no laws abridging these rights.

b. Our determination to maintain these freedoms as the necessary condition for creating new mind (new knowledge, new insights, new attitudes, new beliefs—any new "mental" behaviors) and the realization that whoever to any degree denies any of these freedoms to that degree aborts intelligence.

c. The high valuation we place on accuracy and integrity, based on the realization that false knowledge enslaves the minds of men, leads them into error, and so is injurious to human well-being.

4. We believe in the rule of law: in a written Constitution which brings government and public officials as well as all other persons under the

rule of law; in law which is made by representatives of our own choosing; in law which prevents the exercise of arbitrary power by persons
clothed with the authority of the state; in law which upholds the rights
and enforces the obligations of men in their everyday pursuits and
associations. Our ideal is a self-imposed type of law and order.

5. We believe in the principle of majority rule with minority protection,
that the will of the majority should prevail at any given moment, that
any person or group who believes that the operation of the will of the
majority is inimical to any democratic principle is morally obligated to
attempt to change this will through persuasion based on reason, that
all minorities which seek to change the will of the majority through
persuasion based on reason should be legally sanctioned and fully protected in their right to do so; but that, except for the minimum violation
necessary to induce a test case in the courts, all minorities are obligated
to abide by the will of the majority even while they work to change it.

6. Within our own country, we are determined that there shall be freedom
for peaceful social change, and insist upon the peaceful settlement under
law of all internal disputes; we believe that ballots should be substituted for bullets in resolving internal differences as to policy, and that
men should abide by the decisions of the courts in respect to other disputes which they are unable to talk out.

7. We assert the individual's right to freedom in all respects not injurious
to the common good; we declare that every person has the right to
worship in his own way, think his own thoughts, speak his mind on any
matter not causative of some clear and present danger to others, dress in
any fashion not corruptive of public morals, seek employment in any
lawful occupation of his own choosing, search in whatever social class
he will for a marriage partner, and domicile himself in any state in the
Union.[5]

These working principles are not absolute but change with changing
social circumstances. They have to be reinterpreted, reconstructed, or
in some cases even abandoned, as new conditions require. In a period
of pioneering, when vast virgin territory is being conquered, or in any
highly individualized phase of cultural development, the individual may
be left largely to himself to work out his own destiny. Under such conditions his actions may have little or no effect upon the public at large.
But, in a highly interdependent social system, to respect the individual
by leaving him alone—as in pioneer days—may, and in fact usually

[5] Harold C. Hand, *Principles of American Public Secondary Education* (to be published by Harcourt, Brace & Co.).

does, lead to evil consequences. Under these highly complex circumstances the individual may either suffer from the acts of others over whom he has no control, or he may do things himself that adversely affect other individuals. Hence, in a highly interrelated social scheme, some measure of social control may be essential to the fulfillment of these working principles. Yet people are so accustomed to thinking in the pattern of simple community life, where formal public controls were all but absent, that it is almost impossible for them to conceive of deliberate public control and freedom and equality for the individual as correlative terms.

Despite such variation of interpretation, these principles possess enough uniformity of meaning to serve as the moral bases of social justice, to supply a sense of social direction, and to underwrite a large measure of social stability. They still constitute the highest moral ideals in terms of which institutions, as well as social policies and practices, can be judged. By acting on these principles, the individual can transcend his narrow motives and prejudices in the interest of the common good; and organized groups can subordinate their biases and goals to the public welfare.

Maximum Development of the Individual

The heart of the American value system is faith in and respect for the common man—that is, for the individual irrespective of his religion, color, occupation, political views, or social position. Respect for the individual does not mean that anyone is to be free to exploit his fellows, whether through the subtle processes of the industrial and economic systems or through the more obvious processes of outright suppression by physical force. On the contrary, respect for the individual may, and in fact does, require that some individuals and social groups be deliberately prevented from following social, economic, and political practices harmful to the public. Faith in, and respect for, the common man has at least four interrelated meanings, all of which are essential parts of the central concept. First, the physical and cultural conditions into which an individual is born shall be such as to enable him to develop to his fullest capacity. Second, an individual shall share in the formulation and fulfillment of the policies and programs under which he shall live and work. Third, an individual shall not be used merely as a means to the ends desired by others—or, to put the same idea positively, the individual shall share in determining the ends he shall serve as well as the means he shall employ. And, fourth, an individual shall not be required by social circumstances to live in a state of chronic economic insecurity. Perhaps no one has translated this article of the American Creed into more realistic terms than has Theodore Brameld in the following list of human wants:

Most men do not want to be hungry: they cherish the value of *sufficient nourishment*.

Most men do not want to be cold or ragged: they cherish the value of *adequate dress*.

Most men do not want uncontrolled exposure either to the elements or to people: they cherish the value of *shelter* and *privacy*.

Most men do not want celibacy: they cherish the value of *sexual expression*.

Most men do not want illness: they cherish the value of *physiological and mental health*.

Most men do not want chronic insecurity: they cherish the value of *steady work, steady income*.

Most men do not want loneliness: they cherish the value of *companionship, mutual devotion, belongingness*.

Most men do not want indifference: they cherish the value of *recognition, appreciation, status*.

Most men do not want constant drudgery, monotony, or routine: they cherish the value of *novelty, curiosity, variation, recreation, adventure, growth, creativity*.

Most men do not want ignorance: they cherish the value of *literacy, skill, information*.

Most men do not want continual domination: they cherish the value of *participation, sharing*.

Most men do not want bewilderment: they cherish the value of *fairly immediate meaning, significance, order, direction*.[6]

It is not difficult to see that the social, political, and economic arrangements essential to the satisfaction of these wants will be quite different in a society where individuals are fairly independent of one another and in a society where interdependence has reached an advanced level of development.

[6] Theodore Brameld, "An Inductive Approach to Intercultural Values," *The Journal of Educational Sociology*, Vol. 21, No. 1 (September, 1947), pp. 10–11.

Institutions and the Value System

The core of the American system of values underlies most of the basic institutions of the nation. It is the ultimate justification of the public school system. This core of values leads not only to the belief that every individual can profit from educational opportunity but also to the belief that everyone is entitled to the fullest possible personal development. Of course, universal education can be justified in terms of national interest, or even on religious grounds. In America, however, the single-ladder system of universal education is based upon the doctrine of the supreme worth of the individual as an object of development.

For the same reason, a system of civil liberties is generally accepted by the American people. The right of free speech and assembly is based on the firm conviction that if the people are allowed to know whatever there is to be known they can manage their individual and collective affairs better than anyone else can do it for them. The belief that the people should have the right to know is thus no less firmly held than that the individual should have the right to express and to advocate his views, regardless of how unpopular they may be. Moreover, the legislative system, and the principle of popular suffrage supporting it, go back to the universal faith in the ability of the common run of men to rule themselves, to solve the problems that face them as a people, and to know when those who represent them are serving their interests.

Some critics have decried American ideals as mere talk, and many Americans have supported the critics by honoring these ideals with mere lip-service. It is only fair to admit also that such lip-service—together with the obvious refusal in some responsible quarters to act in the public interest—has tended to make many Americans socially callous and insensitive to gross violations of their professed ideals. It is easy to exaggerate the amount of cynicism among American citizens, however, and to underestimate their capacity for courageous moral action. Nowhere is this courage better demonstrated than in the crisis situation that has existed since the beginning of the Great Depression. During these years of crisis, many changes have occurred in American institutions; and, for the most part, they have been made in the interest of the public. The increasing public control of business, industry, agriculture, and labor, together with the development of social security on a nation-wide basis, are all cases in point. These have been accomplished within the frame of the American Creed and in most respects represent its most promising fulfillment.

It is also reassuring to hear the testimony of one of the leading students of American culture. Writing in 1944 about the alleged hypocrisy of Americans, Gunnar Myrdal said:

This explanation is too superficial. To begin with, the true hypocrite sins in secret; he conceals his faults. The American, on the contrary, is strongly and sincerely "against sin," even, and not least, his own sins. He investigates his faults, puts them on record, and shouts them from the housetops, adding the most severe recriminations against himself, including the accusation of hypocrisy. If all the world is well informed about the political corruption, organized crime, and faltering system of justice in America, it is primarily not due to its malice but to American publicity about its own imperfections. America's handling of the Negro problem has been criticized most emphatically by white Americans since long before the Revolution, and the criticism has steadily gone on and will not stop until America has completely reformed itself.

. . . As a matter of fact, this young nation is the least cynical of all nations. It is not hypocritical in the usual sense of the word, but labors persistently with its moral problems. It is taking its Creed very seriously indeed, and this is the reason why the ideals are not only continuously discussed but also represent a social force—why they receive more than "lip-service" in the collective life of the nation. The cultural unity of the nation is this common sharing in both the consciousness of sins and the devotion to high ideals.[7]

The point of this discussion is that American society, despite the disintegrative tendencies of the past fifty years, still exhibits a few universal ideals by which both public and private policies and programs, as well as institutions, can be evaluated. These ideals, too, are part of the common ground on which the people stand while resolving the issues that divide them. While they are few in number and are not always understood alike by all Americans, they are still the source of the nation's vitality and stability, and the yardstick by which educational and social progress is to be measured.

[7] Gunnar Myrdal, *An American Dilemma* (New York: Harper & Brothers; 1944), Vol. 1, pp. 21, 22. By permission.

5. *The Educational Task*

One of the characteristics of American society is the increasing specialization of interests and social perspectives arising out of modern urbanization, industrialization, and technology. Concurrently with this increasing specialization—and principally as a result of it—has come an
increase in the number of social conflicts involving differences of opinion about the interpretation of the fundamental moral commitments of
the American people. The cultural alternatives that have emerged in
the economic system, in the family, in the community, and in occupational activities have accentuated conflict within the value system and
have disturbed the co-ordination of values, institutions, and social practices. Today, social institutions and moral ideals are increasingly caught
in situations of stress and strain, in which one or the other, or both,
must yield.

The complexity of American society requires that integration be
continuously worked out on various planes: at the level of institutions,
at the level of basic policies, and at the level of fundamental moral
rules. In addition, economic, political, and social practices must be
co-ordinated with these integrations so that what is actually done in
society will conform as nearly as possible to professed ideals and policies. The processes and techniques by which these integrations and
co-ordinations are achieved must be such as to encourage and facilitate
the greatest amount of free participation, for only in this way will the
outcomes represent an uncoerced consensus. The development of these
processes and techniques to the point where conflicts at the level of
values can be resolved is one of the essentials on which the future of
democratic society in America depends. It is one of the tasks of education in this period of maladjustment to develop persons capable of dealing constructively with these conflicts.

Need for a Moral Integration at Fundamental Social Levels

Above all else, it is the task of education to encourage the growth of
fundamental moral agreements among the people. The consensus must
be more than agreement upon the resolution of particular issues. A

genuine consensus reaches down into the common outlooks, values, and aspirations of the people. If agreement on a specific issue is not to be a mere expedient, a mere superficial and temporary compromise, it must be grounded in the common life. As social issues arise in more and more spheres of activity, it is clear that the common ground of the people must become more comprehensive in order to underwrite agreements in all these spheres. The core of democratic ideals must be expanded into an ever-widening set of working principles.

Democracy will always stress methods and techniques of resolving differences of opinion, since one of its commitments is to the widest possible participation of the people in reaching a consensus. But to equate democracy with methods of thinking and working together, in this age of shrinking moral commitments, is no less perilous than to conceive of it merely as a political system. Democracy is more than a method of collective thought and action. It is a set of moral principles, including the principle of free inquiry and deliberation, for the control of every aspect of social life. The primary business of the school is to make these principles clear, to show how they are to be used in social thought and action, and to provide experience in thus using them.

Need for a New Kind of Subject Matter

If the school is to fulfill these obligations it will need to stress a new kind of content. The present curriculum emphasizes descriptive knowledge and facts and all but neglects the moral content of the culture. Everywhere the individual is encouraged to understand things and to practice certain skills. He is continually asked in school such questions as: What is this? Can you describe so and so? Can you explain this? What causes this? Who did thus and so? Where and when did such a thing happen? Why did it happen? Seldom, if ever, is the individual asked whether or not a particular course of action or an event is good or bad, or by what principle he considers it to be good or bad. These questions are thought to be mere matters of opinion about which one person's judgment is as good as another's. Consequently, it is thought that nothing can be gained by studying such matters.

Thus the school has followed a *laissez faire* policy with respect to moral principles, or the rules of the game of democracy. The school must now do an about-face on the place of moral principles in the curriculum. It must no longer shrink from considering questions of value, and it must not tolerate the notion that agreement on values is neither important nor feasible in a democracy. The fundamental principles comprising the core of American culture must become objects of study in the same sense and to the same degree that the principles of science are now studied. Only then can democracy as a value system be understood and used in social action at the level of deliberate acceptance and criticism.

The heart of a culture is its universals. The heart of the universals is the values or, in other words, the rules by which people order their social existence. These rules, when built into the personalities of the individuals comprising the society, create the personality type peculiar to the culture. Hence, the heart of any satisfactory educational program consists of those basic values that give meaning to the purposes, plans, and activities of the individual.

It is now possible to define general education in terms of this analysis. General education is to be defined in reference to the value system of a particular culture. Education in a democratic society is *general* when it is geared to the task of clarifying the democratic value system, increasing the depth and range of these values, and encouraging through concrete activities the realization of these ideals for everyone —a realization that will be brought about by rebuilding institutions to exemplify the desired values more closely.

▶ *Following Up* *This Chapter*

1. Compile a list of inconsistent rules about economic, political, educational, and social questions. Get a number of persons to respond to your list by indicating the statements with which they agree and those with which they disagree. Study their responses to ascertain the extent to which the respondents accept contradictory rules.

2. In terms of your experience, what values do you think the public schools attempt to build? Colleges and universities? How do they try to build them? To what extent are these values compatible with one another? To what extent do they take account of the social realities?

3. Examine recent courses of study to determine whether or not they

provide activities and materials for critical consideration and reconstruction of the student's value system.

4. With a group of individuals explore the following: If the schools were to attempt to be more effective in building a fundamental moral consensus, what changes would they need to make in their purposes? Methods of teaching? Content? Administrative organization?

5. In discussions with other individuals note the points of disagreement on the problems arising in Item 4. Try to ascertain whether your lack of agreement is due to differences of opinion about the facts or to differences in value-beliefs. Note how you attempt to resolve your differences. How can you improve your ability to attain consensus?

▶ *Suggested Reading*

1. An outstanding analysis of American culture by a foreign scholar is Gunnar Myrdal's *An American Dilemma*. Chapters 1, 2, and 3, of Vol. 1, are especially valuable. Robert C. Angell's *Integration of American Society* is helpful on the meaning of cultural integration at the level of values. In Chapter XII the status of the American value system is described. A stimulating exploration of our values is Carl L. Becker's *New Liberties for Old*. A semi-popular discussion of some of our beliefs is found in Barrows Dunham's *Man against Myth*.

2. No list of readings on our value system would be adequate without John Dewey's *The Public and Its Problems* and his *Individualism Old and New*. For the same reason Karl Mannheim's *Diagnosis of Our Time* should be mentioned again. The advanced reader will find Mannheim's *Ideology and Utopia* to be one of the most penetrating discussions of the problem of values to appear in recent years.

3. Among discussions of values from an educational standpoint, the following should be mentioned: "The Public Schools and Spiritual Values," *Seventh Yearbook* of the John Dewey Society; Rugg, *Foundations for American Education*, Chapter XV; Rugg (editor), *Readings in the Foundations of Education*, Vol. II, Part I; Raup, Benne, Axtelle, and Smith, *The Improvement of Practical Intelligence*. See also Educational Policies Commission, *Education of Free Men* and *Education and Economic Well-Being in American Democracy*.

4. The best systematic study of democratic theory from a logico-empirical standpoint is Robert A. Dahl's *A Preface to Democratic Theory*.

Chapter 4

Social Perspective
and the Task of
Curriculum Building

THE PRECEDING CHAPTERS have documented the fact that American culture is in a period of fundamental change. The community pattern, the family structure, the economic system, the governmental pattern, and occupational life are all caught in this social transformation. The value system, too, is undergoing serious alterations. The meaning of these changes for curriculum building has been set forth briefly. The purpose of the present chapter is to indicate the main lines of social development implicit in the changes now occurring in American culture and to make more explicit the meaning of these changes for the task of curriculum reconstruction.[1]

1. *Transition from a* Laissez Faire *to an Interdependent Society*

The main conclusion of all the foregoing discussion can be generalized in one sentence: *The United States is in a transition period from a*

[1] This chapter is adapted from B. Othanel Smith, "Social Perspective as the Basic Orientation of the Curriculum" in *Toward Improved Curriculum Theory,* Virgil E. Herrick and Ralph W. Tyler (editors), Supplementary Educational Monographs, No. 71, March, 1950.

laissez faire *to an interdependent society*. No one can read the enactments of state legislatures, or of the United States Congress during the last twenty-five years, without being impressed by the fact that the American people are demanding more and more public control of human relationships. Even those senators and representatives who cry loudest against government regulations vote for measures creating controls in violation of the principles they cherish. These representatives vote for measures regulating the behavior of men in business, labor, and agriculture, as if they were driven against their will by overwhelming social forces. They frequently talk in terms of ideas and beliefs of an earlier period, but they act in terms of current social realities. Because their beliefs and their acts are often disconnected, their responses to the realities of the day are sometimes unintelligent. So, too, are the responses of their constituents. As someone has aptly phrased this inconsistency, "They have their heads in the eighteenth century and their feet in the twentieth." Perhaps this is inevitable in a period of transition.

No one can forecast with certainty the future form of society. From the discussion in the preceding chapters, however, it is possible to set forth some of the first signs of developments that will probably exercise a major influence in shaping the future. Among these are the following:

1. Interdependence is increasing and spreading into almost every aspect of human activity. It is grounded in the structural foundation of society and not in the desire for co-operation. It is the inevitable counterpart of increasing specialization of labor and responsibility and the consequent complexity of society.

2. Positions from which the entire pattern of relationships among human activities can be perceived without the aid of education designed for that purpose are decreasing, and fewer and fewer individuals are able to reach these positions.

3. Social processes are being increasingly regulated and integrated by deliberate human effort based upon refined social knowledge and insight. Less and less are men depending upon hypothetical natural law and the chance meshing of these processes by conflict and competition for integration of their activities.

4. Democratization with respect to material welfare is becoming a matter of greater public concern, because in a highly interdependent

regime everyone must prosper if all are to attain the level of development of which they are capable. If some people are forced to go hungry, ill-clothed, and ill-housed, all suffer in consequence.

5. The suppressed races and social classes are increasingly asserting their rights to the equalities and freedoms promised by the democratic ideology. These rights are being sought through intellectual, legal, and military means, indicating increasing public impatience with discrimination among people on the basis of race.

6. The development of a world order, strong enough to adjudicate international disputes without resort to war, is already under way. While progress in this direction is slow and faltering, the world is endeavoring to shape itself to this end.

7. The value system of the democratic world is in a stage of thoroughgoing reconstruction. This reconstruction is necessary because the rules by which men regulate their lives must be revised to meet the new conditions wrought by science and technology.

8. Habits of thinking and social skills carried over from earlier cultural phases are undergoing serious transformation in order to enable men to deal effectively with new social and psychological realities.

These are the broad prognostic facts which the curriculum worker can neglect only to the peril of democratic society. No one can know in advance how these incipient developments will work out in detail. Some of them may be crushed by the force of social drift. But in any event, they now lay down some of the conditions setting the limits within which men can mold the human relationships they will either suffer or enjoy. These trends, plus the disintegration of old social principles and practices, constitute the conditions that determine the crucial tasks of education at the present stage of events.

The social pattern emerging along the lines of these social trends will require men with new modes of thinking, ideas, motivations, and social skills. To grasp the magnitude of these demands, it is helpful to refer to earlier periods of cultural transition. There are many instances of these periods in the history of the various peoples of the world.[2] In the Western World some of the more familiar ones are the transition period of Greek civilization—marked by the Peloponnesian Wars, the Decline

[2] Pitirim A. Sorokin, *The Crisis of Our Age.* Karl Mannheim, *Man and Society in an Age of Reconstruction.*

of the Roman Empire, and the rise of Christendom—and the break-down of the medieval world and the rise of capitalism and nationalism. Each cultural synthesis before and after these transition periods was dominated by a particular pattern of beliefs, values, and loyalties. Each produced different types of men. For purposes of illustration, the medieval and capitalistic syntheses will be briefly considered.

The medieval world emphasized status, obedience, and resignation. Serfdom was woven into its fabric and maintained by class distinctions believed to be ordained by God. This world rationalized a subsistence economy. What the lower classes lacked in material wealth was compensated for in the emotional satisfaction of rituals, festivals, and pageantry, and in the promise of a transcendent life. The idea of work was permeated by notions of subsistence and status. It meant doing what was required to procure a full stomach and the material possessions becoming to the individual's social status. The idea of work as a means of personal advancement would have seemed unreasonable, contrary to human nature and the will of God. Prices were considered just or unjust according to the way they affected whatever was necessary to maintain an individual in his ordained status. Anything beyond that was sinful; and any trade that brought a person more was unlawful.

Overspreading and permeating these economic relations was a system of beliefs, rituals, and festivals built upon the Christian epic as interpreted by the Church. The individual was counseled by the Church to remain in the status to which he was born and to assume the obligations which his status required. Within this frame of acquiescence the suffering and striving of the individual had meaning, and through its symbols he transcended his status and worldly existence.

Commerce, industry, and science turned the medieval world upside down within a span of two hundred years. A new frame of acceptance, compounded of political and religious freedoms and classical capitalism, sprang up to animate and rationalize the activities of the new cultural system. In this new constellation of beliefs and adjustments, status was assumed to be a function of individual efficiency rather than the result of accidents of birth. The rights and obligations of contract were substituted for inherited rights and obligations. Obedience and resignation were replaced by ambition and enterprise. Work became a means of personal advancement. Men no longer labored to provide for the needs peculiar to their status but to improve their status, to climb in the economic and social scale. If countless men were overcome in the struggle for gain, if some refused to enter the contest, no one could complain. For the game was on, and all played by the same set of rules. And a man could blame only himself or Dame Fortune for the place he occupied in the scheme of things. Natural law and nationalism supplanted the Church as the integrative force. Protestant sects, which emerged from the breakdown of the medieval synthesis, added their support to this new frame of reference by adding emphasis upon the responsibility of the individual.

This new world required new men, new minds—men who accepted its fundamental postulates and who ordered their daily choices, beliefs, ambitions, and labor by these new rules. It would have been impossible for business and industry to prosper with men molded in the pattern of the medieval synthesis. The ideas of incentives, contractual obligations, and free labor would not only have been strange to them, but would have failed to evoke the labor and industry that the capitalistic period required. For the same reason, people in remote parts of the world today, who have not been influenced by industrial civilization, do not readily respond to these incentives. They do not carry in their personal structures the habit systems upon which such civilization depends.

This frame of conventions, which has formed the character of men for the past two or three hundred years, is already disappearing. Social sanctions brought over from the medieval and protestant outlooks are rapidly dissolving. The structure of classic economic thought is creaking at its joints; it is all but gone as a regulating force in economic life. Even those who appeal to it in theory are forced to deny it in practice. The principles of political democracy formulated in an agrarian, pre-industrial society are in need of serious reconstruction. At the level of high abstraction the people subscribe to these principles. When they come to the task of molding public action, they find that this agreement is only apparent and that sincere democrats exhibit differing and often conflicting interpretations of these ideals. The morality of nation-states, centering in unlimited sovereignty, leads to international distrust and ultimately to war. In short, the structural foundations of industrial society are being transformed. In these new conditions men are creating new rules by which to live.

In the face of this dissolving social synthesis, America is blessed with power in the form of skill, knowledge, resources, productive machinery, and managerial know-how beyond the wildest dreams of the most adventurous of history's speculative minds. Yet in the midst of this unprecedented power and wealth the individual—instead of becoming more secure and more important—is becoming more fearful and, in his own eyes, less and less significant. Industrial man is afflicted with loneliness because, in a world of men highly organized as means in a vast industrial and political system, he is losing his sense of common purpose and outlook.

The political and educational task of the current period is no less than that of helping to build a reintegration of society in which men can find meaning and significance for themselves. Social reintegration will of course occur even without deliberate human effort. It is characteristic of a society per se to seek the integration of its cultural elements. The question is whether or not the reintegration will satisfy the principles of a free society; whether the regulation of society will be based upon democratic or autocratic methods; and whether the new synthesis will occur through the processes of war and revolution, leading to another "dark age," or through the orderly processes of deliberation and consensus.

2. *The Need for Re-education*

Curriculum making in an era of cultural transformation involves problems not encountered in a period of cultural stability. The learnings which the individual acquires informally by cultural induction are usually satisfactory in a static period, for there are few, if any, new cultural patterns and rules of conduct with which they conflict. The development of a consistent point of view and moral character—which is one of the major tasks of education, broadly conceived—is performed in such a period by the processes of cultural induction. There remains for the school the task of overlaying these fundamental learnings with a veneer of skills, information, and technical knowledge. With slight modifications, this is the way the teaching profession has conceived its task throughout the history of American education. Even in the last century, when considerable stress was placed upon moral content, the purpose of the school was to reinforce the teachings of the home and the church.

But in a period of profound cultural change, such as is now witnessed in the United States, the learnings instilled by the forces of cultural induction can no longer be taken at their face value. Most of these learnings belong to old cultural patterns, which have been invalidated in varying degrees by new economic, political, and social realities and must, therefore, be discounted. They are vestiges of prior cultural phases, and many of them have to be removed from the social structure. The individual, too, must be freed of them. Education, then, will be required to penetrate the deeper layers of personality and, thereby, to assist in the reconstruction of the loyalties, aspirations, points of view, and moral ideals of individuals. The task is no less than that of transforming the characters of men—of creating new personality types adequate for the task of controlling the social arrangements emerging from the modern social conditions.

The child comes to school already "educated." He has been learning from his parents, playmates, and the countless social influences that play upon him from the time of birth. On entering school he possesses points of view, rules of conduct, social techniques, mechanical skills, language habits, aspirations, attitudes, and a welter of information. The child does not leave the world behind him when he enters the doors of the school, no matter how isolated from ordinary social activities the educational program may be. He brings his cultural background with him into the classroom and into all the activities in which he participates. He feels, thinks, and reacts in every school situation out of this cultural background. Not that the child sees his life in the school and his life out of the school as one—he may, and frequently does, see them as quite different worlds. This does not, however, alter the basic fact that the way he views the activities of the school, whether or not he sees any value in them, goes back to the cultural roots of his personality.

As long as this out-of-school education is in line with cultural reality, it is the function of the school to reinforce these learnings and to build a richer and more extended education upon them. Unfortunately, such out-of-school learnings—and, it may be added, many school learnings—do not conform to reality, or else they reinforce an undesirable social behavior. This fact is clearly seen in such learnings as those that characterize a criminal, an alcoholic, or a juvenile delinquent. It is now known that these learnings are acquired in the same way as those that meet with general social approval. Each of these kinds of learnings goes back to the influence of the social groups with which the individual is associated. The learned behavior of the social deviate lacks social reality, however, because it fails to take account of what is acceptable, or potentially acceptable, in realms of wider human association. In the groups where these deviate behaviors are acquired, they of course conform to the realities as the group sees them. But the deviate's wants and aspirations, as well as his rules of conduct, are not in accord with those of the persons who constitute the wider society, nor are they potentially acceptable to that society.

It is no less true that much of what passes as normal behavior is out of step with cultural reality. The ideas, loyalties, and information of the individual may not accord with new conditions and rules emerging in society at a particular time. His patterns of thought and action have no roots in reality when the conditions out of which they arose no longer exist. This is just as true of children on first entering school as it is of adults of all ages. A person who believes that all "foreigners" are "reds," that all government restraint on business is evil, that criminals are such because they *will* to be so, or that Negroes should not be allowed to hold jobs which white people want, is out of step with the dominant social rules, constituting the heart of the democratic value system and with the reality of objective facts.

The necessity of attempting to bring the social deviate into line with the facts of society and with what are considered to be desirable social norms is generally recognized. It is also becoming clear that this end can be achieved only through the processes of re-education. It is not recognized, however, that modern cultural change requires an equal emphasis upon mass re-education with respect to ideas, goals, skills, and ideals that traditionally have been considered normal and desirable.

The burden of the preceding chapters was to show that many cultural elements, whose validity in the past has been taken for granted, can no longer be accepted without serious reconstruction, if they can be accepted at all.

Yet these cultural elements are built into the personalities of individuals by the informal processes of induction from lingering social patterns. If this is true, it follows that one of the primary tasks of curriculum development is to build a program in which everyone can learn, through the processes of re-education, to become the kind of person demanded by the cultural patterns and realities now in the making.

3. *Orientation of Curriculum Development*

Turning to the character of the curriculum needed in the current stage of social transition, it is assumed that the educational program should be both conservative and progressive. It should be conservative in that it includes and emphasizes the valid aspects of the passing epoch; it should be progressive in that it stresses those aspects of the culture that are new and that must be understood if men are to adjust themselves to the emerging state of affairs and, within the limits allowed them, to create the kinds of human relationships they desire. More specifically, the task is to design an educational program that will help to create the following:

1. Common social goals, which lend meaning to individual efforts and achievement.
2. A new frame of acceptance—an adequate social and moral orientation.
3. A new conception of human nature based upon modern psychological and sociological knowledge and embracing new insights into personal and social actions and accomplishments.
4. New patterns of thinking, wherein a number of social variables in politics, economics, and the like, are kept in the picture in the process of reaching conclusions about social policies and actions, instead of the prevailing and now obsolete habit of thinking in a linear and compartmentalized fashion (where, for example, the attempt is made to keep political and economic thought in their separate spheres).
5. New methods and techniques of dealing with social conflicts—methods and techniques that will release creative energy rather than give rise to repressive measures.

Need for the Development of Common Social Goals

To have spoken of collective social goals in the early capitalistic period would have been nonsense, because at that time society was highly individualistic and compartmentalized. Economics was separated from politics, politics from religion, and so on. Each activity had its own sphere of influence. In each of these realms—especially the economic—goals were individualized. Each person was influenced by the cultural realities to do what he thought best for himself. This scheme was rationalized by the belief that out of the unhampered striving of individuals would come the greatest good for all. There were no social ends per se, for there was no need of them. The ends of society, when they were thought about at all, were conceived to be nothing more than the coincidence of individual ends.

As has already been observed, one of the basic tendencies of the present stage of industrial society is interdependence. No longer is it possible to keep the various compartments of society separate, one from another. It is also becoming increasingly evident that what one individual hopes to achieve for himself is so conditioned by what other people want and strive for that even individual goals can no longer be treated in isolation. The time has come, therefore, when individuals must think together about the ends they wish to attain, not only as individuals but also as a people.

This does not mean that individuals are to be encouraged to think about social goals entirely beyond their reach. Such speculating may be an interesting enterprise for theorists in a static cultural period, but not for teachers and students in a crucial cultural situation. If goals are not to be mere idle speculation, they must be within the grasp of the generation involved. The actual conditions and means of their attainment must be explored. Not to think realistically about goals is perilous. Psychological research has made it clear in recent years that to build hopes that cannot be realized is one way of creating frustration.[3] If the goals of a whole generation of people are allowed to exceed their reach, the result may be mass frustration accompanied by mass primitivization. On the other hand, to allow this possibility to frighten the teaching profession away from the problem of social goals could be

[3] Newcomb and Hartley (Eds.), *Readings in Social Psychology*, pp. 257–296.

equally disastrous. For, in a period of increasing interdependence, the ambitions of individuals are so easily and unintentionally thwarted by groups with which the individuals are not even associated, that not to plan co-operatively for individual and social action may lead either to extreme aggressive behavior or to lethargy on a mass scale. Whether most frustration arises from extravagant and unrealistic goals or from lack of common goals within which the individual's life plan can be realized, the resulting social situation is fertile soil for the growth of dictatorships.

Need for Study of the Rules by Which Men Live

A second part of the task of education is the study of the fundamental rules by which men live. These rules are understood to mean the deep-lying social constants on which the expectations of the people depend. As they function in conduct they are normative—that is to say, they are the principles by which people play the economic, political, and social games.[4] For example, in the period of classical capitalism prices were fixed by competition on the free market, which was believed to be governed by natural law embracing human nature itself. In the same period the jural laws were formal in the sense that they were constituted of general propositions, which allowed few, if any, exceptions and which in theory applied equally and impartially to all individuals. In the current social phase such principles often arouse expectations that cannot be realized.

In a static period such principles can be taken for granted. In fact, their presence is seldom disclosed except by the most sensitive minds in the social sciences and humanities. The common run of scholars, and the people alike, take them for granted in both thought and conduct. Individuals expect certain events and ways of behaving on the part of others without knowing why. When they attempt any explanation, they usually attribute these things to human nature. In a transition period all this is changed. Then, many expectations are not fulfilled. The people find that some individuals among them tend to vary from time-honored patterns, and a few persons recognize a change in basic principles. Of course, even the people of a relatively static epoch are

---

[4] Karl Mannheim, *Diagnosis of Our Time,* pp. 73–94.

accustomed to certain kinds of novelty. New facts and events emerge from moment to moment. As long as these conform to the old rules and can be rationalized by reference to them, the security of the individual is not touched. When these novel events can no longer be accounted for, however, the individual feels threatened and may be overcome by bewilderment and despair.

The alternative is for the individual to become aware of what is happening and to engage in a collective effort to think through the problems that arise out of this change in fundamental principles. To the extent that opportunity to do this is provided, he can escape the irrational conduct growing out of the feeling that the world is mysteriously caving in. Any such experience should include a factual study of the new state of affairs and an identification and examination of the old principles. It should also include an effort either to reconstruct the old rules or to discern new ones. Further, it is important that the interrelation of the various principles involved be examined, since one principle can seldom be understood except in relation to other principles, and since the interrelations among the emerging principles constitute a sort of structure which foreshadows the social patterns of the future.

All of this means that a new kind of content must dominate the curriculum in the transition period.[5] It will be a social-moral content, because the fundamental rules are basically moral in character. Facts will of course be stressed, but they will be employed in examining and straightening out moral ideas and in evaluating and reconstructing various courses of social action.

There is a tendency in a transition period to think that changes in the rules are the result of the diabolical work of some particular group of people—business and industrial leaders, labor leaders, radicals, socialists, or ambitious politicians. This tendency is partly the result of superficial thinking, from which the schools are not wholly free. Individuals and social groups do, of course, influence the development of fundamental social standards at points where crucial decisions must be made. But they have little or nothing to do directly with the creation of the circumstances that bring the need for new standards into existence.

[5] Bruce Raup, Kenneth D. Benne, George Axtelle, and B. Othanel Smith, *The Improvement of Practical Intelligence*.

Need for Moral Commitments in Learning Situations

Character can be changed only as the individual and his social group are caught in situations that disturb fundamental moral ideas and rules of conduct.[6] This fact points to one of the weakest aspects of prevailing educational practice. The preoccupation of the school with facts, information, and erudition makes it ineffective in so far as the modification of rules and conduct is concerned, for it leaves untouched the character which the individual imbibes from his culture. Current educational practice succeeds only in covering the old personality with a veneer of new words and facts. The individual talks better, he is better informed, but he is essentially what he would have been without the influence of the school.

This condition is adequate for a static period of society; for in such a period the soil that nourishes character is more or less the same from decade to decade. But when the social structure is undergoing change, character is at stake because it is rooted in the existing structure. This is why social changes are so often bitterly opposed by those who think they will lose prestige in the new scheme of things. As emerging social realities begin to give rise to new standards of conduct, many individuals find themselves in conflict with the new rules. Eventually these standards get into their personal structure. Then they find themselves suffering from internal confusion and conflict; they are torn internally between the old and the new. It is, therefore, a safeguard for sound mental and social health that learning situations involve the character of individuals, that they require consideration of the social "constants" —especially if, through group deliberation, a more adequate set of constants can be acquired.

Knowledge of Group Dynamics

It is becoming increasingly evident that the disposition and the behavior of the individual are shaped by the cultural system and groups to which he belongs. As the individual accepts membership in a group, he takes on the value system of the group. If the individual is in a group for which he has no feeling of belongingness, the facts and the

[6] *Ibid.*, Chapters XIII and XIV.

reasoning of the members are likely to have little or no effect upon him.

On the other hand, if an out-group individual projects himself into a group, as teachers frequently do, his activities will have little influence in changing the members in desirable directions. This means that, in a curriculum designed for an age of transition, ways must be provided for building student groups and for creating a sense of belongingness on the part of the members. It means also that ways must be devised by which the teacher can work himself into existing groups, both in and out of school, and by which he can use these groups in rebuilding character. Of course, the teacher must play a number of special roles in the group. For example, he has superior knowledge and, hence, is a resource for the group; he has more effective social skills and intellectual habits, and for this reason he is in a position to help the group with its procedures. He thus supplies a measure of security, which the group would not have without him. Partly for these reasons the teacher will always occupy a different position in the group from that of the other members. Nevertheless, the students must feel that the teacher has at least one foot in the boat with them, or else he will be considered an out-group person and his influence will be restricted.

In such a social group the individual must also feel free to express the social ideas and beliefs to which he adheres, no matter how unpopular they may be or how contrary to the standards of society at large they may appear. Only as the ideas and prejudices cherished by the various members of the group are brought to the surface with complete freedom can group spirit and understanding reach its fullest development. In this way also the individual attains self-objectification, being able fully to take account of and appraise himself.

It now seems clear that under modern conditions of social confusion and conflict, logical approaches by out-group persons to the modification of ideas and values sometimes drive the prejudices under cover or provoke an aggressive defense which further entrenches them.[7] Learning the facts about a belief or acquiring a new principle of behavior does not necessarily lead to changes in attitudes and ways of behaving. It is possible for an individual to study scientific principles in biology or psychology, for example, and yet continue to believe and act in keeping with some previous notions. Facts and logical reasoning influence

---

[7] Kurt Lewin, *Resolving Social Conflicts*, pp. 56–58.

personal structure and behavior only under certain conditions. There must be, among other things, enough common perspective to make the facts and arguments understandable and reasonable, and to create enough confidence in the sources of the facts and arguments to maintain an atmosphere of sincerity. Within the context of a genuine social group it is possible for facts, logic, and other forms of persuasion to regain their influence on personality. The group must seek out its own facts and pursue its own reasoning. Facts and ideas brought in by *total* outsiders will tend to be rejected. When the members themselves bring in the facts, these facts will be accepted as their own. Only if the group has the freedom and encouragement to do this will it accept the conclusions to which it is led by facts and logic.

It is important to bear in mind that American society still enjoys a common perspective at the level of its fundamental norms. To be sure, this perspective is often obscured by confusions and conflicts among competing groups. But an observer who penetrates beneath these confusions and disagreements will find a hard core of common values. It is, therefore, seldom possible to speak of a completely out-group situation. There are always some values common to the conflicting parties. For this reason facts and logic are still potent instruments in the resolution of social issues, especially when they appeal to the level of common values. On the other hand, many situations involve such fundamental disagreements that participants cannot easily discover their common ground. In such cases the parties to the conflict often perceive each other as out-group persons. Under this condition the effects of facts and logic are often greatly reduced.

Such disparity of outlooks is found in the classroom more frequently than is usually believed. Of course, in the classroom the differences in perspectives do not break out into open conflict as often as in society. But this fact does not alter the reality of classroom cleavages. The tendency of the school either to ignore or to suppress the values and viewpoints of children from the lower social strata affords many cases in point.

In such cases it is necessary to restore the situation within which factual and logical persuasion will be effective. In a period of social unrest requiring changes of thought and action, the dynamics of group processes take on great significance. Knowledge of the conditions and principles of group behavior becomes a necessary part of the teacher's professional equipment. In addition, he must possess the human-relations skills essential to the development of effective group processes of thought and action.

Need for the Curriculum to Emphasize
Social Techniques and Procedures

One of the main points of all this discussion is that in a transition period the character of the people must be rebuilt. New social realities require new types of men. These men must have social techniques and procedures appropriate to the problems and human relationships with which they must deal. As people are increasingly brought to depend upon one another in situations that challenge their personal structures, they must employ new procedures and techniques. The procedures and techniques which they now possess are largely those derived from working with things, and from working with other people in periods of relative stability when their characters were not fundamentally involved. They assume that individuals can and should be manipulated much in the same fashion as material things.

If we were dealing with mere things, the techniques of the first instance would be appropriate. Since we are dealing with human beings, these techniques are indefensible. They force personal relationships into mechanical categories. While in a mass society some of this may be unavoidable, that is no reason to accept its use as a matter of course. The most blatant manifestation of the tendency to carry over thing-techniques to human relationships is seen in the growth of propaganda designed to direct overt behavior to the advantage of others. Moreover, language habits, as revealed in round-table discussions, town-hall meetings, and the like, are more suited to winning contests of psychological intimidation than to the resolution of issues by inter-personal and inter-group persuasion that moves toward personal reconstruction.

It will be necessary in the new curriculum to emphasize the cultivation of the techniques of group deliberation and persuasion on a wide scale, to instill the kind of self-discipline that such deliberation requires, and to develop the capacity of sympathetically exploring the frame of mind out of which one's opposition thinks and acts. Only as men learn to escape their own narrow perspectives and to discover or to create new and more comprehensive outlooks can they begin to look back at themselves, to understand others, and to reach agreements with a minimum display of naked force.

The groups that come together in school will have in the personal structures of their members all of the predispositions found in the general population. There will be found the children of laborers, farmers, businessmen, and professional people, the children of all the social classes. They will have the perspectives, ambitions, and antagonisms of the groups and classes from which they come. The social issues dealt with in the school will thus involve and challenge the very characters of the boys and girls. Here then is the time and place for them to begin to acquire the discipline and techniques which proper human relationships demand in this period of transition.

Building Social Patterns to Sustain the New Personalities

For a long time it has been assumed that society could be improved by changing isolated individuals. The theory has been that by educational and logical appeals and other forms of persuasion the individual could be brought to change his attitudes and ideas. Then, from the aggregate of these changed personalities, would come social improvements. There is no reason to believe that this is a universal principle operating independently of a particular cultural reality. It is doubtless valid in a static system where changes do not reach down to the fundamental structure of society and fundamentally new personal adjustments are infrequently needed. But the shortcomings of this view in relation to the current situation are all too apparent. Not only is it too slow for the tempo of events, but it is not in keeping with the actualities of group thought and action. Its greatest defect is that it overlooks the tremendous impact of the lingering cultural patterns upon the individual.

The educational program must now be expanded to include what Lewin called "psychological ecology." Personality structure is sustained by a measure of acceptance on the part of the people among whom the individual moves. Modification of the standards of conduct—the basic elements of character—would be dangerous to the personal stability of the individual if the general social context were seriously contrary to the new norms. The individual would find his own personality threatened and in the long run would be forced either to take on the attitudes and beliefs of the more dominant social patterns or to withdraw from the major activities of society. Therefore, it is clear that in a period of social transition, when the standards are undergoing reconstruction, the educational program must be extended into the community so as to help create the social patterns necessary to sustain the new personalities. To the extent that education is effective in the present social plight, it will embrace the reconstruction of the channels of behavior through which the majority of the people now move. Only as this is accomplished can the needed characters find an atmosphere in which they can survive.

▶ *Following Up This Chapter*

1. Examine some of the more forward-looking curriculums, such as those designed along the lines of core programs or common-learnings programs. Try to determine the extent to which they take account of the six curriculum principles set forth above.

2. With a discussion group, try to think out the changes that would have to be made in the traditional curriculum in order to take fully into account the social conditions discussed in this part of the book.

▶ *Suggested Reading*

In *The Improvement of Practical Intelligence,* by Raup, Benne, Axtelle, and Smith, you will find an extensive discussion of the method and character of an educational program essential to the reconstruction of human character along the lines required by the social realities of our times. See especially Chapters XIII and XIV.

Somewhat similar treatments are to be found in the following: Kurt Lewin, *Resolving Social Conflicts;* Karl Mannheim, *Man and Society in an Age of Reconstruction* (especially Part IV); Karl Mannheim, *Diagnosis of Our Times;* George Soule, *The Strength of Nations.*

See also Educational Policies Commission, *Education for All American Youth.*

PRINCIPLES AND PROCEDURES OF CURRICULUM DEVELOPMENT

Part Two

THE TASK *of bringing the curriculum into line with social and psychological realities requires the use of principles and procedures. These principles and procedures can be organized around certain questions that will inevitably arise as the curriculum worker tries to make significant changes in the curriculum. Among the first questions will be that of how to determine the purposes of the school. Any attempt to improve the curriculum will necessarily raise this question: Why should a change in the curriculum be made? The answer to this question almost always leads directly into the further question of whether or not the proposed change implies a change in educational direction. The curriculum worker must, therefore, have grounds for accepting some purposes and rejecting others.*

Another pertinent question involves selection of subject matter for the educational program. In recent years it has been fashionable to renounce subject matter as belonging to traditional education. Curriculum development, however, cannot avoid the problem of how to determine the content of the educational program. No less an authority than John Dewey has said "that up to the present time the weakest point in progressive schools is in the matter of selection and organization of intellectual subject mat-

ter. . . ." [1] In any case it will be necessary to select the materials of instruction. And the wisdom of this choice will depend in no small part upon the thoroughness with which the various bases and procedures of subject-matter selection have been considered.

Further, subject matter must be selected in terms of whether or not it is within the experience and ability of the learner. No matter how desirable it may be for students to study certain subject matter or to engage in certain activities, these things will be of no avail if the materials of instruction are too far removed from the interests and abilities of the students. The question of adjusting the content of the educational program—problems, activities, reading materials—to the level of the learner's development is one that has claimed, and continues to claim, much attention from curriculum workers, research students, and teachers. This is commonly known as the problem of grade placement and, in more recent curriculum terminology, as the problem of sequence.

Finally, the amount of subject matter and the number of problems, or activities, that will be included in the educational program will depend not only on the ability of the learners but also on the amount of time allotted to the various fields of study, subjects, problems, or activities. How much of the total school time will be allotted to a given field or subject depends in part upon what is deemed to be important and in part upon a judgment of how long it will take the "average" individual to do what is expected of him. In any kind of curriculum, the question of how much time to allot to various aspects of the program will arise.

Part Two is concerned with the following questions:

1. *How can the worth of educational objectives be determined?*
2. *How should subject matter be selected?*
3. *How can the grade location, or sequence, of learning materials be established?*
4. *How can the allotment and distribution of instructional time be decided?*

[1] John Dewey, *Experience and Education*, p. 95. Published in the Kappa Delta Pi lecture series by the Macmillan Company, 1938. By permission of Kappa Delta Pi.

Chapter 5

The Validation of Educational Objectives

T H E   O B J E C T I V E S of education are derived from the culture. Since the culture consists of the ideals, ideas, methods of thinking, skills, attitudes, institutions, and other man-made aspects of environment, whatever ends the school attempts to achieve will be ends recognized as desirable in the cultural system to which the school belongs. In a highly integrated culture a large number of common beliefs constitute the core of the universals. In such a culture there will be relatively few things upon which the people disagree. The objectives of education will be clear, and the people as a whole will be in agreement as to what the objectives should be. In a highly complex culture, in which the common beliefs comprising the core are few in comparison with the number of variable elements, great diversity of beliefs will be found about almost every topic of discussion. In this state of affairs the objectives of education will be controversial.

American society is highly diversified. Few significant aspects of its culture are accepted by all the people, and nowhere is this more evident than in the objectives of education. If all the objectives that have been suggested by individuals and social groups could be realized in a twelve-year program of education—and if these objectives were mutually compatible—little, if any, selection would need to be made. Unfortunately, neither of these conditions exists. It is impossible to organize and conduct the school in such a way as to attain all the objectives set forth in educational literature. And it would be unwise, for lists of objectives are often incompatible or even contradictory, and any attempt to attain them indiscriminately would result in the teaching of conflicting ideas, attitudes, and modes of behavior. The curriculum worker, therefore, needs some satisfactory way of deciding upon the objectives to be achieved by the educational program.

In order to choose among objectives, the curriculum worker requires criteria that are understood and used alike by everyone involved in curriculum building. These criteria will embrace the conditions that worth-while objectives must satisfy. If proposed educational objectives are to be considered sound, they must:

1. Be conceived in terms of the demands of the social circumstances;
2. Lead toward the fulfillment of basic human needs;
3. Be consistent with democratic ideals;
4. Be either consistent or noncontradictory in their relationships with one another;
5. Be capable of reduction to behavioristic terms.[1]

This chapter attempts to make explicit the conditions required by these criteria.

1. *The Criterion of Social Adequacy*

Since the objectives of an educational program are derived from the culture, they will always be related in some degree to the social circumstances currently faced by a people or to those that were faced in the past. In a society that is undergoing little or no fundamental change, objectives usually are closely related to conditions as they now are. However, when a society enters a period of severe cultural change, social ideas and practices tend to lag behind new ways of doing things, and the educational objectives of earlier times are brought into the new period. When this happens the school attempts to educate people in ways of thinking and behaving which belong to an age that has passed away. Yet the old objectives are no longer valid.

[1] Gale E. Jensen, *Methodology and Criteria for the Validation of Educational Aims.* Doctor's dissertation, University of Illinois, 1948.

How Objectives and Social Circumstances Are Related

The way in which the objectives of education become invalid may be illustrated by an example from the field of language. It is generally believed that one of the objectives of education is to develop proficiency in the mother tongue. Yet proficiency in the native language will be defined quite differently from one cultural phase to another, depending upon how the social function of language is conceived. The conception of language proficiency which dominates the educational program today was developed in the eighteenth and nineteenth centuries, out of efforts of grammarians to standardize English usage and to develop elegance of expression, and from the requirements placed on language at that time. The chief function of language, excepting face-to-face communication, was to carry on correspondence for public, commercial, and personal reasons. Telephones and radios had not been developed, and railroads and other present-day means of transportation had not yet concentrated people into great urban centers, where the need for language as an instrument of social control and group deliberation becomes more crucial.

During the nineteenth century, public debates were common, for debate was a useful social tool. With the coming of radio, television, improved transportation, and improved methods of publication and distribution of reading materials, debate has been supplanted by forums, panel and round-table discussions, and the interview. To determine objectives relating to techniques of debate is to subscribe to the "fish-grabbing-with-the-bare-hands" curriculum after the discovery of nets.[2] Yet debate continues to be taught in the public schools, and each year champion debaters are determined in state-wide contests. Objectives resulting in this emphasis in instruction are invalid in terms of the criterion of social adequacy.

During the seventeenth and eighteenth centuries the notion developed that facility in language, especially in niceties of expression, was a mark of social prestige in that it was indicative of gentle breeding. The present emphasis upon the study of grammar and upon the development of literary style arose in this period, when the schools existed primarily for the upper classes, and when nicety of expression was con-

[2] *The Saber Tooth Curriculum*, pp. 33–35.

sidered an essential characteristic of an educated man. When facility in the mother tongue is defined in these terms today—and unfortunately this is often the case—there is reason to ask whether or not this objective takes account of social realities.

Today the social circumstances are quite different from those of the seventeenth, eighteenth, and nineteenth centuries. The schools are now for the masses; the amount of personal correspondence has been materially reduced because of technological developments in communication; secretarial and stenographic employees have increased in number and have assumed many responsibilities of written expression formerly belonging to the correspondent; mass media of communication have grown by leaps and bounds; occupational and social groups representing special interests have multiplied, and, finding themselves in conflict over matters of social policy, resort to the use of language in group situations to resolve their differences. These are new social realities, which require a redefinition of language proficiency as an educational objective. Only as new language skills are developed, and old ones reconstructed to meet the linguistic requirements of current social circumstances, can the objective of language proficiency be socially valid.

Knowledge of Social Realities Does Not Guarantee Valid Objectives

Knowledge of the present state of affairs does not necessarily mean that objectives formulated on the basis of these facts will be socially adequate. Curriculum workers sometimes seek to avoid the dangers they see in present-day society by appealing to ideals and virtues they believe to be eternal or to belong to a historical period superior to the current one. Despite the fact that representatives of these points of view sometimes make keen and generally accurate analyses of the social situation, the educational purposes they propose are rooted in points of view, conceptions, and beliefs brought over from an earlier historical period, rather than in the realities of the present.

Frequently this criticism applies with even more force to the objectives formulated by persons who in no way share the theoretical views of those who appeal to the past or to eternal truth. In this instance the social facts are carefully noted, but the objectives proposed as a result are precisely the ones that have been honored by the educational program of the past generation—thorough mastery of the conventional subjects, emphasis upon the "fundamental skills," stress upon the appreciation of literature, stress upon grammar, and emphasis upon the virtues of honesty, truthfulness, industry, thrift, and responsibility. This response to the social realities of the present has even less to commend it than the position of those who rest their claims upon either eternal truth or the superiority of the past. For the latter have, at least, a well-formulated theory of life and education to support them, whereas those who can conceive no better response to the social transformations now occurring than to do what is already being done seldom have any justification of their position worthy of consideration.

Illustration of Objectives Satisfying the Criterion of Social Adequacy

It is not the purpose of this discussion to set forth the goals of education, but rather to indicate the criteria by which goals may be evaluated. For illustrative purposes, however, it is relevant to indicate an objective that takes due account of the social transformations of today. It was indicated in earlier chapters that—because of the impact of science and technology upon the cultural system—traditional social incentives, social sanctions, and modes of life have been disrupted, and men have consequently become confused about social directions. Old standards of conduct have broken down in almost every aspect of society, so that it is difficult, if not impossible, for men to know in concrete social situations just what they should do. In a conflict between labor and management, should an individual be neutral? Should he be for labor? Or should he be on the side of management? In the struggle between nations, should he be willing to yield a measure of national sovereignty? Or should he strengthen the forces of nationalism by supporting larger armies and other ways of increasing combat potential? Or should he support both of these courses of action? The way he answers these questions will depend, in large measure, upon the kind of social goals he deems desirable and, in equal measure, upon his belief as to the effectiveness of the different courses of action in achieving these goals. Hence, if he is confused about the sort of society he thinks possible and desirable, he will be uncertain as to the course of action to be followed.

It is such questions as these that plague modern man. What should the school do to assist him in dealing with such questions? If the school attempts to teach the old answers and the old standards of judgment, it will fail to give him genuine help; for the old answers and standards are the ones that have failed him. Man is in difficulty, not because he has failed to learn the conventional answers and principles of conduct, but rather because the conditions in which they were effective and valid have passed away. Clearly the school cannot teach him new answers and new standards, for these are in the making. It can help him, however, to discover what the facts are and to perceive what values are at stake. It can help him to build a set of social values and goals by which to judge whatever answers may from time to time be proposed; and it can and must help him to acquire discipline in, and loyalty to, a method of thinking by which differences can be peacefully resolved. Seldom, if ever, does the school attempt to help boys and girls, men and women, to think about the kind of future they should build for themselves, not as individuals, but as a people. In times past this was not so essential; but in a period of social change and in a society where men govern themselves, it is courting social catastrophe to neglect this important educational task.

2. *The Criterion of Basic Human Needs*

It is well established by biologists, psychologists, and cultural anthropologists that man seeks to maintain himself in a state of equilibrium. The absence of equilibrium gives rise to an impulse. For example, an imbalance called hunger gives rise to an impulse, which becomes channeled in the search for food to restore the balance. In like manner, another imbalance, referred to as fatigue, gives rise to acts leading to rest and the consequent restoration of muscular and nervous energy. That which is required to restore the equilibrium is usually referred to as *need*. Certain imbalances and their corresponding objects of restoration are found among men of all cultures. These are called *basic impulses,* or more often *basic needs*. Among the basic needs that have been identified are food, sex, shelter, protection, growth (training), hygiene, movement, and social recognition.

Two Kinds of Needs: Basic and Derived

A cultural system is a particular way in which human beings become organized and carry on activities for the fulfillment of their basic needs. The satisfaction of these needs requires a great variety of materials, processes, ways of behaving, and social institutions. These things and activities that come to be used in the process of satisfying basic needs are themselves considered needs. They are called *derived needs* to distinguish them from basic ones. For example, food is one of the basic needs. But in procuring food people develop agriculture and ways of processing and preserving foods. In addition, they develop methods of distributing food and elaborate ways of preparing, serving, and eating it. An individual, therefore, has many needs growing out of these activities. He develops derived needs such as the need for knowledge and skill in the field of agriculture, need for farm tools, etc. These become indispensable objectives to his social existence.

As an individual grows to maturity, he acquires a personal structure which is conditioned by the position he occupies in the social system. Among the elements of this structure are tastes, likes and dislikes, aspirations, desires, skills and knowledges, all of which directly influence what the individual will need at a given moment. Some derived needs vary from one social group or compartment of society to another. An individual may feel the need to protect himself by skill in physical combat, or by the use of pistols and other instruments of violence. Indeed, he may, as in the case of the gangster, look upon these as means of earning a livelihood and of acquiring a favorable status among his peers. In another social group, the individual may protect himself by skill in business processes and by the accumulation of material wealth. Other derived needs, however, are found throughout a society rather than in a particular group or social level. In American society an individual needs a job, without which he will be unable to purchase food; he needs to cook his food—this need requiring in turn that he have a kitchen and such furnishings as are usually found in an American kitchen.

These derived needs are frequently as imperative in the life of the individual as basic needs. The need for a particular style of dress for a particular occasion may be more imperative for a woman than the need for either bodily protection or food. Yet style is a highly derived need, which is probably compounded of two basic needs—bodily comfort and social recognition.

How Objectives Are Related to Basic Needs

Although all educational objectives are based ultimately upon some conception of human needs, there are practical difficulties in using basic needs to validate educational objectives. Objectives are often connected with basic needs only by a long and tenuous chain of cultural factors. Consider, for example, the objective "to teach children to spell the common words of their native language." How is this objective related to the basic needs of individuals? It is sometimes held that a person must know how to spell in order to secure a job and gain promotions that will enable him to increase his standard of living. This claim would appear to be based on a direct connection between the objective "to learn to spell the common words" and the basic need for food, clothing, and shelter, since a job is needed in order to satisfy these needs. But this connection is by no means established. There are many persons who have good jobs and are poor spellers. Indeed, it may be likely that the ability to spell and the amount of personal income bear little relation to one another.

It is often maintained that the ability to spell the most frequently used words is essential to effective communication and that communication is necessary for the maintenance of the common life through which basic needs are met. But this contention is open to serious objection. In the first place, no scientific evidence is available to show that the ability to spell in accordance with the standards set in school is required for effective written communication. Indeed, it is clear from everyday experience that many individuals in every walk of life misspell words that appear in the standard spelling lists. Yet these individuals do not seem to be impeded in written correspondence. Misunderstandings arising from a failure of communication are seldom caused by poor spelling.

A few students of language instruction have asserted that spelling has little relationship either to earning a living or to communication but that it is closely related historically to social status. Those who advocate this position point out that emphasis upon spelling originated when formal education was largely limited to the upper classes, and facility in language was the primary mark of an educated man. At that time the path from social status to the basic need for social recognition was short and direct. This notion of education, with its social-class overtones, may have been brought into the current period of mass education. Thus spelling is taught, not as an instrument of communication but as a mark of social distinction. This conclusion has some support from the fact that a person who misspells a word does not think that his expression will be misunderstood but that he will be considered uneducated. The same argument might apply with equal force to other objectives of instruction in English. It can hardly be disputed that a considerable number of persons still respect the ability to spell as a mark of an educated person, and that, for the same reason, even those on the lower social planes give at least lip service to the importance of spelling.

What then becomes of the relationship between spelling as an educational objective and the basic needs of people? The foregoing analysis has made clear how circuitous and tenuous is the connection between basic needs and objectives. It has also brought out the fact that, in a society composed of different social strata, an objective may be related to the basic needs of persons on one social plane and not related at all to the basic needs of persons on another plane. For example, it is an undisputed fact that for individuals training to be secretaries or stenographers spelling is essential to vocational success and hence to the fulfillment of the basic need for food and bodily warmth. But when this derived need for spelling is generalized to include all individuals, the connection of the spelling objective with basic needs is broken. Furthermore, it may be that the ability to spell is connected with the need for social status in the case of individuals in the middle and upper classes of American society. While the lack of this ability may be a handicap, success in business or a profession, skill in conversation, and certain personal qualities are usually sufficient to enable even the poorest speller to gain status and prestige in these classes.

Some educational objectives, however, are related to the basic needs of individuals regardless of their social or occupational status. Discipline in the use of language as an instrument of resolving the social problems now facing men in every walk of life is an illustration of a language objective that touches the basic need of all people for food and shelter and for the preservation of life itself. These objectives will require, among other things, the teaching of those language skills that will enable individuals to recognize and understand the points of view of others, to locate and define the issues that divide individuals, to find points of common ground, and to use these in moving toward a resolution of the issues. It seems to be reasonably certain that unless men can learn to do these things their basic need for food and protection can hardly be provided for in the industrialized and multi-group societies of today.

It is now possible to state the factors that must be considered when the criterion of basic needs is used in the validation of educational objectives. (1) The curriculum worker must know what the basic needs are, as described in the research literature of sociology, cultural anthropology, biology, and psychology; (2) he must have the cultural facts that will enable him to connect basic needs to the objectives being evaluated; (3) he must discover whether or not the relationship between basic needs and objectives holds only for individuals occupying a particular social position or for all members of society, regardless of their social status.

3. *The Criterion of Democratic Ideals*

Every social class, in its rise to power, builds an ideological system—a system of social ideals and their rationalization—to support its claims and to guide its struggle to fulfill basic human needs. The ideology of the French *ancien régime* rationalized the superiority of the upper classes, the rule of kings and noblemen, and the inferior status of the lower classes. Communist ideology explains the goals and the strategy of the "working classes" in their struggle for power with the "propertied classes," who are allegedly exploiters of the workers. Fascist ideology, in its German version, rationalized the superiority of the "German race," on the one hand, and the inferiority of the masses, German and non-German alike, on the other. It underwrote an extreme nationalism centering in a theory of racial superiority. Democratic ideology, in its early modern form, was the supreme rationalization of the middle class in its struggle to build a free society against the resistance of the *ancien régime*. More recently it has been expanded to include the economic and social relations of men as well as their political life.

While an ideology is always the instrument of a social class, it is seldom rationalized in terms of advantages to that social class alone. Almost always the aims, methods, and social relations set forth in the ideology are held to be the best for mankind, either because of universal social dividends or because the ideology is in conformity with the laws of nature or the will of God. It is, therefore, no easy task to demonstrate the superiority of one ideology over another, however forcefully a man's faith may drive him to accept one system or another.

In most quarters of the Western World the democratic ideology is believed to be the best that man has been able to devise. The factual and theoretical justification of this position is too long and involved to set forth in a book on the curriculum. In the final analysis the argument rests on the proposition that the democratic system permits the fulfillment of all the basic human needs more completely than any other ideology. From a practical standpoint, however, the important fact is that the democratic ideology is the only one that can be used in validating educational objectives in the United States; for it is the only one to which the American people as well as American teachers will knowingly subscribe.

Since the democratic ideology represents the aims, methods, and social relationships to which the American people are devoted, their social institutions, policies, and practices are shaped in large measure by democratic ideals. It follows that *valid* educational objectives will be consistent with the democratic ideology—and that objectives that lead to modes of behavior incompatible with the democratic value system will be considered invalid.

The democratic ideology has been expressed in many different ways, although in substance all formulations of it are similar. Since its essential elements were set forth in previous chapters, they need not be repeated here save as a summary statement. Perhaps no better digest of the democratic value system has been given than the following passage from the pen of a great political scientist:

1. The dignity of man and the importance of treating personalities upon a fraternal rather than upon a differential basis.
2. The perfectibility of man or confidence in the development more fully as time goes on of the possibilities latent in human personality, as over against the doctrine of fixed caste, class, and slave systems.
3. The gains of civilization and of nations viewed as essentially mass gains —the product of national effort either in war or in time of peace rather than the efforts of the few.
4. Confidence in the value of the consent of the governed expressed in institutional forms, understandings, and practices as the basis of order, liberty, justice.
5. The value of decisions arrived at by rational processes, by common counsel, with the implications, normally, of tolerance and freedom of discussion rather than violence and brutality.[3]

How Objectives and Democratic Ideals Are Related

The problem of validating objectives, in so far as the democratic values are concerned, is one of determining whether or not proposed objectives lead to the realization of these values for the masses of the people. Some objectives contribute to the realization of these values; others make little or no contribution to their fulfillment; and still others lead to anti-democratic attitudes and habits of conduct. To teach an individual that human character is fixed by biological inheritance is to teach not only an untruth but also an undemocratic notion. For if character is fixed by the operation of the genes, the improvement of individuals becomes impossible, and the notion that some persons are by nature morally superior to others is given support. Both of these consequences are contrary to the principles of democracy, which assert as moral ends the improvability of the common man and the equivalence of men. Of course, individuals vary with respect to

[3] Charles E. Merriam, *What Is Democracy?* (Chicago: University of Chicago Press; 1941), p. 8. By permission.

their capacity to take on the attitudes and behavior patterns of the social group, and the limits of such capacity are undoubtedly fixed by heredity. However, the extent to which the capacity of any individual will be realized—and the kind of personal structure and character he will build—are determined by the culture and the position he occupies in society.

The teaching of spelling and grammar may contribute little to the realization of democratic ideals—except as these skills may be required by a few persons for vocational purposes and thus for their well-being in society, as in the case of teachers and clerical workers. On the other hand, mastery of the habits of effective thinking and critical reading and listening is to be rated high on the scale of objectives that satisfy the democratic ideals. For democracy is based on the principle that the common man can manage public, as well as private, affairs if he has a chance to acquire information and to learn to think for himself.

Application of the democratic value system requires that the curriculum worker master the principles of democracy and that he trace with care the relation of objectives to these principles. The principles of democracy are complex and interrelated and are subject to different interpretations. Hence no condensed statement of these principles can be used effectively in the validation of educational objectives by persons not thoroughly versed in their historical development and in their current meaning and interpretation in the political, economic, and social aspects of American culture. For example, the kind of reasoning which asserts that a knowledge of history is essential to the realization of democratic ideals (on the theory that we must know the past before we can understand the present) is the sort of loose thinking that enables justification of anything by recourse to democracy. Before the study of history can be justified by the criterion of democratic ideals, we must know just what aspect of historical knowledge is to be stressed, and just how this knowledge will be used as men move toward a fuller realization of democratic goals. Anything less than the satisfaction of these two conditions, not only for history but for any other aspect of the educational program, will lead to the prostitution of this criterion in curriculum building.

4. The Criterion of Consistency and Noncontradiction

Educational objectives are related not only to the criteria of basic human needs, social adequacy, and democratic ideals but also to one another. They may be neutral, consistent, or contradictory with respect to one another. If an objective is neutral or consistent with others, it is not contradictory. If an objective is not logically related to another objective, as teaching swimming is usually unrelated to teaching appreciation of literature, the relationship is a neutral one. A great number of educational objectives are neutral in this way. If one objective is logically compatible with one another, as teaching the desirability of co-operation is logically compatible with teaching students ways of co-operating, the relationship is a consistent one. A person is guided by incompatible objectives if he teaches an individual that labor and management are partners and that they should therefore work co-operatively together—and, at the same time, condones methods by which either group can exploit the other.

Importance of Logical Consistency of Objectives

In no society, not even in a highly integrated one, is the conduct of an individual always consistent. The elements of a culture never constitute a logical system, nor are they ever entirely mutually adjusted and integrated. In a highly integrated culture, however, the number of contradictory ways of behaving is reduced to a minimum, or else they are insulated from one another by social differentiation. For example, in the rigidly stratified society of the Middle Ages, where the circulation from class to class was more or less closed, different rules of conduct and ways of behaving could exist in the various social strata. The lower classes lived by one set of rules and the upper classes by another, although some principles of conduct were held in common by all classes.

But in a society, such as that in America today, where there is movement of persons from one social class to another and where communication between social classes and between specialized groups is going on from hour to hour, ways of behaving and principles of conduct belonging to the various classes and groups come into conflict. The individual then becomes confused and uncertain, becomes mentally unhealthy.

It is true that American culture is highly compartmentalized, so that a person may act on one set of principles in his family life and on an opposite set in business and professional relations; so that he may follow one set of principles in a political campaign and quite a different set in his private affairs. It is also true that individuals have a remarkable capacity to harbor contradictory principles and ways of behaving. Nevertheless, modern conditions of social mobility and communication force more and more people to become aware of their inconsistent ideas and actions. Failure to resolve these inconsistencies, the inability to gear the industrial machine and scientific resources to the satisfaction of human needs, costs more each year in social tensions, personal maladjustments, and human suffering.

It is, therefore, important that the curriculum worker evaluate educational objectives in terms of their logical relationships. It is unlikely that any set of objectives will be entirely consistent among themselves. In fact, any set of objectives will contain many that are neutral with respect to those that are logically consistent, and there will be some that actually contradict those that hang together logically. But this is no reason for failing to decrease the number of contradictory objectives wherever possible. In a society needing a greater degree of cultural integration, persons who select educational objectives without regard to their internal consistency are apt thereby to accentuate the tendency toward cultural disintegration.

5. *The Criterion of Behavioristic Interpretation*

Objectives must also be capable of reduction to behavioristic terms. In fact, the meaning of an objective is not clear until its meaning in terms of actual behavior is known. If the objective is to develop civic responsibility, the meaning of this objective is not clear until civic responsibility is defined by reference to concrete ways of behaving in actual situations. Of course it is possible to say, as is the ordinary practice, that an individual is acting responsibly when he is doing his duty;

but this definition of responsibility is a verbal abstraction that can mean nearly anything to anybody. Persons who have quite different understandings of this objective can appear to be in agreement. Nevertheless, most formulations of objectives are at this level, which probably accounts for the humorous observation that educational objectives are like New Year's resolutions.

To return to the behavioristic meaning of civic responsibility, the only way to clarify its meaning for practice is to state it in terms of behaviors to be developed. Its definition would then take the following form. If an individual does *this, this,* and *this* in situations of *this, this,* and *this* kind, he is civically responsible. For example, if he reads about the issues in each political campaign, reads about the candidates for each office, and goes to the polls and votes on election day, he is exercising his civic responsibility. It is understood, of course, that a responsible citizen would perform many other functions in addition to these. These few only illustrate the form that objectives must take to be clear and meaningful. Such objectives as the development of integrated personalities, self-realization, independence of thought, economic efficiency, problem-solving ability, critical thinking, appreciation of home and family life, understanding of the rights and privileges of childhood, and appreciation of music and art are apt to be misunderstood until they are reduced to statements of behavior in concrete situations. Objectives that cannot be put in terms of human behavior are invalid.

It is possible for objectives to be put in terms of behaviors to be developed which are beyond the capacity of individuals at all levels of growth. If an objective is to be attainable, it must be reduced to statements of behavior which individuals of a certain level of development are able to achieve. In stating the objective of critical thinking in terms of behavior, for example, it is necessary to consider the maturity of those who are to be taught. This means that the facts concerning the capacity of boys and girls of different ages to think critically will have to be taken into account. Those aspects of critical thinking that appear, in the light of these facts, to be possible of development at a particular level will constitute the behavioristic definition of critical thinking for students at that level.

6. *Application of Criteria*

Efforts to apply the foregoing criteria without thorough consideration of the facts and values they presuppose will lead to the selection of invalid objectives. The use of these criteria will require that the curriculum worker become thoroughly familiar with the knowledge to which each criterion has reference. The criterion of social adequacy, for example, has reference to social conditions. Application of this criterion will, therefore, require that the curriculum worker familiarize himself with social diagnoses made in recent years by competent social scientists. From a study of these diagnoses he will come to understand the culture of the United States and its relations to other cultures; he will learn about the welfare-levels existing in American society and the effects of these levels upon individuals; he will be able to see the ways in which the culture is changing; he will come to see how all of these matters are related to the objectives of education and, correspondingly, what the objectives must take into account if they are to be socially significant.

In like manner and in like degree, the curriculum worker must understand the democratic ideals in both their historical and current forms. He will recognize that this criterion alone, among the five suggested for the validation of education objectives, offers a social-moral direction to curriculum planning. Under the other criteria, considered singly or as a group, it would be possible for the curriculum to be inconsistent with the long-time hopes, dreams, and aspirations of the American people. Careful consideration of the criterion of democratic ideals will assure objectives in keeping with the democratic way of life.

In addition, the curriculum worker must be thoroughly familiar with the literature of human needs; he must understand the socio-psychological investigations of child and adolescent development.

Knowledge of all these matters, however, will only lead to confusion about the objectives of education unless those who are involved in curriculum improvement deliberately attempt to be consistent in their logic and clear as to meanings when dealing with ideas or with the expression of these ideas. To make objectives clearly understood and valid is an important step in the development of a curriculum. It is a step requiring far more study and care than is the general practice in curriculum work.

▶ *Following Up*
This Chapter

1. Choose an objective from any part of a course of study for an elementary or secondary school, and try to show how it is related to the fulfillment of one or more basic human needs. Can you follow the chain of cultural factors connecting the objective to the need? Examine the same objective by applying the criterion of social adequacy and the criterion of democratic ideals.

2. Select an objective from any field of instruction, and try to state it in behavioristic terms. Try to describe the behavior that the objective implies for a particular situation.

3. Select a list of general objectives from a city, county, or state course of study. Try to evaluate the list by applying the five criteria discussed in this chapter.

▶ *Suggested*
Reading

Literature on the validation of educational objectives is scanty. Since objectives of education always involve moral ideas, most of the relevant material is to be found in such related fields as ethics and value-theory. Nevertheless, there are references in the field of education.

1. One of the most balanced treatments of the problem of validating educational objectives is to be found in John S. Brubacher's *Modern Philosophies of Education,* Chapter 4. In this chapter you will find the ways in which various schools of educational thought have attempted to derive and to justify objectives of education. You will find also insightful criticisms of the various positions that have been taken on this problem. For a critical discussion of the relation of "needs" to objectives, see Boyd H. Bode's *Progressive Education at the Crossroads,* Chapters 4–5. Robert J. Havig-

hurst's *Developmental Tasks and Education* sets forth the needs of the individual which emerge in the course of his development. For an excellent discussion of present-day confusion about educational directions, see William H. Kilpatrick (Editor), *The Educational Frontier,* especially Chapter 1. The relation of democratic ideals to the determination of educational objectives is explored in Chapter 9, and the problem of relating the school to social realities is discussed in Chapter 2. See also Chapter 15 of Harold Rugg's *Foundations for American Education.* An exploration of objectives from various standpoints is Lyman Bryson and Others (Editors), *Goals for American Education.* Although this book emphasizes higher education, many of its principles have general application.

2. More fundamental treatments of the problem are to be found in the following: John Dewey's *Theory of Valuation;* Orlie H. Pell's *Value-Theory and Criticism;* F. S. C. Northrop's *The Logic of the Sciences and the Humanities; The Improvement of Practical Intelligence,* by Raup, Benne, Axtelle, and Smith; *De Principiis Non Disputandum . . . ?,* by Herbert Feigl in Max Black's *Philosophical Analysis,* pages 119–156; and *On Grading,* by J. O. Urmson in Antony Flew's *Logic and Language,* pages 159–186. The more advanced reader will find that these references explore various aspects of the problem in such a way as to supply new insights and new approaches. Wayne A. R. Leys' *Ethics and Social Policy* (especially Chapters 1–4) bears directly on the problem. See also "Educational Objectives: Improvement of Curricular Theory about Their Determination" in Herrick and Tyler (Editors), *Toward Improved Curriculum Theory,* pages 26–35.

3. The best classification of objectives as well as behavioristic description of them may be found in Benjamin S. Bloom and others (Editors), *Taxonomy of Educational Objectives.*

Chapter 6

Principles of
Subject-Matter
Selection

ONE OF THE MOST DIFFICULT TASKS of curriculum building is the selection of subject matter appropriate to the objectives of instruction. Changes in objectives require changes in content. Too often objectives are professed only to be denied in practice by inability to select the content upon which their realization depends. Moreover, vested interest in subject matter—the tendency to see values in content that exist only for persons who teach it and who believe that an appreciable change in it will sacrifice essentials of education—is a complicating factor in a problem already fraught with difficulties. Frequently teachers do not understand the role of subject matter in human activities; neither are they always aware of the fact that the subject matter they know and use as teachers is highly selected from a vast store of human knowledge; nor are they ordinarily aware of the biases operating in the selection of the content they teach. Therefore, the wisest selection of subject matter will result from approaching the problem from broad principles concerned with the meaning and source of subject matter and the bases of its selection.

1. *What Is Subject Matter?*

The members of a social group participate in two kinds of activities: first, those such as hunting, selling, farming, and manufacturing, which result in the procurement of food, clothing, shelter, and other necessities of life; second, those involving the common life of the group, such as voting, discussing social issues, appreciating music, and obeying a system of law. From these activities they learn skills, facts, rules of conduct, and aesthetic principles comprising what the social group has learned about the world, about ways of using the world and of improving its beauty, about man himself, and about how to live together. Such knowledge, values, and skills constitute the subject matter of the group.

Subject matter is, however, only a part of the total culture. Subject matter includes what men know and believe and their ideals and loyalties, but not everything they have created. An institution such as the family is not subject matter, but what is known and believed about the family and the ideals we hold for family life are subject matter. Tools and machines are not subject matter, but knowledge about tools and machines—about how they are made, their operation, and their uses— is subject matter.

General and Specialized Subject Matter

Activities involved in government, citizenship, economics, and other areas of common endeavor give rise to shared knowledge and values. Here are found the standards of right and wrong, good and bad, beautiful and ugly upon which members of the group rest their choices; here are found the customs and traditions to which all members are expected to be loyal; here are found the general social goals and sanctions motivating the individual; here are found the institutional procedures and social practices to which all individuals are encouraged to conform. These make up the "common sense" of the group and the body of subject matter which the group insists that all its immature members learn. This teaching is carried on informally in a simple group through shared group life. As the group grows more complex, these common learnings are taught by formal schooling.

A type of specialized subject matter is that knowledge required to satisfy the material needs of life. These activities are the first to be affected by division of labor. Division of labor between the sexes in a primitive social group may delegate knowledge and skill of hunting to men, while knowledge and skill of tilling the soil may be the special concern of women. With the introduction of domesticated animals, hunting is partly replaced by herding and stock raising, and, in highly developed societies, by an elaborate system of farming and animal husbandry requiring much specialized knowledge and ability. Highly industralized societies require more specialization of activities and consequently of subject matter. This content is usually referred to as technical and specialized in order to distinguish it from learnings that are more or less common to all.

Descriptive Subject Matter

Descriptive subject matter consists of facts and principles. Facts are reported in statements about things that can be perceived directly or in principle. If someone says that the thermometer reading is 70 degrees or that there are thirty registered voters in precinct two, he is making factual statements, which can be directly verified by observing and counting. If someone says that George Washington died in 1799, he is also making a statement of fact; however, this one is perceptible only in principle. George Washington's death is not now capable of being observed. Yet his death was observed, and in theory it is now observable in the sense that a person can mentally reconstruct the observation.

Books and other instructional materials are heavily weighted with factual content. Courses in history consist largely of factual statements about what happened, when and where it happened, and who was involved in it. Biology courses contain facts about the structure of plants and animals, about their classification, and about their functions. Indeed, curriculum workers often disagree as to whether there is too much or too little factual content in relation to the corresponding attention given to principles.

Descriptive principles are laws, rules, and theories, such as scientific laws and theories. They indicate how to proceed when in doubt. Boyle's law, for example, tells how to deal with problems relating to the control of a confined volume of gas. It tells us that if the temperature of a gas is held constant and pressure is applied, the volume will decrease or increase as the pressure is increased and decreased. It does not say that people *should* deal with problems involving gases, nor does it say that gases *should* act in this way. It simply indicates how gases *do in reality act*. From this standpoint, these principles resemble facts in that they do not involve values. Hence principles and facts are both called descriptive subject matter.

Normative Subject Matter

Normative subject matter consists of the rules of the game, norms, or standards by which individuals make moral and aesthetic choices. It represents the value standards men have built up through generations. The rules that "the governor should be responsible to the governed," that "those who are affected by policies should have a share in making them," that "one should act toward others as he would have others act toward him" are all examples of normative content. A long list of such normative rules could be cited. The objectives of education, the social-moral controls of economics, the ideals operating in and through political institutions, the legal systems, the rules of acceptable family conduct, the standards for judging the merits of artistic works—all these would be included in such a list, and it would still be incomplete. Normative subject matter abounds in literature and in the writings of political leaders, sages, and prophets. It is drawn from the wisdom of the people. Normative content and descriptive content may be further distinguished by relating them to the kinds of questions that might be asked about an event. What happened? When and where did it happen? Who was involved in it? These questions can be answered only by factual statements.

Why did it happen? What would cause it to happen again? These questions require an explanation for an answer; all explanations take the form of theories and general ideas, using descriptive principles rather than facts to provide the answer. It should be recognized, however, that facts are needed to prove any explanatory principle and that the way in which such a principle works depends upon the facts of the situation.

Was its occurrence good or bad? Should it have happened? Should it happen again? Was it beautiful? Answers to these questions require moral and aesthetic judgments, and hence involve normative content. In general, therefore, descriptive subject matter is used to answer the first two kinds of questions, and normative content to answer the third.

If another question, "What should I do?" had been asked, the answer would require both types of knowledge. The making of such a simple decision as where to eat the evening meal requires facts and both descriptive and normative principles. Facts are gathered about the prices, the cleanliness, the service, the amount of noise, the availability of music, and the distance to travel to reach the restaurant. Descriptive principles are called upon to give these facts meaning. If there are flies and roaches in the kitchen, the food is likely to be unsanitary. If the eating utensils are washed in dirty water, they will be unclean. But the very decision to collect these facts and employ these principles in making the choice of an eating place, as well as the final decision of where to eat, are directed by normative principles. A good restaurant should be clean, economical, should not have unnecessary noise. It should provide good service and should be nearby. It was with respect to these values that the relevant facts were collected and the principles applied. Thus questions with respect to what is best for an individual or a group to do require both facts and descriptive principles, on the one hand, and normative principles, on the other.

Subject Matter as the Content of Subjects

In America today the amount of knowledge about collective activities, to say nothing of specialized activities, is far greater than any one individual can master. Hence the core of common knowledge and wisdom must be selected and organized in order to instruct the immature members. Similarly, knowledge about specialized activities, the technical and scientific pursuits, is selected and organized for instructional purposes.

The subject matter of a school subject is what man has learned about that subject—whether it be agriculture, biology, economics, mathematics, recreation, health, or what not. It is selected from the vast stock of facts, ideas, and values that man has accumulated from his collective and specialized endeavors. The content of a textbook is what an author has selected from man's total knowledge of the subject. Full recognition of this point would perhaps help to break down uncritical attachment to the conventional subject matter of courses.

It is not unusual for teachers and other curriculum workers to accept new objectives and at the same time insist that the subject matter with which they are familiar, if well organized and taught, satisfies the new purposes. Many promising programs of curriculum reconstruction have begun with new objectives and ended in a reorganization of old content. It is as though a physician, on making a new diagnosis, were to prescribe the same medicine, insisting that the trouble was in the way the medicine was given rather than in the medicine itself. Frank recognition that the subject matter of textbooks and courses of study represents deliberate choices, and that the bases of these choices must be discovered and criticized before the new content is accepted, would result in improvements in curriculum rebuilding.

2. Criteria for Selecting Subject Matter

Since only a fraction of the total accumulated experience of a culture can be included in a program of formal education, the curriculum worker is faced with the task of selecting content. How is the content to be selected? What kinds of experiences should be provided?

If the objectives had been carefully chosen to be in keeping with the criteria discussed in Chapter 5, and were thus clearly stated in terms of expected behaviors, a strong theoretical case could be made for determining the worth of subject matter by scientific test. With evidence that certain subject matter reached the chosen objective, that subject matter would be used until scientific study indicated that another was an even better approach to the objective. While such studies have made a few significant contributions to curriculum building, there are at least two important reasons why this approach cannot be the only one used to select content. In the first place, objectives are seldom chosen as carefully or stated as clearly as this method would require. Secondly, educational measurement is a new science, and, even though it is developing and improving evaluative instruments rapidly, there is still a large number of objectives for which no efficient measures exist.

It is clear then that the ultimate basis of subject-matter selection should rest with the determination of objectives. Yet the consideration of social and moral judgment, too, is implicit in the selection, as shown by such questions as, Why should subject matter judged, or even proved, useful, be considered good or valuable? Such questions must be decided and cannot be answered with a scientific test. Of course, these decisions should be made when the criteria for determining objectives are applied. When this is not done, they must be met in the selection of subject matter. To make these decisions and to try to make the content satisfy the objectives is further complicated by the fact that curriculums are seldom if ever reconstructed as a whole, and are already committed to the basic principles of a certain type of curriculum organization as well as to certain objectives in keeping with these principles.

It is in this context of prior commitments with respect to objectives and curriculum organization that several criteria of content selection will be discussed. In question form, the following five standards for subject-matter selection are presented:

1. Is the subject matter significant to an organized field of knowledge?
2. Does the subject matter stand the test of survival?
3. Is the subject matter useful?
4. Is the subject matter interesting to the learner?
5. Does the subject matter contribute to the growth and development of a democratic society?

It should be understood at once that these are not criteria to be applied as standards for all subject matter by anyone engaged in content selection. They are not a set of standards at all in the sense that the criteria for determining objectives were advocated as standards. Instead, these are simply five different single criteria that have been used alone or in combination by different curriculum workers in recent years. As such, no one of them is advocated here as the single best way of selecting subject matter. Nor are they suggested for this purpose. However, it is hoped that knowledge of these currently used criteria will help the curriculum worker in his approach to the problem of content selection. With this purpose in mind the section following the presentation of the five criteria considers some strengths, weaknesses, and underlying assumptions of each. This discussion is intended to enable the curriculum worker to choose more intelligently a criterion or group of criteria for use in subject-matter selection.

Is the Subject Matter Significant to an Organized Field of Knowledge?

Under this criterion subject matter is included if it is thought to be essential to the mastery of the field to which it belongs. The first assumption here is that the entire area of knowledge is worth studying. This criterion further presupposes a program of studies consisting of specialized courses, with each course being followed by a more advanced course. Not all the subject matter of a field, such as mathematics or history, can be included in a series of courses. But according to the criterion the subject matter which a competent student of the field is expected to know should be included.

An idea related to this criterion, and sometimes used as a guide in selecting subject matter, is that of prerequisite knowledge. The content of beginning algebra, for example, is often defended on the ground that it is essential to the study of advanced algebra and calculus. This principle is limited in application and may operate in the process of selection only when an organized field of knowledge has been delimited and the significant subject matter within it has been determined. Then the principle may be used to select the items that are most directly related to advanced study. For example, how much and what part of the content of beginning algebra courses is actually needed in the study of calculus? Rigorous application of the principle in answering this question reveals which mathematical facts and processes are needed in the study of calculus.[1] As a principle of selection, therefore, the idea of prerequisite knowledge is a highly refined phase of the much broader principle of "significance to an organized field of knowledge."

Does the Subject Matter Stand the Test of Survival?

The notion that age is a mark of value is widely accepted and is deeply rooted in human experience. Acceptance of the "old and tried"

[1] F. H. Fagerstrom, "Mathematical Facts and Processes Prerequisite to the Study of the Calculus," *Teachers College Contributions to Education*, No. 572.

is due partly to the sentiments that the antique arouses and even more to the belief that the things that have come down from the past are the product of generations and even centuries of "experimentation." Objects of worth are those that have survived because they have been capable of satisfying the aspirations of mankind for a higher and richer culture. This principle was, and still is, widely used in curriculum building, especially in the field of moral conduct and in the arts of music, painting, and literature. The literary works that have been included in the curriculum, for example, are those whose worth has been attested by the fact that they have been highly prized by generation after generation.

Is the Subject Matter Useful?

The principle of utility may be broadly conceived, as when subject matter is selected because of its usefulness in the performance of activities classified into areas of living. One of the early efforts to set forth such areas was made by Herbert Spencer. In an essay entitled, "What Knowledge Is of Most Worth?" he listed five major areas of human activity, as follows:

(1) those activities which directly minister to self-preservation; (2) those activities which, by securing the necessaries of life, indirectly minister to self-preservation; (3) those activities which have for their end the rearing and discipline of offspring; (4) those activities which are involved in the maintenance of proper social and political relations; (5) those miscellaneous activities which make up the leisure part of life, devoted to the gratification of the tastes and feelings.[2]

Over a score of more recent classifications of activities have been prepared by individuals as well as by educational commissions. Since these more recent classifications are similar in many respects, only one, Bobbitt's list of life activities, will be given:

(1) language activities; social intercommunication; (2) health activities; (3) citizenship activities; (4) general social activities—meeting and mingling with others; (5) spare-time activities, amusements, recreations; (6) keeping oneself mentally fit—analogous to health activities of keeping

[2] Herbert Spencer, *Education* (New York: D. Appleton & Company; 1860), pp. 13–14.

oneself physically fit; (7) religious activities; (8) parental activities, the upbringing of children, the maintenance of a proper home life; (9) unspecialized or non-vocational practical activities; (10) the labors of one's calling.[3]

Subject matter needed in developing the ability to perform these life activities is deemed useful, while that which makes no contribution or only slight contribution to such abilities fails to satisfy the principle of utility.

This criterion is more frequently interpreted in a narrow sense, as when the content of the conventional subjects is studied to determine what items are most useful to adults. For example, G. M. Wilson made studies to ascertain what parts of arithmetic were most useful.[4] In one of these studies children in the sixth, seventh, and eighth grades collected the arithmetic problems encountered by their parents during a two weeks' period. These problems were analyzed to discover the content of arithmetic which their solutions required. Similarly, though by different techniques, spelling lists and basic reading vocabularies have been developed and the utility of the content of courses in history, science, and other subjects has been investigated.[5] In almost every one of these studies utility is defined in terms of frequency of use—those items of subject matter most often used by adults being considered the most useful and, hence, the most desirable as curriculum content.

Is the Subject Matter Interesting to the Learner?

Under the criterion of interest, pupil problems and objectives become the guiding points in content selection. The curriculum should consist of subject matter that is needed in solving pupil problems or in fulfilling pupil purposes or plans.

A common interpretation of this criterion is that the subject mat-

---

[3] Franklin Bobbitt, *How to Make a Curriculum* (Boston: Houghton Mifflin Co.; 1924), pp. 8–9. By permission.

[4] G. M. Wilson, "A Survey of the Social and Business Usage of Arithmetic," *Teachers College Contributions to Education,* No. 100.

[5] National Education Association, Department of Superintendence, *Third Yearbook,* "Research in Constructing the Elementary School Curriculum." See also *Fifth Yearbook,* "The Junior High School Curriculum"; *Sixth Yearbook,* "The Development of the High School Curriculum."

ter must satisfy the *needs* of the learner. When thus interpreted, its meaning hinges on the word *needs*. As used here, it designates a disposition toward the subject matter. If the learner feels that the subject matter helps him to obtain something he genuinely wants, it meets the criterion of interest. If, on the other hand, it is selected because other people think the learner "needs" it—as they may think he needs punishment or that he needs to remove a personality deficiency about which he has no concern—the criterion is violated. In other words, the subject matter included in the curriculum must be interesting to the learner.

Strict application of this principle has led to the conclusion that the curriculum should not be made in advance but should be developed on the spot under the direction of the learner's interests. The subject matter would not be selected and set-out-in-advance to be learned, as in a textbook, but would be sought for as it was needed in solving a problem or in carrying out purposeful activities. When set-out-in-advance, the subject matter becomes so divorced from interests as to appear as though it existed for its own sake. Then, instead of being studied because it is needed in the fulfillment of some purpose, it is studied as if it had meaning in and of itself—or, at best, as if its sole usefulness were in the attainment of marks and promotions.

A less strict interpretation of this criterion holds that there are some more or less persistent and common interests, and that the criterion of interest can be used to choose subject matter far in advance of any actual need of it by the pupils. The criterion can be used to predict the content in which the majority of pupils of a given age range will most likely be interested. Although interests vary from individual to individual, investigations indicate that some interests are more or less common and can, therefore, be employed in the selection of content. Of course, the more uniform the backgrounds and past experiences of persons, the more they exhibit the same interests. It has been found, for example, that most adolescents, especially those from middle-class families, are interested in getting along with others, in choosing vocations, in choosing mates, and in getting along with members of their family. Whatever subject matter will satisfy these interests will be valuable curriculum material for those whose interests are satisfied by it.

Does the Subject Matter Contribute to the Growth and Development of a Democratic Society?

The criterion of social development assumes that society is changing and that men can and should direct these changes toward an even better life for all. It also assumes that the schools can help with intelligent direction of social change by their selection of curriculum content. A careful selection can build the kinds of knowledge and abilities required to deal intelligently with the problems related to social change.

Two unfortunate misconceptions have sometimes been associated with this criterion. One is that curriculum workers advocating this criterion for content selection are claiming that society as it now exists is all wrong and that the schools intend to rebuild it. The second error follows directly—that curriculum workers have in mind some plan of social utopia they would foist upon the public by indoctrinating it in the schools. Both of these are complete distortions of the criterion of social development. Instead, it says that society is changing and that within the limits of irreversible social trends the people of a democracy can direct the changes toward democratic ideals. The schools cannot teach answers to the social problems through which these changes emerge. These answers will be determined by the people as a whole. But the schools can select the kind of content that will enable children and youth to become increasingly able to deal with social problems and issues.

The criterion of social development is not met if content is selected only because it contributes to an understanding of contemporary affairs. This may mean no more than bringing the content up-to-date. The social changes with which this content would deal have already occurred. Rather, the criterion of social development makes the school a positive force in social change. The criterion requires, among other things, that the instructional program focus upon development of moral values, effective processes of thinking, and skills of democratic social processes. Under this criterion subject matter is valuable to the extent that it equips people with the ideals, knowledges, and skills needed to help shape the social changes now taking place and those that will take place in the future.

3. *Choosing among Principles of Content Selection*

Thus far the more significant principles by which content is determined have been described without reference to their worth. The curriculum maker, however, cannot be content with this impartial treatment, for he must choose among the principles as he seeks solutions to the problems of curriculum building. Even if he makes use of most, if not all, of them, as is the usual practice, he will of necessity emphasize some and make little use of others. How then can the worth of these principles be determined? How can he decide which criterion should be the primary basis of subject-matter selection?

The answer to these questions always results from practical judgment rather than from scientific investigation alone. Since dependable, practical judgments are based upon acceptable values as well as facts, the appraisal of each criterion will involve two questions: First, is the criterion adequately supported by facts and sound reasoning? Second, does its use contribute significantly to the realization of desirable educational and social objectives? In the discussion which follows, each criterion will be considered in connection with the objective usually associated with it, as well as from the standpoint of its general dependability.

Criteria Related Primarily to Uncritical Transmission of the Cultural Heritage

It is obvious that the knowledge, skills, and values mankind has created through the ages are vast and that no generation, however gifted, can master the entire cultural heritage. How, then, can the part of the racial experience that is to be singled out for transmission through the school be determined? Indeed, this is the question that all the criteria described in the preceding discussion are designed to answer. But those theories that make the transmission of the culture the primary aim of education answer it by applying two criteria: (1) survival, and (2) significance to an organized field of knowledge.

The criterion of survival will be considered first. The fact that an item of subject matter has been handed down from generation to generation does not make it valuable. Mere age is no more a dependable test of the worth of anything than is pure novelty. Undesirable as well as desirable things survive. History abounds with erroneous ideas and inefficient skills and techniques which endured for generations before they were eliminated. It is necessary only to remember the part superstitions and outworn ideas have played, and continue to play, in all aspects of human endeavor, to realize that mere survival is not an adequate test of what the schools should teach.

Advocates of the principle of survival would be the first to agree that age alone is no indication of worth. In their view, it is not survival alone that marks the value of content, but rather the fact that in its survival the content has proved its worth in instance after instance of human endeavor. This view places the real test of the value of content in the consequences of its past uses. If the consequences have been good, the content is believed to be valuable. This interpretation is clearly stated in H. C. Morrison's definition of a universal institution, which he employs as the basis of common education.

A universal institution is a system of popular usages or beliefs which, originating in human nature, in the common sense and experience of mankind, has survived as a useful form of harmony and co-operation, has become organized, extended, and refined in the course of social evolution, and is, finally, capable of being rationally comprehended as a necessary element in the structure of all advancing societies.[6]

The criterion of survival is thus the historical counterpart of the principles of utility.

No amount of past usefulness, however, can assure the value of subject matter for today. That men have found it worth while to know certain things, or to be able to do certain things, is not sufficient evidence that they will continue to do so. As the aims and conditions of social life change, new knowledge and skills are brought into use, and neglected parts of the cultural heritage are dusted off and used. Reasoning historically to establish the value of subject matter always involves two assumptions: first, that the previous conditions in which the content was found valuable were the same as the present ones; second, that the ends to which men then devoted themselves are the ones to

[6] H. C. Morrison, *The Curriculum of the Common School* (Chicago: University of Chicago Press; 1940), p. 14. By permission.

which men should now be committed. A century ago great stress was placed upon moral maxims such as those in *Poor Richard's Almanac*. Elementary school readers were heavily weighted with stories pointing to these maxims. These have been mostly deleted from the curriculum of the public schools, and persons who contend, on the basis of the principle of survival, that these elements of the culture heritage should be restored must show that the above assumptions are valid with respect to such content. Similarly, persons who believe that more emphasis should now be placed upon the study of grammar—on the ground that in the past such study has produced better written expression—must show that the social importance of good written expression is as great today as in the last century, when grammar played a dominant role in the school's program. They must also show that the conditions making the study of grammar effective—if indeed it was—were the same as those of today.

It is exceedingly difficult to validate these assumptions; hence the criterion of survival is always employed with considerable risk. Partly because of this fact and partly because of the persuasive power of historical reasoning, this criterion is almost invariably used loosely, thus playing into the hands of individuals who defend the existing educational programs. Efforts to change the content of history and literature courses, for example, have often been impeded, if not actually thwarted, by the belief that, since the old subject matter was the tried and true, changes were destructive of genuine education.

Nevertheless, when rigorously interpreted, the principle of survival can play a significant role in the selection of content. This is especially true in the selection of those elements of the culture—such as deep-lying moral principles—that are often the least affected by social change. For example, it will be generally agreed that freedom and equality are still desirable, despite all the social changes of recent years, because societies based upon these ideals have always released the human spirit and have produced the highest development of personality. Yet despite the historical evidence in their favor, these ideals must be interpreted in terms of the complex social conditions of today. They must be judged not only by their history but also by their capacity to guide man in his present quest for deep and lasting satisfactions.

The principle of significance to an organized field of knowledge, like the principle of survival, is related primarily to the notion of cultural accumulation and transmission. The transmission of the cultural heritage is usually thought of as covered by science, mathematics, and English. The subject matter judged important to these subjects is, therefore, accepted as satisfying the aim of cultural transmission. This criterion is used primarily, however, in the selection of subject matter for the purpose of producing scholars and research workers in the various subjects of specialized knowledge. In effect, therefore, the selection of content by this criterion reduces the ideal of cultural transmission to the ideal of specialized scholarship.

This is clear from the fact that the purposes of organized subjects are shaped in no small part by the academic requirements of the graduate school, which is the capstone of the educational structure. The graduate school is a vocational school par excellence. Every graduate student is preparing for a job—to teach, to do research, or to do something else for which his specialized training prepares him. This vocational aim permeates the whole educational system by influencing the choice of subject matter at all rounds of the educational ladder. The content deemed significant in the liberal arts college, for example, is that which prepares the individual for further specialized competence in the fields of his choice. This is also true in diminishing degree at the lower levels of schooling. The conventional courses in high school history or chemistry, for example, are embryonic college courses. Thus, while the criterion of "significance to an organized field of knowledge" is used by those who accept cultural transmission as the main objective, its actual effects in practice are to strengthen the influence of the vocational objective of the graduate school upon the whole educational system.

Criteria related primarily to transmission of the cultural heritage tend to ignore both the nature and the needs of the learner. The learner is not ignored because he is considered unimportant. He is ignored by default. When content is selected primarily because it has survived or because it is significant to an organized field, it follows that the characteristics or concerns of children and youth are considered only after content has been screened on bases unrelated to these matters.

A further criticism of both of these criteria is that they lend themselves to those educational theories that ignore the importance, and indeed the necessity in modern society, of clearly formulated social directions. The mere passing on of the cultural heritage and the mere development of specialized competence, however necessary and desirable these may be, are inadequate purposes of education in an age when many of the fundamental beliefs and institutions of Western society are challenged by social changes. To the extent, therefore, that these criteria help to maintain the curriculum as it is or as it once was—to the degree that they are used to facilitate changes that disregard fundamental social needs—they are to be seriously questioned or actually rejected.

The Criterion of Utility and Social Efficiency as an Educational Aim

All subject matter ever taught in the schools was considered useful. Now, as in the past, if the educational aim is mental discipline, the content believed best fitted to the attainment of that end is selected; if the purpose is to make men obedient to authority, the subject matter believed most instrumental to that objective is included. But, when social efficiency is taken as the purpose of education, the criterion of utility becomes related to the daily activities of men. According to this aim, an individual is expected to participate effectively in political, economic, and social affairs—to be a wholesome member of a family, to protect his health and that of others, to worship, to play, to work, and to do a thousand other things generally expected of a responsible member of society.

Social efficiency as an educational aim is variously expressed—preparation for adult life, civic training, education for social responsibility, and social adaptation. No matter how it is expressed, this aim always calls for a curriculum to prepare the individual to perform the adult activities of collective life in a manner prescribed by the *status quo*. It requires efficiency in current social activities, not in those of the past nor in those of the future. Efficiency means the performance of these activities with a minimum of misunderstanding, fruitless effort, and loss of time and energy, and with a maximum of effectiveness and personal satisfaction.

The subject matter judged most useful in the development of the capacity to perform adult duties efficiently is therefore the most desirable curriculum content.

The employment of the criterion of utility under the general direction of the aim of social efficiency has resulted in some desirable curriculum changes. Much outworn instructional material carried along from the schools of past generations has been eliminated. For example, arithmetic has been simplified by removing unusual and seldom used processes. The more useful concepts and skills are now emphasized. Similar results have been achieved in almost every school program.

Nevertheless, the criterion of utility has been criticized. The point is made that individuals cannot use what they do not know. For example, adults who have never understood decimal fractions will not use them. Data about what arithmetical skills are most useful, derived from a study of such adults, might indicate that decimals should not be taught. It has been estimated that it took almost two decades to get farmers to grow hybrid corn after its superiority had been demonstrated. An activity analysis of corn growing, made before the use of hybrid seed corn became general, would have led to the conclusion that the schools should take no part in instructing farmers about the benefits to be derived from hybrid corn.

Critics have also maintained that the activities of adults are not necessarily desirable, that the things men do are not necessarily what they ought to do. These critics ask how the criterion of utility can serve as a guide in choosing subject matter if it cannot be used to distinguish activities to be encouraged from those to be discouraged. Of course, the reply can be made that those activities most widely and most frequently performed are most desirable and, accordingly, the subject matter involved in them should be included in the curriculum. But do not men frequently do things they should not do? Do they not often try to prevent social changes when those changes are clearly beneficial to nearly all people? Do they not repeatedly try to sell goods and services at unreasonable prices in times of inflation? Do they not continually advocate public policies that would be beneficial to themselves and harmful to others? Moreover, are not many things they do frequently, such as getting dressed or boarding a bus, more or less trivial and comparatively lacking in educational value?

If the curriculum worker went out to apply the criterion of utility without any presuppositions as to what is desirable, would he not discover that many of his findings were contrary to acceptable notions of what is right and wrong, desirable and undesirable? This criticism is partly neutralized, however, by the fact that the criterion of utility is usually employed in the service of the ideal of social efficiency, which prescribes in general language certain current standards of behavior such as the belief that a citizen should take part in the affairs of the government. For this reason, advocates of the utility principle say that it results in the selection of desirable as well as useful subject matter.

When the principle of utility focuses on usefulness in adult life, it ignores facts and principles of child development and those of the psychology of learning as completely as did the principles of survival and significance to an organized field of knowledge. Content is selected because it will be needed later. What the learner needs now, what he is like, and how he learns most efficiently are considered secondarily, if at all.

Perhaps the most serious objection to the criterion of utility as well as to the aim of social efficiency with which it is associated—like the objection to the two preceding criteria and their corresponding educational purposes—is the lack of social direction. This criterion stresses the present state of affairs. It does not indicate the sort of world mankind should attempt to build for itself out of the potentialities of the world as it is. Lacking this sense of direction, it is at best a dubious guide when employed alone in choosing the particular knowledge, values, and skills to be taught.

The principle of utility also overlooks the fact of rapid social change. In periods of gradual change it was fairly certain that what men believed and did, their children would also believe and do when they came of age. The facts, beliefs, and skills used by adults could, therefore, be taught to the youth with the firm conviction that these would be useful to them as adults. But in contemporary civilization, social events occur with great rapidity and result in profound social changes. In such a period the assumption that subject matter chosen on the basis of present value will be needed by children when they come of age can be accepted only after careful study—and even then with reservations.

Intelligent Self-Direction and the Criterion of Interest

The criterion of interest has been most persistently and thoroughly embraced by those who hold intelligent self-direction to be the major aim of education. The capacity of self-direction is best developed, according to this view, by engaging in activities of concern to the individual. As the individual seeks goals to which he feels committed, he learns to think for himself, to weigh and use knowledge, and to be self-dependent. In pursuing his interests, the need for knowledge, skills, and values arises. The subject matter thus needed and used defines the scope of the curriculum.

Two objections to this criterion are worthy of note. Some critics point out that not all the knowledge demanded by modern civilized life can be learned in the pursuit of the ordinary interests of individuals. In what practical activity, they ask, would a child learn that the earth is a sphere, that this sphere revolves around the sun, and that the laws of storms are related to the earth's rotation? And what real-life purpose would motivate such activity? In other words, if the subject matter is restricted to that which the ordinary interests of individuals require, the curriculum would be extremely narrow. This would tend, so the critics assert, to rule out not only the general background of knowledge, which functions more or less indirectly, and hence will likely not be acquired in a curriculum based upon mere interest, but also the content of the fine arts, which is even more remotely related to practical interests and activities.

To this criticism the advocates of this criterion of interest reply that there is no limit to the range and depth of interests an individual will exhibit, provided his interests are recognized and encouraged. The pursuit of one interest leads to other interests; hence, a curriculum that enables an individual to expand and to realize his purposes would build a background of knowledge more extensive, more useful, and more enduring than that attained through a study of content selected by any other principle.

Another important objection is that an interest is not necessarily desirable, that what an individual is interested in is not necessarily what he should be interested in. The criterion here under discussion gives no clue as to how to choose among interests. Taken unqualifiedly, this criterion leads to the view that it does not matter what an individual does, provided he does it with a purpose. This would, according to the critics, make the pursuit of money, the activities of the gangster, and the works of the social reformer of equal worth, provided they were motivated by genuine interests.

This criticism loses much of its effect when it is recognized that the objective with which the criterion is most closely associated is the real basis for determining which interests are to be fostered and which are to be discouraged. The proponents of the criterion reply that those interests that show little or no promise of leading to the capacity of intelligent self-direction would not be nurtured. In positive terms, interests that are most widely shared by the members of society and that lead to full and free interplay of individuals in various forms of association are the ones to be fostered. They lead to intelligent self-direction.

Although the principle of interest is in keeping with the findings of child development and the psychology of learning—and hence is a necessary part of any adequate plan of subject-matter selection—exclusive use of it leads to neglect of fundamental social goals. It is no historical accident that this criterion has been devoted, at least in theory, almost entirely to the development of discipline in the method of intelligence; that is, growth in better ways of thinking. This is a natural result of the fact that those who favor the principle under discussion have equated intelligence with democracy. Now democracy as a set of ideals includes critical intelligence and self-direction, but it is much more than these. It embraces, in addition, socio-economic goals, attainment of which will safeguard free intelligence, and social equality. This tendency of the criterion of interest to be limited to the ideal of intelligent self-direction is, therefore, its most serious defect—especially today when men are troubled, as perhaps never before in modern times, about the social ends they should try to achieve, not individually, but collectively.

Ideals of Democracy and the Criterion of Social Development

The selection of subject matter that makes a maximum contribution to the orderly development of society necessarily commits the curriculum worker to a set of social goals. As social problems are met and resolved, the society changes. It is obviously better for this continuous development to take place with society having a clear vision of the social directions in which change is to be made. The criterion of social development, however, may be the instrument of any set of social goals, depending upon the social ideals motivating its use. In American society it is geared to the democratic ideals, and the subject matter selected in keeping with it will therefore facilitate the attainment of democratic goals. To put the same thing in different terms, certain fundamental human wants, now unsatisfied or only partly satisfied, determine in part the ends for the guidance of social reconstruction. The National Resources Planning Board has stated these wants in the form of rights:

The right to work, usefully and creatively through the productive years.

The right to fair pay, adequate to command the necessities and amenities of life in exchange for work, ideas, thrift, and other socially valuable service.

The right to adequate food, clothing, shelter, and medical care.

The right to security, with freedom from fear of old age, want, dependency, sickness, unemployment, and accident.

The right to live in a system of free enterprise, free from compulsory labor, irresponsible private power, arbitrary public authority, and unregulated monopolies.

The right to come and go, to speak or to be silent, free from the spyings of secret political police.

The right to equality before the law, with equal access to justice in fact.

The right to education, for work, for citizenship, and for personal growth and happiness.

The right to rest, recreation, and adventure; the opportunity to enjoy life and take part in an advancing civilization.

Of course, the ideals of democracy include far more than a system of rights. They embrace with equal force a set of responsibilities. Democracy requires that each individual be disciplined in methods of thinking, in procedures of working with others, and in ethical principles that commit him—for one thing—to protect others against those who would deny them their democratic rights. Democracy requires as much, if not more, social and personal discipline than any other system of human association. To become thoroughly disciplined in these respects and to use these abilities in the interest of the common good is a responsibility of every member of a democratic society.

Application of the criterion of social development would lead to the selection of content that would help people to understand such rights, the ways to get them, and the forces working for and against efforts to attain them. Content that would lead to understanding of, and discipline in, the responsibilities of the individual would be stressed with equal force.

This criterion has been opposed on three counts: first, that social development through the school is neither desirable nor possible; second, that the criterion can be used only in the social studies, and is, therefore, not comprehensive enough for use in a general program of curriculum building; and third, that the criterion is too hazy and nebulous to be used as a basis for subject-matter selection.

Advocates of this criterion point to the part played by the schools in the social progress of Mexico and Turkey to indicate that the view that the school cannot help with social development is no longer tenable. That the schools alone cannot bring about desirable social growth is granted at once. But callous indeed is the person who still insists that the schools cannot exercise a major influence upon social change.

Some who oppose this criterion want the school to be socially neutral by limiting the content to noncontroversial subject matter. Those who defend this criterion hold that this kind of neutrality is impossible, that it is a way of taking sides under the banner of neutrality. For, they point out, society is changing and the content of the curriculum, no matter how it is selected, favors things as they are, things as they were, or things as they might become. None of these positions is neutral, and the curriculum worker would have a more defensible position if he realized this fact, and carefully considered the direction that curriculum content offers to social development.

A second objection assumes that certain subjects, such as biology and chemistry, are socially neutral. It is argued that the objective facts and descriptive principles of these subjects have nothing to do with any social system. They educate neither for nor against democracy or any other social order and therefore contribute nothing either positively or negatively toward the realization of social ideals. Those who defend the criterion of social development claim that the content of these subjects is not devoid of social values, but that the social values related to them have been neglected by the schools. While content drawn from the social sciences to be taught in history, economics, and political science courses is more directly related to social values and social direction, it is difficult to deny the social direction implicit in the content of the sciences. The history of science reveals that even the questions selected for scientific study reflect the preferences of dominant social groups.[7]

It is also apparent that whenever scientific facts and principles are taken one step beyond the laboratory to consideration of how this knowledge is useful, science has entered directly into the realm of social ideals. The science of nuclear fission was motivated by social need; and, once developed, consideration of the use of such knowledge is inescapable. How is it useful? How is it to be used? With the answers to such questions may lie key decisions to the social development of not one but all social systems. It must be clear that the content of science courses selected by the criterion of social development in the interest of realizing a group of social ideas, such as the human rights expressed by the National Resources Planning Board, would differ significantly from content selected by the criterion of "significance to an organized field of knowledge."

A third criticism is that the criterion of social development is so general that it can mean anything to anybody. If it is so general and so hazy a concept that any content might be included as desirable for social development, then not only is it unusable by those devoted to curriculum development, but is actually a hindrance by providing a catch-all category for any content that can't otherwise be justified.

Of course, the answer to this criticism is that there is a clear relationship between curriculum content and social goals and processes. This relationship has not been understood by curriculum workers. However, with as much thought given to the development and use of this criterion as has already been given to "significance to an organized field of knowledge" or to the principle of utility, the criterion of social development would be useful.

Still, this criticism cannot be dismissed lightly. The gap between generalized statements of the democratic ideals and the immediate need

[7] V. F. Lenzen, "Science and Social Context," *University of California Publications in Philosophy,* Vol. 23, pp. 3–26.

to select content for the public schools is a huge one. When one includes equally generalized understandings of the nature of this complex society, the relations of these to the democratic ideals, and the implications of both of these for the selection of content, the criterion is not at all clear. While advocates of the other criteria must defend and strengthen their positions against an immoral or amoral neglect of social direction, the advocates of the criterion of social development must develop their criterion into a more usable form.

4. *Criteria and Schools of Educational Thought*

Each of these five principles of subject-matter selection is employed to some extent in almost every program of curriculum development, but in no program are they emphasized equally. The educational and social goals that guide the program of curriculum development determine which criterion will be given primary consideration. Consequently, the various schools of educational thought tend to stress the principles of selection that most nearly conform to their purposes and social perspectives. Those educational theorists and curriculum workers who follow a conservative path, such as the *Essentialist* school of thought, stress primarily the criteria of survival, "significance to an organized field of knowledge," and utility. The *Progressive* school of thought, on the other hand, stresses the criterion of interest. This school has sometimes been criticized because it appeared to make interest the sole criterion in choosing curriculum content. In recent years, however, this school of thought has tended to emphasize the criterion of social development along with the criterion of interest. This new emphasis is giving rise to a group of curriculum workers whose primary concern is in developing a curriculum for social development along the lines of the democratic tradition in America.

▶ *Following Up*
This Chapter

1. Identify the different kinds of subject matter—descriptive and normative—presented in either a high school or an elementary school textbook. Which kind is stressed?

2. From a study of a textbook, used in either high school or elementary school, find evidence of the principles of subject-matter selection employed by the authors. Do the same with a course of study.

3. Criticize the principles found in this study, and indicate clearly why you accept or reject them.

4. Formulate and justify a theory of content selection satisfactory to you. Try to find out whether or not other persons agree with you. Why do they agree? Or why do they disagree?

▶ *Suggested Reading*

The best exploration of the nature and classification of subject matter is found in *Text Materials in Modern Education,* edited by Lee J. Cronbach, pages 28–58.

It is not easy to find references dealing with the various principles of content selection. The following references have been chosen because each one stresses a particular principle. Perhaps the best and clearest statement of the child-interest criterion is William H. Kilpatrick's *Remaking the Curriculum.* The principle of utility has been set forth by a number of writers. Herbert Spencer's essay *What Knowledge Is of Most Worth?* is still the classic statement of this position, although it was written a century ago. One of the most thorough explorations of the kinds of situations people must meet is to be found in *Developing a Curriculum for Modern Living,* by Florence B. Stratemeyer, Hamden L. Forkner, Margaret G. McKim, and others. The principle of survival has been carefully set forth, with some important qualifications, in *The Curriculum of the Common School,* by Henry C. Morrison, Chapters 1–3. The criterion of "significance to an organized field of knowledge" has been treated in Ernest C. Moore's *What Is Education?* pages 18–24.

For a discussion of the principle of social development and its application in an extensive program of curriculum development, see Harold Rugg's *That Men May Understand,* especially Chapters X and XI. See also his *American Life and the School Curriculum.* This principle has also been clearly enunciated in *Conclusions and Recommendations* of the American Historical Association's Commission on the Social Studies, especially pages 10–19. Of course, the first American writer to make this criterion a significant part of his educational theory was John Dewey in his *Democracy and Education.* See his discussion of this criterion on pages 384–387.

Chapter 7

Procedures of
Content Selection

THE CURRICULUM WORKER must not only choose among the criteria of content selection but also must explore the cultural heritage for the kind of content implied by them. This requires procedures for the selection of subject matter. In some cases these procedures are based almost entirely upon practical reason and judgment, as in the case of those used to satisfy such criteria as survival and social reconstruction. Some of these procedures, however, approach the rigor of scientific investigation, as in the case of experimental procedures and those devised to discover the content or the skills that are most useful in the performance of a particular set of activities. In this chapter the more important procedures will be set forth and related to the various principles of content selection. The procedures to be discussed are as follows: judgmental, experimental, analytical, and consensual.

1. *The Judgmental Procedure*

The judgmental procedure is loosely defined and can be described only in broad outlines. Since it has not been reduced to a set of techniques, successful use of it depends upon the point of view of the curriculum

152

worker. If his social perspective is narrow, and his ideas and prejudices are too little affected by democratic ideals and too closely identified with the interests of special social groups such as industrial managers, business organizations, labor unions, farm organizations, or academic groups, or if he is so occupied with the past that he cannot appreciate the present nor see its potentialities for the future, the curriculum worker's judgment will hardly lead to the best selection of subject matter. The most "objective" selection of content by this procedure requires that his interests, knowledge, and ideals rise above special social groups and embrace the common good. In short, this procedure—perhaps more than any other method of content selection—demands broad social vision and freedom from the restricting influences of partisan rationalizations.

Phases of the Judgmental Procedure

Selection of subject matter by judgment requires the curriculum worker to raise and answer the following questions: (1) What social and educational objectives should be accepted? (2) What is the existing state of affairs in which these objectives are considered desirable and appropriate, and in which they must be realized? (3) What subject matter best satisfies these objectives under the existing conditions? [1] As long as individuals are divided on either the first or second of these questions, they can reach no agreement upon the third. The first two questions, therefore, are the crucial points of the procedure.

If the criteria for the validation of educational objectives described in Chapter 6 have been used with care, the first two questions have been answered well. The criteria of democratic ideals, social adequacy, and basic human needs have demanded answers to the questions of these first two phases of the judgmental procedure. These answers have required thorough study of past and present stages of the development of society. They have called for thorough understanding of the processes of social change and the forces that shape this change. They have demanded understanding of the differences among persons regarding educational and social goals, and mastery of the social and intellectual techniques needed to resolve these differences.

[1] Raup et al., *The Improvement of Practical Intelligence.*

Ways of Preparing for the Questions of the Judgmental Procedure

When the curriculum worker is collecting data to help determine objectives, or when he is using these same data to select content with the judgmental procedure, he is not expected to make original social and historical investigations. The knowledge he needs must be drawn from scholarly works in cultural anthropology, sociology, economics, political science, geography, history, psychology, and social philosophy.

In addition, the judgmental procedure calls for extensive group discussion and deliberation, in which general points of view and personal and group opinions are critically evaluated and reconstructed in the process of agreeing upon social ideals and goals. Curriculum content chosen on the basis of the prejudices and rationalizations of uninformed and uncritical persons will not satisfy the conditions of the judgmental procedure. Nor will the selection of such content improve the curriculum.

Examples of the Judgmental Procedure

The judgmental procedure is best demonstrated when the criterion of social reconstruction is the primary basis of subject-matter selection, although it is also used with the criteria of survival and "significance to an organized field of knowledge." The Virginia Curriculum Program illustrates the selection of subject matter by the judgmental procedure. The educational platform of the Principles Committee was developed to guide those who were to co-operate in developing the new curriculum. The first of these principles suggests the judgmental procedure of content selection:

The school is an agency of society for its perpetuation and re-creation. In its processes the school should:

1. Discover and define the ideals of a democratic society.
2. Provide for the continuous redefinition and reinterpretation of the social ideals in light of economic, political, and social changes.
3. Provide experiences for boys and girls which make possible their greatest contribution to the realization of the social ideals.

From the social point of view this involves: (a) The definition of understandings, attitudes, appreciations, and automatic responses that are necessary for the realization of the social ideals, (b) The selection from the group culture of materials which will assist most effectively in the realization of the social ideals.[2]

This principle makes social development a primary basis of content selection. Now the selection of "materials which assist most effectively in the realization of the social ideals" is a complex task. It requires a judgment of what the democratic ideals are or should be, and a clear understanding of "economic, political, and social changes." Having satisfied these two conditions it is, then, a matter of further judgment—made of course in light of facts and ideals—as to whether a given item or body of content will contribute to the realization of the accepted ideals. It should not be assumed, however, that this is merely a matter of personal choice. On the contrary, in this case, as in all others, the test of the judgment is the extent to which other persons accepting the same ideals, facing the same facts, and possessing the same social understandings would themselves select the same subject matter or agree to its selection.

A superficial form of this procedure is sometimes used in the selection of subject matter on the basis of "significance to an organized field of knowledge." In such cases the first and second phases of the procedure are usually taken for granted. There is little or no discussion, or study, of educational and social goals and little reference to social and educational conditions as factors affecting the selection of content. A common reason for this lack of discussion is that the aim of specialized competence is accepted without serious question; or else, the content selected for that purpose is rationalized on the ground that it contributes to general education or to the cultural development of the individual. Commitment to this aim, or surrender to these rationalizations, makes it easy to ignore social conditions and ideals and to go directly to choice of content. Unexamined educational and social prejudices are thus allowed to influence the selection of subject matter, and the judgmental procedure is violated.

When used with the criterion of survival, the judgmental procedure is usually influenced by historical facts and reasoning—to the neglect of present conditions and future developments. Perhaps the clearest ex-

[2] Sidney B. Hall, D. W. Peters, and H. L. Caswell, *Procedures for Virginia State Curriculum Program.* Bulletin of the State Board of Education, July, 1932, pp. 11–12.

ample of this is the curriculum outline proposed by Henry C. Morrison in *The Curriculum of the Common School*. He sets forth in bold outline a curriculum based upon a notion of universal institutions. These are judged to be good because of their long service to man in his social evolution. Among the universal institutions are Language, Mathematics, the Natural Sciences, the Humanities, Commerce, and Industry. Since these, according to Morrison, are common to all advancing societies and have proved their value in human history, and since they also constitute the arts by which men carry on community life and control the environment, they are the best curriculum for common education.

Such socio-historical reasoning enables Morrison to project a curriculum which neglects the first and second phases of the judgmental procedure and hence reduces the present state of affairs and its potentialities to abstract universal forms called institutions. This leaves open the question of what content is to be included in these various institutions—Language, Mathematics, Natural Sciences, and so on—for it can hardly be supposed that all subject matter related to each of these is of equal worth. Thus the actual selection of content is again left open to the influence of unexamined social and educational prejudices, and the judgmental procedure has again been violated.

These examples should help to indicate that great care must be exercised in using the judgmental procedure. Its successful use requires critical, informed, and judicious persons. In the hands of such persons it can be one of the most dependable methods of content selection. But the curriculum worker cannot neglect any of its phases without the risk of serious misjudgment.

2. *The Experimental Procedure*

The experimental procedure of content selection tries to determine by actual test whether or not subject matter satisfies a particular criterion. It answers such questions as: Is this subject matter interesting? Is this subject matter used by adults? The try-out of subject matter must, of course, be done under prescribed conditions and by techniques that make the procedure as rigorous as possible. Errors due to personal or group prejudices, misjudgment, and outside conditions are reduced to a minimum.

The General Pattern of Experimentation

All experimentation follows the same general pattern: (1) a hypothesis, that is, an idea to be tried out; (2) control of the conditions of the try-out; (3) an objective account of the results; and (4) checking the results against the hypothesis to find whether or not the hypothesis is true.

When these requirements are translated into procedures of content selection, they take the following form:

1. Tentative selection of subject matter in accordance with a criterion.
2. Hypothesis that the tentatively selected subject matter meets the conditions of the criterion (that it is interesting or useful).
3. Prescribed conditions of the try-out (description of children, teacher, classroom, methods of teaching, materials to be used, and other factors affecting the experiment).
4. Objective techniques for determining the results (tests and other observations and records).
5. Checking the results against the hypothesis to find whether or not the subject matter satisfies the criterion.

This procedure has not been used extensively, but its findings have been generally respected. It has been used, for example, in ascertaining the interests of children in poetry and other forms of literature, in music, and in color combinations and arrangements.[3]

An Example of the Experimental Procedure

Huber, Bruner, and Curry conducted an experiment to determine the poetry which should be included in the curriculum of the elementary and junior high schools.[4] The experiment was based upon the criterion of interest, and is an example of the use of the experimental procedure.

[3] Arthur M. Jordan, "Children's Interests in Reading," *Teachers College Contributions to Education*, No. 107. See also G. LaV. Freeman and R. S. Freeman, *The Child and His Picture Book*. B. E. Mellinger, "Children's Interests in Pictures," *Teachers College Contributions to Education*, No. 516.

[4] Miriam B. Huber, H. B. Bruner, and C. M. Curry, *Children's Interests in Poetry*, p. 4

The first step was to make a preliminary selection of poetry suitable for children. The initial selection of poems was on the basis of the opinions of "expert" teachers of poetry, from an examination of 900 courses of study and of the most commonly used textbooks. The 900 courses of study were evaluated by criteria for judging courses of study in literature, and the thirty best ones in each grade from one to nine were selected for intensive study. Also, thirty outstanding textbooks were selected for detailed analysis. On the basis of this preliminary investigation about 100 poems were chosen for each grade. These were prepared as an experimental booklet, which was issued to eleven experimental centers involving some 60,000 children. The hypothesis was that these were poems in which children would most likely be interested, and the experiment was designed to test this hypothesis.

The next step in the experiment was the prescription of conditions under which the interest of children in these poems was to be determined. Control of these conditions consisted of two steps. The first one was the choice of experimental centers in accordance with the following requirements: (1) adequate preparation of supervisors and teachers with respect to the proposed experiment, (2) proper geographical distribution, (3) representation of all types of children—underprivileged, normal, superior, foreign-born, and the like, (4) interest of teachers and superintendents in poetry and poetry teaching, and (5) ability to handle the experiment educationally, statistically, and clerically.

Second, the general requirements for presenting the poems were prescribed as follows: (1) Each teacher was issued an experimental edition of *Children's Poetry* containing the poems she was to use. (2) The time and length of the experiment was indicated—about 18 weeks. (3) During the experiment the children were to read, or the teacher was to read to them, some 60 of the 100 poems selected for the particular grade range. (4) Methods of teaching the poems were left to the choice of each teacher, though some suggestions for teaching poetry were given. (5) Each booklet of poems was used over a range of five grades, two above and two below the particular grade to be taught, thus taking account of the factors of pupil age and maturity.

To check the results, each teacher was supplied with specially prepared "pupil's choice sheets," on which each pupil was to record his choice of poems as the teacher presented them to the class. Also, at the middle of the experiment each pupil was required to record the five poems he liked best; and, at the end of the experiment, the ten best-liked poems. The poems he liked least were also to be reported. In addition, each teacher was given a set of directions for using these "pupil-choice sheets" and recording the results of pupil responses. The results from each experimental center were collected and compiled as a final report. The findings from this compilation enabled the experimenters to prepare a master list of poems for each grade, to eliminate certain poems from the experimental collection because they failed to satisfy the criterion of interest, and to move other poems into grades in which pupil interest in them was higher.

The Experimental Procedure Directly Related to Objectives

While the experimental procedure is most often used to find whether content satisfies a particular criterion, it may be used to relate content more directly to the realization of an objective. When the experimental procedure is used in this way, the intent of the experiment would not be that of finding whether the content was interesting or useful, but instead to find whether the content realized the objective. Of course, the realization of objectives is seldom an all-or-none process, and a more likely outcome would be to find the extent to which the objective was reached.

If the objective were a simple safety practice, and if it were stated behavioristically that "The children look both ways before they cross the street," it would be possible to select content for the realization of this objective by an experimental procedure without definite reference to any of the criteria for the selection of content. It might be hypothesized that this behavior could be taught directly through the use of audio-visual materials and related discussion. Conditions that might affect the experiment would be prescribed, and objective techniques would be devised for determining the results, as in other uses of the experimental procedure. The final step would involve checking the results against the objective to find the extent to which it had been reached. It would be possible, of course, to hypothesize that different content would reach the objective more efficiently, and the experimental procedure might then be used again.

Criticism of the Experimental Procedure

The experimental procedure is open to the objection that not all factors can be controlled; and its findings, therefore, are not entirely dependable. For example, one teacher may be more generally effective than another in getting children interested in poems; or the pupil's interest in a particular poem and his lack of interest in another may be due to the interest and enthusiasm expressed by the teacher. Furthermore, the past experiences of children in literature may have conditioned them for or against poems; hence, the experiment may not reveal the potential interests of children but rather their reactions to previous instruction.

Another criticism is that the experimental procedure assumes an unchanging curriculum in all the aspects related to the one under investigation. One may deny that this is a criticism, but the fact that dependable evidence would require stable conditions in the activities related to the experiment cannot be denied. Were this not so, the experimenter could not know whether his results were due to the conditions of the experiment or to some outside conditions that changed without measurement or control. A related criticism is that holding all the important factors constant would put a stop to lots of other changes that should be going on at this time. It should be recognized that if either of these are valid criticisms, they are criticisms of experimentation with the curriculum and not just criticisms of the experimental procedure of content selection. However, after all criticisms, objections, fears, or dangers have been taken into account, the experimental procedure remains one of the most promising means of subject-matter selection.

3. *The Analytical Procedure*

The analytical procedure [5] is one of the most widely known methods of content selection. It has been closely identified with the criterion of utility, although it has been used with other criteria. In general, it consists of an analysis of the things people do in order to discover the subject matter functioning in these activities.

[5] W. W. Charters, *Curriculum Construction.* See also Franklin Bobbitt, *How to Make a Curriculum.*

General Forms of the Analytical Procedure

There are three forms of the analytical procedure, all following more or less the same pattern. First is *activity analysis,* in which the purpose is to discover the general kinds of activities engaged in by people of a given national group or region. These general activities are reduced to specific activities which form the basis for instructional materials designed to teach proficiency in the general activities. Spencer's five major activities of life (noted in connection with the criterion of utility in the previous chapter) illustrate these general activities. What people do in performing each of these major activities make up the specific activities. The second, *job analysis,* is activity analysis applied to vocational operations.[6] To determine what should be taught in the professional preparation of teachers, for example, an analysis would be made of what teachers actually do, and these activities would become the basis of teacher-education. A third form of this procedure is simply the *analysis to determine the generally useful knowledges and skills.* If the problem is to find what elements of written expression have general use, one procedure would be to analyze such documentary materials as minutes of board meetings or newspapers. The content to be included in a course in grammar might be determined by studying the grammatical forms found in the correspondence of people in general or of a selected group such as college graduates.

Techniques of Analysis

The analytical procedure of content selection consists of the application of certain techniques of fact-finding to the activities under investigation. Therefore, the first step is the selection of the area of human concern, the specific function, or the specialized occupation to be investigated. After one of these has been selected, it is broken down into more specific elements, and an appropriate technique is chosen for collecting facts about these various elements. There are six such techniques in general use. While most of these originated in job analysis, they have been adapted with varying success to the study of major life activities as well as to more specific functions.

[6] W. W. Charters and Douglas Waples, *The Commonwealth Teacher-Training Study.* See also Charters and Whitley, *An Analysis of Secretarial Duties and Traits.*

1. *Interviewing:* The interviewer requests a person on the job, or one who performs certain activities, to name the duties for which he is responsible or the ideas and skills he employs. These are listed by the interviewer and are returned in typed form for the worker to correct. Other persons on the same job, or engaged in the same activity, are also interviewed independently. From these interviews a composite list of duties is made.

2. *Working on the job:* The investigator works on the job, studying the operations required and making a list of them. Since the job is new to him, he is more apt to be aware of the duties than a worker who has become habituated to the job.

3. *Analysis of the job or activity by the worker:* A person who has become familiar with a job or activity is asked to list his duties or the operations he performs. This differs from the preceding technique primarily in the amount of familiarity with the work on the part of the persons involved, the worker being more familiar than the investigator.

4. *Questionnaire:* The duties or operations involved in a job or activity are sought by means of an inquiry blank sent to the workers or persons whose activities are under investigation. This is similar to the interview technique, the latter being more dependable because the investigator can check the responses of the worker by further questioning.

5. *Documentary analysis:* The investigator makes an analysis of magazines, correspondence, public records, and the like, and tabulates the information, skills, or principles found in these documents. These findings throw light on what will be needed by persons who use these documents or who are involved in activities from which they result.

6. *Observing the performance of people:* The curriculum worker, or a group of persons under his direction, observe and tabulate the things people in general, or people of a particular social group, do in their endeavors. This may be concerned with the daily activities of people or it may involve analysis of individuals or groups in certain situations. Children's "needs" as they perceive them may be studied in the classroom or in other group situations in connection with the criterion of interest. Following this type of analysis, content may be selected to meet these self-perceived "needs." [7]

[7] Aleyne C. Haines, *Children's Perception of Membership Roles in Problem-Solving Groups.*

The application of these six techniques yields a list of performances or "needs." The question then is how to determine the relative importance of the items on the list. In some cases this question is answered at the outset by selecting for analysis the activities of highly efficient persons. In other cases some standard is employed by which to judge the relative weight to be given each item. One of the most common standards is frequency of occurrence.

Example of the Analytical Procedure

An example of the analytical procedure is a study of written expression using the technique of documentary analysis. The purpose of the study is to find out what grammar is in current English usage in the United States in order to select grammatical content for English courses. The study is based on the criterion of utility. Two fundamental assumptions of the research are worthy of special attention.

1. It assumes that the only method to attain really good English—effective language nicely adapted in both denotation and connotation to the circumstances of the occasion and the needs of both the speaker and the hearer —demands constant observation of the actual practice of the users of the language together with a *sensitiveness to the suggestions inevitably attached to words and constructions.* . . .

2. It assumes that the most important facts concerning any words, forms, or constructions of language are the circumstances in which they are usually used, because these words, forms, or constructions will inevitably suggest these circumstances. . . . there are language forms and construction that are somewhat limited in their constant use to particular social groups. To use any such forms seriously, whether they be those customary to the "vulgar" or those customary only to precise "school mistresses," helps to give the impression that the common social contacts of the user are with that particular group. This study, therefore, has attempted to find the important matters of American English that thus have distinct social class connotations. Unlike any of the former studies it has not been limited to an examination of the so-called "disputed" constructions and phrases; it has been concerned with a firsthand examination of the grammatical matters that appeared in a large number of carefully selected specimens of the language of several social groups.[8]

[8] C. C. Fries, *American English Grammar* (New York: Appleton-Century-Crofts, Inc.; copyright 1940), pp. 24–25. By permission.

This research emphasizes the social utility of language forms and functions and would eliminate those having little or no use outside the classroom.

The study required an adequate selection of written materials. Certain materials were ruled out. Stenographic reports of court hearings were eliminated because stenographers usually correct the expression of the witnesses. Business correspondence was not considered representative of the range of situations calling for written expression. The materials finally selected for study were those made available from federal government files of informal correspondence. The letters and their authors were required to meet the following conditions:

1. The letters must really contain the language usage of the person whose letter is being analyzed. Hence only those letters were used which were in the original handwriting of the persons selected as suitable subjects.

2. Certain information about the writers of the letters must be available: place and date of birth, place and date of birth of father and mother, present address of each, record of the writer's schooling, occupations in which he had been engaged, and in some cases a confidential report on the family.

3. The written material from each subject must be sufficient to represent a fair sample of his language.

4. A wide range of topics must be covered by the correspondence. Altogether some 2000 letters and excerpts from about 1000 additional letters were used in the investigation.[9]

The persons whose letters were studied were classified into three groups: (1) those who had graduated from a reputable college and whose position was one of recognized standing in the community; (2) those who had not passed beyond the eighth grade and whose occupations were strictly manual and unskilled; and (3) those who fell between those two extremes; that is, persons whose formal education ranged from one year of high school to a single year in college, or technical school, and whose occupations were neither professional nor strictly manual and unskilled.

The correspondence of each of these three groups was examined and the grammatical facts tabulated and classified. These facts fell into three categories. The first one was the *form* of words—for example, the

[9] C. C. Fries, *American English Grammar*, pp. 27–28. By permission.

way in which the word *grew* differs from *grow*. The second category was the *function* of words. Certain words have little meaning except for the grammatical relationship they express—as, for example, the word *with* in "He struck the animal *with* a rod." The third was *word order,* the order in which words appear in sentences. The statistical findings were placed against a historical background of language usage, as a method of evaluating them. The findings of this investigation are extensive and are presented in detail in a series of six chapters of the original report of the study.[10]

Criticism of the Analytical Procedure

Some hold that the analytical procedure breaks operations, skills, and knowledges into such small elements that the real identity of the original process or knowledge is lost, as water is changed, upon analysis, into hydrogen and oxygen. According to this view, if the process of teaching, for example, is broken into its various elements, which are then mastered by an individual, there is no assurance that he will be an effective teacher. It is assumed that the art of teaching is more than the sum of its elements, just as water is more than the sum of the atoms of which it consists. Although this criticism may be valid when analysis has been carried to extremes, it can hardly be held valid in most instances. Analysis is always essential, and there is no justification for wholesale criticism of it. The pertinent questions should always be these: What is the analysis for? Is it sufficient for the purpose?

A second criticism is that the process of analysis yields static results. Analysis of conditions as they now are indicates nothing about what they should be. Hence, the discovery of what is actually done on a job, or the knowledge and skills that people actually use in their various activities, offers no basis for improving performance. When this procedure is used in the interest of the aim of social efficiency, for example, it tends to yield content in support of the *status quo*. But if it is borne in mind that analysis does not yield objectives but the materials by which objectives may be realized, this criticism loses much of its weight.

[10] C. C. Fries, *American English Grammar,* Chapters 5–10.

4. *The Consensual Procedure*

The consensual procedure is a way of collecting people's opinions about what they *believe* the curriculum should be. The three procedures just described represent investigations into the content of activities, objects of interest, and conflicts of ideals and prejudices. The results of the consensual procedure are expressed in terms of the number of persons, or per cent of persons, of a particular community or group who *believe* that such and such should be taught in the schools. This procedure is exemplified in the practice of asking local businessmen to express their opinions about what elements of arithmetic or English should be included or stressed in the curriculum.

Aspects of the Consensual Procedure

The selection of persons whose opinions are to be sought is the first step. Such persons are usually selected because they are (1) outstanding leaders in the fields of industry, business, agriculture, labor, and in the social life of the community, (2) experts and specialists such as physicians, engineers, teachers, artists, and musicians, or (3) representatives of the population of a community or region. The next phase is the development of a method for collecting opinions. Usually a questionnaire is used. In some cases interviews or small group conferences are employed. In any event, precaution must be taken to get the opinion of the subject without influencing his response. The final stage of the consensual procedure is the tabulation and interpretation of the responses.

Example of the Consensual Procedure

Since this procedure of content selection is probably the simplest of all, it has had wide use by both research workers and practitioners. A good example is that followed by The National Committee on Mathematical Requirements in its study of the topics to be included in high-school courses, as presented in its report, *The Reorganization of Mathematics in the Secondary School.* The Committee prepared a list of topics in mathematics, and the list was presented to college teachers prominent in their respective fields. Teachers were asked to assign to each topic an estimate of its value as preparation for the elementary courses in their fields of specialization.

The replies were tabulated and arranged in two groups: physical sciences, including astronomy, physics, and chemistry; and social sciences, including history, economics, sociology, and political science. It was found that high value was attached to certain topics by prominent teachers of both of these science areas. These topics were, therefore, judged to be essential elements of mathematics courses designed for college preparation.

Criticism of the Consensual Procedure

The consensual procedure is perhaps most dependable when it is used with the judgmental procedure. It probably is also more dependable when it is used to determine the content of a very narrow field of instruction, as in the example above. But even in this instance it is subject to the objection that people's replies are too often dictated by vested interests, unexamined prejudices, and occupational biases.

It is also apparent that this procedure results not in consensus (agreement or concord) but in a tabulation of votes. There is no opportunity here, as there is in the judgmental procedure, for group deliberation toward consensus. A related criticism is that the consensual procedure is simply the sum of opinions reached by another procedure. The point here is that those who respond reached their decisions by use of one of the other procedures, and that the consensual procedure obscures the process by covering up the real bases for choice.

▶ *Following Up*
This Chapter

1. Examine each of the following investigations to decide the kind of procedure used to determine the content: Helen Christianson, *Bodily Rhythmic Movements of Young Children in Relation to Rhythm in Music;* Commission on the Social Studies, American Historical Association, *Conclusions*

and Recommendations of the Commission; Ruth Strang, *Subject Matter in Health Education;* Guy M. Wilson, *What Arithmetic Shall We Teach?*

2. Criticize one of the investigations listed above. Make clear the position you yourself assume as you make the criticisms.

3. Assume that you are a member of a committee to revise the curriculum in a field of your choice. Outline a procedure of content selection which you would recommend to the committee. What difficulties would you anticipate in following this procedure?

4. Examine a textbook or a course of study, and try to determine the procedure of content selection which the authors employed.

▶ Suggested Reading

1. The judgmental procedure has never been clearly formulated in curriculum work, even though it has been used for centuries. Perhaps the nearest statement of it, although in a generalized form, is to be found in *The Improvement of Practical Intelligence,* by Raup, Benne, Axtelle, and Smith, especially Chapters V, VI, and VII.

2. The experimental procedure has not been formulated apart from particular investigations. But since it is essentially the same in all educational experimentation, general formulations will suggest the nature of this procedure. See, for example, *The Scientific Study of Educational Problems,* by Walter S. Monroe and Max Engelhart. For applications of this procedure, see references given in the text. See also C. E. Turner's "Description of the Malden, Massachusetts, Experiment in Health Education," *Fourth Yearbook,* National Education Association, Department of Superintendence, pages 233–238.

3. The classic elaboration of the analytical procedure is that of W. W. Charters in his *Curriculum Construction,* especially Chapters I to VI. Part II contains many examples of the application of this procedure.

4. The consensual procedure is set forth in Franklin Bobbitt's *Curriculum Making in Los Angeles* and in his *How to Make a Curriculum.*

5. For an excellent criticism of the various theories and procedures of content selection, see Boyd H. Bode's *Modern Educational Theories,* Chapters II to VII.

Chapter 8

Principles and Procedures for Determining Sequence and Grade Placement

IN THIS CHAPTER attention will be given to the question of how to determine the grade in which an objective or the content selected to reach an objective should be placed. While the question of grade placement will be considered by itself, in actual practice it cannot be separated from the problem of content selection, for any attempt to select subject matter presupposes some age or grade group with whom it is to be used. According to one viewpoint, the problem of grade placement arises only in a rigid scheme of grade levels, promotions, and graduations, and not in a flexible system in which pupils can progress as freely as their growth and development will allow. In any plan of education, no matter how flexible, teachers will be concerned with the relation between the development stage of the individual and the educational experiences he is to have. Moreover, emphasis in recent years upon child development and the cultivation of healthy personalities has given new meaning and additional importance to the problem of grade placement. As one authority has so well said:

A child who has been confused over and over again by the complexity of the material and energy factors met in earlier experience can hardly be expected to mobilize his knowledge and integrate his energy output into effective behavior patterns. Children need to feel adequate in capacity and skill to meet a fair proportion of the situations which they are called upon to face. They need to obtain a fair balance between success and failure in the realization of their hopes and desires.[1]

Some curriculum workers have replaced the term "grade placement" with the term "sequence," because to them "sequence" connotes less rigidity and is less associated with older curriculums. But changing the name does not remove the problem. Whether a person speaks of sequence, or of grade placement, he has reference to the problem of meshing the development of the individual with some order of activities and content. Usually the term "sequence" is used to refer to the order of the learner's experience rather than to the order of logically organized subject matter in the educational ladder. But even so, guide lines to individual development are essential in order to plan for an educational program at all. In the discussion that follows, the terms "grade placement" and "sequence" will be used interchangeably.

The successful curriculum worker will be aware of the factors conditioning what a student can do and learn at any given time in his schooling. This means that the curriculum worker must be familiar with curriculum materials and with particular social and psychological concepts and facts. In addition, knowledge of procedures for determining the grade placement of curriculum materials, or the sequence of activities and experiences, is indispensable.

The curriculum worker meets the problem of sequence in many practical situations. A teacher is assigned to a grade or subject. He asks, "What is expected during this year?" He realizes that the placement of one set of objectives and content affects the placement of others. He knows that some students will drop out and that others will transfer. For those who drop, what is essential to teach before they leave? For those who transfer, what sequence of activities will make their move an easy one? His problem is one of priorities for teaching. What must come first? On one hand is the danger of gaps in the orderly development of experience and on the other is the danger of excessive duplication. This chapter will deal with some of the factors that the curriculum worker must consider in determining sequence and with a few procedures that are used in the study of problems of grade placement.

[1] D. A. Prescott, *Emotion and the Educative Process* (Washington, D.C.: American Council on Education; 1938), p. 123. By permission.

1. *Approaches to Grade Placement and Sequence*

There are only two possible approaches to the solution of problems of grade placement and sequence. *The first* accepts the child as he is and adjusts the experience to his level of development while holding the instructional goals constant. When should the study of a group of skills, facts, principles, or problems begin? Attack on this problem necessarily involves answers to such questions as the following: At what grade level can children learn a given skill or concept, or study a particular problem most readily? Should the learning be placed closest to the time when the child feels a need for it? Should it be placed where it is most interesting? Or should its placement involve some combination of these?

The second approach assumes curriculum experiences to be located at a given grade level and provides learnings to adjust the child to these experiences—that is, to get him ready for the learning. What experiences and materials will best facilitate learning at a given grade level? This question also requires answers to subsidiary ones: What skills and concepts are prerequisite to the desired learning? What experiences will best develop readiness for the desired learning? How can materials be prepared that will bring the child to the place where the desired learning will be an easy and natural next step?

These are, of course, opposing approaches. To accept wholeheartedly the first approach, which emphasizes the nature of the child and regards the curriculum as always flexible enough at each grade level to be bent to the child's needs, is probably unrealistic. And just as unrealistic is the inflexibility of the second approach, which allows objectives and content to be so fixed at any one grade that lower grade experiences must always prepare for this hurdle and later experiences always build upon it. Probably neither of these approaches will be used without consideration for the other, but the advantage of setting the two apart is clear. Here is the child as he is and as he is becoming. What sequence of experiences is to be provided for his optimum development? Then, here is the curriculum as *it* is and is becoming. What earlier experiences will cause the child to get the most from the new experiences? These are the two variables—the child and what is provided for him. It is important to know where the focus is as those two are seen in relationship to one another.

Perhaps these two possibilities may be better understood from questions that could typically be asked about the placement of any learning —in this instance appreciation of literature in the junior high school. Consider, for example, the question of where to place the story *Silas Marner*. Using the first approach, these questions might be asked: What is the reading level of junior-high-school students with respect to the difficulty of material? What will the experience background of a thirteen-year-old child permit him to appreciate? How widely do the members of the class differ in reading ability and in ability to appreciate? How nearly does *Silas Marner* satisfy the conditions embraced by these questions? What changes (in vocabulary, sentence structure, etc.) must be made in this book to enable the majority of students to read and enjoy it?

If the second approach were followed, other questions might be asked: What kinds of experiences must a student have in order to be able to read and appreciate the story *Silas Marner* in the eighth grade? What skills and knowledges are prerequisite to this reading? What reading materials will prepare the class for *Silas Marner*?

The first of these approaches studies the child and adjusts materials and activities to what he is capable of learning at a given period in his growth. The child is accepted as he is, and knowledge of his capabilities is used as a basis for planning future experiences for his continued growth. Thus this method focuses attention upon the child, and the curriculum is adjusted to place experiences at a grade most consonant with the child's level of development.

The second approach assumes grade placement of materials and activities. The child is then prepared for these potential experiences. The grade placement of any given content alters the curriculum of the earlier grades during which the child is made ready. If the readiness program cannot adequately prepare him for the experience, the learning is moved to a more advanced level, and the adjustment process is then repeated. This method focuses attention upon the hypothesis that learning is to take place at a particular time, and the earlier experiences are planned to make this possible.

In either of these approaches, changes in instructional goals may throw new light on problems of grade placement. This is especially true when major goals are kept, but intermediate goals are changed. In some instances an intermediate goal may be beyond a child's present ability and also beyond any reasonable expectation of his future ability. Suppose that a child is to be taught to recognize words independently in his reading, that the intermediate goals include techniques of phonetic analysis, and that this child is hard of hearing and has serious speech defects. Because he is unable to hear or say the phonetic elements, this method of word recognition obviously is not feasible for him. If we assume also that the hearing and speech difficulties cannot be readily corrected, it is not reasonable to expect him to be ready to learn by phonetic analysis for some time. The sensible procedure, then, is to alter the intermediate goal of teaching phonetic analysis to this child but to keep the larger goal of teaching him to recognize words independently in his reading. Instruction would then be planned to emphasize other methods of word recognition.

Another example may be drawn from the consideration of the grade placement of *Silas Marner* as mentioned earlier. As an intermediate instructional goal, should all junior-high-school students try to learn to appreciate *Silas Marner?* Could all students ever learn to appreciate it? If they could, is this intermediate goal worth the instructional effort? Would their appreciation of literature, the larger goal, be reached more readily through other selections at this stage in their development?

However, it should be noted that a change of instructional goals is not a different approach to the problem of grade placement. After the new goals are set, one of the two approaches described earlier, or some combination of the two, is used to attack the problem of sequence. The new materials and activities are then selected to be in keeping with the learner's current stage of development, or are chosen to adjust his background to the anticipated new experiences.

Historically speaking, the earliest attack on the problem of grade placement consisted of attempts to locate materials on the basis of what teachers and subject-matter experts believed children of different chronological ages could do. As research on the problem developed, however, it became clear that children of the same age differed radically in almost every measurable characteristic.

In a similar way, the relative complexity of subject matter has become more and more obvious with discoveries of its intimate connections with the teaching-learning process. At first, subject matter was believed to have some fixed and inherent logical structure, which made the conventional sequence of content both necessary and desirable. Investigations gradually disclosed, however, that there were many different sequences of content and that the way learnings shape up in the learner's experience is not necessarily the same as the order in which they appear in a textbook or in a teacher's presentation. Furthermore, the facts and principles to be taught were found to be either easy or difficult, depending upon methods of teaching and upon whether the materials of instruction were written with the capacities and experiences of children in mind. Simple sentences and a well-chosen vocabulary have brought many facts and concepts, formerly beyond the reach of children, within their easy grasp. Thus the problem of grade placement, complex enough to begin with, has become more and more involved with each new investigation into child development and with each new exploration of content and its relation to methods of instruction.

2. *Factors Involved in Grade Placement*

A number of social and psychological factors are involved in each of the foregoing ways of resolving the problem of grade placement. Among them are maturation, experiential background, mental age, interest, usefulness, and difficulty. Each of these will be discussed as it bears upon the problem of grade placement.

Maturation

Evidence from a number of studies indicates that materials of instruction should be graded with due regard to the maturity of the learner. Children exhibit many behaviors at about the same age, and in about the same order, even though they have experienced very different environments. For example, children begin to walk, to talk, to discriminate among persons, or to exhibit fear of strangers at about the same age. Such growth occurs without the specific stimulation of instruction. Its occurrence at a particular time is due primarily to maturation, which is closely related to the development of the nervous system and other physiological structures.

It is a common observation that most, if not all, changes in behavior result from instruction and practice rather than from mere physiological maturing. Just as no amount of instruction will cause physiological growth, no amount of physiological development will result in mastery of the facts of arithmetic. Learning depends upon specific stimulation such as is found in training and instruction. What an individual learns, therefore, depends almost entirely upon the character and impact of the environment. On the other hand, maturation resulting from internal development makes learnings possible at particular times, and lack of maturation makes them impossible at other times. For example, it would be a waste of time to try to teach a child to walk at the age of six months, no matter what techniques of instruction were used, for the simple reason that the child's growth has not progressed to the point that walking is possible.

The dependence of learning upon maturation has been clearly demonstrated by a number of experiments. This relation is strikingly brought out in an experiment in which identical twin girls were taught to climb a stairway. In this experiment it was demonstrated that one twin improved more with two weeks of training at the age of fifty-three weeks than the other twin improved with six weeks of training at the age of forty-six weeks.[2] The superiority of the second twin is attributed to maturation. Evidence from similar experiments indicates that learning occurs most readily when practice and instruction are correlated with level of maturation.

This relation between learning and maturation also holds in more difficult skills,[3] and in such complex processes as the learning of concepts,[4] social adjustments,[5] emotional reactions,[6] methods of thinking,[7] and the study of one's own problems.[8] Getting a concept of historical time

[2] Arnold Gesell, "The Developmental Psychology of Twins," in *Handbook of Child Psychology*, edited by Carl Murchison, pp. 158–203.

[3] W. C. Olson and S. I. Davis, "The Adaptation of Instruction in Reading to the Growth of Children," *Educational Method*, Vol. XX, pp. 71–79.

[4] F. Pistor, "How Time Concepts Are Acquired by Children," *Educational Method*, XX, 107–112. J. Piaget. *The Moral Judgment of the Child*, pp. 314–316.

[5] S. M. Corey, "The Developmental Tasks of Youth," in *Eighth Yearbook* of the John Dewey Society, pp. 70–99.

[6] Arnold Gesell and F. L. Ilg, *The Child from Five to Ten*, Chapters 11–20.

[7] J. Piaget, *The Language and Thought of the Child*.

[8] R. L. Mooney, "Surveying High School Students' Problems by Means of a Problem Check List," *Educational Research Bulletin*, Vol. XXI, pp. 57–69.

is a case in point. Objective evidence indicates that the "average" child does not acquire before the fifth or sixth grade much understanding of historical time.

In one investigation two equivalent groups of sixth-grade pupils were used to determine the effects of instruction in chronology. One group was taught history and chronology by extensive use of time lines and charts, in addition to regular procedures of instruction. The other group received instruction in history only incidentally as need of it arose in the study of the geography of Europe and Asia. "Time-concepts tests" were administered to both groups before and after instruction. Test results revealed that during the year both "history" and "nonhistory" groups made gains. The gains of the two groups, however, were about equal. Interpretations of the results indicate that maturation, and experience derived from everyday activities, are as influential at this age as formal instruction in history and chronology. On the basis of this evidence, instruction in the elementary grades about historical periods, time relations among events, and geological eras may be much less effective in building up a sense of time than is generally supposed.[9]

Experiential Background

Learning is frequently thought of as a process, but it may also be thought of as a *product*. This is apparent when reference is made to achievement in the form of "knowledge," "understandings," "attitudes," and "skills." We may speak of learning to read as a process and of reading abilities as the products or end results. Learning as a *product* is of primary importance in deciding the grade location of materials of instruction. What an individual can learn is determined not only by his level of maturation but also by what skills, attitudes, interests, tastes, and knowledge he has already learned. If the height of an individual's enjoyment in reading is at the level of such materials as *Donald Duck*, for example, it would be a mistake to begin with *Lady of the Lake* to develop his literary taste.

As a factor in grade placement, learning as a product may be viewed in two ways: first, in the sense of general experiential background, and second, as a specialized achievement in a subject or field of study. The

[9] Pistor, *op. cit.*

first is illustrated in readiness for learning and is significant in determining when the study of a particular subject, skill, or item of content should begin. A specific example is found in the case of reading. Readiness for reading is very complex and is intimately related to mental, physical, emotional, and social growth of the individual. There are many learning products that condition an individual for reading. One authority on the teaching of reading, after calling attention to maturation as a factor in reading readiness, proceeds to point out that readiness results in no small part from experience, guidance, and specific training in the home, the kindergarten, and the early part of the first grade. Some of the factors mentioned are the following: keen interest in reading; reasonably wide experience; facility in the use of ideas; ability to solve simple problems and to do abstract thinking of a very elementary type; ability to remember ideas, word forms, and word sounds; a reasonable range of vocabulary; command of simple English sentences; ability to distinguish word forms and word sounds; emotional stability; and some degree of social adjustment.[10]

Most of these factors are abilities which children can and do learn. Together they represent a general background of attainment, which is of primary importance in determining whether an individual is ready to profit from reading instruction. The practice of beginning instruction with what is familiar to children and moving to the less familiar is a common pattern and has had considerable influence upon the placement of materials and activities in the primary grades. It is not always possible to know the experiential background needed for a particular study, but in all judgments about grade location some idea of the general background of the student or grade group is present.

The second sense in which earlier experience, as a learning product, is used in determining grade placement is that of prerequisite knowledge. When specific knowledge is thought to be prerequisite to a particular study, as algebra is often held to be prerequisite to the study of physics, or history to the study of social problems, this consideration becomes important to grade placement.

Parts of subjects may be related in a temporal sequence; for example, Galileo lived before Newton and the American Revolution took

[10] W. S. Gray, "Reading," *Thirty-eighth Yearbook* of the National Society for the Study of Education, Part I, pp. 195–197.

place before the French Revolution. This kind of temporal relation is often used in history courses, where, according to some critics, chronological sequence has been stressed out of all proportion to its value.[11] The placement of ancient history in the ninth or tenth grade, with medieval, modern, and American history following in order, is based partly upon the supposition that temporal priority is somehow related to priority in learning. There is little or no basis for this assumption.[12] Until the truth of this assumption is established, the placement of historical content in chronological sequence will continue to be an issue.

Content may be logically related also when one idea includes another or is included in another. For example, a theorem about a polygon is logically prior to a theorem about a triangle. This relation, although logical, does not require that a theorem about a polygon be learned before a theorem about a triangle.

Logical relations may be thought of also as an orderly, systematic development of a subject. If the subject is geography, it may be defined at the very outset, distinguishing it from other subjects. Then the key terms upon which the science of geography depends are set forth and defined—pole, equator, longitude, latitude, zone, and so on—moving from the simple to the more complex. This step may be followed by the more concrete content involving the ideas of oceans, lakes, rivers, islands, land masses, and the like.

It is often, and erroneously, assumed that the "logical" relations among these key concepts prescribe a necessary order of learning. The way in which elements of subject matter are thus logically related, however, depends upon the order of presentation, and this order in turn depends upon the purposes, insights, and mental habits of the author. Moreover, the way in which ideas are related in teaching is not necessarily the order in which they will be learned. Nor does it determine the shape such ideas will take in the experience of the learner. Instances in which the order of learning is fixed by an order of presentation are much less frequent than is supposed, and the placement of content on the basis of such logical relations has little to commend it.

The most commonly used relationships of subject matter are those

---

[11] B. Othanel Smith, "Is History a Prerequisite to the Study of Social Problems?" *Social Studies,* Vol. 29, No. 5, pp. 206–210.
[12] *Ibid.*

involving priority in learning. For example, the solving of problems about gases in chemistry requires facility with ratio and proportion; multiplication of large numbers requires mastery of addition; satisfactory work in advanced algebra requires mastery of the first course. Where prerequisite knowledge or skill is established, the curriculum worker must take this into account in grade placement. However, the amount of prerequisite knowledge is probably much smaller than is generally supposed. It is almost impossible to establish enough specific prerequisite knowledge in history or social science to justify a fixed series of courses. The same is true for the natural sciences and English. Perhaps a stronger case can be made for prerequisite knowledge in foreign languages and mathematics,[13] but even here a conclusion should not be accepted without sufficient evidence. The need for caution is shown by the fact that laboratory experiments and classroom practice have demonstrated that the study of grammar as such is not a prerequisite to reading skill in a foreign language.[14]

Mental Age

When the general experiential background of people is roughly comparable by virtue of the fact that they live in the same culture, the mental performance of an "average" member of an age group—such as six-year-olds or ten-year-olds—is taken as the mental age. Mental age is a statistical norm which makes it possible to describe a person's mental performance in terms of the age at which an individual of "average" ability would make the same test score. For example, if a child makes the same score as an "average" ten-year-old, he has a mental age of ten years, no matter how old he is. If his chronological age is also ten, he has "average" mental ability. If his chronological age is eight, he is above "average"; if twelve, he is below "average." Thus, while mental age is a measure of general experiential background, it is also an index of general mental ability.

[13] F. H. Fagerstrom, "Mathematical Facts and Processes Prerequisite to the Study of the Calculus," *Teachers College Contributions to Education*, No. 572. Allan R. Congdon, "Training in High School Mathematics Essential for Success in Certain College Subjects," *Teachers College Contributions to Education*, No. 403.

[14] G. T. Buswell, *A Laboratory Study of the Reading of Modern Foreign Languages*.

Efforts have been made to determine the grade placement of arithmetic topics and reading materials by discovering the mental age at which various processes and skills can be most easily learned. On the basis of these investigations and the experience of teachers, there has been a tendency to shift many topics and materials to higher grades. Algebra, which was ordinarily taught in the ninth grade, is now often taught in the tenth grade; and long division has been moved from the fourth to the fifth grade. However, mental age is only one factor in the placement of materials, and when considered alone it is apt to lead to inadequate decisions. For example, early investigations showed that efficient work in beginning reading required a mental age of six and one-half years. Later investigations have shown that the mental age required for successful progress in reading depends largely upon the simplicity of materials and upon how reading is taught.

Interest

Among some educators, interest has become the chief criterion for placing activities and materials of instruction. Although this view has never been widely accepted, interest is generally looked upon as an important element in adapting materials of instruction to the level of the individual.

It was once a widely held idea that all people are born with certain interests and that the curriculum should be built upon these. This was implied in the Culture-Epoch theory, in favor with many teachers at the turn of the last century. According to this theory, the individual in his development repeats the stages through which the race progressed in its evolution. Thus the human embryo at one stage has gills indicative of the fish stage of evolution. Similarly, the child goes through a period in which he seems to "recapitulate" the savage phase of the race's development. During this period he is innately interested in adventure and in performing the activities of primitive man. At a later stage he becomes interested in the activities of civilized man because he has reached that stage of racial evolution in his personal development. This theory is now discredited. But one of the practical claims of the Culture-Epoch theory persists—that there are areas of interest more or less peculiar to children of different age groups.

There are few, if any, innate interests. Interests are acquired through the impact of the total environment upon the impulses of the individual. However, the effect of the environment upon the individual, and hence upon the shaping of his interests, is conditioned by what the individual is—by his level of maturation and his previous experience and learning.

Even though interests emerge from the interaction of the individual and his environment, certain interests do tend to appear at certain developmental stages. This is probably due to the fact that at any given period of an individual's early life he can know only a certain aspect of the world around him. In the preschool and first grade, the home and immediate community draw the boundaries for things with which the child is familiar, or that his maturational level will permit him to grasp. His interests tend to be focused in the home, school, and community. As he becomes more mature, his interests expand in time and space beyond his immediate environment. His thoughts wander into the past, into other lands, and into the less obvious aspects of his world.

The fact that interests tend to focus in certain areas has led to the practice of determining the grade placement of materials and activities by centers of interest for different grade or age groups. An investigation of 31 courses of study and 163 textbooks in various subjects revealed a number of centers of interest in actual use.[15] These interest centers were evaluated by the following criteria: (1) the center of interest should be a major influence on life; (2) there should be adequate instructional materials of suitable difficulty to develop each center of interest at the grade level indicated; (3) the center of interest should offer opportunity for the pupils to participate in significant undertakings; and (4) the center of interest should provide for the progressive development of the pupils from grade to grade. On the basis of this evaluation the following centers of interest were chosen:

Primary grades: Becoming better acquainted with the physical and social environment; Grade 1—Life in the home and school; Grade 2—Life in the immediate community; Grade 3—Life in the community, state, and nation.

Intermediate grades: Understanding the influence of the physical and social environment on life; Grade 4—Influence of different physical environ-

---

[15] O. I. Frederick, and L. P. Musselwhite, "Centers of Emphasis for Grades One through Twelve," *Journal of Educational Research,* Vol. 32, pp. 123–130.

ments on life; Grade 5—Influence of travel, adventure, and advancing physical frontiers on life; Grade 6—Influence of language, mathematics, governments, social institutions, and social agencies on life.

Junior high school: Adjusting to and using the physical and social environment; Grade 7—Fitting into and using the home, school, and community; Grade 8—Adjusting life to scientific inventions and machine production; Grade 9—Using science and social and governmental agencies for the welfare of the public.

Senior high school: Controlling and improving the physical and social environment; Grade 10—Controlling and improving biological and social conditions; Grade 11—Controlling and improving physical, economic, and business conditions; Grade 12—Understanding major scientific, social, economic, business, and governmental movements and trends.[16]

Such classification of interests is valuable as a partial synthesis of existing knowledge about the interests of children and adolescents. It is thus no wholesale objection to centers of interest, to indicate that evidence concerning the interests of children of various ages is weak and fragmentary. As a consequence, most centers of interest are based more upon what adults believe to be interesting to children than upon facts about children's interests. In the use and interpretation of centers of interest, the close relationship between experiential background and interest should be kept in mind. Children from the lower social strata, for example, could be expected to vary somewhat from middle-class children in their interests.

A few studies of children's interests are general enough to have implications for grade placement in many curriculum areas and yet are specific enough to indicate the kinds of activities or materials in which interest was found. The findings of Jersild and Tasch concerning the most liked and most disliked aspects of school would be pertinent in connection with the factor of interest in grade placement.[17]

Another example of a general approach to children's interests is that of Rudman and Shores.[18] In this study, 6,313 pupils in grades four

16 O. I. Frederick, and L. P. Musselwhite. "Centers of Emphasis for Grades One through Twelve," *Journal of Educational Research,* Vol. 32, by permission.

17 A. T. Jersild and R. Tasch, *Children's Interests.*

18 Herbert C. Rudman, *Interrelationships among Various Aspects of Children's Interests and Informational Needs and Expectations of Teachers, Parents, and Librarians.* Doctor's dissertation, University of Illinois, 1954. J. Harlan Shores, "Reading Interests and Informational Needs of Children in Grades Four to Eight." *Elementary English,* Vol. 31 (December 1954), pp. 493–500.

through eight, 4,531 parents of these pupils, 212 of these students' teachers, and 169 librarians responded to questions about pupils' reading interests and "informational needs." Among the more significant findings with respect to problems of grade placement were the following:

1. As children progress through the grades from four to eight, interest increases in mystery stories and decreases in cowboy stories and fairy tales. As children reach the seventh and eighth grades they are increasingly interested in reading about teenagers and children. Children in grades four through eight are interested in animals. As children move toward the upper elementary grades, interest in reading about various sports and recreational activities increases.
2. There is little difference in the reading interests of children from rural, urban, and metropolitan centers.
3. Children indicate a strong interest in questions related to ethics, values and religion, and become increasingly concerned with these types of questions as they progress through the upper elementary school grades.
4. As children progress through the grades from grade four to eight, they want to ask fewer questions about animals.
5. Children's concerns with their personal problems increase dramatically as they approach puberty. By grade eight, the response increases tenfold over grade four. Interest in this area centers around vocations, and boy-girl relationships.
6. Parents want children to ask about personal problems, and show this strong desire at all grade levels, especially in the upper grades. Parents show a particularly strong desire for children's questions about vocations.
7. Parents of upper-grade children indicate a strong desire for their children to become familiar with current events and social problems.
8. Upper-grade teachers are strong in their desire for children to ask questions concerning their personal problems. Teachers are particularly concerned that children ask questions about how to get along with others.
9. There is little difference between rural, urban, and metropolitan parents concerning what they want children to ask about.
10. Children look up information about animals in decreasing amount as they advance through the upper elementary grades.
11. Children look up information about famous people increasingly through the grades.[19]

[19] Shores, pp. 494–496.

In both the Jersild-Tasch and Rudman-Shores studies, the large number of children involved and the careful design of the study helped to eliminate many of the errors earlier associated with studies of children's interests.

Interests also may be used in a less comprehensive fashion in the grade placement of materials and activities. Many studies have been made of the interests of children, youth, and adults in relation to subject-matter areas. The findings of a study, by Murphy, of the art interests of students illustrate how interests may be used to determine the grade location of subject matter and activities in specialized fields. This study shows that preschool children are likely to exhibit little interest in objects of art as such; they take great pleasure, however, in the exploration of art materials. Five-year-olds ask more specific questions about art and show interest in such objects as pets and zoo specimens. At six years, children reveal interest in homes, in stories about objects observed in the museum, and in dramatizing experiences associated with the museum. Seven- and eight-year-olds are interested in construction activities, such as the making of Indian costumes, pictures, and homes.[20] Such studies enable the curriculum maker to know about the grade level at which activities and materials of instruction may be compatible with the developing of interests of students.

Closely related to the principle of interest are those studies that attempt to discover the problems of concern to youth at different levels of development. With a check list of 330 items, Mooney studied the problems of high-school students. He found that freshmen were concerned primarily about problems of "Health and Physical Development," sophomores with "Social and Recreational Activities," and juniors with "Adjustment of School Work." The problems of seniors were chiefly in two areas: "The Future: Vocational and Educational" and "Personal-Psychological Relations."[21]

Usefulness

Usefulness as a factor of grade placement should be distinguished from utility as a criterion of subject-matter selection. The latter refers

[20] National Society for the Study of Education, *Thirty-eighth Yearbook,* Part I, "Child Development and the Curriculum," p. 178.
[21] Ross L. Mooney, "Surveying High-School Students' Problems by Means of a Problem Check List," *Educational Research Bulletin,* Vol. XXI, No. 3, pp. 57–69.

to the general uses of knowledge and skills in adult life. Usefulness as a factor in grade placement refers to the immediate functional value of materials and activities for children of particular ages. For example, since measles and scarlet fever have a high incidence during the first few years of elementary school, facts concerning the prevention of these diseases can be important subject matter for the primary grades. Again, since many boys and girls begin to drive automobiles at about the age of sixteen, many schools have placed driver-training courses in the ninth or tenth grade. Since even kindergarten children need to know how to cross streets, materials and activities designed to teach this knowledge are introduced early in the program of the school. Many other illustrations of the placement of materials and activities by the criterion of usefulness can be pointed out, but these few instances should make clear this factor in grade placement.

Difficulty

Since schools have been graded, the placement of content has depended largely upon the factor of difficulty; and, even before the rise of the graded system, some judgment of difficulty, inadequate and ill-defined though it was, guided the selection and placement of materials of instruction. In present-day curriculum construction the criterion of difficulty has been applied to almost every form of content from spelling to poetry, from facts to fundamental concepts. It has been rigorously applied to such problems as determination of graded spelling lists, selection of reading materials for different grade levels, and placement of arithmetical processes.

In actual practice, the difficulty of subject matter or activities is relative to the maturation, achievement, and interest of the learners. A reading passage, for example, may be very difficult for one person and very simple for another. For that matter, the same factor—such as technical vocabulary or peculiarity of writing style—may cause it to be difficult for one person but will enable another to read it more rapidly and with better comprehension. Again, the same person may find content beyond his comprehension at one stage of his development and within easy grasp at a later stage.

Nevertheless, subject matter has its own inherent qualities of difficulty. It is generally agreed that content is of different degrees of complexity. Some words are longer, more complex, or otherwise harder to spell than others. Since division involves both subtraction and multiplication, it is considered more difficult than either of these operations alone. One idea may be more complex than another in that it involves more subordinate parts.

In an investigation of the difficulty of geographic content,[22] the following were accepted as indexes of difficulty: (1) the number of lesser relational ideas involved in gaining major geographic ideas, (2) the relative complexity of the relationships between these lesser ideas, and (3) the relative concreteness or abstractness of the particular elements entering into those relationships. Thus the temperature, vegetation, and topography of a region are simple concepts or facts on which more general ideas may rest. These are relatively simple to learn. That logging in a given region is possible because of an extensive forest—or that in another region the growing of olives is possible because of the long, hot, dry summers—are examples of ideas involving one-step relations. A relationship involving at least two inferences is: great forests are possible only where the soil is fertile and the climate is temperate; hence, logging is found chiefly in temperate regions of the earth. Again, people tend to engage in soapmaking when they live near an olive-growing region and can secure large quantities of olive oil cheaply.

Difficulty of content is sometimes defined statistically. If a set of operations in arithmetic, for example, is worked correctly by 90 per cent of third-grade children and another set by only 20 per cent, the first set is said to be less difficult than the second. This way of defining difficulty gives objective results. The conception of difficulty as complexity of ideas, on the other hand, is much less objective, and the results of its application are dependent largely upon the judgment of teachers and subject-matter experts.

3. *Interdependence of Factors*

While these factors in grade placement have been presented separately, they are so inextricably related that in practice consideration of one

[22] National Society for the Study of Education, *Thirty-second Yearbook,* "The Teaching of Geography," p. 124.

includes, at least by implication, one or more of the others. Difficulty of subject matter, for example, depends not only upon the inherent complexity of ideas but also upon the maturity of the individual, his interest or lack of interest, and his past experiences and achievements. In turn, the interest of an individual in a subject matter is affected by his prior achievement, his maturity, and the usefulness of the content. The dependence of learning and interest upon maturation has already been pointed out. All of these—interests, maturation, and prior achievement —are factors in the growth and development of the individual and, by virtue of this fact alone, are involved in the process of education. Any adequate scheme of grade placement, therefore, will incorporate all of these factors, with due emphasis upon each.

The idea of "readiness," once associated almost entirely with beginning instruction in the skill areas, has now been expanded to mean preparation for more advanced learning at any level.[23] Since this concept includes all the factors discussed earlier in connection with grade placement, there is little point in using "readiness" except possibly as a generalized term to recognize the interdependence of the various factors of determining sequence. Another reason for not using the readiness concept in this discussion is its close association with only one of the two approaches to problems of grade placement—that of adapting the learner to a preconceived placement of materials and experiences. It is for this that the learner is made ready.

How Factors and Approaches Are Related

Problems of grade placement, as noted already, may be approached from one of two angles: to change curriculum experiences to fit the child, or to change the child to fit a hypothesis of grade placement. The first of these approaches emphasizes the modification of materials and the adaptation of methods and techniques of instruction to the child's interests and level of development. In order to accomplish this, the curriculum worker must, of course, know the interests, backgrounds, and abilities of the children. For these factors will help to determine the

[23] Nila Banton Smith, *Readiness for Reading and Related Language Arts,* Research Bulletin of the National Conference on Research in English. Chicago: The National Council of Teachers of English, 1950.

selection of materials and methods. Since the second approach emphasizes changing the child to enable him to deal with the materials at the
levels at which they are placed, it emphasizes such factors as prerequisite knowledge and general experience.

However, these approaches are much more likely to be used in conjunction with one another than separately. Unless all the various factors are taken into account, the location of activities and materials in
the program of instruction will stress developmental needs and interests
to the neglect of adequate content; or else it will stress subject matter
without regard to the child and his development.

Appropriate Balance of Factors

Despite interdependence of the factors influencing choice of grade
location, from time to time grade placement has been determined by
emphasizing some factors to the neglect of others. The difficulty of content has been most frequently used to determine grade placement, and
prerequisite learning probably has received only a little less emphasis.
The principle of maturation, on the other hand—which came into educational discussions only about twenty years ago as a result of research
in child development—has only recently become recognized as a factor
in grade placement and has been less generally employed. Experimental schools have tended to emphasize interest as a factor in grade placement, while conventional schools have located skills and content in
terms of their supposed difficulty and importance as prerequisites to
later achievement.

As a matter of good policy, all factors should not be stressed equally;
indeed, certain factors may sometimes be only passively used. There is
good reason at times to give children training in skills for which their
maturation level is inadequate, provided other factors such as interest
and general experience are strong. This is probably true of certain reading and number manipulations, skills which lay the foundations for
later learning and enable the child to extend his experience. Some authorities have gone so far as to suggest a restatement of the problem of
grade placement to throw the emphasis, not upon locating skills and
concepts in terms of maturity, but upon developing methods and ma-

terials most effective in teaching these skills and concepts at various ages or grade levels.[24]

It is a fact that it is quite difficult to determine the precise grade in which a particular skill or concept can first be learned, or at least learned in part. And it is also a fact that studies have shown that certain skills and concepts can be learned in some degree at any grade level. Considered together, these facts suggest—for instance—that, once it has been decided that first-grade children should learn certain knowledges and skills for protecting themselves from disease and traffic accidents, the task of curriculum research or curriculum building would be to determine the materials and methods best suited to teaching these things, even though only partial mastery of them is possible in the first grade.

In a very real sense the idea of precise grade placement of materials or experiences is a misconception—or is, at least, misleading in its implicit denial of the tremendous range of abilities within any one grade. For example, it is common for the reading grade scores of a sixth-grade class to range from grade three to the freshman year in college.

Educational Economy and the Problem of Grade Placement

While the adaptation of materials and methods to the learner has much to commend it—and, in fact, needs to be stressed much more now than it has been in the past—this view cannot be accepted as an exclusive approach. For if it is true that children of any age can make some progress with the concepts and skills required by cultural conditions—and this is a very dubious supposition—the question still remains as to whether or not they can learn enough about them and in brief enough time to repay the effort of instruction. For instance, if it required nine months for fifth-grade children to get only a slight grasp of historical time using the best materials and methods that could be devised, while the same children could gain a fairly adequate concept of it in the eighth grade within four months, would there not be good reason for delaying this instruction until the eighth grade?

[24] National Society for the Study of Education, *Thirty-eighth Yearbook,* Part I, "Child Development and the Curriculum," p. 401.

As a matter of fact, questions about grade placement may be seen as questions of educational economy. Were such questions to be answered strictly upon the basis of ease of learning or height of interest, much of the present curriculum would be offered several years later. Increasing mental age, maturation, and experiential background would loom large in this postponement. However, these factors must be balanced by the early, pressing social need for tools of learning, prerequisite under-standings, and the importance of such instruction as that in health and safety. Thus the question of when the content is easiest and best learned must always be considered in relation to the pressure of social needs.

4. *Procedures of Grade Placement*

Two procedures are usually used to determine grade placement on the basis of the foregoing factors: judgmental and experimental. In addi-tion to these, studies of current practice are sometimes followed. The latter requires an analysis of current courses of study and textbooks to determine the average or most frequent grade location of skills or con-tent. In the last analysis, however, this method is based upon either the judgmental or experimental procedure, since current practice itself has been determined by one or the other. Moreover, the study of cur-rent practice frequently yields disappointing results, since wide varia-tions in the location of content from school to school make it difficult to establish common practice.[25]

The Judgmental Procedure

The judgmental procedure might be called the committee procedure, so much does it depend upon committees for its prestige. It is the most commonly accepted procedure, and the grade placement of most skills and content in the current curriculum has been determined by it. As a matter of fact, the general pattern of the curriculum from the first to the twelfth grade inclusive—especially in the fields of history, English,

[25] As an illustration of this, see George C. Kyte, "Variations in the Organization of the Elementary Courses of Study in History," *Educational Administration and Super-vision,* Vol. 13, No. 6, pp. 361–376.

mathematics, Latin, modern languages, physical sciences, biological sciences, and geography—was shaped largely by the recommendations of two committees, the Committee of Ten and the Committee of Fifteen. The Committee of Ten, appointed in 1892, made its final report in 1893. It was appointed to investigate the nature and scope of the major subjects of study in the secondary school. The Committee of Fifteen was convened immediately following the report of the Committee of Ten. Its duties were to investigate the length of elementary education and to make curriculum recommendations.

Since the 1890's, and increasingly since 1920, a number of national committees have been appointed to study and recommend, among other things, the proper placement of materials in various fields: Latin, science, mathematics, geography, social studies, modern languages, English, and so on.[26] Some of these committees conducted scientific investigations upon which to base their choice of grade location. For example, under the auspices of the *American and Canadian Committees on Modern Languages*, objective investigations were made to determine when the study of foreign languages should begin.

One of the serious criticisms of the judgmental procedure is that committees too often base their decisions upon the prejudices held by persons disciplined in one field of specialization. As a result, recommendations regarding grade placement too frequently rest upon unexamined assumptions and erroneous judgments of such factors as interest and difficulty.

The judgmental procedure should not be abandoned, however, just because it is occasionally abused. Its misuse merely indicates the need for rules by which to safeguard the procedure and to guarantee the best results. An examination of the work of the more effective committees reveals the following guideposts: (1) the bases of the committee's judgment should be clearly stated so that the members can better understand their own procedure, and so that other persons may more easily evaluate the committee's work; (2) the committee should test all of its choices by the available facts and seek new facts when these are needed; (3) it should examine the extent to which the various factors

[26] National Society for the Study of Education, *Thirty-first Yearbook*, Part I, "A Program for Teaching Science." *Twenty-ninth Yearbook*, "Report of the Society's Committee on Arithmetic."

involved in grade location have been considered and try to use them in its judgments; (4) it should take a broad view of the curriculum and the child rather than the narrow view usually associated with specialized teachers and subject-matter specialists; (5) it should make comprehensive, not piecemeal, decisions; that is, it should not be concerned with what should be done at one grade level alone, or with a single activity, topic, or skill, but with all levels of education.

The Experimental Procedure

The experimental procedure is an attempt to make objective investigations into the placement of activities, skills, and subject matter. There are many different patterns of this procedure, depending upon the criteria of placement employed and the breadth of the study. The usual plan is to select as a guide some factor or set of factors such as child interest, difficulty of content, and mental age. The activities, skills, or content to be located are then selected, and a hypothesis is made as to their probable placement. They are then taught to the children in the selected grade, under specified conditions. The tryout is checked by achievement tests, and if a particular percentage of the group—perhaps 75 per cent—succeeds in learning from the materials, they are considered properly placed.

The plan followed by the Committee of Seven, in studying the placement of arithmetic skills and materials, is one of the best illustrations of the experimental procedure. The essential phases of this investigation are as follows:

1. The approximate grade placement of each unit of arithmetic was determined either by current practice or by preliminary experiments in a few schools.

2. Using this approximate location as a "central grade," the topic was taught at the central grade, at one grade lower, or one or two grades above.

3. The mental ages of the children were ascertained by intelligence tests; the existing knowledge of the children regarding the topic to be taught was determined by pretests. Other tests were given to discover whether or not the children possessed the knowledge and skills prerequisite to the mastery of the topic.

4. If the children lacked the prerequisite knowledge and skills, a brief time was allowed for the teacher to try to bring them up to an acceptable

mastery. A second test was then given to see whether or not the prerequisites had been attained.

5. The number of minutes per day and the number of weeks that a topic was to be taught were set by the committee.

6. A general teaching outline indicating methods to be followed was prepared for all teachers engaged in the experiment.

7. Following the period of instruction on the topic being tried out, a final test was given to ascertain the immediate learning. This was followed in six weeks by a retention test to discover the amount of relatively permanent learning.

8. The data were intepreted by plotting the average scores of children on the retention tests against their mental ages, and by plotting the per cent of children making a score of 80 per cent on the retention tests against their mental ages. The latter was considered of more practical value.[27]

As a general rule experimental investigations have been fragmentary, covering only a small aspect of subject matter or involving only one grade level. In most instances they have been based upon consideration of a single factor, such as mental age or child interest, rather than upon the many interrelated factors in the curriculum, the child's development, and the demands of society. However, such criticisms should not be directed at the procedure as such but at the limited purposes and conceptions of those who design the experiments.

Care must be taken in the interpretation of results of grade-placement experiments. Demands of society, or, for that matter, of prerequisite educational experiences, are seldom considered as relevant factors. It is also common practice to freeze instructional method as a nonvariable factor and to assume no change in the earlier instructional program. Thus, an interpretation of the results of such experimental studies *should* read: "Assuming a constant experiential background in all factors relevant to this study, assuming a constant teaching method, considering only a few of the factors relevant to ease of learning, and assuming no pressing educational or social need, we reached the following conclusions."

In practical schoolwork it may never be possible to place materials and activities solely by means of experimentation. There are too many

[27] National Society for the Study of Education, *Thirty-eighth Yearbook,* Part I (1939), "Child Development and the Curriculum," pp. 300–306. Quoted by permission of the Society.

factors necessarily involved in the problem of placement. Furthermore, the relative importance of these factors depends upon the judgment of teachers and curriculum workers. Hence it would seem that the experimental procedure can best be used to find the effects of some combination of factors, whose relative weight in the experimental set-up would have been first determined by judgment.

▶ Following Up This Chapter

1. Examine a conventional course of study for either the elementary or secondary school, and try to determine the procedure that was used to place the materials of instruction.

2. Examine a guide prepared for use in activity curriculums, such as the *California Guide to Child Development: Manual for Kindergarten and Primary Grades*, and try to determine the criteria and procedures employed in deciding the grade location of activities.

3. Study one of the following investigations of the problem of grade placement, and prepare a critique of it. Indicate its assumptions and the defects in its procedure. C. O. Mathews, "Grade-Placement of Curriculum Materials in the Social Studies," *Teachers College Contributions to Education*, No. 241. Adelaide M. Ayer, *Some Difficulties in Elementary School History*. Dorothea A. McCarthy, *The Language Development of the Pre-School Child*. A. R. Dyer, *The Placement of Home Economics Content in Junior and Senior High Schools*, Home Economic Curriculum Study No 1. S. M. Corey, "The Developmental Tasks of Youth," in *Eighth Yearbook* of the John Dewey Society, pages 70–99. Ross L. Mooney, "Surveying High-School Students' Problems by Means of a Problem Check List," *Educational Research Bulletin*, Vol. XXI (March 18, 1942), pages 57–69. Dora V. Smith, "Growth in Language Power as Related to Child Development," in *Forty-third Yearbook* of the National Society for the Study of Education, Part II, Chapter IV.

▶ *Suggested
Reading*

1. In order to gain more adequate understanding of concepts underlying grade placement, such as maturation, mental age, interest, and so on, you should review these concepts in a general educational psychology, such as *Educational Psychology,* by Cole and Bruce.

2. For a general discussion of the problems of grade placement, see Caswell and Campbell's *Curriculum Development,* pages 291–332. The findings of research studies of grade placement are reviewed in Norton and Norton's *Foundations of Curriculum Building.* See their discussion of the problem of grade placement in each chapter that deals with a particular subject of instruction. For a good discussion of some of the more recently considered aspects of the problem of grade placement, see "Sequence and Grade Placement," by Arno Bellack, in *Journal of Educational Research,* Vol. XLI, No. 8 (April, 1948), pages 610–623. See also *Text Materials in Modern Education,* edited by Lee J. Cronbach, pages 71–76.

3. The judgmental procedure, like the scientific procedure, has not been reduced to a "one-two-three" pattern. You can find out something about the general outlines of these procedures, however, by studying intensively the references to these procedures given in the text.

Chapter 9

Allotment and
Distribution of
Instructional Time

HOW MUCH EMPHASIS should be placed upon each part of the instructional program? This is a question of considerable practical importance, and its answer involves at least three related questions. First, how many years of the total educational program should be given to a particular subject or study? Second, how many times each week should it be taught? Third, how much of the school day should be devoted to it?

Another way of looking at this problem is to consider how the total number of years devoted to public education should be used. Communities usually give the schools twelve years to educate the young. If the nursery school, kindergarten, and junior college are included, the total number of years may run as high as seventeen. The question of time allotment is concerned with how these years should be divided among the subjects, fields, and activities. Other questions deal with the distribution of the allotted time. Should the time allotted to a subject be concentrated in a few semesters or distributed over a longer period of time, perhaps over twelve or more school years? This question will involve certain others. How often should a class meet—five times a week, three times, only once? And how long should the class period be? Should it be thirty minutes, forty minutes, ninety minutes?

There is very little research evidence to help answer these questions. Without such evidence, all that can be done is to indicate the way in which time has been allotted in the past and to indicate some of the considerations and the kinds of research studies that should be taken into account when the question of time allotment is to be answered in a particular case. The same observations hold for the problem of determining the distribution of instructional time.

The amount of time allotted in any case is the result of practical experience and a judgment of the relative importance of the objectives to be met through various subjects and activities. Why, for example, is more time given to the study of the mother tongue than to any other subject? The answer is found in the fact that the objectives to be reached through the study of English rank high in the scale of importance, and that much time is needed for its mastery. The relative importance of a group of objectives is determined by the combined judgment of the public and the teaching profession. If the goals to be met through science, history, music, dancing, or any other subject or activity are relatively unimportant in the opinion of the public and the teaching profession, then these subjects will receive comparatively little attention in the educational program. Such judgments, however, are subject to change as new social circumstances call for new knowledge and skills. Therefore, it is not unusual to find that the amount of time given to a subject increases or decreases as the social realities change the goals of people.

The amount of time given content also depends upon how much time is needed to master it. This depends, of course, upon improved methods and materials, and other related factors. It is in answer to questions about these factors that scientific investigation can be of most worth in the determination of time allotment. Too little research has been done on these problems.

As a result, the curriculum worker must depend largely upon the practical experience of the better schools and upon the best established psychological facts and theories.

1. *Time Allotment Practices in the Conventional Elementary Curriculum*

Data on time allotment practices in elementary schools of the early part of the nineteenth century are fragmentary. By combining data from several sources, the following table was developed to indicate a few trends in time allotment practices in elementary schools from 1826 to 1935.

TABLE I

Time Allotment in the Elementary Subjects

DATES	THREE R'S	CONTENT SUBJECTS	SPECIAL ACTIVITIES
1826	91.7%	0.0%	8.3%
1856	70.1	15.7	14.2
1866	63.0	12.5	25.5
1904	61.8	12.3	25.9
1926	51.7	11.8	36.5
1935	51.3	14.5	34.2

Figures are per cent of total school time. Three R's consists of reading, 'riting, and 'rithmetic; Content subjects include such subjects as history, geography and science; special activities consist of music, drawing, recess, and opening exercises, and other content not readily classified under the three R's or content subjects.

Based on data from the following sources: Carleton H. Mann, "How Schools Use Their Time"; C. M. Reinoeld, "Time Allotment of School Subjects and Length of School Days," *Elementary Principal*, Vol. XXIII, No. 5 (June, 1944), pp. 15–18; George C. Kyte and Robert H. Lewis, "Time Tables," *The Nation's Schools*, Vol. 17, No. 1 (January, 1936), pp. 23–25.

From Table I it can be seen that the Three R's and the content subjects have lost and the special subjects and activities have gained in the per cent of time devoted to them. However, the Three R's still occu-

pied the most favored position as late as 1935, since they still consumed over half the time. The most striking change is in the amount
of time allotted to the special subjects and activities. During a period
of approximately seventy-five years, from 1856 to 1935, the time given
to them increased from 14.2 per cent to 34.2 per cent, the special subjects thus becoming second only to the Three R's in the consumption of
time.

These general trends represent changes in the time allotment of various subjects and activities. Mann's study gives more detail about these
general trends.[1] In the period from 1866 to 1926 spelling suffered the
greatest loss. At the end of this period it received about 45 per cent of
the time allotted to it at the beginning of the period. During the same
period the amount of time devoted to arithmetic decreased by approximately 33 per cent. The per cent of time given to reading remained
about the same throughout this sixty-year period. Reading and arithmetic, however, continued to hold first and second place respectively in
time allotment. History showed the greatest gain of any subject; geography showed a slight gain. The time given to music remained practically constant. Art and drawing, on the other hand, made considerable
gain, increasing from 292 minutes to 433 minutes per week over the
sixty years. Manual and household arts came into the elementary curriculum during this time and by 1926 were receiving 146 minutes per
week. Health and physical education also made marked gains.

It would be easy to conclude from the foregoing data that the Three
R's received less attention in 1935 than they did earlier. The per cent
of time devoted to these subjects decreased from 91.7 in 1826 to 51.3 in
1935. However, this is only a decrease in *relative* emphasis. From an
absolute standpoint the *amount* of time given to these subjects was increased. This was due to the tremendous increase in the average number of days of schooling during the period under discussion. This increase and its effect upon the amount of time given to the Three R's
are presented in Table II. Nearly four times as many hours were devoted to the Three R's in 1926 as in 1826, and there is no reason to assume that this ratio changed markedly between 1926 and 1935.

[1] Carleton H. Mann, "How Schools Use Their Time," *Teachers College Contributions to Education*, No. 333, p. 25.

TABLE II

Effects of Increase in Total Time Allowed for Schooling upon Amount of Time Given to the Three R's

DATES	AVERAGE NO. OF DAYS OF SCHOOLING	AVERAGE NO. OF HOURS PER SCHOOL DAY, ELEMEN- TARY GRADES	TOTAL NO. OF HOURS OF SCHOOLING	PER CENT OF TIME GIVEN TO THREE R'S	AVERAGE NO. OF HOURS IN- STRUCTION IN THREE R'S
1826	163	6.25	1,019	91.7	934
1866	523	5.22	2,730	62.0	1,693
1926	1,360	5.07	6,895	51.7	3,565

From Carleton H. Mann, "How Schools Use Their Time," *Teachers College Contributions to Education*, No. 333. Bureau of Publications, Teachers College, Columbia University. By permission.

Reasons for Changes in Time Allotment

It is possible to do little more than speculate on the causes of the changes in per cent of total time given to the subjects represented in Table I (page 198). The shift during the forty years between 1826 and 1866 was probably due largely to the growth of the curriculum and the necessity to find time for the new offerings. Except for physiology and the household and manual arts, which were added between 1866 and 1904, the offerings of the elementary school were almost constant by 1866. Between 1866 and 1904 there was little change in time allotment for any of the categories—Three R's, content subjects, and special subjects and activities.

However, the period between 1904 and 1926 was one of marked shifts in time allotment. This was the period of two great developments in education: first, the rise of educational science and the resulting crusade against educational inefficiency; second, the rise of the activity movement with its emphasis on developing the entire personality, which called for more than academic content and skills. The first development stressed the importance of accomplishing in less time, by more efficient methods and materials of instruction, desirable results in spelling, arithmetic, reading, and other fields. The second emphasized the importance of the arts and other activities related to the development of wholesome habits and tastes beyond the usual academic areas. It is interesting to note that the rapid increase in time allotment for history corresponded with the rapid expansion of the urban population through immigration after the frontier closed in 1890. The need for educating the children of immigrants in the story of the nation thus became of utmost importance.

The amount of time devoted to a subject varies, not only from one historic period to another, but also from school to school within the same period. From a study of the time allotment practices of 444 cities in 1926, Mann discovered wide variations. Reading, one of the oldest and most firmly established subjects, varied so much in its time allotments that some cities were found to give 11.8 times as much time to it as others. Some cities gave 4.4 times as much time to arithmetic as other cities; some gave 14.1 times as much time to language as others; some gave 48 times as much time to spelling as others; some gave 22.9 times as much time to history as others; some gave 144 times as much time to nature study and science as others; some gave 47.6 times as much time to art and drawing as others; some gave 18 times as much time to music as others; some gave 422.5 times as much time to projects and activities as others.[2]

2. Time Allotment Practices in the Conventional High-School Curriculum

Time allotment practices in the high school have usually been expressed in terms of the number of years in which a subject is offered, rather than in terms of the total number of minutes devoted to it over a period of years, as is the case with time allotment practices in the elementary school. For example, the time given to mathematics would be expressed as three years on the average for a particular span of years.

[2] Mann, *op. cit.*, pp. 141–144.

In a comprehensive study of time allotment practices, Stout investigated the development of the high school curriculum in the North Central States over a period of fifty-eight years from 1860 to 1918.[3] The data dealing with time allotment, however, cover only the years from 1860 to 1900.

Stout's study shows wide variation in the amount of time devoted to the various fields over this forty-year period. For mathematics the minimum was 1 year and the maximum 5 years. The average amount of time given to mathematics ranged from $2\frac{1}{2}$ to $3\frac{1}{8}$ years.[4] English showed a greater range of time allotment practices. The minimum time devoted to English was $\frac{1}{3}$ year, the maximum was $6\frac{1}{4}$ years, and the average ranged from $1\frac{1}{2}$ to $3\frac{1}{8}$ years. The minimum time given to science was $\frac{1}{2}$ year, and the maximum was $6\frac{1}{2}$ years. The time allotment in the social studies ranged from $\frac{1}{3}$ year to $5\frac{1}{3}$ years. Foreign languages combined to receive a maximum of 16 years and a minimum of 1 year.

Tendency toward Uniformity of Time Allotment Practices

During the period from 1860 to 1900 there was a slight tendency toward standardization of time allotment practices. Despite the wide variation in time devoted to mathematics and English at the close of the century, Stout's investigation shows slightly more uniformity in time allotment in these subjects than in 1860–1865. In the period 1860–1865 there were seven different time allotments in mathematics in a total of fourteen schools. In other words, every second school had a different amount of time assigned to mathematics. By 1896–1900 there were thirteen different time allotments in mathematics in forty schools; that is, one out of three schools had a different time assignment. The same movement toward uniformity is found in English. Ten out of thirteen schools had different time assignments in English during the period 1860–1865. However, in the period 1896–1900 there were only fifteen different time allotments in forty schools—a little better than one

[3] John E. Stout, *The Development of High School Curricula in the North Central States from 1860 to 1918.*

[4] The range of averages refers to the lowest and highest average allotments calculated by five-year periods.

out of three schools had a different amount of time devoted to English. Stout's data reveal similar tendencies in other subjects.

Uniformity Accentuated by Reports and College Requirements

The tendency toward the standardization of time allotment of high school subjects, begun in the closing years of the nineteenth century, was accentuated by the report of the Committee of Ten on Secondary School Studies in 1894. The Committee of Ten, working on the assumption that the courses offered should be taught extensively enough to make them yield the training they are potentially capable of yielding, recommended a complete high school program of studies, covering the subjects to be offered, the years in which they were to be offered, and the distribution of time for each subject in terms of periods per week.[5]

Uniformity of time allotment was also helped by the standardization of college entrance requirements. Since preparation for college was one of the recognized purposes of the high school, the requirements for college entrance had a definite influence on high school offerings. As the colleges began to agree upon requirements for admission, the number of years devoted to subjects recognized for college entrance tended to become constant. One of the earliest influences in this direction was that of the regional accrediting associations. The North Central Association, founded in 1894, recommended in 1900 that entrance requirements include two years of English, two of mathematics, and one each of science and history. The Committee on College Entrance Requirements of the National Education Association recommended in 1899 "that the number of constants be recognized in the following proportion, namely: four units in foreign language (no language accepted in less than two units), two units in mathematics, two in English, one in history, and one in science." [6] The work of the College Entrance Examination Board, organized in 1900, and that of the Carnegie Foundation for the Ad-

[5] National Education Association, *Report of the Committee of Ten on Secondary School Studies,* pp. 33–53.

[6] National Education Association, "Report of the Committee on College Entrance Requirements," *Proceedings and Addresses,* Thirty-eighth Annual Meeting (Chicago, 1899), p. 661.

vancement of Teaching helped to bring about uniformity of time allotment in subjects recognized for college admission.

By the period 1906–1911 there was a marked degree of uniformity in
the number of years devoted to the various subjects of the high school
curriculum. All but five of the schools studied by Stout offered from
three to four years of mathematics. By 1918 all but three of these
schools were offering from three to four years. This trend is even more
marked in English. In the period 1906–1911, thirty-four of the forty
schools were offering four years of English. The remaining six were offering three or three-and-one-half years. By 1918, all except one were
offering four years of English. This tendency toward uniformity of time
allotment is noticeable in other subjects and fields, but the standardization in them was not as complete by 1918 as it was in mathematics and
English.

Time Allotment for New Subjects

As the psychology of individual differences developed and the public
demands for a broader, more flexible, and more practical educational
program increased, curriculum offerings expanded. Not only were such
fields as music and art—seldom found prior to 1900—introduced in increasing amounts, but well-established subjects were expanded to include new aspects. English, for example, grew to include journalism
and speech. As a result of such innovations, the curriculum of the high
school expanded tremendously during the second and third decades of
this century. During the period 1906–1911 there were 53 courses offered
by the schools Stout studied. Approximately twenty years later, in
1929–1930, Van Dyke found that these same schools were offering 306
different courses, an increase of 475 per cent.[7] This marked enrichment
of the curriculum, however, did not seriously affect the amount of time
devoted to the established fields of mathematics, English, and science.[8]

[7] George E. Van Dyke, "Trends in the Development of the High School Offering,"
I and II, *School Review,* Vol. 39 (November, 1931), pp. 657–664; (December, 1931),
pp. 737–747.

[8] For evidence on this point, see A. K. Loomis, Edwin S. Lide, and B. Lamar Johnson, *The Program of Studies,* especially pp. 125–140.

3. Required Courses and the Utilization of Allocated Time

Up to this point the allotment of time has been considered from the standpoint of the division of total school time among the various subjects and fields in the elementary and high schools. Another aspect of the problem is how the time is used. What the student is required to take, and how much of his school time is used by such requirements, bear directly upon how time is used in various subjects. If a student is required to take American history, for example, he will not be able to take some other subject which he might have preferred, or which might have been more valuable to him. Required courses weight the educational program in one direction or another. Moreover, by this technique the time allotted to some fields, such as English, has been utilized to a maximum, whereas the time allotted to certain other fields, such as the fine arts, where there are no course requirements, has been utilized by only a few students.

Since most of the offerings in the elementary school are required, it seems reasonable to conclude that the time allocated to the various aspects of the curriculum is utilized by most of the pupils. This means that in 1926, according to Table I, nearly all pupils devoted 51.7 per cent of their time to the Three R's, 11.8 per cent to the content subjects, and 36.5 per cent to special subjects and activities. It is, of course, impossible to determine whether individual pupils actually devoted these percentages of their time to these endeavors. Nevertheless, the time was scheduled in these proportions for all students.

During 1929–1931 the junior high school was placing greatest emphasis on these subjects, in the order named: English, social studies, foreign language, mathematics, and manual arts. Fourteen per cent of the total time of the school year was devoted to the study of Engglish in grades 7, 8, and 9; 13 per cent to social studies; 12 per cent to foreign language; 12 per cent to mathematics; and 11 per cent to manual arts—making a total of 62 per cent. The remaining 38 per cent of school time was distributed as follows: Fine arts, 10 per cent; domestic arts, 10 per cent; science, 7 per cent; commerce, 6 per cent; and physical education, 5 per cent.[9]

[9] Loomis, Lide, and Johnson, *The Program of Studies*, pp. 25–27.

Data concerning required courses in the high school before 1915 are not readily available. Stout, however, says of the period 1860–1900:

No subject seems to have been universally required although some were practically so. Algebra and geometry were sometimes not required in commercial courses; but this was not the rule, particularly in three- and four-year courses. English was not required in some of the earlier classical courses, but the later practice was to require something in this field of all students. In science, the rule was to require physics of all students, although exceptions are found. In the field of social studies there seems to have been no one subject universally required of all students.[10]

By 1915–1918, all the high schools studied by Stout were requiring two years of English; about 90 per cent were requiring at least three years; and roughly 50 per cent, four years. Algebra was required in approximately 80 per cent of the schools, and plane geometry in about 60 per cent. About half the schools required two years, one of algebra and one of plane geometry. From one to two years of science were also required by about half of the schools. About 60 per cent required something in the social studies, usually American history.[11]

In 1929–1930, Van Dyke observed the following requirements in the same schools studied by Stout. English was required by all of these schools, American history by 85.7 per cent, physical education by 60 per cent, civics by 25.7 per cent and geometry by 34.3 per cent. Biology was required of all pupils in 8.6 per cent of these schools.

It seems that the "academic subjects" have enjoyed a favored position in school programs for almost three-quarters of a century. The "nonacademic" subjects and fields, on the other hand, have enjoyed a less favorable status. Except for music, which was required by 5.7 per cent of the thirty-five schools covered by Van Dyke's study, the nonacademic subjects have tended to be omitted as requirements of high schools.

With these facts in mind, it would be interesting to know what courses high school students actually take during the four years. How does the time allotted to various subjects actually work out in student

[10] Stout, *The Development of High School Curricula in the North Central States from 1860 to 1918,* Supplementary Educational Monographs, Vol. III, No. 3 (Chicago: University of Chicago Press; 1921), p. 106. By permission.
[11] *Ibid.,* pp. 223–224.

programs? The data bearing on these questions are meager. One of the most comprehensive investigations of this subject involved the graduates of the high schools of nine cities: Denver, Colorado; Washington, D.C.; Joliet, Illinois; Long Beach, California; Providence, Rhode Island; Trenton, New Jersey; St. Louis, Missouri; Sacramento, California; and Springfield, Massachusetts.[12] The average fractions of the total program in six subject fields during the period 1926–1930 are as follows: English, one-fifth; social studies, one-sixth; foreign languages, one-eighth; mathematics, one-ninth; science, one-tenth; and nonacademic subjects, one-fourth.

The data for five of these cities (Denver, Washington, Joliet, Long Beach, and Providence) were complete enough to permit tabulation (see Table III, page 208) of the percentage of work completed in each field. It is clear from Table III that over 75 per cent of the high school student's time is actually devoted to the academic fields, and that such fields as music and art are all but ignored. English enjoys the most favored position, with about one-fifth of the total time, and social studies is second with about one-sixth. These percentage distributions are for large high schools where the programs of study are more likely to be enriched by a wide variety of course offerings than in smaller schools. It is likely that the academic subjects would be even more dominant in the smaller schools.

4. Allotment Practices in New-Type Curriculums

In new curriculums (see Chapters 13 and 15)—organized on the basis of social problems, social functions, or centers of interest—the problem of time allotment deserves separate consideration. The way in which school time is allocated is a reflection of educational theory (methods, materials, goals, etc.) operating in a school. The way in which time is assigned is an expression of what is considered important. And what is thought to be important indicates an educational and social point of view. Hence it is not surprising that the curriculums based upon new educational and social theories have abandoned the old patterns of time allotment based upon educational and social viewpoints no longer acceptable.

[12] Loomis, Lide, and Johnson, *The Program of Studies,* pp. 216–232.

TABLE III

Percentage Distribution of Work Completed by High-School Graduates in Five Cities in June, 1930

	CITIES REPRESENTED					MEAN
	DENVER	WASH-INGTON	JOLIET	LONG BEACH	PROVI-DENCE	
English...............	21.8%	25.4%	21.4%	19.4%	18.6%	21.3%
Social studies...........	18.3	15.1	16.8	18.2	15.4	16.7
French.................	2.2	8.5	1.3	1.8	7.3	4.5
Spanish...............	6.1	3.5	1.9	5.6	1.2	3.6
German...............	.2	.8	.8	.04	2.4	.9
Latin.................	6.3	6.7	3.4	2.0	4.6	4.7
Total foreign language..	14.8	19.6	7.4	9.4	15.5	13.7
Mathematics...........	13.9	14.6	11.3	9.1	12.4	12.4
General science..........	.5	1.3	4.5	1.1	7.7	3.1
Biology...............	3.0	3.7	3.6	5.8	.6	3.2
Chemistry..............	3.0	2.1	1.6	1.3	.6	1.7
Physics................	2.3	1.5	4.5	1.8	.6	2.1
Other..................	1.9	...	6.4	1.6	.5	1.9
Total science..........	10.7	8.6	20.6	11.6	10.0	12.0
Stenography............	2.4	6.1	3.5	1.1	2.4	3.1
Bookkeeping...........	1.4	1.8	2.7	1.9	2.2	2.0
Typing................	2.4	(1)	4.1	2.7	3.1	2.4
Other..................	3.2	3.6	1.8	9.7	9.2	5.6
Total commerce	9.4	11.5	12.1	15.4	16.9	13.1
Home economics	2.9	2.1	3.1	3.1	1.2	2.4
Industrial arts..........	2.7	1.3	5.4	4.4	6.1	4.0
Art....................	1.9	.8	.5	2.8	3.0	1.8
Music.................	2.2	1.0	1.4	6.5	.8	2.3
Psychology.............	1.4	(2)	(2)	.1	.1	.3
Total miscellaneous....	11.1	5.2	10.4	16.9	11.2	10.8
Number of graduates.....	(3) 206	229	200	200	200	1,035

(1) Included in stenography and transcription
(2) Included in social studies
(3) Sampling of Denver graduates in order to avoid weighting the mean unduly.

From A. K. Loomis, Edwin S. Lide, and B. Lamar Johnson, *The Program of Studies*, Monograph No. 19, National Survey of Secondary Education, p. 223.

Daily Program in an Activity Curriculum

TIME

9:00	(Monday through Friday) Informal greetings, reports, observations, rhymes, music, events of current interest, informal activities designed to create a mental set conducive to a happy, profitable day.

9:15	*Arithmetical Enterprises* (Monday through Friday) Playstores, banking activities, handling of school supplies, etc. Although rich in arithmetical content through which the child is trained in skills and abilities, such units also yield abundantly in group and individual situations which develop initiative, responsibility, and co-operation. The flexible period provides opportunity for individual instruction.

10:00	*Healthful Living Enterprises* (Monday through Friday) Physical education enterprises, free play, the nutrition program, and adequate relief periods are provided for daily; units of work such as: "the study of milk," "a balanced meal," etc., provide enterprises which have healthful living as a center of interest but provide situations developmental of social and civic attitudes as well.

10:50	*Language Arts* (Monday through Friday) Oral and written composition, spelling and writing develop from activities rich in opportunities for expression, as the writing of a play to be presented in the auditorium period, puppet shows, the school newspaper, etc. The period should provide opportunity for literary discrimination and original expression; the long period provides for concentration of effort and attention according to individual interest and need.

12:00	(Monday through Friday) Lunch, Rest and Directed Playground Activities

Allotment Practices in the Activity Curriculum

At the elementary level the activity curriculum emphasizes individual and group activities arising from individual and group interests. These activities, rich in opportunities to develop initiative, co-operation, social skills, and personal responsibility, usually take the major portion of school time from grades 1 to 6. Special periods are usually

TIME

1:00	*Avocational Activities*			
	(Monday) Music; Activities, music appreciation, rhythm, harmonica, band, orchestra, etc.	(Tuesday) Nature Club, School museum, aquarium, gardens, terrarium. (Friday) Civics Club Committees responsible for various phases of school life.	(Wednesday) Creative Art and constructive activities in pottery, weaving, painting, drawing.	(Thursday) Use of auditorium for music, dancing, dramatics, projects, stagecraft, related to class activities.

1:50	(Monday through Friday) Recreation and Rest

2:00   *Reading Groups: Library Activities*

(Monday through Friday) Group organization on the basis of reading ability provides opportunity for remedial work with children having reading deficiencies and library guidance to superior readers. The quiet reading period may contribute to the development of information needed in the class activities related to social science, avocational, or health or other interests.

2:50	(Monday through Friday) Recreation and Rest

3:00	(Monday) Social studies activities	(Tuesday) Social studies activities	(Wednesday) Free creative work period	(Thursday) Social studies activities	(Friday) Shop enterprises

From *Teachers' Guide to Child Development: Manual for Kindergarten and Primary Teachers.* Prepared under the direction of the California State Curriculum Commission; Ruth Manning Hockett, editor (Sacramento: California State Department of Education; 1930), pp. 355–356.

assigned to practice work in arithmetic, language skills, and music. There are also special periods for play, lunch, and rest. This pattern of time allotment is illustrated in the program above.

It should be kept in mind that the time schedule in an activity curriculum is always flexible. The amount of time needed for various activities will vary from day to day. New developments in the activities of the group will require new information, new experiences, and new and unexpected activities. A program bound by a rigid schedule cannot provide for these new experiences, and the loss is in individual and group growth.

Allotment Pattern in the Core Curriculum

The allotment of time in a core curriculum is similar to that of the activity curriculum, in that a large block of time is set aside for group experiences. This is illustrated in the following chart.

GENERAL CURRICULUM FLOW CHART

Grades		
Kdg.	Development of an Integrated Program of Knowledges, Skills, and Basic Concepts	*through* Child Guidance and Development of Attitudes and Special Interests
6		
7	Continuation of Common Learnings and Basic Skills	Guidance and Exploration
9		
10	Core Curriculum Constants	Elective Subjects General - Vocational
12		

From *Charting the Curriculum in New York State Schools* (New York State Education Department, 1954), p. 7.

By reference to the chart above it is easy to see that the core curriculum allots a major portion of the total school time to those aspects of the educational program which contribute to the building of a common life. The remainder of the time is devoted to the special interests of students.

In keeping with the psychological fact that growth can be expressed in terms of increasing differentiation of structure and function, special interests are given an increasing amount of time in the junior and senior high schools. This is common practice in charts of time allotment practices in core curriculums. In fact some such charts allot time for the beginning of this specialization in grade one with increasing amounts through the public school years.[13] The way in which this theory of time allotment works out in a daily schedule is illustrated by the following general plan.

Eighth-Grade Core Program, West Junior High School. Kansas City, Missouri, 1951–1952

PERIOD	GROUP A	GROUP B	GROUP C	GROUP D	GROUP E	GROUP F
I...	Common learnings...	Common learnings...	Common learnings...	Homemaking..... Ind. A......	Homemaking..... Ind. A......	Home making Ind. A.
II...	Common learnings...	Common learnings...	Common learnings...	Ph. Ed..... Health.....	Ph. Ed..... Health.....	Ph. Ed. Health
III...	Common learnings... Lunch.....	Common learnings... Lunch.....	Common learnings... Lunch.....	Speech.....	Arith.......	Arith.
IV...	Arith......	Speech.....	Arith.......	Arith.......	Music.. or Art......	Music or Art
V...	Homemaking..... Ind. A......	Homemaking..... Ind. A......	Homemaking..... Ind. A......	Lunch...... Common learnings	Lunch...... Common learnings	Lunch Common learnings
VI...	Ph. Ed..... Health.....	Ph. Ed..... Health.....	Ph. Ed..... Health.....	Common learnings...	Common learnings...	Common learnings
VII...	Speech.....	Arith.......	Band......	Common learnings...	Common learnings...	Common learnings

Groups A, B, and D have speech first semester and the choice of art or music second semester. Groups E and F have the choice of art or music first semester and speech second semester. Group C elected band and has it for both semesters.

From Grace S. Wright, *Core Curriculum Development, Problems and Practices,* Bulletin 1952, No. 5, Federal Security Agency, Office of Education, pp. 65–66.

For a more detailed description of this program, see Roscoe Cramer, "Common-Learnings Program in the Junior High School," Bulletin 35 (April, 1951), *National Association of Secondary School Principals,* pp. 158–166.

[13] "A Guide to a Functional Program in the Secondary School," Bulletin No. 10, Florida State Department of Education, 1940.

The core or common-learnings program of Kansas City's West Junior High School is allotted two and one-half periods of the seven-period school day. These periods were formerly separate courses of social studies and English. Guidance and the routine functions of the home-room are also a part of the common-learnings time allotment. Wright describes the changes of time allocations in this program as a result of earlier trials with it:

During the first 2 years of experimentation in the seventh grade common learnings included arithmetic and met for 3 periods a day. Homeroom was not included. Before the introduction of the new program in the eighth and ninth grades in September 1945, it was realized that some drastic changes in schedule needed to be made.

1. The school day was lengthened from 6 to 7 55-minute periods, 2½ of which were allotted to common learnings. Arithmetic was taken out of the common learnings, the extra half period being allowed for guidance. Ten minutes additional time was added to the first period to provide for the routines of homeroom which it had absorbed.
2. Each teacher of common learnings was assigned 2 classes a day for a to-tal of 5 periods. One period was for lunch and individual needs. The re-maining period was for planning.
3. All common-learnings teachers in a grade were given the *same* period free each day. They meet together about twice a week to plan for the showing of films, taking trips, and anything else they are doing that is similar. Every 2 or 3 weeks the principal and counselor meet with each grade group to provide supervisory help with planning and with com-mon problems. The presidents of each core group also attend these meet-ings.[14]

5. *Distribution of Instructional Time*

Is it more effective to teach the skills in thirty- or sixty-minute periods? What is the best length of class period for history and science? Would students learn as much during daily thirty-minute periods for history as in daily sixty-minute periods? Would it be more effective, other things being equal, to distribute the time over a longer period by offer-

[14] Grace S. Wright, *Core Curriculum Development, Problems and Practices.*

ing the class only two or three times each week rather than daily? Would students learn as much English in three forty-minute periods per week for two semesters as in six forty-minute periods per week for one semester? Would it be more economical in learning and retention to concentrate the time of students upon two subjects for short periods—say, a quarter of the year—than to distribute their time over four or five subjects for a semester? These are but a few of the questions to be answered once a given amount of time has been allotted to a curriculum area.

Distribution of Time Based on Research Findings

The research bearing upon these questions is both meager and inconclusive. The only aspect of the curriculum for which the distribution of allotted time can be decided on the basis of scientific evidence is the skill subjects, when these are taught by repetitive techniques. It is well established that for such development of skills short and frequent periods of practice are more effective than long and infrequent ones. If practice on a skill is concentrated, a point of diminishing return is soon reached. After a short time no further progress is being made.[15]

The general rule that, the more distributed the practice, the more rapid the learning, must be qualified.[16] It is not always true that the shorter and more frequent periods will result in more rapid improvement. The effect of distribution of practice is conditioned by psychological realities and by the skills the individual is trying to learn. A ten-minute period is not always better than a twenty-minute one. In home-economics and industrial-arts skills, ten minutes would hardly allow enough time for the practice to begin. On the other hand, ten minutes of practice with spelling might be desirable.

The time distribution of study has been investigated even less in the content subjects. The length and distribution of class periods usually have been determined with little regard to psychological realities. The most frequent pattern of distribution at the high school level is a fifty- to sixty-minute period,[17] five times a week, for one or more semesters,

[15] R. S. Woodworth, *Experimental Psychology,* pp. 211–216.
[16] *Ibid.*
[17] American Association of School Administrators, "Length of School Sessions and Class Periods in Public Schools, 1938–39," *Educational Research Service,* Circular No. 2, March, 1940.

depending upon the total time given to the subject. The practices of the junior high school tend to follow those of the high school with regard to length of period, but to devote fewer periods per week to a subject. The average number of periods per week varies from two to six, with the traditional content subjects being assigned the more frequent class meetings.[18]

Distribution of Time by Committee Deliberations

The distribution of the time allotted to various subjects has been determined more often by rule of thumb and by convenience. The Carnegie Unit has shaped the time distribution in the high school for the last half century. This unit was defined as "a course of five periods weekly throughout an academic year of the preparatory school."[19] This was the time distribution proposed by the Committee of Ten in 1894 which was endorsed and recommended by the Committee on College Entrance Requirements in 1899, and which was followed by the College Entrance Examination Board from the beginning of its work on admission requirements in 1900. The Committee of Ten suggested four periods per week as a standard number, although it recognized the necessity of varying from this standard when local conditions made it seem wise to do so. But it stressed the suggestion "that all the subjects which make part of the secondary school course should be taught consecutively enough and extensively enough to make every subject yield that training which it is best fitted to yield." [20] It suggested four primary propositions upon which its recommendations regarding time allotment and distribution were based:

1. It assumed that all students "of like intelligence and maturity in any subject study it in the same way and to the same extent, so long as they study it at all."

[18] Loomis, Lide, and Johnson, *The Program of Studies,* pp. 27–28; "Time Use in the Junior High School Program," *Bulletin of the National Association of Secondary School Principals,* Vol. 29, No. 130 (April, 1945), pp. 93–101.

[19] The Carnegie Foundation for the Advancement of Teaching, *First Annual Report,* 1906, p. 38.

[20] National Education Association, *Report of the Committee of Ten on Secondary School Studies.* p. 41.

2. It assumed that the scope and the intensity of instruction are the same from course to course and from period to period.
3. It assumed that the achievement of students in a subject is directly proportional to the amount of time devoted to it, provided that equally good work is done throughout the course.
4. It assumed, as a corollary, that any two subjects are equal in value provided they are given equal time allotments and that the instruction in both is equally good.[21]

These propositions became the principles underlying the unit-of-credit system. On the basis of time allotment, courses became equivalent, and the *unit* then became a sort of "gold standard" of academic exchange. On the basis of these propositions it was easy to claim that if as much time is given to the study of commerce as is given to English, the achievement of students in commerce will be equal to that in English—provided equally good work is done in the two subjects. Hence, equal credit should be given for such courses. Similarly, if twice as much time is given to English as is given to history in a single year, the achievement of students in English will be twice as great as in history, and the history course should carry only half as much credit as the English course.

In the same vein of thought, the Committee on College Entrance Requirements said that its fundamental problem was:

. . . to formulate courses of study in each of the several subjects of the curriculum which shall be substantially equal in value, the measure of value being both quantity and quality of work done. . . . What is to be desired, and what the Committee hopes may become true, is that the colleges will state their entrance requirements in terms of national units, or norms, and that the schools will build up their program of studies out of the units furnished by these separate courses of study.[22]

This was in 1899. The extent to which the hopes of the Committee have been realized is only too clear to those who are familiar with secondary education today.

Even though the unit-of-credit system was developed earlier, the Carnegie Foundation for the Advancement of Teaching did much to

[21] National Education Association, *Report of the Committee of Ten on Secondary School Studies*, pp. 41–51.
[22] National Education Association, *Proceedings and Addresses,* Thirty-eight Annual Meeting (Chicago, 1899), p. 672.

standardize this procedure. Established in 1905 to provide retirement benefits for college teachers, it became involved during the first year of its existence with the problem of defining a college and distinguishing such an institution from a secondary school. For if it was to provide retirement benefits to college professors, the officers of the Foundation must have ways to distinguish a college from a high school. This was especially urgent at this time because it was not uncommon to find high schools bearing the title of college or university.

As a part of the definition of a college the Foundation stated that a college or university "should require for admission not less than the usual four years of academic or high school preparation, or its equivalent, in addition to the preacademic or grammar school studies." The officers of the Foundation further defined "four years of academic or high school preparation" in terms of units, "a unit being a course of five periods weekly throughout an academic year." [23] This same plan had already been adopted by the College Entrance Examination Board. The Carnegie Foundation's endorsement of the plan in order to administer an endowment for aged professors not only provided the unit with the name "Carnegie" but also clinched the general use of this "gold standard" of academic exchange.

The Carnegie Unit and Time Distribution

At first glance the Carnegie Unit appears to have little to do with the distribution of the time allotted to a course. The unit system clearly provides for credit in terms of time spent in class. If a course meets five periods a week for a full year, it carries one unit of credit. If it meets twice a week for the same length of time, the credit may be two-fifths of a unit. How then does the Carnegie Unit control the pattern of time distribution? Suppose a school wants to have courses in English, mathematics, social studies, foreign languages, and so on, meet one hour a day, three days a week, instead of following the present plan of daily meetings. In order to earn four units of credit—the amount he must earn under the unit system in order to graduate in four years—the student will be required to take approximately seven courses each semester. Many teachers would believe, and probably with good reason,

[23] Carnegie Foundation for the Advancement of Teaching, *Annual Report of the President and Treasurer*, 1906, p. 38.

that the pursuit of seven courses at once would disperse the student's interests and energies and thereby reduce the rate of learning.

If a faculty wishes to concentrate upon fewer subjects for a shorter period of time—say, twelve weeks instead of the usual eighteen weeks— the unit system again becomes a barrier. To earn a unit of credit under this plan, a class must meet one-third again as often, or one-third again as much, as would be the case in the semester plan. If there is an optimum number of courses that can be pursued at any one time, and if there is an optimum amount of concentration of experience in a given subject, the unit system sets the limits within which variations in time distribution can occur.

The assumptions underlying the Carnegie Unit have never been validated. In fact, psychological knowledge developed during the sixty-year period since their proposal would cause its validity to be seriously questioned, if not completely rejected. But the system has not been accepted because of its demonstrated educational advantages. It has been adopted because its theory of equivalent units makes it extremely convenient in academic bookkeeping. No one knows the length of class period, nor the frequency of periods, most conducive to learning in any given content course. It may be that just as much could be gained by reducing the time devoted to various subjects and distributing the time to other areas. Could just as much American history be learned in three class meetings per week as in five per week? Could more learning result from two American history classes a week for a year than from five classes a week for a semester? Is the overdependency of students in intellectual matters due in part to the frequency of class meetings and the consequent tendency of teachers to carry the responsibilities of the class?

There are as yet no answers to these questions. Nor is there adequate research bearing upon them. At the present time the entire secondary school system is operating on the basis of a mere convention with respect to the distribution of time. Moreover, the definition of teaching loads is necessarily related to the allotment and distribution of time to the various aspects of the curriculum. If substantial progress is to be made in changing the curriculum, or in adjusting the instructional load that now burdens teachers in almost every school, the present time pattern may have to be reconstructed. No one has attempted to make significant curriculum changes without encountering the bugbears of unit credit and overscheduled teachers. These two barriers to curriculum development are related, and both are intimately related to the Carnegie Unit as the standard of academic exchange.

6. *Time Allotment Procedures*

The question of determining the allotment of time may be answered in two ways: by appealing to present practice or by setting up time allocations and then trying them out.

Determining Time Allotment by Present Practice

In the absence of adequate research on which to base decisions regarding time allotments, and with the Carnegie Unit inhibiting such research, the most frequent practice has been to base time allocations on the practices found in other schools. While this answer is simple, the actual process of ascertaining present practice is somewhat complex. Practices vary widely. Even in spelling, the amount of time given to it in one school may be many times that devoted to it in another. It has been necessary, therefore, to set up some standard by which to choose among the practices. The usual way out of this difficulty is to take the average allotment of time as the best practice.

Studies of time allotment practices, such as those cited earlier in this chapter, are very important in this procedure. Such studies disclose tendencies either to increase or to decrease the amount of time given to various subjects and activities. They thereby afford a rough guide in setting time allotments in a given school. For example, if the Three R's are given, on the average, 51.3 per cent of the school day, then in a school where time allotment practices deviate markedly from this standard, the allocation of time should be examined.

The procedure of determining time allotment by present practice may be useful in keeping the allotment practices of a school from getting too much out of line with average practices. It is open, however, to the objection that an average of present practice lacks any single rationale. Present practice is partly the result of committee reports, such as that of the Committee of Ten; it is partly the result of countless variations due to the pressures of circumstances; and it may be partly the result of numerous judgments made by local school officials and teachers on the basis of ill-considered facts and values. Nevertheless, this procedure is the one most commonly used today, and it will probably continue in wide use until the problems of time allotment have received more research attention.

The Judgmental Procedure for Determining Time Allotment

The judgmental procedure for determining time allotment, like the judgmental procedure for selecting subject matter, has not been clearly formulated. It would appear that its frequent use by committees and by individuals would have drawn attention to the need for careful study of its pattern and techniques. But such a study has not been made. An effort will be made to state the bold outlines of the judgmental procedure and to indicate its adaptations to the problems of determining time allotments.

In the allotment of time by the judgmental procedure, there must be an agreement upon the purposes of the educational program. Since the amount of time allotted to any aspect of the program depends upon what is considered important, agreements upon educational directions are essential to agreement upon time allotment practices. Moreover, agreement upon purposes must be reached at the level of operational meanings as well as at the level of discussion. For it is not unusual to find persons who agree upon purposes when no choices among purposes have to be made. However, differences of opinion about purposes do not have to be settled before other aspects of the problem of time allotment are considered. Such differences must be resolved as the group moves toward a decision about time allotment.

The judgmental procedure requires the use of research findings. As agreement upon educational purposes is reached, it becomes possible to bring research findings to bear upon the question of how much time to give to a particular part of the school program. The relevant research findings fall into three categories. First, there are those studies that show what a given subject matter contributes to the realization of the accepted purposes. Second, there are studies that show the extent to which certain learnings are acquired incidentally. And third, there are studies which show that improved methods and materials of instruction will produce desirable results with a saving of time. Efforts to reach decisions about time allotment will be ill considered unless the results of the studies in each of these categories are thoroughly understood and used.

To report the research evidence bearing upon the problem of time allocation from these three categories would require more space than can be allowed in a general book on curriculum development. Examples of each category will be given to show how the findings bear upon the problem of time allotment.

Consider first an example of those studies that show the extent to which a given subject matter leads to the desired objective. In fixing the amount of time allotted to the study of grammar, it is usually assumed that knowledge of grammatical rules and definitions is essential to the improvement of written expression. If this assumption is correct, and if the improvement of written expression is important, then the time given to the study of grammar can be fixed in terms of how much study is needed to master it. Research bearing upon the time required to learn grammar will then be of great importance in fixing the amount of time to be given to it. The decision thus made will be based upon further assumptions respecting similarity of language backgrounds of students, equality of instruction from teacher to teacher, age of students, and the like.

But what about the truth of the statement that facility in written expression requires knowledge of grammatical principles and definitions? At this point also in the consideration of time allotment, the findings of research are important. Is knowledge of grammar essential? It has been found that knowledge of the definitions and rules of grammar may result in improved usage in the case of fast-learning students.[24] These students, relatively few in number, are able to learn the grammatical elements and to apply them in expression. On the other hand, slow learners find it difficult to learn the grammatical rules and definitions; and after they have acquired some understanding of grammar, they are unable to use it. Slow learners improve more in expression by practicing

[24] Harry A. Greene, "Direct versus Formal Methods in Elementary English," *Elementary English,* Vol. XIV, No. 5 (May, 1947), pp. 273–285.

correct forms than by studying about them—provided the relationship between *meanings* and *correct forms* is made clear at crucial points. Even the fast learners show as much improvement from this procedure as from the study of grammar. If the findings of these studies are accepted, the amount of time allotted to the study of grammar could be greatly reduced without any loss in proficiency of expression.

An example in the language-arts area illustrates research findings of the second kind—those showing that certain learnings are acquired incidentally. The amount of time to devote to spelling in both the elementary school and the high school is a perennial concern to both teachers and laymen. Some would devote far more time to the study of spelling than is the usual practice. Others would be willing to reduce the amount of time usually given to it. This difference of opinion is due largely to differences in the value attached to spelling. Some believe that uniformity of spelling is not very important, except in certain vocations, and that the amount of time now devoted to the development of uniformity in spelling might better be spent in the development of other abilities such as the improvement of thinking.

Assume, for the sake of illustration, that "correct" or uniform spelling is important and that a time allotment is to be made for it. How much time should be given to spelling? The answer to this question depends in part upon whether or not students learn spelling as a sort of by-product of other studies.

A study bearing upon this question shows that sixth-grade pupils learn to spell unusual words—those not commonly found in spelling lists—incidentally to the study of history, geography, and social studies.[25] It also shows that "Wide reading and a great variety of learning activities results in a larger amount of secondary learning of spelling words than does a more traditional type of textbook teaching of history and geography." [26] This finding suggests that pupils may learn to spell a large number of words as incidental learning throughout the grades and high school. A committee of teachers, trying to fix the amount of time to be allotted to spelling, will look differently on the problem if they are in possession of such research findings. Any judg-

[25] I. K. Tyler, "Spelling as a Secondary Learning," *Teachers College Contributions to Education,* No. 781 (New York: Bureau of Publications, Teacher's College, 1939).
[26] *Ibid.,* p. 110.

ment about increasing time given to spelling will be challenged by such investigations. Moreover, the committee will tend to emphasize the importance of pretesting as a technique in the teaching of spelling. Through pretests the words which each pupil has already learned, either by direct instruction or by incidental methods, can be eliminated in the teaching of this subject.

Investigations of methods of teaching spelling can be used to illustrate the third category of research studies. It is clear that investigations demonstrating more effective methods and materials of instruction will make it possible to reduce the amount of time given to a subject, or activity, provided the desired level of achievement is held constant. Thus improved methods and materials of instruction in spelling have led to the reduction of the amount of time devoted to the study of this subject in most schools. It has been estimated that the time now devoted to it is no more than one-fourth the time allowed in 1926—and perhaps not over one-tenth of the time given to it a century ago.[27]

▶ Following Up This Chapter

1. Make a study of the time allotment practices of an elementary or secondary school in a school system of your own choice. Find out how much of the school day is devoted to various activities, subjects, or problems. Try to find why the time is allocated as it is. Are these reasons sufficient to justify the practice?

2. Study the way the time allotted to the various activities, problems, or subjects in a school is distributed. What justification is there for this distribution of time?

3. Study the distribution of courses completed by the last graduating class of a high school. You can make this study by listing the names of students and tabulating the number of units each student has completed in each of the following categories: English, social studies, foreign language, mathematics, science, commerce, home economics, and so on. From these tabulations you should be able to calculate the percentage of the graduates'

[27] J. Harlan Shores, *A Critical Review of the Research on Elementary School Curriculum Organization, 1890–1949,* pp. 16–17.

total time that is devoted to a particular subject. If the school has a core curriculum, or some other new-type program, calculate in a similar manner the percentage of the graduates' time devoted to it. Criticize the distribution of work of the graduating class. What are your own assumptions in this criticism?

▶ Suggested Reading

1. Studies of time allotment are fragmentary and few in number. The most general treatment of the subject is Carleton H. Mann's "How Schools Use Their Time," which is a historical study of time allotment practices. A review of the research on time allotment is found in Norton and Norton's *Foundations of Curriculum Building*. For a general discussion of the problem of time allotment, see Caswell and Campbell's *Curriculum Development,* pages 291–332.

2. For a treatment of factors related to the question of how to distribute instructional time, consult a general reference on educational psychology, such as Cole and Bruce's *Educational Psychology,* and Cronbach's *Educational Psychology.* You should give particular attention to the discussion of the effectiveness of different lengths of drill periods upon the learning of skills.

PATTERNS OF
Part Three CURRICULUM
ORGANIZATION

PROBLEMS *about such matters as grounding the curriculum in the social realities of a particular culture, determining educational aims, and selecting content are logical first steps in the development of any internally consistent pattern of curriculum organization.*

The professional educator is accustomed to thinking in terms of subjects, activities, problems, or some such organizational scheme. It is indeed difficult for him to visualize objectives or content until he can see these in a school program. In fact, he is prone to rush ahead with changes in the organizational structure before he has thought through the new objectives that require new content.

In recent years a number of curriculum organizations have been worked out and now challenge the older subject curriculum. Most of the controversy over the relative value of these different patterns has focused on the subject curriculum and its opposite, the activity curriculum, which is sometimes referred to as the "project" or "experience" curriculum. It is the purpose of Part Three to describe and evaluate the various curriculum patterns now current in educational theory and practice.

In pure form, there are three organizations of the curriculum: subject, activity, and core. In practice, there are all sorts of devia-

tions from each of these types; and a pure example of any one of them, except perhaps the subject organization, is seldom encountered. Nevertheless, in the interest of clear thinking, it is worth while to set forth the characteristics of each of these types. Once these types are clearly defined, it is possible to discuss without confusion the multiplicity of curriculum patterns encountered in practice. It is then relatively easy to perceive that all these different practical schemes are but deviations from one or another of the three fundamental forms.

Each pure type is characterized by only a very few, though basic, features. These features are the ones that mark off one pure type from another. They are called distinctive characteristics. For example, a distinctive characteristic of the subject organization is that the learning experiences occur within the boundaries of conventional fields of knowledge. This feature marks a basic difference between the subject organization and both the activity and the core curriculums. It is thus a distinctive characteristic and provides a basis for exact definition of the subject curriculum.

Beyond these minimum features, which set apart each type as a distinct pattern, each pure type is further known by essential characteristics. These characteristics differ from the distinctive ones in that each may be found in more than one of the pure types. While they are essential to a particular form of organization, they are not distinctive of it to the point of insuring its identity. An activity organization, for example, requires that activities be co-operatively planned by the students and teachers. This is an essential characteristic of the activity curriculum. However, it is not a distinctive feature of this curriculum, since good instructional method may lead to co-operative teacher-pupil planning within the broad-problem areas of a core organization, or even within a subject curriculum. It is sometimes claimed that the provision of experiences common to all students characterizes the core curriculum. But such experiences are an essential rather than a distinctive feature. For the subject curriculum also requires certain experiences of all students, as when it is specified

226

that some subjects be taken by every student. This common-experience feature is said to be essential to both the subject and the core curriculums. But it is not a distinctive characteristic of either.

Unique patterns of curriculum organization will often require differently trained personnel and particular types of materials of instruction and administrative machinery. These have often been regarded as distinguishing marks of a particular type of organization. Staunch defenders of other patterns have taken exception to these claims and have frequently pointed out that their programs make use of these same arrangements. For example, scheduling to provide larger blocks of time than the usual forty- to sixty-minute periods is characteristic of core programs, but these same arrangements may be used to further the ends of broad-fields, or other variations of subject curriculums. Some of these characteristics will be indicated in the description of each pure form under the heading of "Personnel, Materials, and Arrangements Required for Optimum Operation."

Once the features of a pure type have been set forth, it is possible to look at this curriculum pattern critically in terms of its basic theory and in terms of the forms it assumes in practice. The reader is cautioned not to condemn a theory simply because practice claiming to be based on it is not completely in accord with the theory. Translation of theory into practice usually involves behavioral changes in teachers, administrators, parents, and others who are concerned with the school program. Considering the problems encountered in making such changes, it would hardly be understandable if school practice were an accurate reflection of curriculum theory. A pure-form organization is open to criticism only if its basic theory is untenable, or if it is impossible under any condition to translate the theory into practice. Practice, of course, is open to criticism if it departs significantly from the theory.

It is clear from the foregoing discussion that Part Three deals with the following questions:

1. What are the distinctive characteristics to be found in each pattern of curriculum organization?

2. *What essential characteristics may be seen in the various forms of curriculum organization?*
3. *In what way are problems of personnel, administration, and material facilities handled in each pattern of curriculum organization?*
4. *What are some of the chief criticisms directed against each of these curriculum forms?*
5. *What problems remain to be solved within each form of curriculum?*

Chapter 10

The Subject Curriculum:
Its Chief Characteristics

T H E   S U B J E C T is the oldest and most widely accepted form of curriculum organization. Perhaps the earliest example of this organization is the *Seven Liberal Arts,* which were present in an incipient form in the schools of ancient Greece and Rome, and which were offered in a more advanced stage of development in the monastery and cathedral schools of the Middle Ages. The Seven Liberal Arts consisted of two divisions: the *trivium,* which was comprised of grammar, rhetoric, and dialectic (logic) ; and the *quadrivium,* which consisted of arithmetic, geometry, astronomy, and music. These subjects were very broad; grammar, for example, consisted not only of the kind of content found in modern grammar courses, but also of literature studied analytically—that is, from the standpoint of versification, prosody, figures of speech, and vocal expression. Therefore, the Seven Liberal Arts do not conform precisely to modern subjects having the same titles.

In the modern period the *trivium* was further divided to include literature and history as distinct subjects; and the *quadrivium,* to include algebra, trigonometry, geography, botany, zoology, physics, and chemistry. In the last half century the number of subjects offered in the public schools increased by leaps and bounds, so that by 1930 there were over three hundred distinct subjects of instruction. Despite this enormous multiplication of subjects, the Seven Liberal Arts are still the nucleus of the subject curriculum, as a casual survey of required courses will reveal.

1. *Distinctive Characteristics of the Subject Curriculum*

The subject curriculum is an organization of the content of education into subjects of instruction. In its extreme form the subjects are compartmentalized bodies of knowledge, taught in complete isolation from one another, even from those to which they are related—as history may be taught completely divorced from geography, economics, and sociology. Its less extreme forms permit a certain degree of interrelation among the subjects; in a correlated curriculum a subject is taught with reference to the contribution which the content of other subjects may make to the fullest understanding of it.

In the following pages, two distinctive features of the subject curriculum are set forth.

Classification and Organization of Subject Matter

The first distinctive feature is that *the subject matter is classified and organized in accordance with the divisions of labor in research.* From a historical standpoint, the classification of knowledge is a function of the accumulation of knowledge. As men found out more and more about their world, the point was reached at which it became desirable to classify their learning in order to make reference to it more easily, to use it more effectively in further study of their environment, and to explain to others the knowledge they had gained.

In the subject curriculum, the content is selected and ordered in such a way as to discipline the student in those classifications and arrangements of ideas that have proved most beneficial in locating and investigating new problems of specialized research. The knowledge is not classified and ordered with a view to increasing the practical intelligence and wisdom of the learner. In other words, the bearing of the subject matter upon questions of social policy and decision is ignored in both its selection and arrangement. Instead, the content is chosen and organized in accordance with the needs of the scientist or research specialist, who is interested in the subject "for its own sake" and consequently orders facts and principles so as to render them most useful in conducting further research in the subject.

It should not be supposed, however, that this way of organizing the curriculum is purely for the purpose of developing research workers. It is true that this type of organization is designed to advance the growth of research students—to lead to more and more understanding of the ideas and facts embraced by the subject. But the purpose is not exhausted by research interests. The more comprehensive purpose of this type of curriculum is to develop the capacity of any student to take on more and more of his culture under his own steam. By becoming disciplined in subjects such as mathematics, history, English, and science, the student acquires the ideas, facts, and skills by which to continue to grow in the wider society when his school days are over.

It is sometimes thought that a subject consists of one kind of content. But this is an erroneous belief. A subject is very complex. It is made up of many different kinds of content, each kind leading to its own particular outcome of learning. For example, English consists of the principles of grammar and rhetoric, the various selections of literature, words to be spelled, and those materials involved in the development of skills in written and oral expression. The complexity of English is well illustrated in the chart on page 232. Similarly the complexity of all other subjects could be shown.

From this analysis of English, it is clear that specialization is relative. In the public school program the subject of English is very broad. At the college level, however, this subject is usually broken down into its component parts: one finds specialized subjects in literature, speech, journalism, rhetoric, and so on. And at the more advanced levels of the college and university each of these specialized subjects is further divided into courses for intensive study.

Emphasis on Techniques of Explanation

The second distinctive characteristic of the subject curriculum is that *this curriculum emphasizes expository discourse and techniques of*

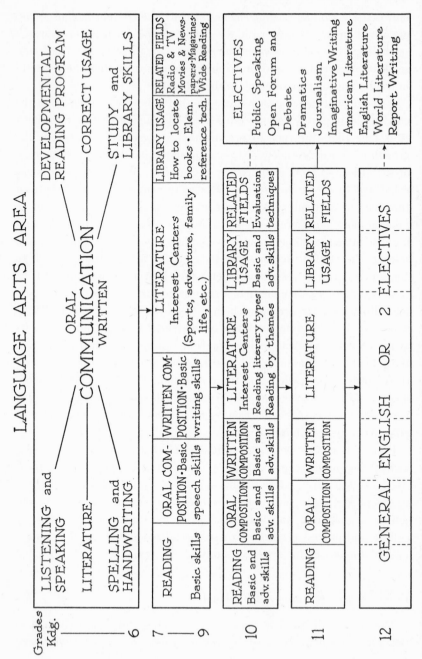

New York State Education Department, *Charting the Curriculum in the New York Schools*, p. 9.

explanation. Exposition is a form of discourse in which ideas are stated and elaborated so that they may be understood. The main ideas are ordered and explored, and, when convenient, illustrated. While the reasons for the truth or falsity of ideas are given, sometimes in great detail, student experimentation except for formal laboratory work is seldom set forth.

At least four kinds of exposition are found in the subject curriculum. The first is that which proceeds from the simple to the complex. The simple is defined as that which contains few elements or subordinate parts, as a one-celled animal is simpler than a many-celled animal, or as hydrogen and oxygen are simpler than chemical compounds. Chemistry and biology courses are frequently organized on this principle; and the organization of many other courses, such as grammar and foreign languages, is influenced by it in more or less degree.

The second is an expository order based upon prerequisite learnings. This principle is followed particularly in subjects consisting largely of laws and principles, such as physics, grammar and geometry. Geometry is organized on the supposition that the theorems bear a particular logical relation to one another and are best learned in that relation.

The third form of exposition is that which proceeds from the whole to the part. Geography frequently begins with the globe, with the idea that the earth is a sphere, because this conception serves to interpret many geographic observations, such as differences in time and seasons.

The fourth kind of exposition is chronological. Facts and ideas are arranged in a time sequence so that presentation of later events is preceded by discussion of earlier ones. This is the organization followed in history courses—and frequently in literature courses, literary selections being arranged in time sequence.

Teaching procedures and techniques are largely based upon language activities—lectures, discussions, questions and answers, written exercises, oral reports, term papers, and the like. Most of these activities tend to emphasize the meaning of terms in their relation to other terms. Hence, the subject curriculum tends not to use such activities as painting, cartooning, modeling, designing, constructing, and the like, for these are seldom suited to the purposes of instruction.

While the subject curriculum stresses explanatory processes, it does not rule out other intellectual activities. There is no good reason why it cannot allow attention to be given to the development of critical thinking. Statements can be examined to ascertain their meaning, their logical grounding, and their factual support. Moreover, problems that fall within the subject can be formulated and studied. Despite these possibilities, however, the processes of mere absorption and memorization have been stressed in the subject curriculum.

That language activities are emphasized in the subject curriculum is further evidenced by the methods conventionally used to evaluate progress in the subjects. These methods commonly ask for facts, principles, and other evidences of understanding and mastery of content, rather than for evidence of growth in habits of effective thinking and skill in social processes.

2. Essential Characteristics

The distinctive features of the subject curriculum were set forth in the preceding section. The following paragraphs describe the characteristics essential to, but not distinctive of, the subject curriculum.

Required and Elective Subjects

The first of the essential characteristics of the subject curriculum is that *subjects may be required of all students, required only for certain specified groups, elected by certain groups, elected by certain individuals, or elected by anyone.* Those responsible for planning the subject curriculum have determined in advance that some subject matter shall be required of all students, while other subject matter shall either be required or elected by specified individuals or groups. Since the subject curriculum is planned in advance, it is necessarily planned for someone. Therefore, the designation of these individuals and groups who are to enter certain courses of the curriculum is only to be expected. It is common practice to have courses in certain subjects required of all students. Other courses are required only of those in a particular program of study, such as the college preparatory sequence or the commercial sequence.

Similarly, certain courses are designed as electives to be chosen by anyone, while other courses are designed only for those following a certain sequence of courses. Beginning typing may be an elective course open to anyone and a required course for those in the commercial sequence, whereas the advanced course in typing may be required of or elected only by commercial students. A third or fourth year of Latin may be an elective only for those in a college preparatory sequence, and only for those individuals in this sequence who have completed two or three previous years of Latin. It is possible to have a subject curriculum in which all courses are required, or one in which all courses are elective. The great multiplicity of courses that has arisen in recent years makes the first of these unlikely; and the current emphasis upon the development of social integration tends to rule out the desirability of a purely elective program.

Some pattern of required and elective courses is an essential characteristic of the subject curriculum. However, such a pattern is not *distinctive* of the subject organization; for the core curriculum also requires certain common areas of experience (although they may not be called courses), and it may have elective areas beyond these required ones.

Constant Subjects as Defining "General Education"

Constant subjects constitute the greater part of the "common learnings" or "general education" program. The program of general education is determined in the subject curriculum by making some subjects constant in all programs of study. These constants do not, of course, constitute all of the common experience areas. There are assembly programs, fire drills, periodic health examinations, and other all-school functions that provide common learnings. Nevertheless, it is true that the required courses do comprise the major share of the general education program. This characteristic is essential, but it is not distinctive, because the core areas of a core curriculum also are required of all students and thus constitute the majority of the common learnings in that type of organization.

Experiences Not Identical

A third essential characteristic of the subject curriculum is as follows: *Requirement of subjects does not mean identical experiences for all students.* It is unfair to accuse the subject organization of attempting to provide identical experiences for everyone studying a required subject. Teachers of a subject curriculum are not untrained in educational psychology. They know about individual differences and understand the necessity of taking these into account in the teaching process. Thus, while the ends of the instruction are still couched in terms of subject matter, the instruction is not planned with either the desire or the hope that all students will leave the courses having had the same experience. In fact, if we assume good explanatory methods—and in judging the theory of the subject curriculum we have no right to assume less—every effort is made to bring the more able students to a better understanding of the facts and principles of the subject than the less able ones could possibly reach.

Planning Programs and Courses in Advance

Required and elective subjects are determined in advance. In order to plan course offerings, it is necessary to determine in advance which courses to offer, the number of sections of each, the people who are to teach them, and the people who are to enroll in them. It is also necessary to decide the grade level at which each course is to be offered and to select the students who are to be required to take or are free to elect each course at each grade level. There are, for instance, certain required courses for juniors in the college preparatory program. These same students are free to elect certain other courses as juniors, and they know in advance which courses will be required and which ones will be electives when they are seniors. This is an essential characteristic of the subject curriculum. Again it is not distinctive, for the same general planning also characterizes the core curriculum.

Provision for Individual Interests and Abilities

A fifth essential characteristic of the subject curriculum is that *elective courses, differentiated assignments, and special programs care for individual differences in interest and ability.* Adjustment of instruction to the interests and abilities of students is made in the subject curriculum partly by elective subjects and partly by differentiation of assignments within subjects. If a boy is interested in farming, he may take courses in agriculture; if a girl is interested in becoming a nurse, she may take courses such as biology and chemistry, which bear upon her special interest.

Within a subject the teacher may adjust instruction to differences in student interests and abilities by differentiation of assignments. One individual may satisfy his particular interest, for example, by preparing and making reports to the class on topics of interest to him, or he may do special projects along the lines of his interests. Variations in ability may be provided for by differentiated assignments in which the faster learners participate in more as well as different activities.

In addition, adjustments are made to individual differences through guidance programs, through diagnostic and remedial programs in the subjects (especially those in the basic skills), and through special care for individuals with serious mental or physical handicaps—for instance, the slow-learning child or the hard-of-hearing child. There is little opportunity in regular classes to care for all of the special needs and interests of slow-learning students. It may be necessary, therefore, to have special classes for youngsters markedly retarded in some of the basic skills. Special classes or individual care must also be provided for children so atypical in vision, hearing, mentality, physical ability, or personality that they cannot learn to best advantage in the regular classes. Teachers, too, are frequently found giving freely of individual instruction to the child who finds a deeper and more sustained interest in a particular aspect of the subject matter than have the majority of the class.

Then, too, there will be those students who indicate interest in activities that do not fit well into the development of any subject. Special provisions are thus made for the model airplane builders, the stamp collectors, the amateur photographers, and other such groups. Provision for these interests often expands the curriculum in actual practice and lengthens the school day without effecting any change in the curriculum as it is described on paper. In actual practice the subject curriculum is often a group of subjects occupying the regular school hours plus an activity program before and after school and sometimes during school hours.

Social Direction

The sixth essential characteristic of the subject curriculum is that *this curriculum may or may not be given deliberate social direction.* It is now generally recognized that it is impossible to teach in a social vacuum. No teacher can carry on the instructional process without moving in some social direction. The first choice of direction is made in the determination of educational goals. If these goals reflect lack of concern for the pressing problems of society and for the democratic resolution of these problems, there is still no neutrality with respect to the social consequences of education. This is true because whatever goals are chosen, whatever values and knowledges are taught, they are either for or against the *status quo* or some special interest group within the society. Were a teacher to succeed in his efforts to be neutral, the effects of his success would be to strengthen the *status quo.* To take no side is, in effect, to throw one's weight to the side of those currently in power.

Although it is impossible to carry on the process of education without social consequences and, hence, without influencing the direction of social change, it is altogether possible to plan a program without being aware of its social effects. Since the subject curriculum emphasizes mastery of the subjects per se, the knowledge and skills contained in them tend to become ends in themselves. For this reason the subject curriculum often lacks deliberate social direction.

It is really not necessary that the subject curriculum be planned without regard to questions of social direction. Whether it is so planned or not depends upon the social sensitivity of those who do the planning and teaching. There is no good reason to suppose that the content of history, English, or even mathematics could not be selected and taught in such a way as to help students to rebuild social values as well as to learn fundamental ideas, beliefs, aspirations, skills, and methods of thinking. In this event, however, questions of "what should be" must be emphasized no less than the accumulation of factual knowledge or the development of skills. It should be noted that such distribution of emphasis is infrequent in the subject curriculum.

3. Personnel, Physical Features, and Administrative Arrangements Required for Optimum Operation

No more of an attempt will be made to include *all* the desirable personnel, physical, and administrative requirements for optimum operation of the subject curriculum than was made to include all the characteristics of such an organization. Only those requirements are discussed that seem especially desirable and most directly related to the goals of the subject organization.

Trained Teachers

Teachers should be thoroughly trained and disciplined in at least one subject. Attention is directed to the dual aspect of this requirement. Teachers should possess mastery of at least one field of knowledge. They should also have adequate training in educational methods peculiarly suited to the presentation of this field. The history teacher will know history and will know how to teach history so that children will learn and remember the facts and understandings comprising the goals of instruction.

The teacher should also know the logic of the subject he is to teach. He should be able to recognize statements such as definitions and other analytic statements which are true without reference to particular facts. He should know the difference between descriptive and normative generalizations as well as the difference between the methods of verification and justification appropriate to them. He should know the levels of knowledge in his subject—that is, he should be able to explain a statement by showing its derivation from other statements. He should know the difference between logical validity and truth and be able to recognize and deal with formal as well as material fallacies. All of these things the teacher should know in the context of his subject. For no matter how much factual knowledge he may possess, the teacher will be handicapped unless he can maneuver logically in the domain of his subject. In order to acquire logical knowledge of his subject, the teacher will need to study logic, philosophy of science, theory of knowledge, and analytic philosophy. Usually some formal work in these studies will be necessary. But in any event, courses in pedagogical method and curriculum development should emphasize the uses of such knowledge.

One Classroom for Each Teacher

Each teacher will have one well-equipped schoolroom. Teachers have found that they can instruct in a subject better if they have a room especially designed and equipped for the optimum development of that subject. The history teacher will be able to teach history more effectively in a room where he has on hand the maps, charts, pictures, and most essential books ready for the job. Similarly, the physics teacher should have a laboratory equipped and arranged to facilitate his own method of teaching physics. Ideally, the chemistry teacher should have a separate laboratory designed for the requirements of his subject.

Transportation for Field Trips

Arrangements should be made for the transportation of classes to centers where the subjects can be enriched and vitalized. The most effective subject-matter teachers have long sought the very best instructional experiences they could devise in the teaching of their subjects. If effective pursuance of the subject requires that the hygiene class go to a hospital, the botany class to the woods, the zoology section to a lake, the art group to a museum, and the English class to the office of the local newspaper, there is no doubt at all that transportation should be readily available for these trips.

One caution comes readily to mind. It would be an error to assume that two groups of children who happened to take a trip to the same place had thus benefited from the same educational experience. No two children can possibly have identical experiences; but beyond this consideration, the purposes for which the experience is designed will determine in large measure the values to be gained from it. A trip taken for the purpose of developing better understanding of a subject would have different values from those gained through a trip to the same place designed to facilitate the solution of a group or individual problem.

Length of Class Periods

A fourth requirement for best operation of the subject curriculum is that *the length of class periods be conducive to maximum progress in the subject.* A subject organization is no more bound by its own administrative devices than is any other type of organization. Spelling, for example, has been taught largely by techniques of memorization, and experimentation with these methods has long indicated that the class period should be fifteen to twenty minutes in length. As a consequence, a short period is the general practice when spelling is taught as a subject. On the other hand, many schools have found that the learnings in certain of the science courses can be developed more efficiently in unbroken time intervals as long as ninety minutes, and such periods are fairly common.

The question of the total amount of time to be spent in any one subject during a week, month, or year, or in the entire curriculum is answered by taking into account the relative value of the subject. Considerations of teaching method shortened the periods for spelling and lengthened those for the sciences. But if spelling instruction is getting less consideration in the total curriculum sequence while science is getting more, it is because other factors besides the effects of the length of class period on achievement have been taken into account.

Providing for Common Needs

As a fifth requirement, *special arrangements should be made for meeting common needs.* In many schools some attention is now given to student needs which do not fit easily into the plan of any of the subjects. Personal and vocational guidance has been devised to care for some of these needs. Health examinations, student government, and social clubs have also been provided. The administrative devices created to meet these needs are numerous. Home-room periods, assembly programs, new courses, reallocation of time in existing courses, and varied types of out-of-school committees are only a few of the diverse administrative plans used to provide for these common needs. Regardless of the scheme employed, it is generally felt that these needs must be met and that the subjects as they are constituted cannot care for them.

▶ *Following Up*
   This Chapter

1. Only the most outstanding characteristics of a subject organization were discussed in this chapter. List other characteristics. Are these distinctive, essential but not distinctive, or are they simply features required for optimum functioning?

2. What do you consider to be the most outstanding advantages of the subject organization? Are these advantages unique to a subject organization?

3. How do you account for the fact that the subject organization has continued for so many years as the most common curriculum pattern?

4. Select a recent course of study from your library. Try to determine in what respects it corresponds to a pure-form subject curriculum and in what respects it departs from the pure form.

5. In what way, if at all, is the course of study you selected superior to the pure form? In what way is it inferior?

▶ *Suggested*
   Reading

The best statement of the theory of the subject curriculum is that set forth by Howard E. Wilson in *The Fusion of Social Studies in Junior High Schools,* pages 168–190. See also *Sixteenth Yearbook of the National Council of Teachers of Mathematics,* pages 8–44, and James L. Mursell's *Developmental Teaching,* pages 1–29. An excellent defense of the subject curriculum is to be found in the report of the Harvard Committee on the Objectives of General Education in a Free Society, *General Education in a Free Society,* pages 103–176.

Chapter 11

The Subject Curriculum: Problems, Practices, and Criticisms

A N Y   F O R M of curriculum organization necessarily rests upon certain conceptions of how individuals learn, how they should be controlled, and what the school should achieve. Any form, therefore, is no more secure than the conceptions that underlie and sustain it. Such underlying ideas are derived from social orientations and from psychological and philosophical thought and investigations.

As new social outlooks and more adequate conceptions of the individual and of the social role of the school emerge, the older forms of curriculum organization become questionable, and new forms begin to arise to challenge them. This is precisely the condition today. For well over a generation the problem of how to organize the curriculum has claimed, and continues to claim, a major part of the thought and practical efforts of the educational profession. The subject curriculum has been at the center of this issue. Accordingly, it is important for the curriculum maker, in determining the most effective form of organization, to consider the more serious indictments of this curriculum.

1. *Indictments of the Subject Curriculum*

The first indictment of the subject curriculum charges that *it is compartmentalized and fragmentary*. The advocates as well as the opponents of the subject curriculum have not been slow to point out that with the rapid increase in knowledge during the last century, the subject curriculum has resulted in an instructional program so divided that all unity has been lost. While this organization may function as smoothly as a machine, teachers seem to possess neither a total picture of what is going on nor knowledge of what it all means. Each teacher is a specialist, taking pride only in the knowledge of his own subject and disclaiming discipline in, or responsibility for, anything outside of his own little garden of subject matter, which he cultivates "for its own sake." In the words of Whitehead:

There is only one subject matter for education, and that is Life in all its manifestations. Instead of this single unity, we offer children—Algebra, from which nothing follows; Geometry, from which nothing follows; Science, from which nothing follows; History, from which nothing follows; a Couple of Languages, never mastered; and lastly, most dreary of all, Literature, represented by plays of Shakespeare, with philological notes and short analyses of plot and character to be in substance committed to memory. Can such a list be said to represent Life, as it is known in the midst of the living of it? The best that can be said of it is, that it is a rapid table of contents which a deity might run over in his mind while he was thinking of creating a world, and had not yet determined how to put it together.[1]

Furthermore, the subject curriculum consists not of a body of knowledge unified by a dynamic purpose, but rather of a collection of fragments of information selected to give the learner an orderly coverage of the various aspects of the different subjects. A course in physics, for example, is but a patch of the total body of physical knowledge, and a course in grammar is but a shred of the theory of language structure. In the subject curriculum, therefore, the learner acquires scraps of information, which in his mind have little or no association with any of

[1] Alfred North Whitehead, *The Aims of Education and Other Essays,* pp. 10–11. Copyright 1929 by The Macmillan Company and used with their permission.

the great divisions of human knowledge save the ones from which the scraps have been gleaned.

Because of the fragmentary and compartmentalized character of the subject curriculum, it is unlikely that the fullest development of the intellectual aspects of personality can be attained with this organization. Narrow and static personalities emerge from an educational program so extremely divided and fragmented. This program is carried on by teachers whose own education is patchy and whose personalities have been partly dwarfed, not only by the curriculum in which they were trained but also by the restrictions imposed upon their own thought and activities by the subjects they teach. If the average pupil ceases to grow intellectually and manifests little or no interest in crucial human problems, and if he remains politically immature, knowing or caring little about social strategy—this stagnation and apathy are probably due in part to the specialized and restrictive character of the subject curriculum.

Neglect of the Learner's Interests and Activities

A second indictment of the subject curriculum charges that *it ignores the interests and activities of the learner*. Since instruction in a subject curriculum must necessarily be directed to the mastery of the subjects as such, only those individuals who are either interested in academic attainment or who seek social approval through marks and promotions show much interest in the learning exercises emphasized by the subject curriculum. Psychological investigations indicate that situations most conducive to growth are those that involve the making of choices and policies of concern to the learner. The inability of the strict subject curriculum to make use of such situations largely divorces it from the concerns of those enrolled. As a result, it incorporates inefficient methods of teaching and learning, depending for the most part upon repetition and *memoriter* drilling. It is interesting to note, in this connection, an observation made by James Harvey Robinson, who can hardly be accused of lack of respect for research and intellectual discipline.

Both the textbooks and manuals used in formal teaching and the various popular presentations of scientific facts written for adults tend, almost without exception, to classify knowledge under generally accepted headings. They have a specious logic and orderliness which appeals to the academic mind. They, therefore, suit the teachers fairly well, but unhappily do not inspire the learners.

When one has "gone through" a textbook and safely "passed" it, he rarely has any further use for it. This is not because he has really absorbed it and so need not refer to it again. On the contrary, it is associated with a process alien to his deeper and more permanent interests. And it is usually found by those who embark in adult education that textbooks make almost no appeal to grown-ups, who are free to express their distaste for them.[2]

In order to compensate for the failure of the subject organization to arouse or to utilize the learner's interest, elaborate systems of motivation have been evolved. Among these are marks, promotions, and graduations—the tangible form of school, family, and community sanctions. The student must, therefore, undertake the learning of facts, principles, and skills, not because these are significant in the activities in which he ordinarily participates, but because acquisition of them is a way of gaining approval. Under such circumstances learning is slow and the outcomes fleeting in tenure.

Moreover, it is now generally known that many things are learned at the same time. While an individual is learning facts, principles, or skills, he is also learning to like or to dislike the subject, the people about him, the school, and so on. These extra learnings are usually referred to as "concomitant outcomes." In the subject curriculum these learnings all too frequently turn out to be undesirable; for when the learner can see little or no meaning in the mastery of content, save as a means of escaping failure and the resulting public disapproval, all sorts of undesirable attitudes are likely to be built into his character.

Inefficient Arrangement of Content

The subject curriculum has been indicted as *an inefficient arrangement of content for learning and use.* The subjects are logically organized and are taught, and supposedly learned, in a logical order. But there is no good reason to suppose that such an arrangement of subject

---

[2] James Harvey Robinson, *The Humanizing of Knowledge* (New York: Doubleday, Doran & Co.; 1924), p. 67. By permission of Doubleday & Company, Inc.

matter is conducive to learning; nor is there reason to suppose that the order of teaching determines the way in which the content will shape up and function in the experience of the learner. It has long been recognized that the order in which learning occurs is different from the order given the content of learning when it is arranged for communication. The order of discovery is different from the order of telling about the discovery. How things are found out, or worked out, is ordinarily referred to as the *psychological order*. How these things are systematically arranged for communication constitutes the *logical organization*. Almost a half century ago Dewey called attention to the importance of this distinction for the organization of instruction.

It may be of use to distinguish and to relate to each other the logical and the psychological aspects of experience—the former standing for subject-matter in itself, the latter for it in relation to the child. A psychological statement of experience follows its actual growth; it is historic; it notes steps actually taken, the uncertain and tortuous, as well as the efficient and successful. The logical point of view, on the other hand, assumes that the development has reached a certain positive stage of fulfillment. It neglects the process and considers the outcome. It summarizes and arranges, and thus separates the achieved results from the actual steps by which they were forthcoming in the first instance. We may compare the difference between the logical and the psychological to the difference between the notes which an explorer makes in a new country, blazing a trail and finding his way along as best he may, and the finished map that is constructed after the country has been thoroughly explored.[3]

How far removed the logical subject organization is from the personal organization of functional knowledge can easily be seen in a person's own experience. Anyone who will take the trouble to examine his own organization and retention of knowledge will find that his useful and effective knowledge has collected about certain poles, or nuclei of interests, which have somehow come to play a significant role in his thought and action. The tearing apart of these centers of interest and knowledge, and the arrangement of their content into a logical system —such as is found in the subject curriculum—constitutes a laborious and painful undertaking. The converse, the breaking up of the subject

[3] John Dewey, *The Child and the Curriculum* (Chicago: University of Chicago Press; 1902), pp. 25–26. By permission.

organization and the mobilization of this content for effective attack on problems, is no less difficult. The plain fact is that the organization of ideas—or for that matter of anything else—depends upon the purpose. Since the purposes of the learner are seldom the purposes implied by the subject curriculum, the organization is of necessity often alien to the centers of interest about which the experiences of the learner crystallize.

Neglect of Social Problems

The subject curriculum is charged with being *divorced from current and persistent social problems*. This is one of the most trenchant criticisms of the school in recent years, and the subject organization has earned a good share of the indictment. It is asserted that because the subject organization consists of an exposition of what has been done in the past and commits the student to a mastery of this knowledge, it necessarily ignores current social issues and conflicts. It is further claimed that discipline in the resolution of these is a major responsibility of the schools. The products of the subject curriculum know more about the crusades than they know about the management of modern industry; more about the structure of the earthworm than about their own bodies and the status of public provisions for their health; more about the exploits of Napoleon than about the nature and workings of their own economic and political systems; more about what a few men have done in the past than about what the social aspirations and commitments of the American people are or should be.

This social isolation is almost inherent in the subject curriculum. It arises out of the fact that the content is taught as a self-contained system. This means that the facts and principles are taught apart from any use they might have in dealing with the confusion and conflicts of today and that their significance must be found in their function in the system of which they are a part, rather than in the activities of the community.

Of course, the content of subjects can be used for social reconstruction just as it can be used for the promotion of further research. It all depends upon whether or not the organized content of subjects is used as a source of information in dealing with problems or as a curriculum to be pursued. If a boy is attempting to devise a microphone, he will find systematic discussion of such a device very helpful, and he will collect and organize information with this activity as a center. But, according to the critics, the adoption of this view of the role of organized subjects in the learning process would require serious departure from the subject curriculum, if not its complete abandonment.

Failure to Develop Habits of Effective Thinking

The final indictment holds that *the subject curriculum fails to develop habits of effective thinking.* This curriculum places emphasis upon mastery of the conclusions of thought rather than upon mastery of the processes by which the conclusions were derived and confirmed. Therefore some critics claim that the subject curriculum is largely responsible for the uncritical tendencies and gullible attitudes of the academic mind and of the people generally. Moreover, the fact that the content of subjects is presented in an expository form has usually meant that the individual learns by repetition and memorization. The subject curriculum is, therefore, in danger of placing relatively little importance upon reflection, especially such reflection as is involved in the critical examination of a conclusion or proposition in the light of its supporting evidence. Nor does an expository presentation attach importance to discipline in the thinking processes by which conclusions are reached and validated. The usual assumption is that anyone who has mastered the facts and principles can think effectively. However, the accumulated evidence of investigations repudiates this assumption [4] and supports the position Aristotle took in the following statement, from *De Sophisticis Elenchis:*

The teaching they gave to their pupils was ready but rough. For they used to suppose that they trained people by imparting to them not the art but its products, as though anyone professing that he would impart a form of knowledge to obviate pain in the feet, were then not to teach a man the art of shoemaking, or the sources whence he can acquire anything of the kind, but were to present him with several pairs of shoes of all sorts; for he had helped him to meet his need, but has not imparted to him any art.[5]

[4] Edward M. Glaser, "An Experiment in the Development of Critical Thinking," *Teachers College Contributions to Education,* No. 843.

[5] Aristotle, *De Sophisticis Elenchis,* translated by W. A. Pickard-Cambridge. *Works of Aristotle,* edited by W. D. Ross (Oxford: The Clarendon Press; 1928).

2. *Defense of the Subject Curriculum*

Supporters of the subject curriculum have not always been quick to reply to these indictments. For one thing, the criticism has often been made obliquely so that it was hard to tell the real point of the objection. For another thing, an entrenched system does not have to defend itself—the habits and dispositions of the people are already on its side. Then, too, alternative curriculum plans have been none too successful in establishing themselves. Nor have they entirely remedied the defects attributed to the subject curriculum.

From time to time there have been replies to the indictments. But they have never rested upon a systematic theory of the subject organization. Indeed, no such theory is to be found in modern literature, except perhaps in Morrison's attempt to ground the subjects in the major institutions of society. Even so, Morrison made no serious effort to answer the critics of the subject curriculum. Nowhere is there anything but particular replies to particular criticisms. There is no wholesale defense.

It is denied by advocates of the subject curriculum that the child's thinking is not improved by it. After all, to take on the ways of thinking characteristic of civilized man is for the individual to become a better thinker. As an individual acquires the knowledge available to him in the subjects, he takes on the ways of thinking peculiar to these subjects. He learns to think as the physicist thinks when he studies physics, as the historian thinks when he studies history, and as the mathematician thinks when he studies mathematics. If he does not learn so to think, the fault is to be found in the instruction and not in the curriculum pattern.

Then, too, according to the proponents of the subject curriculum, the claim that it is fragmentary and compartmentalized is not one that can be leveled at the subject curriculum alone. No one can study every-thing at once. In any kind of curriculum whatever, some things are emphasized and others are excluded. There is always some sort of selection, and whatever is selected is necessarily separated from other things. In a sense anything that is learned is a fragment. It is a part of some larger unity of things. And the kind of situation in which it is learned does not change this fact one bit. If an individual learns that Napoleon was the ruler of France in the first decade of the nineteenth century, he has acquired only a fragment of what is known about Napoleon. If he were to learn all there is to know about Napoleon, he would have acquired only a fragment of French history. And so it goes. It makes no difference whether the individual has learned these historical facts in an activity curriculum or even outside of school, they are still only a tiny part of history.

It may be said that fragmentation refers to the psychological make-up of one's learning and not to the external subject matter. But, in the view of those who accept the subject curriculum, the criticism is thereby made no more secure. The way any item of knowledge shapes up in the head of the learner is controlled by many factors, and no single condition such as the form of the curriculum is decisive. Nor is there any evidence that those who are educated through the subject curriculum have any more unorganized knowledge than those who are educated in other curriculum patterns.

As for the interests of children, there is no ground for the claim that they are neglected in the subject curriculum. At least its defenders say so. From very early years, children express their interests in the questions they ask. They want to know about the animals and plants around them, about people and what they do, about the physical things and gadgets in the home and community, and a little later about people remote in time and space. All these questions fall naturally into subjects of instruction—biology, social studies, physics and chemistry, and history. Of course, the child is not interested in these subjects per se, if indeed anyone ever is. But the subject curriculum does not assume interest in subjects as such. It does assume interest in particular things treated in the subjects. It assumes that the more an individual knows about a subject, the more interested in its contents he may become. The subject curriculum assumes, too, that the subjects are a convenient and efficient way of classifying knowledge for use in helping children learn the answers to their questions and to ask new and more advanced questions.

But even more, it is the function of instruction to push back the horizons of children, to expand their ideas and to show them new possibilities. As they take on new knowledge, children develop new ways of looking at things and new and enlarged interests and ideas. The teacher wants to make certain that the individual continues to grow after he leaves school as well as while he is still in it. What better means could be employed to this end, the defenders ask, than the accumulated knowledge of mankind? Surely one who has acquired the elements of this knowledge is more apt to continue to grow than one who has not done so. And where is this knowledge to be found if not in the subjects of instruction developed through centuries of experience?

3. *Modification of the Subject Curriculum*

Partly in response to criticisms, partly in response to the general feeling of dissatisfaction with the schools on the part of both the teaching profession and the public, and partly as the result of new psychological and educational conceptions, serious efforts have been made to improve the subject curriculum. These efforts have taken various forms, depending upon the diagnosis of the difficulty, and have resulted in at least two modifications of the subject curriculum—namely, the correlated curriculum and the broad-fields curriculum.

The Correlated Curriculum

The correlated curriculum is a subject curriculum in which two or more subjects are articulated and relationships between or among them are made a part of instruction without destroying the subject boundaries. The idea of correlating courses originated in the last century from the psychological and educational conceptions of Herbart. His views laid great stress upon concentration, by which he meant complete absorption in an idea or object of thought, and correlation, by which he meant the reinforcement of the idea by related and supporting conceptions. These conceptions emphasized interest, meaning, and relation, which led his followers to the notion of concentration and correlation of studies. In their view concentration was interpreted as the grouping of subjects around a central study, and correlation was interpreted as the support of the topics of this central subject by related studies.

This interpretation is also the substance of the current significance of correlation. For example, history and geography may be taught so as to reinforce each other, or courses in science and mathematics may be conducted in such a way that the mathematics becomes a useful tool in science, and the scientific data and problems become material for study in mathematics courses. Again, history courses may be made to contribute to the understanding and enjoyment of literature; conversely, the study of literature may be made to contribute to the understanding of historical events and personages. In elementary social studies, stories of early Mediterranean peoples—Hebrews, Greeks, Romans—may be studied in connection with the geography of the Mediterranean area; and the geography of Egypt and the Nile Valley may be accompanied by a study of the early history of the Egyptians.

Three Kinds of Correlation

There are three kinds of correlation, depending upon the kinds of subject matter involved factual, descriptive, and normative. Factual correlation is illustrated in the articulation of history and literature when the historical facts concerning the writing of a piece of literature or the past events upon which an historical novel is based are studied with a view to enriching the enjoyment of the reader. Another illustration is found in the subjects of history and geography when the facts of geography are studied as the setting of an historical event. For example, the geographic facts about the origin and growth of a city may be helpful in understanding the forces determining the location of cities as well as the direction of the flow of a nation's wealth.

Descriptive correlation is illustrated in the use of generalizations common to two or more subjects. Psychology can be correlated with history, or with any of the social studies, by employing psychological principles to explain social events. Conflicts between nations, for instance, are sometimes explained on the principle of frustration and aggression; that is to say, on the theory that a people who are frustrated over a period of time will, under certain conditions, become aggressive and take up arms against other nations. In this way, courses in psychology may be made to contribute significantly to courses in the social sciences. In addition, such subjects as physics and chemistry, biology and psychology, mathematics and sciences can be articulated at the level of descriptive principles as well as through factual relationships. Carried to its logical conclusion, however, correlation through descriptive principles among closely related subjects such as chemistry and physics, or economics and sociology, will result in a fusion course, a form of the broad-fields type of subject organization. The ultimate basis of the unity of subjects is the similarity or identity of their fundamental principles. It follows that a set of principles common to two or more courses, if used as the nucleus about which the factual content is organized, will result in broad, unified courses such as general science.

Normative correlation is attained in much the same way as descriptive correlation, the chief difference being that the principles are social-moral rather than descriptive. For instance, American history and literature may be correlated at some points through the social-moral principles constituting the theory of democracy. Such general ideas as equality and freedom—conceptions essential to the understanding of American history—are equally needed in comprehending and appreciating such American writers as Emerson, Thoreau, and Whitman.

The extent of correlation between subjects depends upon the inherent relations of the subjects, convenience, and the knowledge and wisdom of the teachers. If correlation is not planned for, however, it occurs only occasionally and incidentally. In order to encourage the articulation of courses, they are often scheduled so that related subjects can be taught by the same teacher or by co-operating teachers. Thus, history and literature courses covering the same cultural period are sometimes provided in the same semester. Moreover, it is necessary that teachers work out definite plans for securing the maximum amount of correlation, if a correlated curriculum is to be established and maintained. Sometimes special committees are appointed to plan for desirable correlations among the subjects.

Advantages Claimed for the Correlated Curriculum

It is claimed by advocates of the correlated curriculum that children and youth show greater interest in the conventional subjects when they are correlated and learn more readily than in the conventional program. There is not sufficient evidence to confirm these claims, but as a hypothesis it does seem likely that some increase of interest and learning would result. It is further asserted that greater integration of knowledge occurs; that students see the relationships among subjects so that compartmentalization and fragmentation are reduced. While there is doubtless some truth in this assertion, it should be remembered that correlation leaves the subjects intact and that it requires no reorganization of their content and materials. Correlation requires only that the subjects be articulated through their content and leaves untouched the problem of utilizing the subject matter most directly related to the interests and activities of the learner and to the problems and social issues of today.

It should be pointed out that shifting of factual content, or sharing of descriptive or normative principles across subject boundaries, constitutes no deviation from a pure-form subject curriculum. Whatever form these departures take, however, they are seldom prompted by increased loyalty to the logical exposition of the subject. Such changes are more often indicative of a basic dissatisfaction with the restrictions of the subject boundaries, leading to attempts to achieve results not possible within the earlier definitive subject matter lines. As this dissatisfaction continues and gives rise to one form of slight modification after another, the fact sooner or later becomes apparent that the goals of instruction and the subject organization are no longer in harmony. In other words, the curriculum maker knows that an organization is a means to certain types of learnings, and he now comes to the realization that the goals of instruction are becoming so foreign to the curriculum pattern that both goals and patterns are being twisted out of shape. Since organization is shaped by purposes, it is thus only a matter of time until new curriculum patterns are developed to facilitate changed goals. Thus different kinds of correlation, even though they violate no aspect of the subject curriculum, nevertheless may be beginning steps in the quest for a new curriculum organization.

The Broad-Fields Curriculum

The broad-fields curriculum arose in American secondary schools and colleges, at least in an incipient form, in the second decade of the present century. It began as one or two broad courses, which drew their subject matter from two or more departments of instruction. It developed gradually at the college level into a program of survey courses covering the freshman and sophomore years. In a few elementary schools it came into favor, though much later than in the colleges, as the inclusive pattern of instruction. The high schools, save for a few outstanding exceptions, adopted the broad-fields curriculum only in part by establishing a small number of general courses in certain areas such as science and social studies.

The earliest beginning of the broad-fields curriculum is not found in America but in England, in a course given as a series of lectures by Thomas Huxley to London children at the Royal Institution in 1869 and later published under the title of *Physiography*. The preface indicates Huxley's prophetic views with respect to changes in the conventional subject curriculum. He opposed "an *omnium-gatherum* of scraps of all sorts and undigested and unconnected information." The course was inductively developed and aimed at unity not only by bringing the facts and principles of related fields into juxtaposition but also by choosing the Thames basin and the activities of its people as the unifying factor. This was a happy choice, which anticipated by two generations the regional and community ideas in education.

In 1909 President Lowell of Harvard University called attention in his inaugural address to the need for a comprehensive course in "every considerable field," which would "give to men who do not intend to pursue the subject further a comprehension of its underlying principles or methods of thought."[6] Three years later, in 1912, President Meiklejohn, in his inaugural address at Amherst College went a step further and proposed the divisions of a broad-fields program. "A young man," he said, "must take from a college of liberal training, the contributions of philosophy, of humanistic science, of natural science, of history, and of literature."[7]

Harvard did not act upon President Lowell's suggestion. President Meiklejohn's proposal, however, fell upon more favorable ground and resulted in the introduction, in 1914, of a general course at Amherst College called "Social and Economic Institutions." This appears to have been the first broad-fields course offered in an American college. The

---

[6] A. Lawrence Lowell, "Inaugural Address, October 6, 1909," *Atlantic Monthly,* Vol. 104 (November, 1909), p. 692.

[7] Alexander Meiklejohn, *The Liberal College* (Boston: Marshall Jones; 1920), p. 47.

first complete broad-fields curriculum was introduced at the University of Chicago between 1923 and 1925. It consisted of the following courses: Introduction to Reflective Thinking, the Nature of the World and of Man, Man in Society, and the Meaning and Value of the Arts.

A similar development was taking place in the high schools. General science courses emerged in the early 1900's "to furnish . . . the information and the training in thinking that are fundamental to the special sciences," "to impart information . . . about the useful and interesting things that are all about it," "to give the first-year pupils an attractive view of the content of all the sciences," to free the teacher "from all ambition toward getting college credit for his pupils, and from all attempts to present a 'comprehensive and connected view of the facts and principles' of any one science," so that he may "disregard the logical fences that specialists have for convenience erected between their subjects." [8] In addition, under the stimulus of the report of the Committee on Social Studies in 1916, courses in the problems of democracy began to appear. In many instances these courses covered "problems of democracy" in name only, but they represent some integration and reorganization of social science content.

Courses in the broad-fields curriculum have various appellations, the title depending upon whether one is thinking of the college, the high school, or the elementary school. In the college, they are called "survey" or "comprehensive" courses, and sometimes "general courses." At the high school level they are called "fusion courses" or "general courses," or else they are simply designated by course titles as in the elementary school. The typical broad-fields courses found in whole or in part in the present-day elementary and secondary schools consist of the following: social studies, general science, general arts, health and physical education, general mathematics, and language arts.

Bases of Organization of Broad-Fields Courses

The first broad-fields courses were little more than compressed specialized subjects, brought together into one general course with little or no integration. The first courses in general science, for example, con-

[8] G. R. Twiss, *A Textbook in the Principles of Science Teaching,* pp. 415–417. Copyright 1917 by The Macmillan Company and used with their permission.

sisted more or less of disparate sections drawn from chemistry, physics, zoology, botany, astronomy, and geology. This lack of integration was a cause of dissatisfaction with the early unified courses, for it marked the failure to attain one of the fundamental purposes for which these courses were created—that is, to develop a unified view of the knowledge of a comprehensive field. It gradually became apparent that if this objective was to be attained, the content could not be selected and organized on the basis of a fair coverage of the several specialized subjects from which the unified courses drew their content. Instead, a new synthesis would have to be created; some new principle of organization would have to be found.

Two new types of subject matter integration have developed—the principles type and the history type. These bases of integration have found favor at all levels of the educational ladder.

The Principles Type

Scholars have long recognized generalizations as the basic element of human thought and knowledge. All reasoning depends upon principles, by means of which thought moves safely from one particular fact to another. Without them no one could tell whether a given case is one of a kind, as a dog is one of a kind called collie. Diagnosis would be impossible without them, for in order to tell what the trouble is one must be able to classify it. It is not enough to say that a child is sick; one must be able to say that his sickness is an instance of a kind of malady. The principles of science, mathematics, grammar, social studies, or what not, constitute the instruments of explanation and control when these bodies of knowledge are employed as resources in dealing with problems.

Moreover, some principles are more fundamental than others in the sense that some include others. Boyle's law is an empirical generalization stating that if a confined volume of gas is held at a constant temperature and pressure is applied, the volume varies inversely with the pressure. If we ask why gases behave in this way, the explanation is to be found in the more inclusive generalization, the molecular theory of matter. The molecular theory cuts across the boundaries separating the physical sciences. It explains not only Boyle's law, which is ordinarily included in physics courses, but also the gas law of Charles and the law of partial pressures, which are usually considered to be a part of chemistry. Concepts that are thus basic to two or more disciplines may serve as the pattern of integration.

Efforts to develop curriculums upon such logical integration of subject matter have seldom been successful. The required generalizations are often not available, because the interdisciplinary sciences have not yet developed. For this reason the unifying factor in broad-fields courses is sometimes referred to in educational literature as the "theme procedure."

It is important to note that a theme is not the same kind of statement as a substantive generalization of science. It is more like a topic of exposition than an explanatory statement. Hence, this procedure did not result in a satisfactory logical integration of the content of the broad-fields subjects. Even so, it was a distinct step toward greater emphasis upon large ideas and away from stress upon minutiæ.

The theme procedure stems from the work of Harold Rugg and his research associates at The Lincoln School, between 1920 and 1928. One of these studies, that of Neal Billings, can be cited to illustrate the assumptions and methods employed in all of them.[9] Billings determined, by an extensive investigation of the writings of "frontier thinkers," the generalizations basic to the social studies. From an analysis of a list of authentic books in the field of social science, he compiled a list of 888 generalizations considered useful in understanding modern social life. They were classified under seventy-nine headings, examples of which are agriculture, location of industry, economic interdependence, political democracy, and personality and personality traits.

[9] For the detailed history and documentation, see Harold Rugg's *That Men May Understand*, especially Chapters X and XI. For the full list of basic themes, see his *Culture and Education in America*. The primary research was published in several doctoral studies, as follows:

Neal Billings, *A Determination of Generalizations Basic to the Social Studies Curriculum* (Baltimore: Warwick & York, Inc.; 1929).

John A. Hockett, "A Determination of the Major Social Problems of American Life," *Teachers College Contributions to Education*, No. 281.

C. O. Mathews, "Grade-Placement of Curriculum Materials in the Social Studies," *Teachers College Contributions to Education*, No. 241.

Hyman Meltzer, "Children's Social Concepts," *Teachers College Contributions to Education*, No. 192.

Earle Rugg, *Curriculum Studies in the Social Sciences and Citizenship* (Greeley, Colorado: Colorado State Teachers College, 1928).

He derived 125 major themes from his investigation and proposed them as "summarizing strands around which can be woven the data of the social studies; the data explain the themes, the themes give meaning to the data." [10] The following themes dealing with the development of American life are taken from this list:

1. The tendency of the natural physical environment—geography, climate, etc.—to determine the character of man's economic and social activities.
2. Man's increasing control over nature, including the improvement of means of wholesale mass production, transportation, and communication of goods and persons.
3. The rapid rise of industrialism in Europe and North America and its gradual adoption in the other continents.
4. The transformation in industrial civilization of a self-sufficient people into a fragile world society of interdependent people.
5. The decline in free competition and increased federal control of industry and business.
6. The gradual disappearance in American society of the landed aristocracy and the rise of industrial aristocracy.

The theme procedure was also employed by Rugg in the development of his social studies series,[11] and, in a reduced form, by the State of South Dakota in its course of study in social studies,[12] and by the city schools of Houston, Texas.[13] The South Dakota course of study, for example, employed only five themes for the whole social studies program from grades one to eight, as follows:

1. The increasing interdependence of groups of people.
2. The necessity of man's adaptation to meet the requirements of subsistence, the pressure of competing groups, and the conditions implicit in change.
3. Man's increasing control over nature.
4. Man's tendency to move from place to place in quest of a higher standard of living.
5. The inevitable progress of democracy.

[10] Billings, *op. cit.*, p. 214. By permission of Warwick & York, Inc.
[11] Fourteen volumes, prepared 1921–1937, under the general caption, *Man and His Changing Society*.
[12] South Dakota Department of Education, *Social Studies for Courses of Study for Primary Grades*, pp. 12–14.
[13] Houston Public Schools, *Scope of the Curriculum*, Curriculum Bulletin No. 2.

A similar procedure is followed in the construction of unified science courses. A list of thirty-eight major themes is proposed in the *Thirty-first Yearbook* of the National Society for the Study of Education. The following five items are chosen from this list as illustrations of themes in the field of science:

1. The sun is the chief source of energy for the earth.
2. All life comes from life and produces its own kind of living organism.
3. Through interdependence of species and the struggle for existence a balance tends to be maintained among the many forms of life.
4. All matter is probably electrical in structure.
5. Chemical changes are accompanied by energy changes.

These themes, like the social studies themes, are comprehensive not only in the sense that they involve a number of specialized subjects but also in the sense that they can be developed from grade to grade. Thus they also serve as the basis of vertical integration—that is, the articulation of the instructional programs of different grades.

From the fact that a theme is never completely developed at any grade level, it follows that only aspects of it are studied from grade to grade. This is clearly illustrated in the South Dakota state course of study with respect to the theme, "The Increasing Interdependence of Groups of People." In Grade 1, for example, this theme is studied from the standpoint of the interdependence of the members of a family; in Grade 2, it is developed from the standpoint of the interdependence of the family and the community workers; and in Grade 8, to take a more advanced aspect of the theme, it is studied from the standpoint of the increasing interdependence of communities with one another and with the world at large.

The History Type of Integration

A convenient way of achieving the integration of broad-fields courses is to rely upon historical development. The thread of history is the unifying idea. A choice is made of topics or "problems"—for instance, the family, democracy, international relations, education—and then their development through the ages is traced so that their multifarious forms and their adaptations to varying needs become plainly evident.

This pattern is sometimes found at the college level, especially in the social science field.

Contributions of the Broad-Fields Curriculum

This curriculum varies from the conventional subjects by dissolving certain subject-matter boundaries, by creating a few comprehensive categories to take the place of the multiplicity of specialized subjects, and by adding new content to the broad categories. These variations are concerned primarily with the development of new relationships among the elements of subject matter—especially those relationships that have been neglected because of devotion to specialized interests.

The employment of themes permits greater flexibility within the broad-fields courses; at the same time, continuity and integration are safeguarded. Except in certain elementary schools where activity periods are more popular than unified courses, themes must operate more or less within the boundaries of these major categories. The use of this procedure in the elementary school may tend in the long run to bring the curriculum pattern more into line with either the activity or core curriculum; for the grip of subject-matter boundaries has not been maintained with the same vigor in the elementary school, especially in the primary grades, as it has in the high school and college.

▶ *Following Up*
This Chapter

1. Are all five indictments of the subject curriculum based upon faults inherent in the subject organization? If not, suggest ways of meeting these charges without changing the basic pattern.

2. What do you consider to be the outstanding weaknesses of the theory of the correlated curriculum? What weaknesses would you expect in practice?

3. What do you consider to be the chief obstacles to be overcome in moving from an organization of separate subjects to a broad-fields pattern?

4. What do you consider to be the outstanding weaknesses of a broad-fields organization? Which of these are defects of theory?

5. Select one or more recent courses of study from your library and try to locate evidences of correlation. Try also to find a course of study that attempts to establish broad-fields. Do these broad-fields courses meet the criticisms of the subject curriculum?

▶ Suggested Reading

1. *Readings in Curriculum Development,* compiled by Hollis L. Caswell and Doak S. Campbell, presents a number of excellent short articles in criticism and in defense of various aspects of the subject organization. Articles in Chapter III, "Significant Influences on Curriculum Development"; Chapter VII, "Scope of the Curriculum"; and Chapter X, "Selection of Subject Matter," are especially pertinent.

2. For other criticisms of the subject organization, your attention is directed to James Harvey Robinson's *The Humanizing of Knowledge* and Alfred North Whitehead's *The Aims of Education and Other Essays,* Chapter 1. See also Harold Alberty's *Reorganizing the High School Curriculum,* (Revised Edition), Chapter V.

3. Specific discussion of psychological, as opposed to logical, organization of subject matter is very well presented by John Dewey in *The Child and the Curriculum* and by Boyd Bode in *Modern Educational Theories,* pages 43–72.

4. The correlated curriculum is presented in Chapter X of L. T. Hopkins' *Integration: Its Meaning and Application.* Chapter XI of this book is devoted to the broad-fields curriculum. For further descriptions of correlated and broad-fields programs, see J. Paul Leonard's *Developing the Secondary School Curriculum* (Revised). Chapter 10 presents a fine description and analysis of relationships between subjects and suggests ways to reorganize subjects. For a general discussion of the subject curriculum in which arguments for and against the subject organization are presented, see *Curriculum Planning,* by J. Galen Saylor and William M. Alexander, pp. 253–265.

Chapter 12

The Activity Curriculum:
Its Chief Characteristics

THE CURRICULUM ORGANIZATION to be described in this chapter has been variously called an activity, a project, or an experience curriculum. "Activity curriculum" seems to be the classic term. The other names seem to have been brought about by efforts to escape some ill repute gained by the term "activity curriculum," and then in turn by each of the others, either through misunderstanding of the theory or misuse of it in practice. Inasmuch as the real difficulty is with ideas and not names, and since change of title with no corresponding alteration of meaning is worthless, the term "activity curriculum" will be used.

Although the fundamental conceptions of an activity curriculum have a long history, some of them extending back to Rousseau and others as far back as Plato, the formulation of an activity curriculum is a comparatively recent achievement. Curriculums of this type emerged in a few experimental schools around the end of the last century. The title "activity curriculum," however, did not come into general use before the 1920's, although Dewey had used the expression "activity program," in the sense here implied, as early as 1897 in a talk to the parents and teachers of his laboratory school in Chicago.

The discussion of the activity curriculum is organized to parallel the treatment of the subject curriculum in Chapter 10. Following a description of the development of the activity curriculum, there are sections on its distinctive and essential characteristics and on personnel, physical features, and administrative arrangements.

1. *Rise of the Activity Curriculum*

With the possible exception of the Tuskegee Institute, the first school in America to be set up and operated with an activity curriculum was the Laboratory School, established at the University of Chicago in 1896 as a co-operative venture of parents, teachers, and educators under the direction of John and Alice Dewey.

The Dewey Laboratory School

The curriculum of this school was based upon four human impulses: the *social impulse,* which is shown in the child's desire to share his experiences with the people around him; the *constructive impulse,* which is manifested at first in play, in rhythmic movement, in make-believe, and then in more advanced form in the shaping of raw materials into useful objects; the *impulse to investigate and experiment,* to find out things, as revealed in the tendency of the child to do things just to see what will happen; and the *expressive or artistic impulse,* which seems to be a refinement and further expression of the communicative and constructive interests.[1]

These fundamental impulses are "uninvested capital," as Dewey put it, and the child's growth and development wait upon their use. The curriculum of the Dewey School was designed to utilize in the education of the young these basic impulses toward "saying, making, finding out, and creating." It took the form of certain occupational categories, not of school subjects. In Dewey's language:

The core of school activity was to be found in occupations, rather than in what are conventionally termed studies. Study in the sense of inquiry and its outcome in gathering and retention of information was to be an

[1] Katherine Camp Mayhew and Anna Camp Edwards, *The Dewey School,* pp. 40–41. See also John Dewey, *The School and Society,* Chapter II.

outgrowth of the pursuit of certain continuing or consecutive occupational activities.[2]

The occupations included in the curriculum were cooking, sewing, and carpentry. These should be sharply distinguished from trade and vocational training. They were conceived as embracing man's fundamental relations to his world—as including the activities involved in getting food, in securing shelter and clothing, and in providing the conditions within which the higher interests and values of life may be developed and maintained. As such they required intellectual activities as well as manual manipulations. On the one hand, these occupations gave opportunity for shaping materials, for working with the hands; on the other, they required planning, contriving, experimenting. In addition, they were not studied merely in this contemporary setting but also in the different cultural phases of man's history from primitive times to the present. They were thus enriched and deepened, suffused with the values of social life.

Moreover, these occupations were the means by which the isolation of the traditional school, resulting largely from the subject curriculum, was to be overcome. The experiences arising from a study of these occupations would be useful in daily life, while the experiences the child acquired outside of school could be used in the educative process. The following excerpt from a summary of the first three years of the curriculum gives a glimpse into the operation of the program:

Thus in the first years of his school life the child's play enlarged from the mimic games of his home people to those of the persons who contribute to the daily life of the home. His interests gradually extended to their activities and the things they did, made, or bought. Foods were traced to their sources, and finished products of wood or clothing to their raw materials. So far as he was able, he reproduced these activities and himself learned to shape materials and means to reach his ends or to fashion his ideas. In the shop he was shown from the first the right ways of handling

[2] Katherine Camp Mayhew and Anna Camp Edwards, *The Dewey School* (New York: D. Appleton-Century Co.; copyright 1936), p. 5. By permission.

It is not altogether clear that the Dewey School was based entirely on the activity theory outlined in the present chapter. There are many strands of Dewey's pedagogical theory, and the emphasis on occupations is one that has received little attention. Further exploration of this aspect of his theory might place the instructional program of his experimental school in the category of a core curriculum.

the saw or the plane, as he made from the wood of this tree or that something to use in expressing his ideas. In the textile room he fingered the raw wool, the cotton, the flax, or the silk and compared it with the cloth of his coat or the shining luster of his mother's dress, and the old lure of "the how" and "the why" began to stir. In all the activities which filled his day, spinning, weaving, cooking, shop-work, modeling, dramatic plays, conversation, storytelling, or discussion, he was vitally interested and constantly absorbed knowledge of materials and processes. His activities were always fundamental and typical and, therefore, related and recapitulated his similar previous attempts, enriching and enlarging them into more definite purposes and plans. Thus experience was an onflowing stream continually enlarged from all sides by the pouring in of useful knowledge.[3]

Incentives to learn the fundamental processes—reading, writing, and arithmetical computation—arose out of the activities involved in the occupations. These processes, ordinarily stressed very early in the conventional school, were not taught before the child was ready to learn them. No special effort was made to teach reading to the six- and seven-year-olds unless there were indications that a feeling of need for the reading skills had arisen. It was one of the fundamental ideas of the Dewey School that when and only when the child had acquired a motive for learning a skill—had come to sense something of the significance of the skill—should it be taught to him.

Meriam's Laboratory School

In 1904 J. L. Meriam began the development of a new curriculum in the University Elementary School at the University of Missouri. There was complete absence of conventional subjects in this curriculum. In their place were created four categories of activities—observation, play, stories, and handwork—based upon five principles:

1. The curriculum should provide for meeting the immediate needs of the pupils primarily; only secondarily should it provide for the preparation of pupils for later needs.
2. The curriculum should be expressed in terms of concrete everyday activi-

---

[3] Mayhew and Edwards, *The Dewey School* (New York: D. Appleton-Century Co., copyright 1936), pp. 93–94. By permission.

ties of pupils and adults rather than in terms of generalization such as found in traditional subjects.

3. The curriculum should provide for great individual differences in order to meet varying tastes and abilities of the pupils.

4. The curriculum should be so organized that the various topics may easily be interchanged not only within any grade during the year, but from grade to grade.

5. The curriculum should provide for an acquaintance with both work and leisure.[4]

The general outline of the curriculum based upon these principles is as follows:

1. Observation: In Grades I and II, plant life, animal life, people, earth, and sky. In Grades III and IV, local industries and activities. In Grades V and VI, world-wide activities and industries. In Grades VII and VIII, occupations-vocational intelligence.

2. Play: In Grades I, II, and III, a great variety of games. In Grades IV, V, VI, VII, and VIII, play with nature, electricity, machinery, water, air, etc. All grades: Physical exercise, folk dancing, and free play.

3. Stories: Reading, telling, dramatizing; singing songs; study pictures and drawings; assembly exercises; foreign language.

4. Handwork: A great variety of useful and ornamental articles are made. Only a very few projects are suggested in these outlines. Materials: Paper, cord, yarn, textiles, reed, raffia, wood, metal.[5]

This curriculum, like the curriculum of the Dewey School, makes the skills of the Three R's a means of enriching the activities of children rather than ends toward which the activities are directed. Arithmetic is interesting to the children because it facilitates and enriches the games; the games are not played as in traditional schools, in order to develop the skills. A further similarity between the two schools is the fact that Meriam attempted also to make the school a part of the life of the community, to remove the heavy insulation which the extreme subject curriculum presumably had created between the conventional school and the life of the people.

[4] J. L. Meriam, *Child Life and the Curriculum*, p. 382. Copyright 1920 by World Book Company.
[5] *Ibid.*, p. 383.

Collings' Experimental School

The Dewey and Meriam schools were the forerunners of the activity curriculum. During the second decade of the present century many schools, mostly private ones, experimented with new curriculum organizations, which followed more or less the theory and practice of these earlier educational ventures. It was not until the 1920's, however, that the activity movement reached the public schools. Partly because of the impetus given the movement by the growing number of private and university schools, partly because of the appearance of a clear and stimulating rationale of this new curriculum organization by William Heard Kilpatrick in his brochure entitled *The Project Method,* which appeared in 1918, the number of schools experimenting with some form of activity curriculum increased by leaps and bounds. However, the first significant development in this direction was Ellsworth Collings' experiment with a project curriculum. This experiment was carried on in the rural schools of McDonald County, Missouri, beginning in 1917, a year before Kilpatrick's brochure was published.

The major divisions of the curriculum of Collings' experimental school—closely similar to those of the Meriam school—were: Play, Excursion, Story, and Hand. These categories of activities led to the development of an instructional program believed to be based upon child interests and abilities. The curriculum of the school, in bold outline, was described by Collings in the following way:

1. Play projects represent those experiences in which the purpose is to engage in such group activities as games, folk dancing, dramatization, or social parties.
2. Excursion projects involve purposeful study of problems connected with environments and activities of people.
3. Story projects include purposes to enjoy the story in its various forms —oral, song, picture, phonograph, or piano.
4. Hand projects represent purposes to express ideas in concrete form—to make a rabbit trap, to prepare cocoa for the school luncheon, or to grow cantaloupes.[6]

[6] Ellsworth Collings, *An Experiment with a Project Curriculum* (New York: The Macmillan Company; 1923), p. 48. By permission of the author.

Present Status of the Activity Curriculum

The activity organization of the curriculum has never been widely accepted in comparison with the almost universal acceptance of the subject organization. But since its beginning about fifty years ago, the activity organization has become the curriculum pattern in a number of scattered elementary schools and state and city courses of study. One of the most outstanding of these courses of study is the two-volume manual for kindergarten, primary, and intermediate teachers issued by the California State Department of Education.[7] This curriculum, published in the 1930's, represents an attempt to organize instruction around children's interests and consists largely of activities related to major centers of child interest.

The activity organization has never gained a secure foothold in the secondary school—although it has developed to some extent at this level, and its underlying ideas and some aspects of its concrete forms have influenced high school curriculum improvements, notably the community school developments. This lack of acceptance in the high school is due in part to the fact that high school teachers and administrators are more devoted to the subject organization by training and by teaching habits than are elementary teachers. It is due also to the fact that the subject organization enjoys stronger public support at the secondary level and has the advantages of well-developed materials and accepted methods of instruction.

The discussion of the rise of the activity curriculum has already indicated many of its characteristics. The next question to be taken up is: Which characteristics set it off from other patterns of curriculum organization?

2. Distinctive Characteristics

Three features of the activity curriculum distinguish it from both the subject and the core curriculums.

[7] California State Curriculum Commission, *Teacher's Guide to Child Development: Manual for Kindergarten and Primary Teachers.* See also *Teacher's Guide to Child Development in the Intermediate Grades.*

Children's Interests Determine Content and Structure

The primary principle of the activity curriculum is that *the interests and purposes of children determine the educational program.* What is taught, when it is taught, and the order in which it is learned go back to what is required for the realization of children's purposes.

It is important at this point to indicate that this most basic principle of the activity program refers to the *felt interests and felt needs* of children—the matters with which children themselves find compelling concern—and does not refer to "interest" in the sense of doing something "in the best interests of children." Nor does it refer to adult conceptions of what children should be interested in or what children need. For an adult to determine that a child needs, for example, "to feel secure and happy in the school environment," and then to claim that this is a felt need of the child, is a habit of thought that has led to many misconceptions of the theory of an activity curriculum. The content and the structure of an activity curriculum are determined primarily on the basis of the interests that children would call their own.

According to the theory of the activity curriculum, children are always actively engaged in doing something. Interests do not have to be created *de novo*. Some interests are always present. It is the task of the teacher to discover these and to build educative activities upon them. From these activities new interests arise, which in turn will lead to further activities and so on through the entire career of the child. This fact gave rise to the notion, frequently expressed, that the activity curriculum is characterized by "activity leading to further activity."

Interests and purposes, however, are to be distinguished from whims. The theory of the activity curriculum never assumed that the fancies of children were to be honored. An individual may manifest an interest in doing something and abandon this interest only a few minutes later. Such interests as these are too fleeting to afford the basis of an educational program. It is only as interests are expressed and grow into purposes—that is, intended courses of action, which have been accepted only after their probable consequences have been reviewed—that they are acceptable as the basis of an educational program.

The principle that the educational program is to be shaped by the interests and purposes of those to be educated gives a special place to

subject matter in the educative process. This principle implies that subject matter is a means of fulfilling the purposes and aspirations of the
individual or social group. It denies the traditional notion that the interests and purposes of children are merely aids in learning the subject
matter that adults set out to be learned. In its view, subject matter is
useful in shaping and directing activities in response to the impulses
and purposes of the individual. Knowledge thus originates in actions
devoted to the realization of purposes. Children do not set out to acquire learning as such, but to do things. In the course of doing things,
they have need of subject matter; and as a result of manipulating content and materials in doing these things, they learn.

While the activity theory recognizes the importance of group life and
co-operative activities, it rules out any stifling of individual interests in
attempts at group activities. Within the bounds of group interests and
activities, every attempt is made to allow individual purposes and competencies their full development. Furthermore, the activity program
does not visualize any undue coercing of individuals to follow the interests of the group. If a child found his individual interests compelling,
he would not be forced to go along with the group. In the event of such
an occurrence, he would be helped with his individual purposes. If such
behavior were to develop to the point that the individual had nothing
in common with other members of the group, it is likely that diagnosis
and possibly remedial work would be begun to find the causes of his
isolation and to encourage him to want to work with the group.

The teacher plays a unique role in an activity organization. His first
responsibility is to locate the dominant interests of individuals and of
the group, for the activity program is bound by these no less than the
subject curriculum is bound by subject matter lines. However, once
these interests are apparent, the teacher's influence is felt in co-operatively helping the children to select the most worth while of these for
study. The most worth while are those interests that offer the most
value to individual and social life and those that are pregnant with possibilities of leading to the development and growth of further interests.
Thus teacher guidance would help to sublimate interests that were
either of little value or were dead ends and to encourage the selection of
those that would lead to further rewarding interests.

Common Interests and "Common Learnings"

A second distinctive characteristic of the activity curriculum is that *"common learnings" result from the pursuance of common interests.* Since child interest is the first delimiting factor in determining what to teach, general education, or commonness of education, is possible only to the extent that children have like interests. Curriculum workers have long been conscious of wide differences in the experiential backgrounds of children, even of those found within a single classroom, and of the resulting differences in interests. They have been no less aware of strains of common backgrounds and common interests—witness the almost universal popularity of certain kinds of toys at certain age levels. If the number of such shared interests is sufficiently large, the activity curriculum can provide for common learnings.

On the other hand, this curriculum lacks common learnings to the extent that children lack mutual interests or choose widely different paths in the pursuance of those interests which are shared. Thus, the activity curriculum may or may not have a common learnings program; and the answer to whether such a program is possible or probable depends upon the results of much more conclusive research than is presently available regarding children's interests. Experimental studies of children and their interests have given little tangible evidence concerning how widespread or consuming these more prevalent interests are at different age levels. Location of these common elements and investigation into their nature thus continues to be a major concern of those advocating an activity curriculum.

Since the common elements of both subject and core organizations are rather definite and planned in advance, the activity curriculum holds a somewhat fortuitous position with respect to general or common education. The activity organization is also unique in the source from which the common learnings are derived. Instead of coming from organized fields of knowledge, as in a subject organization, or from problems of social living, as in the core curriculum, the source is the experiences required by the interests and purposes of children. The extent of the commonness depends upon the extent to which these experiences are shared in common by the children.

Children, like adults, usually have mutual interests and individual interests at the same time. It frequently happens that individuals prefer to pursue their personal interests rather than those shared by the group. Again, individuals may not agree as to which of the interests mutually entertained should be followed. At this crucial point in the development of an activity program, the ability to reach agreements about the interests to be pursued will depend upon whether or not the children have enough shared values in which to ground their opinions. It will be readily agreed that to choose deliberately one interest over another requires some standard of judgment. If a group of individuals does not have enough common standards—or if each individual falls back upon the criterion of what is most pleasing to him regardless of what happens to others—then group activities, and consequently common learnings, will be sacrificed. In the final analysis, the common learnings of the activity curriculum depend upon mutual standards of value as well as shared interests.

Preparation—But No Strict Planning in Advance

The third distinctive characteristic is that *the activity curriculum is not planned in advance.* Since child interests provide the starting point for instructional planning, it follows that the activity curriculum cannot be pre-planned. To predetermine the activities would be to assume that all groups of children will find these activities most in keeping with their interests. The errors of adult divination of child interests are too well known for anyone to have confidence in such pre-planning. Children who live in one section of the country are likely to have different interests from those who live in another section. Children who live in underprivileged homes are prone to have different interests from those who live in well-to-do neighborhoods.

While the teacher cannot plan the curriculum in the sense of determining in advance what the children are to do, he is responsible for several major tasks for which planning is necessary. He must work with individuals and groups of individuals to discover their interests; he must guide them in evaluating these interests and in making selections from among those which are considered. Then he must help the individual or group to plan and to carry out the activities required in the pursuit of these interests. Finally, he must guide the individual or group in assessing what they have accomplished. All of these responsibilities require that the teacher make plans for his own activities in the classroom. He must decide how he can best help the children plan what they will do, how they will do it, and how they will evaluate the results of their activities. Such planning requires not only consideration of teacher behavior, of the relative value of possible interests, and of the materials with which children might work, but also keen insight into child growth and development and into group structures and dynamics.

For these reasons those who work in schools where there are activity curriculums want as much information as possible about where the classroom work may lead. Materials and equipment must be available, and possible ways of seeking out the interests of individuals and the group must be explored. As a consequence, those teachers working in an activity curriculum are forever seeking more information about child growth and development. Especially do they need results of investigations that attempt to locate dominant centers of interest at various age levels. Consequently categories of interests based on research studies and practical experience are often included in descriptions of activity programs.

It is well to point out, however, that these categories do not constitute pre-planning of what children are to do. Such categories are the result of investigations of areas in which children at certain ages *may find fundamental interests*. They indicate where to look for individual and group interests; thus they are a guide to the teacher. They are not prescriptions of what the teacher and children must do. They represent possibilities. If the children indicate interests other than those included in the categories, the children's own interests will constitute those for which activities are selected and planned.

3. *Essential Characteristics*

In each pure-type curriculum there are but a few characteristics that set it apart and are not shared at all by either of the two other types. The three characteristics just described provide the uniqueness of the activity curriculum. However, built around these central pillars is a structure of further characteristics every bit as essential to the type but not restricted to it.

Co-operative Planning by Students and Teachers

For the activity curriculum, the first of these characteristics is that
activities are planned co-operatively by students and the teacher. The
theory of the activity curriculum embraces the notion of a group—of
which the teacher is a co-operating member—choosing its own area
for work, defining the problems to be met, planning the activities, carrying out the work, and, finally, evaluating the experiences. This notion
is justified on the grounds that both pupil interest and desirable pupil
growth demand that children take part in the planning of curriculum
projects. Children will, then, see plans take shape for the realization of
their purposes and will at the same time develop the ability to do the
kinds of problem solving and investigation required to meet their needs.
Children are thus engaged not solely for the knowledge gained but also
for the satisfactions, methods, and disciplines resulting from participation in the planning process.

Implied in the notion of co-operative planning is the idea that objectives also are to be determined co-operatively. If this were not so, and
if the objectives were determined instead by teachers, pupil purposes
would be honored only in theory.

Now it may well be that the educators who build, teach, and administer an activity program will see objectives neither stated nor
realized by the teacher-pupil group. These outside objectives may even
be planned for by the teacher and reached during the course of the
activity. However, it is to be understood that such objectives must be
realized within the domain of the children's interests, for deviation
from these would breach the most basic tenet of the activity organization and would defeat it at the level of practice. It should also be recognized that such externally conceived objectives cannot be the ones
that determine the direction of the activities. In order to be in harmony
with child interests and purposes, the directional objectives must grow
from these interests and purposes. Unless outside goals are accepted
and incorporated as group purposes, their realization must be incidental
to the real goals of the group.

At first consideration it may seem that such teacher-pupil co-operation in planning is distinctive of an activity curriculum. In a later
chapter, however, it will become apparent that within the broad prob-

lem-areas of the core curriculum the same sort of co-operative planning may and does take place. Thus this feature is essential to an activity organization but is not a distinctive characteristic of it.

Ambiguity with Respect to Social Direction

The second essential characteristic of the activity curriculum is that *the curriculum may or may not have deliberate social direction.* It has already been pointed out that no educational program is socially neutral. It is impossible to educate in a social vacuum or to maintain any complete neutrality of social position while educating. If education changes behavior—and teaching efforts are futile to the extent that they stop short of behavior changes—then these changes, or the lack of them, are sure to show in the attitudes, beliefs, and actions taken in matters of social concern. Decision, conscious or unconscious, to ignore matters of social concern by not dealing with these in the curriculum, or to study them in the vain hope that pupils can sit high on an impartial judgment seat, is not only ostrichlike but in effect tends to throw the influence of the group toward the maintenance of the *status quo*—another way of lending support to individuals and social groups currently in power. The real question here, as in the subject matter curriculum, is not whether an activity program has a social direction; rather, it is a question of whether this direction is a deliberately considered and consistent one.

The first basis for the selection of curriculum content is the interests of children. These interests have been conditioned by the radio, television, motion pictures, comic books, newspapers, homes, the church, the school, and countless other mind-forming agencies. It would be wishful thinking to expect to find a consistent social orientation reflected in the interests acquired by any elementary school class. All these interests will undoubtedly reflect aspects of living in twentieth-century America. But contemporary society is not characterized by a single environment or a single set of value standards. It is, instead, compounded of many environments and conflicting values, and the interests of children will reflect these differences.

Children often have more interests than they can follow at once, and sometimes their interests are not worthy of the children's efforts to follow them. Hence a second basis for the selection of content is a criterion for choosing among expressed interests. This is a critical point, for the writings of some theorists on the activity curriculum set forth a value framework for use by teachers in helping children to select worth-while interests. Furthermore, some of these frameworks are characterized by a consistent social orientation.

If the teachers in an activity curriculum understood and held such a value system in common, if the teachers alone were making the choice among child interests, and if they used this commonly held value system in the choice, then the activity curriculum would be devoted deliberately to social ends. These suppositions, however, are not necessarily true. Teachers alone do not select the activities to be pursued. As already noted, this selection is a co-operative venture of teacher and pupils. It might be supposed that both teacher and pupils, in reaching an agreement respecting the interests to be followed, would necessarily be in agreement upon social directions. But the fact that two individuals will reach the same decision for quite different reasons is too well known to dispute; hence, there is no good reason to suppose that the activities finally decided upon have been chosen because they serve a set of deliberately selected social goals. Moreover, children's true interests are more likely than not to be violated through attempts to mold them to a consistent social direction. The presupposition is that youngsters are concerned about the social consequences of their interests, and this seems at best a doubtful assumption.

This indecisiveness or ambiguity with respect to social orientation is not a distinctive characteristic of the activity curriculum. It is shared by the subject curriculum, where loyalty to a field of knowledge rather than to the interests of children rises as a barrier to curriculum planning for social reconstruction.

Problem-Solving the Dominant Method

The third essential characteristic of the activity curriculum is that *problem-solving is the dominant method.* When a group or an individual decides to do something, it not infrequently happens that difficulties are encountered. The task of overcoming a difficulty or barrier constitutes a problem. In the activity curriculum, the teaching-learning process consists largely of problem-solving. This is true because in the pursuit of interests and purposes various difficulties will arise, and pupils and teachers will be challenged to find ways of overcoming these obstacles.

In the activity curriculum the learning process is not short-circuited by simply telling children what they want to know or doing for them what they ought to do. While "telling" is used from time to time, it is not the whole of the teaching process and is to be used sparingly and at such times as will best facilitate problem-solving activities. The major values of this curriculum are not to be found in the answers to problems, although these are not unimportant, but in the learnings inherent in the activities of problem-solving by which purposes are realized.

From the fact that problem-solving is at the heart of the teaching-learning process, it follows that subject matter is studied as a means of solving problems and not as an end in itself. It is thus unfair to contend that an activity is carried on without subject matter. Actually, subject matter from almost every field of knowledge is used in the activity curriculum, because the interests of children lead to problems requiring a great diversity of content.

By the same token, skills would be taught and learned as they are needed. It would be contrary to the fundamental premises of an activity curriculum to violate children's interests by insisting on the teaching of skills before children are interested in learning these skills. According to the activity theory, children will learn to read when learning to read becomes a dominant interest. As children pursue their interests, it is presumed that they will find reading a necessary tool for their work. When this interest runs high, learning to read will be one of the activities pursued. Other skills will be mastered in like manner.

Little Need for Extracurricular Features

As a fourth essential characteristic, *children's individual needs and interests are met within the program of the activity curriculum*. In a preceding chapter it was pointed out that the subject curriculum does not readily lend itself to the encouragement of certain interests of children. Hence, special classes and out-of-class activities are often necessary to care for children's individual needs. In marked contrast, an activity curriculum probably has less need for extracurricular features and other special arrangements than does any other curriculum organization. By the very nature of this curriculum, children's interests are not only recognized but are a primary basis of the curriculum itself.

The school recognizes a responsibility to help the child who wants to pursue an interest beyond the domain of a particular project. Every attempt is made to allow this interest full development within the curriculum. A small group may be helped to start a camera club or a model airplane club as additional activities. However, it is altogether likely that the scope of various projects will allow free play of these interests within the curriculum.

Similarly, a handicapped child, or one markedly retarded in some skill, may require special arrangements for his care; but the extreme flexibility of an activity program will provide, without recourse to special arrangements, help for many of these marked deviates. Within any chosen activity there are many opportunities for the play of individual interests and for the care of individual needs.

There is no doubt but that certain needs of children, as determined by adults, must be cared for by special arrangements in the school program. One large category of these needs has to do with the protection of life and health. Children may have little interest in plans to protect them from fire. Yet there must be unannounced fire drills a number of times each year. Children may not find physical examinations at regular intervals in keeping with their felt needs, yet these examinations must be arranged. These constant concerns for life and health may not be in keeping with the interests and felt needs of children, yet the school insists that they be an integral part of the curriculum.

Special Subjects for Special Needs

The fifth essential characteristic of the activity curriculum is that *special subjects provide for specialized interests.* Even in the early elementary school program children's interests and felt needs sometimes fall into areas best characterized by subject matter boundaries. While the individual is motivated to learn the skills of reading, arithmetic, writing, spelling, and speaking by the need to engage in certain activities, activity programs have found need for a time set aside for further development of these skills. Further work may be informally and flexibly scheduled. It should be problem-motivated, and be quite unlike the usual "drill period" in reading, spelling, or arithmetic.

Other subjects are required to provide for the constant and progressive differentiation of interests, needs, and abilities. The primary grades have children who have either already begun or want to begin training in instrumental music. Interests in creative work in the various art mediums are not adequately met within the confines of the group projects. By the time children have reached the seventh year in an activity curriculum, a definite plan to care for the specialized subject-matter needs of the students must be provided. It must be understood that these specialized subjects grow from the demands of pupil interest and need and not from what adults think children need. This is a major distinction between the specialized offerings of an activity curriculum and the elective courses in a subject curriculum. The specialized subjects provide an opportunity for groups of pupils to solve problems dictated by their own interests, and the subjects are merely convenient categories for grouping these related interests.

It is quite likely that some students will have developed only a few specialized interests by the latter years of high school. Some may have acquired none during their school career. Such students would be occupied almost entirely by the nonspecialized activity program. On the other hand, most students would spend a major part of the last year in high school in specialized courses with opportunity for individualized and intensive study.

4. Personnel, Physical Features, and Administrative Arrangements Required for Optimum Operation

These features of an activity curriculum are of a different order from the distinctive and essential characteristics considered above. They are discussed in order to point up a few of the practical implications of previously mentioned characteristics, and to give a better view of what the activity curriculum requires to run smoothly.

Training of Teachers

Teachers should have a broad general education with specialized training in child and adolescent development, guidance, and project methods of teaching. A teacher in an activity curriculum may well have deeper interest and more specialization in one field of knowledge than in others, but there is little need for extensive training in the segmented branches of organized subject matter. Much more vital is broad training in a number of general areas. There should be no great gaps in fields where children's interests might lead.

Another type of training should take teachers into specific interest areas that children are currently exploring in activity programs. In these areas teachers gain familiarity not only with the area and its possibilities but with project methods as well.

It is also essential that teachers in activity programs have a better understanding of child and adolescent development than has resulted from the usual teacher training curriculums. It is truly said that students in colleges of agriculture spend more time studying the characteristics of animals and plants than prospective teachers spend attempting to understand human behavior. To work in close co-operation with children on problems arising from their interests, and to do this in such a manner that maximum growth will ensue, will require thorough understanding of child growth and development. Since work in an activity curriculum is more often carried on in groups than with individuals, much of this psychological training should be concerned with the structure and dynamics of group processes.

Also, the teacher in an activity curriculum must have thorough grounding in those aspects of the philosophical and sociological foundations of education that will insure wise guidance in teacher-pupil selection and planning of activities. The democratic value system and its sociological and psychological justification must be mastered. The guidance skills, in which such a teacher will also be trained, will be subservient to this value orientation.

Physical Features of the School

A second requirement for operation of an activity curriculum is that *building, grounds, and classrooms be large and flexible enough to per-*

mit as many activities as possible. We must remember that the physical features designed to house an activity curriculum cannot be planned for a group of preconceived educational experiences. The activities to be carried on within the school's domain will be as varied as children's interests. Experiences with problem-solving methods in an activity curriculum and a knowledge of children's interests will offer many clues as to building requirements. Every attempt must be made to provide flexibility of use. The rooms will have to be large—probably at least half again as large as the usual classrooms. Furniture must be light-weight and movable. Built-in facilities tend to freeze the room's uses. Plans for space and equipment must be worked out with an eye to the need for construction activities on widely varied individual and group projects. Corridors and general-purpose rooms (auditorium, gymnasium, etc.) will be built to facilitate children's purposes. These will be well lighted and will have ample facilities for displays and decorations devised by the children.

The school grounds should also lend themselves to many uses. In addition to the usual space for games there should be ground for gardening, for outdoor classwork, for growing flowers, for designing the permanent planting, and for countless other outdoor activities in which children may engage as they follow their interests. The realization of these possibilities will require several times the space now given to most school sites. Ten acres would likely be a minimum to meet the needs of an activity curriculum. To those who would claim that such an outlay would be too expensive, advocates of an activity program might reply that there is no such thing as "a good cheap education."

Equipment and Materials in the Classroom

The third requirement is that *equipment and materials be such as will satisfy the interests of children.* An activity classroom would not look like a carpenter's shop, a library, an art studio, a committee room, a science laboratory, or anything else commonly seen; yet it would look something like a combination of all these—and more. An approximate idea of the materials and equipment to be found in an activity classroom may be formed by imagining a combination of many children's playrooms fitted out in the ways children would desire.

It is unlikely that the entire class group would be using the same types of materials at any one time. While some children were using books and reference materials, others would be constructing; still others would be at work on the art aspects of the project; and yet another group would be gathering the materials needed for a display. Incidentally, this brief picture of an activity room at work may have implications for the teaching of skills. Children would have to learn to read, for instance, in the face of many factors hitherto thought to be distracting. The point here is that a picture of an activity program is not one of uniformity of either materials or activities.

Since adults are uncertain about the fundamental interests of children, and since the results of research concerning these are none too dependable, selection of materials and equipment is a problem of no mean proportions. If teachers and administrators should err in their judgments concerning children's needs for materials or equipment—and should then make the further error of attempting to assure the use of whatever purchases they had made—the most basic tenet of the activity curriculum would be violated. In this event, the curriculum would be determined not by children's interests but by mistakes of adults in attempts to prejudge these interests. In other words, a curriculum pattern may be frozen by the materials and equipment provided to facilitate it. This is especially true when the need for economy causes teachers to press "white elephants" into service.

As a rule it is much safer to let the demonstrated interests of children determine equipment and material needs than to attempt to buy for a year on the basis of adult judgments concerning the nature of children's interests. This observation is made with full knowledge of the impossibility of beginning a school year without instructional materials and with full appreciation of the relative ease of budgeting when nearly all expenditures are anticipated well in advance of need. Flexibility in budgeting procedures is a requirement for optimum operation of activity programs. Purchase of equipment in the same manner as that used for a subject curriculum is a practice that would almost surely freeze the activity program into a pattern quite unlike any real conception of an activity curriculum. Above all else, an activity organization must be true to the fundamental interests of children. Materials and equipment should be those best designed to facilitate the solution of problems growing from these interests.

Activity Rooms

As a fourth requirement, *the building should have several activity rooms for general use in addition to the classrooms.* While activities are pursued in each classroom as suggested earlier, numerous problems require several additional general-purpose rooms. It is necessary to have a large workbench with a larger vise and more adequate tools than are found in each room. A kiln for firing clay products, a band saw, or other large and bulky equipment would find many uses in a general room. These and other tools and scientific apparatus are too expensive and infrequently used to justify duplication in each room, yet they find an excellent place in a room shared by several class groups. For an activity program in the secondary school, more of these rooms might be required, and each might meet a more specialized function than the all-purpose activity rooms in an elementary school.

Discussions are frequent as to whether a modern school building should have a separate room for art, music, general science, home economics, shopwork, or some other phase of a program. Labeling of rooms is likely to be a reflection of thinking in terms of the subject matter to be pursued in each and is thus the result of binding the uses of general-purpose rooms to the ends of a subject curriculum. In an activity curriculum these rooms are planned and equipped to provide facilities to meet the problems of children. One room might have more science equipment than another for reasons of convenience, but it still remains an activity room equipped in part or entirely with scientific apparatus. Hence, the number of general-purpose rooms required in a school and the uses to which each will be put are to be decided in terms of the space and equipment needed for activities. Experience with activity programs and findings regarding children's interests and methods of work will provide the bases for the requirements of these rooms—and, for that matter, for the entire building and grounds.

Transportation Facilities

The fifth requirement for the activity curriculum is that *transportation facilities be available to take children to places where their interests lead them.* It will be recalled that transportation is desired in order to enrich and extend the content of the subject curriculum. The activity program has a similar need for transportation but for a different purpose. Solution of problems emerging from felt needs of children requires trips to various places.

In some instances, the mode of transportation may itself be the subject of inquiry and may prompt the trips. Even though school buses are essential for optimum operation of an activity program, it would be an error to think only in terms of this mode of transportation. At different times, motivated by different needs, commercial buses, planes, steam, diesel, or electric trains, subways, elevated trains—or even horse-drawn sleighs, buggies, or wagons—might be used. Perhaps funds and plans for such study of transportation would fall into a different budgetary allotment from that set aside for the prime purpose of transporting pupils.

In the heat of controversy over the relative advantages of different curriculum organizations, it has sometimes been assumed that trips taken in an activity program follow the unplanned whims of children and are thus a waste of both time and money, while those taken in a subject curriculum are carefully planned and are, therefore, a wise expenditure of energies and funds. This is a fallacious argument. The only real differences between the two types of trips are, first, the share that children have had in the planning and, second, the underlying reasons for taking the trip. In both cases the trips are anticipated so that use of transportation facilities will not conflict with other plans and so that objectives of the particular curriculum program will be realized.

The activity curriculum protects itself from goals and subsequent activities established on the basis of mere whims by the teacher's influence upon the pupil when problems are being selected for study. The problems themselves are expressions of genuine pupil interests, but the ones selected for study are those that (1) have possibilities of leading to further interests and (2) have real social and individual significance.

Planning without Rigid Scheduling

Operation of an activity curriculum requires that *time blocks or periods not be decided in advance*. The fact that an activity program is not characterized by the usual "periods," bells to separate activities, and other evidences of rigid scheduling is not evidence of lack of planning. Instead, it is evidence of planning on different bases and by different groups. Plans in an activity curriculum are formulated by a group of children and the teacher in co-operation, and these plans are especially designed to meet the purposes previously determined by this same group. Nothing but trouble and confusion could result from any superimposition of a rigid predetermined schedule upon the plans made within each classroom. Of course there are certain beginning and ending times, times for the lunch period, and scheduled times for fire drills and the like. However, flexibility of time blocks is the rule within these general limits. There are no bells to separate activities.

Children do not take their recesses at scheduled times. Recesses are taken, instead, when the nature of the work causes children and teacher to feel the need of relaxation. Large flexible rooms or covered play areas permit inside games when the weather is bad and when the gymnasium is in use by other groups. It is contended—and it is probably true—that there is much less reason for a conventional recess in an activity program since the nature of the activities allows flexibility of pursuit. That is, if an activity requires close and tedious work, relaxation is provided by a shift to another part of the activity, where big muscle work is required. Rainy days, with their accompanying restrictions of outdoor play, are excellent ones for construction activities.

The general rule is that all scheduling be adjusted to the needs of current activities and be flexible enough to fit as many of these as possible. Within general limits of school hours and considerations for health and safety, the program is scheduled to facilitate activities planned and carried out by pupils and teachers in co-operation.

No Sequence of Grades

As a seventh factor required for optimum operation, *grouping of students is decided on the basis of children's interests.* A program especially designed to care for the interests and needs of its individual members has no need for a sequence of grades. It is thought that six-year-old children will, as a rule, be on about the same level of social maturation. As a consequence of this generalization—and because the curriculum worker has not had dependable ways of classifying children on the basis of their interests—children have more often been grouped by chronological age than by interests and needs. If, after being placed in one group, it is discovered that a child's interests and needs are more in keeping with those of another group, he would be placed in that group.

If a child is less able than others in the group with which he shares his interests, the program is flexible enough to provide tasks at his level and thus to facilitate the next step in his growth. Similarly, a child who is more able than others will also contribute to the group at his own level and rate, and he will grow still more able. Both of these children will be growing and working with interests shared by other children in their group, and both will be learning to work with children of similar interests.

A sequence of grades has generally been based upon the premise that children should have developed certain skills and acquired certain knowledge as prerequisites for the next grade. This premise is foreign to the concepts of an activity curriculum, in which a child grows as fast as he can, not only in knowledge but in ability to pursue his own purposes successfully. The need here is not for him to be grouped with others of similar ability but to be grouped with others of similar interests.

It should be mentioned that marks are also believed to be foreign to the purposes of an activity program. Teachers in an activity curriculum want the children and their parents to know how the children are developing. They feel, however, that description of all-round growth in terms of the objectives co-operatively planned by teachers and pupils is best communicated by letters—or preferably by talks among children, parents, and teachers.

Flexibility in Administrative Arrangements

The eighth requirement for the operation of an activity curriculum is that *all administrative arrangements be flexible.* Anyone trained in school administration or sensitive to some of the problems of a principal or superintendent has probably anticipated this section, in which some of the difficulties thrust upon an administrator by the requirements of an activity program will be discussed. The general rule is flexibility of administrative arrangements, and planning for flexibility is a much more difficult task than planning a relatively inflexible and highly organized program.

One of an administrator's major problems is budgeting. Several large items of recurring expense may be budgeted in advance much as with any other curriculum organization. Salaries, heating costs, general costs of building repair and maintenance, and interest on indebtedness are examples. However, major problems arise in the area of instructional expenses. Even with a curriculum library for the school system, which centralizes the budgeting and distribution of many instructional materials, much of the equipment and material must be bought as the activities progress. It is extremely difficult to budget these in advance. The same type of problem arises with respect to transportation costs when the administrator cannot know how far in advance, how often, or for what length of trips funds must be available.

Still another budgetary problem, though perhaps not as troublesome as either of the former two, is concerned with expense for the improvement of classrooms and grounds. Children frequently find an interest in such improvement. Such an interest may involve money for materials with which to decorate a classroom or money for shrubbery to plant a portion of the grounds. In each of these instances of an indeterminate budget, the administrator may find himself caught, so to speak, between two fires. He is pressed by the school board for a reasonable estimate of annual expense and is embarrassed by either a deficit or a sizeable surplus at the end of a school year. On the other hand, the instructional program will suffer to the extent that funds are not available for the requirements of worth-while projects.

An administrator of an activity program is, by the very nature of the program, beset with many temporary and unanticipated requirements other than those of year-around spending. Class groups must not interfere with one another's plans, yet these cannot be made far in advance. Hence, plans for use of rooms and major items of equipment must be cleared through the administrator's office with maximum efficiency but still with the flexibility prerequisite to successful operation of an activity curriculum.

All-school announcements, functions, or projects must be planned so that they do not disrupt work in the separate classes. In a situation where each class group is organized differently and where it is extremely difficult to find convenient periods in which these all-school activities can be carried out, the task of administering such arrangements is complicated.

Provision for adequate janitorial service is also more of a problem in a school carrying on an activity program than it is in one following a subject curriculum. Children in an activity program will clean up after their work, but the muss of the activities is a minor problem. There are tables and chairs instead of desks; since these are frequently rearranged, the job of cleaning each room is never the same from day to day. The varied paraphernalia and partially completed products of an activity program are sure to complicate the janitor's job. In addition, the janitor assumes a much more vital role in the instructional job than he does in a subject curriculum. The variety of activities requires his help and co-operation much more often than does a less varied program. The requirement of flexibility thus extends to the work of the janitorial staff. The janitor can no longer plan to care for each room at a specified time and in a standardized way. His work will have to be fitted to the types of work being carried out in the various rooms. To revert for a moment to the matter of budgeting for personnel, an activity program is likely to be more expensive than a subject curriculum in terms of provision for janitors. Not only must these men be more able, but the demands upon them will be increased at nearly every point.

Flexibility of administrative arrangements extends as well to the administrator's budgeting of his own time. Inability to plan the instructional program in advance will invariably mean that new demands will be made upon an administrator. While any type of organization demands the administrator's time, a constantly changing school program is especially time-consuming. Children's interests are sure to take them into problems utilizing different community resources and to cause different groups of children to go to the same places for different purposes. Arrangements for these studies place an ever-recurring demand upon administrative time. Constant ordering and receiving of supplies, scheduling of trips, and planning for most efficient use of building and equipment in the light of changing plans are all reasons why the administrator of an activity program must have a flexible arrangement of his time.

▶ *Following Up*
This Chapter

1. What would you consider to be the advantages of the pure-form activity curriculum over the pure-form subject curriculum? In what respects is the subject curriculum superior?

2. Select a recent course of study from your library, and try to determine in what respect, if any, it corresponds to a pure-form activity curriculum.

3. In what respect is the course of study you selected inferior to the pure-form activity curriculum? In what respect is it superior to the activity program?

4. What do you consider to be the one or two most basic weaknesses in the theory of the activity curriculum?

5. How would you account for the fact that few, if any, curriculums in effect today are true to the three distinctive characteristics of an activity curriculum?

6. If you were to spend several days visiting a school which claimed to have an activity curriculum, what would you look for to assure yourself that the curriculum in practice was really true to the theory? List these clues in the order of their cruciality.

▶ *Suggested*
Reading

Classic statements of the theory underlying the activity curriculum are John Dewey's *The Child and the Curriculum;* William Heard Kilpatrick's *Foundations of Method* and *Remaking the Curriculum;* Rugg and Shumaker, *The Child-Centered School;* Lois Coffey Mossman's *The Activity Concept;* and the *Thirty-third Yearbook* of the National Society for the Study of Education, Part II, pages 45–64. The most thorough elaboration of the moral, logical, and psychological principles underlying the Dewey School is Melvin Baker's *Foundations of Dewey's Educational Theory.*

Chapter 13

The Activity Curriculum: Problems, Practices, and Criticisms

IN ORDER to translate the principles described in the preceding chapter into a practical curriculum pattern, two problems must be solved. First, what will be the categories of the curriculum? Merely to say that the activity curriculum will be based upon children's interests does not provide a framework of categories for a curriculum pattern.

Second, how should each of these categories be broken down and arranged for teaching from grade to grade? Growth and development should be planned according to some orderly sequence of experiences. What should be the basis for this sequence in an activity curriculum?

1. *The Problem of Categories*

The activity curriculum has brought to light a new kind of categories, categories which represent wide divisions of interests and activities rather than subject matter. These categories rest primarily upon the theory that children's interests are, for the most part, limited to the present; that their motives are derived from the normal course of their daily living; that they are intensely active in meeting the complexities in the world of their everyday experiences. It is further held that children who are intensely and richly engaged in the process of meeting their felt needs are at the same time receiving the best preparation for dealing with the demands later events will make upon them. Preparation for the future is thus not neglected, according to this theory; for such preparation is the result of effective participation in activities having immediate interest and value. Categories based upon this theory will naturally emphasize those areas of interest in which the activities of children, or individuals for whom the curriculum is being organized, tend to concentrate.

Meriam's "Subjects"

Perhaps the best illustration of such categories is found in the "subjects" of Meriam's school,[1] and in the "project areas" of Collings' experimental rural school.[2] Meriam's subjects, it will be remembered, are observation, play, stories, and handwork. It is well to look at these subjects more closely, for they are more or less typical of interest-centered categories.

1. *Observation.* Children must adjust to the physical and cultural environment into which they are born. They can accomplish this most effectively by studying as directly as possible those aspects of their environment relating to their everyday affairs. Indeed, the environment stimulates them to observe, to ask questions. They ask about trees, plants, insects; about rocks, clouds, stars; about people and the things people do and make.

Observation, as a major category of the curriculum, embraces those activities that have to do with the exploration of the environment and with the adjustment and continual readjustment of children to it. In the first and second grades it embraces activities having to do with plant life, animal life, earth, sky, and people; in the third and fourth grades it includes local industries; in the fifth and sixth grades it embraces activities that extend into the world at large; and in the seventh

---

[1] Meriam, *Child Life and the Curriculum.*
[2] Collings, *An Experiment with a Project Curriculum.*

and eighth grades it consists of activities leading to an acquaintance with the various occupations. On its content side, observation includes materials from the fields of science and social studies.

2. *Play.* Play as a school study will seem the height of absurdity to a person who has given little thought to the role of play in human life. No one can doubt, however, that play is a normal activity of children—and, for that matter, of all individuals, adults and children alike. It is this fact that gives play its significance in the curriculum. As an area of human activity, it should be developed on a parity with any other category of human interests.

This view of play is in sharp contrast to the notion that play is an escape from work, that it is recreation. In Meriam's view, play is not merely recreation; it is not just a means of recuperating from the strains of labor. Nor is it a device for teaching the Three R's, as some conventional schools have suggested. Rather it is a major phase of child life, not because it is a means of relieving fatigue or of escaping the worries of the day but because it is a source of fun.

In Meriam's school the subject of play consists of five classes of games: (1) competitive games of two kinds—relay or group competition and individual competition; (2) games largely of a physical nature; (3) games largely of a mental nature; (4) singing games; and (5) outdoor games. In addition, play activities involving relationships between the individual and the things of his surroundings are stressed in and above Grade IV. The following list of play activities gives a further idea of the potentialities of play as a curriculum category:

Water. Playing with water, pouring, wading, splashing, watching objects in water, throwing objects into water, building dams and water wheels, watching the action of water on land, "erosion models," etc., which develop problems in fluids.

Air. Playing with air, sailboats, kites, windmills, airplanes, which develop problems in air pressure, air currents, wind, temperature, humidity, rainfall, etc.

Heat. Watching fire, making fires, observing friction and heat, playing with toy steam engines, thermometers, which develop problems in heat, combustion, expansion, contraction, and other effects of heat.

Mechanical Devices. Playing with hoops, tops, pulleys, wheels, toy machines, gyroscopes, pendulums, levers, watching thrown objects, balancing objects, etc., which develop problems in motor dynamics.

Sound. Vocalization, beating and drumming, blowing on toy instruments, "listening to shells," speaking-tubes and telephones, experimenting with conduction through air, water, and timbers, with vibrating bodies, echoes, etc., which develop problems in vibration, noises, tones, music, etc.

Light. Playing with reflectors, mirrors, prisms, lenses, water refraction, glasses, telescopes, which develop problems in light, color, optics, time, etc.

Electricity. Experimenting and playing with magnets, batteries, induction coils, telephones, telegraph instruments, dynamos, electric motors, electric lights, etc., which present problems in electrodynamics.[3]

3. *Stories.* The third category in Meriam's curriculum is stories, including music, poetry, and pictures. Stories and leisure are closely related in Meriam's scheme. Leisure is conceived as one of the fundamental phases of civilized life. Leisure, according to Meriam, is coordinate with work. The reason work is not included as a category in his curriculum is that children do not engage in work but spend considerable time in leisure activities. Had his curriculum been developed for adults or adolescents, it is probable that attention would have been given to work activities.

Stories are included as a subject of study because they constitute one of the wholesome ways in which children spend their leisure time. The stories included in the program must be such as will give immediate enjoyment. The general types of reading materials used are indicated in the following list: (1) fables, fairy tales, myths, legends, wonder stories; (2) travel, including sightseeing, exploration, adventure, scenery, manners, and customs; (3) nature; (4) industries, invention, science; (5) history and biography; (6) character study—fiction; and (7) humor. Among the activities included in this category are reading, telling, dramatizing, singing, drawing, and looking at pictures.

4. *Handwork.* Handwork is the fourth subject in Meriam's elementary school. It is based upon the constructive activities in which children normally engage. That children like to make things, to construct, to contrive, is a matter of common observation. Hence, the inclusion

[3] Clark W. Hetherington, "The Demonstration Play School of 1913," *University of California Publications in Education*, Vol. 5, No. 2, p. 273. University of California Press. By permission. Quoted in *Child Life and the Curriculum*, p. 324.

of handwork as a major category is in line with beliefs concerning the normal interests and activities of children. A list of projects using materials as a basis of classification suggests the range of activities covered by this subject:

Cord, yarn, rags: Bags, mats, rugs, holders, hammocks, tatting edging, stocking caps, sailor's knots.

Paper, cardboard: Boxes, poster work, lamp shade, bookmarks, portfolio, covers, blotter pad, reminder pad.

Reed, raffia, tissue-paper rope: Baskets, mats, jardinieres, bird nests, hats.

Textiles: Table runners, whisk brooms, holders, slipper cases, needlebooks, doilies, bookmarks, napkin rings, laundry bags, cushion covers, magazine covers, silver case, wall pockets, articles of clothing, bibs.

Wood: Boxes, spoolrack, necktie holder, footstools, fox and geese board, bread board, boats, water wheel, weathervane, bookrack.

Metal: Pin tray, paper knife, bookmark, blotter pad, lamp shade, paperweight, watch fob.[4]

Recent Tendencies—Centers of Interest

More recent developments of interest-centered categories have tended to stress *centers of interest*. Common observation bears out the fact that children's interests are very diversified and tend to be distributed over a great variety of objects and events. Children show interests in first one thing and then another; they change from one activity to another as their interests lead them, without the least hesitation. To speak of "a center of interest," therefore, is not to describe the way in which children's interests are actually organized but to indicate a particular classification of interests for the sake of reducing the activities of children to manageable terms. Interests may be grouped in a number of ways, depending upon how the activities in which they are reflected are classified.

A fairly typical classification of centers of interest as the major categories of study is set forth in the California course of study for the primary grades. In this outline it is claimed that desirable growth of children is most likely to occur when the children engage in activities within the range of their understanding and with the wholehearted pur-

[4] Meriam, *Child Life and the Curriculum*, p. 377. Copyright 1920 by World Book Company.

posing of the group. According to this course of study, the activities which the young child can grasp and in which he is most apt to be interested are:

The immediate as to space.
The contemporary as to time.
The most recurring in experience.
The most inclusive of the group.
Those representing the real serious business of the child's life. . . .
Those filled with known and familiar personalities, as parents, neighbors, postman, teacher; as against heroic characters brought in for the occasion —Hiawatha, Appleseed John, Mother Goose, etc.
The spectacular when it comes normally into his social experience, as a circus, Santa Claus, a fire, parade, airplane, fiesta, auto show. . . .[5]

The classification of interests based upon the foregoing criteria of what children of the primary grades will find interesting is as follows:

Activities centering in the interests relating to Home Life.
Activities centering in the interests relating to the Natural World.
Activities centering in the interests relating to the Local Community and Common Experiences of Children.
Activities centering in the interests relating to Food, Its Production and Distribution.
Activities centering in the interests relating to Transportation and Communication.
Activities centering in the interests relating to Community Life of Earlier Times.
Activities centering in the interests relating to Community Life of Other Lands and Peoples.
Activities centering in the interests relating to Social Experiences.[6]

Present knowledge of children's interests rests more upon practical observations, shrewd guesses, and empirical generalizations than upon systematic research. This admission, however, does not negate the fact that a considerable amount of understanding of interests has resulted from practical experience in building activity curriculums and in ob-

[5] From *Teachers' Guide to Child Development: Manual for Kindergarten and Primary Teachers*. Prepared under the direction of the California State Curriculum Commission; Ruth Manning Hockett, editor (Sacramento: California State Department of Education; 1930), p. 59.
[6] *Ibid.*, p. 60.

serving the free behavior of children. The activity movement has made it difficult, if not impossible, to ignore interests and purposes in practice while lauding them in theory, as has so often been done in the history of education. For when interests are made the very basis of curriculum organization, as in the activity program, they must necessarily be of major concern.

Criticisms of Interest as the Basis of the Curriculum

The most frequent criticisms of the theory are as follows: First, interest categories sacrifice the subject organization of knowledge and do not replace it with any organization; thus a risk is run of leaving huge gaps in basic experience. Second, there is an apparent lack of continuity of experience. Third, a curriculum based primarily upon interest categories does not provide adequate preparation for the future. Increasing concern over the obvious social ineptitude of the present products of the schools in dealing with current crucial problems makes the latter criticism the most vital one.

The criticism that interest categories do not provide any basis for curriculum organization is ill-considered and unjust unless it can be proved that it is indeed impossible to organize experiences in terms of centers of interest. To indicate that certain activity programs in practice have been disorganized is beside the point. The same could truthfully be said of certain programs under any type of curriculum organization. The point that proponents of the activity curriculum have experienced difficulty in finding suitable categories would probably be granted by its staunchest advocates, but this admission is not the same as the criticism that centers of interest provide no basis for organization. As a matter of fact, centers of interest *have* provided an organizational basis for activity programs. Some of these patterns were illustrated earlier in this chapter.

The second criticism of interest categories is that they do not provide an adequate continuity of experience. The determination of sequence on the basis of children's interests is a considerable problem, and it will be treated later in this chapter.

The third major criticism is that a curriculum based primarily upon children's interests does not provide adequate preparation for the future. In this discussion attention will be directed first to the adequacy of the concept of using children's interests as the basis for the selection of curriculum content. It will then be pertinent to turn to the translation of theory into practice and to question whether centers of interest are adequate means of classifying children's interests.

Sociologists have pointed to the fact that the life of children in modern society is largely divorced from the life of adults—that children and youth no longer have an important function in the socio-economic scheme. Since interests are largely determined by experiences, it is not strange for children to find their fundamental interests outside the major social goals of adults. Then how are the interests of children, at any one time, good preparation for a future characterized by pressing social problems?

It is too easy an answer to point to the teacher's part in the co-operative selection of an activity from among those proposed by the child group. Genuine co-operation in the selection of a problem implies acceptance by both children and teachers of value standards to be used in making the choice. But teachers and children do not always possess the same values. If the children want "to win, to vanquish, to master" one another or to exceed one another in the skills, as Collings and Wilson claim that they do,[7] what happens to the goal of co-operation as a way of life? Without considering the point of how the child became competitive—and without even doubting the truth of Collings' and Wilson's dubious assertion that such competitiveness is a fundamental interest of children, for the example is illustrative only—it is interesting to see where such motives would lead. Collings' and Wilson's conception of the activity program would utilize these motives in such a way as to feed and develop them. The concepts of competition and co-operation are eternally at war, and different kinds of behavior result from instruction in each. If, then, competition in various forms is a real interest of children, and if co-operation is a value possessed only by their teachers, the question becomes one of whether children can learn to value co-operation by engaging in competition. If they cannot learn co-operation in this way, then how are the interests of children to be reconciled with the values of teachers. In other words,

[7] Ellsworth Collings and M. O. Wilson, *Psychology for Teachers* (New York: Charles Scribner's Sons; 1930).

how is the competitive interest going to lead to the co-operative habits so much emphasized in today's society.

It is true that attempts to put into practice the theory of the activity curriculum, with respect to selection and use of interest categories, are open to many criticisms. Even the seemingly sound practice of setting forth criteria by which to select centers of interest for a particular age group runs into difficulties. When the group responsible for the California centers of interest said that an area for study should be contemporary as to time and place, it would seem that this would be a safe criterion.[8] Yet common observation of children's interest in fairy tales, in futuristic stories of the "comic book" variety, and in anticipating school and adulthood leads to the conclusion that generalizations about children's interests are shaky even when based upon our present best, but limited, knowledge.

Centers of interest seem to be formed more from what adults want children to be interested in than from information now available about the interests of children, inadequate though it be. This seems to be a real danger even if criteria are set up in advance for the selection of centers of interest. For instance, the selection of "activities centering in the interests related to community life of earlier times" for the primary grades of the California curriculum probably does not conform to a single one of their criteria for centers of interest. It is not "immediate as to space," "contemporary as to time," "recurring in child experience," "representative of the real and serious business of the child's life," nor "filled with familiar personalities"; and it is extremely doubtful that it is "the most inclusive interest of the group" at that age or "the most spectacular when it comes normally into his social experience." Yet it is in the curriculum and is labeled a center of interest.[9]

The interest categories of activity programs seem to follow more closely the areas in which interests may be easily developed than areas of real and present interests as held by children. Many of the earlier programs, perhaps following the lead of Meriam, concentrated upon interests centering in concrete things.[10] Science activities were strong, while concrete experiences in the social studies were almost entirely

---

[8] California State Curriculum Commission, *Teachers' Guide to Child Development: Manual for Kindergarten and Primary Teachers*, p. 59.

[9] *Ibid.*, p. 60.

[10] Meriam, *Child Life and the Curriculum*, p. 324.

neglected. Yet who can deny the reality or concreteness of the slum? The strong interest of children in people would make it difficult to explain this omission on grounds of lack of interest. Perhaps earlier activity programs conceived both the concreteness and the limits of child interest and experience too narrowly. Meriam taught science and called it play. It is a tribute to his methods that this was no misnomer. However, even in his program the interests attributed to children tended to be the interests adults thought could be developed rather than genuine child interests. Note, for example, the omission from the play category of playing with dolls, bike-riding, and the like.

A major difficulty in the accumulation of research data concerning child interests is the transient character of centers of interest from one decade to another—and almost from one year to the next. This same fact lessens the value and utility of earlier developed interest categories. In 1896, when John and Mary Dewey established the Laboratory School, food and cooking, wood products and construction with wood, textiles and sewing were probably among the most interesting occupations to children. And these, to be sure, far outstrip in interest value the content of many a curriculum in operation today. But we must not forget for a moment that the rush of social and technological change has captured and taken children's interests with it. Automobiles, airplanes, streamlined trains, telephones, radios, television sets, tractors, cranes, power tools, mechanical toys, and countless other seeming miracles are now within the child's world. With this ever-changing mechanical circus showing every day, teachers would be naïve indeed if they could not understand why the everyday occupations of the life of even a few years ago are not as exciting as they once were.

While this observation does not negate the value of such broad classifications of interest categories as the excursion activity, the play activity, the communication activity, and the like, it does indicate that these categories cannot be filled with activities most interesting to a past generation of children. Moreover, in filling in the actual content of these interest categories, more than lip-service will have to be paid to the influence of subcultural impacts. Food has a different interest for the child who has been hungry most of his life than for the child who has only to make his food preferences known in order to have them satisfied.

2. The Problem of Sequence

After the major categories of the curriculum have been determined, the proper distribution of the activities of each category over the various grades or developmental levels of children must be worked out. The activities, the things children can do within each category, will vary in appeal to children of different ages. Children in the first grade may be interested in building and decorating a playhouse, but in the second and third grades these same children may be more interested in building a façade of Main Street and studying appropriate window displays.

The Nature of the Problem of Sequence

Grade placement is usually associated with the subject curriculum; but it is no less a problem in the activity curriculum, where emphasis is placed upon the role of interest in the educative process. Activities are not empty forms; they embody meanings, values, and skills and require all sorts of instructional materials, including books. Hence the placement of activities requires the most careful consideration of the curriculum worker.

It has been noted that the fundamental ideas involved in grade placement are these: maturation, experiential background, prerequisite learning, interest, usefulness, and difficulty. All of these in one way or another have been used in the determination of learning sequence in the activity curriculum. But the problem in the activity curriculum is different from that in the subject organization, in which the curriculum is conceived as a series of well-defined subjects. In the latter case the problem is to determine the grade level at which a given phase of a subject is most readily learned. The difficulties here have never been satisfactorily overcome, despite long study and centuries of practical experience in the development of the subject organization. When the curriculum is thought of as a series of purposeful activities grouped into major categories, the sequential arrangement of the learning experiences raises many new questions for which there are few satisfactory answers. Moreover, the amount of research and practical experience bearing upon these questions is comparatively small.

Practical Plans for Determining Sequence

In the early development of the activity movement, the problem of sequence was considered of minor importance. In fact, it was believed by many that if the teacher and students were free to plan their own series of activities within their own groups, the problem would not arise. It soon became evident that this plan provided for no satisfactory continuity from year to year. Activities carried on in one year tended to be repeated with only slight modifications in the next—or else they tended to result in lack of continuity of learning from year to year.

As a supplement to this plan, the practice was evolved of passing on an instructional log when the children were assigned to another teacher. But teachers were too busy with the day-to-day requirements of teaching to give much attention to the information contained in the log; furthermore, being a mere account of the preceding year's work, the log gave no positive directions as to what the teachers and children should do. This fact led to efforts to establish some scheme to assure continuity from year to year and at the same time to provide for teacher-pupil freedom to plan the sequence of activities within their own group. As a result, a number of schemes have been developed for the determination of year-to-year sequence in the activity curriculum.

There are two more or less distinct patterns of sequential development, depending upon which principles of grade placement are stressed. The first of these is *a sequential order shaped by stages of mental growth*. The plan leans heavily upon the concept of maturation but also incorporates the criteria of experiential background and immediate utility. Sequence in the Dewey School, for example, was based upon three levels of child growth: (1) from the ages of four to eight, a period in which the children are occupied with doing and talking in their home and school life; (2) from eight to ten, a stage in which the need for improved ways of doing things, as distinct from the mere doing itself, becomes important; stress is put upon skills—reading, writing, arithmetic, and the skills of manipulation; (3) from ten to thirteen, a phase in which emphasis is placed upon investigation, reflection, and generalization.[11]

[11] "The University Elementary School. General Outline of Scheme of Work," University of Chicago, *University Record,* Vol. 3, No. 40 (December 30, 1898). n 254.

A recent development of sequence along the same line, though with less stress upon specific stages of development, is found in the curriculum of The Little Red School House.[12] Formal experiences in reading and number work, for example, are delayed until the child has become adjusted to the school, to the immediate community, and to his schoolmates. Still another variation of this general pattern is illustrated in *The Primary Manual* of the Cincinnati Public Schools.[13] A chart is provided which shows the physical, social, emotional, and mental development of the child in terms of needs. These general aspects of development are translated into phases of development in the various areas of instruction. For example, three stages of development in written expression are given: Stage I—Readiness for Written Expression; Stage II—Co-operative Group Composition; Stage III—Individual Composition. All three of these stages may be recognized even in the first grade, as well as in later grades, but the amount of individual composition tends to be increased as the child becomes more and more mature. Thus in the third grade composition receives more stress than in the first grade.

In the second pattern of development, *sequence is determined by centers of interest.* These centers, as they have been worked out in practice, recognize experiential backgrounds and assume that young children are more interested in things, persons, and events in their immediate neighborhood than in remote aspects of the world. Hence, the general pattern of sequence based upon centers of interest has tended to begin in the early grades with things close to the life of the child and to progress gradually to things more remote in time and space. This plan is illustrated in the California course of study discussed earlier in this chapter.[14]

The application of this plan at the secondary school level has not commanded the sanction it has sometimes enjoyed in the elementary school, even though in the intermediate grades the centers of interest tend to become less and less genuine and more and more what adults

[12] Agnes DeLima, *The Little Red School House.*
[13] Cincinnati Public Schools, *The Primary Manual,* Curriculum Bulletin No. 95, 1942, pp. 3–9.
[14] California State Curriculum Commission, *Teacher's Guide to Child Development: Manual for Kindergarten and Primary Grades.*

think children should be interested in.[15] At the secondary school level this tendency becomes accentuated. Perhaps one reason for this is the specialization and individualization of interest as children grow into adolescence—factors that make it exceedingly difficult, if not impossible, to define centers about which their common interests cluster. A few such centers have been ascertained, as for example: how to accept one's physique as well as one's sex, how to develop new relations with one's peers, how to develop independence from parents and other adults, how to prepare for an occupation and for marriage and family life.[16] These are questions in which adolescent boys and girls have keen interest at one time or another. But these are not comprehensive enough in their application to serve as guides to sequential arrangement of learning experiences in a thorough-going activity curriculum.

Criticisms of Plans for Determining Sequence

Each of these schemes of sequence is subject to criticism from two standpoints: first, the validity of the principle underlying the scheme; second, the practical interpretation of the principle as it is exemplified in the actual pattern of sequence. There is little psychological evidence to support the theory that children go through specific stages of mental growth. One of the most thorough-going forms of this theory was the culture-epoch hypothesis, which held that the mental life of the child would be most easily developed if the curriculum took the child through the cultural phases of man's social history. Whatever may be the fortunes of the theory of biological recapitulation, the notion that the individual in his mental development repeats the cultural history of the human race is now completely repudiated.

Another view of developmental stages—which is of considerable theoretical interest as well as of practical importance—is that advanced by Piaget. On the basis of his study of children between the ages of three and nine, he concludes that children are egocentric in thought until about the age of seven, when egocentrism rapidly diminishes. Piaget means by egocentrism "that the child thinks for himself with-

[15] California State Curriculum Commission, *Teacher's Guide to Child Development in the Intermediate Grades.*
[16] Havighurst, Robert J., *Development Tasks and Education,* pp. 30–63

out troubling to make himself understood nor to place himself at the other person's point of view." [17] In this period the child does not feel the need of proof, his reason is limited to isolated or special events, and there are no general propositions in his thought. He therefore has no powers of induction or deduction.

If this conclusion were confirmed, there would be good reason to suppose that activities involving cause-effect relationships, inductive and deductive reasoning, and, in fact, the whole structure of reflective thinking should be postponed for all children until the intermediate grades. This view of child development, however, is by no means established. Indeed, the work of other psychologists has led to the conclusion that children can think reflectively before the age of seven, provided the things they are asked to think about are relatively simple and within the range of their experiences. According to these studies, children of beginning school age can recognize fallacies in logic, make generalizations, and select from a number of generalizations the one that is applicable to a given situation.[18]

On the basis of the evidence now available, some investigators have been led to conclude that there are no mental stages sufficiently well defined to support an educational program erected on a theory of specific stages of development of thought and reasoning in children. The current opinion is to regard the development of various traits or patterns of behavior as partly the result of maturation and partly the effect of environmental stimulation, and to believe that the age at which these traits and behavior patterns appear is so variable that the truth of generalizations concerning the time of their emergence is dubious.

Studies of the maturation of children do indicate that some concepts, skills, and emotional reactions are acquired more readily when the individual has reached certain points of development. Nevertheless, at the present time the evidence does not permit any final conclusion about the dependability of sequence based upon stages of growth. On the basis of present evidence, it must be said that any such plan is largely arbi-

---

[17] Jean Piaget, *Judgment and Reasoning in the Child* (New York: Harcourt, Brace & Co.; 1928), p. 1.

[18] T. V. Moore, *The Reasoning Ability of Children in the First Years of School Life.* See also J. M. Deutsche, *The Development of Children's Concepts of Causal Relations.*

trary, resting more upon convenience than upon actual facts about child growth and development. A great deal of research on problems of maturation will have to be made for specific activities embodying recognized concepts and skills before any final conclusion can be reached about the ultimate validity of the theory of stages of growth as a basis of establishing sequence in the activity curriculum.

Centers of interest for different age or grade groups, like stages of development, are capable of being tested by facts. By various techniques—such as interest questionnaires, interviews, and observation of the free behavior of children—interests can be ascertained and classified by age groups. For example, one study of children's play reveals the play activities that children of different ages like best.[19] If the assumption could be made that their true interests are expressed by the play activities in which they freely engage, it would be safe to assert that such studies would reveal their real interests.

Educators must consider how children's interests are altered by different environmental conditions. Inasmuch as the activity program itself provides conditions which develop interest, centers of interest in later years depend, at least in part, upon centers of interest in earlier years. Moreover, much complication arises because of the fact that the interests of individuals—even individuals in the same classroom—have been and continue to be molded by markedly different out-of-school experiences. Such considerations temper judgments of the value of these and similar studies which have revealed the interests, vocational interests, and social interests of individuals at different ages from the preschool through the high school.[20]

The evidence accumulated from such studies indicates, for example, that elementary school children tend to engage in active forms of play, whereas in the adolescent years their activities become more sedentary and, on the whole, more social. Studies of the isolated interests of individuals, however, will not reveal centers of interest unless the results

[19] H. C. Lehman and Paul A. Witty, *The Psychology of Play Activities,* pp. 59–80.
[20] P. L. Boynton, "The Wishes of Elementary School Children," *Peabody Journal of Education,* Vol. 13, No. 4, pp. 165–174; P. M. Freeston, "Vocational Interests of Elementary School Children," *Occupational Psychology,* Vol. 13, pp. 223–237; A. I. Gates, et al., "Studies of Children's Interests in Reading," *Elementary School Journal,* Vol. 31, pp. 656–670; B. L. Johnson, "Children's Reading Interests as Related to Sex and Grade in School," *School Review,* Vol. 40, pp. 257–272.

of the studies somehow yield definite classes of interests more or less common to children of particular ages and clustering about some significant aspect of the environment, such as the home, the school, or life in the local community.

It is precisely at this point that studies of interests fail to afford adequate information for the curriculum maker. It is, of course, important for him to know the reading interests of children of different ages, their art interests, and so on. But unless these interests can be grouped about some aspect of the environment—so that the curriculum maker will know, for example, that in the primary grades children will on the whole be interested in certain aspects of their world—knowledge then will afford little guidance in the establishment of sequence within and between grades. Individuals have more common interests at the preschool and primary levels than at the higher levels. As individuals progress through the grades to the high school, their interests become more and more differentiated. At the high school level it is exceedingly difficult to locate common interests except in the realm of personal-social relations. This extreme differentiation of interests is probably due to the fact that the culture as a whole provides few common social directions, thus leaving the individual to develop his own independent interests.

Of the two plans for sequence, that based upon centers of interest is most in keeping with the theory of the activity curriculum and seems to offer the best hope for a satisfactory plan. However, further research is needed on children's interests, as they are developed both within and beyond the school program, before the activity curriculum can be placed upon a more satisfactory foundation with respect to sequence.

3. The Role of Organized Subject Matter

The activity curriculum makes extensive use of conventional subjects as represented in books and other forms of organized subject matter. The successful pursuit of any series of activities under the guidance of the learner's interest requires much reading, calculation, study, and thinking. This means that a wide variety of subject matter is used in the activity curriculum and that the learner will have need of all sorts of reference materials. For example, the development of activities or projects to answer the third-grade question, "Why does it rain?" will call for extensive reading from books representing fields of organized knowledge. Study of this question will call for simple books on geography and climatology, or at least books treating the needed aspects of these subjects. According to the theory underlying the activity curriculum, the books will be studied, however, with a genuine purpose in mind—the purpose being to answer questions arising out of the interests of children in exploring their environment.

It should also be pointed out in this connection that the activity curriculum does not deny a place for subjects in the program of the school. First, these subjects are needed in such areas as mathematics and reading because sufficient skill in these fields cannot be developed in the activities and projects carried on in the nonspecialized activity program. The activity motivates study of the skill subject. In the second place, as individuals progress through the educational program, they reach a point at which they differ from each other in knowledge and interests to such an extent that specialized subjects—or at least problems centering in specialized areas—are called for. Both theory and convenience indicate that this point is reached at about the seventh grade for most children, and that some definite plan to care for the specialized subject matter needs of students should be provided increasingly from the seventh to the twelfth grade. By the last year of high school the larger part of the daily program would consist of specialized courses for a large number of students.

Of course, it is quite likely that many students will develop only a few specialized interests, and perhaps some will acquire none at all during their school career. Such students would remain occupied mostly, if not entirely, in the purposeful activities of the activity curriculum. In other words, the theory of individual growth and development underlying the activity curriculum requires that specialization of the curriculum, into areas of more limited scope with opportunity for more intensive study, should grow and be provided only when need of it arises, rather than being forced upon the child's mind before he has matured sufficiently to be interested in specialized studies.

▶ *Following Up*
This Chapter

1. Which of the criticisms leveled at the activity curriculum seem to you most basic? Justify your selection of these over others.

2. If you, as a member of a faculty, were attempting to plan for an activity program, what sort of planning jobs would you advocate for the faculty group?

3. In this faculty planning, what kind of categories would you advocate for the activity curriculum framework? If you were to select one of the several centers-of-interest categories, which one would you choose? Justify your choice.

4. What plan would you advocate as a solution to the problem of sequence in an activity curriculum? Assume the categories you have developed in (3) above.

5. What would you consider to be a good offering of specialized subjects as a part of an activity curriculum in the intermediate grades? In the high school?

▶ *Suggested*
Reading

1. Excellent descriptions of the early beginnings of the activity curriculum and its basic theory are found in John Dewey's *The School and Society* and in the book by Katherine C. Mayhew and Anna C. Edwards entitled *The Dewey School.* J. L. Meriam's *Child Life and the Curriculum,* W. H. Kilpatrick's *The Project Method,* and Ellsworth Collings' *An Experiment with a Project Curriculum* are also fine in this regard.

2. California's *Teacher's Guide to Child Development: Manual for Kindergarten and Primary Teachers,* and *Teacher's Guide to Child Development in the Intermediate Grades* are courses of study exemplifying the theory of the activity curriculum. These are analyzed and appraised in *The Changing Curriculum,* edited by Henry Harap.

3. Criticisms and defenses of the activity curriculum may be found in "The Activity Movement," *Thirty-third Yearbook,* Part II, of the National Society for the Study of Education.

Chapter 14

The Core Curriculum: Its Chief Characteristics

AS IN THE CASE of the activity curriculum, the meaning of the core curriculum has been confused by a multiplicity of definitions. The true nature of the core curriculum demands clarification. It is the purpose of this chapter to set forth a clear-cut conception of the core curriculum. It should be borne in mind that a perfect exemplification of this conception may not be found anywhere. Yet that fact does not negate the need for clarification at the theoretical level; for only as the core curriculum is clear in theory can the curriculum thus conceived be developed in practice.

Before turning to a discussion of the features of a core curriculum, attention is invited to a consideration of some of the roots of this new pattern of curriculum organization.

1. *Beginnings of the Core Curriculum*

The core curriculum grew from two widely different emphases in educational thought, a fact which accounts in part for the confusion about its theoretical meaning and for variations in its practical patterns. The first of these emphases was reaction against the piecemeal learnings accumulated from separate subjects. The organization of subject matter into a unifying core of studies was believed to be a way of enriching the

311

content with greater meaning by making the interrelations of subject matter more evident. This line of development led to core curriculums based upon the unification of subjects as the core of the educational program.

The second emphasis was a change in the conception of the social role of public education. It became clear that as society became more and more fragmented and divided by the forces released by science and technology, the educational program must emphasize the clarification and maintenance of common values and common social perspectives. Thus a different core curriculum emerged, one which sought to give imperative social needs the central place in the curriculum. From this orientation grew such patterns as the social functions and social problems cores. The widely differing intent of these two core curriculums explains the fact that they have little in common other than name.

Early Core Programs

While certain aspects of the unified-core-of-studies idea of a core curriculum—such as the unification of subjects—are new, its essential principle was anticipated in the Herbartian notion of *concentration*. This notion took the practical form of one or more subjects as the center or core. In a paper read before the National Department of Superintendence in 1896, there is found the following definition of the core curriculum which foreshadows some current conceptions of it.

Complete unification is the blending of all subjects and branches of study into one whole, and the teaching of the same in successive groups or lessons or sections. When this union is effected by making one group or branch of study in the course the center or core, and subordinating all other subjects to it, the process is properly called the concentration of studies.[1]

At that time there were two well-known plans for the development of a curriculum in accordance with this definition, the Ziller Plan and the Parker Plan. Ziller was the founder of the radical school of Herbartians at the University of Leipzig. His scheme made the cultural studies—Biblical and profane history and literature—the center, or

[1] Emerson E. White, "Isolation and Unification as Bases of Courses of Study," *Second Yearbook of the National Herbart Society for the Scientific Study of Teaching* (Bloomington, Illinois: Pantograph Printing and Stationery Co.; 1896), pp. 12–13. Quoted by permission of the National Society for the Study of Education.

core, about which all other subjects were organized. These central studies were developed in a sequence determined by the culture-epoch theory. The subordinate subjects depended for their development upon connections with the central subjects, since they had no independent principle to determine their respective roles in the program. The natural sciences, mathematics, language arts, and fine arts were subordinated to or dissolved into history and literature, and the whole scheme developed in a sequence based upon the theory that the child traverses in his own development the periods through which the race has gone in its evolution. Fairy stories formed the chief material during the first year. In the second year *Robinson Crusoe* became the center. The nucleus of the third year was primitive history, the Bible, and literature. History began with myths, legends, heroic tales, then merged into biography, and finally ended in history proper.[2]

Colonel Francis W. Parker's scheme of concentration employed the natural sciences as the core of the program. The subjects comprising the core were mineralogy, geology, geography, astronomy, meteorology, biology, zoology, anthropology, and history. The unification of these subjects was accomplished through their logical and philosophical relations, their unity being based upon the unity of nature. Not the least significant feature of Colonel Parker's plan was the assimilation of reading, spelling, writing, grammar, and arithmetic to the natural science core so that these subjects, which he considered as form rather than content, would no longer exist in the program as formal and isolated studies.[3]

While the theoretical underpinning of this way of organizing the curriculum has changed from time to time, the general pattern persists. But, as will be noted in the next chapter, this idea of the core curriculum is only a radical modification of the subject curriculum.

Later Core Developments

Core curriculums involving the unification of the subjects are still the most prevalent in practice. In recent years, however, a new concep-

[2] Charles De Garmo, "Most Pressing Problems Concerning the Elementary Course of Study," *First Yearbook of the National Herbart Society for the Scientific Study of Teaching* (Second Edition. Chicago: University of Chicago Press; 1907), pp. 19–20.

[3] *Ibid.,* pp. 20–22.

tion of the core curriculum has emerged from diagnoses of society. In the late 1920's, at the height of the controversy between those advocating the activity curriculum and those promoting the subject curriculum, a conception took shape which visualized the school as an instrument for deliberate social reconstruction and reintegration.

Sociological analyses (such as those reported by the Lynds in *Middletown* and by Albert Blumenthal in *Small Town Stuff*) patterned after studies in cultural anthropology, focused attention upon the common activities of men and how well these activities were performed. These analyses were made at a time when the disintegrative tendencies of society were becoming more and more apparent. The studies re-emphasized the importance of building the curriculum around the persistent social problems that arise in the course of carrying on the common social processes of a society. However, the central role of social values was not clearly perceived in this new conception of a core curriculum; and, as will be seen later, this has continued to be one of its chief defects. The theory of the core curriculum that emerged out of these considerations has certain unique aspects, which distinguish it from the subject curriculum, on the one hand, and the activity curriculum, on the other. One of the first efforts to build a comprehensive educational program on this new conception of the core curriculum was the Virginia State Curriculum program which began in the early 1930's.[4]

2. *Distinctive Characteristics*

Two features of the core curriculum distinguish it from all other forms of curriculum organization.

Emphasis on a Core of Social Values

The core curriculum emphasizes social values. The universal elements of a culture give the society its stability and unity. The core of the universals consists of the basic values or rules by which the people govern, or ought to govern, their activities. By these rules they decide what is good or bad, desirable or undesirable. In a period of profound social

---

[4] State of Virginia, *Course of Study for Virginia Elementary Schools.* See also *Tentative Course of Study for the Core Curriculum of Virginia Secondary Schools.*

change such as that now witnessed in the society of the United States, these values begin to erode, and new ones emerge to compete with the old ones in the control of conduct. In such a period the value system must be reconstructed and reintegrated if the culture is to survive. The values that have been taken for granted for decades or even centuries must then become the objects of study and reconstruction; and they must be deliberately applied, in their reconstructed form, to various spheres of social activity.

The values that make up the stable and vital aspects of the universals constitute the heart of the core curriculum. In short, the core of the curriculum consists in large part of the socio-moral rules comprising the core of the culture. In the society of the United States, these rules are chiefly those that constitute the democratic value system. The core curriculum, therefore, places considerable emphasis upon the deliberate study of the moral content of the culture—especially as this content bears upon the resolution of the social issues that divide the people and thereby prevent effective social action.

A social problem, or issue, involves factual content, descriptive principles, and socio-moral rules or values. It is customary to think of social problems as being capable of solution by means of facts and descriptive principles without explicit reference to the values involved. The core curriculum rejects this view and instead makes the value content of a social problem, along with facts and descriptive principles, the object of study. When it is recognized that conflicts over values are as prevalent as differences of opinion about facts and descriptive principles, and perhaps far more serious, it becomes no longer possible to ignore the moral content of the culture in the educational program. It is the chief characteristic of the core curriculum, as a pure type, that the democratic value system is not only taught as the standard of judgment but that it is also deliberately criticized and reconstructed so as to bring it into line with the social realities of today.

The aims of a subject curriculum are conceived in terms of understandings or skills achieved in the study of organized fields of knowledge. The need for these understandings and skills is justified partly on the basis of their value to individuals as specialists. For instance, if a man knows mathematics, he will be able to study physics; then, if he wishes, he can learn mechanical engineering. If anyone should ask what all this means for social progress, he would likely be told that society needs mathematicians, physical scientists, and engineers. As markedly different as the subject and activity curriculums are in many respects, the activity curriculum also tends to state its aims and justify its learnings in terms of what is done for individuals. Thus, a child who is practiced in the solution of his own problems is more likely to be competent to solve the many problems he will face as a youth and as an adult. If anyone asked what this means in terms of a better society, he would be told that society needs people competent to solve their problems—or that a society characterized by persons able to solve problems would not find itself beset by so many social ills.

That a society needs people of many and diverse competencies no one would deny. It needs mathematicians, physical scientists, and engineers. It needs people trained to solve their problems. However, those individuals who favor a core curriculum point out that the satisfaction of these societal needs is not sufficient. In addition, there are broad social problems involving an entire community, a region, a nation, or even the peoples of the world. These are problems that do not grow out of individual needs and cannot be solved by individualized thinking. In neither the activity nor subject curriculum do the proponents of a core curriculum find the development and training of individuals who can understand and deal with these problems involving groups of men. They point to scientists unparalleled in their ability within a field of specialized knowledge who do not see or care about the consequences of their discoveries on the lives of men. They also see men exceptionally able to solve problems relating to their interests or to the interests of the group to which they belong but either uninterested in, or incompetent to deal with, the larger social problems related to the prevention of such social maladies as crime, poverty, depressions, and wars.

In the interdependent society of today, what the individual can do—what he can have and enjoy—depends upon the resolution of broad social issues in which the destiny of all individuals is involved. Even if it were possible to create for him through education a healthy personality, desirable in all respects, he could not long endure without a healthy society to sustain him. In its pure form the core curriculum, therefore, emphasizes a social-centered education. The theory of the core curriculum holds that it is not enough to help boys and girls, young men and women, to understand the conventional subjects; it is not enough that they follow their interests and solve their own problems, however important these may be; it is not enough to help them understand social trends and think about social problems, no matter how thoroughly and critically these things may be done. In addition, youth must be encouraged to project their thinking into the future, to conceive the kind of social ends and relationships it is possible to build within the bounds of basic social trends, and to think constructively and co-operatively in the projection of social goals for these times. Then they must master the social techniques and strategies, consistent with a democratic value system, required for the realization of these goals.

In short, the core curriculum is deliberately and consistently normative in its orientation. All aspects of the common core of educational experience are oriented to the realization of a healthy society, democratically conceived. While no reasonable claim can be made that either a subject or an activity curriculum is oblivious of social needs, it is true that the core program is unique in its insistence that the major goals of education be those reflecting the major needs of the social system.

Structure Fixed by Social Problems

The second distinctive feature of the core curriculum is that *the structure of the core curriculum is fixed by broad social problems or by themes of social living.* Just as the structure of the subject curriculum is shaped by the requirements of explanation and research, and that of the activity curriculum by the interests of children, so the structure of the core curriculum is determined by the way in which social issues are grouped. The core curriculum in its pure form is a refinement and simplification of the basic elements of the culture that all members of the society share. These elements consist of normative rules, descriptive principles, facts, and, in addition, methods of thinking, points of view, and so on.

In the core curriculum these elements are organized into neither subject nor interest categories. Instead, they are organized into social categories based upon the major areas of social activities. In some instances these social categories are conceived in terms of social processes—such as "The protection and conservation of life, property, and natural re-

sources"—in which all members of society are involved. In other instances they are formulated in terms of the "needs" of individuals for
social adjustment in a variety of circumstances, such as those arising in
the areas of personal living, face-to-face relationships, social-civic relationships, and economic relationships.

Descriptions of the core curriculum have often leaned heavily upon
the idea that this program is not definable in terms of conventional
subject-matter boundaries. The truth of this is undeniable. In the core
curriculum, subject matter is employed in defining and solving problems. Study of problems concerned, for example, with conservation of
natural resources cuts at will across even the broad-fields of science,
social studies, mathematics, and the communicative skills. Yet it is
obvious that something new cannot be described with any exactitude by
telling what it is not. The distinctive element is not that a core program
does away with subject boundaries but that it replaces the subject organization with one in which the primary emphasis is upon social living.

It has apparently been easier to visualize the role of subject matter
in the core program than to see the part played by the concerns of students. No one would deny the importance of these concerns in any
curriculum organization. If this be so, how can a core program lend
itself to the interests and needs of children and yet be something different from an activity curriculum? In the core curriculum children's interests are given real consideration; but they do not provide the primary basis for the selection and organization of curriculum content, as
is the case in an activity curriculum. In other words, those who advocate
a core curriculum make the fundamental assumption that the latitude
of a broad area of social living provides ample opportunity for both the
play of children's interests and the satisfaction of their needs. The dic-
tates of teaching method would require that children have a large part
in the location, definition, and selection of problems within an area of
social living as well as in solving the problems. Thus the core curriculum is not an organization that depends upon the interests of children
as its most fundamental organizing principle, although it uses these
interests as a dynamic factor in the educative process.

The social direction of the core curriculum can be lost easily at the
point where the children are having a large role in the location, selection, and planning of specific problems. If their attitudes and beliefs
are not subjected to critical thought during the planning sessions, the

selection and treatment of the problem will be guided more by unexamined prejudices than by any deliberately chosen set of social ideals. It would be an error to minimize the cruciality of this point in the development of a core curriculum. On the one hand, children must have a large share in the location, selection, and planning of the problems they are to study. If they do not, there is danger that the problem will be merely an assigned one. Moreover, the students will miss the valuable training gained through practice in defining and structuring problems for study.

On the other hand, it is extremely difficult for children from homes of diverse social and occupational strata to take the conflicting notions of social right and wrong gathered from the movies, streets, comic books, homes, and churches, and to mold these into some sort of a consistent pattern. If the children do have a real part in shaping what and how they shall study and do not have a common value orientation, or have no opportunity to consider their values, the result is apt to be confusion, conflict, and indecision, pulling the child first this way and then that and developing bases for mental conflict leading to personality maladjustment. The only satisfactory answer to this dilemma is able teacher leadership with constant concern for the critical examination of the values underlying child thought. Normative judgments of *what should be done* are crucial parts of group deliberation in a core curriculum.

3. *Essential Characteristics*

Each pure-type curriculum is set apart from others by a few distinctive characteristics. Those of the core curriculum have been indicated in the preceding section. In addition to these characteristics, there are other features just as essential to the type, but not restricted to it. The core curriculum has four essential features.

Common Learnings

The core areas are required of all students. The core curriculum consists of common learnings. These learnings are believed to be essential for all members of the society, regardless of ability, social status, or vocational plans. Thus the idea that the brilliant, the dull, the maladjusted, or the otherwise exceptional individuals should not take part in the core program is due to a misinterpretation of this curriculum. It is designed to provide all youth with a common social orientation and to foster social reintegration. Those who are so atypical that they must be segregated because they cannot profit from the usual instruction will still be instructed in the core areas within the limits allowed by their extreme variations of ability. The core curriculum provides instruction in communal living, and neither the normal nor atypical individual should be exempt from its requirements.

Co-operative Planning of Activities

A second essential characteristic of the core curriculum is that *activities are co-operatively planned by teacher and pupils*. While the theory of the core curriculum holds that all individuals enter the core areas and learn to share a common regard for matters of social welfare, it insists with equal vigor that the unique value of the individual be recognized and honored in the pursuit of common problems and common goals. For this reason the core curriculum makes provisions for teacher-pupil planning. The idea that children should have a large share in the location, selection, and definition of problems to be studied, as well as in planning the activities by which the problems may be solved, has long been accepted as a sound principle of teaching. Only by such participation do children become proficient in all phases of problem solving. Also, it is only in this way that children accept the problems as their own responsibilities.

When the teacher locates the problems, selects one for study, defines it, plans how it is to be studied, assigns tasks, and then evaluates the learning, it is not strange that the teacher rather than the children has valuable learning experiences. The theory of the core curriculum recognizes the principle of personal involvement as an essential element of effective teaching. Not only does it recognize the twin principles of personal involvement and shared participation but it also recognizes that teacher-pupil planning is required by the value system to which the core curriculum is committed.

The role of the teacher in the teacher-pupil planning of the core curriculum involves more than membership in the planning group. The teacher's role is a combination of the best conceptions of group leader and bearer of expert knowledge. As a group leader the teacher assists the group in every possible manner to reach their goals. As a bearer of expert knowledge and the moral authority of the larger society, the teacher insists upon clarification of goal-seeking and value-orientation by processes of critical thought and by reference to the imperatives of a democratic society.

No claim can be seriously made that teacher-pupil planning in the core curriculum enjoys the same latitude as that in an activity program. The core curriculum tends to restrict planning to certain learnings and abilities in social areas. Thus, while there is considerable latitude for teacher-pupil planning within an area, and although there are no restrictions in terms of subject matter, there are limits beyond which such planning in the core program cannot go and at the same time remain true to its basic principle of organization. However, within the wide boundaries of core areas, the method of problem solving, considerations of sound educational method, and the democratic value system combine to make co-operative teacher-pupil planning an essential feature of the core curriculum.

Provision for Special Needs

The third essential characteristic is that *provisions for special needs and interests are made as these arise.* The core curriculum is a more flexible organization than the subject curriculum. It is, therefore, more responsive to the interest of individuals. By the same token, the structure of the core curriculum is not based primarily upon the interests of individuals, as is the activity curriculum, and thus needs more special arrangements to care for these interests.

Even in the first grade there will be need for some specialization. Perhaps some children will want to learn to play musical instruments; others may want to express themselves in art mediums in ways that cannot be readily admitted in the core areas. The study of radio in the later grades of the core program, for example, may not adequately meet the needs of the boy who wants to have his own transmitting and receiving apparatus and to become a licensed "ham" operator. Each area of the core program is fraught with possibilities for the stimulation of specialized interests, but provision for further development of these specialties is to be found, for the most part, in courses outside the core program.

A careful distinction must be drawn between courses that provide for specialties outside the core areas and the elective subjects of a subject curriculum. The purpose of the core electives is to permit study of individual problems or the pursuance of interests to an extent not practicable within the core program. In these electives, subject matter is a means to the solution of problems rather than an end in itself, and problem solving, rather than the mere study of expository materials, is the primary method of learning. In the core electives, the subject matter of physics will be employed, for example, in the solution of problems about radio and electric power. In the subject curriculum, on the other hand, the elective subjects are studied as ready-made bodies of content to be learned and applied in practical situations. In physics, radio and electric power will be studied to illustrate and to clarify concepts of physics.

The core curriculum includes electives, too, for the individuals who need remedial instruction in such skills as those required in reading and arithmetical processes. Some of these skills can be developed in the activities of the core program, but deficiencies will often need to be remedied by special treatment which cannot be given in core areas. In like manner, personal counseling and guidance can be provided for partly by the core program and partly by special arrangements. Many problems belonging to the sphere of counseling and guidance will come up for study in the core areas; in addition, the staff will take every opportunity to counsel with students. When problems requiring technical knowledge and skill arise, the instructional staff will refer these to individuals who are properly trained to handle them.

Some conceptions of the core curriculum make guidance a central feature of it. As society has become more complex and youth more divorced from the activities of adults, problems of adjustment have become more difficult for the adolescent. For this reason, many schools have sought to work out ways of helping the student to deal with his personal problems. The flexibility of the core curriculum has made it readily adaptable to this purpose. Hence in many schools both group and individual guidance is carried on through the core curriculum. It should not be supposed, however, that because guidance is included in the core curriculum it is a distinctive characteristic of the curriculum. For guidance can be handled in a comparable way in both the subject and the activity curriculums.

The core curriculum does not include a number of activities commonly found in the school. Periodic health examinations, fire drills, assembly programs, student government, and social games are examples of such activities. It is likely that the core program will include study of the social significance of these activities, and development of the skills needed in them. However, personal and public health and hygiene are certain to be studied in the core areas, and it would be a waste of educational opportunity not to use the periodic health examinations as part of this study. Yet it would also be a waste of time to include the data of these examinations regularly in the core areas and thus to interrupt other activities in order to restudy this aspect of social life on the occasion of every health examination.

In the first grade the core areas consume most of the instructional time, while special interests are few and require little time. The number of special interests increases, however, as the individual progresses in the educational program. Consequently, in the high school more than half of the instructional time may be spent in the specialties, while the time devoted to the core areas will be reduced in proportion. Thus the core curriculum, like the activity curriculum and the subject curriculum, provides for alternative specialties as the child progresses in school. This is an essential characteristic of the core curriculum, but it does not distinguish this curriculum from either the subject or the activity organization.

Skills Taught When Needed

The fourth of the essential characteristics of the core curriculum is that *skills are taught as they are needed.* According to the theory of the core curriculum, learning to read, write, spell, use arithmetic, work with others, think effectively, or perform adequately a host of other skills should be motivated by a feeling of need on the part of the individual. Reading, for example, would begin when children want to read or when they see that they must learn to read in order to do the things they wish to do. This generalization with respect to the teaching of skills applies equally to all grade levels. A child would not learn to spell *osmosis,* to read railroad timetables, to use a dictionary, or to compute the area of a rectangle, until the problems with which he is concerned call for the use of these skills. The core program, however, provides the problems and experiences that create the need for various skills. Motivated by this demonstrated need, time would be allocated for the individual to pursue these skills both in the core program and in special periods set aside for that purpose. While the skills will be developed, for the most part, in special classes, their significance and utilization are found in the core areas of the curriculum.

4. Personnel, Physical Features, and Administrative Arrangements Required for Optimum Operation

The characteristics of a core curriculum have been described. The task of the remainder of this chapter is to indicate some of the more important requirements for effective operation of this curriculum.

Training of Teachers

Teachers should have a broad general education and specialized training in the social foundations of education, child and adolescent psychology, the structure and dynamics of social groups, guidance, and problem-methods of teaching. The wide range of problems that must be treated in the core curriculum makes a broad general education indispensable. Yet a general education which is limited to factual information and descriptive principles, such as physical and chemical laws and social generalizations, will not prepare the teacher for the tasks encountered in a core curriculum. This becomes clear when it is recognized that most of the social issues embraced by the core curriculum involve deep-lying cleavages about moral beliefs. These beliefs are fundamental elements of the personal structures of individuals involved in a social issue. The resolution of such an issue, therefore, requires that their personalities be partly reconstructed. The function of the teacher in a core program—since the heart of this program consists of social issues—is to facilitate this process of personal reconstruction. In order to do this the teacher must, of course, have adequate factual information and a thorough knowledge of laws and generalizations. These competencies, however, are not sufficient. In addition, he must be thoroughly disciplined in the socio-moral content of the culture; he must be familiar with the perspectives and strategies of the major social groups; and he must be thoroughly disciplined in methods of thinking appropriate to such socio-moral problems as those that characterize politics, economics, and education.

As the social system becomes more and more interdependent and individuals are consequently thrown together into all sorts of interpersonal and group relationships, it becomes necessary that individuals master the skills of human relations. Unless the teacher has had the opportunity to acquire these skills and to intellectualize them to the point that they have become part of his general store of information, there is little likelihood that he will have mastered them and still less likelihood that he will be able to help others acquire them. It is necessary that a thorough knowledge and mastery of these skills become a part of the equipment of every teacher. Moreover, the teacher must understand children and possess the human relations skills essential to the development of a classroom atmosphere wherein the child feels emotionally secure.

The teacher should also be trained in a specialized field of knowledge. The specialized electives will require that some teachers have specialized training in at least one field. Furthermore, the problems which arise in the core areas frequently require special competencies not ordinarily acquired in a program of general education. It should be noted that teachers who work in the core program are frequently called upon, especially in the smaller schools, to teach in the specialties in addition to their duties in the core program.

Physical Features of the School

As a second requirement for optimum operation, *buildings, grounds, and classrooms should be large and flexible enough to permit pursuance of a wide latitude of group activities.* Buildings and classrooms to house a core curriculum would follow the general pattern of those required for an activity curriculum. In both the activity and the core curriculums, breadth and diversity of activities is the rule. The rooms must lend themselves to whatever problem is studied. Furniture should be strong, light, and easily movable. There should be few built-in features, since these tend to limit the flexibility of a room.

A single blackboard across one end of the room is probably ample. A large workbench and a sink-type lavatory are almost essential. Floor space must be much more ample than in the conventional classroom, for the core curriculum requires workrooms or laboratories for problem solving, and the size and arrangements of these rooms must broaden rather than restrict the possibilities for learning.

The same general principles apply to the building as a whole. It, too, must encourage the varied program envisioned by the core curriculum. Corridors should be large and well lighted and should provide ample space to be decorated by student groups or to display student work and other objects of general interest. General purpose rooms should be centrally located and otherwise easily accessible. It should be possible to pass outdoors from every room with a minimum of disturbance to the work of other rooms, for the core program uses the classroom only as central headquarters and workshop.

The grounds of the school should also be large enough to lend themselves to the varied requirements of a core curriculum. In addition to the usual play area and foundation planting, there should be space for flower, vegetable, and rock gardens and a well-planned area for parking bicycles. When youth is given a part in such planning and improvement, the school building, rooms, and grounds become valuable instructional materials as well as places to work and play.

Equipment and Materials

The third requirement for operating a core curriculum is that *equipment and materials be adequate for and in keeping with the probable scope of the group projects*. The only general rule that should govern the purchase of equipment and materials for a core curriculum is one of functional utility. The core program needs those supplies required by the problems arising within the framework of areas set out by the core curriculum. The demands of the core program in this respect are nearly as diversified as are those of an activity organization. In both programs pupils' purposes play a large part in the determination of the immediate problems for study.

Since problem solving is the dominant method, there will be little occasion for textbooks in the sense of a copy of the same book for each child. Several copies of the most valuable reference books may be required in order that several children can use them for different purposes at the same time. Problem solving places a heavy burden upon the room and school libraries. These must be stocked with books covering a wide variety of topics and useful at various grade levels. Many school systems have avoided the expense of an extensive library in each school through the creation of a centrally located curriculum library, where materials for use in each major area of the core program are collected for distribution as requested. This same arrangement facilitates the handling of visual aids, professional literature for teachers, and infrequently used tools and materials of instruction.

The equipment required for problem solving is also more extensive and diversified than that necessary for learning in the conventional subjects. In problem solving, the nature of the problem determines the materials needed for its solution. Many of these, such as "How to make the local community a more beautiful place in which to live," are problems for which some of the data must be collected from numerous sources before they can be studied. Thus the supplies and the equipment of a core program are as diversified as the requirements of its problems; and these, in turn, are limited only by the bounds of the major concerns of men.

With problem solving as the dominant method in the specialized areas, the equipment and materials needed in the specialized courses will also be diverse. The rooms adapted to these purposes will take on the form of well-equipped laboratories for solving problems in specialized areas. For example, art work would find a good place in the core program, while individual explorations and development of competencies in the field of art would be achieved in the specialized courses. The room equipped for this purpose would need not only the usual clay, paints, easels and all that the art teacher might use as the materials of instruction, but would also have balsam wood, airplane "dope," and other materials with which a child could design and build model airplanes and other objects of his desire.

General Purpose or Activity Rooms

As a fourth requirement of a core program, *the building should have several general purpose or activity rooms.* It is patent that any structure, whether it be a home, office building, store, or school, should be planned in terms of the activities to be carried on there. The building housing a core curriculum needs three types of classrooms. In addition to the previously mentioned core program and specialized classrooms, several activity rooms are needed. These would be useful as places to work on large construction projects, as storage space for bulky materials, and as additional space for jobs too big, noisy, or messy for the classroom.

In an elementary school, where there is little need for many specialized classrooms, these general purpose rooms would house the band saw, lathe, looms, kiln, and other large or expensive equipment which is needed for the entire school but which it would be an extravagant expenditure, as well as a waste of valuable space, to provide for each classroom. The workbench in such a room would be larger, heavier, and better equipped than those in each classroom. Tools for craft work and those required for the encouragement and development of hobbies might also be housed here.

In the secondary school much of the specialized equipment may find a better place in the laboratories or shops equipped to carry on these specialties. However, if these major items are going to be in almost constant use in the specialized room, as easels would be in an art room or as a lathe would be in a wood shop, they should be supplied also in an activity room for use in the core curriculum. Even if these large items can be used as needed in the specialized rooms, several general purpose rooms are still required for additional floor and work space during construction phases of problem solving. The core program needs space to expand when the activities outgrow the classroom. It is also true that much of the equipment required by the core program can be shared by housing it in rooms used in common. A well-equipped curriculum laboratory for an entire school system saves storage space and unnecessary duplication of equipment, but it is no substitute for the increased working facilities provided by several activity rooms.

Transportation Facilities

Requirement number five is that *ample transportation facilities be available*. It is just as true in a core curriculum as it is in an activity program that problem solving will lead the group beyond the school building and into the neighborhood and community. The data and basic learnings for the solution of social problems will require many trips to different parts of a community and to surrounding areas.

Since it is impossible for students to plan a trip for any definite purposes before the analysis of the problem has progressed to the point where they see the need of going, it will be almost as difficult to schedule the use of buses in advance as it is in an activity curriculum. Needless to say, these trips will be planned as far in advance as foresight will allow.

Large and Flexible Time Blocks

As a sixth requirement for optimum operation of a core curriculum, *time blocks must be large and flexible*. Current descriptions of core programs make much of the double- or triple-length periods generally employed to facilitate instruction. This feature is often listed as a distinctive characteristic of the core curriculum. A moment's reflection will indicate that any type of curriculum organization can alter the allotment and distribution of instructional time to its own ends. In fact, it has long been a rather common practice in the subject curriculum of elementary schools to have short periods for spelling and longer, even double-length, periods for shop courses, where much time is needed to get ready for work and to clean up at the close of the period. Thus, the extra-long periods of the core curriculum are not peculiar to this type of curriculum, although they constitute a desirable condition for its proper operation.

Pupil planning and the other varied activities of the core areas require long unbroken time intervals for optimum progress. Such planning and activities would scarcely get started before the usual fifty-minute periods were over. On the other hand, the varied nature of the activities protects the child from long periods of work on tedious or minute tasks. When he reaches a point of diminishing returns on this type of job during any one period, he can shift to other activities.

It cannot be overemphasized that long periods in themselves are no indication of the actual type of curriculum organization. The practice of setting aside a large unbroken block of time for the required-learnings program is becoming a common innovation. In some of these programs the only real change is the absence of bells. The teachers continue to teach the conventional subjects in this longer period. The curriculum retains all the unique and most of the essential features of a subject organization, and lacks all the distinctive and most of the essential features of a core program. The length of period is a very poor indication of the type of curriculum organization in operation.

Flexible Grouping of Children

The seventh requirement of a core program is that *grouping of children by age or grade be flexible*. In many schools where the instructional program is organized according to the basic pattern of a core program, children are grouped for instructional purposes by age rather than by achievement. In other words, continuous or automatic promotion is likely to be the rule in core organizations.

However, the theory underlying the core curriculum is not at all clear upon this point. There is an apparent conflict between the required nature of the common learnings and the provision for flexibility. The core program requires that all youth enter the core areas. The presumption is that there are certain learnings all should have—certain abilities, understandings, attitudes, and skills required by all citizens. Now, if this is true, it would seem that the child who did not have the experiences essential to the acquisition of these learnings (because of illness, mental retardation, emotional instability, or some other reason) would remain at an appropriate level in the core program until these minimum learnings could be assured. On the other hand, advocates of the core curriculum are insistent that the child be adjusted to his group in terms of age, physical and social maturity, and the like. Moreover, great care is taken to provide for individual differences in the course of problem solving. Under such a plan it would seem that a child would move along with the group most compatible to him.

The glib answer to this dilemma is that the child who has missed many of the essential experiences of the core program will be happier and better adjusted if he moves along to the next level with children of his own age. While this may be true in certain cases, it obviously is not true in others. This is a problem that each type of curriculum faces sooner or later. As in the case of so many other problems of curriculum development, the findings of research are still too fragmentary for a solution. In the present state of knowledge, perhaps the most adequate general principle applicable to grouping in the core curriculum is that of flexibility. By this principle, each child would progress through the program in the group with which he could best work. Then, if it were necessary to shift him to another group, the school, in consultation with parents and child, would make the shift.

Flexibility in Administrative Arrangements

Another condition of effective operation of a core curriculum is that *all administrative arrangements be as flexible as possible.* Perhaps one reason for the entrenchment of a subject organization is its relative ease of administration as compared with that of either the activity or the core curriculum. When teachers determine precisely what will be taught and when and how the teaching will take place, problems of budgeting and scheduling can be planned in considerable detail well in advance. However, when children have a major share in the location, selection, and sequence of problems for study, the administrator is forced to make budgetary estimates on the basis of past experience rather than actual data.

Budgeting of instructional costs is not as difficult an administrative task in a core program as it is in the activity program, but the same problems are still troublesome. It is some advantage to know in which areas and with what emphases children will be working in each grade. Equipment and materials of general worth in these areas can then be ordered in advance with fair assurance that they will be needed and used. However, beyond these generally useful supplies, the problems and plans of groups will determine in large measure the materials required. For these unforeseen needs a liberal budget must be allowed.

The administrator's time must also be flexible. He will need to have time to order materials as the need for them arises, to arrange for transportation and clearance for trips as these become necessary, to carry on the public relations program essential to an ever-changing group of instructional experiences—and still have time left for the countless other duties of administering a flexible program.

At first glance it might seem that the provision of a large block of time for the core program would lessen scheduling difficulties. While this is true in the sense that there are fewer time blocks to schedule, difficulties are multiplied many times in scheduling specialized courses and all-school activities around these larger time units. The work of core program groups is likely to be seriously hampered by an assembly program or by the practice of drawing students from the core program groups for one reason or another. The activities of a core program are planned without reference to these interruptions, and the success of these activities often depends heavily upon the participation of particular students at particular times.

To add to these problems, each class in a core program will be engaged in different activities, and it is difficult to determine when the building, transportation, or equipment needs of two or more groups will conflict. Some sort of continuous scheduling of the use of these shared facilities must be accomplished. Again, there will be times when field trips or other needs of the core program will require the entire school day. These and countless other arrangements are demanded by the problem-solving nature of the work in a core curriculum. Nearly all these arrangements require a flexibility of administration that is difficult to achieve; yet such flexibility is essential to the optimum operation of the program.

Public Relations Program

As a further requirement of a core curriculum, *the public relations program of the school must be continuous and effective.* As long as both content and teaching method remain relatively stable for a number of years, public relations with respect to the instructional program are likely to present no major problems. Each subject has its well-established precedent. Parents and members of the community in general have had the same kind of experience in the public schools and have usually come to accept the conventional subjects and methods as the established public school program.

However, when a new organization and new methods are established to replace the ones the members of the community have known so well, the school is faced with a task of adult public re-education. Parents and the lay public have difficulty understanding the values or advantages of pupil participation in the setting of goals, or of problem solving, over an exacting expository presentation of subject matter. Furthermore, unless curriculum building has involved all the teaching staff to a point of thorough understanding and acceptance of the change, the lack of understanding on the part of the public is likely to become active opposition under the leadership of teachers who regard the new program as of doubtful value. Thus both the teaching staff and the public must see the value of the core curriculum.

The basic theory of the core curriculum, emphasizing as it does the primary worth of the individual, requires that those who are being educated have a share in shaping the general nature of the educational program through which they must go. Moreover, the students have been conditioned by past experience to expect certain things of the school. If these expectations are not fulfilled, the students may become insecure and in time militantly opposed to any changes associated with their bewilderment. These two facts mean that where a core curriculum is introduced, the students should take part in a thorough study of the school and its role in modern society and of the nature of the changes to be made in the conventional program. Such study will, of course, be conditioned by the maturity of the students; but, regardless of the grade level, there is little excuse for making fundamental changes in the educational program without student participation.

There are yet other reasons why public relations are especially vital in a core organization. It was mentioned earlier that the core curriculum must have deliberate social direction. Since the core program is primarily concerned with social learnings, and since most of the experiences of this program are concerned with real social problems, study of these problems is certain to result in a definite and rational stand concerning many controversial social issues. These issues are close to the most basic concerns of powerful groups of people. It is partly for this reason that the areas containing them were chosen as essential for study. But this is also a reason why all community groups ought to understand thoroughly that the school *should* study such questions. For the same reason, the need for thorough understanding of the methods to be used in such study should be made clear to the public. Nor should there be any question in the public mind concerning the value system to be used by a class in their attempt to understand and resolve these social issues for themselves.

Still another aspect of the public relations problem is the ever-changing nature of the core program. If the same problems were studied in the fourth grade each year, the community would come to know and accept this program; for while it is true that different groups of parents are immediately concerned each year, general community understanding and acceptance would grow over a period of years. In the core program, the areas of study and the emphases within them may remain relatively constant, but the actual problems are more likely than not to change from year to year. Thus the community must not only understand and approve the general organization and methods but must also see value in the problems under study at any one time. Under these conditions there is no acceptable alternative to a continuous and effective public relations program.

The School as a Community Center

In an effectively operating core program, *the school is a community center*. Instruction centered in the common concerns of people can be very realistic if both the school program and the school building and grounds are an integral part of the vital activities of the community. Not only must the core program develop in close harmony with diverse community groups, but also these groups will want to use and continue the investigations undertaken by the students. In a core program the concerns of the school are the same as those of adult members of the community. What is more natural under these conditions than for the school to provide the facilities for students and adults to study these problems together? Moreover—when a school is freed from the idea that work is by definition unpleasant, and when having fun is considered a worth-while expenditure of time—both adults and students will want to use the school for a hobby center, a place to talk with their neighbors, and a location for games and dancing, as well as for its more serious use as a place to work on social problems.

▶ *Following Up*
This Chapter

1. If you were to advocate change from a subject to a core organization, what would be the major points you would develop to indicate superiority of core theory?

2. What would you consider to be the one or two most outstanding weaknesses of core theory? Are these weaknesses shared by the principles of an activity curriculum? Are they shared by the theory of a subject organization?

3. Select a recent course of study from your library and try to indicate the points at which it is true to core principles and the points of departure from core theory.

4. Compare and contrast the role of student interests in the subject, activity, and core curriculum theories. What do you think should be the role of student interests in curriculum planning?

5. The core curriculum is sometimes criticized on the grounds that children have no business trying to solve the knotty social problems which have defied adult attempts. In what sense is this criticism justified? Can you defend the core curriculum against such a charge?

6. Compare and contrast several definitions of the core curriculum found in recent books concerned with the secondary school curriculum.

▶ *Suggested*
Reading

1. Justification for a curriculum centered about social problems is ably presented in Harold Rugg's *Culture and Education in America* and in George Counts' *The Social Foundations of Education*.

2. An earlier statement of the meaning of the core curriculum is found in L. T. Hopkins' *Integration: Its Meaning and Application*. More recent attempts to define the core curriculum are to be found in J. Paul Leonard's *Developing the Secondary School Curriculum* (Revised Edition); Harold Alberty's *Reorganizing the High School Curriculum* (Revised Edition); *Curriculum Planning*, by J. Galen Saylor and William M. Alexander; and *Developing the Core Curriculum*, by Roland Faunce and Nelson Bossing.

Chapter 15

The Core Curriculum:
Problems, Practices,
and Criticisms

AS IN THE ACTIVITY CURRICULUM, the primary problems in the development of a core curriculum are the determination of appropriate categories to take the place of the conventional subjects and the development of an adequate sequence of potential experiences.

1. *Subject-Centered Categories and Core Theory*

The theory of the core curriculum, like theories in general, does not work perfectly in practice. Any theory, whether in the physical, biological, or social sciences, presupposes ideal conditions which can never be completely realized in practice. Hence, experimental results must always be stated in terms of a margin of error. For this reason, also, practical social plans, such as a curriculum program, can at best only approximate the conditions laid down in their underlying theory. They never look as good in practice as they do on paper.

While none of the plans discussed in this chapter conforms precisely to the theory of the core curriculum, some approximate it. Several of the schemes are related more to the theory of the subject curriculum, or to that of the activity curriculum, than to principles of the core curriculum. But it is helpful in the clarification of the meaning of a core curriculum to review these practical schemes, even though, when critically examined, they may not be core curriculums at all. Accordingly, the subject-centered core programs—some of which were discussed earlier as variations of the subject curriculum—will be treated here only to indicate similarities and differences between these programs and those in closer harmony with the basic theory of the core curriculum.

The Broad-Fields as the Core Areas

In the early development of core curriculums the tendency was to think in terms of a body of facts and knowledge that all individuals should acquire. This body of information was referred to as the "core curriculum." This conception gave rise to the adoption of a number of well-known curriculum practices as illustrations of the core curriculum. Among these was the utilization of broad-fields as the categories constituting the core. When this was done, the core had no special significance, for it was simply an application of the old pattern of constants and variables to the broad-fields type of subject organization—comprehensive subjects being the constants, and specialized courses being the variables. Since the practice of labeling broad-fields courses as core programs has almost disappeared from current educational literature and is now found infrequently in school situations, these courses will be given no further attention here.

Unified Courses as the Primary Categories

About fifty years separate the core curriculum from the programs of Ziller and Parker.[1] Yet these programs have much in common with the curriculum organization referred to as "unified courses." Under this

[1] Charles De Garmo, "Most Pressing Problems Concerning the Elementary Course of Study," *First Yearbook of the National Herbart Society for the Scientific Study of Teaching,* pp. 19–20.

plan the content of certain subject fields such as English and social studies or English and science is fused so as to constitute a new course referred to as the "core program." In one school, for example, an integration of social studies and English in the ninth grade, of biology and English in the tenth grade, and of social problems and English in the eleventh grade is called the "core program." In this program there are no resultant changes in other parts of the curriculum such as the courses in mathematics, art, music, physics, chemistry, and home economics.

The scope of the new program is that of the combined and reorganized separate courses. These unified courses consume from two to three hours of the school day, depending upon the amount of content involved in the unification and upon the grade level at which they are taught. A unified course usually includes a greater variety of content and activities than is ordinarily found in separate English and social studies or science courses. The separate subjects commonly chosen for unification are those required for all students in a particular grade. If literature is the major content of a required English course during the same year that history is required, these two courses will likely be unified without violating the chronological sequence of the history course. The literature of the historical period will be used to enlarge the scope of the unified course and to enrich the study of the history; and the history, in turn, will enrich the literary study.

In another practice, certain aspects of the social studies are unified with a portion of science. In such a course, a unit dealing with "Community Public Health" would include concepts from biological science as well as from the social sciences. It might draw its goals and pattern of sequence from either field, depending upon the emphasis in the unified course. Moreover, the goals and content might change from unit to unit. One unit might be especially designed to achieve the aims of science, while another might emphasize the goals and principles of the social studies. A study of water supply might be designed primarily to teach certain knowledge from biology, geology, and chemistry, while a study of housing might be developed with learnings from sociology and political science foremost in mind. The goals, principles of developmental sequence, and methods of instruction would thus change with the nature of the content and the emphasis desired.

Criticism of the Unified-Courses Organization

The practice of bringing the content of two or more required courses together into a coherent whole is undoubtedly an improvement over the piecemeal presentation of related courses, in which the recognition of interrelationships is left to chance. New relationships among the subject matter are developed, which otherwise might have been long neglected through devotion to specialized interests or through fear of teaching beyond the subject boundaries and thereby getting into another teacher's special domain. One further advantage of unified courses over separate subjects, or even broad-fields, is the considerable degree of teacher-pupil freedom that is possible. In the framework of a unified course, which may include two broad-fields such as social studies and science, teachers and pupils can select topics of interest and concern to themselves.

While the subject boundaries are not as restrictive in these courses as in a traditional subject curriculum, it should be clear that a program of unified courses is really a deviate form of the subject organization. The course boundaries still fix the scope of the program. No essential feature of a subject organization has been omitted, nor has any distinctive feature of the core theory been added. And since the goals and content are expressed in terms of knowledges, skills, and abilities in the organized fields of knowledge, exposition continues to be the primary technique of organizing and presenting learning experiences.

Moreover, there is no clear-cut principle for determining the organization of a unified course. Consequently, one of the subjects involved in the unification is apt to become the frame of reference for the unified course. In the case of the unification of history and literature, the chronology of history usually provides the basis for the organization and sequence of learning experience. Since the course is organized more in keeping with the goals and chronological sequence of history than with those of literature, it is not strange that the literary part of the course often seems to be a hodgepodge. It is difficult to study types of literature and the literature of different countries when this study must be tied to a particular historical period of a particular culture. Nor is it likely that much of the literature formerly studied in a grade would now be pertinent. It is even more unlikely that the literature that is especially illuminating or well adapted to the history would be at the reading or interest level of children in the grade where the history is studied.

The most serious criticism of unified courses, as an exemplification of a core program, is the fact that they are divorced from the social problems now plaguing the world and from any deliberate consideration of values and social goals. The first and most vital of the distinctive elements of a core curriculum is a constant and consistent social orientation—one which requires that democracy as a system of values be apparent in the goals, selection of experiences, and methods of teaching. The program called a "unified-courses core" emphasizes the content of organized fields of knowledge and, like other forms of subject organization, neglects social-moral ideals and social goals.

The content of the history and literature of a period, unified into a single course, has been and often is taught with little or no concern for the rightness or wrongness of the social positions taken by the different groups in the history or expressed in the literature. Even when reference is made—as is sometimes done in the classroom—to the values involved in historical and literary materials, no effort is made to develop critical methods of dealing with conflicts of values. Questions as to what is right and wrong, good and bad, desirable and undesirable with respect to economic, political, and other social issues arise more or less accidentally and are treated as matters of individual opinion. Since the unified courses are not designed to deal with socio-moral issues at the level of conflicting prejudices and values, they could hardly be expected to provide discipline in the construction and examination of values and social goals.

The Cultural-History Core

This subject-centered notion of the core curriculum involves a broader unification than is found in such fused courses as English-Social Studies, or Science-Social Studies. Comprehensive phases of cultural development provide the basis for this broader unification. The unifying factor is some significant phase of cultural development; for example, the Greco-Roman or medieval phase of the growth of western culture. It is at once apparent that history in its broadest meaning, in-

cluding study of art, music, government, literature, and social and economic life, provides both the general sequential pattern of chronology
and the outline of the scope for such a course.

The core of this program is history—a history that includes fewer of
the year-to-year and day-to-day events and more of the various aspects
of cultural periods than does the usual history course. The core would
encompass the literature, art, music, mathematics, science, education,
politics, economics, and sociology of significant cultural periods. The
organizing principles of such a core are the chronological and geographical locations of historical events and the interrelations of these events.

One of the best examples of this type of unification was developed
about two decades ago in the Horace Mann School.[2] In the junior high
school core, the unifying topic was "The Story of Men through the
Ages." The content of such specialized fields as fine arts, science, mathematics, language, and industrial arts was worked into the core program
as these specialties contributed to an understanding of the significant
phases of man's progress through the ages. In the seventh grade, the
cultural phase orienting the content and activities was the period from
primitive man through the ancient world; in the eighth grade, from
the ancient world to the discovery of America; and in the ninth grade,
from the discovery of America to the present-day world. The senior
high school core was built entirely on modern civilizations and cultures,
the tenth grade concentrating on American culture and the eleventh
grade on contemporary issues in American life.

At first glance this program appears to be the same as the unified-
courses core, but closer examination reveals this is not the case. In the
cultural-history type of core organization, the integration of the major
fields of knowledge is much more extensive. The unified courses, as
pointed out above, may be developed with no effect on the subjects outside the core. In this more extensive integration, however, almost any
subject in the program contributes to the core or is directly affected by
it. In studying the topic of housing in the early history of man, for
example, content and activities may be drawn from history, language
arts, fine arts, industrial arts, home economics, and so on. Furthermore,
a greater proportion of the school day is usually given to this kind of
core. The Horace Mann program in the junior high school, for example,

---

[2] Progressive Education Association, *Thirty Schools Tell Their Story,* pp. 395–430.

consumed approximately half of the school day. The core was under the direction of a single teacher, who worked with the teachers of music, science, mathematics, and the like in developing the program.

Criticism of the Cultural-History Core

A core that makes the life of a significant cultural phase or sequence of phases the unifying factor requires that the curriculum be oriented to the past. This preoccupation of the cultural-history core with the past leads to neglect of the conflicts of values and social perspectives now dividing the people. Historical orientation of the core program presupposes that by understanding the cultural phases of man's past, the individual will become more rational and more effective in dealing with the social issues of today. There is little, if any, reason to suppose that ability to deal with the present will result from such study of the past. That knowledge about the past of mankind is important, and indeed indispensable, can hardly be denied. Historical facts and theories are necessary in defining and solving most social problems; but that the relevant knowledge can be determined—and learned in advance of actual concern with such problems—is dubious.[3]

Moreover, this type of core lends itself to the pervasive habit of the occidental mind of thinking of culture almost exclusively in western terms. This is clearly illustrated in the Horace Mann core program, where none of the great cultural systems such as Oriental culture, Mexican culture, and Russian culture is emphasized save as it comes into contact with Western culture. When world understanding and intercultural education at the world level are as sorely needed as they are today, a cultural-history theory embracing as its prototype an evolutionary concept of man's progress in the western world has little to commend it.

The cultural-history core is, in reality, a new history course. It is much more inclusive of the total range of human activities than the conventional course in history. At its best, it deals not only with the factual aspects of a cultural period, such as the medieval culture in the western world, but also with the hopes and aspirations, the value

[3] B. Othanel Smith, "Historical Background and Social Perspective," *Educational Forum*, Vol. 7 (March, 1943), pp. 217–228.

standards, and the achievements of the masses. It emphasizes the structure of a cultural system—its social classes and castes, its occupations, and its institutional arrangements, together with the interrelations of these. In more concrete terms, this type of cultural core would stress the way the people of various cultural phases conceived work, play, achievement, personal greatness, freedom, and the like. It would help the student to see how the various elements of a culture fit together into a pattern, supplying the people with their methods of thinking, personal and collective goods, and basic motivations.

A study of history, thus broadly conceived, has much justification. But it properly belongs in the pattern of a subject curriculum and not in that of a core program. This conclusion follows immediately from the fact that this type of core is only the subject of history broadened to include many more aspects of man's total life than can be dealt with in the time allotted to an ordinary history course. Its goals, regardless of claims to the contrary, are the development of understandings peculiar to the historical content rather than the acquisition of those skills, values, and understandings required by the nature of the issues and conflicts now facing the people of the United States and of the world.

Finally, from a psychological standpoint, the cultural-history theory is open to serious objections. Chronology, the common basis for the determination of sequence in history, provides the sequence of the epochs. Earlier periods are studied before later periods. It is difficult to justify this procedure on the basis of interests or the psychological concept of readiness. The individual spends several years developing background and getting ready to study the current issues in which he is already involved.

2. Individual-Centered Categories and Core Theory

One of the efforts to define the categories of the core program has turned in the direction of the needs and interests of individuals. This development is in danger of becoming another version of the activity curriculum. This way of organizing the core curriculum will be described, and its relation to the core-curriculum theory will be examined.

The Adolescent-Needs Core

In recent years a number of efforts have been made to identify and classify the needs of adolescents. These needs are derived from the fact that the adolescent is developing physically and socially. As a result, he comes up against problems which require that he understand and adjust himself and that he also understand other persons and exercise skill in associating with them. By virtue of the social relationships in which he is unavoidably involved, he comes to feel the need for certain knowledge and skill with respect to personal relations in face-to-face groups and in economic and political activities in the wider social life. Needs based upon this approach are largely individual-centered, although they have reference to the social circumstances in which the adolescent finds himself. One such identification and classification of needs gives six categories which have been used in one form or another as the basis for a core curriculum. They are as follows:

1. Establishing Personal Relationships.
   a. With own sex.
   b. With other sex.
   c. Concerns about superficial mores.
   d. Yearning for understanding friendship.
   e. Confusions arising from different standards in society.
   f. Problems in achieving successful marriage.
2. Establishing Independence.
   a. Father or mother domination—"authority."
   b. Desire to work and achieve independent income.
   c. Compulsory work to support others.
   d. Acceptance on adult level.
   e. Freedom of choice in vital decisions.
   f. Emotional break with dependence on family.
3. Understanding Human Behavior.
   a. Concern over ways people dominate and hurt each other.
   b. Concern over frailties of justice.
   c. General discord between people.
4. Establishing Self in Society.
   a. Desire for acceptance as socially and morally responsible person.
   b. Desire for acceptance of opinions as important by adults and others.

    c. Concern over acceptance of family status by social group.

    d. Concern over status of race or minority group.

    e. Desire to excel in some skill.

5. Normality.

    a. Physical growth.

    b. Mental ability.

    c. Native intelligence.

    d. Emotions.

6. Understanding the Universe.

    a. Sensitivity.

    b. Concern over "authorities" outside experience.

    c. Urge to create as effort to comprehend and express.

    d. Effort to establish security in a world and universe not understood.

    e. Effort to establish philosophy of life.[4]

Another set of major divisions which has received wide attention, and which has been used as a basis for an adolescent-needs core, emphasizes individual needs as they emerge more directly in social relationships.[5] The individual is always involved in a system of social relationships, and out of the necessity of dealing with these relations his needs emerge. If the different kinds of relationships can be searched out and typed, they will afford the categories for the fullest recognition of both personal and social needs.

From studies of case history materials and other sources, three different kinds of relationships were formulated: (1) immediate social relationships, as in face-to-face relations between the adolescent and members of his family; (2) wider social relationships, as in the more abstract relations between the adolescent and all sorts of groups—those he can confront and those remote in space and time; and (3) the relationships involved in personal living, many of which are among the immediate and wider social relations. These types of relationships were expanded into four areas of basic needs: Personal Living, Immediate Personal-Social Relationships, Social-Civic Relationships, and Economic Relationships. One development of these categories reveals the following subdivisions:

[4] Condensed from H. H. Giles, S. P. McCutchen, and A. N. Zechiel, *Exploring the Curriculum* (New York: Harper & Brothers; 1942), pp. 315–320. By permission.

[5] V. T. Thayer, C. B. Zachry, and R. Kotinsky, *Reorganizing Secondary Education.*

I. Personal Living.
   A. Personal Health (Physical and Mental)—
      Heredity, native endowments, habits, learning, intelligence, normal
      variability, eugenics, diet, drugs, developing personality traits, etc.
   B. Man and Nature—
      Man in relation to lower animals, organic evolution, cosmology,
      religion, ethics, anthropology, social philosophy, relativity of
      truth, operational thinking.
   C. Man's Realization of Self through Aesthetic Appreciations, Art,
      Music, Drama, Literature.

II. Immediate Personal-Social Relationships.
   A. The Family in Civilization—
      Problems of individual adjustment, social relations, economic
      problems, budgeting, standards of living, improvement of home
      life, food, clothing, nutrition.
   B. Human Relations—
      Growth and development, sex, mating, dating, petting, problems
      of individual adjustment, social relations.
   C. Living in the School—
      Adjustment to school life, participation, making choices, social
      responsibility, parties, attitudes toward teachers, care of building
      and grounds, participation in curriculum planning, student gov-
      ernment, etc.

III. Social Civic Relationships.
   A. The Community—
      Health, housing, transportation, communication, taxation, govern-
      ment, schools, recreation, beautification, sharing of interests, par-
      ticipation in improving community life, changing concept of the
      community.
   B. Changing Conceptions of Government—
      Government and human welfare, protection of individual against
      exploitation.
   C. Types of Social-Political Organizations—
      Democracy, fascism, communism, etc. Effects upon human wel-
      fare.
   D. Getting Along with Other Races and Nations—
      Internationalism, war, trade barriers, league of nations, courts of
      international justice, treatment of Negro, Oriental, and the In-
      dian, naturalization, citizenship, etc.

IV. Economic Relationships.
   A. Conflicting Economic Systems—
   Capitalism, communism, socialism, trade unionism, consumer co-operatives.
   B. Impact of Technology upon Living—
   Machine age production, communication, transportation, distribution of goods, from scarcity to abundance—"The American Dream," possibilities of improving living in a machine civilization.
   C. Vocational Orientation—
   Study of occupations, professions, social responsibilities, culture through vocation.
   D. Consumer Problems—
   Advertising, installment buying, banking, child labor, sweatshops, consumer co-operatives, laboratory testing.[6]

What does the adolescent-needs approach lead to in practice? The development of this approach would conceivably lead to a number of different practical schemes. One of the best examples of a core program of this type for the junior high school is the one developed by the State of Wisconsin. This curriculum stresses adolescent needs as well as social functions. Only the former will be dealt with at this point. The needs of adolescents are those which emerge from physical and intellectual growth. Aspects of growth which are singled out for special treatment in this curriculum are as follows:

I. Physical growth characteristics
   A. Growth in height, weight, and body proportions
   B. Growth in organs of digestion and respiration
   C. Growth in primary and secondary sex characteristics
   D. Development of physical abilities
   E. Maintenance of physical health and hygiene

II. Social and emotional characteristics
   A. Changing relationships with home and family
   B. Need for affectional relationships outside the home
   C. Substitution of standards of the peer group for those of home and family
   D. Changes in boy-girl relationships
   E. Need for social experience in groups

[6] Giles, McCutchen, and Zechiel, *Exploring the Curriculum* (New York: Harper & Brothers; 1942), pp. 50–52. By permission.

      F. Feelings of social and personal inadequacy
      G. Development of ethical standards and religious feelings

III. Intellectual development and intellectual-cultural interests
      A. Intellectual development
      B. Intellectual-cultural interests [7]

When these characteristics are used to shape the curriculum, it takes the form given below. Only a sample of how each of the three categories was developed is reproduced here.

I. Physical growth characteristics

A. Growth in height, weight, and body proportions

1. Rapid increase in height

**Characteristics and behavior
related to growth**

Almost all girls and boys enter upon or are already in the circumpubertal spurt of growth during junior high school years. Some individuals grow as much as six inches in height in the course of a year.

Girls, on the average, are taller than boys during the junior high school years.

Early maturing boys and girls are apt to experience more intense and rapid growth than later maturing children but often end up shorter in stature than the others.

The rate of growth decelerates rapidly after the onset of puberty.

There is a tendency to awkwardness and postural defects. Lowered resistance is related to acceleration in growth and boys and girls are apt to fatigue easily.

Size and maturity do not necessarily proceed together. The "large" adolescent may be relatively immature and may experience feelings of inadequacy at his inability to live up to adult expectations in performance and behavior.

[7] Wisconsin State Department of Education, *Guide to Curriculum Building*. The Junior High School Level, Bulletin No. 8, January, 1950.

Tasks the pupil faces

To grow normally according to his own growth pattern.

To understand and accept his own growth status.

To understand that individuals differ widely in their maturity levels and rates of growth.

To build good postural habits.

To recognize symptoms of fatigue and learn to plan a balanced program of activity and rest adjusted to his own needs.

To follow a schedule of work and leisure-time activities which allows sufficient time for sleep and rest.

To refrain from making tactless or thoughtless remarks to or about one's companions who are unusually tall, short, clumsy, round shouldered, etc.

What the school can do

Set the level of expectation for each pupil in harmony with his general maturity level (social, emotional, intellectual and physical) rather than in terms of physical size alone.

Provide accurate information and guidance to help the pupil understand his own growth pattern and the often temporary relationship of his height to that of his peers.

Keep adequate individual records of height, weight, posture, and other pertinent factors of growth.

Provide competent medical advice in the analysis of growth records; provide a thorough medical check-up when growth seems abnormal.

Offer a program of physical education appropriate to the physical maturity of each pupil rather than to his chronological age or class membership.

Avoid overemphasis of competitive sports to prevent fatigue.

Provide experiences to help develop correct posture and to improve physical co-ordination (appropriate games, dramatic and social experiences, etc.)

Offer a program of corrective measures for individuals who need it.

Guide the pupil in planning his extracurricular activities in harmony with the energy pattern and resistance level of each individual.

Offer a sufficiently wide variety of activities from which to choose.

Provide seating equipment adjusted to the wide range of individual differences in physical size.

Segregate boys and girls in team sports.

Provide opportunities for boys and girls to learn to be considerate of others and sensitive to their feelings.

Establish a teacher-pupil relationship which will provide security for the pupil who feels markedly different by reason of rapid or retarded growth.

II. Social and emotional characteristics

A. Changing relationships with home and family

1. Elaborate resistance to, yet need for, parent and home control

**Characteristics and behavior
related to growth**

With entrance upon the pubertal cycle there is a tremendous impetus to break away from parent supervision and demonstrate independence. This is perhaps the period of greatest resistance to adult authority, which with some boys and girls takes the form of actual defiance. Young adolescents are apt to be supercritical of parent behavior and appearance, family folkways or household furniture. They tend to resist parental decisions or even advice regarding what they should wear, whom they should choose as friends, when they should go to bed, etc.

At the same time that young adolescents are attempting to break home ties, they often become involved in problems which they do not have the judgment to handle. The affectional security they have in their homes and the fundamental respect they feel for their parents serve them in good stead when they are in trouble. Such affectional support should not hamper them in their efforts to achieve independence but should provide an anchorage when the going gets rough. Young people who do not have this basic security are at a grave disadvantage in handling the baffling situations characteristic of this period.

Lack of parental understanding of the meaning of adolescent rebellion, which may result in efforts to retain too close control, may hamper boys and girls from establishing wider social contacts and the heterosexual friendships which mark the necessary steps toward adulthood.

At this time there is apt to be more warmth between parent and child of the opposite sex. The boy begins to see his mother as a representative of the feminine sex.

The girl views her father as representing masculine characteristics.

Tasks the pupil faces

To gain experience in accepting responsibility and making choices without need for too great reliance on parent authority or supervision.

To experience a type of consistent parent guidance which helps him understand and accept the need for some adult supervision and protection and some rules for governing family life.

To find opportunity to share in making sensible rules for harmonious family living.

To gain some understanding of his parents' motives in attempting to guide him and/or continue to control his activities.

To learn to make reasonable compromises with his parents on matters relating to his activities and behavior.

To continue to respect his parents and value his home while he is struggling to gain some freedom from the protected environment of home.

To retain the love, respect, and understanding of both parents and to feel assured of their affectional support especially at times when he has made mistakes in conduct or judgment and needs their help.

To find in his parents worthy representatives of their respective sex groups and wholesome models for his own behavior.

To receive helpful counseling from teachers or other competent advisers on problems related to breaking home ties.

To receive parental encouragement and helpful guidance in his attempts to broaden his friendships and choose friends from the opposite sex; to learn to choose friends wisely.

To learn to evaluate his home in terms more fundamental than furnishings or equipment; to understand the financial limitations within which the home must be run.

What the school can do

Provide opportunity for boys and girls to study the role of various members of the family; guide them in analyzing their own problems related to breaking home ties.

Encourage them to make an analysis of their present family relations and to plan what they can do to improve home life.

Help them analyze the kinds of situations in which it is important for young people to follow the judgment of their parents.

Encourage the pupils to call in representative parents to present their points of view on problems of family living and suggest ways in which boys and girls can gain their objectives without resort to rebellion or selfishness.

Gain sufficient information about each boy and girl to know what problems he may be facing in his home; establish contacts with the home and parents of pupils who seem to be receiving unwise handling; work with parents for greater understanding of the urge and need for young people to become increasingly independent of parent authority and of ways in which parents can encourage growth in assuming responsibility.

Give counseling on an individual basis to boys and girls who face frustrating problems by reason of overprotection, authoritarianism, or inconsistent discipline in the home.

Guide pupils in evaluating the fine things about their homes and parents.

Help them gain some skills by which they can contribute to the happiness of the family: meal planning and preparation, home decoration, etc.

Help boys and girls plan a program of school activities which will not conflict with family routine or reasonable home responsibilities; club activities or team practice which will get them home in time for dinner, home study which will allow time for helping with the dishes, etc.

Provide many opportunities at school for pupils to accept responsibilities, use initiative, make their own choices, and in other ways demonstrate their readiness for independence.

III. Intellectual development and intellectual-cultural interests

A. Intellectual development

1. Growth in mental ability

Characteristics and behavior related to growth

Up to an undetermined end point (estimates range from 16 to 20 years of age) there is an increase in mental ability with age. Boys and girls are increasingly able to deal with words, ideas, and other symbols of mental ability. Authorities feel that physical growth does not retard mental growth.

Intellectual growth at all ages is affected by stimulations in the environment. The interests, motivations, and experiences of young people affect their performance of intellectual tasks.

The 12 to 15 year old often displays amazing intellectual curiosity and power when not "bogged down" by stereotyped education.

Increased mental maturity is reflected in the growing capacity of junior high school boys and girls to plan their own lives. They are capable of greater insight into themselves and increasing responsibility for self-direction. They desire wider freedom to make their own choices in clothes, amusements, friends, etc.

They experience a growing urge to earn money and be independent in spending it.

They desire and are better able than in younger years to take part in adult discussion and in adult activities. Sometimes their plans are more ambitious than they can carry through.

Tasks the pupil faces

To find sufficient challenge at home and school to make full use of his growing mental ability.

To assume increasing responsibility for planning his own daily program and for being self-directive.

To learn to make realistic plans and carry them through.

To gain experience in sharing in adult discussions and undertakings.

To gain the security which results from having his ideas, immature though they may be, considered with respect by parents and teachers.

To gain experience on his own level of maturity in doing many of the things involved in effective living on the adult level—earning and spending money, planning and using leisure time wisely, assuming responsibility for his health needs and those of the community, accepting citizenship responsibilities, etc.

What the school can do

Recognize that while teen-age boys and girls lack experience, they approach the intellectual ability of adults and should therefore be stimulated accordingly.

Offer learning experiences which are purposeful and challenging to each student—which offer creative and research activities and stimulate thinking rather than put a premium on the passive acceptance of the ideas and conclusions of others and the memorization of required facts.

Provide many opportunities for pupils to share in establishing purposes, making plans, carrying through plans and evaluating outcomes; help them become increasingly self-directive through these experiences.

Provide many learning experiences to help boys and girls use their intellectual powers more effectively; help them become increasingly skillful in communicating ideas through speaking and writing; in gaining ideas from others through reading and listening, interpreting charts, graphs, tables, maps, etc.; in finding reliable sources of information, etc.

Provide many learning experiences to induct boys and girls into the areas of experience and the responsibilities they must assume as adult members of the community, the nation and the world.

Help parents understand the growing capacity of boys and girls for self-direction and their desire to be included in adult discussions and family councils.[8]

[8] Wisconsin State Department of Education, *Guide to Curriculum Building*. The Junior High School Level, Bulletin No. 8, January, 1950, pp. 13, 37, 59.

Perhaps one of the best examples of the individual-centered cores in the senior high school is the one developed at the East High School, Denver, Colorado. The four areas of relationships—Personal Living, Immediate Personal-Social, Social-Civic, and Economic—determine the scope of the program. The sequence of units is suggested on the basis of the experience of teachers with pupil needs at each grade level. Examples of these include:

Grade 10

Orientation to the school building.

Understanding oneself through a testing program in skills.

Exploration of special interest fields (art, music, sports, radio, gardening, crafts, etc.).

Becoming aware of the current scene (world problems, world citizenship).

Orientation to the Rocky Mountain Region (natural, human, and cultural resources).

Learning how public opinion is formed (radio, movies, newspapers, books, folklore, etc.).

Boy and girl relationships and problems of friendship.

Budgeting and spending an allowance or the money one earns.

Grade 11

Studying Denver (health, housing, recreation, government, transportation, education, communication, the arts in Denver, food, water, crime, vocational life).

Recognizing how to deal with consumer problems (quality and taste in buying, advertising, etc.).

Studying the conflicting economic systems of the world and various means of providing for production and consumption of goods.

Understanding democracy (documents, lives of leaders, minority rights, comparative governments).

Understanding and appreciating the American heritage (art, music, literature, religion, ideas, ideals, way of life).

Facing some of the urgent problems in American life (civic irresponsibility, degrading economic inequalities, improving life in machine age, education, the home, unemployment).

Exploring special leisure-time interests.

Grade 12

Developing appreciations of the resources which make life worth living (arts, music, drama, literature, nature, science).

Studying problems of investments, savings, commercial law, and the like.
Exploring problems of philosophy and ethics and attempting to build a
framework for a philosophy of one's own.
Exploring vocational opportunities in the community and nation.
Studying the problems of employment (job training, application for
job, employer-employee relations, cultural aspects of vocational life).
Participating in a vocational trek in the community.
Exploring the problems of living in a modern family.
Taking stock of three years at high school and planning for the years
which follow.[9]

Children's Interests and Needs Core

While the term *core curriculum* was developed in the literature concerned with secondary education and consequently has not been widely
used in reference to organizational plans at the elementary school level,
the core curriculum in practice is exemplified in nearly all its varied
forms in elementary schools. Especially is this true in the more recent
city and state curriculum developments where a core program is advocated from the kindergarten through the junior college years.

The kindergarten program of the State of Wisconsin is an illustration
of a carefully developed core curriculum based upon the interests and
needs of children.[10] It is apparent at once that this curriculum is not an
activity curriculum in disguise and is not so intended. The first mentioned determinant of curriculum content is a detailed analysis of aspects of child development—developmental needs. Following this is an
equally thorough consideration of the demands of a democratic culture,
as a second basis for the determination of content. The third general
consideration, which provides the actual basis of curriculum organization, is the interests and needs of children as suggested by the earlier
analysis of developmental needs and knowledge of child development.
"It is out of this, the child's world—its people, its daily activities, its
natural beauties, its problems and hazards—that we will find appropriate centers of interest for curriculum organization." [11]

[9] Progressive Education Association, *Thirty Schools Tell Their Story* (New York:
Harper & Brothers; 1943), pp. 146–212. By permission.

[10] Wisconsin State Department of Education, *Guides to Curriculum Building, Vol. 1,
Kindergarten Level* (Madison, Wisconsin: State Printing Office, Bulletin No. 12; October, 1947).

[11] Wisconsin State Department of Education, *op. cit.,* p. 107.

The following are listed as an illustration of an appropriate sequence of centers of interest for the kindergarten program:

Year's Problem: What can we learn about the things and people about us?
1. What can we learn to help us in our work at school?
2. How shall we celebrate special days and events?
3. What interesting things are happening because it is fall?
4. How can we care for plants and animals in our schoolroom?
5. How can we make and enjoy our playhouse?
6. How do plants and animals live and grow? [12]

These and other centers of interest are evaluated in terms of the following criteria:

1. Is the center of interest based on the need and interest level of the child of kindergarten age?
2. Is it selected and developed with reference to the social imperatives of democracy and to the characteristic features and cultural needs of the local community?
3. Does the method of expressing each center of interest seem to be the one which will best suggest appropriate experiences, techniques, and procedures?
4. Does each center of interest offer sufficient opportunity for the organization of a rich variety of experiences needed by children of this age and related to the social problems they are expected to solve? Is there sufficient variety and flexibility to adjust to the unique personal and social needs of each child within the kindergarten group?
5. Will the centers of interest for the entire year provide sufficient scope for the accomplishment of all of the developmental and cultural tasks demanded by kindergarten children?
6. Does the sequence of centers of interest provide for continuity in the development of the child?
7. Have the centers of interest been carefully selected and organized with reference to the availability of equipment and materials and the feasibility of weather conditions to carry out the desired experiences?
8. Does each center of interest provide ample opportunity for the children to participate with the teacher in choosing and planning activities? Is there room for pupil-teacher planning? [13]

[12] *Ibid.*, adapted from pp. 112–113.
[13] *Ibid.*, pp. 113–114.

Criticisms of the Adolescent-Needs and Child-Interests Cores

A curriculum organization that employs, as its first criterion for the selection of content, the fundamental interests or felt needs of children or youth has satisfied the first and most fundamental test of an activity curriculum. If the adolescent-needs core is in reality based upon adolescent needs as recognized by the youth themselves, the resultant is simply an activity curriculum with provision for elective courses to care for specialized interests. Such a curriculum could be determined in advance only in so far as the true interests of youth could be prejudged. There would be common learnings only to the extent that interests were shared in common and to the extent that common paths were taken in the pursuance of these interests. All this is in keeping with the unique features of the theory of the activity curriculum—or of any curriculum that employs the fundamental interests of children as the prime bench mark for the selection and organization of content. However, the adolescent-needs categories are not based upon the interests of youth without regard to the demands of society.

This type of adolescent-needs core is an attempt to bridge the major dichotomy of educational theory and practice, arising from the question of whether the curriculum should be based upon interests or social values. Those favoring an activity curriculum hold that curriculum making is, first, a matter of finding out what interests, native or acquired, are available in the learner, and second, a matter of discovering ways in which these interests can be effectively stimulated and directed. In sharp contrast to this view is the theory that the things to be learned should first be chosen, and then the best way of teaching them should be sought for and described. Both of these views have always been seriously opposed by people who believe that neither the interests of the learner nor the judgment of adults as to what the learner should study can be neglected in the construction of a satisfactory curriculum.

Even many advocates of the activity curriculum prefer a more orderly sequence of experiences and a greater safeguard of social values than the wholesale commitment to interest guarantees. And many of those who place their trust in a subject curriculum have seldom felt comfortable about the neglect of interest their position seems to entail. The problem of resolving this dilemma of interest and social values in the practical work of curriculum construction is of primary importance.

The adolescent-needs and the child-interests core begin with the fundamental interests and felt needs of children or youth and attempt to expand these into a study of the major social concerns of the people. Thus, consideration of "budgeting and spending an allowance or earned money" would be expected to lead into study of the "conflicting economic systems of the world" and "degrading economic inequalities." One of the serious problems of such plans is that of providing a basis for determining which of the several allegiances to which the curriculum is dedicated (individual interests and needs, and social realities and values) is to be considered paramount. Are the basic categories to be set up in terms of existing knowledge of needs, or of interests, or in terms of the social realities and the core of values constituting the heart of the culture? How does the curriculum worker know when to emphasize one over the other or how to choose between them when they are in conflict?

It is easy to explain away this conflict between interests and social values by holding that since the interests are always shaped by the relationships which an individual has to things and people, his interests will naturally be in significant social issues and defensible values and goals. If society were all of a piece, much could be said in support of this thesis. Unfortunately, present-day society is differentiated into many social groups and strata. As was made clear in an earlier chapter, the society of the United States has been fragmented into all sorts of social groups and classes—each of which is characterized by its own perception of social realities, the goals for which men should work, the purposes of social action, and the democratic values themselves. These groups and classes shape the needs, interests, points of view, and values of their members. Children and youth will therefore reflect the outlooks, aspirations, and values of the groups and classes from which they come. In any classroom, students will largely be motivated and controlled by the beliefs and hopes that permeate their social medium, rather than by the school. This will be true at least in the early stages of instruction, until the school's program of social education becomes as effective as out-of-school influences.

In the light of these facts, it is relevant to ask how a core curriculum, which purports to be based upon children's needs, also satisfies social demands. The co-ordination of individual needs and social demands has sometimes been accomplished by measures that have not been recognized. In the first place, the values and goals of the middle class have been unwittingly accepted as the standard of worth in judging potential experiences. As a result, all children and youth of the lower classes, except the few who were able to accept the middle class point of view, have been neglected. Most of them drop out of school at the earliest opportunity. Moreover, many upper class youth go to private schools or to public schools located in residential areas so restricted as to make the school population tantamount to that of private schools.

As a result of the withdrawal of these two social classes, the public schools, especially the secondary schools, tend to be primarily the schools of the middle class. This fact has necessarily influenced all curriculum thinking, and nowhere is this influence more apparent than in the child- and adolescent-needs approach to curriculum making. A review of inventories of adolescent needs and problems will indicate that these instruments have been prepared from the standpoint of middle class youth.[14] And the learning activities and experiences planned and carried on in the school are usually those that are compatible with the perspectives, values, and goals of the middle class.

In the second place, it is assumed that all middle class youth see things alike. This is not true. Their views and aspirations go back to the social and occupational associations of their parents and friends. Consequently, interests and needs will vary considerably from individual to individual. There are two ways in which this variation can be handled. First, the instruction can be so completely individualized that each individual pursues his own interests more or less independently of other students except when their interests coincide with his. At least in theory, few, if any, external standards will need to be applied; hence, the individual will not feel himself hampered, in this case, by the demands of the teacher.

Second, only those needs of the individual that do not run counter to the standards accepted wittingly or unwittingly by the teacher would be recognized in the educational program. This would mean that those students whose interests were in conflict with the judgment of the teacher would have to forego these interests and turn to such other interests as would meet with the teacher's approval. Theoretically, not all the stu-

---

[14] For an example, see the list of typical needs of high school youth prepared for the Denver Public Schools, in *Manual for Teachers Working on Core Course,* November, 1938.

dent's interests would have to be forsaken; he simply would be induced
to pursue the ones entertained by himself which were deemed to be of
most worth. The way in which social demands, as reflected by the
teacher, and the interests expressed by the student may be co-ordinated
can be illustrated in the following way. If we interpret the social-centered categories as embracing the things that curriculum theorists think
the individual needs (and designate these with the title *He needs* to indicate that they are the choices of people other than the learner), and
if we further assume that individual-centered categories contain the
things the learner feels the need of (and label these things *I need* to
show that they are the learner's choice), the co-ordinates can be represented by the diagram below:

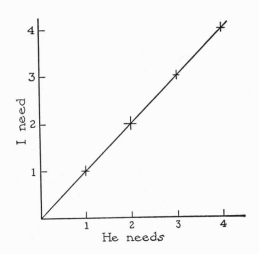

A. *I need*
    1. What does the policeman do?
    2. What does the farmer do with all his corn?
    3. Where does the grocery man get the things he sells?
    4. Where does the doctor get his money?

B. *He needs*
    1. To know about the protection of life, property, and resources.
    2. To know about the production of goods and services.
    3. To know about the distribution of goods.
    4. To know about the consumption of goods and services.

In the primary grades the series of interests and demands (corresponding to the numbers on the axis) satisfying both co-ordinates might be as listed under A and B.

The achievement of such harmonious individual and social demands is obviously not automatic. And when conflict does emerge between the *I need* and *He needs* categories, it is settled either by the curriculum builder in his basic theory or by the teacher in the classroom. If the decision about what is to be studied is made exclusively in terms of the felt needs of youth, then the adolescent-needs core meets all of the essentials of an activity curriculum. If, on the other hand, social functions or social needs provide the real bench mark for determining what to teach and how to classify experiences, the adolescent-needs core is simply a misnomer, and it is in reality a social-centered core. In other words, the adolescent-needs core is either an activity program and not a core curriculum, or it is a social-centered core and is not based primarily upon the felt needs of adolescents.

3. *Social-Centered Categories and Core Theory*

The activities of the people of different societies appear to be very unlike; but this is not true of certain basic categories of life activities such as government, vocational activities, and recreation. The way in which these functions are performed varies enormously from one society to another. The point is, however, that such *functions* are common to all societies. Whether in the primitive villages of central Africa or in the highly developed institutionalized society of today, with its intricate industrial and commercial system, its complex governmental procedures, and its highly specialized professional services—to mention only a few of its infinite varieties—human conduct consists for the most part of variations upon these few major lines of activity. If these major persistent strands could be ascertained, they would afford the centers about which the content of a common education could be organized.

The Social-Functions Core

Fortunately for the curriculum worker, students of cultural anthropology have been accumulating for almost half a century a mass of data

on primitive cultures as well as on the highly developed western societies. Out of these data have emerged certain universal lines of activity. Wissler's list of cultural constants, while somewhat formal, is indicative of the sort of major cultural strands needed in curriculum
integration of the social-functions type:

1. Speech
2. Material traits—food, shelter, industries, transportation, etc.
3. Art
4. Mythology and scientific knowledge
5. Religious practices
6. Family and social systems
7. Property
8. Government
9. War [15]

If these are reduced to their functional equivalents, they will be recognized as fundamental types of activities, common to all people regardless of the cultural pattern into which they are born and in which
they develop. In their analysis of contemporary American culture, as
reported in *Middletown,* the Lynds grouped their data about six major-
trunk activities, which they hold to be common to all cultures: getting
a living; making a home; training the young; using leisure in various
forms of play, art, and so on; engaging in religious practices; engaging
in community activities. It is important to note in this regard that the
fact that these kinds of activities are found in all cultures does not
imply a unified content of study from society to society. Each of these
activities takes markedly different forms in different societies.

The areas of living comprising the categories of the social-functions
core were obtained, as was mentioned above, from years of careful research by anthropologists. Students of education analyzed and sometimes synthesized these categories to make them usable as a basis of
curriculum organization, but this changed them very little. These categories are classifications of man's endeavors throughout recorded history and throughout the wide gamut of civilized and relatively uncivi-
lized societies. They are what men do and have always done regardless
of time, geographical location, religious beliefs, type of government, or

---

[15] Clark Wissler, *Man and Culture* (New York: Thomas Y. Crowell Co., 1923),
p. 74. By permission. See also Malinowski, *A Scientific Theory of Culture,* p. 125.

of social ideals and mores. These, then, are purely descriptive categories and are completely non-moral. There are, as far as the classifications themselves go, no guideposts as to whether the pursuits are or are not worth while; nor is there any value orientation to provide a basis for determining how one ought to behave in any one of these endeavors. They are simply classifications of the kinds of things man has always done and is currently doing.

One of the earliest and most widely known attempts of educators to classify social functions is the "seven cardinal principles" of secondary education: health, fundamental processes, worthy home membership, vocation, civic education, worthy use of leisure time, and ethical character. These have been referred to frequently as objectives of education, but in reality they are areas of activities and social relationships. Over a half century before the seven cardinal principles were propounded, Spencer had formulated a theory of curriculum development based upon a sociological analysis that yielded a list of social functions seldom equalled by more recent studies.[16]

In recent years such classifications of life activities have multiplied by leaps and bounds. From a study of thirty-eight classifications of such activities, Frederick derived nine *areas of living:*

1. Protecting life and health.
2. Living in and improving the home.
3. Conserving and improving material conditions.
4. Co-operating in social and civic action.
5. Getting a living.
6. Securing an education.
7. Expressing religious impulses.
8. Enjoying and expressing beauty.
9. Engaging in recreation.[17]

With slight modifications these major divisions have been widely used in programs of curriculum development. A similar list was derived by the Joint Committee on Curriculum of the Department of Supervisors and Directors of Instruction and the Society for Curriculum Study. This Committee made a synthesis of thirty classifications of life

[16] Herbert Spencer, *Education: Intellectual, Moral, and Physical,* pp. 11–14.
[17] O. I. Frederick and L. J. Farquear, "Areas of Human Activity," *Journal of Educational Research,* Vol. 30, pp. 672–679. By permission.

activities. It was guided by certain criteria, which each category was required to meet. Of these criteria the following are cited as examples: each category must embrace actual activities and not adult abstractions; each must anticipate bodies of experience rather than traditional school subjects; each must admit goal-seeking activities; and each must be capable of being limited in time and space. The categories formulated by this committee, with a brief description of each, follow:

Living in the home includes rearing of children, the maintenance and repair of the home, the management of the home, and family relations.

Leisure includes physical exercise; outdoor activities, including camping and motoring; the handicrafts; the arts and literature; the dance and the theater. These have an amateur creative aspect and enjoyment aspect. Some of these, obviously, are carried on in the home, but for convenience they are classified under the heading of recreation.

Citizenship includes the relation of the individual to government, to civic enterprises, and to world affairs; sanitation; social welfare, social security, and the like.

Organized social life includes the church, social organizations, cultural groups, fraternal organizations, study clubs, discussion groups, luncheon clubs, professional groups, garden clubs, etc.

Consumption includes the selection, purchase, and care of food, clothing, shelter, fuel, and household furnishings; household accounting, insurance; certain social phases of consumption, such as housing, the co-operative movement, and government aid to the consumer.

Production includes earning a living, choosing vocations, the organization of business, banking, agriculture, organized labor, distribution of income, corporate business.

Communication includes the motion picture, the radio, the press, and the postal system.

Transportation includes all of the means in which passengers and goods are transported from place to place, including the railroad, the automobile, the boat, the airplane, and highways. Emphasis here is on the movement of persons, since movement of goods would be handled under the heading of production.[18]

It was pointed out above that the Wisconsin *Guide to Curriculum Building* for the junior high school is based upon two ideas: adolescent

[18] Henry Harap (Ed.), *The Changing Curriculum* (New York: Appleton-Century-Crofts, Inc.; copyright 1937), pp. 96–97. By permission.

needs with respect to knowledge about their own growth and development, and social functions. That part of the curriculum based upon adolescent needs has already been illustrated. Since this *Guide* also affords
one of the best examples of a social-functions core, excerpts from it will
be used to show how such a core curriculum shapes up in practice. The
social functions used in this core are as follows:

1. To keep the population healthy.
2. To provide physical protection and guarantee against war.
3. To conserve and wisely utilize natural resources.
4. To provide opportunity for people to make a living.
5. To rear and educate the young.
6. To provide wholesome and adequate recreation.
7. To enable the population to satisfy aesthetic and spiritual values.
8. To provide sufficient social cement to guarantee social integration.
9. To organize and govern in harmony with beliefs and aspirations.[19]

The following table gives examples of how a selected number of
these social functions are used in shaping the core program.

I. America must keep the population healthy— free from disease, accidents, and inhibiting frustrations

A. Large segments of the population suffer from malnutrition and related diseases. Almost half of the American people consume less milk, egg, and fruits than they need to maintain good nutritional status.

The situation we confront

(In the junior high school years many pupils face for the first time the
problem of personal selection of food in school cafeterias and restau-
rants. A tendency to be dictated by food fads, ignorance of relative
food values, and limited spending money often result in unwise choice.)

What the pupil needs

To be provided enough food at home and at school at short enough in-

[19] Wisconsin State Department of Education, Bulletin No. 8, Jan. 1950, p. 74.

tervals to satisfy hunger and to maintain energy for sustained effort in work and play.

To get up in time to eat a good breakfast.

To know what combinations of foods contain the essential food factors for a balanced diet.

To develop a willingness to choose foods which satisfy basic nutritional needs. This implies a willingness to forego certain less wholesome foods for those which are better.

To try to break faulty food habits such as irregular and inappropriate snacks, rapid eating, etc.

To understand the relationship of the nutritional needs of his age group to body development during this period.

To understand the relationship of good food habits to personal appearance. To see and accept the reason why reducing diets at this age may prove harmful.

What the school can do

Make provision for adequate school lunches at minimum cost. Use the lunch hour as a time for practicing wise selection of food and good eating habits.

Make provision for learning experiences to gain knowledge about and the correct attitudes toward proper nutrition.

Provide for co-operation between the home and the school on matters relating to proper diet for the pupil.

Discourage certain prevalent school practices which are detrimental to the development of good eating habits: selling soft drinks under school auspices during the school day, running the cafeteria along commercial lines, scheduling too short a lunch hour for establishing good eating habits, etc.

Secure the assistance of health specialists in carrying out a nutrition program for pupils who are underweight, overweight, anemic, or give evidence of other special health problems.

Capitalize on the adolescent's concern about personal appearance to show the relationship between proper diet and personal health and attractiveness.

II. America must provide physical protection and guarantees against war

A. The complex and diverse nature of group living in this country makes organized police protection necessary for carrying out the will of the people as expressed by law.

What the pupil needs

To respect the role of law enforcement officers; to co-operate with their efforts and seek their help.

To know the laws which protect him and those with which he must comply.

To understand and accept the reasons for the laws which affect him and grow in desire to comply with them—not to "beat" them.

To develop self-discipline and self-direction and thus have less need to rely upon the restraints of law.

To contribute to "law-making" and "law-enforcing" by participating in student government and/or helping to establish rules to govern his class or club.

To understand the role of law-making and law-enforcing agencies in his community, state, and nation.

What the school can do

Use the local community as a laboratory for studying the relationship of law enforcement to the improvement of group living and individual happiness.

Encourage the pupils to invite local law-enforcement officers to discuss with them the major problems of law enforcement in the community and the role of the pupils in helping to solve these problems.

Provide many self-governing activities which will give pupils opportunity to think and plan in terms of group welfare and to consult and co-operate with school and community officials.

Include as part of teacher-pupil planning in every school situation, setting up some rules or standards to provide optimum working conditions for all.

Give the pupils continuous practice in complying with self-imposed rules.

Guide the pupils in developing increasing responsibility for their own behavior and their own choices. If unwise choices are made, substitute guided self-evaluation and self-planning for teacher-imposed penalties and directives.

Provide learning experiences to acquaint the pupils with the laws which protect them: child labor laws, pure food acts, property rights, safety regulations, health and sanitation measures, etc. Insofar as possible, use the local community to investigate evidence of compliance or non-compliance with law.

Give pupils the opportunity to become familiar with the organization and operation of law-enforcement agencies on the local, state, and national levels. Familiarize them with the safeguards the citizen enjoys against the possibility of high-handed acts by law-enforcement officers. Use court cases of local interest as motivation for studying the jury system and other measures to insure justice.

III. America must conserve and wisely utilize and replace its natural resources

A. Neglect, ignorance, and selfish profiteering have resulted in profligate waste of our natural resources.

The situation we confront

Available supplies of such resources as coal, minerals, water, oil, topsoil, and timber are limited and will become exhausted unless efficient methods of conservation and utilization are understood and employed.

What the pupil needs

To establish basic habits of conservation through learning to plan wisely: in buying food, clothing, insurance, household equipment, etc.

To practice habits of intelligent saving as it applies to school supplies, his own and his family's belongings: saving paper, preparing left-over foods, repairing and renovating clothing and equipment, etc.

To recognize wasteful practices in his own community.

To combat waste and neglect wherever they occur in his own environment. To take an active part in community programs for the saving of resources: collecting scrap metals, helping with programs designed to prevent forest fires, etc.

To take an active part in programs for the replacement of natural resources such as planting cover crop, reforestation, etc.

To assume some personal responsibility for encouraging others to practice better conservation methods.

To begin to understand the relation between the nation's supplies of natural resources and its standard of living.

To understand to what extent natural resources are limited, which resources are exhaustible, which cannot be replaced when used up.

To understand to what extent usable substitutes for exhaustible resources are being developed and employed.

To understand the consequences of continued neglect and waste of exhaustible resources; to know how these resources contribute to human welfare.

What the school can do

Guide boys and girls in developing wholesome attitudes toward the wise use and care of school and personal property with the hope that such attitudes will carry over into wise regard for natural wealth.

Provide learning experiences to help boys and girls budget and buy wisely; clean, repair, and remodel clothing efficiently; become skillful in the preparation of left-over food, etc.

Provide varied source materials for sensitizing pupils to the need for community and nation-wide conservation of scarce and exhaustible materials; encourage reading stories with a conservation theme; show documentary films such as "The River" to dramatize the destruction resulting from unwise use of natural resources, etc.

Provide opportunity for a clear understanding of what constitutes wasteful practice, what is being done or can be done to correct inefficient and wasteful practice; encourage the pupils to meet with community leaders engaged in conservation and learn from them the nature and probable effectiveness of their work.

Provide opportunity for junior high school boys and girls to take an active part in programs designed to promote good conservation practices. (Such activities as school forest planting and care, the distribution of literature concerned with good conservation practices to farmers and others, taking an active part in conservation clubs, 4-H clubs, Trees for Tomorrow, Boy Scouts are examples of some activities within the understanding of pupils of junior high school age.) [20]

Criticism of the Social-Functions Core

The social-functions pattern is clearly neither an activity nor a subject curriculum. Its general scope is determined by broad trunk lines of social activity without reference to individual needs, on the one hand, or to subject boundaries on the other. It thus satisfies one of the characteristics distinctive of a core curriculum—namely, that the basic areas of instruction represent the broad areas of social living.

However, the relation of this type of core program to the core of values constituting the heart of American culture is not so clear. While categories of life functions offer promising possibilities for developing normatively oriented individuals, self-objective and socially critical, there is no assurance that these possibilities will be realized. There is no assurance that study within such areas as "getting a living," "conserving and improving material conditions," or "living in and improving the home" would be oriented to deliberately considered and criticized social values. The study of such areas does not, in and of itself, assume anything in particular with respect to values, standards of right and wrong, or relative worth of several ways of earning a living. It may tell nothing about whether a living earned through teaching, carpentry, manipulation of stocks, or what-not, is conducive to individual or societal good health. Nor does the content of such categories necessarily tell whether earning a living under either fascism or communism is or is not to be preferred over earning a living in a capitalistic democracy.

A social-functions core is, of course, no less likely to be securely tied to the values of democracy than is a subject or activity organization. The point is that there is nothing about any of these curriculums to guarantee that problems centering in conflicts of values will be treated as such.

[20] Wisconsin State Department of Education. *Ibid.*, pp. 79, 88, 94.

When the social-functions core is developed with little or no reference to the conflict in the values that comprise the core of the culture, it fails to satisfy one of the distinctive principles of a core curriculum. The problems that harass the people are precisely those that embrace differences of opinion about questions of the ends to be sought and not merely about the means of action. If the social-functions areas are developed strictly in terms of fact questions, such as "How do we protect property?", "How can we have an enjoyable time?", "How does machine production influence recreation?"—then normative issues will be almost completely omitted; if included at all, they will be dealt with in a loose and opinionated manner. On the other hand, if aspects of social functions are dealt with at the level of value conflict as well as at the level of fact and descriptive principle, so that the students—and, for that matter, the entire class as a social group—are encouraged to consider critically not only what values they should accept but also what social goals they should be committed to, the program would have all the distinctive features of a genuine core curriculum. As will be seen in the next section, the social-functions core can be oriented normatively by the method of fixing the sequential development of the core program. In practice, however, it is easy to ignore this sort of orientation.

The Social-Problems Core

This core is similar to the social-functions core. In fact, more than a casual analysis is required to determine whether or not a particular core program takes its organizational pattern from social functions or from social problems. Yet there is an important difference between these two plans. The social-functions categories are based upon activities believed to be universal. The social-problems categories are derived from classifications of *crucial* social problems. These problems are usually conceived as existing at local, national, and world levels, and as not necessarily universal in scope.

Since *cruciality* is of primary importance, it is relevant to ask what determines the cruciality of a problem. A problem is crucial when its solution is decisive in the life of the people, when it has a significant bearing upon the direction in which a society will move. For example, the question of how the industrial system of the United States is to be controlled and what ends it is to serve is a crucial problem; for the solution that is finally worked out will be decisive with respect to how people live for generations to come. The same thing can be said for such questions as whether or not there should be universal military training in the United States and whether or not an adequate system of world government can be worked out.

How can the curriculum worker know which of the many problems facing the people at a given time are crucial? The cruciality of social problems can be determined by competent scholars in the social sciences—by social analysts who are on the cutting edge of social thought. This means that curriculum workers must analyze the writings of social scientists—specifically, those judged by their peers to be outstanding students of society—to ascertain the problems about which these scientists are most concerned. From such an analysis can be ascertained a group of problems, which can be classified into categories. These groups, or classes of problems then constitute the categories of the social-problems core.

The twelfth-grade program in Eugene, Oregon, illustrates the social-problems core. Ten problems are listed in the scope and sequence chart, as follows:

1. School Government: How can the principles of democracy be applied to the school and to the classroom?
2. Standard of Living: How can the American standard of living be improved?
3. Unemployment: How can we eliminate unemployment?
4. Consumer: How can we become intelligent consumers?
5. Propaganda: How can we recognize and deal with propaganda?
6. War: How can war be eliminated?
7. Crime: How can crime be prevented?
8. Religion: How can we provide for the religious and spiritual needs of youth?
9. Marriage and Family: How can marriage and family life be made more successful?
10. Social Reform Movements: How can various programs for social reform aid in solving our social and economic problems? [21]

[21] Eugene, Oregon, Public Schools, *Tentative Scope and Sequence Chart*, 1940.

These problems were selected because they were deemed to be of crucial importance to the United States and to the world. It was suggested that in the study of these problems emphasis be placed upon the scientific method—analysis of problems, determination of the difficulties to be overcome in solving them, and the formulation and evaluation of ways of overcoming the difficulties.

The problems serving as organizing centers in grades nine through twelve of the Santa Barbara, California, program also indicate concern about the pressing problems of contemporary society.[22] Illustrative of these problems are the following, selected from those suggested for grades nine through twelve: Making Our Water Supply Serve Human Needs; How Can We Better House the Nation; Influencing Public Opinion; Promoting International Understanding; Conserving Our National Resources; Providing for National Defense; Appreciating the Contributions of Other Cultures; Making Machines Serve Mankind; Protecting Civil Liberties; Keeping the Government Responsible to the People; Improving Relationships between Racial and Cultural Groups.

The Meaning of a Social Problem

The extent to which these examples satisfy the conditions of a core curriculum depends upon the conception of social problems they embrace in practice. There are three conceptions of a social problem found in social-problem cores, only one of which is in full accord with the theory of the core curriculum. The first of these conceptions makes a social problem synonymous with a topic. This way of looking at a problem is well illustrated by the teacher who begins with the question, How can we eliminate unemployment? and proceeds to guide the students in a study *about* unemployment. The students learn about different kinds of unemployment, the amount of unemployment at different times, the "causes" of unemployment, the effects of unemployment insurance, and the like. From this exploration they acquire considerable knowledge about unemployment in American society in precisely the

---

[22] Santa Barbara County, California, *Santa Barbara County Curriculum Guide for Teachers in Secondary Schools,* pp. 41–42.

same way and to the same extent they would have done had they studied the topic, "Unemployment and Its Prevention." At no time do the students become involved in the real problem.

The second conception identifies a problem as completely outside of persons and social groups. Like a problem in the physical sciences, it is *out there* somewhere in the environment, more or less remote from the person or social group. As a result, it is something to be studied in an objective and detached manner. Moreover, this notion of a problem reduces the difficulty to one of finding the proper means of reaching goals which are assumed to be agreed upon by all persons concerned. A group viewing a problem in this manner might begin with the question: How can we eliminate unemployment? They would then study the proposed solutions to the unemployment problem in the light of the facts. They would consider the probable effect of these solutions on industry, taxpayers, laborers, and others affected. The analysis would stop at this point with no explicit reference to the prejudices operating in the thinking of the members of the class with respect to the unemployment question. Nor would the study involve any explicit concern for broader social goals or values to which the various solutions might contribute.

A social problem, according to this view, should be studied factually; for, since goals are not in doubt, no serious attention need be given to values nor to the determination of social goals. In consequence, little reference is made to the future, and even less in the sense of trying to visualize a future state of affairs to be deliberately created. Preoccupation with means tends to reduce all considerations of the future to mere imaginary rehearsals of the probable consequences of different plans of action. Deliberation upon social goals as deliberate projections of a more desirable state of affairs tends to be sacrificed in the interest of things as they are. When there is no real consideration of value questions—and thus no fundamental reconstruction of personalities—the likely alternatives are (1) an easy solution that does not face social facts, or (2) a refusal to consider possible solutions, because these may conflict with unexamined values.

The third notion of a social problem, and the one the theory of the core curriculum assumes, makes the critical construction of social goals and social values a central feature in the exploration and resolution of crucial problems. According to this conception, social problems are as much ends-problems as they are means-problems. A group employing this approach might consider the same problem: How can we eliminate unemployment? The group would undoubtedly find need to learn about unemployment (kinds of unemployment, amount at different times, "causes" of unemployment, effects of unemployment, and the like) as was done in the case of the first view of a social problem. They could not, as in the second approach, be tied to an impersonal study of unemployment, because the group is concerned not only with what *is* but also with what *should be.*

What will this plan mean in terms of the way people live? Is this plan more or less in accord with what we believe is the right way for people to live? Do we believe that some people are born lazy and worthless, or do we believe that, within broad physiological limits, people are the products of their culture? Do we believe that the "down and almost out" unemployed person should be the concern of all people who are employed, or do we believe that anything he gets he should get by himself? These are but a few illustrations of questions which this view of a social problem insists must be considered.

This third conception of a social problem recognizes that problems arise, in large part, because individuals and social groups, desiring different outcomes, conceive the difficulties differently, and, in consequence, advocate opposing solutions. Moreover, since desires and values of individuals are tied up in any social problem, these become factors in the definition and solution of the problem. Only as these conflicting elements of personal structure are somehow reconciled can social problems be solved. This means that the resolution of any social issue usually entails modification of the personal structures of those persons who are parties to the issue.

Method and the Social-Problems Core

This notion of a problem requires that attention be given to the following phases of thought in the study of any crucial social issue: (1) the formulation, through mutual interpersonal persuasion, of a concerted idea of the state of affairs the students desire to have established in the future with respect to that aspect of society which the problem embraces; (2) an exploration of existing conditions and their connection with the ends projected and desired; and (3) the charting of a plan of action leading through existing conditions to the projected state of affairs.[23] This way of conceiving and exploring a social problem is normatively oriented. It is this normative orientation that lies at the heart of a core curriculum and distinguishes it most significantly from other curriculum patterns.

Perhaps the best illustration of a genuine social-problems core is that developed at Floodwood, Minnesota. In this program there were three areas—economic-political, art and science, and education and human relations—all of which were centered in one theme, "Design for America." The following description of the program indicates its general nature and normative orientation.

The Students Vote to Try It. One morning about a year ago fifty boys and girls, members of the junior and senior classes in a small, fairly typical rural community school at Floodwood, Minnesota, met for discussion with the superintendent of schools, the English teacher, the social studies teacher, and a visiting member of the University of Minnesota faculty. The students were asked whether they would enjoy embarking upon an educational adventure. Instead of studying literature of the past, the institutions and practices of yesterday and today, why not turn to the future for a change? Why not try to answer the question, "What kind of society do we as young citizens want to build for tomorrow?"

The discussion did not, however, go into detail regarding the "design for America" that they would construct. Indeed, this would have been premature, for the construction would take place by co-operative effort from step to step. The teachers did try to suggest that the great changes taking place everywhere in society, the dangers and uncertainties of the immediate and long-range period after World War II, made such an effort significant and challenging. They further pointed out that, if the project were to succeed, it would be better for them not to think in terms of departments and standardized courses, since they would want to turn for their design to whatever areas of knowledge and experience seemed important to the welfare of people like ourselves.

After listening with both interest and skepticism, the students adjourned to discuss the proposal at lunch time. They then returned to bombard the

[23] Raup et al., *The Improvement of Practical Intelligence,* pp. 10? ff.

teachers with questions. What would happen to the regular courses for which this new plan would be a substitute? What kind of materials would they study? Was it practical? And so on. The answer was that probably some of the traditional subject matter in such courses as American literature would be retained, and that certainly practice in speaking and writing would be provided, but that both content and skill would be gained primarily as pertinent to the over-all purpose of the experiment rather than for their own sake or otherwise in isolation. But every student was urged to be critical and not to be influenced merely by the instructors' convictions. Accordingly, when they were ready to make a decision, they did so by secret ballot: three voted against trying the experiment, the rest were in favor. But since all had previously agreed to abide by the decision of the majority, the dissenters remained in the project and their identity was never learned.

They Seek to Agree on the Kind of Society They Want. Four and one-half months, two hours a day, five days a week, were devoted to the project. An orientation-motivation period of four weeks focused upon two problems: Is it important to build a plan for the future of America? and Is it possible to get the goals of such a plan so clear that the plan itself, in form and content, will be definitely indicated? In answering the first question, the students found themselves turning both to history and to their own community. From history, particularly that of the past quarter-century, they saw what had happened when America failed to plan after a previous great war. From their community, where in teams they interviewed many typical citizens, they found deep fear and uncertainty over the impending period of demobilization and reconversion. Gradually their own indifference and easy optimism that "everything will turn out all right" were quite markedly replaced by concern over their own stake in the future.

The second of the two questions led them to seek an understandable, tangible standard of a desirable society. They compared fascism and communism with democracy, and above all they tried to determine which basic type of society would be most likely to provide the widest opportunities for satisfaction of their own essential desires. At this point, then, they were compelled to examine their own desires and to locate those which were most common to all of them. Gradually they prepared a master list, and with it they tested the democratic and antidemocratic alternatives. When at last they reached a consensus that democracy alone could guarantee satisfaction not only of such "needs" as food and shelter, but also of such "wants" as participation and creative education, they were at least in some degree the possessors of a criterion with meaning and vitality in their own terms.

They Examine Existing Conditions and Consult Those Who Have Vital Ideas about Them. Following the orientation-motivation period, the students turned to the major areas which are relevant to a design for America. Several weeks were devoted to economic reconstruction, each of the major roads to "prosperity" from the extreme right to the extreme left being followed in turn and each being tested ultimately by the norm which they had already tried to establish. Pamphlet materials from such organizations as the National Association of Manufacturers, Co-operative League, Congress of Industrial Organizations, and from New Deal agencies were read and discussed, and finally the group sought the largest possible agreement among its members as to the most promising direction for economic planning to take.

The same general method was followed in studying politics, education, art, science, and "human relations." The present structure of public education, for example, was studied with a view to determining its effectiveness for the future democratic society—a process which led these high school students not only to rather devastating criticisms but to an appreciation of education as a necessary force within a larger context of institutional forces. So also with science and art. With the help of the science teacher, who co-operated in this part of the experiment, the group came to think of science as a social function (they read chapters from Bernal's *Social Function of Science*) with enormous possibilities for good or evil in the future of civilization. With the help of the English teacher, they considered poetry, music, architecture, city planning, until again they saw, however imperfectly, that art also is a social power important in any design for America.

They Check Their Design against the Criterion of Democracy. The closing weeks of the project were devoted to review, with the purpose, first of all, of appreciating the interrelationships of each area with the others. Returning frequently to their original criterion of democracy as the chief principle of synthesis, they saw how politics and economics become allies, they saw art and science co-operating in the building of cities, they saw intercultural and interracial democracy expanding through good education.[24]

Criticism of the Social-Problems Core

A social-problems core provides an excellent medium for learning value standards and how to use these in the process of critical thought.

[24] Theodore Brameld, *Design for America* (New York: Hinds, Hayden, and Eldredge; 1945), pp. 159–162. By permission.

However, the fact that vital social problems determine the scope of the content is in itself no guarantee at all that a value orientation will be deliberately used and taught. Of course, it is true that the solution of problems is impossible without the employment of values, at least in implicit form. Nevertheless, it is altogether possible to attack and to solve problems without clarifying and reconstructing confused and conflicting values. When the social-problems core neglects the study and explicit grounding of thought in a value orientation, individuals and groups are developed who are unable to think consistently, who are without bench marks for their decisions of right and wrong, and who are constantly at variance with themselves. On the other hand, a social-problems core that provides for the development of a consistent orientation to democratic standards is in complete accord with core theory and promises to develop individuals consistent in their methods of thinking and in their social-moral behavior.

The solution to a social problem requires the reconstruction of the personalities of individuals involved in the problem. If more adequate health services are to be provided, for example, all persons involved must undergo changes in the way they look at the matter. This means that their wants will be modified, that they will be willing to forego certain freedoms of social and psychological movement in order that all may enjoy more freedoms of activity with respect to health services.

A solution requires even more than that. Since the individual is inextricably woven into various groups that also exercise social pressure for or against the improvement of health services, these groups must also be modified. Indeed, it is likely that changes in the individual will be slow—or, if they are made at all, that they will not be sustained without changes in what the various groups define as their policies. It is thus a hard fact that the resolution of a social issue requires the achievement of enough social consensus among conflicting groups and individuals to sustain a course of social action. And this consensus, if it is an uncoerced one, will rest upon modifications of personal structures and group pressures.

From this way of looking at social problems, it is easy to see that children and teachers are limited in their capacity to solve them. To be sure, the resolution of a social issue always requires changes in persons, and for this reason it is educative. But school education can seldom be geared directly to the resolution of such issues. To do so on a large scale would result in turning children and teachers into politicians. There is, of course, nothing wrong with being a politician, and both teachers and students could learn a lot from engaging in political activities. But it would be difficult to justify building an educational program upon the thesis that education is politics.

The social-problems core must, therefore, place emphasis upon the rigorous study of problems and the consequent development of habits of effective thinking. It will, of course, encourage students to solve social problems and to act upon their conclusions in cases where the problems fall within their power to act.

4. The Problem of Sequence in the Core Curriculum

After the categories have been determined, the curriculum maker must then decide what aspects of each category are to be developed for each grade. The task of determining these aspects involves the problem of sequence. The structure of a core program is well illustrated by the following scope and sequence design, from the Santa Barbara County, California, program.

Scope
1. Developing and Conserving Human Resources
2. Developing, Conserving, and Intelligently Utilizing Non-Human Resources
3. Producing, Distributing, and Consuming Goods and Services
4. Communicating
5. Transporting
6. Recreating and Playing
7. Expressing and Satisfying Spiritual and Aesthetic Needs
8. Organizing and Governing
9. Providing for Education

Sequence
Integrating Theme for Kindergarten, Grades One, Two, and Three:
  Guiding the growth of children toward living more effectively in their immediate and expanding environment (home, school, neighborhood, and community), through participation in activities involved in carrying out the basic functions of human living.
Integrating Theme for Grades Four and Five:
  Guiding the growth of children toward living more effectively in a chang-

ing world and understanding it through investigating man's relationship
to his physical environment, comparing and contrasting our increasing
control of the environment with the simpler adjustment techniques
utilized by people of simpler cultures.

Integrating Theme for Grades Six, Seven, and Eight:
Guiding the growth of children toward gaining increasing effectiveness
in carrying out the basic functions of human living through developing
the ability and desire to react to the total environment according to a
pattern which is based upon (1) an adequate understanding and appreciation of scientific principles and methods involved, (2) an understanding of the resulting increased possibilities of control, and (3) an understanding of resulting rapidity of change.

Integrating Theme for Grades Nine and Ten:
Planning with respect to educational, vocational, personal, and social
goals, and gaining in understanding of the relationship between the problems of the individual and those of the school, community, state, and
nation.

Integrating Theme for Grades Eleven and Twelve:
Developing in understanding of the ways man has met and is meeting
his major problems with emphasis upon the solutions now proposed and
upon the historical foundations of present problems.

Integrating Theme for Grades Thirteen and Fourteen:
Developing in understanding of democratic ideals and their implications
for social organization.[25]

The problem of sequence is the problem of grade placement in a new
form. Instructional guides will usually contain many suggested problems, activities, and materials. But these may be developed in many
different ways by teachers and students, depending upon the status of
the classroom group at a given time. These details of the categories,
together with their sequence, will be shaped by conceptions of what
students at different ages can do successfully, the kinds of things they
will be interested in, and what is deemed to be of social importance.
In short, determination of sequence suggested for a core program rests
upon two sets of facts, one *psychological* and the other *sociological*. In
addition, a third factor, *temporal order,* is sometimes appealed to, but
it is of no particular importance in the core curriculum.

In an earlier discussion of grade placement it was pointed out how
such factors as maturity, experiential background, prior learnings, in-

[25] Santa Barbara County, California, *Santa Barbara County Curriculum Guide for
Teachers in Secondary Schools,* 1941.

terests, and difficulty underlie the grade placement of problems, activities, and materials of instruction. These same factors are no less related to the determination of sequence in the core program. In the activity curriculum, the experience and the interest of the students tend to be the factors most compatible with the activity theory. While these are always important factors in any form of curriculum organization, they are never used exclusively in the determination of sequence in a genuine core program. Such a procedure would tend to convert the core program in practice into an activity curriculum.

In addition to these factors, the solution of the problem of order in a core program always relies heavily upon such sociological strands as life in the home, school, community, and the wider society, including the peoples of the world with their diverse cultures but common problems. These strands include, consecutively, the individual's immediate environment, the expanding social and scientific world, and the development of the means and conditions of orderly social change. It is worthy of note that these constitute the integrating theme of each grade as well as the means by which the work of each grade is related to that of the preceding grade.

The Virginia course of study represents a pattern of sequence based upon a consideration of such sociological factors as well as interests and maturation. While the sequence of topics in this program is expressed as progressive development in centers of interests, in reality the grade topics suggested for the years beyond the third grade bear little relationship to the interests of students. The sequence of topics is as follows: Grade I, Home and School Life; Grade II, Community Life; Grade III, Adaptation of Life to Environmental Forces of Nature; Grade IV, Adaptation of Life to Advancing Physical Frontiers; Grade V, Effects of Inventions and Discoveries upon Our Living; Grade VI, Effects of Machine Production upon Our Living; Grade VII, Social Provision for Co-operative Living; Grade VIII, Adaptation of Our Living through Nature, Social and Mechanical Inventions, and Discoveries; Grade IX, Agrarianism and Industrialism and Their Effects upon Our Living; Grade X, Effects of Changing Culture and Changing Social Institutions upon Our Living; Grade XI, Effects of Continuously Planning Social Order upon Our Living.[26]

[26] Virginia State Board of Education, *Tentative Course of Study for the Core Curriculum of Virginia Secondary Schools*, pp. 16–19.

These guides to the integration of the work of each grade and the sequential arrangement of learning experiences are more the expression of what a committee of curriculum workers believes to be socially important and within the capacities and potential interests of students than reflections of research findings on the actual interests of children and adolescents. This observation, however, is in no way a criticism of the core program, since its basic theory emphasizes the sociological frame of reference.

Another illustration of the same kind of curriculum structure is that presented in the Santa Barbara City curriculum. It is expressed in terms of a general scope and a series of controlling themes for each grade, as follows:

Scope
1. Developing and conserving personal resources
2. Developing and conserving other than personal resources
3. Producing, distributing, and consuming goods and services
4. Communicating
5. Transporting
6. Recreating and playing
7. Expressing and satisfying spiritual and aesthetic needs
8. Organizing and governing

Sequence
Kindergarten and grade one:
   Growth in effective living through self-adjustment within the immediate environment.
Grade two:
   Growth in effective living through adjusting to the community.
Grade three:
   Growth in effective living by further adjusting to the community through the development of insights into the manner in which the natural and controlled environment is contributing to life in our community.
Grade four:
   Growth in effective living by further adjusting to the community through developing insights into the manner in which the present culture-groups are adjusting to life in our community.
Grade five:
   Growth in effective living through developing insights into the manner in which present as compared with former culture groups carry on the basic functions of human living in Santa Barbara and California.

Grade six:
  Growth in effective living through problem-centered experiences directed toward understanding how modern techniques are being utilized in carrying out the basic functions of human living in the United States.
Grade seven:
  Growth in effective living through problem-centered experiences directed toward understanding the interdependence of individuals in our school, our community, the regions of our nation, and in the countries of our American neighbors.
Grade eight:
  Growth in effective living through problem-centered experiences directed toward understanding how man's courage, knowledge, discoveries, and inventions have affected his way of living.
Grade nine:
  Growth in effective living through problem-centered experiences directed toward understanding and appreciating the individual's privileges and responsibilities as an American citizen.
Grade ten:
  Growth in effective living through problem-centered experiences directed toward happy, effective, personal, spiritual, social, recreational, and vocational living in the home, school, and community.
Grades eleven, twelve, and beyond:
  Growth in effective living through problem-centered experiences directed toward achieving the highest possible quality of experiences through striving for social, political, and economic democracy in local, state, and national setting and for peace and co-operation on the international scene.[27]

The problem of sequence in a normatively oriented core program—a program that places emphasis upon problems centering in the question of what social values and goals should guide public thought and action in dealing with social issues—is one that has not been solved. Some progress toward a solution has been made in such programs as the Virginia core program and the Santa Barbara City and County programs. In these programs, "centers of attention" from grades one to twelve advance from factual analyses of conditions, in the earlier grades, to social values and social planning in the eleventh and twelfth grades. These programs, however, fall short of deliberate projections of future

---

[27] Santa Barbara (California) City Schools, *Developmental Curriculum,* Bulletin No. 1, Revision No. 1, November, 1941, pp. 22–24.

social arrangements worthy of human striving and capable of giving explicit direction to present social action.

The genuine core program requires the sort of sequential arrangement of problems and materials described by Harap as characterized by "progress toward a social ideal." He continues:

This pattern of sequence is used in programs which move toward the development of a social ideal. The attainment of the goal is dependent upon growth in social understanding. For example, the Santa Barbara sequence for secondary grades builds successively toward a cultivation of a willingness to participate in improving the social order. This involves understanding of biological and physical progress; which is followed by an analysis of social organization. At this stage the pupil grasps the need for improvement in social organization; this leads, finally, to the planning of a better society.[28]

▶ *Following Up*
  This Chapter

1. Make a list of categories that you would be willing to defend as being in keeping with the principles of a core curriculum.

2. What do you see as desirable intermediate steps or phases of change between a pure-form subject organization and a pure-form core curriculum? List the major features of each of these phases.

3. To what extent should the categories of a core curriculum reflect concern for problems that seem to be more or less peculiar to the local community?

4. Assume that you were able to observe a core curriculum in practice for as long a period as was necessary in order to determine the extent to which it was in agreement with your standards of the very best core curriculum. List the standards you would apply in approximate order of their importance.

5. Select from your library a recent course of study which seems to have some of the characteristics of a core curriculum. Are its basic categories subject-centered, individual-centered, or social-centered? What plan of

[28] Henry Harap (Ed.), *The Changing Curriculum* (New York: Appleton-Century-Crofts, Inc.; copyright 1937), p. 108. By permission.

sequence was used? What is especially good in this plan? What are its outstanding weaknesses?

▶ *Suggested*
Reading

1. Examples of core programs are described in *Exploring the Curriculum*, by H. H. Giles, S. P. McCutchen, and A. N. Zechiel. More complete accounts of these same programs are given in the Progressive Education Association's *Thirty Schools Tell Their Story*. Both of these volumes were published in conjunction with the Eight-Year Study of the Progressive Education Association.

2. In addition to the core programs described as a part of the Eight-Year Study, attention is specifically invited to the programs advocated by the state of Virginia and by Santa Barbara County, California. See *Course of Study for Virginia Elementary Schools*, Grades I–VII; *Tentative Course of Study for the Core Curriculum of Virginia Secondary Schools; Santa Barbara County Curriculum Guide for Teachers in Elementary Schools*, Vol. II; *Santa Barbara County Curriculum Guide for Teachers in Secondary Schools*, Vol. IV. See also The University School, Ohio State University, *A Description of Curricular Experiences: The Upper School*.

3. A good description of the Horace Mann culture-epoch core is provided in *Thirty Schools Tell Their Story*. Bases for the adolescent-needs core are found in Giles et al., *Exploring the Curriculum* and in *Reorganizing Secondary Education*, by V. T. Thayer, Caroline B. Zachry, and Ruth Kotinsky. Social categories are described by O. I. Frederick and Lucile J. Farquear, *Journal of Educational Research*, Vol. 30, pages 672–679. A slightly different grouping is reported in *The Changing Curriculum*, Henry Harap, editor.

4. Perhaps the most exhaustive classification of the various core programs found in schools throughout the country is the U.S. Office of Education Bulletin 1952, No. 5, *Core Curriculum Development: Problems and Practices*. The most exhaustive treatment of needs as the basis of the school program is found in "Adapting the Secondary-School Program to the Needs of Youth," Part I, *The Fifty-Second Yearbook of the National Society for the Study of Education*.

Chapter 16

Experimental Appraisal
of Curriculum Patterns

IN PREVIOUS CHAPTERS the basic principles of the subject, activity, and core curriculums were described, and these three curriculum patterns were analyzed from the standpoint of the forms they have assumed in practice. Each pattern was found to have unresolved problems, resulting either from defects in its basic theory or from difficulties in the translation of the theory into practice. The question to be explored in this chapter is whether or not it is possible, on the basis of experimental evidence, to say that one of these pure-form curriculums is better than another.

A considerable number of experiments bearing upon this question have been conducted in the past two decades. Since these research studies have been the object of much criticism, some attention will be given to the development of a set of criteria against which to judge the studies themselves. Then the more important studies will be briefly reviewed. After this review, a short critique of the studies will be made.

1. *Conditions Required for*
Experimental Investigations

It is much easier to describe the conditions for research studies designed to ascertain the relative effectiveness of curriculum patterns than it is to create these conditions in an actual investigation. In order to set up these conditions assumptions must be made with respect to the values, beliefs, and skills of all individuals—children, teachers, administrators, parents, and other members of the community—who influence the effects of the school's instructional program. The validation of such assumptions is an almost impossible task. Nevertheless, granted the limitations imposed by these difficulties, the curriculum worker needs the best experimental evidence he can get concerning the behavior resulting from experiences under the various plans of curriculum organization.

In order to appraise experimental studies of curriculum patterns, it is necessary to understand the conditions that must be satisfied by any dependable piece of research on this problem. Succinctly, these conditions are as follows:

1. The theory of the curriculum pattern to be tested must be stated unequivocally.
2. The conditions (social, psychological, educational, and physical) under which the curriculum pattern is tried out must be described in detail.
3. The anticipated results of the curriculum theory must be stated as hypotheses derived from the theory.
4. Data must be collected to ascertain whether or not the hypotheses derived from the curriculum theory were borne out by observed facts; for as these hypotheses are tested out, confirmed, or invalidated by observation, the theory is affirmed or denied.

Assuming there were no logical errors in the derivation of the hypotheses and that only minor errors have been made in the observations, an experimenter is permitted to make certain statements when these four criteria have been satisfied by an experiment. He can say, for example, that this kind of a curriculum will yield these results under these specified conditions. He can also say that if these results were not obtained, then the specified conditions were not present. On the other hand, he is not permitted to make certain other statements. He cannot say that such results as those issuing from this experiment can be obtained *only* with this kind of a curriculum. For there may be some other way by which the same outcomes can be secured. Nor can he say that this kind of a curriculum yields these results in less time and with less expenditure of effort than some other curriculum. For, again, there may be other and more efficient ways of attaining the same ends.

If an investigator wishes to make comparative statements—for example, that a core curriculum is better in certain regards than a subject curriculum—his inquiry must satisfy certain conditions in addition to those listed above. He must run two independent experiments in which the conditions are exactly alike in all relevant respects, except that the curriculum theory and pattern will be one kind in one of the experiments and another kind in the other. Then the hypotheses by which the two theories are being compared will be tested in each experiment by careful observations. And that pattern which excels in the most significant ways will be judged superior.

Curriculum Theory Must Be Clearly Stated

It is important in any experimental investigation to know what is being tested. One of the ways of meeting this requirement here is to state clearly the curriculum theory to be used in constructing the program of action to be tried out. Only if the theory is unequivocally stated can another investigator, or for that matter anyone else, determine whether or not the propositions experimentally tested were derived from, and only from, the curriculum theory presumably involved in the experiment. The experiment itself merely demonstrates that if certain educational procedures are used under a defined set of circumstances, then certain specified results follow. Hence, unless the essential logical connection is clearly established between a given curriculum theory and the educational procedures used in the experiment, it is impossible to make any valid assertion whatever about the curriculum theory on the basis of the results obtained in the experiment.

Thus it is not possible to assert, on the basis of evidence secured from experimental investigation, that the core curriculum, for example, will yield such and such learning products, unless the operations performed in the experiment are precisely, without addition or subtraction, the operations logically implied by the core-curriculum theory. Obviously, the first step in meeting this requirement is a full and accurate statement of the theory itself. Apart from an unequivocal statement of the core theory, no one can ascertain with precision what the experimenter means by a core curriculum and to what extent, if at all, the operations actually employed in the experiment deviated from the operations logically entailed by the theory. Hence, no one can say whether or not the results obtained by the experiment—assuming that it is sound in other respects—can be ascribed to the core curriculum so as to confirm or refute the claims made by its advocates. Consequently, a full and precise statement of the theory is the first requirement of sound curriculum research.

For this reason curriculum research based on one of the pure-type curriculums will have greater value for the curriculum worker than research not so grounded. If, under practical circumstance, the precise operations prescribed by a pure-type curriculum cannot be rigorously carried through, then the experimenter should clearly detail both the nature and the amount of deviation from the pure type.

The general conditions of any complete theory of curriculum organization involve such a multitude of variables that research workers may choose to test only one or two aspects of a curriculum pattern. In this instance, countless other variables are still operative, and those that are instrumental in determining the results of the experiment must be described in tangible terms. If the curriculum organization to be tested, for example, were a pure-form subject curriculum, but one in which problem solving rather than exposition were used as the primary method, it would be the responsibility of the research worker to describe precisely the points and amounts of deviation in this regard from the pure-type subject organization. In this way anyone reviewing his research would know, by reference to the theory of the pure-type, just what principles had actually been tested.

Conditions of the Experiment Must Be Described in Detail

The conditions of any experiment are defined by two different sets of facts. The first is comprised of all those facts that constitute the experimental features of the inquiry. In the case of an experiment on curriculum patterns, these facts consist of those that characterize the curriculum plan—the scope and sequence of the curriculum, the units and methods of instruction, and the like. The second set of facts, referred to as conditioning factors or circumstances, consists of those that make up the conditions under which the experiment must be conducted. It is clear that the curriculum pattern cannot operate in a vacuum—that it can be put into practice only in some set of circumstances capable of being factually described. Since these circumstances influence both the practice and what results from it, it is necessary that these conditioning circumstances be known and described as accurately as possible.

Among the facts describing the circumstances under which the experiment must be carried on are those that have to do with the personalities of the children—values, felt needs, attitudes, abilities, knowledge, skills, emotional behavior, health, and the like; those that have to do with the personalities of teachers—values, attitudes, instructional skills, knowledge, and the like; and those that characterize the human situation in the school and classroom. The reader can easily suggest other factors likely to affect the results of curriculum experimentation.

When these two sets of conditions are fully and accurately described, it is possible to determine whether or not the results secured in the experiment should be ascribed to the specified curriculum pattern when the latter is applied in the combination of conditioning circumstances under which the experiment was conducted. In the absence of such knowledge it would not be intellectually feasible to attribute the outcome to anything in particular.

Moreover, the use of experimental results in the determination of educational practice requires that the conditioning circumstances as well as the curriculum pattern be duplicated as nearly as possible. Practitioners have frequently attempted to apply the results of experiments without creating the conditions within which the new technique, or procedure, could yield the results claimed for it in the experiment. A comparable case would be that of a soap manufacturer who proceeded to produce soap by mixing the chemicals used to make soap experimentally while at the same time ignoring the conditions of temperature, moisture, and the like adhered to in the experiment. In defense of the practitioner it should be pointed out that reports of educational experiments are often so lacking in detail that the practitioner cannot find out the conditions under which the results were obtained.

Furthermore, so long as the research in any field is in its early stages, the variables that determine the results cannot be isolated, measured, or otherwise described with exactitude. This is the general situation with respect to curriculum research. It has seldom been proved that any one variable—mental age, chronological age, learning materials, methods of teaching, socio-economic status of parents, or any other factor—is, or is not, a major determinant of the results of an experiment. This is especially true in the case of experimentation on curriculum designs.

Research Design Should Include Hypotheses

The experimenter must be aware of, and state accurately, not only the factual conditions of an experiment but also the consequences which, if the theory involved is sound, must follow from the execution of the experimental operations. This statement of the consequences anticipated from the application, under a given set of conditions, of a particular theory—in terms of the present case, a curriculum theory—is called a hypothesis. It usually takes the form of an "if . . . then" proposition. If such and such things are done (first set of facts discussed above) in such and such conditions (second set of facts discussed above), then such and such behavior will be developed in students. The "then . . ." part of the last sentence expresses the anticipated consequences; the "If . . ." part of the sentence expresses the conditions under which the consequences are expected to occur.

Hypotheses tend to orient and sharpen the investigation by indicating both its scope and its direction. Without these aids it is difficult to know precisely what to investigate, what to look for, and how to determine when the study has been completed in a satisfactory manner. In addition, the careful delineation of a hypothesis is a check on the understanding of the theory to be tested. In curriculum research the specific hypotheses are stated behaviors to be expected as a result of the application of at least some portion of a curriculum theory. For example, the theory of a core curriculum emphasizes a focal cluster of social values, which it claims to develop in the behavior of individuals. A hypothesis derived from statements about this feature might be: "If a group of children (accurately described) have gone through the experiences provided by a pure-type core curriculum (under specified conditions), then they will make social-moral decisions in conformity with the value system in the particular version of the core curriculum em-

ployed in the experiment." The proof, or disproof, of this hypothesis
would be a direct test of this particular claim and, indirectly, a test also
of the core curriculum theory.

Hypotheses Must Be Checked by Records of Behavior

After the hypothesis drawn from curriculum theory has been clearly
stated in terms of expected behavior, it is necessary to test the hypothesis. This test can be made by checking the predicted behaviors against
the observed behaviors of students who have gone through the experimental curriculum. The record of behavior must be broad enough to
cover the hypothesis. It is fairly common for experiments in curriculum
development to postulate broad hypotheses and then to use only the
limited facilities afforded by pencil-and-paper tests. The curriculum
investigator should seek any and all valid evidence bearing upon the
particular hypothesis under scrutiny.

2. *Problems Involved in Making Comparative Judgments*

The curriculum worker is usually interested not only in the learning
products resulting from a new curriculum design but also in a comparison of these products with those resulting from some older and
better understood alternative plan. Thus investigations are common
which attempt to compare "traditional" and "new-type" curriculums
with respect to their effects upon student behavior. The group experiencing the "traditional" pattern is usually called a "control group,"
while those working under the new program constitute the "experimental group."

It should be noticed that this procedure embraces not one but two
experiments, carried on simultaneously, and that the "new" and "old"
curriculum patterns can be compared, with respect to their effects, only
if the conditioning factors of the two experiments are comparable. Let
it be assumed, for instance, that two groups of students are equated
with respect to intelligence, achievement, emotional reactions, attitudes,
interests, and so on. Assume also that the teachers of the two groups

are equated with respect to intelligence, interest, teaching ability, and the like. In addition, assume that the school and classroom "atmospheres" are alike—except as different atmospheres are a direct result of the educational procedures prescribed by the respective curriculum theories involved—and that the community influences on teachers and students are comparable for the two groups. In short, let it be supposed that the two groups, and the circumstances within both the school and the community, are the same in all relevant respects except for the curriculum patterns. Where these suppositions are true, then the two experiments, at least in theory, can be compared; and the differences in results can be ascribed to the differences in curriculum theory and practice.

Unfortunately, it is not now possible to know all of these conditions. Even if they were known at a given moment, it would be impossible to keep them from changing during the course of an experiment. Partly for this reason, and partly for other reasons that cannot be discussed here, experiments to determine the effectiveness of curriculum designs, to say nothing of those to ascertain the comparative effectiveness of two or more designs, are always subject to criticism—and, in some cases, to repudiation.

To continue the analysis, suppose that the foregoing requirements have been met, that the facts have been collected, and that comparisons of the resulting behaviors have been made. For example, it has been shown that the students in the "old" curriculum have acquired more skill in arithmetic and less ability to engage in co-operative activities than the students of the "new" curriculum. On the basis of such comparisons as these, would it be possible to decide which curriculum is the better? While such a decision would be possible for an individual, he would not attain agreement with other persons unless they were in substantial agreement with him upon the objectives of education. In order to compare two or more curriculum patterns, therefore, it is necessary to take into account not only the consequences of each pattern under comparable circumstances but also the value system used in making the comparative judgments.

With all the foregoing considerations of an adequate experimental appraisal of curriculum patterns in mind, attention is now directed to a review of some of the more significant curriculum experiments.

3. Six Major Curriculum Experiments

The six studies to be reported briefly are not meant to include all of the significant researches concerned with appraisal of curriculum designs.[1] However, they are among the most significant investigations of curriculum organization conducted within recent years and are generally representative of both the types of research and the findings in this field. These studies—three conducted in the elementary schools and three in the secondary schools—were planned with considerable care and, as a group, have exerted a marked influence upon programs of curriculum development.

The New York City Experiment

A large scale six-year experiment involving 75,000 children and 2,500 teachers was conducted in the elementary schools of New York City.[2] "Typical schools throughout the city were designated as 'activity schools' and were encouraged to develop a program based upon units of pupil activity as a substitute for, and supplement to, the traditional textbook learnings." [3] The experimental and control schools were paired on the basis of national or social background, socio-economic status, location in the city, and intelligence of pupils.

In an experiment involving as many schools and teachers as did the New York City study, it would be almost impossible either to hold the experimental and control conditions constant from school to school and classroom to classroom or to describe in any detail the exact nature of the instructional program carried on with any one group. As a consequence only the major differences between the experimental and control groups were reported. Jersild and his associates describe these in the following words:

Activity classes, on the whole, exhibited more participation by the pupils in the planning and direction of some or all the features of the work of the

---

[1] See "Suggested Reading," p. 422.

[2] A. T. Jersild, R. L. Thorndike, B. Goldman, and J. J. Loftus, "An Evaluation of Aspects of the Activity Program in the New York City Public Elementary Schools," *Journal of Experimental Education*, Vol. 8 (December, 1939), pp. 166–207.

[3] *Ibid.*, p. 166.

class (partly by way of pupil chairmanships, committees charged with responsibilities and duties of various kinds, etc.), more freedom on the part
of the pupils, individually or in small groups, to work on projects of their
own: more freedom (usually during some periods of the day more than
others) to move about, to consult with other pupils, to approach the teacher
and converse with her; more opportunity for the pupils to evaluate and
criticize the performance of members of the class; more apparent opportunity for individual pupils to exercise and obtain recognition for their own
interests and aptitudes, including the opportunity to do "research" on special aspects of subject matter that is being considered by the class as a
whole, and encouragement to tap sources of information outside the traditional textbooks by way of bringing in reports, illustrations, clippings, etc.,
from sources not assigned to the class as a whole; more emphasis on field
trips.

Features which especially seemed to distinguish the "average" activity
from the "average" control class, are, first, more outward appearance of
pupil self-direction; second, more diversity and a larger range of occupation, especially during certain periods of the day; third, more projects of
the sort that correlate various enterprises and skills as distinguished from
the study of isolated subject matter; fourth, a considerably larger display
of pupils' handiwork (drawings, models, workbooks, posters, class journals,
class anthologies, etc.).[4]

In reporting the results of this study the investigators concluded:

Accordingly, the picture as far as it emerges from the lines of investigation mentioned above shows that while the control children seem to have
a slight but statistically unreliable advantage as far as achievement in
academic subject matter is concerned, the activity children surpass the
controls in the frequency with which they exercise such presumably wholesome activities as leadership, experimentation, self-initiated enterprises,
participation in oral discussion, and the like. The activity children have
more experiences and show more tangible accomplishments in the fields of
the arts and crafts. The activity children as already noted also tend to be
superior in tests that call for intellectual operations. . . .[5]

[4] *Ibid.*, p. 196.
[5] Jersild et al., "A Further Comparison of Pupils in Activity and Non-Activity
Schools," *Journal of Experimental Education,* Vol. 9 (June, 1941), p. 308.
  The superiority in intellectual operations referred to was in the Wrightstone tests of
working skills, explaining facts, applying generalizations, current events, what you
believe, and personality.

In his review of the New York City experiment Morrison summarizes the findings as follows:

In the mastery of knowledge and skills three conclusions are supported by the data reviewed . . . : (1) the only statistically reliable differences between the two programs favor the activity procedure and are found in those areas affected by the latter's emphasis upon developing skill in critical reading, in the use of elementary research techniques, and in the development of civic attitudes and understanding of social relationships; (2) in all but three of those areas of knowledge and skills wherein the difference favored the regular program, improving the sampling of the activity program tended to lessen or to eliminate the difference; (3) the activity program may be continued and improved with reasonable assurance that children will gain as thorough a mastery of knowledge and skills as they would in the regular program.[6]

Morrison also commented upon the fact that, contrary to many verbal claims made before this experiment, the activity group tended to excel in respect for school authority. Children in the activity classes also liked school better.

There is no good reason to doubt either the conclusions drawn by Morrison or the results described by the experimenters. They are based upon observations of what particular children actually did. However, the question remains as to whether or not these results can be attributed to the differences in curriculum patterns used in the experiment. There is no guarantee that the conditioning circumstances were held constant from classroom to classroom throughout the investigation. Nor is there sufficient reason to suppose that the instructional procedures characteristic of either the "activity classes" or the "control classes" were followed precisely from day to day.

While there was doubtless something operating to produce the reported results, what this something was remains a mystery. Neither is there any certainty that the same results would be obtained again were the investigation to be repeated. While there is no doubt that the reported facts are correct, the explanation of the facts in terms of the superiority of a particular curriculum pattern is by no means established.

[6] J. Cayce Morrison et al., State Education Department, *The Activity Program; A Survey of the Curriculum Experiment with the Activity Program in the Elementary Schools of the City of New York* (New York State Education Department, 1941).

Turning now to the question of whether or not the experiment demonstrated the superiority of the activity curriculum, it is apparent at once that the term "activity classes" as used in this study is not synonymous with the term "activity curriculum" as a pure form. While the majority of the features of an "activity class" in the New York City experiment would be present in a pure-form activity curriculum, they could also be found in an enriched subject organization. The first, and most distinctive, characteristic of the activity curriculum is the effort to base the educational program squarely on the interests of children. But in this experiment no thoroughgoing and sustained attempt to ground the school program in the interests of children appeared among the conditions of the experiment. Hence the logical grounds for the claim that this experiment demonstrated the superiority of the activity curriculum are insufficient.

Pistor's Experiment

The experiment conducted by Pistor [7] in the experimental school of Ball State Teachers College differs in many respects from the New York City experiment. Pistor used two groups of students. One of the groups had been in a "progressive" program for two years—grades three and four. During the first two years of school the pupils of this group had been in a "traditional" public school program; hence, their first four years of school were divided equally between traditional and progressive programs. The other group had been in a traditional public school program for all of the first four years. The experiment covered grades five and six. With respect to previous school experience, therefore, the two groups differed at the beginning of the experiment by two years of time spent in the traditional or in the progressive program.

The achievement of the two groups was tested at the beginning of the experiment, midway through the experiment, and then again at the end. In addition, individuals selected from these two groups, for comparative purposes, were equated on the basis of mental age, chronological age, motor ability, ratings of social qualities (co-operation, initiative, and popularity), and home training.

[7] F. A. Pistor, "Evaluating Newer School Practices by the Observational Method," *Sixteenth Yearbook* of the Department of Elementary School Principals (Washington, D.C.: National Education Association; 1937), pp. 377–389.

Furthermore, the experimental techniques included controlled observation of thirty-eight "trait-actions." These were selected on the basis of "yes" or "no" responses of professional educators to a questionnaire asking whether or not the respondent "Believed that encouraging fifth- and sixth-grade children to perform the action would help to develop a certain general trait such as 'initiative,' 'work spirit,' 'reliability,' and so forth." [8] One hundred such questionnaires were sent to professional educators. At least forty-eight of the seventy-three persons responding to the questionnaire voted "yes" on the thirty-eight trait-actions finally selected. In order to check these particular actions, each group was observed during two-week periods (alternating with two-week periods of no observing). Six different pupil activity periods—practice or drill, conference, problem solving, creative work or construction, directed study or research, and before-school periods—were observed from two to six times each week during the two-week periods.

Pistor describes the following four types of work units in the experimental program:

1. Studies of the environment, consisting of activities which called for a resynthesis of subject matter from the more vital phases of the conventional content subjects.

2. The creative arts, consisting of activities dominated by the play impulse, and utilizing aspects of music, fine arts, dramatics, literature, writing, and construction.

3. Maintenance and self-government activities, which were the children's attempts to assume responsibility for the recurring affairs of the day. . . . The duties were performed by twelve committees.

4. The tool subjects, which were considered as byproducts of the units of work in the other three fields. They included the specific learnings in reading, language, spelling, penmanship, and computation which were needed in the other activities of the children.[9]

A more complete insight into the learning conditions in the experimental school is afforded by the following description of the ways in which units of work were selected.

1. The teacher began with no definite idea for the unit, either as to subject matter content or methods of carrying it out. He listed the suggestions

[8] *Ibid.*, p. 381.
[9] Pistor, *op. cit.*, pp. 379–380.

for a unit made by the pupils and helped the children prepare lists of possible contents for the proposed units. These contents were in the form of things to do, places to visit, and questions to answer. Each group presented to the whole class for its consideration a proposed unit and its possibilities. As this went on, the teacher called the attention of the pupils to criteria for selecting a worth-while unit. As the attention of the class gradually focused on the units which seemed most worth while, the activity of sponsors for units based on cursory, temporary, and capricious interests subsided. After several days of campaigning, the final selection was made by class vote.

2. The teacher began with no definite idea for the unit. He listed the suggestions of the pupils, which were immediate or remote experiences of interest. As these suggestions were made, the teacher led the group to explore them. In so doing, he was able to determine the intensity of group interest in a particular suggestion. When enough incipient interest was manifested toward a proposed unit, the teacher attempted to arouse activity with respect to the unit. If the interest subsided, the teacher turned to another suggested unit and repeated the process of orientation. Thru a period of several weeks there emerged a permanent interest which the teacher capitalized into a unit of work.

3. The teacher selected and prepared a unit in advance because he believed it fell within certain areas in which the genuine interests of children at that age are usually located. He suggested the unit and showed its possibilities to the class, permitting the group to suggest its own ways of carrying out the project. When tentative plans were completed, each child was permitted to vote for or against the plans. If not enough children voted for the plans, the latter were either modified or the teacher suggested another unit.

4. The teacher selected and prepared a unit in advance after examining the previous educational experience of the group and deciding that the unit was necessary to give richness or breadth to their experience, or to fill what appeared to be important gaps. He suggested the unit, outlined its possibilities, and led the pupils to give reasons why it should be undertaken. These reasons were often similar to his own. Tentative plans were made co-operatively, and the group was given opportunity to vote for or against the unit.

5. Short-time and minor units were selected less formally and in proportionately less time.[10]

[10] Pistor, *op. cit.*, p. 380.

At the beginning of grade five the experimental group was superior in all thirty-eight positive trait-actions. However, the differences were statistically significant in only fourteen of the comparisons. While both groups showed marked improvement, the experimental group made far greater improvement. At the end of grade six all the differences continued to favor the experimental group, and in all but four of the thirty-eight comparisons these differences were statistically significant.

Both groups were tested on academic achievement at the beginning of grade five, during the first month of grade six, and again in the ninth month of grade six. The experimental group made higher average scores during each of these testings in reading, language usage, literature, history, geography, hygiene, arithmetic, and in all subjects combined. In dictation (spelling) the two groups were equal on the first and last testings. On the test given at the beginning of the sixth grade the traditional group slightly excelled the experimental pupils in spelling. At the end of the experiment, differences between the two groups, on the basis of average grade equivalents, favored the experimental group by a year or more in reading, literature, history, hygiene, and arithmetic. It is interesting to note that the experimental group excelled the traditional group by exactly one year in literature and hygiene at the beginning of the experimental testing. In the final test the experimental group tested one and two-tenths years better in literature and one and one-tenth years better in hygiene, thus showing a gain of two-tenths of a year in the first instance and one-tenth in the second.

It is at once apparent that the organization of learnings in Pistor's experimental school approximates much more closely the characteristics of a pure-form activity program than did those of the New York City experiment. However, since content in the form of units was selected in five different ways in the experimental classes, it is likely that the program conformed more closely to the basic principles of an activity curriculum at some times than at others. The fourth method of selecting units described above is not wholly in keeping with the fundamental postulates of activity theory. A school program cannot be regarded as an activity program in the full sense of the term unless it is based primarily upon the interests of children.

Since both the traditional and experimental school groups shared the experimental school conditions during grades five and six, the critical point of any comparison is the difference between the school experiences of the two groups in grades three and four. It can be assumed that the third- and fourth-grade learnings in the experimental school approximated those described in grades five and six. Unfortunately, however, the nature of the experiences afforded the traditional school group in grades three and four is not described.

Wrightstone's Appraisal of Elementary School Practices

The investigation conducted by Wrightstone in selected "newer-type" and "conventional" elementary schools has some features in common with both the New York City and Pistor studies. Individual students from the newer-type schools were matched with those in conventional schools on the basis of intelligence (I.Q.), chronological age, and socioeconomic status. The conventional and experimental schools were equated in terms of general community characteristics of wealth, socioeconomic status, and type of population.

Wrightstone's description of the conventional school follows:

The practices of the conventional elementary school . . . are founded upon an educational theory which has the following principles or hypotheses: First, the classroom is a restricted form of social life, and children's experiences are limited therein to academic lessons and allied supplementary subjects and activities. Second, the quickest and most thorough method of teaching is to allot a certain portion of the school day to instruction in separate subjects, such as reading, phonics, word-drill, language, arithmetic, history, geography, health, gymnasium, music, drawing, and literature. Third, children's interests which do not conform with the set curriculum should be disregarded. Fourth, the real objectives of classroom instruction consist to a major degree in the acquisition of the content matter and skills of each subject. Fifth, teaching the conventional subjects is the wisest method of achieving social progress. . . .

Materials and content of study are assigned by the teacher and all pupils study identical assignments and recite on them. . . . Pupils are permitted to exert little or no influence in forming or developing the curriculum. . . . Little attempt is made to correlate or integrate the various subjects of the curriculum. . . . The content of each subject which is to be taught during stated periods is specified in a definite course of study. During class recitations the teacher tests the pupil's mastery of assigned skills, habits, and knowledge, and, if such a test reveals that the pupil lacks mastery in any of these fields, the teacher's role is to correct any deficiency by drills and suggestions.[11]

While such a description may apply to the programs of the schools chosen for Wrightstone's inquiry as conventional schools, he does not indicate that this characterization actually described the programs of these schools, individually or as a group.

According to Wrightstone, the newer-type school has the following characteristics:

There is no fixed succession of subject matter in the grades of newer schools. Units of work adapted to children's interests and experiences include subject matter appropriate to the pupils' needs and abilities. The units have certain common factors or component structural elements. These elements, or steps, have been organized for convenience into the following categories: (1) stimulation, or identification, of interests; (2) formulation of aims, activities, and methods; (3) investigation and collection of data: (4) integration, or correlation, of data; (5) culmination of activities; and (6) evaluation of outcomes.

Co-ordinate pupil activities and services such as assembly, clubs, pupil councils, library, health services, and child guidance services, are closely related to the classroom programs in the newer-type schools. Many assembly programs, for example, grow out of the classroom activity—usually a dramatization or other culminating activity in a unit of work. In like manner the library may become a center—co-ordinate with the classroom—for solving, by means of pupil investigation, problems in social studies, natural sciences, and the arts, as well as a place to enjoy literature.

In the schools employing newer instructional practices the educational, personal, and social adjustments are regarded as important aspects of the teaching process. Educational adjustment for low ability or performance in reading, for instance, is made with a proper regard for concomitant factors in a child's personality, such as eyesight, interests, emotional stability, home conditions, and adjustment or integration of personality. Records and reports also play an increasingly important role. The records and reports, however, grow from the philosophy and purposes of the school so that they reflect valid and reliable continuous evidence about the growth and development of pupils toward the avowed objectives of the school.

[11] J. W. Wrightstone, *Appraisal of Newer Elementary School Practices* (New York: Bureau of Publications, Teachers College, Columbia University; 1938), pp. 40–41. By permission.

The formulation of cardinal objectives for elementary education has tended to be stated in terms of major purposes of the school's instructional program. The objectives accepted as a basis for gathering evidence in this study were those formulated and published in recent bulletins by teachers and school officials of New York, California, and Colorado. In these states the major objectives of public elementary schools are to help every child:

1. To understand and practice desirable social relationships.
2. To discover and develop his own individual aptitudes.
3. To cultivate the habit of critical thinking.
4. To appreciate and desire worth-while activities.
5. To gain command of the common integrating knowledges and skills.
6. To develop a sound body and normal mental attitudes.

These objectives, when defined in terms of typical pupil activities, may well become the basis for evaluating the newer practices in elementary education.[12]

By the process of equating individuals from newer-type schools with those from conventional schools and then statistically treating the differences among them with respect to achievement along specified lines, Wrightstone obtained the following results:

1. The experimental school pupils were significantly superior on a test of information about current social, economic, and aesthetic problems, and noted personalities.
2. More broad-minded interpretations and more tolerant attitudes toward social and economic affairs were demonstrated by the experimental school pupils. These differences were statistically significant.
3. On the self-marking tests the experimental school pupils were found to be significantly more honest than those in conventional schools.
4. There was a statistically significant difference favoring the experimental pupils in the number of acts defined as "self-initiated." Experimental school pupils performed more "critical" and "experimental" acts and about an equal number of "co-operative," "leadership," and "work spirit" acts.
5. Experimental school pupils had significantly better average ratings based on judgment scales in both creative language arts and creative graphic arts.

[12] Wrightstone, *op. cit.*, pp. 212–214. By permission.

6. Experimental school pupils were, on the average, better on the art judgment tests, but the difference here was not statistically significant.

7. All differences between means of the two groups on the three measures of critical thinking favored the experimental school pupils. However, these differences were statistically significant only in "obtaining facts." Tests of "explaining facts" and "applying facts" fell short of statistical significance.

8. Although the difference was not a statistically significant one, the conventional school pupils showed a considerable average advantage in tests of health information.

9. The advantage of experimental pupils in physical capacity, as measured by a physical fitness index, was statistically significant.

10. The experimental school pupils were significantly better in measures of both personal and social adjustment.

11. Results of a questionnaire regarding leisure-time activities gave the experimental group a statistically significant advantage in eight of the eleven interest categories.

12. Experimental school pupils in the primary grades were significantly superior in standardized tests of reading, language, and spelling. While their mean score in arithmetic was also better, the difference here was not a statistically significant one.

13. Differences in average scores on tests of reading, language, and arithmetic in the intermediate grades favored the experimental school pupils, but none of these differences were statistically significant ones.

This investigation is subject to some of the same objections as those raised in the case of the New York City study. From a strictly logical standpoint Wrightstone's investigation does not conclusively demonstrate the superiority of an activity curriculum in any regard. His description of newer practices is strikingly similar to the pure-form activity curriculum. Likewise his account of conventional practices corresponds in most regards to the subject pattern. But these observations do not mean that the programs of the new-type and conventional schools correspond in every regard to these descriptions. Wrightstone did not claim that every teacher in each of the experimental schools employed, to an equal extent, the educational principles and techniques outlined in his description of new practices. Nor did he claim that every teacher in each conventional school taught in the precise way indicated in his account of conventional procedures. There is every reason to suppose that in actual practice the new-type programs varied markedly from the pattern laid down by Wrightstone in his ideal description of these programs. Moreover, it is equally certain that the new-type programs varied from school to school and from classroom to classroom. Similarly, the correspondence between his description of conventional schools and what actually went on in these schools was undoubtedly more marked in some schools and classes than in others.

Consequently, the kinds of educational programs compared in the investigation are uncertain. Moreover, the conditioning circumstances were not necessarily comparable from school to school. Although an effort was made to equate both the pupils and the schools with respect to certain factors, there were many other apparently relevant conditions, such as teacher personality, which were not taken into account. Thus it hardly seems reasonable to suppose that the evidence from this investigation is conclusive.

Wrightstone's Secondary School Experiment

Wrightstone's appraisal of experimental high school practices [13] employed the same experimental design as that used in the elementary school experiment just described. A group of conventional and experimental practices were generally defined. Several metropolitan communities with conventional schools were matched by communities with experimental schools on the bases of type of community (suburban residential, industrial residential, etc.), wealth, educational expenditure, type of population, and socio-economic status and background. Teachers in the two types of schools were equated on the bases of training and preparation, experience, salary, and teacher-pupil ratio. Individual pupils from experimental and conventional schools were matched on the bases of chronological age, intelligence (I.Q.), socio-

[13] J. W. Wrightstone, *Appraisal of Experimental High School Practices* (New York: Bureau of Publications, Teachers College, Columbia University; 1936).

Attention is directed to the fact that Wrightstone's secondary school experiment was actually reported two years prior to his elementary school study. They are reviewed here in reverse order for the purpose of reporting the three elementary school experiments as a group, to be followed by the three in the secondary schools.

economic status of parents, and number of semesters' study in certain fields. Students in these two groups were then compared on a variety of measures of significant outcomes.

A few selected quotations from Wrightstone's comparison of the nature of conventional and experimental high schools may serve as a description of the differences between the types of curriculum offered in these schools.

In conventional high schools learning is often based upon an assumption of specificity of behavior. . . . Generally teachers in the experimental high schools interpret the individual as an organism in interaction with the environment. . . . Learning is always multiple, and multiple values must be considered and safeguarded. Not merely an individual's progress in subject matter mastery but also his mental health, safe-confidence, and other attitudes toward social and scientific processes, toward classmates, teachers, and himself are aspects of the educative process. . . . Experimental high schools have moved toward reduction of separate and compartmentalized courses by correlating or integrating conventional subject matter from several courses around a class or an individual problem or need. Subject matter thus tends to become a means rather than an end of instruction. Several patterns of correlation or integration among the school subjects have begun to appear in the experimental practices of some schools. Perhaps the most common form of integration is that in which the various elements of social studies, English, and art are woven into a more or less unified fabric. This pattern of correlation operates in this manner: The teachers in the various subjects who are teaching the same pupils meet and co-operate in co-ordinating the work of all the subjects around certain more or less major themes. . . . Because its context is not as essential to the solution of present-day problems as in other knowledge, there are evident two tendencies toward adapting mathematics to the needs of the pupil. The one tendency is that of the conventional schools toward addition and specialization of courses in mathematics. The other tendency—toward integration—is sponsored by the proponents of the experimental schools who feel that the interrelationships of the sciences and mathematics with other parts of the curriculum should be emphasized.

In foreign language instruction the conventional schools tend to retain the grammatical and syntactical approach with intensive reading. Experimental schools have accepted and emphasized the major aim of extensive reading of a foreign language with only incidental and functional grammar, especially during the first two years of instruction. The major point of issue is the validity of the extensive reading with functional grammar approach versus the intensive reading with systematic grammar approach. Other points are the understandings and appreciations of peoples and their cultures.

The health and physical education program in the conventional schools usually is not adapted to the needs of the individual boys and girls. Quite frequently there are no means or instruments for ascertaining the abilities or disabilities of the pupils; hence there is no remedial program of a systematic sort. Slight correlation exists between the health instruction and physical education features of this program. Correlation with other areas of information and knowledge, especially the physical and biological sciences in the curriculum of the school, is nonexistent.

The physical education programs of the experimental schools of this study have for a long time comprised informal activities in the gymnasium and on the field adapted to pupils' interests and needs. . . . Calisthenics and formalized class drill have been eliminated. . . .

Attempts are frequently made to correlate aspects of health and physical education with the natural sciences, especially biology and physics. . . . Correlation with the social studies is maintained.[14]

By comparing students from the experimental schools with students from the conventional schools with respect to certain achievements, the superiority of one type of school over the other was ascertained. For convenience, Wrightstone's findings regarding the relative superiority of these two types of schools are summarized as follows:

1. In social studies, English, and fine arts, the experimental pupils were significantly superior in recall of facts in literature, working skills, interpreting facts, civic beliefs, and in number and quality of self-initiative and co-operative activities.

The experimental pupils did only slightly better, on the average, in recall of facts in social studies, on the art judgment test, and in ability to apply generalizations. These differences were so slight that they fell far below the level of statistical significance.

Experimental pupils had the edge in organizing skills, but the difference here also fell short of statistical significance.

Recitational activities had slightly greater frequency per pupil in the conventional schools.

[14] Wrightstone, *Appraisal of Experimental High School Practices,* pp. 186–189. By permission.

2. In the natural sciences and in mathematics, experimental school students were significantly superior in recall of facts in physics and chemistry, in ability to apply generalizations, on tests of science beliefs, and in achievement in plane geometry.

Results of tests in general science, biology, working skills, interpretation of facts, and algebra favored the experimental school pupils. These differences, however, were not statistically significant.

Both quantitative and qualitative analyses of self-initiative and cooperative activities indicated significant superiority in the case of the experimental group.

The conventional school reported a significantly greater number of recitational experiences per pupil.

3. Experimental pupils were significantly superior in tests of French reading, French grammar, and in the total French tests. Their superiority in French vocabulary approached statistical significance.

In Latin, experimental pupils were superior on the average in reading, vocabulary, and the total of test scores. However, the conventional school pupils were superior in Latin grammar. None of the differences in Latin were statistically significant.

4. Both boys and girls in the experimental group were significantly superior to their corresponding conventional school group in a battery of physical fitness tests.

Experimental school pupils were slightly superior in the personal adjustment questionnaire, and conventional school pupils were slightly superior in social adjustment. Both of these differences were so slight that the best interpretation is one of no difference between the two physical education groups on adjustment factors.

Did this investigation test the effectiveness of two different kinds of curriculums or only variations of a single curriculum pattern? From Wrightstone's description of the conventional and experimental schools, it is clear that these schools did not differ in their basic curriculum structure. Differences in goal orientation, integration, care for pupil interests and needs, and especially in teaching methods were often quite marked, but both types of schools were organized in terms of the boundaries of knowledge defined by subjects. Hence the investigation is more a comparison of the different possibilities within the subject organization than it is a comparison of essentially different organizational patterns.

Furthermore, it is apparent that there are marked differences among the various conventional and experimental schools. The conventional schools were not all "conventional" in the same way or to the same degree. Nor did the experimental schools all "experiment" in the same way or to the same extent. It would probably be reasonable to assume that all the conventional schools followed to some extent the basic theory of a subject curriculum. On the other hand, it is altogether likely that some of the experimental schools departed from the basic principles of the subject curriculum little, if at all, while others may have had features in common with the activity and core curriculums.

This investigation is subject to the same criticism as the preceding inquiry into newer practices in the elementary school. There were differences between the experimental schools and the conventional schools. This much seems to be established factually. But, as in the preceding study, the explanation of these differences is by no means clear.

The Kight and Mickelson Experiment

The experiment by Kight and Mickelson attempts to determine the relative efficiency of problem-centered as against subject-centered instruction. A problem is defined as "A situation in which action is involved, the learner is the agent of the action, and he has some difficulty or blocking in regard to the action." According to this definition, "The presentation of units of instruction must focus the factual information presented on the pupils' difficulty in such a manner as to relate this information directly to the action which pupils must take in order to overcome their difficulty or to solve their problems." In sharp contrast to this position, the advocates of subject-centered instruction hold that if "The learner is in command of the essential facts supporting a given action, this action can be expected naturally to follow." These contrasting statements define the essential distinctions employed by Kight and Mickelson to classify problem-centered and subject-centered units of instruction.[15]

[15] S. S. Kight and J. M. Mickelson, "Problems vs. Subjects," *The Clearing House,* Vol. 24, No. 1 (September, 1949), pp. 3–7.

Eight problem-centered and eight subject-centered units were con-structed by the investigators and were taught according to a rotation technique, by twenty-four regular teachers, to ninety-six classes in eleven different secondary schools in the Los Angeles area. The 1,415 pupils involved were measured with respect to both factual informa-tion and rules of action learned. The units of instruction were in the areas of English composition, life science, social studies, and English literature.

Kight and Mickelson summarize their findings as follows:

1. Pupils learned significantly more rules of action, regardless of subject-matter field, with the problem type.

2. Pupils in the I.Q. range of 62 to 85 learned significantly more rules of action with the problem type.

3. The findings indicate, but do not conclusively prove, that pupils in the I.Q. range of 115 to 143 learned more rules of action with the problem type.

4. In terms of the total combined results, pupils learned significantly more factual information with the problem type; but in terms of the results by subject-matter fields and I.Q. levels, these findings were not in all cases statistically significant.

5. Pupils made significantly more connections of specific rules of action with their corresponding facts with the problem type, regardless of subject-matter field or I.Q. level.

6. When facts learned were compared with rules of action learned *within* the problem type of presentation, there was no statistically significant difference between the amount of rules of action and factual informa-tion learned regardless of subject-matter field or I.Q. level.

7. When facts learned were compared with rules of action learned *within* the subject-matter type of presentation, pupils learned significantly more factual information than they learned rules of action, regardless of subject-matter field or I.Q. level.[16]

It is at once apparent that the Kight and Mickelson study is not de-signed to compare the subject and activity, or the subject and core curriculums. Hence, this experiment cannot be used to describe the resultant learnings within any one of these organizations in its pure form This investigation was set within the framework of broad-fields

[16] S. S. Kight and J. M. Mickelson, "Problems vs. Subjects," *The Clearing House*, Vol. 24, No. 1 (September, 1949), p. 7.

and separate subjects, both of which are forms of the subject curriculum. The significance of the study for present purposes lies in the fact
that it attempts to test one of the distinctive features of the subject
curriculum—namely, the instructional method. The method of instruction associated with the subject curriculum is carefully defined and
tested against the instructional method used in both the activity and the
core curriculums. But in any attempt to use this study to compare the
effectiveness of different curriculum patterns, it should be remembered
that method of instruction is only one aspect of such patterns. Hence,
the results obtained with this limited operation may be quite at variance with those obtained when the total curriculum patterns are tried
out on a comparative basis.

Eight-Year Study—College Follow-Up Experiment

It should be understood at once that the Eight-Year Study [17] was not
designed to evaluate, except in one respect, different patterns of curriculum organization. The initial concern of the Commission on the
Relation of School and College of the Progressive Education Association was with college entrance requirements. How would the graduates
of schools unhampered by college entrance requirements, and differing
in at least several respects from the more traditional high school, fare
in college? While the Eight-Year Study grew to include most of the
aspects of an extensive curriculum-building and evaluation project in
the thirty selected secondary schools, the only comparison between
graduates of the traditional and experimental schools was with respect
to their relative success in college.

It should also be clearly understood that the graduates of the thirty
experimental schools had not experienced anything like a common
curriculum pattern. They represented at least thirty different programs.
Some of these programs differed little from those of the traditional
schools with whose graduates the "experimental" students were compared. Other programs represented marked deviations from the ortho-
dox program of college preparation.[18] Since each of the Thirty Schools
developed its curriculum independently and with no common orienta-

[17] Dean Chamberlin, Enid Chamberlin, N. E. Drought, and W. E. Scott, *Did They
Succeed in College?* (New York: Harper & Brothers; 1942).
[18] *Ibid.,* Preface, pp. xix–xx.

tion or design, it is not possible to group them in any manner to indicate superiority of any particular curriculum organization.

The report entitled *Did They Succeed in College?* sets forth the research method and findings in such an excellent and concise manner
that the description will be quoted here with no attempt at further
condensation.

An intensive study has been made of 2,108 graduates from the Thirty
Schools which, under an agreement with more than 300 colleges, had been
freed from the necessity of meeting the usual unit or examination requirements for college admission. Of these Thirty Schools graduates, 1,475
were matched, student for student, with graduates of conventional schools
in terms of scholastic aptitude, interests, and socio-economic background.
This report deals primarily with these 1,475 matched pairs of college students. In general, these students were fairly representative of the student
bodies in most of the colleges where the Study was undertaken.

Four classes were included in the Study: the classes entering college in
1936, 1937, 1938, and 1939. Data were gathered on the first class for four
years, on the second for three, on the third for two, and on the last for one
year. The follow-up was carried on in 38 colleges of four types: the northeastern men's colleges, the northeastern women's colleges, coeducational
endowed colleges and universities, and middle-western state universities.

Success in college, as defined in this Study, included grades earned;
certain "intellectual characteristics" which are not necessarily measured
by grades; citizenship in the college community as indicated by extent
and quality of interest in extra-class activities; and the attainment of
personal goals as revealed by the nature of vocational orientation, concern
about the contemporary scene, attitudes toward and relation to contemporaries. In effect, these criteria represent success as judged by college
standards, by the students' contemporaries, and by students themselves.

Data were gathered from regular interviews with students, questionnaires, records of reading and activities, reports from instructors, official
college records, and comments of college officers, house heads, and others
who had contact with the students. Summaries were made of grades
and of questionnaire responses. In addition each student was judged for
each year in college in some 60 separate areas including his quality of
thinking, extent of participation in each of a series of organized activities
and leisure time interests, personal-social relationships, problems, and a
number of others. All available data for each student in a given year were
used in arriving at such judgments.[19]

[19] Chamberlin et al., *op. cit.*, pp. 206–207. By permission.

General Findings

A comparison of the 1,475 matched pairs reveals that the Thirty Schools graduates

1. earned a slightly higher total grade average;
2. earned higher grade averages in all subject fields except foreign language;
3. specialized in the same academic fields as did the comparison students;
4. did not differ from the comparison group in the number of times they were placed on probation;
5. received slightly more academic honors in each year;
6. were more often judged to possess a high degree of intellectual curiosity and drive;
7. were more often judged to be precise, systematic, and objective in their thinking;
8. were more often judged to have developed clear or well-formulated ideas concerning the meaning of education—especially in the first two years in college;
9. more often demonstrated a high degree of resourcefulness in meeting new situations;
10. did not differ from the comparison group in ability to plan their time effectively;
11. had about the same problems of adjustment as the comparison group, but approached their solution with greater effectiveness;
12. participated somewhat more frequently, and more often enjoyed appreciative experiences, in the arts;
13. participated more in all organized student groups except religious and "service" activities;
14. earned in each college year a higher percentage of nonacademic honors;
15. did not differ from the comparison group in the quality of adjustment to their contemporaries;
16. differed only slightly from the comparison group in the kinds of judgments about their schooling;
17. had a somewhat better orientation toward the choice of a vocation;
18. demonstrated a more active concern for what was going on in the world.

Some of these differences were not large, but wherever reported, they were consistent for each class. It is apparent that when one finds even small margins of difference for a number of large groups, the probability greatly increases that the differences cannot be due to chance alone.

It is quite obvious from these data that the Thirty Schools graduates, as a group, have done a somewhat better job than the comparison group whether success is judged by college standards, by the students' contemporaries, or by the individual students.

The Thirty Schools differed widely in the extent to which they experimented. A special analysis was therefore made of the graduates of the six schools whose programs differed most sharply from the conventional. A corollary study was made of the graduates from the six schools which departed least from a traditional approach. Each of these groups was contrasted with its respective comparison groups.

The graduates of the most experimental schools were strikingly more successful than their matchees. Differences in their favor were much greater than the differences between the total Thirty Schools and their comparison group. Conversely, there were no large or consistent differences between the least experimental graduates and their comparison group. For these students the differences were smaller and less consistent than for the total Thirty Schools and their comparison group.

Finally, a study was made of the graduates of two schools which were among the most progressive. Again, these students were contrasted with their matchees. The superiority of these progressive students over their comparison group was greater than any previous differences reported.

Clearly, among the Thirty Schools, the more experimental the school, the greater the degree of success in college. Furthermore, although students of high aptitude seem to have profited most from experimental education, students of low aptitude profited as much from experimental programs as their matchees did from conventional schooling.[20]

The part of this investigation most relevant to the present discussion is that which compares the graduates of the schools exhibiting the most extreme departures with graduates of schools having the most conventional programs. The findings show that the graduates of these most novel schools excel those of the most conventional schools—and excel them more extensively than the graduates of the remainder of the thirty experimental schools. Conversely, the graduates of schools manifesting the least innovation showed the least gain over the graduates of the most conventional schools.

These results are encouraging, for they indicate that improvements in the educational program can be made. But again the nature of the changes to be made in order to secure such improvements is not clear

[20] Dean Chamberlin, Enid Chamberlin, N. E. Drought, and W. E. Scott, *Did They Succeed in College?* (New York: Harper & Brothers; 1942), pp. 207–209 [italics in original]. By permission.

from this investigation. Valuable as the inquiry is in other connections, it gives no clear insight as to what changes to make in conventional programs. In other words, the explanation of the observed superior results, in terms of any specific set of operations and conditions, is not available from the reports of the investigation.

4. *Critique of the Experimental Evidence*

Regardless of the reasons advanced to explain the fact, it is still true that curriculum research, as exemplified by the six prominent studies reported here, falls considerably short of meeting desirable standards of research design. In general, neither the curriculum theories under test nor the logical connection of the hypotheses with these theories were made explicit. As a consequence, those who examine this research have difficulty in knowing just what propositions were proved or disproved.

Neither is it possible to discover the precise conditions obtaining in either the experimental or control classrooms. Thus it is not possible to say under what conditions the results reported occurred or could be expected to occur. It is even likely that conditions neither described nor controlled were responsible in part for the experimental results. Consequently, there is no conclusive evidence to indicate that a program based primarily upon children's interests—or, for that matter, a program based upon any other characteristics—is or is not superior, in terms of any set of criteria, to some other sort of a program.

That these six studies do not follow rigorously the research standards set forth earlier in this chapter is probably due to several important factors. First, it is almost impossible to design research in a practical situation in terms of acceptable standards. It is exceedingly difficult to find or to formulate clear and concise statements of the basic theory of any pure-type curriculum. It is still more difficult to establish in experimental schools even an approximation of the essential conditions of any one curriculum theory. Further, the numerous variables in the learning situation make control or adequate description of many of these experimental determinants a tremendous task. Again, since difficulties are encountered in stating curriculum theory precisely, hypotheses based upon such theory cannot be sharply drawn.

Another practical problem centers in a lag in fundamental research in evaluation. It was necessary in most of these studies to do research in evaluation concurrently with research in the curriculum. New techniques of evaluation were developed in these studies, but these techniques were often relatively crude. Many additional methods were needed, but they could not be devised under the pressure of experimental schedules.

Still another trouble, ascribable in large measure to practical concerns and growing out of the complexities already mentioned, is that the experimental and control schools, or classes, are really not comparable under the conditions affecting curriculum research. The effects of many of the variables, generally thought to be significant in determining the outcomes of curriculum research, cannot be accurately isolated and described.

A second reason for deviation from the highest standards of research design may lie in the fact that these investigations were not actually planned for the purpose of accumulating knowledge about the curriculum by testing basic principles. This is certainly true of the Eight-Year Study, which made freedom from college entrance requirements the major difference between the experimental and control groups. Other investigations seemed more intent upon testing a general hypothesis—that something new, especially an innovation in the direction of pupil freedom, is superior to something old and familiar—than upon testing hypotheses drawn from a particular curriculum theory.

Other deviations from the research design suggested in this chapter may be due to an attempt on the part of several of these studies to include a large population and to conduct two or more experiments simultaneously. To point out that individual schools and individual classes are, in some respects, unique is to deal in platitudes. Yet it is this undeniable fact that causes experimental conditions to vary within a population of a large-scale investigation and leaves practitioners who would use the results in doubt as to what the conditions really were. Single experiments with smaller populations, with one set of well-defined hypotheses, and with much more thoroughly described experimental conditions, would probably offer more dependable and more valuable knowledge.

5. *What Conclusions May Be Drawn?*

The value of studies such as those reported above does not depend entirely upon the generalizations that may be legitimately drawn from the experimental evidence. For the studies are also important as pioneering investigations, clearing the way for new areas of research and study. In this sense their value consists primarily in the fact that they have indicated the possibilities of a broadly conceived program of research, which deals with curriculum patterns as a whole rather than with isolated issues and problems.

It is as unsound to lump together indiscriminately, in summary form, the results of experiments carried out under different conditions as it is to base extensive comparisons upon the results of such experiments. At the same time, it is interesting to note that the experimental innovations described in these six experiments do seem to have a few common strands. The existence of certain elements that seem to be common to the "nontraditional classes" in these six experiments indicates nothing, of course, about the extent to which these elements were operative in producing the results. Furthermore, there are marked differences from experiment to experiment and within the bounds of a large-scale investigation with respect to both the form and amount of these common factors. Nevertheless, the following characteristics seem to be common to the "experimental classrooms."

1. At least a portion of the program relied upon problem solving rather than purely expository methods of teaching. This is a distinctive feature of no curriculum organization. However, it is an essential element in both the activity and core programs and is not an essential feature of an organization by subjects.

2. Some attempt was made to appeal to the interests and felt needs of students. If the content was determined primarily on this basis, as it may have been in certain classes in Wrightstone's elementary schools and at times in Pistor's study, the curriculum employed was an activity curriculum. On the other hand, if children's interests and needs were used merely as a source of motivation, the curriculum involved would have been either a core or a subject curriculum. From the reports of

these studies it is not possible to tell how interests and needs were used.

3. Students generally had some part in planning and evaluating their work. This is, of course, an essential characteristic of both activity and core curriculums, but it is not an essential feature of the subject organization.

4. The materials of learning, methods of study, and experiences were more diversified than those provided in a subject curriculum. Although this diversification is neither a distinctive nor an essential characteristic of any curriculum, it would logically follow from the characteristics set forth as essential to the activity and core programs.

In general, curriculum research tends to support the position (although it does not offer conclusive proof) that curriculum change is desirable even though the nature of the change takes many forms and varies widely in extent. The innovations seem to have resulted in little loss to the realization of conventional objectives; in some cases, these objectives have actually been achieved more effectively by these innovations. Moreover, the attainment of so-called intangibles such as cooperative behavior, critical thinking, and intellectual independence is greater in the new-type curriculum practices.

Yet the plain fact is that the curriculum worker still does not have experimental evidence to indicate the specific curriculum conditions from which specified behaviors can be expected. He does not have conclusive empirical evidence that a pure-form subject curriculum is inferior—or superior—to a pure-form activity curriculum, or to a pure-form core curriculum. Nor does he have experimental proof of the relative effectiveness of either a pure-form activity or core curriculum.

While the evidence is not yet conclusive, it is still legitimate to point out that these studies do support the proposition that the newer curriculum practices, generally characterized by the four points outlined above, usually secure results equal to the older practices so far as subject-matter objectives are concerned and that they appear to achieve additional results not ordinarily included in the ambit of the more traditional curriculums. The issue of the best form of curriculum organization is not fully settled, and the need for research is urgent. Even so, the weight of experimental evidence has now shifted the burden of proof to the defenders of traditional practices.

▶ *Following Up*
This Chapter

1. From the basic theory of the subject, activity, or core curriculum derive a list of hypotheses that should be tested in curriculum research. State them as definite hypotheses in a form to be proved or disproved.

2. List the factual conditions that should be described as variables in curriculum research. Suggest possible ways of describing each condition or variable.

3. Using the ideas in items 1 and 2 above, set forth the general outlines of a satisfactory curriculum experiment. Indicate the general steps to be taken to carry out this research.

4. Select from your library the report of an experiment dealing with some broad aspect of curriculum organization (one of the six reported in this chapter, or another) and review this study critically. What, if anything, is proved by this study? What hypotheses does it suggest for further testing? How could this experiment be improved if it were to be redesigned?

▶ *Suggested*
   Reading

1. For reviews of and citations to curriculum research, see *An Evaluation of Modern Education,* edited by Paul Leonard and Alvin Eurich. *Encyclopedia of Educational Research,* edited by Walter S. Monroe, will also be beneficial for these brief reviews and citations. J. Harlan Shores' *A Critical Review of the Research on Elementary School Curriculum Organization, 1890–1949,* offers a very brief account and extensive bibliography of curriculum research in elementary schools.

2. For help on problems of experimental methodology, see F. Stuart Chapin's *Experimental Designs in Sociological Research,* especially Chapters 1, 2, and 7. See also "Science of Education," by B. Othanel Smith, in *Encyclopedia of Educational Research* (Revised Edition). If you wish to go more deeply into the meaning of scientific method, see Cohen and Nagel's *An Introduction to Logic and the Scientific Method,* especially Chapters XI, XII, XIII, XIV.

HUMAN RELATIONS

Part Four | # IN CURRICULUM

DEVELOPMENT

PART THREE *of this book explored various conceptions of the curriculum, but nothing was said about how any of these curriculums might be put into practice. To know* what *to do is not the same thing as knowing* how *to do it. It is, of course, important—indeed indispensable—that a faculty, especially its leadership, know clearly the changes they desire to make in the educational program. Unless the changes are clearly understood in terms of the practical operations they require and in terms of the direction in which they lead, a faculty need not be surprised if its efforts go astray. There is no substitute for* thinking through *a change before it is made, if risk is to be reduced to a minimum.*

Clearly, however, the execution of what is thought through and planned is just as important as the thinking and planning. Fully as many curriculum programs have collapsed because of faulty execution as from inadequate understanding of the changes to be effected. The plain fact is that far less attention has been given to the question of how to make changes in the educational program than to the formulation of the changes themselves. Hence, there is need for intensive exploration of the problems of human and social engineering—problems inevitably encountered in a program of curriculum development. Everyone knows how easily the best laid plans are wrecked for lack of know-how.

The science of social engineering has hardly reached the infant stage of development. Know-how is still largely based on common sense and techniques derived from trial and error. Nevertheless, a few promising theories, supported by research evidence, are beginning to bear fruit in many areas of human relations, especially in the field of industry. Furthermore, some of these ideas are being tried out in social work of all kinds, particularly in education. The purpose of the next four chapters is to explore the theory and the techniques of inducing and controlling educational change, in the hope that more adequate know-how can be developed. There is far more knowledge and skill now available than is sometimes supposed—certainly far more than is used.

The development of a systematic program of curriculum change will require modification of many ideas about human behavior and of many human-relations skills. This means that educators must re-educate themselves for the tasks of curriculum development. If their efforts to change the educational program are to be effective, they must change themselves. No one would propose to improve his efforts to use a typewriter without developing new skills or improving the ones he has already. Yet men repeatedly attempt to improve their efforts to teach, to work with others, and to mediate human relations with the same attitudes, knowledges, and skills that led to inadequate results in the first place.

These four chapters will take up such questions as these:

1. What does a change in the curriculum involve with respect to relations among pupils, teachers, administrators, and parents?
2. How can we know where to begin in making a curriculum change?
3. How can the change be introduced?
4. How can the change be controlled once it is begun?
5. How can the new curriculum be sustained so that it will not change back to what it was before the change was made?
6. What is the role of leadership in educational engineering?
7. How can consultants be used effectively?

Chapter 17

Curriculum Development as Educational Engineering

AS INDICATED in preceding chapters, curriculum building involves the task of determining the objectives and content of the educational program together with the way the content is to be organized and taught. No less important, as a phase of curriculum building, is the task of altering the existing curriculum.

The problem of how to change the curriculum has seldom been solved successfully. Everyone who has been involved in programs of curriculum development knows that all sorts of resistance to curriculum changes arise from parents, teachers, students, administrators, and organized groups of the community, and from outside educational agencies. Attempts to carry out plans of curriculum change have often failed when faced with these resistances. In some cases superintendents, principals, and teachers have lost their jobs because of public reaction against curriculum innovations they were attempting to introduce. In the more fortunate situations the resistances were dissolved or else converted into actual support for the new program. In other instances, even where curriculum changes have been made on paper, and new and up-to-date courses of study printed and issued to teachers, opposition has permitted little or no change at the level of classroom practice.

More frequently, the resistances have been overcome temporarily only to emerge later in a stronger form to force the curriculum to revert to its former state. A letter to a school system in which such regression has occurred is likely to be answered as follows: "A few years ago when Mr. Johnson was here we were doing some of the things you asked about. But now we are doing about what we were before he came."

Those who attempt to change the relations among individuals, or the structure and processes of a social institution, are involved in "social engineering." If dependable principles and techniques are employed, and if skill is exercised in using them, the anticipated results will be obtained. All those who engage in educational work—like political and economic leaders, labor leaders, and so on—are either good or bad "social engineers," depending upon their knowledge of valid principles and techniques and their skill in applying them. When the principles and techniques of social change are applied to the problem of inducing, controlling, and maintaining changes in an educational system, the process is referred to as "educational engineering."[1] It is the purpose of this chapter to set forth the bold outlines of curriculum development from this standpoint.

1. Well-Known Approaches to Curriculum Change

Before turning to an analysis of the task of inducing and controlling change in the educational program, the commonly used approaches to curriculum change will be set forth.[2]

In the history of curriculum development three approaches have been employed: the administrative approach, the grass-roots approach, and the demonstration approach.

[1] Herbert A. Thelen, "Engineering Research in Curriculum Building," *Journal of Educational Research,* Vol. 41, No. 8 (April, 1948), pp. 577–596. See also *Progressive Education,* Vol. 26, No. 7 (May, 1949). The entire number is devoted to a discussion of educational engineering.

[2] For discussion of these types, see William M. Alexander, "State Leadership in Improving Instruction," *Teachers College Contributions to Education,* No. 820, and J. G. Saylor, "Factors Associated with Participation in Co-operative Programs of Curriculum Development," *Teachers College Contributions to Education,* No. 829.

The Administrative Approach

As the first move in the administrative approach, the superintendent of schools, recognizing the need for curriculum development, sets up machinery for accomplishing the needed revision. He arranges for faculty meetings in which the need for curriculum improvement is presented, and he asks the board of education to approve a curriculum development program. Then a steering committee is appointed, consisting of administrative officers and teachers. This committee, working closely with the superintendent, performs a number of functions: it formulates general plans; it develops guiding principles; and it usually prepares a statement of general objectives covering the entire school system. These formulations become the curriculum development manual for the remainder of the faculty.[3]

In addition, the steering committee may, and usually does, work out plans for training teachers in curriculum work. It determines the number and kind of consultants to be employed and the kinds of activities best calculated to familiarize teachers with the theory and practice of curriculum building. The steering committee may also set up advisory committees or councils, composed of laymen, to work with the steering committee in the formulation of plans, principles, and objectives.

The plans finally worked out by the steering committee usually provide for a number of committees, consisting largely of teachers and referred to as "production committees," to prepare new courses of study in keeping with the objectives and guiding principles laid down by the steering committee. In the high school, these production committees are usually appointed for each subject. In the elementary school, they may be appointed by subjects or by grade levels. They work out the objectives of their respective subjects and suggest methods of teaching and materials of instruction. All these objectives and plans go into the preparation of courses of study, which are the chief obligations of the production committees.

When the courses of study are completed, they are reviewed either by the steering committee or by a committee created especially for that purpose. The purpose of the review is to perfect the co-ordination of the work of various departments and of separate grades, to edit the expres-

[3] L. T. Hopkins, *Curriculum Principles and Practices,* pp. 287–513.

sion and form of the courses of study, and to make such other changes as may be required in the preparation of the materials for publication.

Finally, the courses of study must be tried out and installed. This responsibility is ordinarily assumed by an installation committee. This committee interprets the new courses of study to teachers and principals who were not directly involved in the preparation of the new guides. Teachers and principals are made acquainted with the techniques and purposes of the revised curriculum by discussions, by class visitations, and by such other devices as may seem to be effective. As the new courses of study are tried out, they may be modified as classroom experience indicates.

The direct approach to curriculum building was developed in the early days of the curriculum movement. One of the first places to use it was the city of Denver, in its program of curriculum revision initiated in 1923. This approach was used quite generally in the 1920's and is found not infrequently today. While it has resulted in some improvement in the schools when employed under favorable circumstances, it has not succeeded in bringing about and maintaining educational changes commensurate with expectations. Partly for this reason—and partly because it was conceived, initiated, and directed from the top, and thus judged to be undemocratic—it has been abandoned in theory and, in many places, in practice.

The Grass-Roots Approach

Failure of the administrative approach was attributed largely to the fact that it did not enlist the interests of teachers in the task of curriculum revision. The teachers did not become personally involved in such a way that changes in the curriculum were perceived by them as being of constructive consequence to themselves and their work. Those who developed the grass-roots approach attempted to find ways of involving all members of the staff in the problem of curriculum building, from the first to the last stages of the process. In its most comprehensive form the grass-roots approach is community wide. It embraces not only teachers but also students, parents, and other members of the community.[4] This approach is based upon a few general propositions, among which are the following:

[4] Helen F. Storen, *Laymen Help Plan the Curriculum.*

1. The curriculum will be improved only as the professional competence of the teachers improves.
2. The competence of teachers will be improved only as the teachers become involved personally in the problems of curriculum revision.
3. If teachers share in shaping the goals to be attained, in selecting, defining, and solving the problems to be encountered, and in judging and evaluating the results, their involvement will be most nearly assured.
4. As people meet in face-to-face groups, they will be able to understand one another better and to reach a consensus on basic principles, goals, and plans.

When this approach is employed in its broadest form, these principles apply also to the students and to the lay members of the community.

In sharp contrast to the city-wide or state-wide programs associated with the administrative approach, the grass-roots procedure begins with individual schools in each neighborhood. Each school is encouraged to work as a unit in the development of a new program. Perhaps the most important feature of this procedure is that the teachers, administrators, students, and parents of a particular locality can work face-to-face on their common problems. In this way the remote and impersonal problems encountered in the administrative procedure are eliminated. This is deemed to be a distinct gain, since teachers will be more interested in problems of their own school or neighborhood than in those of city-wide scope. This approach also precludes the problems of curriculum installation faced in the administrative procedure. Since the teachers of each school co-operatively work out their own programs of instruction, they do not have to put into use courses of study worked out by other teachers and by administrators.

In this pattern of curriculum development the function of the central administration is to provide stimulating leadership, free time, materials, and whatever else the various schools may need. A number of techniques have been used to encourage individual schools to improve their programs. One of the most successful is the workshop technique, which provides opportunities for teachers to engage in co-operative curriculum planning. Some workshops are provided by local school systems, and here administrators, teachers, and laymen work shoulder to shoulder planning and developing changes in the educational program. These workshops are frequently arranged as preschool-year conferences. Where teachers' salaries are maintained over a twelve-months' period, one or more weeks before the opening of school are set aside for curriculum planning. Then again a brief work-conference may be scheduled at the end of the school year to review and to evaluate the year's work and to plan for the next workshop in the fall.

In other cases workshops are operated by universities and colleges as part of their summer-school programs or as part of their off-campus programs in the regular academic year. In a few states, the state departments of public instruction have taken the leadership in developing and operating workshops. These workshops ordinarily are organized for a special purpose—to work on problems in the language arts, the sciences, and so on; to work on problems in guidance; to deal with problems in evaluation; to work out materials and procedures for a core curriculum. Participants are expected to work on problems that are significant to them and to resolve these problems in such a way as to deal with them effectively in their own schools.

The grass-roots approach also makes wide use of consultants, as well as of bulletins and study guides issued by the central administration on such topics as child development, community needs and resources, social and economic conditions, and innovations in curriculum theory and practice. The study guide issued by the Illinois Secondary School Curriculum Program, for community co-operation in educational planning, is illustrative of this kind of material. It suggests that the youth, the school, and the community be studied along the following lines:

The Program and Methods of Your School

The Guide does not purport to indicate all the types of information about your school that would be desirable as a basis for curriculum improvement. All of the following questions are significant; undoubtedly, others will be suggested as your study progresses.

1. What is some local problem that the faculty thinks needs attention? What are the curriculum implications of this problem?
. How well is the school at present meeting the needs of youth and of society outlined on pages 15–17?

    a. Through the subject-matter content of courses required of all students.

    b. Through the provision of elective courses.

    c. Through teaching methods.

       (1) Do students know why they are doing what they are doing?

       (2) To what extent is teacher-pupil planning followed?

       (3) How effective are the classroom discussions, questioning, reports, and the like?

       (4) How effectively are audio-visual materials and other teaching aids being utilized in meeting the needs of youth?

       (5) To what extent do the evaluative instruments in use measure the purposes of instruction as defined in terms of pupil behavior?

    d. Through the functioning of the guidance organization.

    e. Through the program of extracurriculum activities.

    f. Through the provision and maintenance of appropriate building facilities, supplies, and equipment.

    g. Through knowledge gained from socio-metric tests.

3. What relationships exist between the school and the homes of the students?

    a. What do teachers actually know about home conditions of individual students?

    b. Is the system of reporting pupil progress to parents (grade cards) consistent with the youth needs described on pages 16–17?

    c. To what extent have parents become aware of the purposes of the school and its program for achieving these purposes?

4. What relationships exist between the school and agencies, employers, and other groups in the community?

5. What percentage of the high school graduates of the past ten years have entered college? What have they taken? How well have they succeeded?

6. What provisions have been made for a year-around program including such activities as summer camps, planned vacations, co-ordinated work experiences, and recreational activities?

7. To what extent has the program of this school been planned in co-operation with neighboring elementary and secondary schools?

8. What are the educational needs of out-of-school youth and adults which the local school should attempt to meet?

9. What do the high school students, recent graduates, and former students who did not graduate think the school should do that it is not now doing?

Youth in Your School

A careful analysis of the students is very important in a program of curriculum improvement. This information should be available insofar as possible for both the students actually enrolled in school and those who have discontinued attendance. The following questions should be answered for both individual students and groups:

1. What is the health and physical status of students?
2. What is the family background?
   a. Social.
   b. Economic.
   c. Cultural.
   d. Religious.
3. What is the record on appraisal instruments?
   a. Interest inventories.
   b. Adjustment inventories.
   c. Personality scales.
   d. Aptitude measures.
   e. Attitude scales.
   f. Socio-metric tests.
   g. Achievement tests.
   h. Psychological tests.
4. What is the school record in terms of achievement in both formal and informal activities? What examples of unusual success or failure may be noted?
5. What are the characteristics of the out-of-school life of students?
   a. Work experience.
   b. Recreation.
   c. Group and individual contacts.
   d. Special interests.
6. What is the citizenship record both in and out of school?
7. What is the record with respect to regularity and punctuality of attendance?
8. How effective are youth as consumers of goods and services?
9. What are the personal and group goals of students?

Your Community

In considering curriculum improvements it is important to have readily available significant information of a sociological nature about the community in which the school is located. The answers to questions such as those given here provide fundamental information for the common learnings area of the curriculum as well as for other areas. These questions all are significant; undoubtedly, other important ones will occur to you as you conduct your community survey.

1. What is the present status and what future developments are contemplated in the field of community planning?
2. What are the population trends in the community? What is the population make-up of the community by age groups, ethnic backgrounds, religious preference, and the like?
3. How is the community meeting housing problems?
4. What provisions does the community have for coping with problems of delinquency and crime?
5. What provisions are made for leisure-time activities?
6. What methods are used in dealing with the economically dependent?
7. How are the socially maladjusted treated?
8. How are family welfare problems being met?
9. What improvements in health and sanitation have been made in the past 20 years?

Jobs in Your Community

Basic to planning the program of occupational adjustment is knowledge of the vocational life of the community your school serves. Here are significant questions to be answered in this occupational survey of your community; other questions will probably occur to you as you plan your survey.

1. What do the 1940 census data indicate regarding occupational opportunities?
   a. Distribution of workers among occupational groups.
   b. Trends as shown by comparisons from 1910, 1920, 1930, and 1940 figures.
   c. Comparisons by sex.
   d. Comparisons with other sections of the state and nation.

2. What does each of the following studies of high school graduates of the classes of the past ten years reveal?
   a. Occupational distribution of graduates by sex.
   b. Geographical distribution of graduates gainfully employed.
   c. Relationships between occupations followed and high school curriculum choices and scholarship.
   d. Subjects for which graduates would return to school for additional training in evening school or other adult programs.
3. What do the data found above under No. 2 show for students who withdrew from school before graduation?
4. What are the occupational choices, occupations of parents, training requirements, and part-time work needs of the present students in school by grade and sex?
5. What is the present status of local industries including those engaged in production as well as those engaged in distribution of goods?
   a. Different types of employees with number in each classification by age and sex.
   b. Number of beginning employees and annual turnover in employees.
   c. Types of training programs now in effect.
   d. What the school needs to do to train workers in regular and part-time educational programs.
   e. Ways of entering and advancing in different jobs.[5]

Procedures are suggested for answering some of these questions. The suggestions have been published in a series of bulletins.[6] In local communities, committees composed of teachers and laymen may be appointed to study these questions and to make their findings available to all citizens. Each committee is, of course, expected to consult with as many members of the community as possible and to invite general criticism of its work at every stage of its procedure.

Whatever techniques may be employed, the primary contribution of the grass-roots approach is the broadening of the base of deliberation and action with respect to educational problems. These problems can

[5] *Guide to the Study of the Curriculum in the Secondary Schools of Illinois* (Springfield, Illinois: State Department of Public Instruction; August, 1948), pp. 29–33. By permission.

[6] C. M. Allen, *How to Conduct the Holding Power Study;* H. C. Hand, *How to Conduct the Hidden Tuition Costs Study;* H. C. Hand, *How to Conduct the Participation in Extra-Class Activities Study;* H. D. Lovelass, *How to Conduct the Study of the Guidance Services of the School.*

thus be seen in a larger social context and from various perspectives. In consequence, there is greater assurance that educational problems will be solved in the public interest.

The Demonstration Approach

A school-wide change in curriculum is not feasible in some communities because of strong resistances, especially from faculty members who believe that their security and prestige will be threatened. The demonstration approach has been contrived to introduce changes in the regular program on a small scale, thereby holding the disturbance of the faculty and community to a minimum. Since this approach discovers the consequences of a proposed change on a small scale before making the change in the whole school, it reflects the sort of caution associated with an experimental attitude.

There are two forms of this approach. The first is an experimental unit within a school. A separate faculty and administration are set up deliberately to operate the experimental project. This plan is illustrated by the New School, established in 1937 as an experimental unit in the Evanston (Illinois) Township High School. Its purpose was to develop new programs, methods, and materials in the hope that the whole school would be influenced by them.

The second form of this approach is the same as the first in purpose; but the lines separating the experimental project from the rest of the school are not as clearly drawn—or, in most cases, not drawn at all. There is no experimental faculty designated as such, nor is the project under a separate administration. A few teachers who are dissatisfied with the regular program—and who are, therefore, most enthusiastic for curriculum change—are given an opportunity and the encouragement to make innovations. The number of teachers involved may vary from one or two, representing a single grade level or area of instruction, to a considerable number, representing two or more grades or instructional areas. This more limited form of the demonstration approach is illustrated by a number of schools in the Thirty Schools Experiment; for example, the programs developed by the Altoona, Pennsylvania, High School, the junior high schools of Tulsa, Oklahoma, and the Roosevelt High School in Des Moines, Iowa.[7]

[7] Progressive Education Association, *Thirty Schools Tell Their Story.*

As already indicated, the demonstration approach is characterized by the development of new programs on a small scale. The first step in the procedure is taken by the administrative staff, usually by the principal and the curriculum director, who identify those teachers who wish to improve the existing program. Customarily they are teachers who hold a common concern for improving the curriculum and are interested in trying out new ideas. These teachers are provided with enough free time, leadership, and materials to develop new programs at the level of classroom practice. It is assumed that these new developments, if they prove to be successful, will influence less enthusiastic teachers to re-examine the regular program and to modify it. In this way the results of the new program may influence the whole school.

This procedure combines features of both the administrative and grass-roots approaches. It capitalizes on the initiative and resourceful-ness of teachers, and it gears the administrative resources to the needs and interests of teachers in the development of new programs. It avoids the danger of a head-on collision with the major resistances to cur-riculum change. Yet the demonstration procedure creates new resist-ances in the place of those it circumvents. Teachers who are outside the experimental program tend to develop negative attitudes toward the new practices and toward the teachers involved in the project. They tend to regard the experimental teachers as the "fair-haired lads," "well-meaning but misguided young men (or women)." These resentful teachers frequently influence both students and parents to be unsym-pathetic toward innovations. As a result, advocates of this approach now stress the improvement of communication between the new-pro-gram teachers and the remainder of the faculty. Through explanation of the new program to faculty, parents, and students, and by wide-spread participation of these groups in the process of setting up the new program, it is believed that new resistances to the program will be prevented from developing; or, should they develop, it is believed that they will be reduced in number and strength.

2. *A Systematic Approach to Curriculum Change*

The chief weakness of all three of the procedures just discussed is that they attempt to change human relations and institutional structures by rule-of-thumb methods. Systematic methods have been employed in solving such curriculum problems as the grade placement of materials, the identification of child and adolescent needs, and the development of effective methods of teaching such skills as reading and arithmetic processes. But even a cursory review of efforts to change educational programs at the level of practice will indicate that problems arising in this connection are handled by common-sense procedures and techniques. Sometimes these procedures and techniques prove to be adequate. Just as often, however, they fail to produce the anticipated results. In either case the reasons for their success or failure are unknown.

Of course, explanations are always given. In the event of failure, the tendency is to assume that either the superintendent or the principal, or else the curriculum director, was not capable of handling the situation, that he was too autocratic in dealing with teachers, or that he did not offer the needed leadership. Success, on the other hand, is likely to be attributed to the fact that the schools were blessed with a competent group of teachers and a dynamic and democratic superintendent or principal. Just what was done by the teachers and superintendent or principal to produce success or failure, as the case might be, is not clear. Since there is no clear-cut rationale, those who participate in the program must "play by ear." Like a pianist who plays by ear and is unable to tell others the secret of his success, so those engaged in effective curriculum work are often at a loss to explain their achievements.

It would be a serious error, however, to assume that no progress toward a more adequate plan of curriculum change has been made. As a matter of fact, many techniques worked out in connection with the approaches outlined above can be utilized in any effective scheme of educational engineering. Moreover, considerable experience by which to evaluate various procedures and techniques has accumulated from the last three decades of curriculum work. What is needed at the present time, however, is not only the evaluation of techniques, but also a rationale of educational engineering by which to attack the problems of curriculum change more systematically and in terms of which to select and to contrive additional procedures and techniques.

Fortunately, it is not necessary to start from scratch in the development of a rationale of educational engineering. During the last twenty years a considerable amount of knowledge has been accumulated respecting the problem of inducing and controlling changes in the structure of social institutions. It has been developed from sociological studies, psychological investigations of social structures and forces, research in industrial relations, public opinion surveys, and practical curriculum work.[8] It is now possible, on the basis of this knowledge, to sketch the bold outlines of social engineering as it is applied to public education with special reference to curriculum development.

The Social Nature of Curriculum Change

Until recently it was thought that curriculum change consisted largely of developing and installing new courses of study. It is now recognized that curriculum change is a process involving the personalities of parents, students, and teachers, the structure of the school system, and the patterns of personal and group relations among members of the school and community. Curriculum change is social change.

When an individual acts in accordance with, or in opposition to, the expectations of some other person or social group, his behavior is social. As long as an individual's expectations are realized, life goes along smoothly, and he feels more or less secure. But when expectations are thwarted over a considerable period of time, he becomes uncertain. His morale may drop if the uncertainty continues, and this will lead to the decrease of productive efforts. In addition, personal conflicts will increase, and social tensions of all sorts will be brought to the surface.[9]

When members of a community go to a medical doctor, for example, they expect him to behave in certain ways. If their anticipations are not fulfilled, they are disappointed; and, unless these established expectations are somehow modified, the public will not patronize the

---

[8] Samples of these developments are as follows: K. Lewin, "Frontiers in Group Dynamics; I. Concept, Method, and Reality in Social Change," *Human Relations*, Vol. 1, No. 1, 1947, pp. 5–41. "Frontiers in Group Dynamics; II. Channels of Group Life, Social Planning and Action Research," *Human Relations*, Vol. 1, No. 2, 1947, pp. 143–153. F. J. Roethlisberger and W. J. Dickson, *Management and the Worker*. G. Watson (Ed.), "Civilian Morale," *Second Yearbook of the Society for the Psychological Study of Social Issues*. T. Newcomb and E. L. Hartley (Eds.), *Readings in Social Psychology*. G. Myrdal, *An American Dilemma*, Vol. 2, pp. 1027–1070. H. C. Hand, *What People Think about Their Schools*. A. Miel, *Changing the Curriculum: A Social Process*.

[9] Kurt Lewin, *Resolving Social Conflicts*, pp. 110–112.

physician. In like manner, every member of the community looks for certain things from the church, the family, business establishments, and the school. They have a picture in their heads of what and how the school teaches, of the way in which children are dealt with, and of a thousand other things that a school is supposed to do. Likewise, students and teachers have sets of expectations peculiar to their respective positions in the educational and social scheme. Teachers, parents, and students are usually well aware of what each is supposed to do. The "good" teacher tries to fulfill the parent's expectations, as he perceives them. The "good" parent attempts to do likewise with respect to the teacher. The "good" student tries to meet the expectations of his teachers and his parents.

From a socio-psychological standpoint the educational program is set in an extensive web of expectations among members of the community. Any significant change in the educational program will, therefore, upset the established anticipations of behavior that members of the community entertain with respect to one another. Effective educational engineering will attempt to identify the points at which these expectations are most certain to be disturbed when an educational change is made and will attempt to help individuals to build new anticipations in terms of which to approach the school and its problems.

No less important in curriculum change is the social organization of the school. The school has a social structure which tends to shape the attitudes of teachers toward curriculum change as well as their perception of what is educationally possible and desirable. It also determines in large measure the kind of co-operation that is possible in the faculty and the kind of persons who will attain positions of responsibility.

Examination of the social structure of any school will reveal individuals and groups of persons, associated together in educational tasks, behaving toward one another and the tasks at hand in accepted and prescribed ways. Their behavior, to be sure, will vary somewhat from person to person because individuals occupy different positions in the school structure and hence perceive the tasks somewhat differently. Individuals in the higher brackets of the school structure will often perceive the problems of the school in ways that make little sense to those in the lower echelons.

The lack of homogeneity of behavior will be intensified by the fact that various individuals will be more closely associated with some groups or cliques in the faculty than with others. A teacher of English, for example, will try to live up to the expectations which his fellow English teachers have with respect to him and their work. In other words, he is a bearer of certain values, which are shared by his colleagues. Moreover, the English teacher, as in the case of any other teacher, will react to the principal in one way, to vocational teachers in another, and to his colleagues in English in still another. He will be governed by different sentiments and expectations, depending upon the position, power, and anticipations of the persons involved. To continue the example, the acts of the head of the English department toward a member of his department will tend one way in the presence of the principal, another when they are alone, and still another when they are in a meeting of the department. The teacher's behavior will vary from one of these situations to another no less than that of the department head.

Teachers who have grown accustomed to the relationships by which their status is defined and maintained will be upset by real or imagined curriculum changes, especially if these changes involve modifications of the school structure, as is frequently the case. Any change tending to alter their status, especially if it is perceived as an adverse alteration, will be viewed with alarm and met with resistance. This is no less true of administrative officers and supervisors than of teachers.

To summarize the foregoing discussion, the modern school as well as the modern community is comprised of a number of working groups. Between these groups and between members of the groups, there are patterns of relationships expressing social position, expectations, and sentiments. The curriculum is inextricably woven into these relationships, and it cannot be torn apart from its social context to be treated as a thing in itself. In order to change the curriculum, the social fabric must be changed—more at some points than others, but changed nevertheless. Broadly conceived, then, the problem of curriculum change is a problem in social engineering.

The Concept of Social Equilibrium

If a social institution is studied over a considerable period of time, it will be discovered that the institution performs its functions in about the same way and at about the same level of efficiency year after year. The school bears out this observation. It has been estimated that under "normal" circumstances it takes seventy-five years for a new idea to become incorporated in educational practice from coast to coast. The ordinary explanation of this lag of practice behind theory is that teachers are conservative, timid souls who make changes only when they have to. However true this judgment of the teaching profession may be, it is a gross oversimplification of the situation. The fact of the case is that there are scores of social and psychological forces playing upon the school with respect to the educational program. Some of these forces are tending to change the program, while others, acting in the opposite direction, are tending to keep the program as it is, if not to drive it to a lower level of efficiency. When the resultant of these opposing forces is zero, the level of educational practice tends to remain about the same. When these opposing forces become "frozen," so that they remain nearly the same from year to year, it is customary to speak of the educational program as the "conventional" or "traditional" curriculum. A state of affairs such as the one just described, in which the resultant of the opposing forces is zero, or so near zero as to allow little appreciable change, is referred to as *social equilibrium*.

The concept of social equilibrium is a very useful one in curriculum development. A change in the curriculum can be made only by upsetting the old equilibrium and by establishing a new equilibrium at another level of educational practice. Only as those engaged in curriculum work ascertain the constellation of forces in the school-community situation can they know the realities with which they are working. Those involved in curriculum work have too often seized upon one or two forces, and at best only a few of the forces of a total situation, and have neglected the remainder. Then, too, the forces identified have usually been selected without reference to their influence in the total constellation. Frequently the more powerful ones have thus been overlooked until the whole program of curriculum development was threatened by the forces of reaction.

Changing an Established Social Equilibrium

The problem of changing the curriculum of a school is one facet of the general problem of how to change an established social equilibrium.

The changing of an equilibrium to a higher level of social practice requires that changes be induced in the prevailing constellation of forces, that these changes be controlled and directed, and that a new constellation of forces be established and maintained at the level where the new equilibrium is desired. In the words of Lewin, "A successful change includes . . . three aspects: unfreezing (if necessary) the present level, moving to the new level, and freezing group life on the new level." [10]

Of course it is possible to upset an existing equilibrium without any clear notion of the amount and direction of the change desired or even of the forces involved. The hoped-for change may get off to a good start; but within a brief period the enthusiasm of individuals and groups wanes and the practices fall back to the old level. Or worse, the change may get so out of hand that unforeseen consequences threaten to depress even the old equilibrium.

This often happens in curriculum development. The principal, superintendent, or curriculum director, as the case may be, gives the faculty a "shot in the arm" by such techniques as high-powered speakers, workshops, and exciting written accounts of new practices. The faculty is motivated to move in an ill-defined direction without any clear notion of the amount of change ultimately required. Soon the initial enthusiasm of the faculty is spent. Tensions created by incipient changes emerge in the school and community and are released through aggressive behavior. Morale is consequently further depressed. The restricting forces are multiplied and increased in strength. As a result, the "curriculum bubble" bursts, and the whole educational program is fortunate if it does not fall below the old level. In the more extreme cases, when the social and psychological forces get completely out of hand, those associated with the program of curriculum development may have to be replaced in order to restore even the old equilibrium.

It frequently happens that a disequilibrium respecting the curriculum occurs in a community without deliberate effort on the part of the profession. A group of individuals becomes dissatisfied with aspects of the existing curriculum and attempts to bring about changes in it by bringing pressure to bear upon the school. The pressures sometimes act

[10] Kurt Lewin, "Group Decision and Social Change," in *Readings in Social Psychology*, T. Newcomb and E. L. Hartley (Eds.) (New York: Henry Holt and Co.; 1947), p. 344.

in directions indicated by the best professional knowledge. More often, however, they tend to move the curriculum in directions which the profession cannot support. In either case the professional leadership will do well to take account of disequilibriums and by effective procedures and techniques turn them to good account.

Deliberate social change, whether in the realm of economics, politics, or education, must be planned if the risk of "social abortion" is to be reduced to a minimum. It is, of course, impossible to reduce the risk to zero in any engineering discipline. The engineer who plans the construction of a bridge, skyscraper, tunnel, or what not—like the well-trained farmer who plans his crops in the light of available scientific knowledge—must take calculated risks. Since not all the forces can be ascertained and controlled, there must be an element of adventure in any engineering enterprise. When a practical enterprise such as education, medicine, or economics moves from a common-sense to a professional level of knowledge and skill, the risk entailed in any particular task is reduced to a "calculated" amount rather than eliminated.

Returning to the problem of modifying an existing equilibrium, there are two basic ways in which an equilibrium can be changed: (1) by removing or reducing the strength of restraining forces; and (2) by adding to or strengthening the driving forces. The curriculum can be moved in the direction of a core curriculum, for example, by eliminating or reducing the strength of one or more of the restraining forces. It can also be moved in the same direction by strengthening the driving forces or by adding forces in this direction. In either case, the resultant of the constellation of forces will be in the direction of the new level. The core curriculum may be reached by either or both of these procedures.

The concomitant results, however, will be very different when the new program is attained by strengthening the driving forces rather than by weakening the resisting ones. When the driving forces are increased without a reduction of the resisting forces, tensions between and within individuals and social groups for and against the change will be increased in both number and intensity. Moreover, the strength of the resisting forces is likely to increase as the level of curriculum development moves from the conventional level toward the new curriculum. A little change in the new direction will likely be met with weaker resistance than a marked change. It is to be expected, therefore, that individual and group tensions will be further accentuated as the curriculum change progresses in the desired direction. Because a marked increase in tension, especially above a certain degree, is likely to be attended by aggressive behavior and ineffective work, an educational program brought about by this method is apt to be very unstable and fleeting in tenure. On the other hand, the reduction of the resisting forces—accompanied by a gradual increase of the strength of the driving forces—is a procedure that avoids high tensions and emotional conduct.

Phases of Systematic Curriculum Change

The foregoing analysis of social equilibrium, and of how such an equilibrium may be modified, suggests a method of curriculum change. This method can be reduced to four phases, as follows:

1. A diagnostic study of the school-community situation to ascertain the constellation of forces that maintains the present curriculum.
2. The induction of change in the existing equilibrium so as to loosen up the established constellation of forces.
3. The control of various forces in order to move the level of curriculum practice in the desired direction and to the desired amount.
4. The establishment of the new constellation of forces to sustain the new curriculum.

The analysis of curriculum change into these phases is, of course, an oversimplification. It would be difficult, if not impossible, to separate them in actual practice so as to say that here one phase begins and another ends. Indeed, only in a very rough sense is it possible to speak of a phase either following or preceding another. The procedures for inducing change are identical in some respects with diagnostic procedures, since fact-finding to ascertain what the situation is may also serve to induce changes in the existing state of affairs. Moreover, diagnosis of the situation must be made at almost every point where major alignments and modifications of forces occur. Unless a diagnosis is made at such points, those involved in the program of change will not know what they are dealing with in the new state of affairs. Likewise, the induction of changes and the control of forces must go on at every point in the development of a curriculum.

Nevertheless, in any large-scale operation such as curriculum change, it is helpful to back off from the operations themselves and to take a broad, analytical perspective of the total picture. In this way, the individual can see the total pattern and the main points in the general outline of activities. For this purpose the overlapping of activities can be neglected to a considerable extent without sacrificing essential factors.

3. *Curriculum Change as Action-Research*

Thus far curriculum change has been viewed in a formal rather than in a functional sense. The yield of the formal analysis is an outline of the major phases of curriculum engineering. The way these phases fit together and are used over and over again in the process of changing the curriculum can be seen only by reference to a functional analysis of educational engineering. When such engineering is analyzed functionally, it turns out to be a form of action-research.

Since curriculum development can hardly begin with everything at once, it must begin with a selected aspect of the total school-community situation. Usually it will begin with some specific situation that requires attention because it is disturbing to the professional personnel. As this specific situation is analyzed, it will become obvious that it has a multitude of connections with other things in the total school-community situation. Then, in order to understand the specific situation that is of immediate concern, a more comprehensive diagnosis, such as that discussed in Chapter 19, becomes necessary. When a faculty has had little experience in solving problems co-operatively, or when it has had the experience of failure rather than success in co-operative ventures, success in dealing with specific problems, no matter how insignificant they may appear to outsiders, is necessary for the growth of the staff in skill, understanding, and confidence.

Hence, a specific situation, such as the feeling of need for a new report card or for a change in methods of assigning playground responsibilities, may well become the sole object of study. Where circumstances permit, the situation may be expanded so as to require a broad school-community diagnosis. In either case, a group of persons will be formed to deal with the situation. The work of this group, if it is to be successful, will take on the character of action-research. The group will survey the specific situation to identify the difficulties together with the forces and conditions that must be dealt with in order to overcome the difficulties. It will devise ways of dealing with the difficulties, and, after critically evaluating these plans, it will try them out to see whether or not they work as anticipated. The group will secure data bearing on the success, or failure, of the plans as tried out. If the plans do not work according to anticipations, they are then revised. Thus, the process of action-research continues until a satisfactory solution is found. This cycle of research will characterize every phase of the master plan of curriculum change outlined in the preceding sections of this chapter. The problems that arise in diagnosing the school-community situation, in inducing change in the equilibrium of forces, and in controlling these forces will each be handled as a problem for action-research.

Since research is ordinarily conceived of as something carried on in a laboratory—the results of which make no immediate difference in what people do but are written up and published for future use—some attention should be given to consideration of the nature of action-research in curriculum development. The chief aim of action-research, in contradistinction to theoretical research, is the immediate modification of social practices. It attempts to investigate situations in which social action is required and to effect changes in the action. Such research is like that carried on at the engineering level of any field of intellectual endeavor. If a man is going to build a suspension bridge, for example, his intellectual activities will be largely in the realm of action-research. He will investigate the total state of affairs to determine the proper location and the difficulties that will be encountered in building the bridge at a chosen spot. He will lay plans for constructing the bridge so as to circumvent or to overcome these difficulties. Moreover, at various points in the construction work he will reassess his plans and his diagnosis of the difficulties. Perhaps no one has described the pattern of action-research more simply than Lewin, in his discussion of the role of research in social planning:

Planning starts usually with something like a general idea. For one reason or another it seems desirable to reach a certain objective. Exactly how to circumscribe this objective, and how to reach it is frequently not too clear. The first step then is to examine the idea carefully in the light of the means available. Frequently more fact-finding about the situation is required. If this first period of planning is successful, two items emerge: namely, an "over-all plan" of how to reach the objective and secondly, a decision in regard to the first step of action. Usually this planning has also somewhat modified the original idea.

The next period is devoted to executing the first step of the over-all plan.

In highly developed fields of social management, such as modern factory management or the execution of a war, this second step is followed by certain fact-findings. For example, in the bombing of Germany a certain factory may have been chosen as the first target after careful consideration of various priorities and of the best means and ways of dealing with this target. The attack is pressed home and immediately a reconnaissance plane follows with the one objective of determining as accurately and objectively as possible the new situation.

This reconnaissance or fact-finding has four functions. First, it should evaluate the action. It shows whether what has been achieved is above or below expectation. Secondly, it gives the planners a chance to learn, that is, to gather new general insight, for instance, regarding the strength and weakness of certain weapons or techniques of action. Thirdly, this fact-finding should serve as a basis for correctly planning the next step. Finally, it serves as a basis for modifying the over-all plan.

The next step again is composed of a circle of planning, executing, and reconnaissance or fact-finding for the purpose of evaluating the results of the second step, for preparing the rational basis for planning the third step, and for perhaps modifying again the over-all plan.

Rational social management, therefore, proceeds in a spiral of steps each of which is composed of a circle of planning, action, and fact-finding about the result of the action.[11]

The character of curriculum change, as a form of action-research, can be further clarified by reference to the accompanying diagram. From this diagram it can be seen that curriculum change begins with a situation requiring action. This situation is set in a web of school-commu-

[11] Kurt Lewin, *Resolving Social Conflict* (New York: Harper Brothers: 1948), pp. 205–206. By permission.

Cycle of Co-operative Action-Research

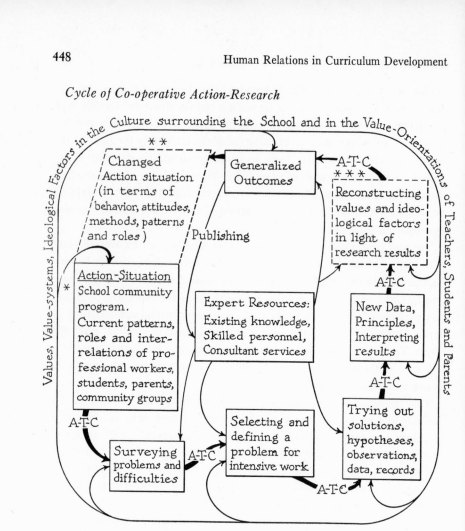

A—Action
T—Training
C—Change

* Begin here. Read counterclockwise.

** Since change in the action-situation is involved at all points in the research process, the situation from which a new cycle of research will start is different from the situation in which the original problem was located and defined.

*** Values and ideological factors which surround and condition the entire process of research are brought in, at points where they have been challenged by research findings, for direct examination and revision.

Prepared by Kenneth D. Benne and Hubert Evans in connection with the work of the Horace Mann Institute of School Experimentation. Reproduced by permission of the authors.

nity and interpersonal relations. This web of relationships is in turn conditioned by the value system and beliefs operating in the culture. The boundary of these is represented by the outer circle. How these relationships are perceived, and the relative importance attached to them, will depend not only upon the social position of the individual but also upon the particular set of values and beliefs he happens to share. Under the influence of a context of values and interpersonal relationships, the group of persons involved in the improvement of the situation surveys the problems and difficulties. At this point, as indicated in the diagram, training of personnel in the techniques of surveying will be required. In addition, expert assistance in the form of consultant services, respecting knowledge and skill, may be needed.

After the survey of the existing state of affairs has been made, the group is ready to select and define a problem for intensive exploration. A probable solution to the problem is formulated and tried out. A new survey is then made to ascertain new data to determine the success of the proposed solution. The proposed plan is reassessed in the light of facts and values and, if need be, is reshaped until it finally operates in the changed action-situation. Thus the process of curriculum engineering, like social engineering in general, moves around the cycle to the new state of affairs. At every step there is a two-fold task—deciding *what* is to be done and *how* it is to be done. And each of these involves action, fact-finding, value-judging, training in know-how, and change.

▶ *Following Up*
This Chapter

1. State the reasons for the interpretation of curriculum change as a form of social change.
2. What is a social equilibrium and how can it be changed? Describe a social practice involving yourself and a number of other persons. Try to think of some of the opposing forces making up the social equilibrium that sustains the practice. Indicate how you might proceed to induce change in this equilibrium.
3. How does action-research differ from other forms of research? What are its chief characteristics?

▶ *Suggested*
Reading

1. The administrative approach to curriculum change has been ably described by L. Thomas Hopkins in his *Curriculum Principles and Practices,* although the view set forth in this reference is not now held by its author. See especially pages 287–513. Helen F. Storen's *Laymen Help Plan the Curriculum,* a pamphlet of about seventy-five pages, gives an excellent exploration of the grass-roots approach.

The theory of the systematic approach has been worked out in industrial relations and in connection with problems of effecting changes in food habits and other group behavior. The most thorough formulation of the theory is to be found in two articles by Kurt Lewin: "Frontiers in Group Dynamics; I. Concept, Method, and Reality in Social Science; Social Equilibria and Social Change," *Human Relations,* Vol. I, No. 1, 1947, pages 5–41; "Frontiers in Group Dynamics; II. Channels of Group Life: Social Planning and Action Research," *Human Relations,* Vol. I, No. 2, 1947, pages 143–153. See also Lewin's *Resolving Social Conflicts,* which is an excellent reference. See especially Chapters 2, 4, and 8.

2. When curriculum change is seen as social engineering, it becomes necessary to understand action-research, since it is through such research that social engineering is carried on. For a simple discussion of action-research, see Lewin's *Resolving Social Conflicts,* pages 201–216. The most important reference on action-research, as it has been developed in school projects, is Stephen M. Corey's *Action Research to Improve School Practices.* For an insightful discussion of curriculum development as social change, see Alice Miel's *Changing the Curriculum: A Social Process.* An extensive collection of readings on group dynamics and curriculum development is *Human Relations in Curriculum Change,* edited by Kenneth D. Benne and Bozidar Muntyan.

For a description of action-research in the development of a general course in "Basic Living," see "Co-operative Research and Curriculum Improvement," *Teachers College Record,* 51:474, April, 1951. This is a progress report on an experimental project developed in the Battle Creek, Michigan, schools. Perhaps one of the best explanations of action-research in curriculum development is "Educational Change and Social Engineering," *Progressive Education,* Vol. 26, No. 7, May, 1949 (entire issue).

Chapter 18

The Organization and Function of Personnel in Curriculum Change

IN ORDER to initiate and develop curriculum change, the personnel to be involved in the engineering project must be organized, supplied with effective leadership, and, where necessary, trained in the skills and procedures essential to success. The question of how the personnel of the school and members of the community are to be organized for curriculum development can be answered either in terms of a specific situation or in terms of a set of principles. Since the pattern of school-community relationships varies widely from one locality to another, an organization suitable for one locality might not be appropriate for another. For this reason it seems better to set forth guiding principles for the organization and operation of personnel than to describe concrete plans. Accordingly, the discussion will be directed to the guiding ideas that should be taken into account as the school-community personnel go about the task of curriculum change.

1. *The Principle of Community Participation*

The systematic approach to curriculum change is a form of engineering research designed to ascertain and to control the forces that maintain the existing curriculum and that can be used to modify the curriculum in desired directions. Since these forces are community-wide—embracing, as they do, the school and the community—the research will be most effective when it is carried on co-operatively. Lay members of the community, as well as teachers and students, should therefore have a responsible share in the process of defining the problems to be studied, collecting and interpreting data, and doing whatever else may be necessary to modify the curriculum and the forces that sustain it.

Why Community Sharing Is Necessary

The principle of widespread participation rests upon three considerations. The first consideration is that changes are apt to enjoy longer tenure if they are understood and supported by the public. Since curriculum change is a form of social change, any modification of the curriculum will affect the wider community. To the extent that the community shares in determining the changes, and, in so doing, foresees the possible consequences, it will be prepared to absorb the shock of unforeseen effects.

The second consideration is that those who are affected by a policy or program of action should share—to the extent of their ability to do so intelligently and responsibly—in shaping the policy or program. This principle is a special case of the more general notion of the inherent worth of the individual and the consequent demand that he be respected. To refuse to allow the individual to share, even indirectly through representatives, in making policies and programs under which he must live is to violate him as a person.

The third consideration is that all persons involved in engineering research, especially those directly involved in it, must share in planning it, or else the program developed by the research may not work in practice. A full exploration of this idea would take the present discussion too far afield, but a few observations will clarify the point for present purposes. Assume that a program of curriculum development is designed by the upper strata of school personnel, so that students and teachers simply follow plans formulated by these persons. Under this condition there would be certain outcomes in the form of student learnings. In addition, the teachers would build up attitudes for, or against, the new program, depending partly upon their respective positions in the school structure and partly upon their personal structures.

Now suppose that in the course of time the teachers and students come to recognize more completely what was involved in the original planning, including its purposes. They may come to believe, for example, that the program was "put over" on them and that it is not as "good" as the old program. On the other hand, the teachers and students may come to see new and desirable meanings in the new program and thus become enthusiastic supporters of it, whereas before they were passive toward it. In either event, a new set of factors would have been injected into the situation so that earlier results, either anticipated or real, would be significantly modified. If the teachers and students share in planning the program from start to finish, new factors of this type are not so likely to arise. In consequence their attitudes toward the new program will be more stable, and the outcomes of the program of change will be more dependable.

2. *Leadership by the Profession*

It is often assumed that expansion of the processes of curriculum change, so as to include lay persons and to place greater responsibility upon teachers and students for the formulation of policies and programs, reduces the need for careful planning and for professional leadership. As a matter of fact, the expansion of the processes of curriculum engineering makes far greater demands upon leaders of the profession. Not only must the leadership be clear on matters of curriculum theory and techniques, but it must also be thoroughly disciplined in the theory and practice of social change, including human relations. For, in the absence of such knowledge and skill, the resources latent in the members of the community and in the school personnel will not be released except by accident. Moreover, the process of change is apt to become hopelessly snarled and, in consequence, dissipate in personal and group conflicts.

In almost every step of curriculum change, working committees composed of appropriate members drawn from laymen, teachers, and students will be directly engaged in fact-finding, value-criticism, and policy-making. These committees will need an adequate perception of their roles in the total plan, a clear sense of direction, and adequate technical help. These requirements can be met by involving laymen, teachers, and students not only in the task of determining the changes to be made in the educational program, but also in the crucial problems of working out the ways in which these changes can be made and sustained. But this *involvement* of persons on a community-wide basis can lead to success only if the profession is clear as to its leadership responsibilities.

Spheres of Professional Leadership

The leadership function of the profession is limited to four spheres of knowledge and skill: technical skills and knowledge of education, knowledge of intellectual disciplines, knowledge of social and educational values, and knowledge and skill in educational engineering. As professionally trained persons, members of the teaching profession possess knowledge of and skill in educational processes and procedures over and beyond those possessed by the laymen. Members of the profession know more about such things as the teaching of reading and other subjects, what the curriculum should embrace, and how the school should be operated. In other words, the profession, by the nature of its training, is supposed to be better informed about the means of education and more disciplined in the necessary skills than the layman. The teacher's expertness in these matters rests upon the fact that he is the bearer of knowledge and skills established either by scientific investigation or by the refinement of professional activities through the application of psychological and educational theory to the practical problems of the school.

In the next place, it is generally recognized that the teaching profession should have greater mastery of the intellectual disciplines than is ordinarily found among laymen. The teacher is presumed to be a competent student of those aspects of the cultural heritage to which he has devoted himself. His scholarship is supposed to be of higher order than that of the layman. This does not mean that the teacher, or the profession, knows more about everything than the public. Indeed, there are many aspects of the community and the wider social scene about which the teacher is much less informed than many laymen. Nevertheless, the claim of the teacher to competence in his field of study—and his responsibility to conduct himself in such a way as to safeguard the claim—can hardly be denied.

The two spheres of professional competence and leadership just discussed have long been recognized by the great bulk of the profession. However, comparable status of the profession with respect to the other two realms—social and educational values, and educational engineering—has neither been claimed nor sought until quite recently. Even yet the competence of the profession in these two areas is woefully lacking—a fact that goes a long way toward explaining the failure of so many curriculum ventures.

Values are involved in almost every controversy, and certainly they are involved in every act of teaching and every curriculum change. The selection of educational objectives, the materials and methods of instruction, and the administration and operation of the school necessarily require choices among values. As the profession begins to work with members of the community in the development of the curriculum, it quickly discovers that many of the problems arise at the level of conflicting choices among values. Some persons will want one thing and other people will want something else. Since it will frequently be impossible to have both, a choice has to be made by those concerned—or else the claims and counterclaims must be reconstructed so as to reach a compromise, or better, a consensus. It is, therefore, important that the profession be as competent as possible in ferreting out and helping to resolve value conflicts among persons and social groups.

Competence in the area of value conflicts requires two things of the profession: first, that it be disciplined in judgmental method such as that discussed in the chapters on procedures of curriculum development; and second, that the profession have mastery of democratic ideals at both the conceptual and operational levels.

It may be asked why the teaching profession should be more competent in this area than other members of the community. Surely the teaching profession has, and should have, no monopoly on the meaning of democracy. This is readily granted. Every member of society should be thoroughly trained in democratic concepts and judgmental method. Indeed, that is one of the purposes of education. But if this purpose is to be realized, the teaching profession must promote it in the school and in the community. This promotion requires that the competence of the profession in this regard excel those for whose education it is responsible.

In the final analysis, the teaching profession is responsible to the community, not in the sense of a local community, but in the broad sense of the common life of the total people. Now democratic ideals are the most pervasive and deepest convictions of the people. They cut across local communities and permeate the structure of institutions that synthesize and channel individual and public activities. While these ideals are always growing and being reinterpreted as conditions change, a certain degree of continuity of meaning is always preserved. They therefore supply the most reliable guideposts by which the profession can tell whether or not it is serving the total public good. Whatever change in the curriculum serves to clarify the democratic values and to extend them to all the people is in the public interest. Whatever curriculum change prevents this extension of democracy is against the common welfare. It follows that in the resolution of value conflicts over changes in the educational program, it is the obligation of the profession to move the resolution in the direction of democratic ideas and practices.

It is one thing to know *what* to do; it is quite another thing to know *how* to do it. The profession may be exceedingly competent in technical educational knowledge and skill, in intellectual disciplines, and in social and educational values. Yet the profession may be unable to use these accomplishments in the development of a more adequate curriculum for the simple reason that it does not know how to get the people of the community to work together effectively. Hence the profession should possess expertness in human-relations skills. It should know how to work with individuals and groups, how to diagnose and overcome difficulties in group processes, how to help laymen to learn to make factual surveys and to think through other kinds of research procedures and techniques that may be required in curriculum development.

The systematic method of curriculum revision requires that the profession either possess the competencies just enumerated or that it acquire these abilities in the course of a program of curriculum development. Indeed, the recognition of this area of competence in curriculum change is one of the distinguishing features of the systematic method. The grass-roots approach, while emphasizing wide participation of laymen and students, neglects the task of planning the procedures, strategies, and techniques required by curriculum engineering. In this regard, it is similar to the administrative approach, which it was designed to replace. The systematic approach, on the other hand, stresses not only wide participation but also the use of psychological knowledge and human-relations skills in planning and controlling the processes of curriculum change. It is important, then, that professional leadership possess or acquire discipline with respect to curriculum engineering.

While the profession's knowledge and skills excel those of the laymen, it should go without saying that such professional competence should seldom, if ever, be used arbitrarily. It is not within the ethics of the profession to dictate to the public what the schools are to be. Rather, the leadership of the profession should be employed in such a way as to enable the community to understand and to assume its educational responsibilities in working with the profession to shape the educational program.

In cases where the local community stands for anti-democratic social practices or for educational practices contrary to scientifically established principles and techniques, it may be desirable for the local profession to exercise its power, as an organized group, in an effort to open such practices to discussion and deliberation and to maintain the conditions for such deliberation. It is the obligation of the profession to create and maintain the conditions for growth on the part of the community. To acquiesce in anti-democratic social practices and in the use of repudiated educational methods would be to close the door to community growth. It is also the responsibility of the total professional group of the nation to support the local profession where it is engaged in the enterprise of keeping dubious practices under discussion.

Local Leadership Essential

It has been assumed all too frequently that in order to change the curriculum of a school system it is necessary to bring in curriculum experts to initiate and carry out the program. In this case, the "spark plug" of the whole development is imported, and the leadership function of the local professional group is surrendered. The local group, in the person of the superintendent and ultimately the board of education, retains little more than veto power as to how far the experts can go in changing the program. There is little reason for surprise, therefore, that when the outside support of the new program is withdrawn, as it must necessarily be, the program almost always undergoes a period of rapid regression. Within a short while the curriculum practices are back where they were before the program of development began. Naturally, when the props are removed, the structure will collapse.

Of course, there is a place for consultant services in connection with any engineering enterprise, whether it be education, industry, agriculture, or business. The nature and use of such services in curriculum development will be treated later. The point of the present discussion is that it is a perversion of consultant services to convert them into agents of change. The function of consultants is to supply expert knowledge and skill. The responsibility for their effective use rests with the local professional group. The dynamic factor in curriculum change must be in the local school-community situation and focused in the local professional leadership. Unless this condition is met, it is useless to call in expert assistance. The local professional group must have studied its situation enough to know its basic problems, its local resources for dealing with these problems, and the kinds of consultant services it must engage from time to time in order to round out its personnel resources. If the local profession cannot do these things, it would be wise to forego the launching of a program of curriculum development until it can do them.

3. Leadership: Its Nature and Function

Thus far leadership has been discussed as the function of the local professional group. This is the way leadership should be perceived when the work of the profession is defined in terms of its unique responsibilities in the community. By virtue of their training and experience, the teachers of the community are especially equipped to do certain things that the rest of the community delegates to them. But leadership can also be perceived as a function within the profession. Within the local professional group one teacher or another will be cast in the role of leadership from time to time, for that role must be filled if the professional group is to serve its leadership function in the community.

The Meaning of Leadership

The common notion is that leadership consists of certain qualities inherent in some individuals and that an individual who possesses these qualities is a leader. In any situation he will be able to command the confidence and respect of his fellows and to induce them to follow his policies and to accept his plans and decisions. Research on the nature of leadership has helped to explode this common-sense notion.[1] Nowadays leadership is not conceived as a set of qualities, traits, or abilities inherent in the individual and remarking him as a leader. Rather, it is conceived as a functional role of a group member, played by an individual at a particular time in a particular group of people. In the language of Benne and Sheats, leadership is to be conceived "in terms of functions to be performed within a group in helping that group to grow and to work productively." Then they go on to say: "No sharp distinction can be made between leadership and membership functions, between leader and member roles. Groups may operate with various degrees of diffusion of 'leadership' functions among group members or of concentration of such functions in one member or a few members." [2]

In other words, leadership is being exercised when a group member is helping the group to define and to meet its needs. And that person is the leader who at a given moment is most effectively helping the group in these respects. Of course, a small subunit of members, as well as individual members, may exercise leadership. It follows from what has been said that leadership in a group may pass from person to person as the group deals with different problems or with different aspects of a single problem. For no individual will know more about every problem than other members of the group. Nevertheless, there are usually some persons who are more adept than the rest of the group at

[1] Theodore Newcomb and E. L. Hartley (Eds.), *Readings in Social Psychology,* pp. 403–436.

[2] Kenneth D. Benne and Paul Sheats, "Functional Roles of Group Members," *Journal of Social Issues,* Vol. IV, No. 2 (Spring, 1948), p. 41.

sensing the group's needs and at serving as a means by which the group can realize its goals. These individuals are more frequently cast in leadership roles than are other members of the group.

Functional leadership, as just discussed, is to be distinguished from status roles. The faculty of almost every school system is organized into a line and staff pattern. There is the superintendent at the top; then there follow, in the order named, the principals, department heads, and teachers. This order of personnel constitutes the line that defines the channel of official power and communication. The staff comprises the supervisors, research workers, curriculum directors, and the like. It constitutes the advisory body within the faculty. All of this is nothing more than the A, B, C's of administrative organization of the school. To be sure, the line and staff organization has been criticized, and in some quarters condemned, as a barrier to democratic administrative practices. The line and staff organization is doubtless in need of reconstruction to bring the administrative pattern into accord with democratic ideals. Nevertheless, the line and staff organization is inherent in every school system; hence, it is necessary to distinguish between functional roles and status positions, between functional leaders and status leaders.

Individuals occupying the top echelons of the line organization are usually perceived as leaders and as occupying positions of leadership. These positions are clothed with official power and prestige; and, since this is the case, individuals who occupy them are able to encourage or to discourage, to initiate or to stop, any change or any course of action. Such individuals, by virtue of their position, are key persons in an educational system. They are status leaders occupying status positions.

Status leaders may or may not be functional leaders. When leadership is defined functionally, as the role of a group member in helping a group to define its needs and in acting as a positive force in the direction of the group's goals, the individual who plays this role is a leader in a functional sense. Measured by this definition, it is not difficult to understand that a status leader may be a barrier to the group, rather than a means, in its efforts to clarify and to satisfy its needs. Whether a status leader is a barrier or a positive force in the eyes of the group does not depend upon his official position, but upon his capacity to serve the group as it seeks to clarify its sense of direction and its problems, and to work out ways of moving in the direction the group sets for itself.

If persons in official positions are also able to play the role of functional leaders, curriculum development by the school-community personnel will be in large measure assured. But if these persons lack the understanding and skill to do the things required of them in the role of functional leadership, any improvement of the curriculum will be unlikely; or, at least, it will be seriously impeded until the official leaders have begun to acquire the know-how of functional leadership. Unfortunately, the demands made upon the status leader by the board of education and by many members of the faculty as well as the community—demands that he be the "boss," that he "run" the school, that he have the answers—drive him in the wrong direction when he lacks the know-how of functional leadership. Instead of trying to diagnose his own needs for further knowledge and skill, and then attempting to satisfy these needs, he turns to the use of his official position and power to accomplish objectives he would not attain with his limited abilities. Recourse to official power feeds upon itself, one act of power leading to another. Thus step by step the status leader, unless he acquires the know-how of functional leadership, goes down the path to outright autocracy or to a milder form called paternalism. His only alternative is to refuse to use official power or, if used, to employ it sparingly. The school system then drifts into a sort of *laissez faire* administration, lacking any common direction and any sense of group effort and achievement. In either case, curriculum change will be unlikely; if it occurs, it is apt to be fleeting in tenure.

Requirements of the Functional Leadership Role

The abilities required by the role of functional leadership are difficult to specify. In general, it can be said that this role requires a high degree of professional knowledge with respect to the school and the field of social influence within which it operates. But the role demands equally that the persons who are to play it be thoroughly disciplined in knowledge of, and skill in, human relations and social diagnosis and communication. Of course, an individual can be a functional leader from time to time without these particular competencies, as, for example, in the case of the member who perceives that the group needs a rest and suggests that it take ten minutes out to relax. If a person is to combine functional leadership with status leadership, however, these abilities are indispensable. For in this case status behavior must be consistent with functional leadership. The status leader cannot assume the functional leadership role one minute and forget about it the next, as other members of the group can do. He cannot, except in unusual circumstances, readily pass back and forth between the authority of status leadership and the co-operative assistance of functional leadership.

More specifically, an individual must have, among others, the following competencies in order to fill the role of functional leadership while holding a status position.

Competencies needed in working in face-to-face situations:
1. Skills in handling group processes; e.g., dealing with group conflicts, identifying group needs, identifying points of view, guiding group planning, establishing action-goals, following the logic of discussion.
2. Skills in presenting reports, representing opposing points of view, explaining difficult points, and the like.
3. Skills in helping others learn the techniques of group processes.

Competencies required by the processes of fact-finding:
1. Skills in making surveys to ascertain facts about school problems— constructing and administering questionnaires and other survey instruments, tabulating and interpreting responses.
2. Skills in making surveys of various aspects of the community to ascertain the power fields conditioning the schools, and to find facts about any educational problem involving aspects of the total community—constructing and administering questionnaires and other survey instruments, tabulating responses, interpreting findings.
3. Skills in helping laymen and teachers learn how to conduct school-community surveys.

Competencies required by the processes of mass communication:
1. Skills in preparing informational reports and releasing them to the community through the press and radio.
2. Skills in assessing the effects of mass communication.

3. Skills in helping teachers and laymen to learn the skills of mass communication.

Competencies needed in the job of selecting individuals to do particular tasks:
1. Skills in identifying and keeping records of the activities and achievements of school and community personnel.
2. Skills in judging the interests and capabilities of individuals on the basis of data bearing on their activities and achievements.

4. Principles of Personnel Organization

Turning from leadership to the kind of organization of personnel conducive to curriculum development, certain principles of organization can be identified. These principles embrace the general conditions that an effective organization must satisfy.

Curriculum Tasks Integrated through Community Councils

The organizational structure should provide for an advisory council including both teachers and laymen. This council should function as an advisory body on matters of educational and social policy. It would help the faculty and the administration to think through such problems as those of procedure and strategy, diagnosing and formulating school-community needs, planning and executing proposed educational changes. However, the council would not be a policy-making body, although it might suggest policies and procedures for the faculty and the administration to consider.

An advisory council should be set up only with the approval of the local board of education; and, while its membership should be recommended by the administration, actual appointment to the council might more appropriately be made by the board of education. Since the membership is very important, persons to be recommended for appointment to the council should be selected with great care, preferably on the basis of sociometric data.

The council must solve its own problems concerning its functions, its procedures, and the limits of its field of operations before it can ful-

fill its purposes. It will therefore be necessary for the council to turn
to the tasks of formulating its own methods of working, defining its
relationship to the faculty, community groups, and the board of education, and working out the limits of its powers. These formulations of
the council should be understood and approved, first, by the faculty
and, finally, by the board of education. Then, and only then, will the
council be free to take up matters that the faculty and administration
may lay before it. Of course, not all the rules and procedures can be
worked out at once. These will gradually evolve as the council con-
fronts new problems. Nevertheless, a minimum clarification is necessary at the outset. Later changes in policies and procedures, like the
earlier ones, should have the consent of the faculty and the board of
education.

Dimensions of the Organizational Structure

The organization of the professional personnel will have two dimensions: a vertical, or hierarchical, dimension and a horizontal dimension. The first of these will define the "official" channel through which
the influences flow from the bottom to the top of the organizational
scheme, and vice versa. The horizontal structure will provide ways
whereby persons, and groups representing different interests, may get
together to achieve a meeting of minds at the various echelons. For
example, teachers of English, teachers of social studies, and other secondary school personnel may need to work together in developing a
core program. The horizontal dimension of the administrative structure must make it possible for this sort of bilateral communication to
occur without too much expenditure of time and energy.

At this point, conventional departmentalization becomes a barrier
to effective co-operation among staff members. It would not be amiss
for a faculty and its administrative arm to re-examine its assumptions
regarding departmentalization. It has long been assumed that those
parts of the curriculum required of all students are the special property
of the fields of specialization into which they fall. Although English is
required of all students, it is thought to be the exclusive property of
the English Department, and likewise for other required courses. Even
core programs have frequently been considered as belonging to special

groups of teachers. It would be more in keeping with accepted principles of curriculum development to proceed on the assumption that whatever is required of all students is the property of the faculty and not the exclusive concern of a particular department or any special group of teachers. Departmentalization would seem to be applicable to elective work and to the various fields of vocational study. In practice, this principle would require that all core programs, required subjects, and the like, be established by the faculty and that the purpose and content of these categories be subject to faculty criticism and approval.

What has just been said does not mean that the faculty as a whole will constitute the teaching staff of these common requirements. At any given time only part of the total faculty will be actively engaged in the common areas of instruction. Nevertheless, it is not unreasonable to expect any member of a faculty to be competent in the areas required of all students. To think otherwise is to condone the incompetence of a faculty with respect to the general education it conceives to be desirable for every citizen. Of course, as in all things, there will be some persons better qualified than others in these general areas. These persons might be given major responsibility for carrying on the work, but no staff member should be exempt, on the grounds of incompetence, from sharing the instructional burden of the common program.

The Role of the Faculty in Policy-Making

The organizational structure should provide for minimum restraint of thought and expression and for uncoerced acceptance of points of view, values, ideas, and facts. This principle will require that persons occupying status positions be perceived by others as persons who reach decisions by fact and reason rather than by personal interests, unfounded prejudices, and response to pressures and "wire pulling." It will require that the presence of status persons in a group be perceived as a positive resource rather than as an official power to which others must accommodate their behavior. As long as persons in positions of official power are perceived as barriers to change, or as bent on making changes in their own way, the conditions of free expression and uncoerced decision will not exist.

A rigid vertical organization, in which policies and decisions are made at the higher levels and passed down to the lower levels, will restrain creativity and lead to conformity. Persons must have a check upon policies and decisions affecting them, or else they will not believe that efforts on their part to improve things beyond their immediate activities are feasible. The power in most schools is concentrated too much at the top for the development of any effective plan of curriculum development. If curriculum development is to succeed, this power must be distributed so that the faculty can share responsibility in policy-making.

The principle just enunciated requires, among other things, that the administration take no policies before the board of education except those fashioned by faculty deliberation and accepted by the faculty after free and open discussion. Where the administration is forced by law to perform certain responsibilities, it is the obligation of the administration to explain these impositions upon the administration. It is then the responsibility of the faculty to respect these obligations and, when possible, to assist the administration in fulfilling these duties. On the other hand, all matters not expressly covered by legal requirements or by state and local regulations should be the concern of the faculty. The end toward which the administration should work is that of identifying itself with the faculty in such a way as to become its spokesman.

Unfortunately, a faculty that has accommodated itself to autocratic practices over a long period of time will possess members who will react against the responsibility of policy-making. Their personal structures are incompatible with the kinds of behavior these new responsibilities will demand. Such persons must unlearn their habits of conformity and irresponsibility and acquire positive attitudes and habits of co-operative work before they can feel emotionally toned to the new responsibilities placed upon them by a program of curriculum change. Frequently they must experience success in many small changes before they can successfully undertake a major operation.

It should be remembered, however, that not all opposition to curriculum change can be attributed to teachers of this strict conformist type. Every teacher is already burdened with either a large number of classes or a large number of students—and usually with both of these—as well as extracurricular activities; and he has little time to devote to problems of curriculum improvement. Thus, the teacher's lack of interest in curriculum problems is often but a reflection of his necessary preoccupation with the daily tasks.

Administrators have recognized this lack of time and have attempted to arrange the necessary leisure by two procedures. The first is that of freeing a number of teachers, at the expense of the board of education, to carry on curriculum study during the regular school year. A more recent plan is that of extending the employment of teachers by at least a month, and in some instances to an entire year. This arrangement allows teachers to devote the summer months to curriculum study. In some cases such study is facilitated by local workshops and before-school planning conferences. Although these practices may represent an advanced step, the lack of time in the daily program for teachers to work continuously on curriculum problems continues to be a serious handicap to curriculum development.

One of the first things a faculty should do, as a prelude to curriculum development, is to assess, and if need be to perfect, its own procedures of working together as a faculty. For a faculty cannot hope to succeed in working out a more adequate instructional program, nor can it expect to succeed in co-operative work with an advisory council and other community groups, as long as its own operating machinery is in need of repair. It should, therefore, examine its machinery for policy-making, for resolving differences of opinion about important educational issues, for assuming its share of administrative responsibilities, and for engaging in numerous other activities. It may be desirable to elect a policy committee to work with the administration in setting up policies and other measures for the faculty to consider. The faculty may need to consider the creation of other standing committees. In addition, it most certainly will need to decide some of the limits of its powers and duties and to learn to distinguish, as clearly as possible, between the executive function, which is delegated to the administration, and the policy-making function, which belongs to the faculty. In short, a faculty must get its own machinery in working order before it can succeed in the performance of tasks requiring united effort. The initiation of programs of curriculum improvement without first perfecting the machinery by which a faculty can work co-operatively and efficiently is closely associated with failure in curriculum development.

Need for a Plan of Communication

The organization of school-community personnel for curriculum work must provide maximum communication between groups, and especially between levels of the line of authority. Few things, if any, are more important than clear channels of communication in an operation involving a large number of people. In a military operation, if persons in different positions do not know what persons at other points are thinking and doing, the whole plan breaks down. And a military operation is a highly centralized one, in which individuals at the lower levels have little or no choice as to what they shall do. In a plan of curriculum change, where the success of the operation is dependent upon both information about and acceptance of the plans, communication is doubly important.

Perhaps the most difficult task is the communication of perspective. Persons in the hierarchical structure will have perceptions, corresponding to the positions they occupy, of what is going on throughout the system. Those at the top will perceive some things that persons at other levels will not see at all, and vice versa. Even those things that are perceived in common by persons at different levels will be weighted differently in the scale of importance. Therefore, the task of communication is more than that of passing on conclusions and other distilled items of information from one level to another in the system. The perspectives belonging to the various levels must also be communicated. Only as individuals become aware of the perspectives operating at different levels and in various groups can they come to understand one another and to share a difficulty from a common standpoint. As a common perspective emerges, problems can be defined alike by persons occupying different positions in the scheme of things and can be solved by them to their mutual satisfaction.

The task of keeping all persons informed about what is going on in a program of curriculum development requires a plan of communication. In a small school-community situation, in which most of the activities can be shared in common, there may be little justification for a communication plan. In a highly complex situation, in which many diverse interests are represented and opportunities for each problem to be shared by all are very limited, a plan of communication is essential. In this case, difficulties of communication should be anticipated and overcome in such a way as to bring the deliberations of each group to all persons. Thus each person will be able to perceive the curriculum program as a whole and thereby maintain his sense of direction.

It is frequently assumed that adequate communication is provided by representatives—that a person representing a lower-level group, for example, will be able to convey the thinking of the higher-level group to the members of the lower group and that he can inform the higher levels of the feelings and thoughts of his constituents. The inadequacy of this assumption is a source of misunderstanding and confusion in programs of curriculum development. Intergroup communication is a difficult art, for it requires not only skill in language but also, and more especially, a thorough grasp of the psychological and social realities of the groups involved in the process of communication. If the problems of communication are to be solved, it may be necessary for the faculty to establish a committee on communications. The faculty should realize, as it establishes such a committee, that the membership will in all probability need to acquire special training under the direction of expert guidance.

5. The Functions of Consultants

The use of consultant services has been given too little attention in programs of curriculum development. This neglect is due partly to the mistaken belief that an expert knows best how to use his time in a practical situation, rather than in a long-range developmental program. Another source of this neglect is the fact that the functions of consultants were established by trial and error when the administrative approach to curriculum development was the accepted practice.

Be that as it may, consultants continue to be used in the newer approaches to curriculum change much in the same way as they were in the administrative approach. This approach required that the pattern of curriculum development be worked out at the top and handed down to those of lesser rank. The consultant was usually employed to assist the administration and to help teachers, especially production committees, at points where the execution of plans was difficult. The consultant's activities were necessarily related to the problems that arose out of the administrative approach. He was expected to help in the campaign to enlist the interest and support of parents and teachers. It was his duty to advise the steering committee in setting up the machinery for curriculum study and change and to help the committee in determining the objectives of education and in performing its other functions. The consultant was also expected to advise production committees on problems of reducing general objectives to classroom activities, procedures, and materials. Finally, he was expected to advise the administration on the formulation of ways to inaugurate the new curriculum.

The chief characteristic of the consultant's services was that they were directed to the task of helping the local professional group, and especially the administration, to solve their problems rather than to learn *how* to solve their problems. In other words, the activities of the consultant tended to build dependency relations between the consultant and the local professional groups. Instead of the local group gaining power to go ahead on its own steam, it tended to increase its inability to meet its problems.

A New Role for the Consultant

The systematic approach to curriculum development requires a reconsideration of the role of the consultant. If curriculum change is viewed as a form of action-research, then the local professional group, as well as the laymen who work intimately with it, will be oriented to the task of defining and solving educational problems. Since consultants have no ready-made solutions to local problems—indeed, there can be no such solutions—their functions must be defined in terms of the needs of the local group. The consultant will then be concerned primarily with

"training situations and activities" by which teachers and laymen learn
to perform the various techniques needed in the research enterprise and
to understand the principles essential to the proper use of these techniques.

At every stage of curriculum change the group will be concerned not
only with *what* to do, but with *how* the *what* is to be done. A survey of
a particular situation will require careful planning with respect to how
and by whom the survey is to be made. Among the questions that may
be considered are the following: What facts should be sought in the
survey? How can such facts be secured—by interview? by questionnaire? or by some other technique? Who should conduct the survey?
For what purpose will the facts be used? How can they be classified
and interpreted for this purpose? What training will be needed by the
survey staff in the procedures and techniques of surveying? What human-relations knowledge and skill will be needed by the staff? The same
kinds of questions will be faced in every phase of curriculum change—
when dealing with problems having to do with the induction of change
in an equilibrium of forces, when formulating plans for controlling
various forces, when evaluating the effects of the plans. Few school systems can boast of enough persons sufficiently trained in research procedures and techniques to carry on a program of curriculum development
without the aid of consultant services. In the systematic, action-
research approach, the consultant will, therefore, be required to provide
on-the-job training in both research and human-relations procedures
and techniques—training at points where it is needed and when it is
needed. His services will then be such as to enable the local professional staff to become less and less dependent upon him for the development of their program.

In addition, other services of the consultant are frequently needed.
In any program of curriculum development there will arise technical
questions about basic principles and procedures of curriculum construction, about the determination of the scope and sequence of the curriculum, and about many other matters. At certain points in the consideration of these questions the local staff will wish to seek expert resources.
Where possible, such resources should be made available. But no matter
how much help the local staff may receive on these technical questions,
it will be of little avail unless the staff becomes proficient in the re-

search techniques and procedures by which changes in the school-community situation can be brought about and sustained.

When Should the Consultant Be Used?

The question of the most propitious time to call in a consultant is difficult to answer. The practice of summoning a consultant without any local preparation for his use hardly seems to be the best way to employ his abilities. It is not unusual for a consultant to appear on the scene with little information beyond the fact that he is to meet with a group of people who are to work on some aspect of curriculum development. Frequently he finds that the group does not know what its problems are and that they have as little orientation as the consultant himself. The exact time at which outside services should be obtained cannot be determined in the abstract. The matter has to be left to the judgment of the local professional group. However, this much can be said: consultant services can be used most effectively if a local staff has defined its problems with care and has reached the point in its deliberations at which it has clear-cut questions on which it can use expert resources.

Need for a New Kind of Consultant

If the foregoing discussion of the consultant's role is correct, a new kind of consultant is required. In his new role the consultant must be competent not only in the technical aspects of curriculum building but also in the theory and practice of action-research, including human-relations. In the administrative approach, curriculum change was conceived largely as an administrative responsibility in which teachers, and sometimes laymen, participated. The whole enterprise was primarily perceived as a task of working out a new program rather than as a problem in social change. As a result, the consultant had little reason to give attention to problems of human-relations, except occasionally when the human situation became threatening, and still less reason to consider the problems of social engineering. The curriculum consultant can no longer enjoy the luxury of ignoring these problems, because the engineering view of curriculum change makes it necessary that the consultant change the conception of his role.

The behavior of the consultant in his new role has not yet been adequately defined, but a few of its characteristics have been ascertained. When a consultant is called into a local situation, he will do well to discover, as early as possible, the "perceptual fields" of those with whom he is to work. The situation with which the local group is concerned may appear quite different to them, individually and collectively, and to the consultant. Now the consultant cannot understand their problem until he gets inside their perspectives so as to see the situation as they see it. He will try to understand what needs of the group are involved, what difficulties the various members see as standing in their way, what possibilities they see in the situation, and what fears and hopes they have with respect to creating a new state of affairs in keeping with their desires. At the same time, he will try to keep his own understanding of the situation somewhat in the background—at least until he has acquired an adequate understanding of the group's perception of the situation and has established favorable relations with the group. If he tries to impose his own perspective, he will fail to understand the situation himself, inasmuch as the point of view of those with whom he works is part of the situation. Moreover, his proposals are likely either to be ignored or to be accepted passively.

As the group comes to accept him, the consultant can begin to explore the members' "perceptual fields" with them. But even then he must avoid making an outright analysis of the situation and a statement of his own view of the problem. As a matter of fact, his own view, as well as any solution he might propose, would probably be inferior to what the group will work out anyway. Rather, he will encourage, through his technical knowledge and skill, a mutual exploration of the situation, helping the group to formulate its own difficulties more adequately and to work out plans for dealing with them. At this point, the consultant can be of great help by suggesting ways of gathering and interpreting needed data, by aiding the group to see the need for training in the required techniques, and by suggesting alternative ways of proceeding. But he must avoid at all cost any behavior that might be interpreted as an attempt to impose his own solution. He must avoid such behavior not only for the sake of a better quality of human-relations but also because the group will probably work out a better solution than any he might try to impose.

▶ *Following Up*
  This Chapter

1. Observe a group of persons working on a problem. Make a record of the behavior of each member—what he says, to whom he responds, and how often he participates. Using the concept of functional leadership, who are the leaders in this group? How do you decide on the basis of your data? What evidence, if any, did you note that would indicate a status role was played in the group?

2. Find a number of organizations of school-community personnel in programs of curriculum development. These are usually suggested in administrative guides to curriculum development issued by city and state curriculum programs. Evaluate each of these plans from the standpoint of the principles set forth in this chapter.

3. From your study of the literature cited on pages 474–476, make a list of human-relations skills that you believe to be conducive to effective curriculum work.

4. Plan and act out a sociodrama to show how a consultant has been used in a particular situation. Then criticize the use made of the consultant, and show how he might have been used more effectively. Note also the use and misuse of human-relations skills in the situation. For details on how to plan a sociodrama, see pages 514–518.

5. Using a sociodrama, depict the status leader, and analyze the situation to indicate how his behavior affects the group.

▶ *Suggested*
  Reading

1. The nature of leadership has been given considerable attention in the last decade. Despite this fact there is still a lack of systematic treatments of the subject. Perhaps the best practical reference is *Instructional Leadership,* by Gordon MacKenzie, Stephen M. Corey, and associates. One of the earliest and still one of the best discussions of leadership in group situations is in Mary P. Follett's posthumous book, *Dynamic Administration,* edited by Metcalf and Urwick. The leadership function, as related

to followership and certain socio-psychological conditions, is ably discussed by a number of authors in *Readings in Social Psychology*, revised edition, edited by Theodore M. Newcomb and Eugene L. Hartley. Perhaps one of the best short essays on the subject is "Leadership: A Conception and Some Implications," by Irving Knickerbocker, in the *Journal of Social Issues*, Vol. No. 3 (Summer, 1948), pages 23–40. See *Education*, Vol. 24, No. 5 (1948), and Paul Pigors' *Leadership or Domination*.

2. Explorations of the nature and function of advisory councils are to be found in Herbert M. Hamlin's *Agricultural Education in Community Schools*, pages 111–135, and in "Citizen Cooperation for Better Schools," Part I, *The Fifty-Third Yearbook of the National Society for the Study of Education*, sections II and III. The Advisory Council movement was pioneered by students of vocational education, and, while this council was designed to meet the needs of vocational teachers, there is no reason to suppose that its more general application would meet with less success. See also Helen Storen's *Laymen Help Plan the Curriculum*. For an illuminating analysis of different kinds of administrative structures and processes, see *Organizing for Curriculum Improvement*, by Ronald C. Doll, Harry A. Passow, and Stephen M. Corey; and George Koopman, Alice Miel, and Paul Misner's *Democracy in School Administration*. See also *Supervision*, revised by William H. Burton, and Leo J. Brueckner, for an extended discussion of the line and staff structure.

3. The role of the consultant in a line and staff system is ably discussed by Douglas McGregor in "The Staff Function in Human Relations," in the *Journal of Social Issues*, Vol. IV, No. 3 (Summer, 1948), pages 5–22. For another insightful treatment of the consultant's job, see Alice Miel's *Changing the Curriculum*, pages 124–128. The relation of the consultant to the social practitioner, particularly in the process of action-research, is ably discussed in Ronald Lippitt's *Training in Community Relations*, especially pages 1–15, 240–264. See also "The Use of Psychodrama for Group Consultants," by Leland P. Bradford, in *Sociatry*, Vol. 1, No. 2 (June, 1947), pages 1–6. In this brief article there is an excellent discussion of the ways consultants can be more effective in their work.

4. Turning now to the problems of training in human-relations skills and in other techniques of the social practitioner, the best literature on this subject has come from the National Training Laboratory in Group Development and from those who have been associated with this project. The following references are especially valuable: Leland P. Bradford, "Human Relations Training," *The Group*, Vol. 10, No. 2 (January, 1948), pages

4–10; in the same issue are "Research and Training," by Ronald Lippitt and John R. P. French, pages 11–15, and "Principles of Training Method," by Kenneth D. Benne, pages 16–22. These and a number of other essays on related subjects have been issued as a reprint under the title *First National Training Laboratory in Group Development, Group Growth and Educational Dynamics*, Bulletin No. 2, Department of Adult Education, National Education Association. See also *National Training Laboratory in Group Development, Report of the Second Summer Laboratory Session*, Bulletin No. 3, 1948. The most thorough piece of research on the problem of training community leaders is Lippitt's *Training in Community Relations*. You should study this reference with care.

5. A few references on the complex problem of group process and the human-relations skills appropriate thereto are listed as an introduction to the subject: "The Dynamics of the Discussion Group," the theme of the Spring, 1948, issue of the *Journal of Social Issues*, Vol. IV, No. 2. This issue contains a number of excellent articles on group processes and skills; Leland P. Bradford and Ronald Lippitt, "Building a Democratic Work Group," *Personnel*, Vol. 22, No. 3, pages 2–12. The application of knowledge about group structures and processes to the problems of planning and operating conferences is a subject that has been given much attention in certain quarters. Much that can be applied to faculty and civic conferences in local communities can be learned from "A Tale of Three Conferences," *Adult Education Bulletin*, Vol. XII, No. 3 (February, 1948), pages 67–96. See also *A Thousand Think Together*, National Nursing Council, New York City, a report on three regional conferences, indicating the structure and operation of these conferences.

An excellent account of human-relations skills in action is to be found in *Group Dynamics and Social Action*, by Benne, Bradford, and Lippitt. See also *Group Process in Supervision*, by Cecil Parker and William Golden.

6. Illustrations of how teachers, pupils, and parents plan together in curriculum development are found in *Human Relations in Action: Pupils, Parents, and Teachers Work Together*, Denver Public Schools. *How Can We Organize for Better Schools?*, by the National Citizens Commission for the Public Schools, is an excellent guide for those who wish to carry on cooperative curriculum planning.

Chapter 19

Diagnosing the
School-Community
Situation

IN ORDER to proceed intelligently with the modification of an educational program, the faculty and other persons concerned need to know the various social forces that must be taken into account. Otherwise, they will be forced to make social displacements without knowing the realities of the situation. In this chapter an effort is made to set forth some of the procedures and techniques for diagnosing a school-community situation.

By diagnosis of a school-community situation is meant the identification of the forces that maintain the curriculum at its present level of development and the location of the channels through which the forces act. The identification of such forces and the location of their channels presuppose a theory of social action. If a curriculum worker or any other educational worker were to start out to ascertain the forces operating in a given school-community situation, he would encounter a multiplicity of forces acting in many directions. Only part of these forces would be considered relevant to the task at hand, and even some of these would be conceived as more important than others. The theory of social action that the curriculum worker brings to the diagnosis constitutes the intellectual grounds for choosing among the forces.

1. *Aspects of the Diagnosis*

It is outside the scope of this discussion to set forth a theory of social action. It will suffice for present purposes to state the main contours of a theory as they bear upon the task of identifying the constellation of forces constituting an equilibrium. It is clear that the forces under discussion act in and through human beings. It is equally clear that human beings never act in a social vacuum—that they are always in some sort of social structure, some network of human relations, which moves them to act in one direction rather than another. Hence, any effort to change the curriculum will encounter the forces of educational and social structures through individuals affected by the change.

The amount of influence an individual exercises is dependent in part upon his position in these structures. One who is at a lower level of the line and staff organization—a teacher, for example—will exercise less social power than the superintendent or any other who occupies a higher position in the system. Moreover, he will be subjected to structural forces different in kind from those that play upon individuals in the higher echelons. As a result, he will tend to perceive change in a somewhat different light and to weigh it differently in the scale of importance. The principle that the behavior of an individual—and what he will work for or against—is dependent in part upon his position in a social structure, holds for individuals in the social and economic scheme as well as for those in the educational structure. No less significant is the fact that the behavior of each individual is influenced by the tensions, fears, anxieties, values, ideas, and skills that have become part of his personal structure from prior experiences.

Five Areas to Be Explored

In the light of this brief review of influences that play upon individuals, it is possible to state some of the more important areas in which the forces sustaining a given level of curriculum development may be sought.

1. The opinions of parents, children, and educational personnel regarding the adequacy of the educational program.

2. The relations between the social strata to which individuals belong and their opinions about the school.
3. The channels of community influence.
4. The human situation and faculty morale.
5. The extra-community influences, such as legal rules, under which the school operates.

Diagnosis of a situation by an exploration of these areas will serve three purposes. First, it will establish the field of forces with which those who undertake curriculum change must deal. Second, it will help to establish a common perception of the situation for all persons involved in the change. As will be seen in the next chapter, this is one of the primary conditions for orderly educational developments. It is a well-known fact that individuals react to situations not as they actually are but as they believe them to be. As long as one group of individuals believes the actual state of affairs to be one thing and another group believes it to be quite different, little change can be made by common consent. A diagnosis, such as here suggested, will lead to wider agreement as to what the actual situation is and what needs to be done in order to improve the educational program. Third, diagnosis will reveal points at which to induce change in the equilibrium of forces and will provide a fulcrum for prying loose some of the persistent influences.

2. *Opinions of Parents, Pupils, and Educational Personnel*

Since any curriculum change will affect parents, pupils, and teachers, and since the opinions of these groups are already acting as forces both for and against the existing program, their opinions should be ascertained as part of the diagnosis. In any school-community situation there will be points of both satisfaction and dissatisfaction among parents, pupils, and teachers regarding the school. The satisfactions usually act as forces in restraint of efforts to modify the existing equilibrium. Dissatisfactions, on the other hand, can be represented as forces in the direction of a new educational program. They indicate points at which change may be induced with less resistance.

Questionnaires and Interviews

The simplest way of ascertaining the opinions of parents, pupils, and teachers is through the use of questionnaires and interviews. While polling procedures and techniques, like all other scientific instruments, are subject to error and misuse, they have been employed successfully in several fields of investigation. They have been used by business concerns to ascertain their potential markets and the extent to which customers are satisfied with their products. They were employed extensively during World War II to keep account of the state of morale in the branches of the armed services. The application of these procedures and techniques to educational questions has spread rapidly in the last few years.

One of the most comprehensive sets of questionnaires suitable to the problem of diagnosis here under discussion is that designed by Hand, Finlay, and Dolio and described by Hand in *What People Think about Their Schools*. There are four inventories in this battery, as follows: *A*. Illinois Inventory of Parent Opinion, *B*. Illinois Inventory of Pupil Opinion (for upper elementary years), *C*. Illinois Inventory of Pupil Opinion (secondary school form), *D*. Illinois Inventory of Teacher Opinion.

Each of these inventories is constructed so as to enable the respondent to record his opinions about certain components of the school and its program. For the parent inventory some of these components are as follows: treatment of children by teachers and other school officials, help with schoolwork, help in resolving personal problems, value of schoolwork, adequacy of the school's offering, participation in student activities, work load, teaching methods, teachers' attitudes toward parents, new curriculum services favored by parents. Among the components incorporated in the pupil inventory are the following: feeling of belonging, fair treatment by teachers, attitude toward value of studies, relationship of schoolwork to real-life needs, help with personal problems, help from teacher with schoolwork, pride in one's school. Some of the factors in morale sampled in the teacher inventory are as follows: acceptance by fellow faculty members, treatment by administrators and supervisors, consultation regarding school policies, satisfaction with assignment, work load, worth-whileness to pupils of the school's program.

Similarity of components in these inventories facilitates comparison of the opinions of pupils, teachers, and parents so as to ascertain the points on which there is either common perception or the lack of it. This sort of information can be used effectively, as will be indicated in the next chapter, in the process of "unfreezing" an equilibrium.

Another battery of inventories prepared by Hand is designed to obtain the opinions of recent graduates, teachers, pupils, and parents as to how well the school is meeting the needs of youth.[1] These inventories go directly to the heart of the curriculum problem. They include questions on such needs as preparation for marriage and home and family living, how to use leisure time wisely, developing satisfactory social relations, and preparing for a vocation. Like the preceding inventories, these questionnaires are useful in discovering the forces acting either for or against the existing curriculum as well as the degree to which groups of persons see the school program alike. They are described more extensively in the next chapter.

Social Strata in Relation to Opinions about the School

In curriculum engineering it is important to know not only the opinions of individuals but also the social context in which these opinions arise. The parent inventory just discussed asks the respondent to indicate his occupation. Now occupations—when classified into the following categories: professional, proprietary, clerical, skilled, semi-skilled, and unskilled—bear significant relations to the educational attainments, economic status, and social position of individuals. The parent inventory thus permits the curriculum worker to discover whatever relationships may exist between the opinions of individuals about the school and the welfare levels of the respondents.

It is important to know at what points on the welfare scale either the satisfactions or dissatisfactions tend to concentrate, or whether or not either of these types of responses tends to be equally distributed over the occupational gradient. Such knowledge can be used in locating the social status of those parents who resist curriculum change as well as the social position of those who support new developments. The curriculum worker and the faculty will thus be able to plan more intelligently the control of the various forces once the equilibrium has been

[1] See Chapter 20, pp. 506–510.

loosened up. For example, they will know whether or not to plan for more activities to be beamed at one socio-economic group than at another.

3. *Locating Channels of School-Community Influence*

The social forces acting in a community at a given time are channeled through persons or small groups. For example, in the case of food habits, Lewin found that the housewife, as the buyer of the family food, was the control point on which the various forces acted in determining what foods would reach the family table.[2] In order to change the food habits of the family it was therefore necessary to change the food choices of the housewife. He called such a person a *gatekeeper*.

Examples of Gatekeepers in School and Community

There are many gates and gatekeepers in every school-community situation. The superintendent and the principal are gatekeepers. They stand at the entrance to the channels through which the forces from the community flow into the faculty. The heads of departments are gatekeepers who stand at the gates leading from the principal to the teachers—but, more significantly, from the teachers to the principal and the superintendent and through them to the public. Likewise, teachers are gatekeepers in so far as the passage of instructional materials and methods to the classroom is concerned. It is also true that the officers of a teachers' organization are gatekeepers. For example, whatever information goes officially to the public or to school officials must clear through the officers. In addition to gatekeepers who stand at strategic points in the formal channels of influence, there are persons who exercise influence by virtue of their position in informal groups and cliques of the faculty and of the community. No less important as gatekeepers are such organized groups as associations of businessmen, labor unions, and religious bodies.

[2] Kurt Lewin, "Forces Behind Food Habits and Methods of Change," *Bulletin of the National Resources Council,* 1943, CVIII, pp. 35–65.

It frequently happens that once a proposed change gets by the gate-keeper, some forces either lose their strength or change their direction. For example, in one locality where racial segregation was practiced in the schools, the question of competitive athletics between the Negro and white schools was under consideration. One of the strong forces acting against the proposed games was the belief on the part of school leaders that the fans would not stand for competition between Negroes and whites, that interracial conflicts would result in the community. For a long time the principals of both Negro and white schools would not allow the games to be played. When a game between a Negro and white school was finally played, there was no public disturbance. The sportsmanship of both teams was excellent. This contributed to the friendly social atmosphere of the entire situation. The fear of unfavorable public reaction, which had acted as a force against the game, now was so reduced in strength that many persons who had expressed this fear warmly supported further games.

Identifying the Gatekeepers

The gatekeeper stands at a strategic point. What he does may determine whether or not a proposed change, or forces in the direction of a change, will enter the channels leading to those persons who are responsible for considering the change further and executing it. In making a curriculum change, therefore, it is important to know what psychological and social forces play upon the various gatekeepers. The curriculum will not be changed until the forces that shape the decisions of the gatekeepers are changed. The identification of the gatekeepers is the first step in that direction.

It is frequently assumed that a community or neighborhood is unstructured and that its social and psychological forces flow through no regular channels. Nevertheless, there are many channels, hidden and ill-defined, through which driving and restraining forces respecting the school are routed. This is shown by the way lay members of school councils and committees are frequently selected. Since there are no clearly recognized gates and gatekeepers for the various social components of the community, these members are usually chosen by applying one or more of the following criteria: the place the individual occupies in a social group, his prominence in civic activities, and the degree to which he is considered an outstanding citizen whose perspective transcends special interests.

This method of choosing lay members serves certain purposes, but it has two serious limitations when used in systematic educational engineering. First, it lacks techniques for applying these criteria. Second, it often results in the selection of the "big names" and the "prestige bearers," rather than the persons through whom the genuine personal and social needs of the people could be realized.

In a neighborhood or a community, individuals tend to group themselves according to the way they feel toward one another. As a result, an ill-defined structure of human relationships emerges which is the genuine psycho-social structure of the neighborhood or community. Because of their capacity to help others see through their problems and to meet their personal and social needs, certain individuals come to be the centers of these ill-defined structures. These persons are not necessarily popular, as the term is used in common parlance, nor are they necessarily prestige bearers. They may be, and frequently are, simple individuals who stand in a substantial way, though unobtrusively, for the things that satisfy the needs of others.[3] They are able to rise above their own personal problems and to encompass other persons' fears, hopes, and problems in such a way as to hold the confidence of a large number of their fellows. These individuals are the "natural" gatekeepers, whose influence does not come from the position they occupy in an institutional structure but from the free interaction of community members. The natural gatekeeper in a neighborhood may be a cobbler, grocer, barber, housewife, physician, or anyone else.

If the curriculum is to be changed, it is important that these unobtrusive gatekeepers, as well as the prestige bearers, be identified. The natural gatekeepers are the individuals through whom educational ideas can best be channeled to the various sections and social layers of a community. The fears and misgivings of community members will reach them, and their reactions will tend to shape the attitudes of the people of their sections toward curriculum innovations. If there is a public meeting to discuss curriculum changes, the people of the various sections and social strata are more apt to perceive changes in a favor-

[3] Helen Hall Jennings, *Leadership and Isolation.*

able light if their "chosen" leader is responsibly involved than if the meeting is entirely under the influence of big names and prestige bearers.

Sociometric Techniques for Locating Channels of Influence

The location of these gatekeepers is too important to leave to guess-work. While present methods are still crude, they represent a marked improvement over judgments based upon a few passing observations or the opinions of one or two persons. The method now most promising is an adaptation of the sociometric techniques used to locate "stars" in social groups.

Only a few efforts have been made to study the channels of influence in community life. One of the best known of these studies is the one carried on in "Southtown," a southern city of about 6,000 population.[4] In this study, a questionnaire was used as a guide in interviewing residents of the city. The questionnaire was designed to locate the top people with respect to influence in the community. While it is open to criticism from certain technical standpoints, the questionnaire represents a long step away from the "guessing procedures" usually employed to locate persons of influence in the community structure. The following fifteen items constitute the inventory:

1. Have you given advice to anybody at all recently?
   (1) On what kinds of things?
   (2) Can you give me some other instances?
2. With whom would you talk it over if you wanted to get a job or start a business? (If respondent is a professional, change questions: "to open a new office or make some changes in your practice?")
   (1) Why would you talk to him (or her)?
   (2) Are there any others to whom you could go for that kind of help?
3. Who do you think could give good advice on some problem of education?

[4] Frank A. Stewart, "A Sociometric Study of Influence in Southtown," *Sociometry*, Vol. X, No. 1 (February, 1947), pp. 11–31. "A Study of Influence in Southtown," *Sociometry*, Vol. X, No. 3 (August, 1947), pp. 273–286. See also Bartels and Stewart, "How Briarcliff Manor Took Inventory," *The American City*, Vol. 63 (September, 1948), pp. 104–105. R. K. Merton, "Patterns of Influence; a Study of Interpersonal Influence and of Communications Behavior in a Local Community," in *Communications Research, 1948–1949*, by P. F. Lazarsfeld and F. N. Stanton, pp. 180–219.

(1) What makes him (or her) a good person to consult with on such a problem?

(2) Are there any others who could give good advice on some educational problem?

4. When people you know have some personal trouble, to whom are they most likely to turn for advice?

(1) Why do you think they would go to him (or her)?

(2) Are there any others to whom they might turn with such problems?

5. Who around here knows the most about political matters (local, national, international)?

(1) What gives you the impression that he (or she) knows the most?

(2) Who else knows a lot about political matters?

6. Who do you think would best be able to get people to co-operate in a War Bond Drive, in Civilian Defense, and so on?

(1) What makes you think he (or she) would be the best person for such things?

(2) Who else would be a good person to get people to co-operate in a War Bond Drive, etc.?

7. Who is the all-around best-informed person you know?

(1) In what way is he (or she) well informed?

(2) Who else is well informed?

(If nobody is mentioned as well informed about national and international affairs, ask: Who is well informed about national and international affairs?)

(3) What gives you that impression (that X knows a great deal about national and international affairs)?

(4) Who else knows a lot about national and international affairs?

8. Who would make you want to go out of your way to see a motion picture if he or she told you it was unusually good?

(1) Whom else's suggestions about movies would you be likely to take up?

9. Who would make you want to read a book or an article if he or she told you it was particularly good?

(1) Who else is likely to have good suggestions about books to read?

10. Who around here has very good taste in house furnishings?

(1) What gives you that impression (that he [or she] has good taste)?

(2) Who else has good taste in that respect?

11. Who around here shows especially good taste in clothes?

(1) What gives you that impression?

(2) Who else shows good taste in clothes?

12. Who would you say are the important people in town? (Ask for each name given the indicated follow-up questions. Be sure to ask, "Any others?" until the respondent has mentioned at least 5 persons. If he finds it difficult to name more than one or two persons, probe by asking, "Are there any others like Mr. A or Mr. B.?")

    (1) In what ways is Mr. A. important?

        (If this question proves too vague for the particular respondent, ask "What makes you think of Mr. A. as important?")

    (2) Now that you stop to think about it, how do you suppose Mr. A. came to be important?

    (3) Who else is important in town?

13. Who would you consider the most important women in town?

    (1) In what ways is Mrs. A. important?

    (2) How do you suppose Mrs. A. came to be important?

    (3) Which other women are important in town?

14. Who has recently become more important than he (or she) used to be?

    (1) What makes you think of him (or her) as having become more important recently?

    (2) Who else has recently become more important?

15. Who do you think is promising, and might be an important person in town ten years from now?

    (1) What gives you the impression that he (or she) is promising?

    (2) What other people do you think of as promising in this way? [5]

It is interesting to note that the relation between the persons of top influence, as revealed by the interview technique, and the holders of office in civic organizations was lower than is ordinarily supposed. Of the 55 top influentials, 38 per cent held no office, 18 per cent held 1 office, and 44 per cent held 2 or more offices each. There were 141 persons who held office in civic or social clubs. Forty-three of these held 2 or more offices each. Fifty-six per cent of the 43 who held 2 or more offices each were among the top of those judged by a cross section of the city to be highly influential citizens. The remaining 44 per cent received only 2.4 mentions each in the cross-section survey, when 10 or more mentions were required to make the list of top influentials. This would seem to indicate that the practice of selecting people as influential because they hold office is not a dependable procedure. It may result in a list of per-

[5] Frank A. Stewart, "A Sociometric Study of Influence in Southtown," *Sociometry*, Vol. X, No. 1 (February, 1947), pp. 13–14. By permission.

sons who enjoy status but who lie outside or on the edge of the channels of influence.[6]

This kind of investigation of the influence structure needs to be extended into the lower levels of influence. It is important to know all those persons who have influence potential. It is equally important to know the channels through which their influence is felt in the different social and occupational levels of the community and to know how these different levels exert their influence on the total community structure. In short, the technique of identifying persons of influence still leaves undescribed the channels through which the various social forces operate. Further research at this point is sorely needed in the present phase of development of curriculum engineering.

4. *The Morale of the Faculty*

What any group of individuals can do in a given situation depends in large measure upon how they feel toward one another, toward their superiors, and toward the job itself. For example, if they feel that they have the approval and support of their superiors, if they feel that they know what is going on about them respecting the system in which they work, they will be more productive than if the opposite of these conditions obtains. Likewise, their attitudes toward change will be related to the way they perceive the human situation in which they work. It is therefore necessary, for effective curriculum development, that the human relations existing in the school system be known as accurately as possible.

It is too often assumed by principals and superintendents, and no less by curriculum workers, that they know the human factors involved in the school system. They tell themselves and others that the faculty of their school works hard, that it likes its work, and that there are no cleavages. Of course, they will admit under questioning that there are a few dissatisfied persons, but after all they are to be found in all schools. It is too much to expect everybody to be satisfied. It is not assumed in this discussion that administrators and curriculum workers know nothing about the human situation in their schools. They are in

[6] Stewart, *Sociometry,* pp. 18–20.

daily contact with teachers and pupils and in consequence observe behaviors that reflect all sorts of attitudes toward individuals within the system. But these observations are sporadic and the interpretations placed upon them are "intuitive" rather than analytical and are seldom checked by further observations. What is needed in curriculum change is a more systematic diagnosis of the human situation.

A school system, as was indicated in preceding chapters, is a social system comprised of individuals related to one another in ways determined by the administrative structure and by the in-school groups—cliques, working groups, and the like—to which individuals belong. The individuals thus related are also embedded in a network of underlying sentiments, loyalties, and beliefs, some of which are deposits from personal history while others are inductions from the human situations in the school.

Relations between Superiors and Subordinates

Further analysis of the school as a social system will reveal that individuals (as in the case of persons in industrial organizations) are influenced in their behavior, and in their beliefs, sentiments, and loyalties, by the conduct of three classes of persons—superiors, subordinates, and associates.[7]

These classes represent dimensions of the social system along which the diagnosis of teacher morale may be made. The way in which the reactions of subordinates are dependent upon their relations to superiors will indicate the significance of these categories for diagnostic purposes. Whether in the case of the principal and the superintendent, the department head and the principal, teachers and principal, or any other subordinate-superior relationship, the subordinate is always dependent upon his superior for the fulfillment of certain needs. He looks to his superior for increases in salary, for status within the system, and for continuance of his employment. In order to get these things, the subordinate must gain the approval of his superiors.

In some school systems efforts have been made to distribute the power of superiors, in such matters as promotions and salaries, by the

[7] Douglas McGregor, "Conditions of Effective Leadership in the Industrial Organization," in Newcomb and Hartley (Eds.), *Readings in Social Psychology,* p. 427.

establishment of faculty committees to make decisions in these areas. But the effect of this procedure on an individual's dependence upon his superior is by no means clear. It has been assumed that it increases the subordinate's independence, that it relieves his fears and raises his expectations of fair play. But research evidence on this point is practically nonexistent. In the absence of such evidence, it appears on deductive grounds that whatever the advantages of these procedures, they either expand or shift the superior-subordinate relationship from a person-to-person to a person-to-committee basis. For all that is known at the present time, it may be that the way in which the superior does things is more important in promoting morale than whether the superior is a person or a committee.

With respect to superior-subordinate relationships, McGregor has proposed three conditions, for industrial organization, which would seem to have application in educational systems.[8] First, the subordinate must feel that he has the genuine approval of his superior. If he feels that such approval is doubtful, or that his superior disapproves of his work, he will be insecure. Continued insecurity will lead to less and less effectiveness in his work and finally to resistance and antagonism. Second, the subordinate must know what is expected of him by his superiors. This condition includes a number of items, among which are the following: knowledge of general school policy, of the subordinate's duties and responsibilities, of the superior's opinion of his work, of the personal peculiarities of his superiors. Third, the subordinate must be certain that he will have the complete support of his superiors so long as he is doing what is expected of him within the area of his responsibility.

In a given school system the principal and the superintendent may believe that these conditions are met. That belief should be checked by questionnaires designed to ascertain the genuine opinions of the entire personnel with regard to various aspects of these requirements. Only then can there be reasonable certainty of what the human situation in the school looks like from this point of view.

The Illinois Inventory of Teacher Opinion includes some items on the subject of subordinate-superior relationships. A few of these are quoted below as illustrations of the type of questions that may be used:

[8] McGregor, *op. cit.*, pp. 429–432.

55. a. In general, do you feel that you are or are not sufficiently consulted about proposed school policies that affect you and your work? (Check one.)

— 1) I am always or nearly always consulted sufficiently.

— 2) I am usually consulted sufficiently.

— 3) About half the time I am consulted sufficiently.

— 4) I am seldom consulted sufficiently.

— 5) I am never or almost never consulted sufficiently.

b. If you are consulted in this regard, how often are your wishes given as much consideration as they merit by the administration? (Check one.)

— 1) Always or almost always.

— 2) Usually.

— 3) About half the time.

— 4) Seldom.

— 5) Never or almost never.

c. If you are not consulted in this regard, do you think you should be? (Check one.)

— 1) Yes, definitely.

— 2) Yes, but I don't feel strongly about it.

— 3) I don't care either way.

— 4) No, I would rather not be consulted.

— 5) No, definitely not.

56. a. In general, are you satisfied or dissatisfied with the way your supervisor(s) treat(s) you? (Check one.)

— 1) Very well satisfied.

— 2) Satisfied.

— 3) About half and half.

— 4) Dissatisfied.

— 5) Very much dissatisfied.

b. If there are things your supervisor(s) does (do) that you don't like, tell what these things are you don't like _____.

62. a. All things considered, are you satisfied or dissatisfied with the way you are treated by the "administration" of your school? (Check one.)

— 1) Very well satisfied.

— 2) Satisfied.

— 3) About half and half.

— 4) Dissatisfied.

— 5) Very much dissatisfied.

    b. If there are things that the administration does that you don't like,
       tell what these are _____.
64. Are you satisfied or dissatisfied with your prospects for advancement
    in the teaching profession? (Check one.)
    __1) Very well satisfied.
    __2) Satisfied.
    __3) About half and half.
    __4) Dissatisfied.
    __5) Very much dissatisfied.
    __6) I have no particular desire to improve my present status.
    __7) I do not intend to remain in the teaching profession.[9]

It should be pointed out that superiors are affected by the attitudes
subordinates have toward them—or by their beliefs as to what these
attitudes are. Many individuals occupying the higher echelons are extremely insecure and have quite as much need of support from their
subordinates as the latter have need of favorable recognition from
those in higher positions. Any adequate analysis of staff morale will,
therefore, include the administrative and supervisory staff in its scope.

Relations among Associates

Another dimension along which diagnosis of faculty morale may be
made is the relationship existing among associates—that is, among individuals at the same level in the line and staff hierarchy. Individuals
are associated as their common work brings them together. For example, mathematics teachers experience interpersonal relations because
they have certain values, sentiments, and problems in common. In like
manner, other teachers and staff members are associated in work groups.

In addition, members of the faculty will be related to one another
through free associations, not because they are engaged in the same
work but because of personal affinities. These associations have been
referred to by Jennings as *psyche-groups*, to distinguish them from
work groups, which she labels *socio-groups*.[10] Individuals gravitate to-

    [9] Harold C. Hand, *What People Think about Their Schools,* pp. 213–214, 216. Copy-
right 1948 by World Book Company.
    [10] Helen Hall Jennings, "Leadership and Sociometric Choice," in Newcomb and
Hartley (Eds.), *Readings in Social Psychology,* pp. 407–413.

ward one another and thus form psyche-groups because they satisfy each other's personality needs. In these associations the individual is recognized and appreciated as a person rather than as a teacher or as a member of a department. "Membership" in these informal groups may, and usually does, cut across socio-groups; thus persons belonging to various departments—and even those on different levels of the line and staff structure—may be related through these free associations. Psyche-groups meet informally and without call in various places—in the teachers' lounge room, at the table in the faculty lunchroom, and so on. Sometimes they are called cliques, especially by outsiders.

Since the psyche-group is usually not problem-centered, though it frequently discusses "sore spots" and incipient dissatisfactions, it can permit a wide range of behavior, including impulsive conduct. It is more tolerant of the individual as a person than the socio-group; as a result, the individual more freely expresses himself and more frequently reduces his tensions in a psyche-group. It is important to the mental and social health of an individual that he have access to such free associations.

The degree to which a teacher or any other member of the school staff enjoys a feeling of belongingness is dependent in large part upon his status, not only with his superiors but also with his peers in both socio-groups and psyche-groups. Individuals will feel different degrees of belongingness to these groups. For example, in the case of psyche-groups some persons will feel that they have no status at all, some will feel that they are on the fringe, while a few will feel that they are at the center of things. The individual's reaction to change will be shaped, to some extent, by the way his group perceives the change and by how much a part of the group he feels himself to be. If he believes he is in the same boat with others, he will be more apt to consider a situation rationally than if he believes himself to be a lone wolf with only that measure of security which he fights for and wins alone.

A thorough diagnosis of the human situation in the school will include an exploration of human relationships, of satisfactions and dissatisfactions, from the foregoing standpoint. Sociometric techniques have been devised for ascertaining relations among individuals in both socio-groups and psyche-groups. They measure the relations among individuals in a group in terms of the frequency of specified types of actions toward one another. The actions most commonly indicated are those embracing choice of companions. The questionnaires employed are usually based upon variants of such questions as, "With whom would you rather do so and so?" Most of these instruments have been worked out for research purposes, for industrial use, and for determining the social atmosphere of the classroom.[11]

The Illinois Inventory of Teacher Opinion taps more directly the feelings of teachers regarding their status in the school. Since this inventory was prepared to sample teacher opinion about a wide variety of things concerning the school and the teacher's work, it devotes fewer items to this aspect of the human situation than is required for a thorough analysis. But a few items from this inventory will illustrate one type of question that may be used in gathering facts about human relations as they relate to teacher morale.

33. How would you rate your own morale at the present time? (Check one.)
    —1) Very high.
    —2) High.
    —3) Fair.
    —4) Low.
    —5) Very low.

34. In general, do you feel that you are "one of the gang" so far as the faculty of your school is concerned? (Check one.)
    —1) Yes, I feel that I "belong," that I "count" for something, and that I am "wanted."
    —2) Yes and no; I wonder about this; I am not certain.
    —3) No, I feel that I am more or less of a "nobody" or an "outsider" and that I don't "count."

35. All things considered, are you satisfied or dissatisfied with the way you are treated in the school in which you teach? (Check one.)
    —1) Very well satisfied.
    —2) Satisfied.
    —3) About half and half.
    —4) Dissatisfied.
    —5) Very much dissatisfied.

[11] Helen Hall Jennings, *Sociometry in Group Relations*. Conrad M. Arensberg and Douglas McGregor, "Determination of Morale in an Industrial Company," *Applied Anthropology*, Vol. I, 1942, pp. 12–34.

60. To what degree do unpleasant personal relationships among the members of your teaching staff interfere with the effective functioning of the school? (Check one.)

___1) A great deal.

___2) Considerably.

___3) Some.

___4) Little or none at all.

___5) I am not aware of any unpleasantness in these relationships.[12]

Relations of Teachers to Students

A person's morale also depends upon the quality of his relations with subordinates. This is especially true of the teacher, for his perception of his success is related to how he thinks his students feel toward him and how they act toward him. Practically no attention has been given to the task of devising techniques of collecting data bearing upon the quality of the relations between students and teachers. Perhaps the best technique thus far devised is the rating scale by which students can express anonymously their judgment of the classroom instruction. As long as these rating devices are used by the teacher to diagnose his own classroom situation and thereby to improve his work, much can be said in their defense. But when used to rate teachers on a comparative basis, these rating scales are of doubtful value.

5. *Extra-Community Influences*

Several forces originating outside the local community impinge upon the existing curriculum to keep it at its present level of development. There are state laws specifying that certain things be taught, rules and regulations of state departments of education concerning what will be accepted for credit and under what conditions it will be accepted, requirements of accrediting and certificating agencies, and admission requirements of colleges and universities. Then there are state-wide and nation-wide pressure groups, which frequently influence the school against making changes believed to be detrimental to these groups.

[12] Harold C. Hand, *What People Think about Their Schools*, pp. 207, 215. Copyright 1948 by World Book Company.

These requirements and influences can be represented as forces opposing certain curriculum changes. Frequently these forces can neither be changed in direction nor reduced in strength so far as the local school personnel is concerned. This is especially true of the requirements of state laws, of state departments of public instruction, of accrediting and certificating agencies, and of universities and colleges. In these instances, the outside influences must ordinarily be taken as part of the given circumstances within which curriculum change must be made, if it is to be made at all.

It would ordinarily be supposed that members of the teaching profession would be thoroughly familiar with the conditions laid down by the state and by other outside influences such as universities and accrediting agencies. Comparatively few school people have taken the trouble, however, to study these requirements to discover their restrictive powers as well as their permissive aspects. For the most part, administrators are acquainted with these requirements. Yet teachers, and often curriculum workers and supervisors, know little about them. For example, in a state where the board of education requires three years of English for graduation from high school, a number of teachers and even some administrators have been found to argue that the requirement is four years. This lack of familiarity with general regulations is probably due to the fact that so long as the school is operated in the traditional way the problems that arise do not ordinarily require reference to laws and other outside influences.

When curriculum change is to be induced, however, the entire staff should have a thorough knowledge of general influences. It is sometimes necessary for a faculty committee to make an exploration of these. It is important for the staff to know what outside forces are fixed in strength and direction; and it is equally important to know what relatively fixed forces will permit in the way of curriculum change. The way relatively fixed forces are perceived by a faculty may determine in large measure what, if anything, can be done under them. If the faculty sees them merely as restraining measures, whatever potential these forces may have for change will be missed. If they can be perceived as permissive forces, or at least as nonrestraining forces, their direction may be changed to conform with driving forces.

6. Need for Continuous Diagnosis

Since curriculum change necessarily disturbs interpersonal relations and all sorts of personal securities in the school and community, diagnosis of relevant aspects of the school-community situation must be made in every phase of curriculum change. As soon as the first change has been made, the fears and uncertainties, the satisfactions and dissatisfactions, of all those concerned should be ascertained. This sort of diagnosis should be kept up throughout the entire span of change, down to and including the point at which the new equilibrium is finally established. Any operation, especially if it includes large numbers of people, must have continuous reconnaissance service. The facts that reconnaissance yields enable a faculty to take stock of its procedures and plans at every step and to change them as the circumstances may require. It is folly to proceed without knowing what is happening. The task of continuous diagnosis is to supply this knowledge in every phase of curriculum change.

▶ *Following Up*
  This Chapter

1. In a program of curriculum development, what use could a faculty make of the following kinds of facts: (1) opinions of parents, teachers, and students concerning the educational program, (2) extra-community influences, (3) the influential people of the community, (4) the social strata to which various members of the community belong? In each case give an illustration of how the facts might be used.

2. Design a brief questionnaire to find out the facts about some curriculum problem with which you are concerned. Try the questionnaire out on a few individuals and have them criticize it. Revise it in the light of their criticism and use it in trying to solve your problem. Try to determine how you will use the responses before you construct the questionnaire.

3. What criticism can you make of the sociometric techniques of selecting community leaders?

▶ *Suggested*
Reading

1. Due to the recent development of this field, reading materials on the subject of diagnosing the school-community situation are scarce. Some of the best references are those that have come out of the Illinois Secondary School Curriculum Program. These materials are in the form of bulletins describing how to make various kinds of factual studies. Since the titles are indicative of the kinds of studies covered by these pamphlets, they are listed without further comment: Charles M. Allen, *How to Conduct the Holding Power Study.* Harold C. Hand, *How to Conduct the Hidden Tuition Costs Study.* Harold C. Hand, *How to Conduct the Participation in Extra-Class Activities Study.* Harry D. Lovelass, *How to Conduct the Study of the Guidance Services of the School.*

2. There has been rapid growth in the use of opinion polls in almost every aspect of society—industry, business, politics. This technique is now being used in educational circles. Its application to the field of curriculum development has been pioneered by Harold C. Hand. Some of the results of his work are reported in *What People Think about Their Schools.* For another discussion of the use of questionnaire techniques in the exploration of opinions among teachers, students, and parents, see *A Look at Springfield Schools,* especially Chapters 4, 5, 6, 11, and 13.

3. A number of outstanding works on morale in industry which have appeared in recent years are rich in suggestions of procedures and techniques applicable to curriculum change. Among these works are F. J. Roethlisberger, *Management and Morale,* and F. J. Roethlisberger and William J. Dickson, *Management and the Worker.*

Chapter 20

The Induction and Control of Curriculum Change

A N Y P L A N to change the curriculum of a particular school will not only include diagnostic procedures and techniques but also ways of inducing change in the system of forces that maintains the present curriculum. The curriculum worker, therefore, will want to consider such questions as the following: How can I know what forces should be changed? How can these forces be changed in strength and direction? A few techniques for dealing with the problems raised by these questions have been worked out. Although these techniques are still inadequate for the task of curriculum development, the curriculum worker will do well to understand them and to use them wherever they are applicable.

This chapter will deal with five topics: the selection of starting points; the analysis of selected forces; techniques of involvement; conventional ways of initiating change; and control of curriculum change.

A change in the curriculum involves the dislocation of the frame of reference that serves as the teacher's guide to action and as a reference system for meaning. Such a fundamental change must be handled with care. The pace of change must be slow enough to allow the free participation of the faculty in deciding what the change shall be and how it shall be made. The change must be gradual enough to allow the teachers to adjust emotionally and to acquire the skills and knowledge required by the new program. Yet curriculum development that moves too slowly, and without a definite time schedule, will likely lose momentum and spend itself before anything has been accomplished.

1. *Selection of Starting Points*

In order to facilitate the choice of forces to be modified, the faculty, or a faculty committee, should construct an "equilibrium diagram" [1] from diagnostic data showing the driving and restraining forces in the school-community situation. The general form of this diagram is shown on the following page.

This diagram will enable the staff to see at a glance the total pattern of forces with which they must deal. Unfortunately, techniques for measuring the strength of these forces have not been developed; hence the faculty will estimate their comparative strengths and weaknesses as best they can from the data made available by the diagnostic study and from their general knowledge of the total situation.

Four Categories of Forces

An analysis of the equilibrium diagram will reveal four categories of forces, as described in the pages that follow.

1. *Those forces that are crucial.* No displacement of the curriculum can be made in the desired direction so long as the crucial forces remain unmodified. In case the core curriculum is the desired goal, for example, one of the crucial restraining forces would be the fear and insecurity of teachers arising from their lack of knowledge, skill, and instructional materials required by the new curriculum. Another example would be the resistance of parents because they perceive the

---

[1] David H. Jenkins, "Social Engineering in Educational Change: An Outline of Method," *Progressive Education,* Vol. 26, No. 7 (May, 1949), pp. 193–197.

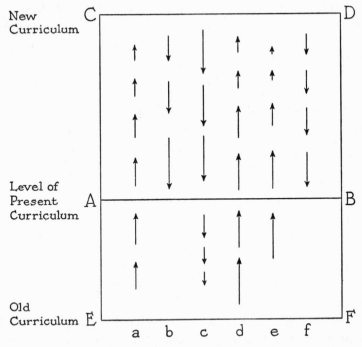

The line AB represents the present level of curriculum improvement in the direction of CD. The forces and their direction are indicated by arrows. The length of the arrow indicates the strength of a force. A minimum number of forces is represented in this diagram. These forces are as follows:

a. Many parents insist upon a more effective program of training for citizenship.

b. Many teachers fear that pupils will not do well on college board examinations if the new curriculum is developed.

c. Teachers and principals fear the criticism of conservative parents.

d. Many teachers accept a "progressive" theory of education.

e. Most of the pupils desire more freedom in making choices.

f. Many teachers feel insecure because they lack skill in planning with pupils.

new curriculum as the surrender of educational and social values important in their frame of conventions.

2. *Those restraining forces that can be reduced with the least effort.* Sometimes one or more crucial forces will fall into this category, being both crucial and easy to deal with; but ordinarily this will not be the case. However, there will be a number of less important resistances that can be handled with relative ease. For example, teachers as well as administrators will sometimes oppose curriculum change in the mistaken belief that the new program will allow no place for the systematic development of skills. Resistances such as this one can be easily overcome by correcting these erroneous impressions of the proposed program. Success in modifying these forces is of psychological value since it gives a sense of achievement.

3. *Those resisting forces that can be changed in direction.* Some forces of resistance can be changed by converting individuals' perception of the change into one that incorporates values they recognize and accept. For example, many persons in the community may hold the view that education should prepare students to meet life needs and responsibilities. At the same time they may hold that the present school program serves this purpose for most students. If it can be shown that the graduates of the school do not consider that the present curriculum prepared them to meet the demands life makes upon them, and if it can be shown further that the proposed curriculum is designed to improve the effectiveness of the school in this regard, many persons will change from active opposition to active support of the new program.

4. *Those augmenting forces that can be increased.* In every situation there are forces acting in the direction of an upward displacement of the curriculum. For example, in the case of displacement toward a core curriculum, one of the driving forces will be the desire on the part of a large number of teachers to make their courses more interesting and meaningful to the students in life situations. If it can be shown that the proposed curriculum change will increase the opportunity to realize this desire, the driving force in the direction of the curriculum change may be increased.

Only a few guide lines can be suggested for deciding which of these categories is most strategic for inducing change. As indicated in an earlier chapter, if the reduction of restraining forces is the main point of departure, there will be less increase of emotionality and less irrational conduct than if the strength of the driving forces is increased at the outset without a corresponding reduction of the opposing forces. Therefore, it would seem the better part of wisdom to begin with the reduction of resisting influences. Teacher and parent insecurities are crucial factors, and since no upward displacement of the curriculum can be made without the alleviation of these psychological realities, it would appear that conditions and factors related to them should be dealt with early in the process of change. Of course, these forces cannot be dealt with and removed entirely from the constellation of influences. They will persist in greater or less strength throughout the entire process of change—their strength at various times depending upon the way the new program works out in terms of student reactions, amount of time and energy demanded of teachers, and a number of other factors. As a consequence, diagnostic measures must be constantly invoked, just as repeated examinations are made by a physician to discover the effects of treatment on a patient.

In cases where teacher morale is discovered to be low, it may be wise to delay curriculum change per se and to begin instead with problems that lie close to the teachers' "sore spots," especially those on which discernible progress is likely. A series of successes at these points will probably increase the staff's confidence in itself, and in the administrative leadership of the school, and will result in less opposition to changes in more difficult areas. In some faculties a great deal of "healing" must occur before any program of change can be undertaken successfully. In any event, it is only sound common sense to make a careful analysis of the forces in the school-community situation before initiating change. Failure to do so probably accounts for the outcome of many ill-fated curriculum ventures.

2. *Analysis of Selected Forces*

It is important that the forces selected for modification be understood. This will require just as much consideration by the faculty as was demanded by the process of selecting the forces in the first place. If the faculty wishes to reduce the resistance of parents to a proposed change or to change the direction of the parents' influence, it is important to know the components of the resistance. For example, it is important to know in what social strata, if any, the resistance is concentrated, to know on what the resistance rests—whether it is based on misinformation, on vested interests of organized groups, on a considered opinion, or what not. Whatever the case, the faculty can hardly plan to work effectively with parents unless they know not only the objections of the parents but also how the objections are rooted psychologically and socially.

The development of plans to work with parents will encounter many of the same resistances that are found in the diagram of forces on page 501. Such plans will necessarily require group work involving parents and teachers. It is to be expected that many members of the faculty will feel a keen sense of inadequacy with respect to the knowledge and skills required by the problems arising in the organization and functioning of the group and in the thinking of the parents and teachers. Many teachers will feel insecure and will be reluctant to proceed with plans to work with parents. An analysis of this resistance will then be required, and plans will have to be worked out to provide training in group processes for the faculty.

3. Techniques of Involvement

One of the facts that must be taken into account is the complacency of individuals about curriculum change. Of course there are always a few individuals who are dissatisfied with existing conditions and will readily exert effort to change them. The dissatisfaction of a few individuals, however, is not sufficient to sustain a program of curriculum development. These persons can be of great help in stimulating and directing the change, but if they become the center of the movement and begin to make changes without the sanction of the faculty, they are likely to lose status with their peers. It is important, therefore, that the whole faculty become involved.

The task of involving the faculty is rendered difficult by the fact that the majority in most situations will ordinarily be more or less complacent. While complacency may be due to a number of things, one of the most important reasons is that the existing system appears to be satisfactory from the complacent person's standpoint. An individual always adjusts to a situation in terms of how he perceives it, how he believes it to be. As long as the complacent person's perception of the circumstances is undisturbed, he is apt to remain indifferent to the need for change.

The Need for Modifying Perception

The fact that individuals differ in their perceptions because of differences in social position has been pointed out a number of times. Teachers, parents, students, and administrators will perceive the same event differently in accordance with their respective orientations. Any contemplated change will be received differently by each of these classes of persons. Each class will be for it, against it, or indifferent toward it, depending upon what they believe the situation to be and what they expect the consequences to be. In order, therefore, to secure common understanding and concerted action in the selection and modification of forces, a considerable degree of common perception must be established.

The effect of change of perception upon behavior is sharply depicted in an interesting story by Kurt Koffka.[2] He tells of a man on horseback who rode up to the front of a country home on a wintery day when the countryside was blanketed with a heavy snow. On being asked the direction from which he came, the rider pointed toward the open landscape. When he was told that he had ridden his horse across a large lake, he was overcome by fright. Most persons are riding across lakes much of the time, for they are not seeing things as they actually are.

The modification of perception is one of the most effective ways of inducing change. A number of techniques have been worked out for modifying perception. Most of these techniques are based on the assumption that if individuals of a given persuasion are confronted by the opinions of persons in quite a different social position, their certainty will be shaken by the incongruous perspectives thus revealed; in consequence, they will be more willing to consider the situation at hand problematically.

2 Kurt Koffka, *Principles of Gestalt Psychology.*

Survey Techniques

Let it be assumed that a considerable proportion of the faculty of a high school believes the present curriculum gives no real-life help to students. Or assume that a large number of faculty members believe the curriculum does not meet the life needs of youth and have no clear idea of how much the needs are neglected. Or assume that they consider satisfying needs is not an important function of the school. As long as any of these beliefs persists, little if any change will be made in the direction of meeting the life needs of youth. In all probability, many teachers who hold these views believe that other people—parents and recent graduates, for example—hold similar ones.

Survey techniques can be used to bring together the opinions of different groups of persons bearing upon a particular question. The amount of agreement and disagreement among individuals of varying perspectives can then be ascertained by tabulating and comparing the responses. Three techniques can be adapted to this purpose: questionnaires, interviews, and recordings. On the following pages will be found descriptions of these techniques and comments on their employment.

Surveys by the Questionnaire Technique

A set of questionnaires designed by Harold C. Hand for the Illinois Secondary School Curriculum Program is based upon the following classification of needs:

A. EARNING A LIVING
   1. The problem of obtaining adequate information about vocations.
   2. The problem of discovering one's own vocational interests and abilities.
   3. The problem of making a wise vocational choice.
   4. The problem of preparing (training) adequately for one's chosen vocation.
   5. The problem of developing good work habits.
   6. The problem of getting a job and making good at it.

B. DEVELOPING AN EFFECTIVE PERSONALITY
   1. The problem of acquiring good manners, poise, and self-confidence.
   2. The problem of improving one's personal appearance.

3. The problem of controlling one's emotions and conduct.
4. The problem of acquiring the ability to speak more effectively and enjoyably.
5. The problem of acquiring the ability to write more effectively and enjoyably.
6. The problem of acquiring the ability to read more effectively and enjoyably.
7. The problem of acquiring the ability to get along happily with other people.
8. The problem of developing intellectual interests in order to become a more cultivated and cultured person.
9. The problem of acquiring the ability to distinguish right from wrong and to guide one's actions accordingly.
10. The problem of securing help in solving one's personal problems.

C. LIVING HEALTHFULLY AND SAFELY
1. The problem of acquiring the ability to care for one's health and of developing good health habits.
2. The problem of selecting a "family doctor" and acquiring the habit of visiting him systematically.
3. The problem of selecting a "family dentist" and acquiring the habit of visiting him systematically.
4. The problem of learning how to prevent accidents to oneself and to others, and of acquiring safety habits.
5. The problem of learning how to drive and care for an automobile.

D. MANAGING PERSONAL FINANCES WISELY
1. The problem of acquiring the ability to spend money wisely.
2. The problem of learning how to use the facilities of a bank and of developing habits of thrift.
3. The problem of providing for the future through learning how to buy insurance and other securities wisely.

E. SPENDING LEISURE TIME WHOLESOMELY AND ENJOYABLY
1. The problem of learning to play athletic games and sports.
2. The problem of developing one or more outdoor activity hobbies (gardening, camping, fishing, etc.)
3. The problem of developing one or more "making thing," "make it go," or "tinkering" hobbies.
4. The problem of developing one or more "art" hobbies (sketching, painting, designing, collecting art objects, etc.)

5. The problem of learning to sing and/or play a musical instrument.
6. The problem of acquiring the ability to select and enjoy good music.
7. The problem of learning how to get the best out of the radio.
8. The problem of acquiring the ability to select and enjoy good motion pictures.
9. The problem of acquiring the ability to select and enjoy good books and magazines.
10. The problem of acquiring the social skills of dancing, playing party games, doing parlor stunts, etc.
11. The problem of acquiring the ability to take an enjoyable part in dramatic activities.
12. The problem of learning how to select and enjoy good plays.

F. TAKING AN EFFECTIVE PART IN CIVIC AFFAIRS
1. The problem of acquiring the ability to conduct a meeting properly.
2. The problem of becoming a more co-operative, community-minded person.
3. The problem of learning how to live democratically with one's fellows.
4. The problem of ridding oneself of religious and racial prejudices.
5. The problem of developing an interest in economic, social, and political problems.
6. The problem of acquiring the ability to study and help solve economic, social, and political problems.
7. The problem of making oneself a well-informed and sensitive "citizen of the world."

G. PREPARING FOR MARRIAGE, HOME–MAKING, AND PARENTHOOD
1. The problem of developing and maintaining wholesome boy-girl relationships.
2. The problem of preparing for a wholesome courtship.
3. The problem of acquiring the ability to manage a home intelligently.
4. The problem of preparing for intelligent parenthood (sound sex education, rearing children intelligently).

H. MAKING EFFECTIVE USE OF EDUCATIONAL OPPORTUNITIES
1. The problem of choosing appropriate school subjects.
2. The problem of choosing appropriate out-of-school activities.

3. The problem of developing good study habits.
4. The problem of deciding whether or not to attend a trade or other vocational school.
5. The problem of choosing a trade or other vocational school if attendance at such an institution is intended.
6. The problem of deciding whether or not to go to college.
7. The problem of choosing a college if attendance at such is planned.
8. The problem of securing adequate preparation for successful college work if attendance at such an institution is planned.[3]

Five inventories based on this classification of needs have been prepared for the Illinois Secondary School Curriculum Program:

1. *What Do You Think?* This inventory is designed to ascertain whether or not a) the parents and other laymen, b) the teachers, and c) the pupils think that the secondary school should give help in reference to each problem included in the list above.
2. *How Much Real-Life Help Did They Get?* This is designed to find out how much help in connection with each problem listed above the teachers think was typically received by the members of the last graduating class.
3. *How Much Were You Helped by Your High School?* This questionnaire asks the recent graduates of the school to tell how much, if any, of the help they needed was received from their high school in connection with each real-life problem.
4. *What Has Become of the Members of Your High School Class and What Are They Doing?* This is constructed to find out how many of the graduates have encountered each of the real-life problems indicated above.
5. *How Well Equipped Are You for Effective Living?* This is designed to secure data for evaluating the effectiveness with which graduates are meeting the real-life problems.[4]

Since these inventories are based on a master list of life problems, the responses of students, parents, teachers, and recent graduates to any problem can be readily compared. This makes it possible to discover

---

[3] "Problems of High School Youth," prepared for the Illinois Secondary School Curriculum Program by Harold C. Hand. (Springfield, Illinois: Office of the State Superintendent of Public Instruction; 1949.)

[4] Adapted from mimeographed materials describing the inventories and how to use them.

whether or not a consensus exists among these groups with respect to a given problem and to find out how much difference there is and between whom the difference exists. For example, the teachers in one community where these inventories were used believed that students wanted help with personal problems and that parents did not want the school to include instruction on sex problems. Responses to the inventories showed that both parents and students in overwhelming numbers wanted the school to give sex education and that fully half of the students did not want help on personal problems. These inventories unmasked an existing consensus about which teachers had no knowledge. Indeed, teachers had been led by their fears to believe the exact opposite of what the situation actually turned out to be. Likewise, a lack of consensus was revealed where the teachers had assumed one to exist.

Surveys by the Interview Technique

The interview technique is more time consuming than the questionnaire technique. Moreover, it is by no means clear that persons feel as free in responding to an interviewer as in filling out an inventory anonymously. However that may be, the interview technique can be applied without too much burden upon a faculty by using volunteer interviewers—in which case it would have the added advantage of *involving* a considerable number of lay people in school problems who otherwise might remain unconcerned. If this plan is followed, interviewers should be selected from all socio-economic layers of the community. Housewives are usually freer than other persons to assist the school in this capacity because their time schedules are more flexible. The interviewers need no prior skill, since in any case they must be given a period of training for the work.

The interview schedule must be carefully worked out by the faculty in accordance with the purposes for which the data are to be collected. As a rule, the schedule should contain few "open-ended" questions, since the volunteer interviewers will not be prepared to engage in the probing to which such questions may lead. All questions should be simple and carefully worded, so that the interviewer will not be required to reformulate questions on the spot. In order to secure as much rapport as possible between the interviewer and the respondent, it is best for interviewers to work with respondents of their own social group or status.

The training of interviewers should take place in a series of meetings planned to cover the following purposes:

1. To explain the purpose of the survey, the kind of facts it is designed to collect, and the informants to be reached.
2. To explain the function of the interviewer and to supply each interviewer with instructions on procedures of interviewing.
3. To study the interview schedule, question by question.
4. To encourage the interviewers to engage in practice interviewing with friends at home.
5. To provide role practice designed to deal with typical interview problems.[5]

If the interview schedule is correctly designed, the results can be used to compare or contrast the perceptions of different groups in the community regarding important curriculum problems. As in the case of inventories, it can be ascertained from interviews whether or not the beliefs of teachers about the opinions of parents and nonparents is based upon realities or fears. The results of the interviews should be compiled and discussed so as to bring out the data and their meaning. The initial forum for the discussion of the results should include the interviewers, members of the faculty who are directly involved, and other persons who have been associated with the conduct of the survey. The initial discussions should center upon the interpretation of the findings and plans to present the results to the faculty and to members of the community.

Surveys by the Recording Technique

The third technique—recordings—is for "spot surveys" rather than for comprehensive ones. It is more limited in scope than either the inventory or the interview. In reality it is an adaptation of the interview technique. Instead of the reactions of the respondents being writ-

[5] Adapted from Margot H. Wormser, "The Northtown Self-Survey: A Case Study," *Journal of Social Issues*, Vol. V, No. 2, 1949, p. 13.

ten down by the interviewer, they are recorded on a wire or tape. The recording situation can include either a group of persons or a single individual. The recording technique has two important advantages. In the first place, it reports the reactions of individuals directly. At the same time, it preserves a sort of "objectivity," since it is more difficult to react emotionally to what a machine says than to what a person says. In the second place, the recordings can be repeated time and again, thus making possible a careful study of the reactions.

An illustration of this technique will help to clarify its usefulness. The teachers of English in one school maintained that they needed to give more time to grammar and written expression. It was suggested by another faculty member that the opinions of graduates would not support this view. The department of English decided to find out. A group of graduates who had made good grades in English were called together to discuss informally the work they had had in English during their high school years. They had not gone to college but were employed in the community. They knew that their discussion was being recorded and that it would be played back to the members of the English department. It was explained to them that the English teachers wanted to improve their program and that the opinions of the graduates with respect to the strong and weak points of the work in English would be helpful in making future plans. Some of the areas of concern to the faculty were suggested to the group, but they were told not to confine their discussion to these matters.

When the discussion was played back it was discovered that these graduates believed ample time had been given to grammar and written expression when they were in school. But, in their view, not enough time had been given to the development of tastes and standards of judgment in such areas as leisure reading, moving pictures, and radio programs; nor had enough stress been placed upon oral expression in group situations. The fact that the graduates thought these things does not mean that they were correct, nor did the teachers change their program because of these reactions. The significance of the study is that the complacency of the teachers with respect to certain areas of English instruction was disturbed. What should be done following this upset would depend upon further study and upon the strength of other forces playing upon members of the English department.

Individual Study by Projective Techniques

Projective techniques have been used extensively in recent years to explore the personalities of individuals. These techniques are based on the assumption that an individual reveals genuine and deep-lying aspects of his personality by his responses to a situation, by what he sees in a given set of circumstances. The possibility of revealing hidden perspectives of individuals with respect to resistances to curriculum change has only begun to be recognized. Projective techniques are most valuable in the cases of individuals under the influence of attitudes of which they are not aware or the existence of which they are loath to admit to themselves or to others.

This technique may be illustrated by the case of a group of persons who claimed to have no prejudice against Negroes when the question of fair employment practice was up for discussion in a group of workers. The discussion leader could elicit no discussion since the workers saw no reason to discuss a question on which they felt themselves to be clear. The discussion leader, anticipating this reaction, had come prepared to shake the group into an awareness of its actual beliefs. He flashed on the screen a cartoon of a Negro and a white man fighting. After a second the cartoon was removed, and the group was asked which one had the razor, the Negro or the white man. More than 80 per cent said the Negro had the razor. Then the picture was returned to the screen, and it was clearly evident that the razor was in the possession of the white man. After that the group did not have to be convinced that it was the victim of a stereotype concerning the Negro.

Projective techniques are rich with possibilities of revealing biases of administrators, teachers, parents, and students concerning interpersonal relations in the operation of the school. Many examples will readily come to mind. It is not unusual for persons in administrative positions to believe that the failure of committee and faculty meetings is due to the inertia and unwillingness of the faculty to take responsibility. As a rule, these persons do not think of themselves as responsible for the ineffectiveness of these meetings. They are reluctant to admit this fact.

A slide showing a faculty meeting being conducted by a principal could be prepared and shown on a screen to a group of principals and teachers, who would be asked to write a story about the picture. An expert analysis of these stories would doubtless uncover hidden beliefs and prejudices about such meetings and the human relationships involved in them. Extensive research along these lines is needed for the advancement of techniques of curriculum change.

Sociodrama as an Involvement Technique

The central feature of the sociodrama technique is the assigning of roles to individuals to act out a problem situation. In this way the work of a principal with a group of teachers or parents, or the behavior of a teacher in a guidance situation, can be presented to a group of persons as a "case" to be analyzed and discussed. Since individuals in the drama are taking the roles of others, they are freer—less involved—than they would be in an actual situation where the playing is "for keeps." Moreover, since what the individual does in the role may reflect the other person rather than himself, the role he plays can be criticized and evaluated with less emotional disturbance. In other words, the sociodrama yields a measure of detachment in both the participants and the audience, even though members of the audience may see themselves in the drama.

Although it is still an open question as to how much the individual enters into the role he plays, there is considerable agreement that an individual playing the role of another comes to get the feel of the other person—to get inside his perspective, his world, and to see things through his eyes. In addition, members of the audience may become identified with various roles so that they, too, get inside the framework of other persons.

If the preceding observations are true, the sociodrama can be effectively adapted to help individuals in various positions (teachers, principals, parents, students) to see themselves as others see them—or, to put the same idea in another way, to see that their perception of a given situation is not shared by persons in other positions. The use of the sociodrama for this purpose is illustrated in a summer workshop for school administrators where there was a tendency to deal superficially and somewhat defensively with problems of relationships between administrators and teachers. The first day was spent in an attempt to explore the problems about which the administrators were concerned. There was a distinct tendency to blame the teachers for poor teacher-administrator relations and to assume that poor faculty meetings were to be attributed to the teachers. The second day's session was therefore designed to help the members of the workshop to see the total situation with respect to staff meetings instead of the partial view resulting from the single perspective of the administrator. The leaders then agreed that the next meeting of the group would be focused upon the four objectives listed below. A record of part of the session follows the list of objectives.

1. To enlarge the perception of the group to a point where they would see what teachers thought about and wanted from staff meetings.
2. To shock their complacency that any problem arising in leading meetings resulted from others' mistakes.
3. To bring about a realization of how really productive staff meetings can be.
4. To practice better ways of leading staff meetings.

At the opening of the second session one of the leaders quickly summarized the progress of the preceding day's session and pointed it toward further analysis by suggesting that now they would want to go right down to the heart of the problem of getting teachers to show greater interest in staff meetings. He pointed out the difficulty of their problem and indicated that some fairly deep analyses of the whole situation would need to be made. He suggested that perhaps a small experiment might get them started and that they pick one of their best administrators for this experiment. The group quickly focused on one individual and the leader then asked if he would step out of the room for a moment.

The leader then suggested to the rest of the group that it might be interesting to see how the person sent out of the room would react if he listened to a number of teachers talking about a staff meeting he might be going to lead. Five or six administrators from the group were asked to volunteer as teachers. A quick briefing meeting was held, with help from the entire group, as to how these "teachers" would act and as to what personalities they would assume. Then the person out of the room was called back in. He returned to find the half dozen persons sitting in a group up in front of the rest of the group. At the same time he saw a single chair set apart from the small group, but also in front of the larger group. The leader then instructed him as follows:

LEADER: You are the principal of a school and you are sitting at your desk (points to the solitary chair) and you have just had installed an inter-communication system to enable you to listen to each room or to speak to each room. You plan, at this hour, to tune in Miss Smith's class in history. Unfortunately the mechanic made a mistake and you get the teachers' lounge room instead. You quickly recognize the voices of some of your teachers and, because of what the first says, you continue to listen. (The "principal" nods that he understands, sits down on the chair to the side, and turns an imaginary switch.)

TEACHER A: Another staff meeting this afternoon; I suppose it will be as useless as the rest.

TEACHER B: He'll spend an extra hour getting nowhere—just wasting time pretending he's democratic when all the time he called a meeting just because he has some order to give. He never really wants us to get at our problems.

TEACHER C: He thinks he kids us about his policies. In the first meeting this year he gave a talk about wanting to maintain high professional standards for the school, and last meeting he told us to raise all the grades so parents wouldn't complain.

TEACHER D: What really irritates me are those two stooges he has. That new blonde and the old war horse who has always been here. He can always count on them to back him up.

TEACHER A: I know he isn't interested in our problems and so I wish he wouldn't pretend to be. I'd rather we never had any meetings than the kind he has.

TEACHER D: But think of his reputation as a democratic school princi-pal. (A few more comments such as these and the leader cuts the scene. He turns to the principal.)

LEADER: Well, you have now a pretty good idea of what your teachers think of staff meetings. However, you still face the staff meeting you had planned for this afternoon. Certainly after hearing these comments, you are having quite a few thoughts. Suppose you think out loud now, both as to how you feel about what you heard and as to any re-thinking you may want to do about this afternoon's staff meeting.

After a slow start, and aided by a few probing open-ended questions by both leaders, the "principal" began to soliloquize concerning his reactions to the previous scene. Both from his reactions and from expressions on the faces of many in the total group, there was evidence that "seeing it from the teacher's side" was quite a shock and was bringing thinking on a much deeper level than had been true the day before. Furthermore, the shock was produced by themselves. It was they, in the role of teachers, who had opened up another perceptual dimension.

The soliloquy was continued only long enough to make certain that "how the teachers felt" was seen as a major factor in planning for a staff meeting. After this, a staff meeting situation was quickly set up and led by the principal. This scene showed evidence of the shock of the preceding scene in the efforts of the principal to bend over backward in his efforts to seek out teacher problems. However, this effort became so distorted that the meeting quickly degenerated into a laissez-faire situation with discussion merely wandering without direction.

After this scene was cut the two leaders were able to lead a very intense discussion, in which the majority of the group participated, on staff meetings. The leaders were able to help the group see the difference between autocratic, laissez-faire, and democratic groups. Suggestions for conducting staff meetings were measured against "what the teachers thought" in the first scene. Little of the defensiveness of the preceding day was seen. The discussion went deeper into basic causes of group problems than had been true the previous day. Furthermore, question and discussion probed toward what kind of help to school administrators in the area of human relations was needed, and where such help could be secured. There was evidence of a much more serious approach to the problems of in-service training of teachers. All in all, evidence accumulated during the latter part of this session of the effectiveness of the complacency shock administered.[6]

The sociodrama can be used to initiate change either by strengthening or reducing a force or by changing its direction. In the foregoing illustration it was used to increase the tendency toward better faculty meetings and to reduce resistance arising from unsatisfactory relations between teachers and administrators. In addition, it may be used merely to point up and make real the problem to be discussed.

The planning of a sociodrama for any of these purposes should be carefully done. A sociodrama can be planned and conducted in many ways. The following is descriptive of one of the common procedures.

After the purpose has been decided upon in terms of the forces to be dealt with, a committee under the guidance of a leader may work out

---

[6] Leland Bradford and Paul Sheats, "Complacency Shock as a Prerequisite to Training," *Sociatry*, Vol. 2, Nos. 1 and 2, 1948, pp. 38–42. By permission.

the general outlines of the drama to be presented. This task will entail certain steps:

1. Give a brief description of the general area in which the forces to be dealt with lie and hold a short discussion of the problem related to the area.
2. Decide upon the problem situation to be dramatized. Members of the committee should be encouraged to tell about cases illustrative of the various aspects of the problem chosen for dramatization. These cases very often point up the problem, make the forces more explicit, and provide excellent material for the drama.
3. Select individuals who are to play the different roles. Some of the role-players may be chosen from the planning committee and others from the larger group. Try to select persons who will most readily enter into the spirit of the situation.

Then the committee is ready to report its plans to the larger group and to continue step by step until the drama has been presented. The presentation will require the following additional events:

1. Send the role-players out of the meeting room. Describe to them the problem situation and decide (with their help) the role each is to play. Give them a few minutes to think through their roles and, if they are to depict a particular situation, to receive instructions in the character of the roles.
2. Describe to the larger group the problem situation to be acted out. Give background material sufficient to make the problem live in the mind of the "audience." Describe the setting of the play, indicating whether it is in the principal's office, a classroom, a lounge room, or what-not. Arrange available furniture—tables, chairs, and the like— to make the situation as definite as possible.
3. Call in the players and have them take their places and begin the play.
4. Let the play continue until the "director" feels that the intended results have been accomplished.
5. Open the meeting to general discussion. The players may now enter the general deliberations at appropriate points, but ordinarily they should keep their positions on the "stage." This keeps the problem situation alive to the "audience."

4. *Conventional Ways of Initiating Change*

It has been recognized for a long time that since curriculum change requires the re-education of administrators and teachers, methods of motivation essential to such re-education are important. It has been maintained, not without good reason, that, since curriculum change is a form of learning, it proceeds best when teachers become involved in problems that to them are real. The initiation of curriculum development has tended, therefore, to emphasize a number of ways by which a faculty can involve itself in problem situations. A few of these are involvement techniques; but a great number of them are nothing more than different forms of the ancient "study" approach, which is based on the erroneous assumption that correct knowledge and firsthand experience necessarily lead to changes in ways of doing things.

The following list, compiled by the Committee for the Illinois Secondary School Curriculum Program, suggests both involvement and academic study techniques. The accompanying introductory note indicates the function of the various approaches as "psychological levers."

There are many ways of getting underway in a program of curriculum revision. The important thing is that we need to pry ourselves loose from the present situation. Maybe one lever will do the prying loose; perhaps it may require several.

Here are some "psychological levers" that have been used by other schools. These levers include carrying on such activities as studies, visits, readings, and self-surveys by local faculties, and then utilizing the resultant data as a basis for arousing discontent with the existing program and encouraging a desire to do something constructive by way of change.

Pick your lever(s) and let's get started:

1. Have the faculty apply the "Evaluative Criteria" (prepared by the Co-operative Study of Secondary School Standards Committee) to your school.
2. Engage some outside agency (e.g., a university survey committee) to survey the curriculum.
3. Have the faculty survey the school's curriculum.
4. Encourage the faculty to visit, or otherwise discover, what was done in one or more schools which have successfully initiated a program of curriculum development.

5. Interest the faculty in examining the "literature of high school criticism" in order to determine for itself which of these criticisms are valid, and consider which of the valid criticisms could be honestly applied to the local school.

6. Read and discuss with the faculty one or more idealized descriptions of imaginary (e.g., "Education for All American Youth") or real (e.g., "Learning the Ways of Democracy") curricula, comparing the resultant "picture" with the practices of the local school.

7. Enumerate with the aid of the faculty the full range of the major types of learning experiences and services (e.g., help in choosing an appropriate vocation, learning how to spend money wisely, preparation for wise parenthood, acquiring a variety of avocational interests and skills, placement service, etc.) which they think the local school should ideally provide.

8. Cast the enumeration noted in Method 7 above into a formal questionnaire and give this inventory either to former or present students, or both, in order to discover how much, if any, of each type of help was or is being received.

9. Encourage teachers to attend summer school curriculum courses.

10. Encourage teachers to attend curriculum workshops.

11. Encourage teachers to attend state, regional, and national conferences of leaders in their respective school enterprises (e.g., National Council of Teachers of English, National Vocational Guidance Association, etc.).

12. Encourage teachers to attend curriculum conferences held by universities or other agencies.

13. Have a study made in which the socio-economic status, and the "IQ" status of the pupils in each year of the high school are compared with similar data for the fifth-grade populations of all "feeder" schools.

14. Have a study made to determine the socio-economic status of all pupils who "belong to" or who "take part in" each classroom or student activity of the school.

15. Have a study made of cost to pupils (e.g., books, fees, dues, etc.) attending the school, projecting these findings against the average family income in the community.

16. Have some member of the faculty report to his fellows the findings of the published researches bearing upon the types of data noted in Methods 13, 14, and 15 above, inviting the staff to estimate the degree to which these findings are probably true of the local situation.

17. Have the faculty familiarize itself with recommendations of the various national professional organizations which concern themselves with any aspect of the secondary school curriculum.

18. Encourage teachers to make intensive case studies of a small number of pupils—"normal" as well as "problem" children—in order to discover the ways in which the school is and is not meeting (it may even be operating in contradiction to) the needs of these few youngsters.

19. Have the felt needs and problems of all (or a substantial representative sampling of all) youth in the school studied through appropriate inventories.

20. Have the faculty thoroughly study the social and psychological foundations of secondary education in order to determine *what* responses the school should induce and *how* these can most effectively be engendered.[7]

5. *Control of Curriculum Change*

One of the most systematic procedures for inducing and controlling curriculum change is that worked out in the Illinois Curriculum Program. This procedure is referred to as the Consensus Study procedure. It is designed to enlist laymen, pupils, and teachers in the task of assessing the curriculum and of working out a more satisfactory program. The assumptions underlying this procedure are:

1. That, although good teaching can be done by teachers working in the face of the uninformed indifference of their colleagues, the *best possible* program in any given subject or service area of the school is likely to be initiated or to endure to the degree that its purposes and program are understood, accepted, and supported by the *entire* faculty; i.e., by *all* the teachers in *all* the subject and service areas of the school

2. That, as matters now stand, secondary school teachers typically understand (and hence are capable of intelligently accepting and effectively supporting) the purposes and programs of but one or two, or at best but a very few, of the "other" subject and service areas of their school

3. That, in consequence, secondary school teachers too frequently not only fail to support but at times even unwittingly hinder or obstruct the

[7] *Guide to the Study of the Curriculum in the Secondary Schools of Illinois* (Springfield, Illinois: State Department of Public Instruction; 1948), pp. 25–26.

desirable things which their fellow teachers are attempting to do in or through the "other" subject and service areas

4. That, in order to improve the curriculum materially, it is therefore necessary for the *entire faculty,* under the leadership of the principal and the tutelage of the teachers directly concerned in each instance

   a. *To decide together* the purposes of each of the subject or service areas of the school

   b. *To decide together* which of the accepted purposes of *each* subject or service area *are* and which *are not* currently being embodied in the the program of the school

   c. *To decide together* what can and should be done to implement those of the accepted purposes in *each* subject or service area which are currently being neglected

5. That it is equally essential that patrons and pupils understand, approve, and support the program of the school; that, consequently, it is essential that at least a panel of pupils and patrons join with the full faculty in these deliberations.[8]

The Consensus Study procedure employs a set of four inventories. The character and purpose of these instruments are indicated in the following account:

In order to make explicit the design of the ISSCP series of Local Area Consensus Studies, let us take for illustrative purposes some *one* of the nineteen parts of this local action study—say mathematics. The reader can then quite readily generalize for science, social studies, industrial education, modern foreign language, camp experience, or any other subject or service area in which he may be interested.

To illustrate, we shall describe as briefly as possible the procedure which will be followed in the case of mathematics. Some recognized leader in this curriculum area will be asked to draw up a concise statement of the principles which would probably govern, and of the chief purposes which would probably be striven for, in the mathematics program of a really up-to-date high school. This will be done in nontechnical language; it will be in terms which can be understood by parents and pupils. This formulation will then be criticized and amended by a jury made up of said leader plus at least two teachers selected by the Illinois Council of the Teachers of Mathematics, plus a representative from the Office of the State Superintendent of

[8] Harold C. Hand, *Prospectus of the Local Area Consensus Studies,* p. 9.

Public Instruction, plus a generalist in the person of a high school principal or superintendent, plus a specialist or two in mathematics education from one or more of the higher institutions in Illinois. If experience to date means anything, this jury will probably require a half dozen or so all-day, face-to-face meetings to accomplish this task.

The amended formulation of principles and purposes will then be cast into a simple inventory (Inventory A) to be used (a) by *all* (not just the mathematics [9]) teachers in the local high school, and (b) by a panel of pupils and patrons. In Inventory A, each respondent will be asked anonymously to do two things in reference to each principle and purpose proposed by the leader-and-jury group: [10] First, he will be asked to indicate whether or not he believes that his school should accept and act upon or strive to accomplish the principle or purpose; second, he will be asked to estimate the extent to which he thinks his school is currently acting upon or accomplishing the principle or purpose.

The data yielded by Inventory A will then be tabulated locally and utilized as the basis for whatever number of full faculty-pupil-patron discussions the local faculty group may deem desirable. The principal purpose of these faculty-pupil-patron discussions will be to argue the pros and cons of each principle and purpose (under the leadership and tutelage of the local principal and mathematics teachers) with a view to building the broadest possible basis of faculty-pupil-patron consensus in understanding support of a good mathematics program. A secondary purpose will be that of enabling the total faculty and the patron and pupil representatives to arrive at a realistic appraisal of the strengths and weaknesses of the current mathematics program of the school.

After these teacher-patron-pupil discussions have been held, the local school will be supplied with a second instrument known as Inventory B. This inventory is also to be administered to all three groups (the total faculty and the panel of patrons and pupils). The purpose of this simple instrument is to find out what the consensus of the teachers, patrons, and pupils is after their discussions based on Inventory A have been concluded. In addition, in Inventory B, each respondent will also be asked to indicate which, if any, of the principles or purposes of its mathematics program he believes his school should attempt better to implement or achieve.

[9] The teachers of mathematics and the principal of the local school will be supplied with examination copies of Inventory A as a basis for deciding whether or not to involve their school in this local area consensus study.

[10] It will of course be understood that the local teachers may add any other principles or purposes which they believe should be included.

With the locally tabulated data yielded by Inventory B before them, the mathematics teachers and the principal of the school (plus any other persons they may see fit to include in decision making) will then decide which, if any, of the principles and purposes noted in the inventory are to be made the objects of serious attempts at curriculum development in their school. This decision will then be communicated to the central leader-and-jury group.

If this decision is to attempt nothing in reference to improving the mathematics program (a very unlikely supposition), that will of course be the end of the matter so far as the central leader-and-jury group is concerned. If, as is almost certain to be the case, this local decision is to attempt seriously to improve various named aspects (i.e., designated principles and purposes) of the local mathematics program, the central leader-and-jury group will then supply the school in question with an instrument designed to enable the local school to work out *its own plan* of concrete and specific ways of making each of the desired improvements in its mathematics program.

The use of this inventory will not be restricted to the teachers of mathematics; instead, it will be utilized by all the teachers in the school who feel that any of the desired improvements should involve some modification of one or more of the subjects they are teaching. With the aid of the inventory just noted, these affected teachers would constitute a special committee who would draw up a concrete and specific plan for making the desired improvements which they believe would be workable in their school. This proposed plan would then be brought before the total faculty and the pupil and patron panel for interpretation, criticism, possible modifications, and adoption.

Then the plan would be put to work. Since it will deal with improvements believed by the school (not just by the mathematics teachers) to be desirable, since it will take account of pertinent local considerations, since it will embody nothing that the school does not believe workable in the local situation, and since it will be made—and hence believed in—by the persons who are to carry it out, there is every reason to believe that this plan of action would work, and work well.[11]

A similar procedure can be followed in making changes in any other subject or in changing a subject curriculum into either a core or an activity curriculum.

[11] Harold C. Hand, *Prospectus of the Local Area Consensus Studies*, pp. 10–12.

▶ *Following Up*
  This Chapter

1. Try to find illustrations in your own experience of how changes in the perception of an individual were accompanied by changes in his attitude toward situations.

2. Describe different ways of helping an individual to change his "field of perception." Try some of the more simple ways on persons with whom you are associated. Note the results, if any.

3. Plan and carry out a sociodrama designed to help a group of persons to become aware of their own perspectives and biases. Use the same procedure to help individuals perceive their human-relations skills.

4. The sociodrama has been criticized as creating an artificial situation and hence as being ineffective. To what extent, if at all, do you think this criticism is justified? Why do you think as you do?

▶ *Suggested*
  Reading

1. Perhaps the best treatment of the problem of inducing change in a social equilibrium is found in Kurt Lewin's investigation of methods of changing the food habits of families. See his "Forces Behind Food Habits and Methods of Change," *Bulletin of the National Research Council,* 1943, pages 35–65. The investigation is reported also in *Readings in Social Psychology,* edited by Newcomb and Hartley, pages 330–344. The most significant study of the problem of training community leaders for dealing with the task of changing community life is Ronald Lippitt's *Training in Community Relations.* For excellent readings on various aspects of the problem of inducing and controlling curriculum change, see *Human Relations in Curriculum Change,* edited by Kenneth D. Benne and Bozidar Muntyan.

2. Principles and techniques of community self-surveys are set forth in the Spring Issue, 1949, *Journal of Social Issues,* Vol. V, No. 2. The entire number is devoted to this subject. For a discussion of the sociodrama, see "Reality Practice as Educational Method," by Alvin Zander and Ronald

Lippitt, in *Sociometry*, Vol. 7, No. 2, 1944, pages 129–151. See also "The Psychodrama in Leadership Training," by Ronald Lippitt, in *Sociometry*, Vol. 6, No. 3, 1943, pages 286–292. The principle of the projective technique is discussed in any standard work on psychology. See Boring, Langfeld, and Weld's *Foundations of Psychology*, pages 495–497. One of the best treatments of the subject is *Projective Techniques*, by L. K. Frank.

3. The ethics of systematic curriculum change have been questioned, by a few persons, as being undemocratic. This issue has been ably discussed by Kenneth D. Benne in "Democratic Ethics in Social Engineering," *Progressive Education*, Vol. 26, No. 7 (May, 1949), pages 201–207.

4. Curriculum change from the point of view of the school administrator is discussed by Van Miller and Willard B. Spalding in *The Public Administration of American Schools*. See especially Chapters 10 and 11.

5. The use of the questionnaire in inducing and controlling curriculum change is well illustrated in the Consensus Studies of the Illinois Curriculum Program. The rationale of these studies is found in *Prospectus of the Local Area Consensus Studies*, by Harold C. Hand, Illinois Curriculum Program, Bulletin No. 15. Plans for making consensus studies in various school subjects are available.

THEORETICAL

Part Five | CURRICULUM

ISSUES

WHEN *the curriculum worker, whether superintendent or principal, director or teacher, begins to revise or develop a curriculum program, he is confronted by a host of theoretical issues. It is not hard to discover the reason for this. The curriculum is the set of pupil activities and experiences by which the educator seeks to achieve his purposes. It is, therefore, education viewed from the standpoint of means. Education, moreover, involves far more than the intellectual training of youth. In its fullest sense, it is the shaping of character, including attitudes, habits, and beliefs. Hence, to develop a curriculum is to touch at every point the complex web of moral and intellectual purposes and beliefs which ultimately define the political, economic, and social arrangements of any society. For this reason, ever since the days of Plato and Aristotle the greatest masters of political science and of education have insisted that to mold the character of education is, in the long run, to mold the character of society.*

In a relatively unchanging and stable society, where substantial agreement exists with respect to basic intellectual and moral beliefs, the educator can, to a marked degree, take for granted the answers to many of the crucial questions underlying the curriculum. For in such a society, the primary function of education is clear. It is simply to shape the personality and character of the student in accordance with the attitudes and beliefs prevalent in the society. Technical and professional issues, dealing for the most part with the best means of achieving this purpose, will of course emerge. But fundamental questions concerning the nature of the curriculum or of the ends it should serve will not arise, since these questions are authoritatively answered in advance by the common beliefs of the society.

In highly dynamic societies, curriculum problems are more complex. Since the educational program must make some allowance for the element of change, it is no longer possible simply to induct the young into the ways of the past. Nevertheless, as long as the people are in substantial agreement about the intellectual and moral beliefs that should guide and direct individual and social action, the educator is not compelled to face and answer questions respecting the foundations of the curriculum. But where this agreement has been disrupted, the educator can no longer concern himself merely with the technical problems involved in the construction of a curriculum. Unless he is content to drift with the tide, he must face and answer certain theoretical questions before he can begin to develop a curriculum at all. These issues will be analyzed in this section.

Chapter 21

The Source of Authority
in Curriculum Building

T H E F I R S T of the issues underlying curriculum building is the problem of authority. Shaping the character and personality of the young is an exceedingly serious business, involving moral responsibility of the highest order. Certainly no thoughtful person can engage in this task without a rigorous examination of the nature and source of his authority to educate in one way rather than in another. Legal control of the public schools in the United States is vested in the governments of the various states. Hence, the teacher derives his legal authority from the state. But education is a significant moral affair. The educator must consider the question of his moral authority as well as the question of his legal authority.

Legal Authority and Moral Authority

The distinction between legal and moral authority is a commonplace in American thought. Nevertheless it may be wise to outline briefly the grounds upon which it rests. Legal authority, of course, is that derived from the formal acts of the duly constituted organs of government operating within the sphere of their constitutional functions. It represents organized political power exercised in accordance with constitutional and legal forms. Hence, the criterion of authority here is formal in the sense that it is concerned with the legality of an act rather than with the moral and practical import of the act. That is to say, the sole question involved is the extent to which the act is performed in the legally prescribed manner by a legally competent person or body.

Moral authority, on the other hand, is derived from fundamental principles of right and wrong. It represents the power of conscience and moral obligation, embedded in the character of persons and ultimately grounded in the premises of some ethical system. Consequently, the criterion of moral authority is substantive in that it is directly concerned with the moral quality of an act—that is, the extent to which it conforms to accepted moral principles and leads to moral and practical consequences that are judged to be good or bad.

A given act, of course, may possess both legal and moral authority. Except in those societies prepared to define morality solely in terms of the commands of the sovereign power, however, the legality and the morality of an act constitute distinct questions to be answered in accordance with quite different criteria. In American thought, as in that of the Western World generally, moral authority has been traditionally regarded as superior to legal authority. Moreover, it is commonly recognized that both private citizens and public officials have many moral obligations that have never been embodied in the law.

This distinction has sometimes been used, as in the case of the American Revolution or of Northern resistance to the fugitive slave act, to justify illegal acts. Except in extraordinary cases, however, Americans have usually held that the citizen has a moral, as well as a legal, obligation to obey the legal commands of duly constituted governmental authorities. The obligation to obey in such cases is based, not on any assumption that the acts of government are necessarily right and just, but on the grave moral consequences inherent in widespread disregard of law. The obligation to obey, however, is not an obligation to accept. On the contrary, the citizen has the duty, as well as the right, to oppose by legitimate political means—and where possible to reverse—governmental decisions and acts that he regards as immoral. In extreme cases, particularly where the democratic processes of revision and repeal are not open, public opinion may even sustain the citizen in passive or active resistance to the law itself. Thus the American people have generally thought that Gandhi was morally justified in his policy of non-co-operation with the British government in India, just as they earlier sympathized with the efforts of oppressed people everywhere to overthrow tyrannical and arbitrary governments.

There are those who argue that the state has the moral right to define the content and purposes of education. Since this is one of the important answers to the question of authority in education, it will be considered in the course of the discussion. But most people, at least in the United States, do not believe that the state has the moral right to determine the character and personality of its citizens or to prescribe the details of the curriculum. Moreover, while legislatures have occasionally interfered with the conduct of the public schools, they have, for the most part, confined themselves to the establishment of the legal framework within which public education is to be carried on. Certainly, up to the present time, there has been little or no attempt to prescribe alternately Democratic or Republican curriculums with every turn of the political wheel.

Yet, if the educator is something more than a mere servant of government, he must face the question as to the source and character of his moral and intellectual authority. For the nature of his commission necessarily influences the type of education he seeks to give.

1. *Divine Will as the Basis of Educational Authority*

The first answer to this question is to be found in the position that the educator derives his authority from the revealed will of God. A distinguished Catholic layman, F. J. Sheed, argues that before we can educate we must know the purposes of life. For the individual teacher to undertake to determine these purposes on his own responsibility is imposition of the rankest sort. But the Catholic educator, Sheed continues, knows—not of himself but directly from the revealed word of God—what the purposes of life are.[1] Hence, he has a certain and authoritative answer to the first problem in education—that is, the ends

[1] F. J. Sheed, "Education for the Realization of God's Purpose," *The Social Frontier*, Vol. I, No. 4 (January, 1935), pp. 10–11.

and purposes it should seek to serve. Sheed, of course, is speaking for the Catholics, but a substantially similar position has sometimes been taken by Jewish and Protestant educators.

This is an ancient position, and even today it has a powerful appeal for most people. What higher or more certain grounds could the educator discover on which to erect the edifice of public education? Yet a moment's reflection will reveal that public education cannot be based on religious authority in a society composed of divergent religious groups. Originally, education in Colonial America was regarded primarily as a religious affair. But the diversity of religious opinion in the United States compelled the American people to secularize education as they moved to establish a public school system for all the children of all the people.[2] For the same reasons, many states have been forced to adopt constitutional provisions forbidding the importation of religious beliefs into the public schools. The secularization of instruction in state-supported schools is merely the educational corollary of the American doctrine of the separation of Church and State. Hence, the educator in the public school cannot ground his authority in religious tenets without violating this principle.

2. *Education Grounded in Eternal Truth*

A second group has sought the solution to the problem of authority in education in eternal and absolute truth revealed by human reason and embedded in the great literature of the past. This group, whose members usually call themselves humanists, contains within itself several varieties of educational thought and is represented in America by a number of able scholars. Perhaps the most important and best-known statement of this position has been made by Robert M. Hutchins.[3]

[2] Ellwood P. Cubberley, *Public Education in the United States,* pp. 171–181. An excellent presentation of the reasons behind the secular character of the American public school will be found in Conrad H. Moehlman, *School and Church: The American Way.* The recent Supreme Court decision in the case of McCollum vs. Board of Education, Champaign, Illinois, vigorously confirmed the conclusion that the American doctrine of the separation of church and state means that public education must retain its secular character.

[3] Robert M. Hutchins, *The Higher Learning in America,* pp. 59–87.

Truth Discovered and Ordered by Reason

All truths, Hutchins declares, do not stand on the same level; that is, they are not all equally important. Hence consistency and unity in education depend upon a proper ordering of truth. The ordering of truth must be achieved, first, by discovering the principles that lie at the base of all knowledge; second, by deducing secondary truths from these first principles; and finally, by arranging secondary principles in a logical series under first principles so that knowledge represents an orderly procession from truth to truth. The discovery and ordering of truth demands both a method and a principle of consistency and order. Hutchins discovers these in reason and in the first principles or axioms of all being.

It is important to note that Hutchins is using the term *reason* in its classical sense. In this sense reason does not mean thinking, but *a particular kind of thinking*. The distinguishing characteristic of the axioms or first principles, in terms of which all truths must be ordered, is that they are prior to and independent of human experience. Hence they cannot be discovered by the ordinary processes of human thought. Facts and experiences are useful in everyday affairs and so are desirable. But they lead only to an inferior and secondary kind of truth, which lacks both the certainty and the significance of the eternal and absolute truth. Precisely because it is this eternal truth that lends order and meaning to education, Hutchins asserts that man needs a method that will enable him to transcend—that is, to rise above or go beyond—experience and fact. This method, as was suggested above, he finds in reason, which is defined as the intuitive grasp of the first principles or axioms of thought and the logical deduction of other truths from these first principles, very much after the manner of geometry. Once these eternal and absolute truths are discovered and ordered, they provide the educator with the consistent body of knowledge which it is his office to communicate to his students.

This position, like the preceding one, represents an ancient viewpoint, which has had a long and distinguished career in the Western World. Indeed, it is sometimes, as in the case of the philosophy of Saint Thomas, combined with the first position—that the source of authority is the Divine will—in a theory recognizing both the principle of faith and the principle of reason, holding that faith goes beyond reason but is not contrary to it.

Objections to Hutchins' Theory of Eternal Truth

In the last analysis, the heart of Hutchins' theory, by which it must stand or fall, lies in its ideal of a body of fixed and eternal first principles, which are discovered by man's "intuitive reason," and to which all other truths are subordinate. Despite the long and honorable career of this viewpoint and the eminent character of the scholars who uphold it, it is open to four serious objections.

In the first place, this conception of the nature of truth and of the method by which it is won is sharply opposed to the spirit and method of modern science. It is true that logical deduction, particularly in the form of mathematical development of scientific theory, is an important part of the scientific method. Hutchins, therefore, is quite justified in his opposition to the false conception of science as the mere collection of isolated and meaningless data. But not since the time of Galileo and Newton has intuitive and deductive demonstration, however exact, been accepted in science as the final test of truth. For in science the final test is always found in empirical investigation and experiment. Historically, the conception of truth and of the means by which it is discovered and tested, as advocated by Hutchins, has been abandoned in field after field of inquiry. Moreover, it is significant that it is exactly in those fields in which it has been most completely abandoned that man has been most successful in his search for a dependable body of knowledge. "By their fruits shall ye know them."

In the second place, the conception of eternal and absolute truth independent of human experience is essentially authoritarian. This conclusion may not be immediately apparent, since theoretically the method of reason is open to all and its conclusions are the same for all. Actually, however, this is not the case. At bottom, Hutchins' theory depends upon the intuition of first principles, and the cold fact is that men do not and have not everywhere "intuitively" grasped the same first principles. Hence, this method inevitably leads to rival sets of first principles, each claiming to represent eternal and absolute truth. The result is either intellectual anarchy or an appeal to a "supreme court" of reason to decide which set of rival axioms is to be accepted as true. In the latter case, the significant question becomes: Who is to constitute this supreme court? In practice, almost the only body of principles accepted by free men has been established by experience and the experimental method.

In the third place, Hutchins' theory of truth and reason leads to a sharp separation between the ideal and the practical, and between knowledge and experience. The validity of ideals and principles is made to depend, not upon their consequences for human life but upon logical demonstration apart from, and independent of, consequences. Hence, both ideals and principles are severed from the actual affairs of life, with the result that they are honored in theory but ignored in practice.

Moreover, when abstract general principles are used to guide and evaluate the conduct of life, they must be translated into means and measures of actions. This requires that they be brought into relationship with the facts and practices of everyday life. When principles are so related, they are always modified and reinterpreted in terms of the way they work in practice. The axiom, "Thou shalt not kill," for example, becomes in practice, "Do not kill except under certain circumstances." Even greater modifications are made in the rule, "Thou shalt love thy neighbor as thyself." These changes, inevitable whenever absolute moral laws are translated into the operating rules governing human behavior, are of major importance.

This process of translation and modification of principles goes on in any case. But it is important that it go on with intelligence and with relevance to the interest, not of particular men and groups of men, but of all those affected by the action. Wherever ideals and principles are regarded as independent of experience, the inevitable process of reconstruction and adaptation is ignored, condemned as an unholy compromise with evil, or deplored as a necessary concession to imperfect human nature. Even in the latter case, these concessions, although necessary, are not regarded as intelligent and rational adaptation of theory but as the irrational consequence of man's lower appetites. Consequently, the full resources of human intelligence cannot be harnessed to the vitally important task of applying general ideals and principles to the actual conduct of life.

This separation of principles and ideals from needs and interests, and the evaluation of human institutions from their actual impact on flesh and blood human beings, has often led to a marked tendency to shield unjust and oppressive social arrangements from needed criticism and reform. Existing institutions are defended on the basis of idealized concepts having but little relation to the concrete institutions that actually govern the lives of men. Hence, it is insisted that these institutions are sound in principle, while the apparent inequities and injustices found in experience are regarded as the inevitable results of a faulty and imperfect human nature or, at most, as abuses due to the misdeeds of individual men.

Finally, the theory of authority in education set forth by Hutchins provides an inadequate basis for education in a dynamic society. For the heart of the conception of fixed and absolute truth is that the world, in all essential matters, is the same yesterday, today, and forever. The concept admits that there is a world of change, but this world is a superficial world of appearances and nonessentials. The denial of fundamental and significant change contained in this position is not a denial of the obvious facts of experience. What is denied is that changes in the economic, social, and political conditions of life, however extensive, necessitate or justify changes in the realm of principles and ideals. The fundamental principles underlying ethics, law, politics, and economics are, it is asserted, independent of changes in the material world. Human nature, moreover, is regarded as fixed and constant. Its essential elements are, as Hutchins said, "the same in any time or place." [4]

Were it not for the fact that this doctrine of a constant and unchanging nature is so firmly fixed in our culture, it would hardly be necessary to point out that it has little basis in the scientific study of human conduct. It is true that all men have basic biological elements in common. All men share the nervous and bodily structures peculiar to the species *homo sapiens,* in the absence of which the development of a human being is impossible. They share, also, certain more or less well-defined mechanisms of action, as well as certain biological needs. But man by virtue of his biological nature is merely a certain type of animal. It is by virtue of a culture that he becomes a human being. The fact is that human nature, if by human nature is meant the ideals, the

[4] Hutchins, *The Higher Learning in America* (New Haven: Yale University Press; 1936), p. 66.

beliefs, the interests, the motives, and the habits that determine character and personality, is a product of a particular way of life. Human nature, therefore—far from being an unchanging entity, the same in any time or place—is capable of almost infinite variety.

The doctrine of absolute truth and of unchanging human nature not only fails to take seriously the facts of a changing world and of cultural differences; it also serves as a bulwark of conservatism and reaction. The dogma of eternal verities and of a fixed human nature has always been the ultimate justification of the *status quo* and of vested interest in every field. Nevertheless, this doctrine, while particularly adapted to the maintenance of the *status quo,* can be used to justify radical social innovation. Existing institutions, in such cases, are declared to be contrary to the law of reason and human nature. Yet the new regime, once established, is just as absolute and rigid as the old regime ever was in its heyday. It is regarded as final and as built on the eternal principles of God and man.

Hence, this doctrine cannot be utilized to further the continuous reinterpretation and reformulation of social ideals and principles and the continuous reconstruction of the social order that are demanded by a changing world. Instead, the rigid and unchanging character of the social ideals and the intellectual principles underlying human action is insisted upon so strictly that the changes demanded by the actual conditions of life can be achieved only by revolutionary measures. Consequently, the practical result of the dogma of eternal principles and an unchanging human nature is a long period of extreme conservatism culminating in a shorter period of violent and unregulated change.

3. *Science as the Source of Educational Authority*

A third school maintains that the educator receives his authority from the method of science. This group holds with Hutchins that truth is the source of authority in education, but it differs from Hutchins in insisting that the scientific method is the only reliable means of establishing truth.

Truth, of course, is a source of authority in teaching. The viewpoint just stated, moreover, is in line with the criticisms that have been made of the preceding position. In the matter of materials and techniques of instruction as well as in a number of such things as school finance and school buildings, science enables the educator to make valid judgments. By scientific procedures he can find out what kinds of materials are effective and he can discover more effective techniques of teaching. In fact he has used the method of science to improve the materials of instruction in all fields. He has also used the scientific method to improve methods of teaching, especially in such skills as reading, spelling, and arithmetic. In this respect the educator is in the same position as any other professional worker who depends upon science.

The chief difficulty with the concept of science as the source of authority lies in the realm of values and aesthetics. This third school insists that education can concern itself with ethical and aesthetic judgments only if those judgments can stand the test of scientific verification. If this meant that moral and aesthetic judgments are grounded in human experience and are tested by it, the appeal to science would be acceptable. However, the term *scientific method* can be used in a broad and in a narrow sense. In the broad sense, it means the rigorous use of man's empirical reason, starting with the examination of all available evidence and reserving the final test of the conclusions so reached to the way these conclusions actually operate in human life. In the narrow sense, scientific method means the mathematical and precision techniques so successfully employed in the physical sciences. It is in this latter sense that the group under discussion usually employs the term.

Unfortunately, up to the present time, no way has been found to apply these techniques successfully to morals or to aesthetics. Accordingly, the scientist in education has undertaken to deal with values in one of three ways. He has, first, refused to consider them at all, on the ground that they represent subjective judgments, which cannot be verified. This point of view has been carried so far that an able American philosopher, Arthur Murphy, has aptly remarked that some social scientists "would rather be caught with an incendiary bomb than a moral preference." [5]

[5] Arthur E. Murphy, *The Uses of Reason,* p. 212. Copyright 1943 by The Macmillan Company and used with their permission.

Second, another group of scientists, insisting that the first group has been unduly restrictive in barring all value judgments from the purview of science, has argued that values can be objectively treated on the descriptive level. Accordingly, it has undertaken to discover and describe the various, and sometimes conflicting, values that men cherish. But this group has refused to express any decision as to the relative significance and validity of these values. This decision, it insists, being clearly a subjective choice, must be left to the unaided judgment of the student.

Finally, a third group has sought to establish objectively the values education should attempt to inculcate in the learner, by discovering what values are dominant in the society for which the student is being educated. Underlying this position is the assumption that, on the whole, the prevailing opinion defines both the right and the beautiful.

None of these ways of dealing with the problem of values in education is satisfactory. The first undertakes to exclude the question of value in education altogether—except, of course, the values embedded in the scientific search for truth. This position is untenable; for to educate is to shape character, and the shaping of character in one way rather than in another involves moral and aesthetic choice. The second position is likewise untenable. It too ignores the fact that the educator unavoidably makes ethical and aesthetic choices in the process of education. It also puts an intolerable burden of choice on the unaided judgment of the immature child. The third position avoids these difficulties, but it does so at the price of accepting existing evaluations as final. Hence, this solution of the problem of authority in education, like the doctrine of eternal truth advocated by Hutchins, puts a heavy premium on the *status quo*. Consequently, it too fails to provide an adequate basis for education in a period of rapid social change.

4. *Education as a Social Agent*

The fourth and last position to be considered is that the school is the agent of and derives its authority from the society that maintains it. In the words of the Commission on Social Studies of the American Historical Association, "Being a form of social action, education . . .

is a function of a particular society at a particular time and place in history; it is rooted in some actual culture and expresses the philosophy and recognized needs of that culture."[6] Behind this conception is the belief that the school is first of all an agency established by society for the purpose of preparing the young to live in the society. Consequently, the teacher is necessarily the vicar of the community.

Three Views of Society as the Authority

Within the framework of the general agreement expressed in the above paragraph, there are several different versions of this position. The first version holds that the school is maintained by the state and that the teacher is the agent of the state. Hence, the educator derives his authority from the state and is properly subject in his teaching to the will of the state. This view rests on the assumption that the state is the authorized voice of society and that its commands express the will of the national community. While this notion of the office of the state has been widely held by political scientists, it is by no means universally accepted either by the political scientists or the peoples of the world. On the contrary, it has been pointed out that at any particular time the state operates through a limited body of men called the government; and, at best, this government never represents more than a part of the community.

This view of the state is the one that has always prevailed in the United States. The people of this country have never been willing to delegate to any government the definition of the moral and social ends of American society. Neither have they been willing to accept the position that the teaching in the public schools should be dictated by the existing government. From the beginning, the founding fathers insisted that in a democratic community the public school exists for the enlightenment of citizens, not for the inculcation of the particular beliefs of the government in power.[7] Accordingly, the thesis that the

---

[6] American Historical Association, Report of the Commission on the Social Studies, *Conclusions and Recommendations of the Commission* (New York: Charles Scribner's Sons; 1934), p. 31. By permission.

[7] For the attitude of the founding fathers toward education, see *First Yearbook* of the John Dewey Society, W. H. Kilpatrick (Ed.), "The Teacher and Society," pp. 4–12.

educator derives his moral authority from the state cannot be maintained in the United States, for that view is incompatible both with the expressed will of the people and the principles of a democratic community.

A second variety of the position that educational authority is grounded in society maintains that the teacher's authority rests upon the consensus of opinion in the local community in which he teaches. Unlike the other viewpoints which have been considered, this position has rarely been formally stated and defended. But it is implicit in the statements of a large number of school men. Indeed, it is not unlikely that the majority of the educational profession in the United States consciously or unconsciously holds this view. It is in line with the long-standing American tradition that the primary responsibility for the schools should lie in the local community.

But this view overlooks the fact that the local community is a part of a larger national community. It also overlooks the fact that at any given moment the prevailing opinion in the local community may represent, not the considered judgment of the people, but a temporary conclusion based on prejudice, passion, and ignorance. All too frequently the school administrator has mistaken the voice of the dominant group in the community for the voice of the united community. While the wise educator will never ignore the viewpoints and opinions held by the people of the locality which he serves, he cannot accept those opinions and viewpoints as the final definition of his moral authority and responsibility.

The third version of the theory under discussion—that the educator derives his authority from the society he serves—holds that this authority resides not in the commands of the state or in the partial and transitory opinions of the local community, but in the moral and intellectual commitments constituting the core of the culture. The quality that distinguishes a society from a mere collection of individuals or groups is precisely this common participation in a vital community of feeling and belief. Only as the child shares in the life of society can he become either a responsible member of it or grow into his fullest stature as a human being. Apart from this participation, he will be little more than a biological animal. It is by means of his membership in the common life of the social group that he learns the attitudes, the motivations, the language, the patterns of thought, the standards of judgment, the skills, and the ways of acting that constitute his *human*, as distinguished from his biological, nature. But the child really shares in the life of the society only as he comes to share in the common ends and purposes by virtue of which the society is a society rather than a mere random collection of individuals. Hence, the induction of the young person into society means, first of all, his transformation into a human being who has built into the warp and woof of his personality the intellectual and moral commitments characteristic of his society.

The Democratic Tradition as the Source of Moral Authority

Applying this principle to American society, it is clear that the educator derives his moral authority primarily from the democratic tradition. For that tradition undoubtedly represents the deepest moral and intellectual commitments of the American people. It is true that many individuals in our society would, as individuals, feel that their commitment to their religious beliefs is even more fundamental than their commitment to the democratic ideals. Yet the American people as a nation have committed themselves to no one particular religious belief. Fortunately, the ethical cores of the majority of religious traditions present in America are, by the statement of their own adherents, largely compatible with the central ethical conception of democracy.

In accepting the democratic tradition as the basis of his authority, the educator must guard against two major fallacies in interpretation. To say that the educator derives his authority to teach from the intellectual and moral traditions of the people has frequently meant that the chief business of the school is to indoctrinate youth in the tenets of a final conception of the good and of the true received from the past. This interpretation assumes that the tradition is absolute and unchanging. But it is one of the characteristics of the democratic tradition that it is, by its very naure, a growing and changing ideal. Furthermore, it is an ideal based on the intelligent participation of all the people. The democratic educator must not be more concerned with the making of adherents, even of adherents to the democratic creed itself, than he is with the development of intelligent individuals able and willing to evaluate, choose, and judge for themselves.

On the other hand, the democratic tradition does represent a definite intellectual and moral orientation. It is not equally hospitable to all ideas or to all types of behavior. The democratic educator must not make the error of assuming that he can be indifferent to the character and the beliefs that the students acquire in his school. The conduct of the school involves the making of choices and decisions. Hence, it involves a certain amount of indoctrination, if only as a result of the way the school is organized and conducted. The democratic educator will make these choices and decisions, and shape the character of his school, in a manner compatible with democratic ideals and practices.

5. *Two Bases of the Educator's Authority*

It is clear from the preceding discussion that the authority of the educator ultimately rests upon two distinct but related bases. As an expert, his authority rests on his verified and tested knowledge in those areas in which his services are needed both by society and by his students. This expertness is derived from two sources: his knowledge of the needs and interests of children and of the way the learning process can best be conducted to attain the ends of education; and his knowledge of the materials and techniques required by the students in their growth and development. In both cases, it is important to note that expert authority is limited by the extent to which the teacher possesses tested and verified knowledge. It is also limited by the extent to which this knowledge coincides with the needs and purposes of society and of the learner. Expert authority, in other words, does not extend to the determination of purposes, except in so far as tested knowledge is a factor in the determination of purposes.[8]

Beyond the range of expert authority, the authority of the teacher rests on the intellectual and moral commitments of the society he serves. In our society, the teacher's authority is based on the American democratic tradition. The American educator, in the last analysis, is commissioned to educate in the spirit of this tradition; whatever authority he possesses must be interpreted primarily in its terms. It is

[8] For an able discussion of both expert and pedagogical authority, see Kenneth D. Benne, *A Conception of Authority*, pp. 34–48, 70–113.

on the basis of this tradition that he is at times justified—nay, obligated—to oppose and resist either the arbitrary actions of governments or the partial and temporary opinions of local citizens when they affect the work of the public school to the point that it can no longer effectively perform the vital function assigned to it.

This right and obligation of the educator, however, does not endow him with final authority in the determination of the ends, the processes, or the content of education. Final authority in all these respects rests with the enlightened and informed judgment of the whole people. The educator's duty consists of the right and obligation to appeal from the arbitrary decision of a particular government or of a particular locality to the mature judgment of the national community. In the performance of this duty, he will call the attention of the public to the application of democratic principles and of verified knowledge to the educational issue in dispute. In the long run, however, the educator as educator, whatever his judgment as a person, is bound by the considered decision of the national community.

As the above discussion suggests, these two bases of the educator's authority are not of equal scope and significance. His authority as the vicar of the community is both broader and deeper than his authority as an expert in the field of education. It is from the former rather than from the latter that he derives the ends and the purposes that shape the entire educational enterprise. Indeed, it is true that, in a democratic society, expert authority can be derived from the democratic ideal. Expertness has a certain status in any society, but the fullest respect for true and verified knowledge is possible only in a society in which decisions are, in theory at least, based on the informed judgment of the people.

▶ *Following Up*
This Chapter

1. The issue raised by this chapter grows out of the fact that teaching, if it has any effect at all, always shapes the character and personality of the learner in one way rather than another. What is meant by the words

personality and *character* as they are used in the above sentence? Do these two words, as used here, mean about the same thing, or do they refer to quite different aspects of human behavior? Check our use of these words against the way they are used in other books on education.

2. Remind your friends, parents, and neighbors that effective teaching does influence the development of the character and personality of children and young people. Then ask them where the teacher should go in order to find out what kind of character and personality he should try to develop in his pupils. Compare their answers with the positions outlined in this chapter. Look especially to see if any important answer to the question has been overlooked in our discussion of the problem.

3. Using the materials collected both from your interviews and from your reading, make a chart listing the arguments for and against each of the positions that you have identified.

4. Try to visualize as exactly as you can what each of the positions would mean in terms of the kind of educational program in the public schools you would favor if you accepted that position. What, if any, differences do you find between these various positions at this point?

5. You might like to participate in a class, small group, or panel discussion of the central problem raised in this chapter. In this case you may find that your understanding is sometimes broadened if you play the role of advocate for one of the positions you are inclined to reject. In any event, as the discussion proceeds try to note (1) the points on which there is general agreement, (2) the points at which significant differences still remain, and (3) the way in which the various arguments advanced seem to stand up in the face of competition and criticism.

6. In not more than four sentences each, state (1) your position on the primary issue explored in this chapter, (2) the educational meaning of this position, and (3) your basic reason for tentatively accepting it.

▶ *Suggested Reading*

1. The best general statement of the problem of authority in contemporary life and education may be found in Kenneth D. Benne's *A Conception of Authority,* pages 1–28. Benne's book also contains an excellent discussion of the nature of expert authority (pages 34–48) and the pedagogical

authority of the teacher as the vicar of the community (pages 70–113). An excellent exploration of the teacher's authority is set forth in *Education as a Profession*, by Myron Lieberman. A good account of the clash of doctrines in American education may be secured in R. Freeman Butts, *The College Charts Its Course*, pages 1–16, 269–426; John S. Brubacher, *A History of the Problems of Education*, pages 1–51, and *Modern Philosophies of Education*, pages 24–100.

2. For explicit and clearly formulated statements of the position that the authority of the teacher is ultimately derived from authentic expressions of the Divine Will, see: Jacques Maritain, *Education at the Crossroads*, pages 1–28; William McGucken, "The Philosophy of Catholic Education" in the *Forty-first Yearbook* of the National Society for the Study of Education, Part I, "Philosophies of Education," pages 251–288; and J. D. Redden and F. A. Ryan, *A Catholic Philosophy of Education*, pages 3–52, 86–101, 368–387. Conrad H. Moehlman's *School and Church: The American Way* states the case for the traditional American separation of church and state in the conduct of public education. The most thorough exploration of the principle of separation of church and state is R. Freeman Butts, *The American Tradition in Religion and Education*. Every curriculum worker should read this book with care.

3. Robert M. Hutchins' *The Higher Learning in America* (pages 59–119) ably sets forth the claim that educational authority is grounded in rational and eternal truth. A similar point of view is expressed by John T. Foudy in *The Educational Principles of American Humanism*, pages 68–98; by Mortimer J. Adler in his essay "In Defense of the Philosophy of Education," *Forty-first Yearbook* of the National Society for the Study of Education, Part I, "Philosophies of Education," pages 197–249; and by Joseph Justman in *Theories of Secondary Education in the United States*, pages 12–22. An interesting and instructive debate between Hutchins and John Dewey on this subject occurred in the pages of the *Social Frontier*, December, 1936, and January, February, and March, 1937.

4. The view that scientifically established truth is the basis of pedagogical authority, while widely held, has not been as frequently detailed in educational literature as is the case with some of the other positions discussed in this chapter. *The Higher Learning in a Democracy*, by Harry D. Gideonse, is a spirited reply to Hutchins' *The Higher Learning in America*. Gideonse clearly takes the position that education must be based upon truth warranted by the method of modern science. Charles A. Beard has written an eloquent defense of the ideal of scientific truth in his *Charter for the Social Sciences*, pages 1–21. Florjan Znaniecki's *The Social Role of*

the Man of Knowledge is a more technical and thorough defense of the thesis that educational authority springs from scientific truth (see especially pages 164–199). Truman L. Kelley's *Scientific Method: Its Function in Research and in Education* offers another able statement of the view that education must be based squarely upon scientific research. John Dewey and Frank N. Freeman have briefly explored, from somewhat different standpoints, the problem of the relationship between science and philosophy in the determination of the ends of education. See the *Thirty-seventh Yearbook* of the National Society for the Study of Education, Part II, "The Scientific Movement in Education," pages 471–495. Finally, a trenchant criticism of certain aspects of the scientific movement in education can be found in Boyd Bode's *Modern Educational Theories*, especially pages 73–94, 171–192, 329–348.

5. The position that the teacher, as the vicar of the community, receives his commission to educate from the society he serves has been elaborated and developed in a large number of articles and books on American education. Benne has cogently presented the arguments for this position in his *A Conception of Authority*, pages 70–113. A similar point of view has been expressed in George S. Counts' *The Social Foundations of Education*, pages 1–6; American Historical Association, Report of the Commission on the Social Studies, *Conclusions and Recommendations of the Commission*, pages 30–43; and in the *First Yearbook* of the John Dewey Society, "The Teacher and Society," pages 3–67, as well as in a host of other books. The idea that in our country the educator derives his authority from the American democratic tradition has also been widely and vigorously urged. The Educational Policies Commission's *The Unique Function of Education in American Democracy* and their *The Education of Free Men in American Democracy* may be taken as typical of this point of view.

6. For comparison and criticism of major theories underlying education, see Theodore Brameld, *Patterns of Educational Philosophy*.

Chapter 22

Educational Objectives:
Individual or Social

A N O T H E R underlying curriculum issue is that of the nature and source of educational objectives. Granted that the educator in our society derives his moral authority from the democratic tradition, the problem raised by this issue may be stated as follows: Is the educator in a democratic society primarily concerned with the development of the potentialities and capacities of the individual, or is he primarily concerned with certain social objectives? Put another way, are educational objectives to be determined by the needs and interests of the student or by the needs and interests of society?

1. *The Society-Centered Position versus the Child-Centered Position*

Three major positions have been taken with respect to this problem: the *society-centered,* the *child-centered,* and the *interactive* positions.

The Society-Centered Position

Advocates of the society-centered position hold that the objectives of education are primarily social. The purpose of education, they insist, is to prepare the individual to live in a certain kind of society. Educational objectives will be found in the beliefs, attitudes, knowledge, and skills required for effective participation in the common life of the social group. The individual interests of the child should not be wholly neglected, but these interests are not of primary importance. The important thing is that he shall become the kind of person desired by society and that he shall acquire the outlooks, knowledges, and skills demanded by it. Consequently, emphasis is placed on discipline and on the mastery of a curriculum determined almost exclusively by social rather than by individual objectives.

The Child-Centered Position

A second major group takes an almost diametrically opposed position. The ultimate purpose of education in a democracy, they argue, is the development of the individual. At the present time there are at least two significant variants of this theory.

The first holds, in effect, that the primary purpose of education is that of preparing the individual to achieve maximum social and economic success. This first variant is progressive in the sense that it seeks to utilize public education as a means of aiding individuals to rise above the social and economic status of their fathers. It is conservative in the sense that it accepts prevailing social arrangements as final and, hence, as definitive of the framework within which individual success must be won. This view assumes, for the most part, that the curriculum materials the child should study are determined by the accepted practices of adult society. In this respect it is in substantial agreement with the society-centered position. Nevertheless, it is essentially a variation of the individualistic wing in American education, since educational aims are stated in individualistic terms and since subject matter is selected on the basis of its contribution to individual success.

This point of view is rooted in the individualistic and competitive conception of democracy that has long been dominant among the American people. It is not surprising, therefore, that many parents and students, as well as certain educators, have conceived education primarily in these terms. Yet, whatever the prominence of individual success among the motivations influencing parents and students, the notion that

personal economic and social success is the fundamental objective of
education has never been accepted by the majority of American educators nor by American society as a whole.[1]

Emphasis on Capacities and Needs of Children as Individuals

The second variation of the individualistic wing in American education—usually called the child-centered school—insists that education,
in both purpose and content, must be based on individual needs, capacities, and interests. It has not, however, conceived individual needs and
interests primarily in terms of economic and social success. Almost
without exception the adherents of this school of educational thought
have emphasized the development of intelligent, rich, and well-balanced
personalities; and many of them have been keenly interested in far-
reaching social reform designed to produce a more democratic society.

Influenced by recent discoveries in child growth and development,
they have argued that an education built upon adult purposes and interests is inadequate. Children are not small and immature adults but
persons in their own right. As such they have capacities, needs, interests, and purposes of their own, which can be ignored only at the risk
of retarding the development of intelligent and healthy personalities.
Hence, the educator must recognize that the needs and capacities as
well as the purposes and interests of children are different from those
of adults.

Moreover, this group contends that while it is true to a certain extent
that these capacities, needs, and interests are common to all children
at any given level of maturation, it is also true that every child is in
some sense unique. Differences in original nature are compounded by
differences in experience and circumstances. Children, as well as adults,
vary widely in their interests, abilities, and temperaments. To insist
that every child pursue the same educational program in the same way
is simply to sacrifice the needs of the growing personality to the Pro-
crustean requirements of a rigid and authoritarian educational system.

Accordingly, the child-centered educator argues, the curriculum
cannot be derived solely, or even primarily, from the demands and re-

[1] John Dewey Society, *First Yearbook,* W. H. Kilpatrick (Ed.), "The Teacher and
Society," pp. 3–25.

quirements of society without doing violence both to the normal processes of maturation and to the facts of individual differences. Learning, properly understood, is not the mastery of the product of other people's learning but progressive growth in the intelligent direction of purposeful activities. The heart of the curriculum in the public schools should consist of a wide variety of purposeful activities based on the present capacities, interests, and needs of the learner. The demands and requirements of society must naturally be taken into account. But the educator must never forget that his first duty is to help the child, at each stage of his development, to live as richly and completely as possible in order that his capacities and abilities may reach their fullest stature.

2. *The Interactive Position*

Except at the extremes, the differences between the society-centered and the child-centered positions probably have not been as sharp in practice as they have been in theory. Most educators, whatever their formal educational philosophy, have found some place for both the demands of adult society and the interests of children in their educational programs. Nevertheless, as pure types, these two schools of educational thought represent diametrically opposed theoretical positions. Further, as differences in emphasis, if not as mutually exclusive educational programs, they have had a significant impact on educational practice.

Individual Interests and Social Values Recognized

Advocates of the interactive position have sought to formulate a consistent educational theory which would include in a coherent system the essential values of both the society-centered and the child-centered approaches to curriculum building.[2] Representing an important wing of the progressive education movement, the group holding the interactive position shares with the individualistic wing the emphasis upon growth, interest, and purposeful activity in education. It insists that

[2] V. T. Thayer et al., *Reorganizing Secondary Education,* pp. 25–51

education must have meaning for the child in terms of his own experience rather than simply in terms of the requirements and activities of adult life. At the same time this group is impressed by the patent evidence that human personalities are shaped—and their destinies primarily determined—by the nature of the social institutions and of the group structures characteristic of the society in which they live.

The interactive group rejects the basic assumption of the child-centered school—that the needs and purposes of children come from the natural unfolding of an innate, private, inner personality, expressing itself largely in terms of demands on the environment. On the contrary, this group asserts that the interests, the purposes, and the needs of children are governed, for the most part, by the way the child is related to the social groups in his society and to the occupations, institutions, and social ideals of that society.

Those who support the interactive theory agree with the contention of the society-centered school that the ends of education cannot be comprehended in purely individualistic terms. Man is a social animal, living in and through the cultural framework of his society; and his human, as distinguished from his biological nature, is a social product. Hence, that which the members of a society share in common—and which is essential if any society at all is to be possible—is fully as important as the fact of individual differences. America needs rich and varied personalities. But they must be rich and varied personalities willing and able to share in the common purposes, concerns, and problems of the nation as a unified social group.

Finally, this position holds that there is no contradiction or inconsistency in its dual emphasis on the child and on society since both individualization and socialization are complementary aspects of the same process. Indeed, the members of this group insist, the fundamental error of both the society-centered and the child-centered schools is that they have separated, each in its own way, these two aspects of a common process. The society-centered school has undertaken to drill the child in the patterns of adult behavior, without reference to the needs and interests generated by his experience. In other words, they have not taken into account the fact that children and adults are differently related to the social groups, the activities, and the institutions of society. The child-centered school, on the other hand, has attempted to define growth primarily in terms of the inner nature of the child, without reference to the demands and problems of society. The society-centered group has been so intent on the requirements of adult society that it has ignored the growing, developing self with its insistent, present needs, interests, and purposes. The child-centered group has been so insistent upon protecting the growing self from premature and unwise impositions of adult patterns of behavior that it has tended to overlook the fact that selfhood is a product of responsible participation in the purposes, activities, and attitudes of a particular society.

In short, if the child-centered school has failed to recognize the essentially social character of human experience, the society-centered school has not understood the educative process. That is, the society-centered school has mistaken habituation and memorization of pre-digested material for the thoughtful participation in group activity and the purposeful reconstruction of experience in genuine problematic situations by which the immature child gradually becomes a disciplined, intelligent, self-directed adult.

Objectives of Education Are Social

According to the interactive position, education begins with the needs and interests of individual children; and it proceeds primarily by means of purposeful activity in which children must have a responsible share, including planning and evaluation. While children's interests do determine the starting point in education—that is to say, they indicate the present drives and motivations of the learner with which the educator must work—they do not determine the ends of education. The ends and objectives of education are social ends and objectives, having their source not in the purely private needs and interests of individuals but in the ideals and demands of society. At this point the interactive position agrees wholly with the society-centered school against the child-centered school. Therefore, it is basically a society-centered position.

Nevertheless, it is a very different type of society-centered position from that traditionally assumed by the society-centered school described above. The interactive position, despite its insistence that educational objectives are socially determined, agrees with the child-centered school that the objective of education in a democratic society is the development of the potentialities and capacities of every individual. This appears to be an exercise in inconsistency, but actually it is not. The decision to emphasize the supreme moral worth of individuals is a social decision, derived from the democratic ideal dominant in our society. What constitutes full or desirable development of the potentialities and capacities of a given individual is also determined with reference to accepted social standards. The cardinal error of the child-centered position is not that it emphasizes the development of the individual but that it defines that development in purely private and individualistic terms.

3. *The Educational Significance of the Interactive Position*

Educationally, the interactive position has three significant connotations. It means, first, as opposed to the child-centered school, that the needs of children must not be identified exclusively with their present interests or felt needs. Needs represent lacks as well as desires, lacks being defined in the light of socially desirable characteristics and behavior. An important aspect of any good educational program, therefore, is designed to reconstruct the interests and attitudes of the learner, just as other aspects of the program are designed to reconstruct his overt behavior or his intellectual beliefs. Thus it is impossible to construct an educational program solely from the felt needs and interests of children.

At the same time, the interactive theory also means, in opposition to the traditional society-centered position, that the felt needs and interests of the learner cannot be ignored. These needs must be satisfied or redirected if the child is to achieve a wholesome, integrated personality; and his unique interests and capacities must likewise be developed in a socially desirable way if his potentialities, as a citizen and as a person, are to be realized. Even that portion of his education designed to cultivate the common rather than the unique, to reconstruct his interests, and to supply his lacks, must be related meaningfully to his present interests and drives if it is to be effective. This linkage is possible because his present interests are largely a social product, which may be altered by different social experiences and demands, and which, since they are social products, possess a certain continuity with the interests society wishes to develop in him. The linkage is difficult, if not impossible, when a curriculum based on the demands of adult society is imposed without regard to the interests or needs of the child personality.

Consequently, the interactive position insists that the curriculum—the educational experiences through which the schools seek to direct the growth of the child—must be selected with reference to both the present desires of the child and the demands of society, rather than with reference to either of these criteria alone. In other words, it holds that the school should provide those educational experiences that will, in any given case, best utilize the present drives and motivations of the learner in activities designed to direct his growth toward the ends desired by society.

4. *Problems of the Interactive Position*

It would appear from the preceding discussion that the interactive position is, in principle, substantially correct. The emphasis upon education as preparation for adult life, without regard for the interests and needs of the growing child, is no longer tenable in the light of modern psychology. The educational program typically advocated by adherents of the society-centered theory, in its traditional form, is in conflict with the findings of modern psychology both in its neglect of the active and purposive character of learning and in its disregard of basic personality needs.[3] The disregard of the unique capacities, interests, and concerns of individual children, implicit in the conventional society-centered theory, is no more compatible with the democratic belief in the supreme moral worth of individuals than it is with the psychological facts of individual differences.

On the other hand, the predominantly individualistic approach to the ends of education inherent in the child-centered school is not warranted either by the facts of child growth or by the requirements of a

[3] See Gates et al., *Educational Psychology,* pp. 324–329, 335–337, 626–721; Ronald Lippitt, *An Experimental Study of the Effects of Democratic and Authoritarian Group Atmospheres,* pp. 43–195; Lippitt and White, "The 'Social Climate' of Children's Groups" in Barker et al. (Eds.), *Child Behavior and Development,* pp. 485–508.

democratic society in an age of cultural transition. Recent research in anthropology, sociology, and social psychology has confirmed the ancient dictum of Aristotle that man is a social animal.[4] He lives in and through a particular culture. Hence the ends of education are inherently social ends, determined by the requirements, the problems, and the aspirations of the society of which the child is a member. This truth is the rock on which education always rests. If possible, this truth acquires additional significance in a period of profound social change, of deep-seated social conflict, and of at least partial cultural disintegration. The very life of society is at stake in such periods—and never more so than in the case of a democratic society, which depends for its existence on the co-operation and intelligence of its citizens.

Furthermore, in periods of change the welfare of the individual, no less than the preservation of democracy, demands the development, through education, of a high degree of social intelligence and of a common intellectual and moral orientation. Studies in sociology and in personal integration alike demonstrate that either the continuation of institutional maladjustment and social conflict or their resolution by totalitarian dictatorship is fatal to the growth of vigorous, healthy, and well-adjusted personalities.[5]

Gap between Children's Interests and Social Needs

However sound the interactive position may be in theory, one caution must be observed in its practical applications to educational problems. This theory bridges the gap between social requirements and individual interests by pointing out that individual interests are culturally built. This is unquestionably true. Nevertheless, it may be a mistake to assume that there is not at certain crucial points in our society an almost unbridgeable gulf between the interests of particular children and the social requirements of our time.

[4] Ruth Benedict, *Patterns of Culture;* C. H. Cooley, *Human Nature and the Social Order;* W. G. Sumner, *Folkways;* J. S. Plant, *Personality and the Cultural Pattern.*

[5] Eric Fromm, *Escape from Freedom.* See also Peter F. Drucker, *The End of Economic Man,* and F. Alexander, *Our Age of Unreason.* For evidence of the close relationship between personal and social disintegration, see R. Bain, "Our Schizoid Culture," *Sociology and Social Research,* Vol. 19, September–August, 1934–1935, pp. 266–276; Mabel A. Elliott and Francis E. Merrill, *Social Disorganization* (Revised Edition), pp. 61–82; and Karen Horney, *The Neurotic Personality of Our Time,* pp. 13–40, 281–290.

In the first place, as previous chapters have indicated, American society is to some extent a splintered and divided society. And it is, to a marked degree, a society based upon an elaborate division of labor. Hence, all men do not bear the same relationship to their institutions; and since they belong to groups cherishing different aspirations, beliefs, and attitudes, they develop somewhat different mentalities and dispositions.[6]

In the second place, modern industrial and urban society has progressively excluded children from the major concerns of human life. Traditionally, as they have grown older, children have increasingly shared in the daily activities and tasks of community and family life. This sharing, coupled with the expectations of other people and the children's own desire for social status, produced a group atmosphere and a way of life that shaped the interests of the young in accordance with the dominant patterns of behavior in the society of which they were a part. Thus the frontier boy prided himself on his growing mastery of the manly arts and skills needed and honored in frontier life. As urbanization, specialization, and industrialization have transformed our way of life, the participation of children in the daily tasks and activities of the home and community has steadily declined.

The result has been the creation of a special world of childhood, isolated from the serious concerns of the community and nation at many crucial points. Status in this child-world has come to depend on behavior which, in many respects, does not reflect the standards and activities of adult society—or else reflects them in a distorted fashion. This tendency has been reinforced by the fact that certain of the expectations and demands of adult society, as they impinge upon childhood and youth, represent conduct that adult society itself does not honor or practice. This is particularly significant in relation to the work of the school, which for most children represents the only serious occupation of childhood. Parents typically demand "good grades," yet American society neither honors nor rewards scholarship.

Traditionally minded laymen and educators, in the course of their vigorous polemics against progressive education, have pointed to the transitory, frivolous, and superficial character—as they prefer to term it—of the whims of children. The charge is grossly exaggerated, as any

[6] Robert C. Angell, *The Integration of American Society,* especially pp. 190–220.

careful student of child behavior can testify. To the extent that the charge is true, the unsatisfactory character of children's interest can probably be better accounted for in terms of the isolation noted above than it can in terms of "the inherent defects of childhood" or of "the weakened moral fiber of modern youth."

It must be added that the educational difficulties created by this gap between the worlds of childhood and adulthood have been further aggravated by the prevailing notion that formal education ends upon the induction of the young into adult life. The failure to develop an extensive system of adult education has meant that the school must choose between omitting highly important problems and topics from the student's program of education or introducing them long before the student has felt the need for them or has acquired an adequate basis in experience for their study.

Division between Social and Educational Values

Finally, in significant respects, American society has created a gulf between certain of the values it seeks to inculcate in schools and those it incorporates in its way of life. The standards of literary and artistic taste that the schools undertake to inculcate have never been built into the warp and woof of American life. These standards have been typically regarded by the great majority of Americans as a form of highbrow and somewhat artificial pretension, suitable only for women, the members of a decadent leisure class, or artistic cranks of doubtful virility, morality, and intelligence. This tendency has been so strong that a standard test of personality adjustment has included an interest in poetry or painting, on the part of males, among the items possibly indicative of serious personality maladjustment.

On the intellectual side, American society has fostered a separation of theory and practice which, in the American environment, encourages the belief that theory is impractical and useless. This is partly a continuation, with a peculiar twist, of the classical aristocratic doctrine of the two educations: a program of cultural studies divorced from the practical concerns of life for the children of the leisure class, and a program of purely practical subjects for the children of the common people.[7] For the most part, however, this belief is simply a reflection of the scorn for theory generated in a society in which most of the major posts of power and prestige have been held by men of action, who have frequently emerged from the ranks without the benefit of very much formal education and who have almost always been unconscious of the theoretical basis of their beliefs and practices. This split between theory and practice, with its concomitant neglect of theory in the practical concerns of life, has been reinforced both by an increasing complexity in modern life and by a *laissez-faire* social philosophy hostile to all systematic attempts at social planning and control. For these two factors, since they have operated to obscure many of the consequences of action, have conspired to prevent the development on the part of the average American of any clear perception or understanding of the wider significance and import of either his own or his neighbor's actions.

Felt Needs and Social Requirements Not Always Correlative

As a result of these divisions in American life—between classes and groups, between the world of the child and the world of the adult, and between certain of the values sought by the school and those actually current in American society—the educator cannot assume that child interest and social demands can always be brought into a working alignment by skillful educational planning and teaching. Ideally, any conflict between these two poles should be resolved by closing the gaps in the student's experiences. In cold fact, educators must recognize that no educational program will be fully effective until this has been accomplished. But the actual achievement of this goal assumes a power over the social environment of the learner that the educator frequently does not possess. It assumes also—as in the case of conflicting ideas and aspirations of the various groups and classes in America—a knowledge of the exact way in which these conflicts should be resolved. Unfortunately, such knowledge is not at the present time possessed by the educator or by anybody else in American society.

[7] There is a sense, of course, in which the type of education described here is highly practical for the upper classes in that it becomes the mark of the cultivated gentleman. Those that aspire to that status must secure the appropriate type of education, since it is the gateway to many posts of honor and profit.

The educator who is genuinely concerned with the social goals of education will be forced, however reluctantly, to set for his students problems not directly related to their felt needs and interests. At the same time, because of the mis-educative aspects of our culture, students will sometimes develop interests and felt needs that are not in harmony with the social goals of education as these goals are envisioned by the educator. This situation will compel compromises and adjustments that would have no place in an ideal educational program. These compromises and adjustments should be made with due consideration for the very real importance of both individual needs and interests and the demands of the social situation. It is essential that they be made with full recognition of the fact that, under existing conditions, no complete reconciliation between felt needs and social requirements is possible. Where reconciliation is impossible, the teacher who is concerned with educational requirements of crucial social problems will employ the best techniques of involvement at his command.

▶ Following Up This Chapter

1. As you look back over your educational experiences in the past, do you think your teachers had a society-centered, a child-centered, or a personal success conception of the basic aims of education? What view do you think your parents held?

2. Get a small group of your classmates together, and try to figure out what a high school program honestly based upon the *felt* needs and interests of high school students would look like. Compare this program with the program of the high school you attended. Taking into account both the nature and the extent of the actual learning that would occur under each of these programs, which do you think would produce the best citizens for our society today? Why?

3. To what extent, if at all, do you believe that children live in a world of their own, largely isolated from the major concerns of adult life? What is the educational import of your conclusion?

4. Make a chart listing the arguments for and against each of the four positions discussed in this chapter. After discussing these arguments with your classmates, make an honest effort to evaluate them. To what extent does your evaluation of each of these arguments agree with that made by

the other members of the group? Where does it differ? How do you account for the differences?

5. In not more than four sentences each, state: (1) your position on the primary issue raised in this chapter, (2) the educational meaning of this position, and (3) your basic reason for tentatively accepting it.

▶ Suggested Reading

1. You can get a good general picture of the conflict between the individual and the social in American education—particularly as it relates to discipline, freedom, and education for personal success—from R. Freeman Butts' *The College Charts Its Course,* pages 309–329, 358–378.

2. Harold Rugg has written two excellent accounts of the rise and development of the child-centered school—one in his *American Life and the School Curriculum* published in 1936 (pages 339–359); the other in his recent *Foundations for American Education* (pages 540–570). Although he is properly regarded as a member of the interactive school, William H. Kilpatrick, in *Foundations of Method,* pages 1–231, ably states the underlying theory upon which the child-centered school is built. *The Child-Centered School* by Harold Rugg and Ann Shumaker affords a friendly analysis and criticism of the child-centered approach to education. Hughes Mearns' *Creative Youth* is a graphic description of a brilliantly successful child-centered program in the teaching of English. Rupert C. Lodge's *Philosophy of Education,* while written from a philosophical point of view different from that espoused by many of the members of the child-centered school, nevertheless will give the discerning reader the spirit and feel of the child-centered position. See pages 43–54, 124–141, 208–212. Finally the student should look for one of the major roots of this theory of education in the growing literature on child growth and development.

3. The view that the fundamental purpose of public education is to prepare the student for personal economic and social success in a competitive society is widely scattered throughout the literature on education. It is, for example, clearly evident in the idea of the public school as "the ladder of opportunity." A good contemporary exposition of this position may be found in Warner, Havighurst, and Loeb, *Who Shall Be Educated?* pages 141–172.

4. The society-centered position does not represent a unified body of educational theory. It is held together as a *position* only on the basis of

the conviction that, if the child is to develop into a civilized human being and a useful citizen, he must be disciplined by means of methods and material selected with reference to the standards of adult society rather than with reference to the felt interests of children or the conditions of economic success. In detail, this position varies from Robert M. Hutchins' insistence on the discipline of the intellectual virtues (*The Higher Learning in America*) to George S. Counts' demand that the schools rebuild the social order (*Dare the Schools Build a New Social Order?*). The references suggested at the close of Chapter 23 define the minimum reading list required to show something of the range of educational thought included under the society-centered conception of the purposes of education. A moderate and reasonable statement of the general position taken by the society-centered educator, however, may be found in I. L. Kandel's *Conflicting Theories of Education*, pages 116–129. *Readings in the Foundations of Education*, prepared by the Staff of Division I, Teachers College, Columbia University, has made available a number of statements from outstanding educational leaders emphasizing the social ends of education. See Vol. I, pages 179–226. You may also wish to read comments of a number of educational leaders on the activity movement, contained in Chapters V and VI of the *Thirty-third Yearbook* of the National Society for the Study of Education, Part II, "The Activity Movement," pages 77–143. Chapters VIII, IX, and X (pages 167–208) of this yearbook might also prove interesting and instructive.

5. Thayer, Zachry, and Kotinsky, *Reorganizing Secondary Education* (pages 3–87) is an excellent statement of the interactive position. Part II (pages 91–354) undertakes to outline the meaning of this position for the course of study in the secondary school, while Part III (pages 359–472) indicates its meaning for school administration. The *Third Yearbook* of the John Dewey Society, "Democracy and the Curriculum," is written largely in the spirit of the interactive school. William H. Kilpatrick's chapters (pages 291–313 and 346–378) contain a clear and simple description of the basic cultural theory of human personality upon which the interactive position rests. More extensive treatments of this theory may be found in Kilpatrick's *Selfhood and Civilization* and in the reading suggestions offered at the close of Chapter 1 of this book. Fairly extensive excerpts taken from the work of a number of distinguished scholars and writers bearing on the relationships between culture and personality are included in *Readings in the Foundations of Education*, Vol. I, pages 125–178. Somewhat briefer quotations on the same subjects are available in W. H. Kilpatrick, *Sourcebook in the Philosophy of Education*, pages 143–161.

Chapter 23

The Social Function of Education

IF EDUCATION is a social affair—that is, if its ends and purposes are primarily social ends and purposes—the curriculum worker, in order to perform his tasks intelligently, must proceed on the basis of some conception of the social function of education. Here again he faces, not a unified consensus but a welter of conflicting points of view. Fortunately, some of these views, such as the doctrine that the social function of education is the inculcation in the masses of a social philosophy appropriate to the interests of a ruling elite, can be eliminated, since they are incompatible with democratic principles. Even after these positions have been eliminated, the curriculum worker is confronted with at least four different conceptions of the social function of education—each, in the eyes of its adherents, not only compatible with but also essential to the preservation of American democratic ideals.

1. *Education for Christian Citizenship*

The first of these views maintains that the social function of education is the development of cultivated Christian men and women, fit for citizenship in a Christian society. This is a corollary of the position that the supreme moral authority in education is to be found in the tenets of the Christian faith. This view has, in the past, been tinctured with the thesis that only a relatively few individuals are, in any real sense, educable. But this particular thesis is a reflection of aristocratic notions in no way either essential to, or restricted to, the view that the ultimate social purpose of education is the creation and maintenance of a Christian society. In any case, the contention that only a select few can profit from real education, as distinct from mere training, is incompatible with the democratic faith in the potentialities of the common man.

The heart of the case against the thesis that education in American society should be grounded in the dogmas of a particular religious faith —that so to ground education is contrary to the American doctrine of the separation of church and state—has already been presented in some detail.

Democracy and the Christian Ethic

Nevertheless, there is one aspect of the argument that has not been dealt with and that demands consideration at this point. It is frequently asserted that democracy is an outgrowth of the Christian religion and, hence, can be maintained only in an essentially Christian society. Basically this contention rests on two theses: first, that democratic principles are directly derived from the Christian ethic and have no meaning apart from this ethic; and, second, that moral character can be developed only through the context of religious teaching.

There is a significant grain of truth in the first thesis. The fundamental democratic principle of the supreme moral worth of individual men and women is intimately related to the Christian emphasis on the supreme value and dignity of the human soul. It cannot be denied that, in Europe and America, Christianity has been a major source of inspiration in the development of democracy. Nevertheless, it is not true that Christianity and democracy are identical. This is evident on two counts:

First: The Christian doctrine of the supreme value and dignity of the human soul can be, and has been, interpreted in ways that are incompatible with a democratic society. No less a Christian philosopher than Maritain has said:

The Christian religion is annexed to no temporal regime; it is compatible with all forms of legitimate government; it is not its business to determine which type of civil rule men must adopt *hic et nunc;* it imposes none on their will nor, so long as the higher essential principles are respected, does it specify any particular system of political philosophy, no matter how general, such as that system (democracy) which occupies us at the moment.[1]

In another book, he writes:

One can be a Christian and achieve one's salvation while militating in favor of any political regime whatsoever, always on condition that it does not trespass against natural law and the law of God. One can be a Christian and achieve one's salvation while defending a political philosophy other than the democratic philosophy, just as one was able to be a Christian, in the days of the Roman Empire, while accepting the social regime of slavery, or in the seventeenth century while holding to the political regime of the absolute monarchy. . . . It was not given to believers faithful to Catholic dogma but to rationalists to proclaim in France the rights of man and the citizen, to Puritans to strike the last blow at slavery in America, to atheistic Communists to abolish in Russia the absolutism of private profit.[2]

Second: Without denying or disparaging the contributions that the Christian ethic has, in historical fact, made to the development of democracy in western Europe and America, Christianity is in no sense essential to democracy.[3] It is true that democracy is impossible apart from a profound belief in the dignity and worth of individual men and women. But Christian dogma is not the sole repository of that belief. Other faiths, some of them secular, have asserted the supreme moral worth and dignity of human beings. As a matter of historical fact, the first systematic statement of democratic theory arose not from Chris-

---

[1] From *The Twilight of Civilization,* by Jacques Maritain, Copyright, Sheed & Ward, Inc., New York, 1943, p. 60.

[2] Jacques Maritain, *Christianity and Democracy* (New York: Charles Scribner's Sons: 1944), pp. 36–38. By permission.

[3] Since Maritain was quoted to support the first part of this argument, it is only fair to indicate that he would not accept this point. He holds, apparently, that while democracy is a secular ethic in no wise necessary to Christianity, it is an ethic that can develop only under the inspiration of the Christian faith. With all due respect to the undoubted sincerity and ability of Maritain, the facts do not justify this conclusion

tian but from Athenian political philosophy several centuries before the founding of Christianity.[4]

The second thesis advanced to support the contention that democracy is possible only in a Christian society is that moral character can be developed only in the context of religious teaching. But this argument has even less warrant than the first. Even if it were true, it would not mean that Christian teaching is necessary to the development of moral character. But it is not true that character can be built only in the context of religious teaching. This statement is not intended to deny the validity of the moral insights of any religious faith. Nor does it deny that a religious faith, when taught as a way of life rather than merely as an intellectual creed, does mold character. What has already been said about the way in which the cultural system shapes the character of the young is sufficient to indicate that moral character is the result of participation in a way of life, religious or otherwise. Nor can it be said that moral standards emerge only from religious teaching. It may be true, although as a historical and anthropological fact it would be difficult to prove, that originally all fundamental moral ideals did emerge in close conjunction with some religious faith. But the historical fact—if established—would not mean that they could arise only in this manner. More important, it would not mean, once the notion of moral standards has arisen, that moral development or evolution is bound to any particular set of religious dogmas.

The assertion that moral standards and moral character depend upon Christian teaching amounts to saying that only Christian ethical principles are valid—or, rather, that only the particular interpretation of these principles accepted by some specific sect or variety of Christians is valid. This may be true. But unless we are to abandon the historical American doctrine of the separation of church and state, the public school cannot base its moral teachings on this premise. The moral teachings of the public school must be based on a secular ethic upon which the vast majority of Americans, whatever their personal faith, can agree.

[4] John L. Myres, *The Political Ideas of the Greeks,* pp. 319–390. Competent scholars have regarded Pericles' defense of democracy in his celebrated Funeral Oration as one of the finest statements of democratic theory in existence. See Irwin Edman, *Fountainheads of Freedom,* p. 17. The Funeral Oration is reported in Thucydides, *The Peloponnesian War,* pp. 111–118.

This ethic is to be found in the democratic ideal—an ideal which, as Maritain correctly asserts, is rooted in the secular conscience of the American people. Fortunately, as the preceding discussion has demonstrated, there is no *necessary* conflict between the democratic and the Christian ethic. Fortunately, in a world split into many conflicting faiths, democracy is not exclusively limited to the Christian ethic, still less to any particular interpretation of it. For all men are not Christians and all Christians are not democrats; nor are all interpretations of Christianity equally compatible with democracy.

2. *Education as Development of the Rational Man*

A second view holds that the primary function of education is the development of the rational man. At first sight it would seem that this view is simply a reiteration, in another form, of the individualistic interpretation of education. A second look, however, will dispel this notion. For the education proper to man, on the basis of the position now being considered, is that which unites man with man rather than that which stresses the development of individual differences.[5] This view differs from the social interpretation of education advanced in the last section in that it points, not to the cultural molding of human personality, but to the existence of an essential humanity, prior to and independent of the mutations of any particular culture, and by virtue of which man is man. The essence of this common humanity is to be found in the rational faculties of man. Hence, the basic objective of education in any time or place is the cultivation of these faculties.

Adherents of this position do not deny the obvious fact that societies differ nor that the specific problems confronting men in different societies vary with cultural circumstances and arrangements. Nor do they deny that education is concerned with the development of the citizen. What they assert is that these problems must be understood in terms of universal and eternal first principles, discovered and confirmed by the application of rational faculties common to all men. Hence, the first duty of education, and its greatest contribution to the development of intelligent citizenship, is to concern itself with the mas-

[5] Robert M. Hutchins, *The Higher Learning in America,* p. 73.

tery of first principles and with the cultivation of the rational faculties —never more so than in a period of rapid social change.[6] They also assert, first, that rationality is defined by the intellectual processes found in the dialectics of deductive reasoning; and, second, that these processes, when properly disciplined by formal exercises, are available for use in any situation calling for rational analysis and thought.[7]

This theory of the social function of education is, of course, derived from the position that the ultimate source of authority in education is to be found in eternal and absolute truths, discovered and verified by man's intuitive and deductive reason. As previously indicated, it embodies conceptions—of the nature of man, of the meaning of truth, and of the way truth is discovered and verified—that are incompatible with the spirit, the method, and in some instances, the conclusions of science. As a subsequent discussion will show, it also embodies a false conception of the nature of learning. There is, however, another aspect of this position that deserves some consideration at this time.

Defects in Hutchins' Notion of the Common

The theory under discussion, it will be remembered, insists that education is primarily concerned with that which unites man with man; in short, it asserts that its chief, if not its sole, purpose is the development of a common orientation and point of view. This emphasis upon a common orientation and outlook as the fundamental goal of education is quite sound. But it must also be remembered that man's common humanity, according to this position, is grounded, not in common purposes and goals growing out of shared experience, but in the original nature of man—specifically in his rational faculties and in the eternal truths revealed by them. Hence the function of education is to cultivate rather than to create the common.

The primary issues raised by this conception of the common are those to which reference has already been made—issues of the nature of man and of truth, and of the way in which man discovers and verifies truth. But this conception also raises some other issues which are of considerable importance.

[6] Hutchins, *The Higher Learning in America*, pp. 62–68.
[7] *Ibid.*, p. 63.

In the first place, it will be noted that this position assumes that the cultivation of the common is, for all practical purposes, the sole function of public education. Hutchins says:

In general education we are interested in drawing out the elements of our common human nature; we are interested in the attributes of the race, not the accidents of individuals.

He quotes with approval the statement of Whewell:

Young persons may be so employed and so treated, that their caprice, their self-will, their individual tastes and propensities, are educed and developed, but this is not Education. It is not the Education of a Man; for what is educed is not what belongs to man as man, and connects man with man. It is not the Education of a man's Humanity, but the Indulgence of his Individuality.[8]

Although it may be granted that the development of the common is the first purpose of education, still it must be said that the development of individuality is also a major purpose of education. In fact, the democratic doctrine of respect for personality would seem to require that, in a democratic society, education should seek to produce rich and varied human personalities, which, within the community of feeling and purpose that transforms a collectivity into a society, enhance the quality of the common life with their unique gifts and perspectives.

There is also ample historical and sociological warrant for the assertion that progress, while it degenerates into chaos where no element of the common is present, is born of difference. It is significant in this respect that the Aristotelian philosophy, on which Hutchins' position rests, not only endowed the universal with far greater reality and worth than the concrete individual but also erected static stability into the final criterion of the good society. On both these counts it is in direct contradiction to the democratic tradition. For the fundamental principle of the democratic ethic is that the locus of supreme moral worth is to be found, not in social institutions nor in an abstract universal humanity, but in concrete human beings. Democracy, whatever else it may be, is a declaration of faith in the possibility and the de-

[8] Robert M. Hutchins, *The Higher Learning in America* (New Haven: Yale University Press; 1936), p. 73.

sirability of social progress. The democratic educator, therefore, must reject Hutchins' contention that the social purposes of education are restricted to the cultivation of the common.

In the second place, Hutchins' definition of the social function of education is exclusively intellectual. "If education is rightly understood," he says, "it will be understood as the cultivation of the intellect." [9] Certainly no educator committed to the democratic tradition can deny that the formation and growth of intelligence is a primary end of education. Neither can any educator who is aware of the significant psychological discoveries of the last century accept the contention that education is to be understood solely as the cultivation of the intellect. For this thesis subordinates, where it does not ignore, the emotional, aesthetic, and moral aspects of education. Hutchins allots no place whatever, either in his educational theory or in his prescriptions for educational practice, to considerations bearing on the emotional adjustments of persons, save as these may perchance be influenced by the cultivation of the intellectual virtues. He recognizes, with the possible exception of literary excellence, no aesthetic goals for education beyond the austere but authentic beauty of logical precision.

Moral considerations fare somewhat better. For Hutchins admits that the study of ethics, as a normative science, has a legitimate place in the educational program. But morals are sternly subordinated to intellect. Moral discipline is merely a means to facilitate the cultivation of the intellect; and ethical principles are derived solely from intellectual considerations. It must be observed that there is a vast difference between the position here assumed by Hutchins and the entirely reasonable position that ethical principles are properly subject to rational criticism and verification. The latter recognizes that ethical principles have their foundation in the irrational—not necessarily antirational—biological, aesthetic, and social preferences of man. On the other hand, Hutchins' position undertakes to establish ethical principles by sheer deduction from intellectual premises, without regard to human preferences or character or to the way the ethical principles so derived would impinge, in practice, on the biological and social needs of man. The ultimate error of the purely intellectualistic interpretation of education is that it severs the intellectual from the aesthetic

<hr>

[9] Hutchins, *The Higher Learning in America*, p. 67.

and emotional nature of man. Such dualism, once it is accepted, necessarily engenders an insoluble and unnecessary conflict between reason
and impulse.

Problems Involved in Developing a Common Orientation

In the present context perhaps the most serious defect of Hutchins'
conception of the common is that it obscures both the difficulty and
the character of the problems involved in developing a common intellectual and moral orientation in a period of rapid social change. It
is true that men, by virtue of their membership in a specific biological
species, share both certain basic bodily needs and certain more or less
well-defined mechanisms of action. But, in the first place, Hutchins'
insistence that the foundations of common beliefs and loyalties are to
be found in a common human nature is grounded, not in these biological needs and mechanisms but in the assertion that man possesses,
a priori, a common reason. In the second place, these needs and mechanisms do not specifically insure that men living under different cultural
influences and circumstances will develop similar patterns of belief and action. At best these needs and mechanisms simply insure common potentialities of growth and development. Since the potentialities
of human growth and development are rich and varied to an extraordinary degree, men living under different circumstances and conditions
and in the midst of different attitudes and beliefs will develop different
minds and characters.

Fundamentally there are two issues involved: First, is human nature,
in its essential elements, relatively fixed and constant, or is it, within
very broad limits, plastic and varied? Second, is human reason (mind
in both its logical and its ideational dimensions) innate or built? These
issues are crucial for education in an age of profound social change.
On the basis of Hutchins' position, confusion and disintegration are
merely the results of an educational system that has failed to elicit
man's common humanity. But, as here assumed, confusion and disintegration are the results of divisions and conflicts in our society, which
have produced different minds and characters. Consequently, the re-
establishment of consensus with respect to basic beliefs and objects of
allegiance involves both the reconstruction of persons and of society.

3. *Education as an Instrument for the Preservation of the Existing Social Order*

The position now to be discussed takes full account of the differences between human societies and of the relationship between social arrangements and personality. Convinced of the soundness of Aristotle's dictum that "the adaptation of education to the form of government" is everywhere the best guarantee of the "permanence of constitutions," and convinced, also, that stability is the greatest of all possible social goods—this view insists that the primary social function of education is to insure the development of the type of human personality required to perpetuate and maintain the mores and institutions of society. This thesis accurately describes the actual operating objective of practically every known educational system—past or present—regardless of the form in which it has preferred to couch its avowed purposes. It is substantially correct up to a certain point.

It is true that this position has been sharply condemned in recent years by those who feel that it represents a prostitution of education by directing it exclusively to the maintenance of the *status quo*. But, in the first place, human life demands a certain degree of stability and continuity, and to educate at all means to induct the young into some moral and intellectual order. What order is to be used if not that approved by the society of which the children themselves are members and in which they must live? In the second place, where criticism of and change in social institutions and arrangements are a part of the socially approved moral and intellectual order, as in a democratic society, the contention that the primary social function of education is the maintenance and perpetuation of this order is not tantamount to an unyielding defense of the *status quo*. Rather, as both the extreme right and left have tended to forget, education to maintain the existing social order, where that order is a democratic one, represents an effort to institutionalize criticism and change within the fundamental framework of democratic methods and ethics.

Nevertheless, this position, as the authors of the Harvard Report have stated, does assume, even in its democratic form, that the standards of the good are defined by the traditions of the past.[10] It is true that in ordinary times tradition does serve as the primary criterion of the good; and there is a considerable degree of continuity in beliefs, as well as in institutional and customary behavior, even in the most revolutionary age. It is a mistake to assume that a wholesale repudiation of the past is the primary characteristic that distinguishes the great transitional eras of history from periods of less fundamental social change. Such acts of total renunciation never occur. If they did, their only effect would be to reduce man to the level of the brute. What does distinguish transitional eras is the fact that in these periods the standards of the good and the foundations of social organization are undergoing alteration and reconstruction.

Need for Critical Examination and Reconstruction

It is precisely this fact that underlies the inadequacies of the position that, in a period of profound social crisis and change, the purposes of education can be conceived primarily in terms of the preservation of the existing intellectual and moral tradition. For in such periods this order has itself begun to crumble, not because of the willful neglect of a perverse generation but because it is no longer able, just as it stands, to interpret and order the experience of a people living under drastically altered circumstances and conditions. Thoroughgoing reconstruction becomes the only viable alternative to social chaos and revolution. Critical examination rather than the inculcation of traditional ideals and conceptions must constitute the core of an educational program designed for a period characterized by widespread intellectual and moral confusion and conflict. Fundamental reconstruction of the tradition is hardly possible within the framework of a theory which holds that tradition itself is the final measure of the good. The thesis that the standard and test of value is to be found in the past offers at best only a static criterion of the good. It provides no means by which the valid can be separated from the invalid aspects of the cultural tradition.

The democratic tradition may be a self-reforming and self-correcting

[10] Harvard Committee on the Objectives of Education in a Free Society, *General Education in a Free Society,* especially pp. 3–102.

tradition. If so, it is precisely because the standard of the good which it embodies is a standard based upon an emerging social consensus as it is tested and verified by experience rather than by reception from the past. An educational system grounded in the democratic tradition will seek to preserve the democratic way of life. But the democracy it seeks to preserve is a revitalized and reconstructed democracy valid for the times, not a static and moribund democracy sanctified only by the passage of years.

4. Education as Reconstruction

The fourth position is that the social office of education is to foster a continuous re-examination and reconstruction of our social ideals, beliefs, and institutions. This school of thought accepts the contention that the educator derives his moral authority from the ethical and methodological tenets of the American democratic tradition. It therefore holds (in substantial agreement with the democratic wing of the position that the primary social function of education is the perpetuation of the cultural heritage) that the first duty of the public school is to maintain and promote the democratic way of life. It differs from that view both in its interpretation of the democratic tradition and in its interpretation of the present social situation.

With respect to the first divergence, those who emphasize reconstruction point out that the final criterion of the good embodied in the democratic tradition is not that of appeal to accepted values of the past, but of the welfare of men and women as verified and confirmed by their own experience. The democratic ethic, unlike purely traditional ethics, includes within itself provisions for its own re-examination and reconstruction. With respect to the second point, those who stress reconstruction find that in the altered world created by the scientific and technological revolutions, certain of the traditional conceptions of democracy no longer work as they had been expected to work. Some persons persist in holding on to these conceptions in their original form, while others seek to discard them in the interest of new and more workable conceptions. Consequently, sincere democrats have now become divided and confused with respect to the meaning of the democratic tradition for the modern world.

Under such circumstances, clarification and definition of the meaning of the democratic tradition for an interdependent industrial civilization are imperative if that tradition is to give birth to a new intellectual and moral consensus capable of molding and directing the social transformations now clearly under way throughout the modern world. On both these counts the theory of reconstruction holds that the educator's commitment to the democratic tradition means, not simply the inculcation of traditional points of view but the re-examination and reconstruction of the cultural heritage in the light of new problems and conditions.

Probably enough has already been said to indicate that the reconstruction theory represents the only definition of the social function of education which, in a period of social crisis and transition such as the present, offers any hope whatever that education may play a significant role in the uncoerced resolution of social conflicts and problems. And if it is true, as many have believed, that education is the only alternative to force, then it would appear that the public must espouse the educational adventure implied by this position—or else abandon the attempt to re-establish consensus through reasoned discussion and consent rather than through civil strife and dictatorship.

In accepting the thesis that continuous re-examination and reconstruction of social ideals, beliefs, and institutions constitute the primary social purpose of education, three rather serious errors of interpretation, current among adherents as well as opponents of this conception, must be avoided.

Reconstruction, not Repudiation, of the Cultural Heritage

Reconstruction does not mean wholesale repudiation of the cultural heritage. For, if reconstruction implies change, it also implies continuity. In fact this position is conservative, in that it holds that the democratic tradition is at once so precious and so deeply ingrained in American character that it affords not only the sole basis upon which moral and intellectual consensus can now be re-established by mutual consent and persuasion but also the sole basis upon which any really satisfactory social order can be built. This theory, however, is realistic enough to recognize that in periods of profound social change reconstruction is the price of survival; and it is radical enough to insist that necessary changes in beliefs and institutions must be vigorously carried through while there is yet time.

But the fundamental spirit of reconstruction is that of preservation, extension, and improvement. In a very real sense it is but the dynamic form of the view that the primary purpose of education in American society is the preservation of a democratic social and moral order. This emphasis is important. For it is clear that the advocates of the third position outlined above (namely, that the function of education is to preserve the existing social order) are fundamentally correct. Societies establish educational systems to preserve, not to destroy, their moral and institutional order. Consequently, it is only in terms of the democratic and dynamic form of that position, particularly adapted to periods of rapid and fundamental social change, that the theory of reconstruction can be defended.

Deep Conviction Not Precluded

To clear up a second erroneous view, continuous reconstruction does not mean that everything is to be changed at once or that all views are to be held so tentatively that they provide no basis for firm and vigorous action. The presumption is always with established beliefs and institutions; re-examination and reconstruction are properly demanded only at those points where serious problems and conflicts emerge. Moreover, critical thought and reasoned discussion are not incompatible with conviction. There is no more grave or erroneous perversion of the democratic creed than the idea that all beliefs must be held so tentatively as to preclude action. Democratic survival demands deep commitment and vigorous action no less than it demands re-examination and reconstruction. The preservation of democracy now requires the development of persons capable of yielding the same devoted loyalty to reasoned convictions and to the method of experimental thought and discussion that they formerly granted only to rigid and dogmatic creeds.

This loyalty to the method of intelligence and mutual persuasion, however, must not be so absolute as to preclude the capacity to fight, on occasion, for democratic ideals. Reason and persuasion, coupled with a marked strain toward genuine consensus, would represent the first impulse and resort of a democratic personality. But in an imperfect democracy—and human democracy will always remain in some respects imperfect—political and even economic conflict, in conjunction with free and open discussion, majority decision, and the right of the minority to examine and criticize in an effort to force reconsideration, are accepted and necessary techniques. Democratic citizenship frequently involves the willingness and the ability to modify conflict in the direction of consensus, where consensus appears possible. But it also involves the ability to analyze and evaluate the issues implicit in social conflict. Where genuine consensus appears impossible, it likewise engages the capacity to participate actively in social conflict.

Democratic citizenship may even involve the willingness and the capacity to employ armed force where intransigent and undemocratic social groups persist in preventing by force the operation of democratic processes of discussion and decision. In short, devotion to democratic ideals and processes does imply a strong preference for reasoned discussion and mutual agreement. But it also means that democratic personalities will vigorously oppose, by the accepted democratic processes of public debate and political action, undemocratic proposals and policies. Devotion to democracy certainly does not mean that democrats must passively accept the arbitrary refusal of entrenched ruling classes to permit the introduction of democratic processes or that they must sit idly by while undemocratic social groups undermine, by force and violence, the foundations of a democratic society.

Reconstruction Not Purely Intellectual

Turning to a third error in interpretation, reconstruction must not be conceived in purely intellectual terms. Actually the task involves much more. Ideals and ideas are meaningless unless they are employed as guides to action. There is little point to intellectual and moral reconstruction unless it is accompanied by a corresponding institutional reconstruction. Behind the contemporary social crisis—and hence behind the threat to the democratic way of life—lies the fact that in certain respects our social institutions are not, under the altered conditions of modern life, functioning as they had been expected to function. To take a single example, in so far as political and economic institutions harbor the idea of unrestricted national sovereignty, they are clearly incompatible with human security in an interdependent world armed with the highly destructive weapons created by modern science and technology. The crisis can be expected to continue until institutional structure is again able to function satisfactorily.

In a very real sense the difficulty is to be found in the partial disintegration of social consensus under the impact of changing conditions and institutional malfunctioning. But it is precisely at the point of institutional arrangements that intellectual and moral confusion and disunity come to a focus. It is in the context of institutional reconstruction that social consensus must be rebuilt if it is to be anything more than a spurious verbal agreement, which will promptly disintegrate at the first contact with reality. Furthermore, any society requires and, at the same time, builds a particular type of personal structure. Intellectual, moral, and institutional reconstruction inevitably involves the reconstruction of the character of persons.

If reconstruction is to proceed by mutual consent, these three aspects of reconstruction cannot be conducted separately. Attempts to remake personal character in isolation from institutional reconstruction have always failed because they have not taken into account the fact that institutional arrangements mold and shape human personality. On the other hand, it is possible, under certain conditions, to alter social institutions prior to a wholesale reshaping of personality. Where this is done deliberately and on a large scale, it entails an iron dictatorship established and maintained by a small and compact minority. In a less systematic and deliberate way institutions (particularly in a highly dynamic society) are often changed by the sheer pressure of events, prior to any thoroughgoing reconstruction of personal structure. Deliberate *and* democratic social reconstruction, however, is an interrelated affair, involving co-ordinate changes in intellectual beliefs, personality structures, and social arrangements.

Educational Implications of the Interrelated Nature of Reconstruction

The fact that democratic reconstruction is an interrelated process is replete with educational implications. It means, in the first place, that education is not something that goes on only within the four walls of the classroom. Educators must take account of, and concern themselves with, the educative effects of social conditions, institutional structures, and group atmospheres as these impinge upon the character and personality of students. Conversely, they must relate the work of the school to the society of which it is a part. On the one hand, they must aid students to comprehend and analyze the major forces operating in society and the major problems which confront it. On the other hand, they must assist students to master the techniques and acquire the attitudes appropriate to democratic participation in society. Hence the educator and the public must abandon the notion that the curriculum can be limited to the traditional purposes and content of the academic subjects. They must abandon, too, the idea that the school is properly a cloistered academic retreat, separated from, and above, the conflict and turmoil of life.

The fact that deliberate and democratic reconstruction always involves co-ordinate changes in beliefs, personality structures, and social arrangements also means that education is an affair of the whole person and not merely of the intellect. Democratic citizenship and democratic reconstruction require a high degree of intellectual understanding. They require also a certain kind of moral commitment and a certain type of personality structure. Intellectual analysis and comprehension can play a significant role in shaping and reshaping personality and character. Democratic character, in fact, cannot be built at all apart from intelligent criticism and understanding, since there is a significant element of self-direction and control in every democratic person.

But the data of the psychological and social sciences indicate that character and personality are, first of all, the products of group atmospheres and behaviors and of the ways in which the physical and psychological needs of the individual are met or thwarted. Charged with the development of democratic persons, the school must give extensive attention to the quality of its functioning as a social group and to the extent to which, as well as the methods by which, personal and group needs are satisfied. For identical reasons, the school must concern itself with the factors of family, neighborhood, community, and institutional life. In short, nothing that is germane to the life of its students or to the society of which they are members is foreign to the work of the school.

Finally, the co-ordinate character of the changes involved in democratic reconstruction means that such reconstruction cannot be fostered by the public school in isolation from the rest of society. There can be no question of the school's inability to remake, purely on its own initiative and by its own unaided efforts, the prevailing pattern of beliefs, institutions, and personality structures of any society. No society will be indifferent—nor can any society afford to be indifferent—about the quality or the tendency of its educational system. No school system will be granted complete autonomy with respect to its major purposes or policies. Even if this were not the case, no school system either would or could remold a society single-handed. Teachers, for the most part, are members of the society in which they teach. Like other men, they cannot escape its molding influence. Where a society is united and certain about its major premises, teachers would share the common faith as a matter of course. In any case, the school, powerful as it is, is so small a part of the total educative influences of society that its teachings would be relatively impotent against the united impact of all the rest.

The Educator as a Statesman

The arguments above have frequently been advanced, by radical as well as by conservative educators, to demonstrate the absurdity of the theory of reconstruction. The arguments are sound, but they are also irrelevant. They assume both a condition that does not exist and a proposal that has not been advanced. The theory of reconstruction does not suggest that the school, on its own authority and by its own unaided effort, attempt to build a new social order. Nor is modern society a unit with respect to either its moral and intellectual postulates or its institutional arrangements. If it were, reconstruction would not be necessary or possible, but neither would it be an issue. The fact is that the modern world is in a period of crisis and transition, in which it is compelled by the march of events to engage in a major task of reconstruction. The American people, in common with the rest of the world, are not wholly agreed upon the direction that reconstruction should take. There are those, indeed, who are not yet fully convinced that reconstruction is necessary. All are aware, however, that the times are seriously out of joint, and many are frankly confused and disturbed.

In this situation those who advocate reconstruction are not embarking on a dubious conspiracy to seize control of the public school. They are making a proposal to the American people. Their proposal is not that the public school should undertake to build a wholly new moral and intellectual order through crass indoctrination. The proposal holds, first, that the school should endeavor, along with other agencies, to clarify and where necessary to reconstruct, through study and mutual agreement, the intellectual and moral order to which America, in its greatest moments, already stands committed. And, second, that the school should strive to explore, again in co-operation with other agencies and through the democratic processes of study and discussion, the implications of this order for the institutional structure of society under the conditions set by modern science and technology. Admittedly, this is a vigorous and far-reaching proposal. But the depth and gravity of the situation preclude puny and superficial measures. In the long run there is no more dangerous disability than the incapacity to project remedies commensurate with the diagnosis of the problem.

This proposal, however bold it may be, is neither impossible nor undemocratic. On the contrary, it is conceived in the spirit of the democratic belief in progress and of the democratic faith in education as a means of progress. As such it will, if educators but make clear its meaning, receive enthusiastic support from substantial elements in American society. Even those who oppose it will frequently do so with uneasy minds and divided souls. For the American people, while they have often denied and flouted their faith on particular occasions, are nevertheless sincerely committed to the thesis that study and discussion rather than violence and coercion are the basic techniques by which social conflicts should be resolved.

In making this proposal the educator must carry a substantial majority of his community with him. He must abandon the cloister for the burdens and responsibilities of educational statesmanship; and he must broaden his concept of education to include adult education in all of its forms. Like other statesmen, he must learn to analyze the trends and forces operating in his community and to ally himself with those groups that are seeking to broaden and extend the democratic foundations of society. The challenge is not without its difficulties and its risks. Perfect safety and security are impossible in the midst of a profound social crisis. It is at least possible that at the present time the dangers of inaction may far exceed the risks of action. To reject the proposal on the ground that it entails responsibility and risk is to reject any democratic or creative leadership whatever for education in an age of social transformation. It is probably tantamount to a rejection of the only means by which men may reasonably hope to re-establish in these times an uncoerced community of persuasion. Democratic reconstruction is the business of education—or, rather, it is the educative process itself. Whatever else educators may do, they cannot afford to abdicate nor to let the battle for democratic reconstruction go by default.

▶ *Following Up*
  This Chapter

1. What conception of the fundamental *social* purposes of education do you think was held by the faculty of the high school from which you graduated? Did the program of the school tend to actualize these purposes? If you believe that your high school faculty had no clear notion of the social purposes of education, can you figure out what social goals the program of the school actually served? Apply these questions to your elementary school.

2. Remind your friends and neighbors that any educational program will in the long run make a significant difference in the character of our society. Then ask them what they think the social purposes of the public school should be. If their answers are stated in very vague or general terms, try to find out what it is that they really mean. Compare the answers you get with the positions outlined in this chapter. Has any significant point of view been overlooked? If so, add it to your list of positions requiring study and examination.

3. With the aid of a small group of your classmates, try to visualize the kind of society—within the bounds of the possible—in which you would like to live. Then try to discover the kind of educational program that would result from the general acceptance of each of the different conceptions of the social purposes of education which you have identified. Finally, taking into account the actual learning products you think these various educational programs would induce in students, try to decide which of them is most likely to produce or preserve the kind of society you desire.

4. What do you think the school should do in a situation where different groups of people hold different views about the fundamental social purposes it should serve?

5. In not more than four sentences for each, state (1) the heart of *each* of the four positions examined in this chapter, (2) the position to which you yourself incline, including your most basic reason for tentatively accepting it, and (3) the central educational meaning of the position you have accepted.

▶ *Suggested Reading*

1. Extended excerpts from the work of several writers taking different points of view on the issues considered in this chapter may be found in William O. Stanley et al., *Social Foundations of Education,* Chapter 12.

2. Good general discussions of the issues explored in this chapter are available in R. Freeman Butts' *The College Charts Its Course,* pages 269–308, 330–357, 379–416; John S. Brubacher, *Modern Philosophies of Education,* pages 140–244, 309–323; John S. Brubacher, *A History of the Problems of Education,* pages 1–51, 612–642; Paul H. Sheats, *Education and the Quest for a Middle Way;* and Theodore Brameld, *Philosophies of Education in Cultural Perspective* and *Toward a Reconstructed Philosophy of Education.* Hollis L. Caswell and Doak S. Campbell, *Reading in Curriculum Development* (pages 1–101) and *Readings in the Foundations of Education,* by the Staff of Division I, Teachers College, Columbia University (Vol. I, pages 899–986), offer a rich collection of fairly extensive selections, bearing on questions of the social function of education, culled from the work of some of the leading educators of our time. A good use might also be made of the shorter quotations in William H. Kilpatrick's *Sourcebook in the Philosophy of Education* (use Index and Table of Contents to locate items of interest).

3. The best, although by no means the only, expressions of the view that the development of Christian citizenship represents the primary social function of education are found in Roman Catholic writings on education. Of these, Jacques Maritain's *Education at the Crossroads* is outstanding for its urbane and liberal Catholic scholarship. See also William McGucken, "The Philosophy of Catholic Education" in the *Forty-first Yearbook* of the National Society for the Study of Education, Part I, "Philosophies of Education," pages 251–288. William J. Sanders, "Spiritual Values and

Education" in the *Seventh Yearbook* of the John Dewey Society, "The Public Schools and Spiritual Values" (pages 80–101), and J. D. Redden and F. A. Ryan, *A Catholic Philosophy of Education* (pages 3–52, 86–101, 368–387) may also be consulted with profit. Arnold S. Nash, *The University and the Modern World* (pages 252–292) presents a liberal Protestant version of the argument for Christian citizenship as *the* social end of education. For criticisms of this conception of the social function of education, see John Childs, "Spiritual Values of the Secular Public School" in the *Seventh Yearbook* of the John Dewey Society, pages 58–79; V. T. Thayer, *American Education under Fire,* pages 97–115; and Conrad Henry Moehlman, *School and Church: The American Way.*

4. Robert M. Hutchins' *The Higher Learning in America,* and Mortimer J. Adler's "In the Defense of the Philosophy of Education" in the *Forty-first Yearbook* of the National Society of the Study of Education, Part I (pages 197–249) are basic references for the position that development of the rational man defines the social function of education. See also Joseph Justman, *Theories of Secondary Education in the United States,* pages 12–22, 55–71; and John T. Foudy, *The Educational Principles of American Humanism,* pages 68–98. For criticisms of this conception of the social purpose of education, see Harold Rugg's *Foundations for American Education,* pages 613–627; Harry D. Gideonse, *The Higher Learning in a Democracy;* and John Dewey's articles in the *Social Frontier,* December, 1936, January, 1937 and March 1937.

5. In actual practice the preservation of the existing social order, with or without a measure of social reform and progress, has always been the primary social purpose of education. Even today it is probably true that most American educators support it in one form or another. Plato's *Republic* (Book IV, 423E–425C, pages 145–147 of the Modern Student Library Edition published by Charles Scribner's Sons) states this position in a bald and unyielding form. The report of the Harvard Committee, *General Education in a Free Society* (pages 3–102) takes the same position with a much greater emphasis on the factor of progress and innovation.

The Social Evolutionists (see Chapter 25 of this book) in particular have worked out systematic defenses of the thesis that the proper social task of education is the development of civilized human beings through the mastery of the social heritage.

6. The basic concept of the social-reconstructionist theory of education was worked out by John Dewey and elaborated in rather general and abstract terms in his *Democracy and Education* (see especially pages 89–116). W. H. Kilpatrick's *Education for a Changing Civilization,* his *Edu-*

cation and the Social Crisis, and a volume he edited, *The Educational Frontier* (especially pages 32–72, 287–319) continued the exploration of the theoretical bases of the social-reconstructionist conception of education. An analysis of contemporary society from the viewpoint of social-reconstruction theory will be found in *Education and Social Integration* by William O. Stanley.

Harold Benjamin's *The Saber-Tooth Curriculum* is amusing and hard hitting. Important also are: American Historical Association, Report of the Commission on the Social Studies, *Conclusions and Recommendations;* I. B. Berkson, *Preface to an Educational Philosophy* and *Education Faces the Future,* pages 241–259; John L. Childs, "Should the School Seek Actively to Reconstruct Society?" in the *Annals of the American Academy of Political and Social Science,* Vol. 182 (November, 1935), pages 1–9; John L. Childs, "A Preface to a New Philosophy of Education" in *Thirteenth Yearbook,* Department of Superintendence of the National Education Association, pages 113–139; George S. Counts, *Dare the School Build a New Social Order?* and *The Social Foundations of Education,* pages 532–563; National Education Association, Committee on Social-Economic Goals of America, *Implications of Social-Economic Goals for Education;* Jesse H. Newlon, *Educational Administration as Social Policy,* pages 1–77, and *Education for Democracy in Our Time;* Progressive Education Association, Committee on Social and Economic Problems, *A Call to the Teachers of the Nation;* Harold Rugg, *Culture and Education in America,* pages 3–15, 259–401, and *Foundations for American Education,* pages 674–813.

Chapter 24

Criteria of Content: Non-Sociological Theories

THE PERSISTENT and decisive questions that confront the curriculum maker, wherever he ventures to probe beneath the surface of his task, cluster around two great problems—that of authority and purpose in education and that of the nature and character of the learning process. At a less ultimate level, however, there is another cluster of issues that cannot be ignored—those focusing on the criteria utilized in the selection of curriculum content. In some instances the proposed criteria are obvious deductions from more fundamental positions respecting the ends of education and the nature of the educative process. In other cases the connections are neither as clear nor as direct. If only because the selection of content lies at the very heart of the curriculum worker's assignment, it seems wise to make a separate and distinct analysis of the major criteria that have been employed for this purpose.

1. *The Disciplinary Subjects*

Remote as it may now seem from the practice of American high schools and colleges, Greek, Latin, and mathematics were, within the memory of men now living, almost universally regarded as the essential core of the curriculum of secondary education.[1] In our own time Hutchins has substituted grammar, rhetoric, and logic for Greek and Latin. While Hutchins' proposal would alter the subject matter of the traditional curriculum—in the direction, incidentally, of a return to the classical *trivium*—the purpose and the method of education as he conceives it would remain substantially the same as they were in the days of our grandfathers: the discipline of the intellectual virtues through formal and rigorous exercise upon difficult and exacting intellectual material.

It would be possible to find, in this conception of the curriculum, a primary emphasis upon the mastery of certain intellectual skills—an interpretation that, in the case of Hutchins, may be fundamentally correct. So interpreted, this theory has the merit of recognizing, as other conceptions of the curriculum frequently do not, the importance of intellectual skills in education. But it is subject to two major criticisms. First, it has erected a necessary end of education into a sufficient end of education. Second, it has identified intellectual skills solely with the skills appropriate to deductive reasoning. The disciplinary theory has not only unduly narrowed the scope of education but has also restricted thought to the processes of deduction.

Inadequate Notion of Mind

Behind the disciplinary conception of education—in the case of most of its adherents, and probably in that of Hutchins himself—lies a theory of mind and of learning. For want of a better term, this theory may be called "faculty psychology." The heart of this theory may be stated in five basic propositions: (1) that man, unlike the lower animals, is endowed at birth with an immaterial substance, properly called mind or soul, which is the source of his unique mental and spiritual powers; (2) that this substance operates through distinct and unitary faculties or powers, such as reason, will, memory, and observation, which constitute the basic forms of mental activity; (3) that, although these powers are present at birth, they can be developed, improved, and disciplined by exercise; (4) that certain subjects—Greek, Latin, and

[1] John S. Brubacher, *A History of the Problems of Education*, pp. 256–258; R. Freeman Butts, *A Cultural History of Education*, pp. 460–462.

mathematics, or, in the Hutchins version, grammar, rhetoric, logic, and mathematics—are peculiarly fitted, because of the nature of their content, to provide the material for such exercise; (5) that, since each of these faculties is a unitary power, it can, when properly disciplined, be utilized with equal facility on any appropriate material.[2] (For example, having developed and disciplined the reason upon such material as grammar, logic, and mathematics, the mature student is equipped to reason cogently in any field of endeavor requiring reason as soon as he has mastered the facts relevant to that field.)

Most adherents of this theory would add to the discipline of the faculties the formation of taste and character, and the mastery of eternal truth, through intensive study of literary classics. The group espousing these two criteria—frequently entitled American Humanists—argue that these criteria represent the most that the school can possibly achieve in the field of general education.

Knowledge has now developed to such a degree that no man can hope to become a universal scholar, still less to perfect himself in all the multifarious techniques, skills, and facts demanded in a complex civilization. Consequently, the attempt to define education in terms of the information and skills required in practical affairs, or in terms of the subject matter of the research disciplines, leads either to a smattering of knowledge in many fields or to a narrow and dehumanizing specialization in a particular area.

The educational theory presented by the formal disciplinist affords a systematic and coherent program of education. Yet, even with the inclusion of an added objective—study of the "great books"—it is a narrow program. For it includes within its ambit only the deductive and the literary, the intellectual and the general. No place is provided for individual and personal objectives of education, for the nonintellectual aspects of education, or for the inductive, the scientific, and the practical modes of thought. Moreover, as the previous chapters have indicated, the program embodies within itself a theory of the nature of truth, and of the method by which truth is discovered and verified, that is contrary to the spirit and method of modern science.

[2] See Frederick Eby and Charles F. Arrowood, *Development of Modern Education,* pp. 414–424; Butts, *A Cultural History of Education,* pp. 460–462; Brubacher, *A History of the Problems of Education,* pp. 135–140. See also Hutchins, *The Higher Learning in America,* pp. 58–87.

False Conception of the Learning Process

Quite apart from these considerations, the disciplinary criterion of curriculum content rests upon a conception of the learning process that is no longer tenable in the light of modern psychological knowledge. Experimentation in transfer of training provides conclusive evidence that the complete and unitary transfer of training within the limits of a particular mental faculty, assumed by the disciplinary theory, is an illusion. Formal exercises designed to discipline the reason, the memory, or the observational power have produced, at best, only small and irregular gains when these functions were tested upon different kinds of material requiring their use. Frequently the results show either no gain at all or a decrease in ability.[3] Moreover, the study of particular school subjects, often quite effective in increasing competence in their respective areas, has but little effect upon "general reasoning power." [4]

There is very little support in these conclusions, which have been confirmed by a host of similar investigations, either for the claim that Latin and mathematics possess a peculiar and extraordinary disciplinary virtue or for the thesis that formal exercises in any school subject contribute to the development of what have been called the "general powers of the mind." [5]

It is true that, to a considerable degree, the failure of the various subjects to enhance the student's capacity to reason in other fields is due primarily to the way these subjects are usually taught. Systematic abstraction and generalization of the principles, logical processes, and intellectual skills implicit in any competent study of many of these

---

[3] For representative examples of this research, see T. H. Briggs, "Formal English Grammar as a Discipline," *Teachers College Record*, September, 1913, Vol. 14, No. 4; L. W. Kline, "Some Experimental Evidence in Regard to Formal Discipline," *Journal of Educational Psychology*, 1914, Vol. 5, pp. 259–266; E. L. Thorndike and R. S. Woodworth, "The Influence of Improvement in One Mental Function upon the Efficiency of Other Functions," *Psychological Review*, 1901, Vol. 8, pp. 247–261, 384–395, 553–564; W. G. Sleight, "Memory and Formal Training," *British Journal of Psychology*, 1911, Vol. 4, pp. 386–457. Excellent critical summaries of the experiments on transfer of training can be found in C. M. Norem, "Transfer of Training Experiments Revalued," *University of Iowa Studies in Education*, 1933, Vol. VIII, No. 6, pp. 3–55; and P. Sandiford, "Transfer of Training," *Encyclopedia of Educational Research* (First Edition), pp. 1306–1313.

[4] E. L. Thorndike, "Mental Discipline in High School Studies," *Journal of Educational Psychology*, 1924, Vol. 15, pp. 1–22, 83–98.

[5] C. R. Griffith, *An Introduction to Educational Psychology*, pp. 481–484.

subjects would increase both the scope and the amount of transfer to other situations and areas where these principles, procedures, or skills are applicable.[6] This procedure involves a highly significant form of mental discipline. But it is not the kind of mental discipline invoked by the theory that unitary faculties of the mind can be sharpened and strengthened by formal exercise upon the material provided by certain hallowed subjects. It is, on the contrary, a discipline based upon the recognition that—where the material and logical principles, skills, and procedures required in the study of one problem or subject have an application extending beyond the problem or subject in question—the student can, by proper teaching, be given some degree of insight into the circumstances and conditions in which these principles, procedures, and skills possess a wider validity.

Although the tenets of faculty psychology have proved to be untenable in the light of modern psychological knowledge, there is no reason to conclude that principles and procedures learned in one situation will never be used in other situations. Recent psychological investigations have revealed that transfer depends, not upon the existence of abstract and unitary powers in the mind but (1) upon the applicability to two or more situations of similar principles, procedures, and skills and (2) upon teaching procedures that develop in the students both a conscious understanding of these principles, skills, and procedures, and an insight into the kinds of situations in which they are likely to be useful.[7]

2. The "Great Books" Criterion

The disciplinary subjects constitute only one aspect of the humanist's program of secondary education. To the humanist, it is fully as important that the education of the young should include an intensive study of the great classics of Western literature. In its most significant and

[6] P. T. Orata, *The Theory of Identical Elements*. See also C. H. Judd, *Educational Psychology*, pp. 509–514, and M. C. Barlow, "Transfer of Training in Reasoning," *Journal of Educational Psychology*, 1937, Vol. 28, pp. 122–128.

[7] See P. T. Orata, *op. cit.*, for an excellent discussion of the theoretical bases of transfer. A convenient summary of the pertinent facts can be found in Robert S. Woodworth, *Experimental Psychology*, pp. 167–207.

logical form this conception of education rests upon three basic propositions: first, that there exists a body of eternal and absolute truth, valid under all circumstances and conditions; second, that the mastery of these truths constitutes the core of any educational program, in any time or place, since they define not only the great and permanent principles of right and justice but also the major premises in terms of which all empirical, and hence changing, human knowledge must be understood; third, that these truths can best be taught through the study and analysis of the great literary classics, which embody, in their purest form, these fundamental and eternal truths.[8]

In this form the great books criterion needs little discussion since its basic premises have already been considered. The first of these propositions embodies a conception of truth, and of the means by which it is discovered and verified, which has been examined at some length in the preceding discussion of the sources of educational and intellectual authority. With the rejection of the first proposition, the second and third cannot be maintained.

The "Great Books" as the Repository of Human Wisdom

It is possible, however, to hold that the study of the great classics of Western thought properly constitutes the core of general education without espousing the theory of an absolute and eternal truth revealed and verified by man's intuitive and deductive reason. It is possible, in short, to argue simply that these books are classics because they represent the noblest and best thought so far attained in our civilization, and hence that any complete and significant education must include a mastery of them.

Several objections can be urged against this position. It must be observed, however, that one of the most common—the contention that the classics are too difficult for the average student—is by no means decisive. The humanist might, like Irving Babbitt, insist that only a chosen few can really understand the great books. Or he might, with Hutchins, proclaim that, where they are properly taught, the classics can be mastered by the vast majority of the students in our public

---

[8] See Hutchins, *The Higher Learning in America*, pp. 59–119; John T. Foudy, *The Educational Principles of American Humanism*, pp. 10–34; Butts, *A Cultural History of Education*, pp. 599–601; Butts, *The College Charts Its Course*, pp. 269–274, 288–360.

schools. In any case he could argue, correctly, that the unwillingness or inability of lazy or intellectually inferior youth to comprehend the classics, however regrettable it may be, is no reason to assert that education is something that it is not or to deprive the able and industrious student of the opportunity to secure it. The argument from the standpoint of difficulty is relevant and sound only if it can be shown that there are two or more routes—the classics and one or more ways that are easier—to the values inherent in a good educational program.

The pertinent question is whether the study of the classics represents the only way or the best way to those values. The answer to this question will depend to a considerable degree upon the values it is believed education should inculcate and develop. For, quite apart from their theory of truth, most humanists are convinced that the spirit of the western literary tradition is itself the most precious of all education values. This is, in part, a continuation of the ancient ideal of the cultivated and urbane gentleman equally at home in the salon, the study, or the councils of government. As such it is an undemocratic and aristocratic ideal, which regards education as the prerogative and mark of birth, wealth, and talents. But it is more than that. There is also a conviction that mind, character, and taste are best developed through intimate and sustained contact with the great literary products of the past.

Granted that reliable knowledge about material facts can be secured only through scientific investigation, the humanist argues that a true understanding of human values and of the basic principles of right conduct can be acquired only by a rigorous literary discipline. To a considerable degree this is simply a belief that correct thinking in these important matters is a product of the absorption into the personality of the values and principles embedded in the classics—a point which will shortly come in for further discussion. In addition, there is the feeling, not always overtly stated but clearly implied, that human thought, except in the physical sciences, is primarily a literary discipline. The intimate relationship between thought and language is beyond dispute. It is a fact that clear and precise expression in written form is always a mark of clear thinking. It is also a fact, all too frequently neglected in American schools, that rigorous analysis of written arguments is an essential aspect of good intellectual training.

Thinking Involves More than a Linguistic Discipline

Nevertheless, thought is more than a linguistic exercise. For the art of thought is not that of literary expression or of literary vision. Rather, the art of thought is the application of logic and fact to hypotheses derived from the logical implications of systematic theory or from a careful analysis of concrete cases. Practice in the production and analysis of written documents, however important it may be in the development of critical thought, is hardly the whole or even the major part of a program of instruction designed to discipline the student in the habits and methods of good thinking.

Intellectual analysis, moreover, is not identical with literary analysis. In fact, these two types of analyses share in common simply an emphasis upon a clear understanding of an author's meaning. Even in this instance it should be borne in mind that there is frequently a sharp difference between intellectual and literary meaning. Indeed, some literary products of high quality have little or no intellectual meaning. Intellectual meaning is concerned with the logical relations and probable consequences of propositions, whereas literary meaning is often, if not usually, concerned primarily with the symbolic expression, contemplation, and celebration of emotions and attitudes. Intellectual analysis may, and in certain instances must, deal with attitudes and values. But it deals with them in a distinctive mood, that of critical examination and evaluation. Intellectual analysis never deals with attitudes and values in their pure form but as intellectual propositions entailing logical relationships and factual consequences. Literary analysis, on the other hand, is not limited to this mood. All this discussion may mean that art and literature form an essential part of a well-rounded educational program. Who, indeed, has ever denied it? But the discussion also means that there are valid differences between intellectual and literary education.

Finally, it must be noted that the criteria of sound thought and of good literature are by no means identical. The literary merits of Shakespeare's *Macbeth,* for example, are quite independent of the scientific accuracy of the historical and psychological propositions embedded in it. Moreover, the standards of judgment are different. The literary form in which error is expressed may be—as it repeatedly has been—as clear, as beautiful, and as moving as that in which truth is clothed. Nor is literary genius any assurance that the ideas advanced by those who possess it, even in a superlative degree, are valid. For truth is not simply vision; it is vision warranted and tested by logic and fact. As to the cultivation of insight, we have it on the authority of Aristotle, fully confirmed by the subsequent experience of Galileo, that insight is the product of long and patient examination of the facts in a particular area. If the argument of the last few paragraphs is sound, then there would appear to be no solid ground for the contention that a curriculum composed of literary classics offers, in any unique sense, a superior discipline in the habits and methods of thought.

"Great Books" Will Not Build Democratic Character

There remains the contention that the study of the classics is the supreme vehicle for the cultivation of character and taste. This thesis assumes that personality structure is, first of all, a product of literary study—an assumption that is, to say the least, open to question. Even granting that intellectual and literary study mold character and taste, as they certainly do in some degree, there is still the question as to what kind of personality would be built by an educational regimen consisting primarily of the philosophical and literary classics of the past. And here the facts are clear. For, despite notable exceptions, the spirit of the classics is overwhelmingly the spirit of aristocracy; the values they embody and the virtues they inculcate are the values and the virtues of a secure and cultivated ruling class. In its literary form, although by no means always in its concrete historical manifestations, this spirit was that of a humane and enlightened aristocracy; and it was unquestionably the expression of great and noble ideals. But whatever the balance of its virtues (and into the scale must be thrown the squalor, ignorance, and misery that the common man endured for centuries) and whatever the values that may be lost with its passing, the fact remains that the social order out of which this spirit grew, and whose standards it so brilliantly and beautifully formulated, has passed from the stage of history.

A humane and cultivated aristocracy can exist only when its prestige and authority are grounded in common consent. Nowhere in the Western World today are the masses of men prepared to yield that consent. The time has come when the only viable form of aristocracy is that of a totalitarian elite, able and prepared to maintain its position by force and suppression. The world today has no place for an education designed to build humane and cultivated aristocrats. What is now needed is an educational program that will produce democratic character. Many of the virtues and values embedded in the great books, once they are stripped of their aristocratic connotations, will find a significant place in that character. But the tradition in which the education of the future must be grounded is the democratic tradition. While the democratic tradition has now and again found its way into the great books as defined by the humanists, these books are not, as a unified literary tradition, adapted to the development of democratic character. Hence, from the standpoint of personality formation, the objection to the thesis that the classics should provide the core of the curriculum of general education is not that they are too difficult, but that they do not offer a useful vehicle for the development of democratic personalities.

"Great Books" a Poor Gateway to Study of the Present

It is possible to argue that the great books should be utilized for another purpose. There is a sense in which they are, in sober reality, the *great* books; for whatever else they may be they are certainly the outstanding landmarks in the development of Western thought and culture. Is not their study, therefore, the best, if not indeed the only, means by which the student can really understand the conflicts and problems of his own time? The heart of the issue raised by this question is one of focus and emphasis. There is no doubt that the major problems of our time have historical roots, which must be understood before the problems themselves can be fully comprehended. There is considerable doubt, however, that a prolonged study of the literary classics of the past offers the best introduction to an analysis of the problems of the present—and still more doubt that it is a competent substitute for such analysis.

The present is a product not of these classics but of the life out of which they sprang. Their use as the gateway to the present assumes, first, that the great books adequately reflect the major historical forces that shaped the life of the period in which they were written, and, second, that they will be taught in a manner designed primarily to identify and emphasize these forces. The second of these assumptions is by no means always valid, and the truth of the first, to speak bluntly, has not been established. Granted that the classics are the work of genius and that a genius, by definition, is a man who sees more deeply into the problems and spirit of his times than other men. Granted, further, that the list of classics is composed, not simply of the works of genius but of the outstanding works of those geniuses whose writings, in the judgment of subsequent generations, have had the greatest impact on the development of Western culture and thought. Nevertheless, they were written by men who were the product, not only of a particular age but also of a particular class; and by men, moreover, who did not have the benefit of subsequent thought and experience.

Plato and Aristotle were the representatives, not of all Greece but of the aristocratic party in Athens; St. Thomas, of medieval scholasticism as it faced the task of reconciling Aristotle and St. Augustine; John Locke, of the insurgent middle class as it sought to overthrow the aristocracy of nobles and prelates. All these men, like their counterparts in other periods, transcend in some measure the limitations of class and time. But they did not wholly escape them; far from being purely universal geniuses they did not even encompass the whole of the age in which they lived. Nor is this defect adequately corrected by the total balance of the classics.

Certainly the list of great books, as presented, overemphasizes the ancient and the medieval as against the modern in the weighing of moral and intellectual significance; the aristocratic as against the democratic in tone and in economic and social, if not in political, theory; the intellectual and the literary as against the economic and the social in the interpretation of human thought and action; the idealistic as against the realistic and the pragmatic in philosophical and ethical thought; the logical and the a priori as against the experimental and the empirical in methodological discussion and procedure; and the static as against the dynamic, both in the delineation of human nature and in the analysis of history.

These biases, moreover, are as inherent in the criterion employed as they are in the predilections of those who selected the lists. Many of the significant forces that have shaped the contours of the modern world have not found expression in the literary landmarks of the past. They must be discovered, if they exist at all in literary form, in the forgotten manuscripts of the dispossessed or the half-articulate protests of the submerged. More often they must be carefully reconstructed, piece by piece, from the dusty and sober records of government, countinghouse, shop, and farm. If the present is to be understood through the past, a strong case can be made for the proposition that the works of modern historical scholars offer a better and more inclusive instrument than the great books.

Finally, in so far as the purpose of study is an understanding of the problems and issues of the present day, there is a question of methodology as well as of content. Two considerations are important here. Pedagogically, the study of the present by means of the classics represents, in an extreme form, an abstract and bookish procedure of doubtful validity for the great majority of students. It is at this point, of course, that the full weight of the argument of difficulty considered above becomes pertinent and significant. For the approach to the present through the great books of the past places a heavy and unnecessary premium on a type of intelligence and interest possessed, in a high degree, only by a tiny minority of students. It may be granted that this minority will, for the most part, provide the scholars of tomorrow. Nevertheless, the fact remains that the insistence that important issues and problems be studied exclusively, or even primarily, by a prolonged preoccupation with the literary products of the past, means that millions will be denied this component of an adequate general education. Nor can it be said that they would be denied in any case. For it is a fact that many who lack the highly specialized interest and ability required to master the literary tradition can, by a more concrete and direct approach, achieve a general understanding of the problems and issues that affect their daily lives.

Moreover, there is ample reason to question the thesis that, even for those students endowed with a higher order of abstract verbal intelligence, a study of the literary products of the past offers, from a methodological standpoint, the best approach to the comprehension and examination of the problems and issues of the present. Each age sees the past through its own glasses; here, in fact, is the primary meaning of the familiar statement that the historical record is rewritten in each generation. This is particularly true when, as the case is now, man is passing through one of the great transition periods of history. The reason behind this phenomenon is that only a particular type of scholar is interested in the past for its own sake. The concern of most men is with the past as it bears upon the present. This means, of course, that functional history is always selective in terms of the interests and problems of a particular period. The classics of literary tradition were not written from the standpoint of the concerns and issues of today but of other days and generations.

A measure of truth may be granted to the contention that the great books are classics because they deal with persistent problems of permanent interest to mankind. But if this is true at all, it is true only in a very general sense. In detail—and generalizations are of a very abstract order indeed without a considerable degree of detail—these problems, as they appear in the classics, were worked out under different circumstances and conditions by men who cherished not only different conceptions of man and of society but also different aspirations and fears. Consequently, with respect to the element of universality in the classics—an element not nearly so pervasive as it is sometimes assumed to be—the student is confronted with a diversity, within identity, which can be very suggestive to the mature and discriminating mind. But it is extremely misleading both to the immature mind and to the mind that is so impressed by identity that it is unable to grasp the crucial significance of diversity.

Study of Traditions Not a Substitute for Study of Current Problems

All of this does not mean that the intellectual tradition of the Western World has no relevance to the problems of modern man. But it does mean that a study of the tradition cannot be substituted for a study of those problems in their concrete reality. It is within the context of such a study that the intellectual tradition, and history itself, find their import and function. As far as the tradition is concerned, that function is one of a vast and rich storehouse of intellectual and moral resources, to which men can turn for inspiration and suggestion.

It is significant that this is precisely the method utilized, on the intellectual side at least, by the authors of the classics. Plato, Aristotle, St. Thomas, Locke, and Darwin, for example, were neither the curators nor the preceptors of ancient doctrines. On the contrary, they were creative thinkers seeking satisfactory solutions for pressing problems and conflicts of their day and generation. As such they did not ignore the tradition, but neither did they mirror it. For in every case the essential task of these thinkers has been to reconstruct the tradition in the light of the problems, the conflicts, and the conditions with which they, and the society of their time, were confronted. In this very fact lie both their primary significance in the history of human thought and their greatest contribution to the solution of one of the cardinal educational problems of the current world.

The induction of the young into the culture of their society is, in every age, the fundamental office of education. In a democratic system, this office requires the instruction of youth in the problems and the conflicts, as well as in the common beliefs and patterns of conduct, of their society. And in our time, as in the time of Plato and Aristotle, the time of St. Thomas Aquinas, and the time of John Locke, the reconstitution of the common sense of mankind defines one of the central moral and intellectual problems—and, hence, a central educational problem. The restoration of order and clarity, in education no less than in society, requires something more than recapitulation. It requires, to be sure, a knowledge of the tradition, but of the tradition in relationship to the problems, the conflicts, and the conditions of the modern world. This knowledge cannot be secured from a curriculum composed in major part of a study of the classics. At an appropriate level of intellectual maturity and capacity, a meticulous examination of great books, ancient or modern, that bear in a significant way on an important current issue, may indeed illuminate the path of reconstruction. But it does not constitute that path.

The Importance of Tradition, History, and Theory

Accordingly, a curriculum based solely, or even primarily, on the classics is inadequate, whether it is viewed from the standpoint of the development of intellectual capacity, of the molding of character and taste, or of the induction of the young into the spirit and the problems of their society. In adopting this conclusion, however, it is essential to guard against the narrow immediacy that is today the hallmark of a shallow but popular cult, that of the "practical man." For, whether the cult finds its expression in the disregard of history or in the scorn of theory, it is the herald of a superficial and inadequate educational system. The institutions, the beliefs, the conflicts, and the problems of the present have their roots in the relevant past, and their import cannot be fully grasped apart from an examination of these roots. The fact that history can be a mere series of more or less interesting anecdotes strung on a chronological string, or a pedantic preoccupation with concerns of the past, must not be allowed to obscure the fact that it is, when properly utilized, an indispensable tool in the analysis and comprehension of the present.

It is even more important to understand the role of theory and of theoretical analysis in the educational program. All practice is, consciously or unconsciously, based on theory. Blind and unintelligent practice, therefore, is in every age the price of ignorance or neglect in the realm of theory. In a period compelled, by the inexorable march of rapid and profound technological change, to reconstitute both its institutional structure and its pattern of common sense, the neglect of theory is but the prelude to disaster. Moreover, it is the death of morality. For it is the essence of such periods that traditional morality, however valid its basic premises may be, is no longer adequate in many of its details. Whatever else morality may be, it is the working out in practice of a theory of human relationships.

Apart from the philosophical questions raised by the humanist's position, the issues posed by the great books criterion are, as stated above, issues of focus, of proportion, and of educational method. On all these counts the great books criterion has been found to be inadequate. These books cannot, therefore, constitute the curriculum. But they are a part of the vast cultural resources upon which the school can draw. They are, almost without exception, distinguished literary products; in many instances they are, as historical documents, parts of the relevant past; and in certain instances they furnish classical statements of significant theoretical positions, which are directly pertinent to issues with which the school must deal. Whether, and at what point, they are utilized for these purposes is primarily a pedagogical matter—a matter of pertinency, of relative adequacy and availability, and of intellectual maturity and capacity. Judged by these standards, it is fair to say that they are, in general, useful only with relatively advanced students.

But the important point in the context of the present discussion is that students, within the limits of their capacity, maturity, and interest, do need to read good literature; they do need to explore the relevant past in connection with their study of the present; and they do need to analyze, as rigorously as possible, vigorous and able statements of the various theoretical positions pertinent to the issues and problems they are studying.

3. Child Interest and Need as the Criterion of Content

A third position finds the criterion of curriculum content in the needs and interests of the child. Learning, from this point of view, is a matter of personal growth, which proceeds best (if indeed it proceeds at all on any other basis) where the activities of the pupil are vitally engaged in the learning process. This involvement can occur only as the learning itself is related to the needs and the interests of the learner.

The thesis that felt needs and interests of the pupil constitute the criterion of curriculum content stems, of course, from the child-centered school of educational thought. The fundamental strengths and weaknesses of this position have been indicated in preceding chapters. It is necessary, at this point, to call attention to the fact that every criterion of curriculum content implies some conception of educational purpose. The purpose espoused by the child-centered school is the maximum development of human personality. That objective is sound in a democratic system of education.

The difficulty with felt needs and interests as the measure of curriculum content is that this criterion assumes that growth and development are inherently individual affairs. In the child-centered position there is a strong tincture of the Froebelian notion that growth is an unfolding of latent inner capacities, which define their own ends. But, as has been previously noted, the growth of human personality is a social affair. It occurs in a social context, and the standards of desirable development are, in the last analysis, social standards. The felt needs and interests of the individual indicate the existing character of the personality, but they do not, in and of themselves, indicate desirable directions of growth and development. Consequently, since curriculum content is a significant aspect of the means of growth, and since ends and means are always correlative, felt needs and interests alone cannot serve as the criterion of content.

Nevertheless, felt needs and interests do furnish one of the criteria of content. For it is the function of means to mediate between the existing state of affairs and the desired future state of affairs. Effective means are always selected with reference both to the present status and to the end in view. Hence, there is a substantial element of truth in the child-centered school's contention that learning should always be rooted in the needs and interests of the learner.

Moreover, there is a sense in which the needs and interests of the individual afford clues for the determination, in the concrete, of the ends and purposes of education. A democratic system of education, particularly in a divided and confused society, dares not ignore the common, but neither can it neglect the personal. Men exist in a system of social relationships by virtue of which they attain the status of human personalities. Needs and interests are shaped by cultural forces, satisfied by social means in a given social context, and judged by socially derived standards. Yet there is a sense in which they are intensely personal; they are the needs and interests of a particular personality. Despite their social base they are in some measure unique, especially in a highly complex and diverse culture.

Democratic respect for personality, and the security of society alike, demand that the school concern itself with these needs and interests in their personal and unique aspect. In so far as these needs and interests represent something more than passing whims and fancies, they must be satisfied if healthy and integrated personalities are to emerge from the educative process. This does not mean, of course, that the school must tolerate, much less foster, anti-social behavior. Nor does it mean that needs and interests must be satisfied in precisely the form in which they appear at any given moment. But it does mean that needs and interests cannot safely be ignored and that repression alone is never adequate. The individual must be shown how to satisfy his needs and interests in socially desirable ways.

A democratic society requires—and by virtue of its basic ideals must foster—the unique as well as the common in its citizens. The development of the common is the essential condition of any ordered society; and an ordered society is an essential condition of healthy and integrated personalities. This aspect of education is fundamental at any time, but it is particularly crucial in a period of crisis and confusion. A rich and varied culture demands the cultivation of unique talents and interests. To the extent that it is democratic, this cultivation of the unique must embrace, within the limits set by original nature, all men alike. Indeed, in the last analysis, the democratic faith is not simply a belief that each man should and can participate in the common decisions and activities of society. It is also a conviction that each person can and should contribute something to the total life of society that only he is able to contribute.

Consequently, if the needs and interests of the individual learner are not a sufficient criterion of curriculum content, they are a necessary criterion. For they define the present status of the learner's personality and hence one of the poles of the educational process. Furthermore, they are a factor in the definition of the ends and purposes of education in its personal and unique aspect. Finally, they are a central factor in the determination of the standards by which the quality of education, in the public school and in other institutional arrangements of society, must be judged. For whatever else the criteria of a good educational and social system may involve, they must, in a democratic society, include the development and satisfaction of the needs and interests of human beings.

4. *Content Defined by the Great Research Disciplines*

A fourth measure of curriculum content—by all odds the most pervasive and influential in American educational practice, if not in American educational theory—has been found in the great research disciplines, such as history, mathematics, and physics, into which scientific scholarship in the modern world has been divided. Asserting that education is simply the imparting of knowledge and that the research disciplines offer the only reservoir of organized and verified knowledge, the adherents of this standard insist that the problem of what to teach has already been determined. To be sure, selection is necessary, since the total body of any science is too great for any schoolboy to master. But the principles upon which selection must be made are determined by the order of sequence and importance implicit in the logic of the subject itself. The task of the curriculum worker consists of the preparation of this material for teaching purposes. Aside from a thorough knowledge of the subject, the proper performance of his task is primarily a matter of pedagogical method and of grade placement; and even in these aspects of curriculum construction the inherent logic and order of the subject is at least as decisive as the facts of child psychology.

Many educators, including those who regard revelation and intuition as authentic ways of knowing, would not accept the thesis that the research disciplines are the sole repository of systematic and tested knowledge. From the standpoint of the position assumed in this text, however, there is no reason to quarrel with the contention that the research disciplines are the source of all systematic and tested knowledge. Nevertheless, the view that the content of the research disciplines—or rather a simplified and summarized version of that content—properly constitutes the curriculum of the public school, is questionable. The dissemination of knowledge, although a part of education, is by no means its essence. Fundamentally, education is the formation of character and personality. It is within this process that the acquisition of knowledge finds its importance and significance. The notion that education consists of the mastery of subject matter is seriously defective even on the intellectual side; for the attitudes and the methodology appropriate to the scientific enterprise are, at the very least, fully as important as the accumulated findings of the various sciences.

Order of Exposition Not the Order of Learning

Even if it were true that the imparting of knowledge comprised the substance of education, it would not necessarily follow that the organized subject matter of the various research disciplines should constitute the curriculum of the schools. For, as indicated in Chapter 11, it does not follow that the logic and sequence of learning is necessarily identical with the logic and sequence of exposition.

Problems of the Citizen Not Identical with Problems of the Scholar

Moreover, it does not follow that the sequence appropriate to the problems of the research specialist is necessarily identical with the sequence appropriate to the citizen. The organizational pattern adopted by the research disciplines was designed for a definite and highly specialized purpose. The scholar's problem is primarily intellectual, the discovery and verification of further knowledge. He has accordingly organized his material in a way calculated to promote inquiry in a particular area of human knowledge—ideally, in such a way that each proposition is derived from other propositions and leads to still other propositions. The very existence of subjects is due to this enterprise. There are no subjects save as scholarly abstractions useful in inquiry. For the purposes for which it was intended, this organization, especially in the physical sciences, is unquestionably one of the most brilliant achievements of man. The fact remains that it is an organization adapted to the specialized problems of the research scholar.

The problems of the man and the citizen, on the other hand, are practical problems. As such they are primarily concerned, not with the discovery of knowledge but with the making of decisions and the formulation of policy. Accordingly, material must be organized on the basis of the relationship between ends and means, rather than on the basis of the logical relationships between propositions. This does not mean, of course, that practical judgments do not involve the use of propositions or that they can ignore with impunity the demands of logic. But the focus of the practical judgment is the working out of a solution of a practical problem. The difference, therefore, is that between the organization of material appropriate to the development of a systematic body of theoretical knowledge and the organization of material appropriate to the application of knowledge to the control of some practical human enterprise. In the first case, the logical relationship between propositions properly supplies the basic principle of organization. But, in the second case, it is the end or purpose that provides the controlling principle.

Largely as a result of this difference in focus, the issues arising in the exercise of the practical judgment almost invariably cut across the boundaries of the research disciplines. Thus the control of atomic energy, to take a single example, is a moral, economic, and political as well as a physical and chemical problem. It is important to note, however, that it is a single problem with many facets rather than an additive cluster of many separate and distinct problems—a generic characteristic which, *mutatis mutandis,* is present, to a greater or lesser extent, in almost all practical problems. Consequently, the research disciplines, with their deliberate concentration on the theoretical problems within a specific field of intellectual inquiry, are not equipped, individually or collectively, to deal with such questions. From the standpoint of practical problems the research disciplines represent indispensable sources of relevant principles and data, but they do not provide ready-made answers or solutions.

Finally, the problems of the man—and to an even greater extent those of the citizen—typically involve significant human relationships. They are concerned, in a unique sense, with human values and attitudes. Psychology, ethics, and the social sciences deal with values and attitudes. But, except for clinical psychology, they deal with them as intellectual abstractions. The practical judgment, however, must deal with values and attitudes in their concrete form, as they are embodied in particular individuals and groups. Hence the solution of practical problems frequently, if not usually, entails the reconstruction of personalities. In part, of course, this is a pedagogical matter. But it is also a methodological affair in a broader sense. For the solution of a practical problem involving vital human relationships is never an affair of logic and fact alone. On the contrary it is always, in part, an affair of conflict, of adjustment and compromise and, at its best, of a persistent search for consensus. Where these processes go on peaceably, they proceed by means of group discussion and interpersuasion employing a methodology different, in certain crucial respects, from the strictly logico-experimental method of the research disciplines. But it requires a no less rigorous discipline—a discipline that cannot be acquired in schools where the consideration of practical problems finds no place in the curriculum.

Education Not Mastery of Information

The advocates of a curriculum composed of elementary and condensed reproductions of the contents of the various research disciplines ignore these distinctions between the problems of the scholar and the problems of the man and the citizen. Consequently, they have confused general education with a summation of elementary courses selected from the various scholarly disciplines. And they have often confused verbal mastery of propositions embodying information with functional and meaningful knowledge. Accordingly, a compartmentalized and multi-headed curriculum—consisting, in practice, of a thin and truncated copy of the education appropriate to the training of research scholars in the various areas of intellectual specialization—has been substituted for a curriculum designed to create intelligent and wholesome personalities.

The premise upon which the criterion of research disciplines rests is the notion that general education consists of an encyclopedic mastery of scholarly information. A moment's reflection will reveal the fatal error in this position. For, entirely apart from the false pedagogical assumption that the acquisition of information ultimately produces intelligent thinking, it is obvious that the bulk of scholarly erudition has now become so great that no man can hope to comprehend it adequately. A modicum of knowledge in selected fields is the most that can be expected. Unfortunately, as the advocates of the subject curriculum are constantly insisting, even this limited and circumscribed goal is not usually achieved. The fact of the matter is that the vast majority of pupils cannot and will not learn in this way. They could, of course, be compelled to work harder by more vigorous teaching—provided that they did not drop out of school.

Presumably, if pushed harder, the majority of students would be able to pass stiffer examinations and might even be able to recall a considerable proportion of the learned material in later years. It is highly doubtful, however, that the information so acquired would be translated into genuine knowledge. Only in exceptional instances would students pursue any subject long enough to acquire the habits, the methods, or the outlook of scholarship. On the other hand, the information they absorbed, since they did not learn it in the context of practical problems, would rarely be functional in their daily lives. In part, of course, this would be the result of their failure to comprehend the practical implications of their verbal formulas—which is merely another way of saying that they did not really comprehend them at all. But it would also be due to the fact that the modicum of knowledge, in each of the various disciplines, to which they had been exposed was too fragmentary and compartmentalized to be really usable in the solution of practical problems. Even under a stern and unyielding discipline, the subject curriculum, in the usual case, would produce neither fish nor fowl, neither trained scholar nor intelligent citizen. And it would, as any child psychologist can testify, exact in direct proportion to the rigor of the discipline a high price in terms of the personality and mental health of the child.

It is important to note that it is not hard work nor even the discipline that is at fault here. Children thrive on hard work, the harder the better, provided it is within the limits of their capacity and is undertaken with due regard to their health and other concerns of child growth and development. They can also take discipline, provided that it is, in some measure, a self-imposed discipline. The difficulty here is that a stern external discipline is employed to compel children to learn material that they do not comprehend and that has, in terms they can grasp, very few roots in their daily lives.

▶ *Following Up*
This Chapter

1. With the aid of a small group of classmates, try to construct a course of study for high school students based upon the disciplinary conception of the curriculum. In this connection you will probably want to consider the following questions: What is meant by the disciplinary subjects? Why do the adherents of this theory believe that these subjects should constitute the heart of the curriculum? What conceptions of mind and of learning lie back of the disciplinary theory?

2. Secure from the library a list of the great books used at St. John's College. Note the books on the list that you have read, and look through some of the others. On what ground do the adherents of the great books criterion claim that the study of these books constitutes the most important

part of general education? To what extent, if at all, is the great books theory of the curriculum justified?

3. Work out, with the assistance of a small group of your classmates, the kind of teacher training curriculum you would set up provided you were free to outline a course of study based squarely on your own felt needs and interests. Compare this program with the teacher training course used in your own school, as well as with those of several other institutions whose catalogues are available to you through your library. As you examine these curriculums, what strengths and weaknesses do you see in your own proposal?

4. How do you understand the distinction between the problems of the specialized research scholar and the problems of the citizen? Formulate several problems of each type.

5. In not more than four sentences each, state the heart of each of the four criteria of curriculum content explored in this chapter.

▶ Suggested
Reading

1. Harold Rugg's *Foundations for American Education* (pages 605–718) provides an indispensable background of criticism, evaluation, and principle for the study and discussion of the issues raised in this and the next two chapters. Samuel Everett (Editor), *A Challenge to Secondary Education* projects several plans, prepared by various educational leaders, for a new type of secondary school curriculum. The concluding chapter (pages 339–353) is devoted to a statement of the major challenges and issues emerging from an analysis of these plans. Stephen M. Corey et al., *General Education in the American High School* (pages 82–104) contains a good discussion by Gordon Mackenzie of some of the emerging curriculum concepts that are challenging the older notions of the proper subject matter of education. Specific examples of such curriculums used in various schools throughout the United States are available in Harold Spears, *The Emerging High School Curriculum* (pages 73–320) and in Samuel Everett (Editor), *The Community School*. The latter book also contains a chapter (pages 435–462) calling the attention to some of the curriculum issues growing out of the community school program.

Hollis L. Caswell and Doak S. Campbell, *Curriculum Development* (pages 248–290) and John K. and Mary A. Norton, *Foundations of Cur-*

riculum Building (pages 24–91) set forth some of the major issues and approaches involved in the selection of curriculum content. Interesting and valuable discussions of clashing points of view with respect to the kind of subject matter that public schools should emphasize will be found in R. Freeman Butts, *The College Charts Its Course,* pages 253–416; John S. Brubacher, *Modern Philosophies of Education,* pages 245–268, 278–308; John S. Brubacher, *A History of the Problems of Education,* pages 249–317; and J. Paul Leonard, *Developing the Secondary School Curriculum,* pages 73–168, 245–285. The Staff of Division I, Teachers College, Columbia University, *Readings in the Foundations of Education* (pages 523–588) and Hollis L. Caswell and Doak S. Campbell, *Readings in Curriculum Development* (pages 152–176, 269–332, 410–456) contain important and fairly extended statements culled from the work of leading educators representative of different points of view with respect to principles that should govern the selection of curriculum content.

2. The disciplinary criterion of subject matter selection, in the form in which it is now debated in American educational circles, has been stated and advocated by Robert M. Hutchins in *The Higher Learning in America,* pages 59–87. Boyd Bode's *How We Learn* (pages 82–106) outlines and criticizes the doctrine of formal discipline. Arthur I. Gates et al., *Educational Psychology* (pages 504–542) summarizes the verdict of modern psychology on the disciplinary theory, together with the evidence upon which that verdict is based.

3. Mark Van Doren's *Liberal Education* (pages 71–168) and Robert M. Hutchins' *The Higher Learning in America* (pages 59–87) eloquently present the case for the great books criterion. Boyd Bode's *How We Learn* (pages 36–82) both states and criticizes the classical conception of education from which the great books criterion is derived. Harry Gideonse, *The Higher Learning in a Democracy* offers a sharp repudiation of Hutchins' educational theories.

Defenses of the classical tradition in education are available in Irving Babbitt, *Literature and the American College* and *Democracy and Leadership;* Norman Foerster, *The Future of the Liberal College* and *The American State University;* Paul Elmer More, *On Being Human;* Everett D. Martin, *The Meaning of a Liberal Education;* and John T. Foudy, *The Educational Principles of American Humanism.*

4. The general theory upon which child interest as the criterion of curriculum content is based has been ably stated in William H. Kilpatrick, *Remaking the Curriculum;* William H. Kilpatrick, *Foundations of Method,* pages 1–216; and Harold Rugg and Ann Shumaker, *The Child-Centered*

School. Description and examples of educational programs built on this criterion are obtainable in a large number of books on the curriculum, especially those dealing with the elementary school. Among these sources may be mentioned the Rugg and Shumaker book just cited; Harold Alberty, *Reorganizing the High School Curriculum,* pages 119–149; J. Murray Lee and Dorris May Lee, *The Child and His Curriculum,* pages 62–132; and Freeman Glenn Macomber, *Guiding Child Development in the Elementary School,* pages 1–92, 304–318. For longer treatments the student may consult Lois Coffey Mossman, *The Activity Concept* and Robert Hill Lane et al., *The Progressive Elementary School.*

5. The best statement of the theory behind the research discipline conception of the curriculum has been made by Howard E. Wilson in *The Fusion of Social Studies in Junior High Schools.* All of this penetrating study is excellent for the purpose, but pages 168–190 are especially pertinent and useful. You might wish to consult also the chapters by Guy Thomas Buswell and Ben A. Sueltz in the National Council of Teachers of Mathematics, *16th Yearbook,* 1941, "Arithmetic in General Education," pages 8–44; and James L. Mursell, *Developmental Teaching,* pages 1–29. Harold Alberty's *Reorganizing the High School Curriculum* (pages 95–118) provides a brief but good analysis of the arguments for and against the subject-centered curriculum. The report of the Harvard Committee on the Objectives of General Education in a Free Society, *General Education in a Free Society* (pages 103–176) offers a good defense of the subject curriculum. Finally, Boyd H. Bode's penetrating chapter on the logical and psychological organization of subject matter, in his *Modern Educational Theories* (pages 43–72), is at least as favorable to the claims of the research disciplines as it is to the activity program.

Chapter 25

Criteria of Content:
Theories Based upon
Sociological Analysis

AN IMPORTANT GROUP of theories undertakes to find the test of curriculum content in some aspect of social reality. Like the humanistic position, these theories, with one possible exception, assert that the curriculum is grounded in the nature of things. The pertinent question, therefore, as the ablest exponent of one of them has repeatedly said, is what the curriculum actually is, not what it ought to be.[1] But since these theories, again with one possible exception, assume that the adaptation of the young to the social order is the primary task of the school, they may be regarded as squarely in the society-centered tradition.

1. *The Curriculum Determined by Analysis of Current Social Practice*

The first, and in many respects the simplest, of these theories rests on the thesis that social efficiency, in terms of the existing social order, defines the objective of education. Accordingly, the adherents of this

---

[1] H. C. Morrison, *The Curriculum of the Common School,* pp. 17–18.

point of view—job analysis—take current social practice as the measure of curriculum content.

The job of the curriculum maker, according to this theory, is first, to discover exactly what functions the adult citizen is expected to perform; second, to ascertain precisely what attitudes, information, and skills are involved in the best existing performances of these functions; and, third, to develop, with due regard to maturation and abilities of children, a graded curriculum designed to produce the indicated attitudes, knowledge, and skills.

It would not be fair to say, as certain critics of job analysis have said, that the effect, if not the purpose, of the curriculum theory proposed by the job analysts would be to freeze existing practices. On the contrary, it would in effect, as in purpose, improve society by substituting best practice for average practice. But it is fair to say that it assumes the essential structure of the existing social order. In this sense the controlling thesis of job analysis is to accept in principle but improve in detail—to do better that which we are already doing.

The job analysis theory of curriculum construction has also been accused of a narrow utilitarianism, which ignores spiritual and cultural values, and of an atomistic and mechanistic conception of learning, which conflicts with the findings of modern organismic psychology. Both of these criticisms are probably justified, as applied to certain formulations of this theory, but they are not necessarily applicable to the theory itself. Job analysis is essentially a theory of curriculum determination, not a statement of the methodology of teaching. Organismic as well as atomistic conceptions of learning could find shelter beneath its wing. Moreover, to the extent that spiritual and cultural values are actually embedded in the best practices of society, the job analyst will, if he is true to his basic principle, take full account of them in his work. In theory at least, job analysis can be charged with ignoring only those cultural and spiritual values that are in no way reflected in current social practice.

The primary objection to the job analyst's interpretation of the curriculum is that it is not adapted to the requirements of a society caught in the grip of social changes which penetrate to the level of the institutional and ideological structure of society. For this reason those who believe that the United States, in common with the rest of the civilized world, is passing through a transitional era, will not find in job analysis an adequate test of curriculum content.

2. The Curriculum Defined by Universal, Fundamental, and Comprehensive Institutions

In a second and more fundamental form, the belief that the measure of curriculum content is to be found in society itself eventuates in a curriculum theory that, for want of a better term, may be called "social evolutionism." [2] According to this view, at least in so far as Morrison's formulation is taken as representative of it, the curriculum consists of the study of the universal, comprehensive, and fundamental institutions which make up the fabric of all progressive civilizations.[3] Since these institutions are present in all progressive societies, the curriculum is universal and constant. This statement, however, will be grossly misunderstood unless several significant distinctions are carefully noted. These institutions will not be found in all societies but only in those societies in the main trunk-line of social evolution—that is, in those societies whose institutions have been fruitful of further growth rather than stagnant or abortive. Moreover, it is the institutions themselves that are universal, rather than the particular form they take in a given society. Government, to take a single example, is present in all progressive societies, but the particular form or type taken by this institution will vary with different societies.

Finally, the curriculum must not be confused with the course of study. The curriculum denotes that which is to be learned; the course of study is the sequence of courses by which the learnings are secured. The curriculum is universal and constant, but the course of study will vary both with the form universal institutions take in a given society and with the pedagogical knowledge and practice in that society. Behind this conception of the curriculum lies a theory of society, grounded in the social psychology of Wilhelm Wundt and the sociology of Her-

[2] The term is borrowed from Justman's work. See Joseph Justman, *Theories of Secondary Education in the United States*, pp. 22–32.

[3] See Morrison, *The Curriculum of the Common School*, pp. 1–35, for a brief but excellent statement of this position. A more elaborate exposition may be found in his *Basic Principles of Education*.

bert Spencer and William Graham Sumner, but ultimately resting on an extension to social reality of Darwin's principles of biological evolution.

Particular social orders or societies, according to this theory, are going concerns based upon common estimates and expectations. These expectations and estimates are the folkways and the mores hammered out in the daily processes of group life. They are reinforced, and enforced, by those modes of group behavior that we call customs. In time, certain folkways, mores, and customs cluster about one of their number in such a way as to form an organized and rational system of social behavior and belief. Such integrated intelligible systems, of course, are institutions. Hence institutions always represent refined and tested crystallizations of human experience.

Universal institutions have successfully met another test—they have developed in every society that can be placed in the mainstream of social evolution. It must be noted that this testing is both historical and rational. Universal institutions have emerged and survived in every progressive society. But they are intelligible—that is to say, when they are studied, it is possible to see why they are an essential element in the life of a progressive society. Universal institutions are right, but not because they have survived. They have survived because they are right. Finally, the civilized person is one who has mastered the art of living with others in harmony and co-operation. But since the universal institutions are, in every progressive society, the means of co-operative life, the civilized person is one "who is in possession of the universal institutions of his time." [4]

The social structure, of course, is a product of learning; but the learning involved in the formulation of folkways, mores, customs, and institutions is social rather than individual learning. It follows not the rational method of thought, but the method of social evolution—variation, selection, transmission, and survival. The conscious deliberate instruction of the individual, on the other hand, consists of his induction into the ways of society. Accordingly, education may be defined as the absorption, into the individual's personality, of the arts, the sciences, and the moral attitudes that make up the fabric of civilization—in short, the mastery of the universal institutions.

[4] H. C. Morrison, *The Curriculum of the Common School* (Chicago: University of Chicago Press; 1940), pp. 17–18.

Universal Institutions Formal and Abstract

Obviously this theory can be criticized in several ways. The universal institutions to which it points may have some basis in fact. A number of able anthropologists, among them Clark Wissler, have identified a universal pattern of human cultures not unlike Morrison's list of universal institutions.[5] However, these institutions are not the concrete institutional forms found in any actual society, but abstract and formalized categories. They are universal only in this formalized and abstract sense. Consequently, to speak of a universal and constant curriculum based upon a study of universal institutions means simply that there are universal, but abstract and formal, categories under which the concrete content of instruction may everywhere be organized. Such rubrics, however useful they may be in the organization of the curriculum, do not define the actual subject matter of instruction. Children cannot learn language or ethics in general; they must learn some specific system of language or ethics. Nor can they, while life remains relatively brief, learn all possible systems. Morrison, of course, recognized this; it is, in part, the reason for his distinction between the curriculum and the course of study.

Nevertheless, the fact remains that the curriculum worker needs some criterion or principle by which he may select the concrete material of instruction. In the formal sense no such criterion is offered by the social evolutionists. Actually, however, they both imply and utilize such a principle. The concrete content of education, as they envision it, consists of the principles, skills, and attitudes embodied in the particular forms assumed by the universal institutions in the society served by the school, supplemented by such other forms as time and estimated importance indicate. While this shift does provide a definite criterion, it also entails a surrender of the universality and rationality upon which the validity of the curriculum, according to this theory, ultimately rests. The particular form taken by the universal institutions in a given society is not itself universal, nor can it be said to be an essential prerequisite to civilized existence. It has, of course, met the test of survival. And, it can be said, except in a seriously disintegrated society, to be right and good in the sense that it is sanctioned by the mores.

[5] Clark Wissler, *Man and Culture*, pp. 73–97.

The erection of sheer survival in a given society into a sufficient criterion of validity, however, conflicts with the obvious fact that not all survivals are good. It also involves an ethical relativity and a deification of particular existences, both of which are quite foreign to Morrison's thought. It is, indeed, tantamount to an assertion that whatever is, is right for that culture. This thesis, of course, is open to serious objections in any society. But it is patently fatal in a society whose basic problems arise from the fact that it is undergoing rapid and profound social change. Morrison can establish a case for the universality of certain human institutions—but only at the price of an order of abstraction that renders them practically useless to the curriculum worker in determination of the actual content of education. Put another way, his distinction between the curriculum and the course of study reduces the former to a mere system of empty and formal rubrics, since the concrete stuff of education is a property of the latter.

At best, his constant and universal curriculum based upon universal institutions tells us simply that government, language, and mathematics, for example, are necessary elements of the program of studies. It does not tell us what language is to be studied, how it is to be studied, or, since not everything known about any language can be learned by all, what aspects or portions of the chosen language are to be selected for inclusion in the common curriculum. In short, it leaves all of the major problems of curriculum content unanswered.

Inadequate Notion of the Common

The formal and abstract character of Morrison's universal institutions points to the second, and perhaps the most crucial, of the major defects in his curriculum theory. The social evolutionists are, correctly, concerned about the development and maintenance of a common orientation. Indeed, like the humanists, they insist upon the common to the practical exclusion of individual needs and interests. The common orientation, however, according to Morrison's theory, is to be attained by assimilation into the personality of the learner, through the study of universal institutions, of the arts, sciences, and moral attitudes comprising the fabric of civilization. Moreover, Morrison specifically states that there can be only one civilization on this planet.[6]

6 Morrison, *The Curriculum of the Common School,* pp. 17–18.

Unfortunately, perhaps, for the world in a period of threatening atomic warfare, Morrison is mistaken at this point. The art of peaceful co-operation, which Morrison terms civilization, rests, as he has correctly indicated, upon common estimates and expectations. And common estimates and expectations depend, not upon formal and abstract universal institutions, but upon the mores, customs, and operating institutions in a particular society. Consequently there are as many civilizations as there are cultures—a conclusion confirmed by the tragic cleavages and conflicts in the contemporary world.

These cleavages cannot be bridged by a curriculum based upon universal institutions. In the first place, the issues that divide the globe do not concern institutions in their universal aspect. No one questions the necessity or validity of government, of ethics, or of economics in the abstract. What divides men is the nature of these institutions and the ends they are to serve. In the second place, the concrete material of education—the course of study—is, as already pointed out, primarily the particular form the universal institutions assume in a given society. In actual practice, therefore, an educational system based upon the social-evolutionist theory of the curriculum is an education adapted to the civilization of a particular culture rather than to a universal civilization embracing all peoples and all creeds.

Furthermore, there is but little reason to suppose that, in a period of crisis and partial disintegration, such a system of education would develop effectively an uncoerced consensus at the national level. Common estimates and expectations are, at bottom, the product of a common way of life. Men always disagree in detail, and this is particularly true where intellectual and political freedom is found in conjunction with a plastic and changing society. Such disagreements are stimulating as long as they occur within a framework of fundamental agreement.

Prolonged and bitter disagreement about fundamentals, however, leads to a type of noncommunal conflict that threatens to disrupt society. Wherever such differences appear it means, first, that institutions are no longer working well, and, second, that men are so differently related to these institutions that deep cleavages have occurred in the character of their experience. Under such circumstances the restoration of consensus demands both the reconstruction of the institutional structure and the re-establishment of a common way of life. Neither of these objectives, however, is fostered by an educational system confined to the assimilation of the intellectual and moral attitudes appropriate to the historical institutional forms that have dominated the society in the past. Such a system ignores the underlying causes of the difficulty, and amounts, in effect if not in intent, to a defense of the *status quo*. Consequently it tends, not toward an uncoerced restoration of consensus, but toward a multiplication of confusion from which only extreme and violent solutions of the social crisis can profit.

Consider, for example, instruction in language. Here, at first sight, is a neutral and highly important bond the possession of which should go far to bind together diverse factions. A common language not only means a common literary heritage; it means also a common instrument of understanding and discussion—and so it is, within certain limits. But, at the very points where consensus has broken down, the common language ceases, in fact, to be a common language. Ultimately, the meaning of words depends upon experience; and where experiences are significantly different the same words are used with subtle and significant differences in meaning. Liberty, for instance, meant one thing to members of the National Association of Manufacturers and quite another thing to members of a labor union struggling for recognition. These groups are, for the most part, sincere; they use the "same" terms and appeal to the "same" values; but they define the situation, the terms, and the values differently. Hence these groups tend, as an able sociologist has shrewdly remarked, to accuse each other of dishonesty and distortion.[7]

The study of a common language, unless it comes to grips with these cleavages in human experience, fails to provide a common medium of understanding and discussion at precisely those points where genuine communication is most needed. And so with the study of any aspect of culture in an age of transition. As long as it is studied solely in its traditional forms, it will, at best, promote confusion rather than consensus. For, whatever else an age of transition may portend, it certainly entails a period of revision and reconstruction in institutional arrangements, and in social and moral orientations.

[7] Robert C. Angell, *The Integration of American Society,* pp. 212–215.

Social Evolution Orients Education to the Past

The failure of the social evolutionist's theory of the curriculum to comprehend the actual character of the problem of consensus in a period of social crisis leads to the heart of its third defect: the attempt to orient education to the past rather than to the future. At first sight, the premise behind this attempt would appear to be simply a denial of significant change, coupled with a reassertion in another form of the doctrine of eternal verities—a conclusion not without a certain warrant in the language employed on occasion by Morrison and Bagley. The theory under consideration, however, is an evolutionary theory based squarely upon the reality of significant change. Even in the case of universal institutions it is not denied that their forms change and develop. Indeed, the ultimate ground for their validity is found in their capacity for continuous growth and development. Hence, despite certain personal predilections based upon an ingrained conservatism, social evolutionism cannot be classified with those theories that deny the reality of change.[8]

There is, of course, a type of social evolutionism that, for all practical purposes, achieves the same results by another route. That is to say, it asserts the reality of social change in historical terms. But, where social change is fundamental or significant, it is conceived as the product of a long and gradual process of historical evolution barely perceptible in any one generation. The social evolutionism of Bagley, Morrison, and Judd, however, is not of that type. On the contrary, it is explicitly based upon a theory of emergent evolution that recognizes abrupt as well as gradual change. Both Judd and Bagley, moreover, have on numerous occasions reiterated their belief that contemporary society has reached a crucial stage in its evolution.

Inadequate Conception of Social Change and of Education

The basis of the social evolutionist's insistence that education must be oriented to the past cannot be found, therefore, in a denial either of significant or of abrupt change. It will more probably be found in a

---

[8] In Bagley's case this conservatism was an educational rather than a social conservatism; in Morrison's case it was both educational and social.

combination of their conceptions of the historical and educative processes. The fact is that the social evolutionist, even of the emergent type, has little faith in the capacity of man to direct the processes of social change. Social change is, of course, a product of human action. People can, by patient and intelligent effort, do a good deal to solve particular human problems. New social orders are not designed, however. They evolve from the unplanned interaction of countless thousands of individuals and groups, each seeking to achieve, under the altered conditions of the time, its own ends and purposes. In the course of this interaction, new institutional forms and new mores emerge by the usual evolutionary processes of variation, selection, transmission, and survival.

In periods of severe social crisis, when the need for adjustment is both great and sharp, social evolution assumes an emergent rather than a gradual form. Such emergencies are by their very nature unpredictable. Social change on the grand scale, represented by the rise of a new social order, is always deeper and wider than a legislative act. It is the product of the unconscious, almost automatic, adjustment of many diverse and contradictory interests confronted with great and impersonal historical forces—a process pregnant with the wisdom of the race, but rarely comprehended, and never controlled, by the conscious intelligence of any individual or group.

Hence—the social evolutionist says—there is little or no point in the attempt to educate directly for social change, even in an era of fundamental transformation. The danger in such periods is that the essential bonds of social stability, order, and discipline will crack under the stresses and strains of the social crises. To a greater extent than in ordinary times, therefore, the task of education is that of molding, through the assimilation of the social heritage, intelligent and disciplined personalities able to maintain their sense of order and direction under the difficult conditions imposed by the character of the times in which they live.

This analysis of the reasons behind the social evolutionist's insistence that education should be oriented to the past is confirmed by the conception of the learning process embodied in their educational theory. The capacity for independent thought, they assert, is the mark of mature and disciplined personalities, achieved only after a long and arduous process devoted to the mastery and assimilation of the cultural heritage. "Thought," says Morrison, "is not mental but cultural. We do not learn to think; we learn thought." [9] To the limited extent, therefore, that man can consciously direct the course of social change, that task is properly a function of adult society. The function of the common school, at all times, is the instruction of youth in the knowledge and arts, the attitudes and skills appropriate to life in a civilized society.

In a very significant sense, the theory that the study of universal institutions defines the curriculum entails the assumption that it is possible to build, in a period of social transformation, integrated personalities endowed with a sense of stability and direction through an uncritical mastery of the cultural heritage. This assumption is remarkable, to say the least, in view of the fact that the uncertainty and confusion characteristic of a transitional era are the direct results of the failure of the cultural heritage, in its traditional form, to order and rationalize the altered conditions of life moving behind the crisis.

Men cannot secure direction and stability from an appeal to institutions and principles that have themselves broken down. To say that we know precisely what is sound in the cultural heritage is tantamount to the assertion that order and clarity have already been achieved. This is simply another facet of the failure of the social evolutionist's theory of the curriculum to provide a sound foundation for the restoration of consensus in an age of social disintegration and reconstruction. The logical conclusion from the premises of this school of thought is that, beyond the elementary knowledge and skills involved in routine affairs of life, education is helpless in such periods. For, if social reconstruction is necessarily a function of unconscious historical processes, the outcome of which cannot be predicted or controlled, then education in the interval between two social orders can derive direction and clarity from neither the old nor the new.

An honest critic must admit at the outset that, in historical terms, the social evolutionist is correct. No social crisis, of the type encountered in one of the great transitional eras of history, has ever been resolved through the conscious and co-operative efforts of the entire social group. In the past, deliberate social reconstruction, where it has

[9] Morrison, *The Curriculum of the Common School,* p. 35.

occurred at all, has been limited to the last stages of the crisis, following a successful seizure of power on the part of a revolutionary class bent upon shaping the future in accordance with its own specifications.

The resolution of a major social crisis through the automatic interaction of impersonal historical forces, accompanied by an unremitting struggle for power on the part of contending social groups, has always been an exceedingly costly affair. The costs, moreover, are not limited to immediate evils exacted by a prolonged period of confusion, decimation, and struggle. They are reflected also in the quality of the social order that emerges at the conclusion of the process. For neither the blind operation of impersonal forces nor the bitter struggle of contending groups offers any assurance that important human values will not be destroyed or ignored in the formulation of the new order. Indeed, there is no assurance that, left to themselves, impersonal forces and contending groups will create a social order capable of sustaining civilized existence in any form. The fact that great civilizations have, in the past, collapsed under the strain of comparable crises suggests that, from the human point of view, the automatic processes of history fail as often as they succeed.

It is an open question, therefore, whether, in a highly interdependent industrial culture, endowed by the rapid advance of science and technology with a destructive potential never before possessed by mankind, society dare adopt a policy of historical *laissez faire*. Such a policy does not mean that no efforts will be made to shape the course of events. But it does mean that such efforts will be made, not by society as a whole but by conflicting and contending groups engaged in a desperate struggle for power.

Dangers in a Laissez Faire Policy

In the past no other policy than *laissez faire* was possible. For, in preceding crises of comparable scope and depth, men possessed neither the knowledge of historical processes nor the scientific and material resources required to deal with the complicated problems of social change. Today, however, the situation is somewhat different. Many have fully recognized the character of the period in which they are living, and almost everyone has sensed it in some degree. Moreover, for the first time in human history, society has at its command material resources and technical competence adequate to the solution of any purely technical social problem. What is lacking is the will to employ these material and technical resources—a condition due simply to the fact that men are not agreed upon the ends for which they should be employed. A fundamental problem of today, therefore, is achievement of some degree of consensus respecting the ends and purposes that should guide and direct social policy.

Of course, neither the blind operation of impersonal social forces nor the struggle of contending social factions for power can be entirely replaced by conscious and co-operative social action. But within the limits set by historical imperatives the operation of social forces can, to some extent, be controlled and directed, as the engineer controls and directs the forces of nature. And the struggle for power can, to a considerable degree, be transformed from an affair of force and violence to one of peaceful persuasion and social action.

It is possible that men may refuse to make the attempt or may fail if it is made. But the very existence of our world is threatened both by the periodic recurrence of total war on a global scale and the constant strain of internal dissension growing out of race and class differences. Hence, it is not too much to say that the preservation of our democratic and humanitarian heritage—and possibly of any industrial civilization whatever—depends upon the success of the attempt to modify, through conscious and deliberate social control, the struggles and rigors that always accompany a great transitional era of history. Ultimately, the problem must be solved, if it is solved at all, in the realm of ideas. For we live in an age of clashing ideologies; and ideas, unless their adherents are totally destroyed, can be finally uprooted only by better ideas, which are able to command general assent. Under such circumstances, and in such an age, the major assumption of the social evolutionist—that processes of history are beyond conscious human control—becomes a deadly handicap, which modern civilization, in its fateful race with catastrophe, cannot afford to carry. If education in our society is to be, in any significant sense, related to the social realities of our time, then the rejection of the thesis that social change is the exclusive product of blind historical forces carries with it the rejection of any educational program primarily oriented to the past.

In the light of the preceding discussion it is clear that the criterion of curriculum content projected by the social evolutionists—that of universal, fundamental, and comprehensive institutions—fails on at least three counts to provide standards of selection and choice adequate to the needs of the curriculum worker.

In the first instance, universal institutions, in so far as they exist at all, are simply generalized and abstract rubrics embodying within themselves no principle of choice or selection in the concrete material of education. Nor do they, in the second instance, contain any principle upon which an educational program, directed toward the establishment of a vital social consensus, can be built. The social controversies of our day are concerned, not with institutions in their universal aspect but with the specific forms they should now take and the social purposes they should serve. Hence, preoccupation with universal institutions obscures both the problem created by the disruption of social consensus and the nature of the causes which have produced it. In the third instance, the criterion proposed by the social evolutionists—oriented as it is to the past and grounded in the premise that rational and deliberate social reconstruction is impossible—offers no basis for an educational program adapted to the social realities of a society caught in the grip of a transitional era.

3. *The Curriculum Defined by Current Social Trends*

The third theory recognizes the difficulties inherent in social evolutionism. It undertakes to overcome these difficulties by substituting social trends for universal institutions as the measure of curriculum content. There are at least two ways in which an analysis of current social trends may be used in curriculum construction. The analysis can be used to uncover social conditions which any group and any educator must take into account in the determination of social and educational choices. In this sense the study of social trends is an indispensable aspect of any educational theory that holds that the school should be an agent of social reconstruction. So defined, the analysis and projection of social trends becomes a part of the working equipment of all

educators who believe that the core of the curriculum should be prem-
ised upon a study of significant social problems—a position explored in
the next section of this chapter.

The present section, however, is concerned with an examination of a
second way of using an analysis of current social trends. In this case
the analysis is regarded not as a condition of choice but as a substitute
for choice. Hence, existing trends are taken, in and of themselves, as
conclusive both for the ends of education and for the content of the
curriculum.

According to this school of thought the curriculum worker must first
discover and document the major social trends now under way in our
society. Then he must construct a curriculum designed to prepare the
young to live in the world indicated by a reasonable projection of these
trends. In short, it is the dynamic form of the job analysis theory of
the curriculum, which has been previously examined.

This view recognizes not only the importance and reality of social
change, but also the fact that education can and should do something
about it. It also represents one interpretation of the theory that a primary social purpose of education is a continuous reconstruction of the
ideological and institutional structure of society. However, that reconstruction is limited to an adaptation of the character and personality of
the young to the social reality defined by a projection of existing social
trends. It is true that even this form of the theory recognizes that the
continuation of these trends will create certain technical and social
problems, which demand examination and criticism in the classroom,
as in the study and the forum. But the trends themselves are taken as
immutable facts.

Up to a certain point this attitude is undoubtedly justified. History
is not completely fluid; some social trends are, practically speaking,
irreversible by deliberate human action. But by no means all discernible social trends are of this order. And, even in the case of those that
are correctly regarded as irreversible, they may, within limits, be de-
flected in this or that direction. To take a single example, the fact that
technological and industrial progress has now created a situation in
which autonomous national sovereignty is incompatible with civilized
existence neither precludes a degree of choice with respect to the form

the world order shall take nor robs this choice of a very considerable degree of moral and practical significance. Consequently, the indubitable necessity of correctly defining and adequately taking into account the direction and force of existing social trends is not tantamount to a rigid obligation to regard these trends as the complete and final arbiters of the future.

On the contrary, while they define the conditions under which deliberate social action must proceed, they do not wholly determine the course events must take. In the last analysis, the social-trend school shares with the social evolutionists both the delusion that the curriculum must be defined in terms of a fixed content, rather than in terms of problems requiring solution, and the erroneous notion that man is incapable, in any real sense, of altering or influencing the course of history. It represents, to borrow a phrase employed by John Dewey in a somewhat comparable case, "the last infirmity of the mind" in its transition from a negative to a positive estimation of the role of intelligence in social change and from a static to a dynamic conception of education.

4. The Curriculum Premised upon Significant Social Problems

The fourth and last curriculum theory predicated on social reality takes the position indicated by the criticism of the previous theories. It defines the curriculum in terms of the significant and persistent social problems of the society in which the school is located. The way in which a group conceives its problems, however, is always relative to its interests and goals. Since the aspirations and purposes of a people are both revealed and shaped by their intellectual and moral commitments, the definition of the significant and persistent problems of any society always entails a determination of the ideological basis of its culture. The resolution of social problems, moreover, is an affair of knowledge and fact. But judgments respecting social policy inevitably involve standards of the good and of the just which, in their turn, are grounded in the ethical and intellectual commitments of a people. Hence both the definition and the study of social problems are intimately related to these commitments.

The adherents of the social-problems theory, in common with many other social realists, locate this basic commitment in the American democratic tradition. The term *tradition* must be employed with considerable caution in this instance. The American democratic faith is traditional in the sense that it has historically represented the supreme social and political allegiance of the American people. It is not traditional in the sense of being traditionalistic; its tenets have never been regarded as immutable, nor have they been validated primarily by an appeal to antiquity. On the contrary, the democratic doctrine, on its own terms, is a growing and developing faith, resting its case on human reason and experience. Accordingly, the adherents of the social-problems school of curriculum determination have usually recognized that, in an age of social transformation, the democratic tradition, if it is to retain its vitality and strength, must be redefined and reconstructed in terms of the problems and conditions of the time. In short, while the democratic tradition is accepted as the ultimate standard that gives point and direction to the selection and study of social problems, that tradition is regarded as problematic in some degree—and, hence, as an object of critical study and revision. This position logically demands the acceptance of the thesis that a growing and changing faith can, at the very time that it is undergoing reconstruction, serve as the touchstone of intellectual and moral judgment.

The major principle espoused by the social-problems school of curriculum construction is, then, that the curriculum should be organized around the problems encountered by a democratic society, compelled by profound scientific and technological changes to adapt its thinking and its institutions to the requirements of a highly interdependent and industrialized world order. This means, of course, that the school must become a laboratory engaged in the analysis and study of the issues and problems involved in social reconstruction through democratic, as opposed to authoritarian and violent, methods. This conception of the curriculum represents the view that a paramount purpose of the school is to develop in the young the understanding and the attitudes required to facilitate social reconstruction along democratic lines and by democratic means.

Difficulty of Studying Social Problems in the School

An educational conception of this type places a heavy burden upon the schools. Yet it is a burden that cannot be avoided save at the price either of arbitrary imposition or of confusion and disorder in education. For, as the previous analysis has revealed, the school in a transitional era is caught between the partially disintegrated conceptions of the old order, not yet wholly dead, and the emerging conceptions of the new society, not yet fully determined or established. Under these conditions the school must seek order and clarity in education in a method of dealing with the confusions and conflicts of the time.

The task of the school can be simplified. The issues and problems encountered in the course of democratic social reconstruction are, in detail, multitudinous and complex. They come to a focus, however, in two great questions, which, from a democratic point of view, define a major task. First, upon what principles and by what means can the consensus required to hold society together be restored, along essentially democratic lines, under the conditions imposed by an interdependent and industrialized world order? And, second, in what ways and by what methods can the institutional structures of society be reconstructed so that they are both compatible with the democratic faith as defined by the emerging consensus and capable of smooth and efficient operation under the conditions set by modern technology? At bottom the criteria of democratic compatibility and efficient operation, measured by democratic goals, are intimately related. Institutions are merely the means by which a society realizes its ideal ends. Hence, any institutional structure which, under a given set of conditions, is incapable of effectively actualizing democratic goals for the vast majority of the population cannot, in that situation, be regarded as efficient.

In the solution of the two basic problems—restoring consensus and reconstructing institutions—almost every phase or aspect of organized social life is potentially involved in one way or another. Three such aspects, however,—world organization, economic structure, and class and race relationships—appear particularly crucial. The disruptive influences of war, of prolonged economic dislocation and depression, and of race and class dissension are so great that it is probably not too much to say that the ultimate destiny of the democratic way of life

depends primarily upon its ability to restore, by peaceful and democratic means, consensus and order in these vital areas of social life.
The successful achievement of this triple task entails technical issues of
a high order—not the least important of which is the discovery of more
adequate means of individual participation in the control and direction
of group activity on a large scale.

Skill in Group Deliberation and Action

It would be difficult to exaggerate the significance of this problem.
Group activity is becoming increasingly important in modern life—so
much so that many students of society have declared with Woodrow
Wilson that the fundamental relationships of men are now with groups
rather than with individuals as such. Moreover, it is clear—documented
by a trend that has persisted for more than fifty years—that the conditions of modern life will require more, not less, group control and
action. Under such circumstances democracy can be destroyed by a
theory that equates democracy with purely individual choice and action. It can also be destroyed, no less effectively, by a theory that defines democracy in terms of individual participation in group decision
and action, in the absence of adequate machinery and techniques
through which individuals may actually participate in group deliberation and choice. Yet it could hardly be maintained that existing techniques are fully satisfactory, even in the case of small and intimate
groups. Where major decisions must be made, as frequently happens in
a modern society, by large groups scattered over a considerable territory, the machinery and techniques now available are grossly inadequate. On the technical side, therefore, the discovery of vastly improved techniques of group deliberation and decision is probably the
most significant problem of democratic reconstruction (unless it is the
problem of insuring that the people have full access to real facts on any
issues that concern them—a problem that is, at bottom, simply a phase
of the larger problem of group control and action).

Despite the great importance of these technical problems, the major
difficulties, as the previous discussion has indicated, are not technical.
They are moral and intellectual, growing directly out of conflicting
conceptions of the ends of social policy.

The significance of this analysis for public education is relatively clear. A school designed to grapple with the problems of democracy in the present crisis must undertake to develop three qualities in its pupils: first, a democratic personality and character; second, a clear understanding of the major issues involved in the restoration of intellectual and moral consensus and in the reconstruction of the institutional structure of society, particularly with respect to the three areas noted above; third, a considerable facility and skill in the use of democratic techniques of group deliberation and action.

Accordingly, the social-problems criterion must be construed in these terms. It does not imply a narrow study of particular social issues considered in isolation from the social context and from one another. Rather, it calls for a curriculum that would provide the student with the necessary bases for intelligent thought and action, in a period of social transformation, by providing him with the experiences and the materials required to develop a broad and penetrating comprehension of the present social situation, with its trends, its problems, and its potentialities. Nor does the social-problems criterion imply a curriculum limited to intellectual understanding alone. On the contrary, its meaning must be interpreted in such a way as to include also within its purview the experiences and materials required to build democratic personalities skilled in techniques of group deliberation and action.

▶ Following Up This Chapter

1. With the aid of several of your classmates, make an exploratory job analysis of current citizenship practices in the United States. What would this analysis reveal as important content for a high school course in citizenship? Where, in your judgment, would this content fall short?

2. What do the social evolutionists mean by a course of study based upon universal institutions? What are the assumptions upon which this theory rests? How would you restate these assumptions in order to make them acceptable to you?

3. With the assistance of some of your friends, see if you can figure out some of the important content that would be included in a high school or

elementary school course of study based upon the social-trend criterion. What are the strengths and the weaknesses of this type of curriculum as you see them?

4. Formulate several important social problems. What difficulties do you see in organizing instruction in the public schools around problems rather than topics? What place would a subject matter specialist have in such a curriculum?

5. In not more than four sentences each, state (1) the criterion or criteria of curriculum content that makes the most sense to you at the present time, (2) your basic reason for accepting this criterion, and (3) its central educational meaning.

▶ Suggested Reading

1. You will not have had time to read all the general discussion of the issues related to the selection of curriculum content suggested at the close of Chapter 24. Since many of those references also deal with the positions considered in this chapter, you may wish to read some that you had to omit before.

2. For clear-cut and vigorous defenses of the social-practice criterion of curriculum content, see: Franklin Bobbitt, *How to Make a Curriculum,* pages 1–62; W. W. Charters, *Curriculum Construction,* and Charles C. Peters, *Foundations of Educational Sociology,* pages 315–353. Boyd H. Bode's *Modern Theories of Education* (pages 95–121) offers a sharp and highly critical dissection of the social-practice criterion.

3. The principle that the curriculum is scientifically determined by the discovery of the comprehensive and fundamental institutions universal to all progressive societies is not simple or easy. Perhaps the most explicit and understandable account is that of Henry Clinton Morrison in *The Curriculum of the Common School,* pages 1–35. Morrison has developed this theory at greater length in *Basic Principles in Education,* but this book is not recommended to any but the exceptionally able, interested, and patient student. Charles H. Judd's *The Psychology of Social Institutions* (pages 1–76, 323–340) and William C. Bagley's *Education and Emergent Man* represent this conception of education in a somewhat less clear-cut fashion than Morrison. A good secondary account of the general theory upon which the institutional criterion of curriculum content is based can be

found in Joseph Justman, *Theories of Secondary Education in the United States,* pages 22–32, 71–88, 144–168, 227–246, 318–339, 410–423.

In the last analysis, the social-evolutionist theory of education grows out of a theory of society that has been best expounded by William Graham Sumner in *Folkways,* pages 1–100. A brief critical summary of Sumner's *Folkways* is available in "Reactions Against Social Atomism: Sumner's *Folkways,*" by Kenneth D. Benne and William O. Stanley, *The Educational Forum,* Vol. VII, No. 1 (November, 1942), pages 51–62.

4. For an excellent statement of the social-trends criterion of curriculum content, see Leon C. Marshall and Rachel Marshall Goetz, *Curriculum-Making in the Social Studies,* pages 1–22.

5. The major sources outlining the basic social and educational theory underlying the contemporary-social-problems criterion of curriculum content have already been suggested to you at the close of Chapter 23 under the heading of the social-reconstructionist position. If you have not already done so, you might like to read Harold Benjamin's brilliant little book *The Saber-Tooth Curriculum.* Harold Alberty, *Reorganizing the High School Curriculum* (pages 398–418) has a good chapter on the teaching of controversial issues in the classroom.

Harold Hand (Editor), *Living in the Atomic Age* offers an example of a resource unit on one of the most dramatic of current social problems. William Van Til's *Economic Roads for American Democracy* is an ably written textbook for the study of what is perhaps the most controversial of all contemporary social issues. Further examples of research and teaching units can be found in two series: National Association of Secondary School Principals and National Council for the Social Studies, *Problems in American Life,* Units 1–15, and North Central Association of Colleges and Secondary Schools, *Unit Studies in American Problems.*

Chapter 26

Critique of the
Social-Problems Criterion

IN THE LAST ANALYSIS the social-problems criterion of
curriculum content is a corollary of the conception of the function
of education embraced by the theory of education as social reconstruction. While this theory of education has been previously discussed,
no formal statement of the basic tenets comprising it has yet been made.
The theory is based upon John Dewey's famous definition of education
as the "continuous reconstruction of experience." [1] To that definition
has been added an emphasis, by no means foreign to Dewey's thought,
on the social character of experience.

In terms of the curriculum issues indicated in the last five chapters,
the social-reconstruction position may be defined as that curriculum
theory which unites in one coherent pattern of thought the following
propositions:

1. The belief that the moral authority of the teacher ultimately rests
   upon the democratic tradition regarded as a growing and developing
   ideal rather than as a fixed and final dogma.
2. The conviction that the ends of education are essentially social ends,
   coupled with the further conviction that, to the extent that society
   is democratic throughout, opposition between the social purposes of

[1] John Dewey, *Democracy and Education* (New York: The Macmillan Company;
1916), pp. 89–92.

education and the needs and interests of children will be reduced to a minimum.

3. The contention that the basic social purpose of education cannot be comprehended simply as the perpetuation of the *status quo*. The purpose must include, as its central focus, that continuous reconstruction of ideas and institutions required to make society a more and more perfect embodiment of the democratic way of life under the conditions prescribed by historical imperatives.

4. The thesis that the *core* of the curriculum of the public schools should consist of a careful study of the significant social problems now confronting the people, ordered and arranged with due regard for the abilities, interest, and needs of children, and managed in such a way as will best develop the capacity of the learner to think, judge, and act intelligently.

As already noted, social-reconstruction theory has been subjected to sharp and varied criticisms. Some of these criticisms—notably the contention that man cannot direct the course of social change and the thesis that the rigorous mastery of the content of the research disciplines offers the best possible training for intelligent social action—have already been considered. Other criticisms, fully as important, require examination here.

This chapter will discuss five arguments that have been directed against social-reconstruction theory. Each of these challenges is expressed in the form of a question.

1. *Are Democratic Standards Adequate?*

One of the most trenchant and persistent of these criticisms challenges the adequacy of the standards proposed. The determination of social policy, it is asserted, can properly proceed only from premises supplied by stable conceptions of right and wrong. The standard of judgment employed by the social-reconstruction theory is admittedly a changing and developing standard. Hence, its opponents insist that this theory is undertaking to build upon a foundation of shifting sand. This objection is ultimately grounded in the previously rejected theory of eternal and absolute truth.

In the present context, however, the objection to changing and relative standards is burdened with an additional disadvantage. For, in periods of social transition, the intellectual and moral premises of society, as well as its institutional structure, are called into question precisely because the old standards, just as they exist, are no longer adequate. In a transitional era the only alternative to a growing and developing standard is the substitution of one absolute for another, a course that has usually been followed in preceding crises of this nature.

But the substitution of one fixed and final canon for another involves a far sharper break in historical continuity than that entailed by the reconstruction of the existing rule. It involves, also, a clash of absolutes, which almost inevitably leads to the substitution of violent for peaceful methods of social change and control. Moreover, the foundations of the new order, once it is established, will prove as rigid and unyielding as the old, with the result that changing conditions will, in time, create a new crisis necessitating yet another moral and intellectual revolution. The theory of absolute and eternal truth can be adjusted, as it has been, to the requirements of any particular historical crisis. What it cannot do is to facilitate that continuous reconstruction of ideas and of institutions that will prevent the development of a major social crisis.

Able adherents of the doctrine of eternal verities, fully aware of the nature of the present period, have undertaken to meet this difficulty by indicating that, while the substance of fundamental intellectual and moral truths does not change, their application necessarily varies with changing conditions. This position is not without its degree of merit. Centuries of human study and experience have produced intellectual and moral concepts which, whatever their imperfections, contain a core of solid virtue. Nevertheless, significant differences in application are always tantamount to subtle changes in the rule itself. In fact, the actual meaning of any canon of conduct can only be determined in terms of the type of behavior to which it would lead if it were adopted as the guide and measure of action. The attempt to graft changing applications upon unchanging standards typically engenders a casuistry which, quite apart from the encouragement it frequently affords to moral cynicism, submerges significant issues in a sea of sophisticated dialectic and brings genuine intellectual and ethical inquiry into serious disrepute.

The truth embodied in the position that, while applications change, fundamental truths do not, is the recognition that intellectual and moral reconstruction does not necessarily imply a complete flux in which no element of stability exists. This fact can be better served by a conception of a growing and developing standard than it can by a doctrine of fixed and final truth that somehow turns out to be, in practice, changing and variable. The capacity for growth and development inherent in the democratic tradition affords the best guarantee that its concepts may prove adequate to the task of comprehending and ordering the altered conditions of life imposed by modern technology.

2. Is the Social Heritage Neglected?

A second criticism, that the social-problems criterion ignores the importance of the social heritage, is based upon a serious misunderstanding. No responsible educator, however misleading his language may have been at times, ever really proposed for education a sheer immediacy, which would deny any significant value or role to the social heritage. Such a position, if it were possible at all, would be utter nonsense. The real issue involved is not that of the importance of the social heritage but that of the way in which the heritage is important. Many educators insist that education is the mastery of the social heritage. The theory of social reconstruction, on the other hand, holds that the use of the heritage as a tool in further inquiry and problem solving defines the essence of the educative process—a process in which the heritage itself, in the only genuine sense of the term, is really mastered. The objection that the social-problems criterion ignores the social heritage loses its point when the issue is correctly joined.

3. Can Children Profitably Study Social Problems?

The third major objection leveled at the social-problems criterion of curriculum content is that it assigns to immature children tasks that are appropriate only for mature scholars and adults. In a certain superficial form this objection, too, is based on a misapprehension. No one seriously proposes that children should reconstruct the social order—although within the limits of their capacity they might, with profit to themselves and to society, participate in such an undertaking. What is proposed, of course, is that children can best come to understand the society in which they live through a study of the problems with which it is confronted. It may be readily granted that this study, if it is genuine and thorough, involves a reconstruction of the normative principles of society as they are taught to the young and that it would, in time, lead to significant changes in institutional structure. The fact remains, however, that the social-reconstruction theory of education does not imply that the direction of social change or of social controls should be determined by children.

The Capacity of Ordinary Citizens to Think

At a deeper level this objection raises two important issues. The first concerns the capacity of ordinary citizens to think intelligently about basic social problems. Even in the United States a considerable group argues that only a relatively small intellectual elite is capable of comprehending and dealing with such problems. They contend that it is sheer folly to introduce young children to problems that are too difficult and complicated for the vast majority of the adult population. The most that can be done is to give the pupils in the public schools such an elementary knowledge of sound moral and social principles as will enable them to choose, with some degree of wisdom, among competing groups of experts.

This view, as was previously suggested, misconceives the function of the expert in the determination of social policy. It is one thing to say that complicated social problems cannot be adequately solved apart from the utilization of expert knowledge. It is quite another thing to assert that the solution of such problems must be relegated entirely to a selected group of experts. A more important objection to this position is that it represents a direct challenge to the democratic premise that, in the realm of social policy, the decisions of the whole people, where they have full access to the facts, are in the long run typically wiser than those made by any single class or group. The cult of the expert is but the prelude to some form of authoritarian society.

Were we able to grant the truth of the thesis urged by this cult, the fact still remains that the masses of people, unless they are to be denied any participation in social control, must learn to choose among experts. On what basis are they to judge if not upon an appraisal of the program recommended by the expert? But an appraisal of the program implies an understanding of the problems for which the program is designed. The only alternative that can be proposed is that the selection be made on the basis of reputation and character. Reputation and character, however, offer no certain guarantee of correctness in any particular issue. Nor do they afford any ground for choice between competing experts of equal reputation and character. The fact is that education for intelligent followership is not different in kind from that required for intelligent leadership.

Learning to Think through Problem Solving

The second issue concerns the way in which man learns to grapple successfully with problematic situations. According to the doctrine espoused by many of the opponents of the social-reconstruction theory, the capacity to think is an emergent capacity, depending, apart from differences in native ability, upon a thorough mastery of existing knowledge. Hence, to ask children to grapple with social problems is to get the cart before the horse. The primary task of the school (these critics argue) is to ensure that pupils learn the facts and principles warranted by established knowledge. Until this is done, the pupil is not capable of critical or original thought. Since the time that can be allotted to the education of the average child is woefully inadequate for the achievement of the primary duty of the school, no extensive place can be found in the public school curriculum for the study of social problems.

This criticism is, in part, a repetition of the doctrine advanced by the research-discipline and social-evolution theories. It is not a complete repetition because those theories asserted that a particular type of knowledge is the precondition of significant thought, while the contention here is limited to the more general proposition that men learn to think through the mastery of existing knowledge.

This position, however, is untenable. While it is true that the ability to think is an acquired ability, it is not true that school children cannot think or that, within the limits of their experience, their thinking is different in kind from that of adults.[2] This capacity has been acquired, moreover, not as a result of a formal study of organized subject matter but of efforts of the young to share in the social life of the group of which they are a part. Critical thought does demand some capacity for theoretical analysis as well as comprehension of relevant principles and facts. But critical thinking is not the typical result of prolonged practice in the assimilation of other people's thought. When students are encouraged to think for themselves, even to the extent of assisting in the selection of problems for study and in the organization of learning activities, they typically respond to the challenge with vigor and intelligence—provided they have not been conditioned by years of exposure to the deadly routines of lesson learning. Even in the teaching of number combinations, understanding gained through experience and problem solving has been found superior to sheer drill. Indeed, there is some evidence that memorization of number combinations does not readily occur until the child has found meaning for them.[3] Whatever the case with respect to routine computation in mathematics, it is clear that the general rule that people learn what they practice applies to development of the capacity to think accurately in any field.

Children Capable of Studying Social Problems

It is possible to accept the principle that thinking is learned through problem solving and still reject, on the ground that school children are not equipped by training or experience to deal with such problems, the thesis that the curriculum should be built around the study of crucial

[2] For evidence on this point, see: T. M. Abel, "Unsynthetic Modes of Thinking Among Adults: A Discussion of Piaget's Concepts," *American Journal of Psychology*, 1932, Vol. 44, pp. 123–132; C Burt, "The Development of Reasoning in Children," *Journal of Experimental Pedagogy*, 1919, 5, pp. 68–77, 121–127; J. M. Deutsche, *The Development of Children's Concepts of Causal Relations;* V. Hazlitt, "Children's Thinking," *British Journal of Psychology*, 1929, 20, pp. 354–361; and T. V. Moore, *The Reasoning Ability of Children in the First Years of School Life.* Contrary to the above evidence, Piaget holds that the reasoning of very young children is quite different from that of adults and that the young child is unable to think from the standpoint of a general proposition or to examine critically either his own or another's conclusions. But even on the basis of Piaget's findings—which do not agree with the bulk of the evidence—this difference disappears at about the age of seven or eight.

[3] W. A. Brownell, *Development of Children's Ideas in the Primary Grades.*

social issues. This objection derives its cogency from the fallacious notion that the child must be able to comprehend all the ramifications of a complex social problem before he is able to consider intelligently any aspect of it. The principle that students should not be asked to tackle problems beyond their comprehension is sound. But a correct understanding of this principle does not indicate that children, even young children, should not study social problems. It rather indicates that the problems, or aspects of problems, selected for study must fall within the range of their experience and understanding.

There is no dearth of such problems. Home, neighborhood, and school abound with issues well within the grasp of the child's experience and understanding. The study of these issues will contribute to the development of democratic attitudes and modes of thinking, to the clarification of the meaning of democratic principles and ideals, and to the comprehension of the impact of modern interdependence and technology upon contemporary life. It is a mistake to think that, in order to build a curriculum organized in terms of significant social problems, the third-grade child must be asked to grapple with all the intricacies of world government or economic structure—just as it also is a mistake to suppose that all aspects of these problems transcend the capacities of the third grader.

It may be argued that the inability of the young student to follow immediately all the ramifications of complicated social problems invalidates the results of any partial study of them. This objection might be sound if it were applied to the work of the research scholar or the legislator, although any study implies some degree of delimitation. However, the immediate purpose of study in the public school is growth and learning, not legislative action. From this point of view, it is a decided asset that the study of any significant social issues extends in many directions. Of course, the student will find that, as the result of further study, he must revise his earlier conclusions. But the capacity to correct and reconstruct previous views, whenever new evidence and thought justifies such revision, is one of the abilities desperately needed in a democratic society caught in the grip of social change. Habituation and skill in this process are important educational products of the type of curriculum embraced by the social reconstruction theory.

4. Does the Social-Reconstruction Approach Recognize the Common and the Settled?

The decision that the study of social problems, when properly conducted, is within the capacity of students in the public schools does not end the debate. For, from a fourth angle, comes the charge that the social-reconstruction theory inevitably leads to an extreme emphasis upon the elements of uncertainty and conflict in our society, accompanied by a grave underestimation, if not a complete neglect, of the settled and the common. Thus it presents to the immature child a crabbed and warped picture of American life, which not only distorts his judgment but also tends to undermine his sense of security and well-being.

Fortunately, the charge is not necessarily true. The solution of any problem is impossible without the recognition and utilization of both the common and the settled. Moreover, the purpose of study in any problematic situation is, in part, to extend the area of the common and the settled. It is sometimes true that, in the study of social problems, issues are sharpened rather than resolved. But this is either a necessary stage in the discovery of a satisfactory solution, or it is a clear indication that no substantial element of common interest and persuasion is present. In the latter case, the remedy is not a refusal to study but an effort to create, through group discussion and action, a sound basis for community of interest and feeling. The effort may fail. But if it does, the fault lies with the realities of a divided and segmented society; these realities are revealed, not created, by intelligent analysis. Nor should anyone forget that, where action is necessary, the only alternative to action based upon intelligent study and analysis is blind and impulsive action. Despite the fact that critical study of pressing social problems sometimes serves to sharpen issues, reasoned discussion and study still offer the best chance of resolving such difficulties without wholesale resort to force and violence.

Nevertheless, it must be admitted that, unless particular care is taken to emphasize not only the elements of the settled and the common present in each of the problems studied but also the role of established knowledge and consensus in the technique of problem solving, a curriculum composed primarily of a study of social problems might create the impression that there is no significant component of stability and unity in American life. Such a result would be more than unfortunate. In an age of social transformation every element of common agreement and of settled knowledge, provided that it is pertinent and genuine, becomes a basis for democratic and peaceful reconstruction, both in the ideological and the institutional realms. The advocates of the social-problems curriculum must not neglect or underemphasize this essential aspect of study and problem solving. The recognition of the inevitability of change—and, hence, of the need for a curriculum based upon a critical examination of vital social problems and issues—does not entail the assertion of an utter flux devoid of any degree of continuity and stability.

5. Can Schools Study Social Problems?

Finally, the critics of the social-problems criterion of curriculum content insist that this criterion, and the theory of education on which it is based, assumes that the school has a degree of freedom that, in fact, it does not have. This criticism has two aspects, either of which, in the view of the critics, is sufficient to invalidate the position.

Schools Can Influence Attitudes and Beliefs

The first aspect calls attention to the fact that the school is merely one of the educative forces of society and, hence, that it cannot educate effectively against the entire pressure of the social order. The answer to this argument is that, particularly in a transitional era, the educative forces of society are not a monolithic unit. Some aspects of the culture in such periods educate in one way, some in another. This is the necessary educative counterpart of a society caught in the grip of a major social crisis. The result is that individual and group perspectives are impregnated with conflict, confusion, and doubt. In this situation the public school, as the primary social agency of deliberate and conscious instruction, can, by clarifying the issues at stake, and by throwing its

weight one way rather than another, influence the thinking and behavior of its pupils.

While it is ridiculous to speak of the school as remaking society in
any total sense, it is quite possible to say that the school may play a
significant, or even a decisive, role in shaping the attitudes, the beliefs,
and the perspectives that will govern the conduct and behavior of persons in the face of the problems and issues of social change and reconstruction. In the long run, these attitudes and beliefs cannot be maintained unless they are supported and confirmed by actual changes in
the structure and customs of society. While thought and action cannot be separated without grave injury to both, there is a sense in which
moral and intellectual reconstruction must precede sociological reconstruction if the latter is not to be automatic and blind. It is this
prior function that defines the primary task of the school. In a period when some type of social reconstruction is inevitable in any case,
there is but little danger, if the work of the school is well done, that its
teachings will be repudiated and undermined by the emerging social
order.

Public Will Permit Study of Social Problems

There is a second aspect of the argument that the schools do not have
the freedom the social-problems criterion assumes. This aspect asserts
that, because the school is effective in molding the character and beliefs
of persons, no body of educators will be permitted to indoctrinate the
young with attitudes and convictions subversive of the existing social
order. The answer to this argument is that the social-reconstruction
theory of education does not contemplate the use of the school as an
instrument of subversion and revolution. Instead, it would utilize the
school as a way of preserving and extending the democratic values and
ideals to which the American people are now committed.

The advocates of the social-reconstruction theory are not trying to
destroy the old order. Rather, they are attempting re-examination and
reconstruction of it because the old order, already seriously undermined, is in imminent danger of collapse. Such a catastrophe would
gravely jeopardize, if it did not destroy, the most precious values embedded in the old order itself. It may be admitted that this distinction

holds but little meaning for those adherents of the old order who are certain that it is still substantially sound. But it is important for many Americans who are convinced that something is seriously wrong and who are entirely unwilling to espouse authoritarian and totalitarian revolutions.

Moreover, apart from the development of intelligent, democratic personalities committed to the ideals and methodological procedures of democracy, the social-problems criterion of curriculum content calls for study, not indoctrination. It is true that study is not completed until a conclusion has been reached, nor can students be left entirely free to draw any conclusion that seems good to them. This does not mean that the school should undertake to dictate the results of study or to frame issues and evidence in such a way that the student is manipulated into accepting a position desired by the school. Such a course would contravene the canons of honest inquiry, prevent the full exercise of the student's capacities of critical judgment, and stunt the growth of his intelligence. In short, it is tantamount to an exploitation of the student wholly out of place in a democratic society. But the school must insist upon certain standards of logical analysis and of evaluation of evidence. To fail in this respect is to honor prejudgment, ignorance, and shoddy habits of thought rather than to develop the student's capacity for mature judgment and choice.

Furthermore, the educator must impose certain conclusions upon the students. If they are to learn at all, young children must be taught principles and attitudes, the full implications of which they cannot grasp until they attain a considerable degree of intellectual maturity. The selection of issues for study, the choice of methods of study, and, above all, the atmosphere and discipline of the school represent subtle but significant ways in which the school inevitably shapes the mind and personality of the young. Students can be asked to participate in the determination of these matters to a certain extent, and at an appropriate age they may be encouraged to examine the principles upon which these choices were made. Such considerations should not be allowed to conceal, however, the inexorable fact that to educate at all entails decisions and choices, which are imposed upon students and which inevitably operate to influence their behavior, attitudes, and beliefs.

On the other hand, the recognition of this fact should not lead to the erroneous conclusion that all education is indoctrination in the usual sense of that term. For there is patently a vast difference between the type of education here described and that which relegates teaching to the inculcation of dogma. The difference is not that the democratic school is indifferent to the character and beliefs of its students, whereas the authoritarian school seeks to build a particular type of character and belief. On the contrary, the democratic school is fully as much concerned with the molding of democratic character as the fascist or communist school is concerned with the production of fascists or communists. The difference lies in the fact that the democratic faith, unlike every type of authoritarianism, contains a respect for personality, differences of opinion, and the method of intelligence. Nevertheless, it is a mistake to believe that democracy is compatible with every type of character and belief or that the democratic school should be neutral.

The fundamental answer to the objection that society will not permit indoctrination of the young with attitudes and beliefs critical of the existing social order is to be found in the suggestion that a school endeavoring to base its curriculum upon a study of crucial social issues cannot proceed in isolation from the rest of society. The educational statesman, like any other statesman in a democratic society, must carry at least a substantial majority of the community with him. The fundamental argument on this point has already been made. However, it may be indicated again that the proposal to resolve, wherever possible, and by means of study and discussion, the confusion and conflict now evident in American life, is inherently a democratic proposal. It may be pointed out also that the school that is seriously considering embarking upon such a program might well consider both the extent to which adult education is a major obligation of the school and the extent to which lay participation in curriculum construction should be encouraged.

6. Conclusion

The tenor of the above discussion will doubtless have revealed the conviction that the core of the curriculum in the public schools should be built around the study of crucial social issues. That conviction does not mean that the social-problems criterion should be erected as the sole criterion of curriculum content. The curriculum must be rounded out by various other types of study.

Core of the Curriculum Not the Whole of the Curriculum

The core of the curriculum, although of first importance, is not the whole of it. A well-rounded education should result in several types of learning products: skill in the manipulation of things; skill in the manipulation of ideas, in the sense of logical analysis; skill in the processes of group discussion and co-operation and in personal relations with others; the understanding of ideas, both in the sense of their consequences in action and of their place in a conceptual system; appreciations, in the sense of adequate standards of the good and the beautiful and of sound personal tastes and enjoyments. Undoubtedly, much can be done in the core program to develop these capacities and skills. Some of them, however, require specific attention outside the core. The development of sound personal tastes and enjoyments is one such case. Skill in the intellectual, as well as the physical sense, requires practice and drill that cannot be obtained incidentally in the core program. The principle that skills should be learned in connection with use is sound doctrine, but that principle does not preclude special periods devoted to practice of needed skills and abilities.

The rejection of the subject curriculum based upon the research disciplines, moreover, does not mean that these disciplines have no place in general education. The scientific method and enterprise are very important aspects of modern civilization—in many respects, perhaps, its most important aspects. The intelligent citizen should understand their basic spirit and import. This understanding can best be secured by a generalization of the method and role of science based upon an intensive examination of one or more of its particular manifestations.

This study would emphasize method and function rather than content—although it must be recognized that, in detail, method cannot be wholly separated from subject matter. For obvious reasons, a systematic study of a particular research discipline should come rather late in the student's program of general education, and it should be chosen with reference to his interest and abilities. But with certain limited exceptions, students should be expected—in addition to the core composed of crucial social problems—to elect one or more research disciplines for systematic and intensive study.

Equally important is the recognition of the need of curriculum material based upon personal and individual needs, interests, and capacities. A democratic society needs rich and varied personalities, able and willing to contribute their unique talents and perspective to the common fund. Moreover, a society can remain democratic only to the extent that it provides abundant opportunity for all of its members to develop all their capacities and abilities. The rejection of the child-centered school does not carry with it the rejection of the thesis that there is a place in the school program for activities based primarily on the needs and interests of children—even the needs and interests of particular children.

Social-Problems Criterion Not the Sole Criterion

It must be recognized that the social-problems criterion, although basic, is not the sole criterion of curriculum content even in the core program. The study of social problems, as it has frequently been projected, is seriously defective at a number of points. It has often been associated with immediacy, which has ignored the significance of the cultural heritage, and with a conception of change that emphasizes sheer flux and conflict at the expense of any element of stability or unity. To an even greater extent it has neglected significant methodological considerations. The study of social problems, for example, has often been conceived in terms of a crude empiricism that has overlooked the need for logical analysis and a study of the canons of evidence and validity. Until very recently almost no consideration has been given to the development or use of adequate techniques and standards in group discussion and persuasion. Finally, very little attention has been paid to the relationship between the study of practical social problems and the research disciplines. These disciplines are an indispensable source of data and principles. The student working on social problems must tap, through study of particular points, the funded intellectual capital represented by the organized findings of the research disciplines.

Opponents of the social-problems conception of the curriculum have entered the objection that untrained laymen can neither discover nor interpret the relevant portions of these disciplines. This objection seriously underestimates the extent to which ordinary people can understand scientific material when it is directly related to their concerns. It overlooks, also, the extent to which this ability can be developed by practice and experience under skillful tutelage. Yet, unless specific attention is given to this aspect of problem solving, growth in this capacity will be considerably less than it should be. Moreover, even under the most favorable circumstances, there is a measure of truth in this objection. There are aspects of the research disciplines that require expert knowledge in their application to practical affairs. The remedy, however, is not that the ordinary citizen should undertake to become a universal expert, still less that he should surrender control of such matters entirely to the expert. Rather, he should learn how to utilize expert advice and assistance. One of the strong points of a curriculum based upon a study of the problems of the man and the citizen is that it helps both expert and layman to understand the role of the expert in group deliberation. Here again, this understanding will not be fully developed unless this function of the expert is made an object of study and analysis.

All of these requirements may properly be regarded as aspects of the social-problems criterion since they are essentially conditions of an adequate study of social issues. It has seemed wise to underline them by specific mention because they have been so frequently overlooked. It is well, also, to note the presence, in the social problems context, of important considerations that rival criteria of curriculum content have sought to promote and safeguard.

When the social-problems criterion is properly construed, it is still inadequate to the definition of the content of the curriculum. Whatever their social significance, problems cannot be assigned to children without considering the interests, experience, and intellectual maturity of the learners. The prejudices, interests, and attitudes of teachers, parents, and the community must likewise be taken into account; so must a host of other factors, including such considerations as the availability of suitable instructional material.

The determination of curriculum content is a complex affair, which cannot be judged wholly in terms of any single criterion. The most that can be said is that, in the core program, the social-problems criterion—with due consideration for the interests, experience, and maturity of the learner and for the prejudices and wishes of the community—constitutes the primary measure of curriculum content. In the other aspects of the curriculum, the personal needs and interests of children, the logic, spirit, and function of science as represented in a chosen research discipline, and the development of specific skills needed by the child in any aspect of his life and work, form the dominant considerations that should, in their respective areas, govern the selection of curriculum content.

▶ *Following Up*
This Chapter

1. Evaluate as carefully as you can all the major criticisms of the social-problems criterion position and the replies to these criticisms. Discuss your evaluations with several of your friends.

2. What should be the relationship between the core and non-core, the common and the special in the curriculum? With some of your friends, try to work out a curriculum that takes due account of these factors.

3. What do you understand the meaning of indoctrination to be? Should the schools indoctrinate?

4. In a brief paragraph state (1) your own position with respect to the social-reconstruction proposal and (2) your basic reason for taking this position.

Bibliography

NOTE: This Bibliography gives publication data for all references mentioned in the text, the footnotes, and the "Suggested Readings."

ABEL, T. M. "Unsynthetic Modes of Thinking among Adults: A Discussion of Piaget's Concepts," *American Journal of Psychology*, 1932, Vol. 44, pages 123–132.

ADAMS, JAMES TRUSLOW. *The Epic of America*. Boston: Little, Brown & Company; 1931.

ADLER, MORTIMER. "In Defense of the Philosophy of Education," in National Society for the Study of Education, *Forty-first Yearbook*, Part I, "Philosophies of Education." Bloomington, Illinois: Public School Publishing Company; 1941.

ALBERTY, HAROLD. *Reorganizing the High School Curriculum*. Revised edition. New York: The Macmillan Company; 1953.

ALEXANDER, FRANZ. *Our Age of Unreason*. Philadelphia: J. B. Lippincott Company; 1942.

ALEXANDER, WILLIAM M. "State Leadership in Improving Instruction," *Teachers College Contributions to Education*, No. 820. New York: Bureau of Publications, Teachers College, Columbia University; 1940.

ALLEN, CHARLES M. *How to Conduct the Holding Power Study*. Circular Series A, No. 51, Illinois Secondary School Curriculum Program Bulletin No. 4.

Office of the State Superintendent of Public Instruction, Springfield, Illinois; May, 1949.

American Association of School Administrators. "Length of School Sessions and Class Periods in Public Schools, 1938–39," *Educational Research Service, Circular No. 2*, March, 1940.

American Historical Association. Report of the Commission on the Social Studies, *Conclusions and Recommendations of the Commission*. New York: Charles Scribner's Sons; 1934.

ANDERSON, HOWARD R. (Editor). *Teaching Critical Thinking in the Social Studies*. Washington, D. C.: National Education Association; 1942.

ANDREWS, T. G. (Editor). *Methods of Psychology*. New York: John Wiley & Sons, Inc.; 1948.

ANGELL, ROBERT COOLEY. *The Integration of American Society*. New York: McGraw-Hill Book Company, Inc.; 1941.

ARENSBERG, CONRAD M., and McGREGOR, DOUGLAS. "Determination of Morale in an Industrial Company," *Applied Anthropology*, Vol. I, 1942, pages 12–34.

ARISTOTLE. *De Sophisticis Elenchis*. Works of Aristotle, edited by W. D. Ross. Oxford, at the Clarendon Press, 1928.

AYER, ADELAIDE M. *Some Difficulties in Elementary School History.* New York: Teachers College, Columbia University; 1926.

BABBITT, IRVING. *Democracy and Leadership.* Boston: Houghton Mifflin Company; 1924.

———. *Literature and the American College.* Boston: Houghton Mifflin Company; 1908.

BAGLEY, WILLIAM C. *Determinism in Education.* Baltimore: Warwick & York, Inc.; 1928.

———. *Education and Emergent Man.* New York: Thomas Nelson & Sons; 1934.

BAIN, READ. "Our Schizoid Culture," *Sociology and Social Research,* Vol. 19, September-August, 1934–1935, pages 266–276.

BAKER, MELVIN. *Foundations of Dewey's Educational Theory.* New York: King's Crown Press; 1954.

BARLOW, M. C. "Transfer of Training in Reasoning," *Journal of Educational Psychology,* 28, 1937, pages 122–128.

BARR, A. S.; BURTON, WILLIAM H.; and BRUECKNER, LEO J. *Supervision.* New York: D. Appleton-Century Company, Inc.; 1947.

BARTELS, ROBERT, and STEWART, FRANK A. "How Briarcliff Manor Took Inventory," *The American City,* September, 1948.

BEARD, CHARLES A. *Charter for the Social Sciences in the Schools.* New York: Charles Scribner's Sons; 1932.

———, and BEARD, MARY F. *The Rise of American Civilization.* New York: The Macmillan Company; 1930.

BECKER, CARL L. *New Liberties for Old.* New Haven: Yale University Press; 1941.

BELL, H. M. *Youth Tell Their Story.* Washington, D. C.: American Council on Education; 1938.

BELLACK, ARNO. "Sequence and Grade Placement," *Journal of Educational Research,* Vol. XLI, No. 8 (April, 1948), pages 610–623.

BENEDICT, RUTH. *Patterns of Culture.* Boston: Houghton Mifflin Company; 1934.

BENJAMIN, HAROLD. *The Saber-Tooth Curriculum.* New York: McGraw-Hill Book Company, Inc.; 1939.

BENNE, KENNETH D. *A Conception of Authority.* New York: Bureau of Publications, Teachers College, Columbia University; 1943.

———. "Democratic Ethics in Social Engineering," *Progressive Education,* Vol. 26, No. 7 (May, 1949), pages 201–207.

———. "Leaders Are Made, Not Born," *Childhood Education,* Vol. 24, No. 5 (1948).

———. "Principles of Training Method," *The Group,* Vol. 10, No. 2 (January, 1948).

———; BRADFORD, LELAND P.; and LIPPITT, RONALD. *Group Dynamics and Social Action.* New York: Anti-Defamation League of B'Nai B'Rith; 1950.

———, and EVANS, HUBERT. *Methodology of Coöperative Research.* (To be published.)

———, and MUNTYAN, BOZIDAR (Editors). *Human Relations in Curriculum Change.* Illinois Secondary School Curriculum Program. Springfield, Illinois: Office of the State Department of Public Instruction; 1950.

———, and SHEATS, PAUL. "Functional Roles of Group Members," *The Journal of Social Issues.* Vol. IV, No. 2 (Spring, 1948).

———, and STANLEY, WILLIAM O. "Reactions against Social Atomism: Sumner's *Folkways,*" *Educational Forum,* Vol. VII, No. 1 (November, 1942), pages 51–62.

BERKSON, I. B. *Education Faces the Future.* New York: Harper & Brothers; 1943.

———. *Preface to an Educational Philosophy.* New York: Columbia University Press; 1940.

BERLE, ADOLF A., JR., and MEANS, GARDINER C. *The Modern Corporation and Private Property.* New York: The Macmillan Company; 1933.

BILLINGS, NEAL. *A Determination of Generalizations Basic to the Social Studies Curriculum.* Baltimore: Warwick & York, Inc.; 1929.

BLAIR, JOHN M. *Seeds of Destruction.* New York: Crown Publishers; 1938.

BLOOM, BENJAMIN S. and Others (Editors). *Taxonomy of Educational Objectives.* New York: Longmans, Green and Company; 1956.

BLUMENTHAL, ALBERT. *Small-Town Stuff.* Chicago: University of Chicago Press; 1932.

BOBBITT, FRANKLIN. *Curriculum Making in Los Angeles.* Educational Monographs, No. 20. Chicago: University of Chicago Press; 1922.

———. *How to Make a Curriculum.* Boston: Houghton Mifflin Company; 1924.

BODE, BOYD H. *Modern Educational Theories.* New York: The Macmillan Company; 1927.

———. *Progressive Education at the Crossroads.* New York: Newson and Company; 1938.

BORING, E. G.; LANGFELD, H. S.; and WELD, H. P. *Foundations of Psychology.* New York: John Wiley & Sons, Inc.; 1948.

BOYNTON, P. L. "The Wishes of Elementary School Children," *Peabody Journal of Education,* Vol. 13, No. 4, pages 165–174.

BRADFORD, LELAND P. "Human Relations Training," *The Group,* Vol. 10, No. 2 (January, 1948).

———. "The Use of Psychodrama for Group Consultants," *Sociatry,* Vol. 1, No. 2 (June, 1947).

———, and LIPPITT, RONALD. "Building a Democratic Work Group," *Personnel,* Vol. 22, No. 3.

———, and SHEATS, PAUL. "Complacency Shock as a Prerequisite to Training," *Sociatry,* Vol. 2, Nos. 1 and 2, 1948.

BRAMELD, THEODORE. *Design for America.* New York: Hinds, Hayden & Eldredge; 1945.

———. "An Inductive Approach to Intercultural Values," *Journal of Educational Sociology,* Vol. 21, No. 1 (September, 1947).

———. *Patterns of Educational Philosophy.* Yonkers, New York: World Book Company; 1950. See *Philosophies of Education in Cultural Perspective,* Dryden Press.

———. *Philosophies of Education in Cultural Perspective.* New York: Dryden Press; 1955.

BRIGGS, T. H. "Formal English Grammar as a Discipline," *Teachers College Record,* Vol. 14, No. 4, 1913.

BROWNELL, W. A. *Development of Children's Number Ideas in the Primary Grades,* Supplementary Educational Monographs, No. 35. Chicago: University of Chicago Press; 1928.

BRUBACHER, JOHN S. *A History of the Problems of Education.* New York: McGraw-Hill Book Company, Inc.; 1947.

———. *Modern Philosophies of Education.* New York: McGraw-Hill Book Company, Inc.; 1939.

BRUNER, HERBERT B. *Place of Units in Course of Study Construction.* South Dakota Curriculum Bulletin No. 2. Pierre, South Dakota: State Printing Office; 1930.

BRYCE, JAMES, VISCOUNT. *The American Commonwealth.* New York: The Macmillan Company; 1893.

BRYSON, LYMAN, and Others (Editors). *Goals for American Education.* New York: Harper & Brothers; 1950.

BUCHANAN, NORMAN S., and LUTZ, FRIEDRICH, A. *Rebuilding the World Economy.* New York: The Twentieth Century Fund; 1947.

BURT, C. "The Development of Reasoning in Children," *Journal of Experimental Pedagogy,* 5, 1919.

BURTON, WILLIAM H. and BRUECKNER, LEO J. *Supervision.* New York: Appleton-Century-Crofts; 1955.

BUSWELL, G. T. *A Laboratory Study of the Reading of Modern Foreign Languages,* Publications of the American and Canadian Committees on Modern

Languages, Vol. II. New York: The Macmillan Company; 1941.

BUTTS, R. FREEMAN. *The College Charts Its Course.* New York: McGraw-Hill Book Company, Inc.; 1939.

————. *A Cultural History of Education.* New York: McGraw-Hill Book Company, Inc.; 1947.

————. *The American Tradition in Religion and Education.* Boston: Beacon Press; 1950.

California State Curriculum Commission. *Teachers' Guide to Child Development in the Intermediate Grades.* Sacramento: State Department of Education; 1937.

————. *Teachers' Guide to Child Development: Manual for Kindergarten and Primary Grades.* (Ruth M. Hockett, Editor.) Sacramento: State Department of Education; 1930.

Carnegie Foundation for the Advancement of Teaching. *First Annual Report of the President and Treasurer.* New York: Carnegie Foundation for the Advancement of Teaching; 1906.

CASWELL, HOLLIS L., and CAMPBELL, DOAK S. *Curriculum Development.* New York: American Book Company; 1935.

————. (Editors). *Readings in Curriculum Development.* New York: American Book Company; 1937.

CHAMBERLIN, DEAN; CHAMBERLIN, ENID; DROUGHT, NEAL E.; and SCOTT, WILLIAM E. *Did They Succeed in College?* New York: Harper & Brothers; 1942.

CHAPIN, F. STUART. *Experimental De.igns in Sociological Research.* New York: Harper & Brothers; 1947.

CHARTERS, W. W. *Curriculum Construction.* New York: The Macmillan Company; 1925.

————, and WAPLES, DOUGLAS. *The Commonwealth Teacher-Training Study.* Chicago: University of Chicago Press; 1929.

————, and WHITLEY, ISADORE B. *An Analysis of Secretarial Duties and Traits.* Baltimore: The Williams & Wilkins Company; 1924.

Charting the Curriculum in New York State Schools. Albany, New York: New York State Education Department; 1954.

CHASE, STUART. *Democracy under Pressure.* New York: The Twentieth Century Fund; 1945.

CHILDS, JOHN L. *American Pragmatism and Education.* New York: Henry Holt & Co., Inc.; 1956.

————. "A Preface to a New Philosophy of Education," in *Thirteenth Yearbook,* National Education Association, Department of Superintendence. Washington, D. C.; 1935.

————. "Should the School Seek Actively to Reconstruct Society?" in *Annals of the American Academy of Political and Social Science,* "Education for Social Control," Vol. 182 (November, 1935). Philadelphia: American Academy of Political and Social Science.

————. "Spiritual Values of the Secular Public Schools," in John Dewey Society, *Seventh Yearbook.* New York: Harper & Brothers; 1944.

CHRISTIANSON, HELEN. *Bodily Rhythmic Movements of Young Children in Relation to Rhythm in Music.* New York: Teachers College, Columbia University; 1938.

Cincinnati Public Schools. *The Primary Manual.* Curriculum Bulletin No. 95, 1942.

CLAPP, ELSIE RIPLEY. *Community Schools in Action.* New York: Viking Press, Inc.; 1940.

COHEN, MORRIS R., and NAGEL, ERNEST. *An Introduction to Logic and the Scientific Method.* New York: Harcourt, Brace & Co., Inc.; 1934.

COLE, LAWRENCE, and BRUCE, WILLIAM. *Educational Psychology.* Yonkers, New York: World Book Company; 1950.

COLLINGS, ELLSWORTH. *An Experiment with a Project Curriculum.* New York: The Macmillan Company; 1923.

————, and WILSON, M. O. *Psychology for Teachers*. New York: Charles Scribner's Sons; 1930.

CONANT, JAMES BRYANT. "Public Education and the Structure of American Society," *Teachers College Record*, Vol. 47, No. 3 (December, 1945).

CONGDON, ALLEN R. "Training in High School Mathematics Essential to Success in Certain College Subjects," *Teachers College Contributions to Education*, No. 403. New York: Bureau of Publications, Teachers College, Columbia University; 1940.

COOLEY, CHARLES H. *Human Nature and the Social Order*. New York: Charles Scribner's Sons; 1902.

COREY, STEPHEN M. "The Developmental Tasks of Youth," in John Dewey Society, *Eighth Yearbook*, "The American High School: Its Responsibility and Opportunity." (Edited by Hollis L. Caswell.) New York: Harper & Brothers; 1946.

————, and Others. *General Education in the American High School*. Chicago: Scott, Foresman and Company; 1942.

COUNTS, GEORGE S. *Dare the School Build a New Social Order?* New York: The John Day Company, Inc.; 1932.

————. *The Social Foundations of Education*. Part IX, Report of the Commission on the Social Studies, American Historical Association. New York: Charles Scribner's Sons; 1934.

CRAMER, ROSCOE. "Common-Learnings Program in the Junior High School," Bulletin 35, *National Association of Secondary School Principals* (April, 1951).

CRONBACH, LEE J. *Educational Psychology*. New York: Harcourt, Brace & Co., Inc.; 1954.

————. (Editor). *Text Materials in Modern Education*. Urbana, Illinois: University of Illinois Press; 1955.

CUBBERLEY, ELLWOOD P. *Public Education in the United States*. Boston: Houghton Mifflin Company; 1919.

DAHL, ROBERT. *A Preface to Democratic Theory*. Chicago: University of Chicago Press; 1956.

DAVIS, ALLISON; GARDNER, BURLEIGH B.; and GARDNER, MARY R. *Deep South, a Social Anthropological Study of Caste and Class*. Chicago: University of Chicago Press; 1941.

————, and HAVIGHURST, ROBERT J., *Father of the Man: How Your Child Gets His Personality*. Boston: Houghton Mifflin Company; 1947.

DE GARMO, CHARLES. "Most Pressing Problems Concerning the Elementary Course of Study," *First Yearbook of the National Herbart Society for the Scientific Study of Teaching* (Second Edition). Chicago: University of Chicago Press; 1907.

DE KRUIF, PAUL. *Hunger Fighters*. New York: Harcourt, Brace & Co., Inc.; 1939.

————. *Microbe Hunters*. New York: Harcourt, Brace & Co., Inc.; 1939.

DE LIMA, AGNES. *The Little Red Schoolhouse*. New York: The Macmillan Company; 1942.

DENNIS, LAWRENCE. *The Coming American Fascism*. New York: Harper & Brothers; 1936.

Denver (Colorado) Public Schools. *Manual for Teachers Working on Core Course*. November, 1938.

DEUTSCHE, J. M. *The Development of Children's Concepts of Causal Relations*. Monograph Series No. XIII. Minneapolis: University of Minnesota Press; 1937.

DEWEY, JOHN. *The Child and the Curriculum*. Chicago: University of Chicago Press; 1902.

————. *Democracy and Education*. New York; The Macmillan Company; 1916.

————. *Experience and Education*. New York: The Macmillan Company; 1938.

————. *How We Think*. Boston: D. C. Heath & Co.; 1910. Revised Edition, 1933.

————. *Individualism Old and New*. New York: Minton, Balch & Company; 1930.

DEWEY, JOHN. *Logic: the Theory of Inquiry.* New York: Henry Holt & Co., Inc.; 1938.

———. *The Public and Its Problems.* New York: Henry Holt & Co., Inc.; 1927.

———. *The School and Society.* Chicago: University of Chicago Press; 1900.

———. *Theory of Valuation.* Chicago: University of Chicago Press; 1939.

———. *The Way Out of Educational Confusion.* Cambridge, Massachusetts: Harvard University Press; 1931.

DEWHURST, J. FREDERIC, and Associates. *America's Needs and Resources.* New York: Twentieth Century Fund; 1947.

———. *America's Needs and Resources: A New Survey.* New York: Twentieth Century Fund, 1953.

DOLL, RONALD C., PASSOW, HARRY A., and COREY, STEPHEN M. *Organizing for Curriculum Improvement.* New York: Bureau of Publications, Teachers College, Columbia University; 1953.

DRUCKER, PETER F. *The End of Economic Man.* New York: The John Day Company, Inc.; 1936.

DUNHAM, BARROWS. *Man against Myth.* Boston: Little, Brown & Company; 1947.

DYER, ANNIE R. *The Placement of Home Economics Content in Junior and Senior High Schools.* New York: Bureau of Publications, Teachers College, Columbia University; 1927.

EBY, FREDERICK, and ARROWOOD, CHARLES F. *The Development of Modern Education in Theory, Organization, and Practice.* New York: Prentice-Hall, Inc.; 1934.

ECKERT, R. E., and MARSHALL, T. O. *When Youth Leave School.* New York: McGraw-Hill Book Company, Inc.; 1938.

EDMAN, IRWIN. *Fountainheads of Freedom.* New York: Reynal & Hitchcock; 1941.

'Educational Change and Social Engineering," *Progressive Education,* Vol. 26, No. 7, May, 1949 (entire issue).

Educational Policies Commission. *Education and Economic Well-Being in American Democracy.* Washington, D. C.: National Education Association; 1940.

———. *Education for All American Youth.* Washington, D. C.: National Education Association; 1944.

———. *Education of Free Men in American Democracy.* Washington, D. C.: National Education Association; 1941.

———. *Learning the Ways of Democracy.* Washington, D. C.: National Education Association; 1940.

———. *The Unique Function of Education in American Democracy.* Washington, D. C.: American Council on Education; 1937.

EDWARDS, NEWTON, and RICHEY, HERMAN G. *The School in the American Social Order.* Boston: Houghton Mifflin Company; 1947.

EDWARDS, V. *Group Leader's Guide to Propaganda Analysis.* New York: Institute for Propaganda Analysis; 1938.

ELLIOTT, MABEL A., and MERRILL, FRANCIS E. *Social Disorganization,* Revised Edition. New York: Harper & Brothers; 1941.

Encyclopedia of Educational Research. (Edited by Walter S. Monroe.) New York: The Macmillan Company; 1941. Revised Edition, 1950.

Eugene, Oregon, Public Schools. *Tentative Scope and Sequence Chart,* 1940.

EVANS, HUBERT M. (Editor). *Coöperative Research and Curriculum Improvement.* New York: Bureau of Publications, Teachers College, Columbia University; 1950. (Reprinted from *Teachers College Record,* Vol. 51. No. 7.)

EVERETT, SAMUEL (Editor). *A Challenge to Secondary Education.* New York: D. Appleton-Century Company, Inc.; 1935.

——— (Editor). *The Community School.* New York: D. Appleton-Century Company, Inc.; 1938.

———. *School and Community.* New York: Hinds, Hayden & Eldredge; 1948.

FAGERSTROM, F. H. "Mathematical Facts and Processes Prerequisite to the Study of the Calculus," *Teachers College Contributions to Education,* No. 572. New York: Bureau of Publications, Teachers College, Columbia University; 1933.

FAUNCE, ROLAND, and BOSSING, NELSON. *Developing the Core Curriculum.* New York: Prentice-Hall, Inc.; 1951.

FAWCETT, HAROLD P. "The Nature of Proof," *Thirteenth Yearbook* of the National Council of Teachers of Mathematics. New York: Bureau of Publications, Teachers College, Columbia University; 1938.

FEIGL, HERBERT. "De Principiis Non Disputandum . . . ?" in Max Black (Editor). *Philosophical Analysis.* Ithaca, New York: Cornell University Press; 1950.

FINER, HERMAN. *Road to Reaction.* Boston: Little, Brown & Company; 1945.

FOERSTER, NORMAN. *The American State University.* Chapel Hill: University of North Carolina Press; 1937.

————. *The Future of the Liberal College.* New York: D. Appleton-Century Company, Inc.; 1938.

FOLLETT, MARY P. *Dynamic Administration.* (Edited by Metcalf and Urwick.) New York: Harper & Brothers; 1942.

FOUDY, JOHN T. *The Educational Principles of American Humanism.* Washington, D. C.: Catholic University of America; 1945.

Francis W. Parker School Yearbook, "The Course in Science," Vol. V (July, 1918).

FRANK, LAWRENCE K. *Projective Techniques.* Springfield, Illinois: C. C. Thomas; 1948.

FREDERICK, O. I., and FARQUEAR, LUCILLE J. "Areas of Human Activity," *Journal of Educational Research,* Vol. 30, pages 672–679.

————., and MUSSELWHITE, L. P. "Centers of Emphasis for Grades One through Twelve," *Journal of Educational Research,* Vol. 32 (October, 1938).

FREEMAN, G. LA V., and FREEMAN, R. S. *The Child and His Picture Book.* Chicago: Northwestern University Press; 1933.

FREESTON, P. M. "Vocational Interests of Elementary School Children," *Occupational Psychology,* Vol. 13, pages 223–237.

FRIES, C. C. *American English Grammar.* New York: D. Appleton-Century Company, Inc.; 1940.

FROMM, ERICH. *Escape from Freedom.* New York: Farrar & Rinehart, Inc.; 1941.

GALLOWAY, GEORGE B., and Associates. "Education and Planning," *Planning for America.* New York: Henry Holt & Co., Inc.; 1941.

GATES, ARTHUR I., and Others. *Educational Psychology.* New York: The Macmillan Company; 1942.

————. "Studies of Children's Interests in Reading," *Elementary School Journal,* Vol. 31, pages 656–670.

GESELL, ARNOLD. "The Developmental Psychology of Twins," in *Handbook of Child Psychology.* (Edited by Carl Murchison.) Worcester, Massachusetts: Clark University Press; 1931.

————, and ILG, FRANCES L. *The Child from Five to Ten.* New York: Harper & Brothers; 1946.

GIDEONSE, HARRY D. *The Higher Learning in a Democracy.* New York: Farrar & Rinehart, Inc.; 1937.

GILES, H. H.; McCUTCHEN, S. P.; and ZECHIEL, A. N. *Exploring the Curriculum.* New York: Harper & Brothers; 1942.

GLASER, EDWARD M. "An Experiment in the Development of Critical Thinking," *Teachers College Contributions to Education.* No. 843. New York: Bureau of Publications, Teachers College, Columbia University; 1941.

GOODSON, MAX R. "Learning to Think about Power," in *Student Teaching,* by C. W. Sanford and Others. Champaign: Stipes Publishing Co.; 1940.

GRAY, W. S. "Reading," in National Society for the Study of Education, *Thirty-eighth Yearbook,* Part I. Bloomington, Illinois: Public School Publishing Company; 1939.

GREENE, HARRY A. "Direct versus Formal Methods in Elementary English," *Elementary English,* Vol. XIV, No. 5 (May, 1947), pages 273–285.

GRIFFITH, COLEMAN R. *An Introduction to Educational Psychology.* New York: Farrar & Rinehart, Inc.; 1935.

HAINES ALEYNE C. *Children's Perception of Membership Roles in Problem-Solving Groups.* Doctor's Dissertation, University of Illinois; 1952.

HALL, SIDNEY B.; PETERS, D. W.; and CASWELL, HOLLIS L. *Procedures for Virginia State Curriculum Program,* Bulletin of the State Board of Education, July, 1932.

HAMLIN, HERBERT M. *Agricultural Education in Community Schools.* Danville, Illinois: Interstate Publishing Company; 1949.

HAND, HAROLD C. *How to Conduct the Hidden Tuition Costs Study.* Circular Series A, No. 51, Illinois Secondary School Curriculum Program Bulletin No. 4. Springfield, Illinois: Office of the State Superintendent of Public Instruction; May, 1949.

———. *How to Conduct the Participation in Extra-Class Activities Study.* Circular Series A, No. 51, Illinois Secondary School Curriculum Program Bulletin No. 5. Springfield, Illinois: Office of the State Superintendent of Public Instruction; May, 1949.

——— (Editor). *Living in the Atomic Age.* Urbana, Illinois: Bureau of Research and Service, University of Illinois; 1948.

———. *Principal Findings of the 1947–1948 Basic Studies of the Illinois Secondary School Curriculum Program.* Circular Series A, No. 51. Illinois Secondary School Curriculum Program Bulletin No. 2. Springfield, Illinois: Office of the State Superintendent of Public Instruction; May, 1949.

HAND, HAROLD C. *Principles of American Public Secondary Education.* New York: Harcourt, Brace & Co., Inc.; 1957.

———. "Problems of High School Youth." Prepared for the Illinois Secondary School Curriculum Program. Springfield, Illinois: Office of the State Superintendent of Public Instruction; 1949.

———. *Prospectus of the Local Area Consensus Studies.* Springfield, Illinois: State Department of Public Instruction; 1951. (Illinois Secondary School Curriculum Program Bulletin No. 51.)

———. *What People Think about Their Schools.* Yonkers, New York: World Book Company; 1948.

HANNA, PAUL R. *Youth Serves the Community.* New York: D. Appleton-Century Company, Inc.; 1936.

HARAP, HENRY (Editor). *The Changing Curriculum.* New York: D. Appleton-Century Company, Inc.; 1937.

Harvard Committee on the Objectives of Education in a Free Society. *General Education in a Free Society.* Cambridge, Massachusetts: Harvard University Press; 1945.

HAVIGHURST, ROBERT J. *Developmental Tasks and Education.* Chicago: University of Chicago Press; 1949.

HAZLITT, V. "Children's Thinking," *British Journal of Psychology,* 20, 1929, pages 354–364.

HERRICK, VIRGIL E., and TYLER, RALPH W. (Editors). *Toward Improved Curriculum Theory.* Supplementary Educational Monographs, No. 71. Chicago: University of Chicago Press; 1950.

HERSKOVITS, MELVILLE. *Man and His Works.* New York: Alfred A. Knopf, Inc.; 1948.

HETHERINGTON, CLARK W. *The Demonstration Play School of 1913.* University of California Publications in Education, Vol. 5, No. 2. Berkeley: University of California Press.

HOCKETT, JOHN A. "A Determination of the Major Social Problems of American Life," *Teachers College Contributions to Education,* No. 281. New York: Bureau of Publications, Teachers College, Columbia University; 1927.

HOCKETT, RUTH M. (Editor). *Teachers' Guide to Child Development: Manual for Kindergarten and Primary Teachers.* Sacramento, California: State Education Department, 1930.

HOLLINGSHEAD, A. B. *Elmtown's Youth, the Impact of Social Classes on Adolescents.* New York: John Wiley & Sons, Inc.; 1949.

HOOD, FRED C. *Developing the Ability to Assess the Results of Thinking.* Urbana, Illinois: Office of the High School Visitor, University of Illinois; 1949.

HOPKINS, L. THOMAS. *Curriculum Principles and Practices.* Chicago: Benjamin H. Sanborn & Co.; 1929.

———. *Integration: Its Meaning and Application.* New York: D. Appleton-Century Company, Inc.; 1937.

HORNEY, KAREN. *The Neurotic Personality of Our Time.* New York: W. W. Norton & Co., Inc.; 1937.

Houston Public Schools. *Scope of the Curriculum.* Curriculum Bulletin No. 2. Houston, Texas; 1933–34.

HUBER, MIRIAM B.; BRUNER, H. B.; and CURRY, C. M. *Children's Interests in Poetry.* Chicago: Rand McNally & Company; 1927.

HUDSON, WILLIAM HENRY. *A Traveller in Little Things.* New York: E. P. Dutton & Co., Inc.; 1921.

HUTCHINS, ROBERT M. *The Higher Learning in America.* New Haven: Yale University Press; 1936.

HUXLEY, THOMAS. *Physiography.* New York: D. Appleton and Company; 1879.

Illinois, State Department of Public Instruction. *Guide to the Study of the Curriculum in the Secondary Schools of Illinois.* Springfield, Illinois, August, 1948.

Illinois Survey Associates. *A Look at Springfield Schools.* Champaign, Illinois: Stipes Publishing Company; 1948.

JACKMAN, W. S. "Francis Wayland Parker," *Report of the Commissioner of Education, 1902.* Washington, D. C.: United States Government Printing Office; 1903.

JENKINS, DAVID H. "Social Engineering in Educational Change: An Outline of Method," *Progressive Education,* Vol. 26, No. 7 (May, 1949), pages 195–196.

JENNINGS, HELEN HALL. *Leadership and Isolation.* New York: Longmans, Green & Company; 1943.

———. "Leadership and Sociometric Choice," in *Readings in Social Psychology.* (Edited by Newcomb and Hartley.) New York: Henry Holt & Co., Inc.; 1947.

———. *Sociometry in Group Relations.* Washington, D. C.: American Council on Education; 1948.

JENSEN, GALE E. *Methodology and Criteria for the Validation of Educational Aims.* Doctor's Dissertation, University of Illinois; 1948 (unpublished).

JERSILD, A. T.; THORNDIKE, R. L.; GOLDMAN, B.; and LOFTUS, J. J. "An Evaluation of Aspects of the Activity Program in the New York City Public Elementary Schools," *Journal of Experimental Education,* Vol. 8 (December, 1939), pages 166–207.

JERSILD, A. T., and Others. "A Further Comparison of Pupils in Activity and Non-Activity Schools," *Journal of Experimental Education,* Vol. 9 (June, 1941).

John Dewey Society. *First Yearbook,* "The Teacher and Society" (Edited by William H. Kilpatrick). New York: D. Appleton-Century Company, Inc.; 1937.

———. *Third Yearbook,* "Democracy and the Curriculum." New York: D. Appleton-Century Company, Inc.; 1939.

———. *Seventh Yearbook,* "The Public Schools and Spiritual Values" (Edited by John S. Brubacher). New York: Harper & Brothers; 1944.

———. *Eighth Yearbook,* "The American High School: Its Responsibility and Opportunity" (Edited by Hollis L. Caswell). New York: Harper & Brothers; 1946.

JOHNSON, B. L. "Children's Reading Interests as Related to Sex and Grade in School," *School Review,* Vol. 40, pages 257–272.

JONES, ARTHUR J.; GRIZZELL, E. D.; and GRINSTEAD, WREN J. *Principles of Unit Construction.* New York: McGraw-Hill Book Company, Inc.; 1939.

JORDAN, ARTHUR M. "Children's Interests in Reading," *Teachers College Contributions to Education,* No. 107. New York: Bureau of Publications, Teachers College, Columbia University; 1921.

JUDD, CHARLES H. *Educational Psychology.* Boston: Houghton Mifflin Company; 1939.

———. *The Psychology of Social Institutions.* New York: The Macmillan Company; 1926.

JUSTMAN, JOSEPH. *Theories of Secondary Education in the United States.* New York: Bureau of Publications, Teachers College, Columbia University; 1940.

KANDEL, I. L. *Conflicting Theories of Education.* New York: The Macmillan Company; 1939.

KARDINER, ABRAM. *The Individual and His Society.* New York: Columbia University Press; 1939.

———. *Psychological Frontiers of Society.* New York: Columbia University Press; 1945.

KELLEY, TRUMAN L. *Scientific Method: Its Function in Research and in Education.* Columbus: Ohio State University Press; 1929.

KIGHT, STANFORD S., and MICKELSON, JOHN M. "Problems vs. Subjects," *The Clearing House,* Vol. 24, No. 1 (September, 1949), pages 3–7.

KILPATRICK, WILLIAM H. *Education and the Social Crisis.* New York: Liveright Publishing Corporation; 1932.

———. *Education for a Changing Civilization.* New York: The Macmillan Company; 1927.

KILPATRICK, WILLIAM H. (Editor). The *Educational Frontier.* New York: D. Appleton-Century Company, Inc.; 1933.

———. *Foundations of Method.* New York: The Macmillan Company; 1925.

——— (Editor). John Dewey Society, *First Yearbook,* "The Teacher and Society." New York: D. Appleton-Century Company, Inc.; 1937.

———. *The Project Method.* Bulletin, 10th Series, No. 3. New York: Teachers College, Columbia University; 1918.

———. *A Reconstructed Theory of the Educative Process.* New York: Bureau of Publications, Teachers College, Columbia University; 1935.

———. *Remaking the Curriculum.* New York: Newson & Company; 1936.

———. *Selfhood and Civilization.* New York: The Macmillan Company; 1941.

———. *Sourcebook in the Philosophy of Education.* New York: The Macmillan Company; 1934.

KLINE, L. W. "Some Experimental Evidence in Regard to Formal Discipline," *Journal of Educational Psychology,* Vol. 5, 1914, pages 259–266.

KLUCKHORN, CLYDE. *Mirror for Man.* New York: McGraw-Hill Book Company, Inc.; 1949.

———, and MURRAY, HENRY A. (Editors). *Personality in Nature, Society, and Culture.* New York: Alfred A. Knopf, Inc.; 1948.

KNICKERBOCKER, IRVING. "Leadership: A Conception and Some Implications," *Journal of Social Issues,* Vol. IV, No. 3 (Summer, 1948), pages 23–40.

KOFFKA, KURT. *Principles of Gestalt Psychology.* New York: Harcourt, Brace & Co., Inc.; 1935.

KOOPMAN, GEORGE; MIEL, ALICE; and MISNER, PAUL. *Democracy in School Administration.* New York: D. Appleton-Century Company, Inc.; 1943.

KOOPMAN, MARGARET O. *Utilizing the Local Environment.* New York: Hinds, Hayden & Eldredge; 1946.

KYTE, GEORGE C. "Variations in the Organization of the Elementary Courses of Study in History," *Educational Administration and Supervision*, Vol. 13, No. 6 (September, 1927), pages 361–376.

————, and LEWIS, ROBERT H. "Time Tables," *The Nation's Schools*, Vol. 17, No. 1 (January, 1936).

LANE, ROBERT HILL, and Others. *The Progressive Elementary School*. Boston: Houghton Mifflin Company; 1938.

LASKI, HAROLD. *The American Democracy*. New York: Viking Press, Inc.; 1948.

LAZARSFELD, PAUL F., and STANTON, FRANK N. (Editors). *Communications Research, 1948–1949*. New York: Columbia University, Bureau of Applied Social Research Publications; 1949.

LEE, J. MURRAY, and LEE, DORRIS MAY. *The Child and His Curriculum*. New York: Appleton-Century-Crofts, Inc.; 1950.

LEHMAN, HARVEY C., and WITTY, PAUL A. *The Psychology of Play Activities*. New York: A. S. Barnes & Co.; 1927.

LENZEN, V. F. "Science and Social Context," *University of California Publications in Philosophy*, Vol. 23, 1942, pages 3–26.

LEONARD, J. PAUL. *Developing the Secondary School Curriculum*. New York: Rinehart & Co., Inc.; 1946.

————, and EURICH, ALVIN C. (Editors). *An Evaluation of Modern Education*. New York: D. Appleton-Century Company, Inc.; 1942.

LEWIN, KURT. "Forces behind Food Habits and Methods of Change," *Bulletin of the National Resources Council*, Washington, D. C., 1943, Vol. CVIII, pages 35–65.

————. "Frontiers in Group Dynamics; I. Concept, Method, and Reality in Social Science; Social Equilibria and Social Change," *Human Relations*, Vol. I, No. 1, 1947, pages 5–41.

————. "Frontiers in Group Dynamics; II. Channels of Group Life; Social Planning and Action Research," *Human Relations*, Vol. I, No. 2, 1947, pages 143–153.

————. "Group Decision and Social Change," in *Readings in Social Psychology* (Newcomb and Hartley, Editors). New York: Henry Holt & Co., Inc.; 1947.

————. *Resolving Social Conflicts*. New York: Harper & Brothers; 1948.

LEYS, WAYNE A. R. *Ethics and Social Policy*. New York: Prentice-Hall, Inc.; 1941.

LIEBERMAN, MYRON. *Education as a Profession*. Englewood Cliffs, New Jersey: Prentice-Hall, Inc.; 1956.

LINTON, RALPH. *Cultural Background of Personality*. New York: D. Appleton-Century Company, Inc.; 1945.

————. *The Study of Man*. New York: D. Appleton-Century Company, Inc.; 1936.

LIPPITT, RONALD. "An Experimental Study of the Effect of Democratic and Authoritarian Group Atmospheres," *University of Iowa Studies in Child Welfare*, 16 (1940), No. 3, pages 45–193.

————. "The Psychodrama in Leadership Training," *Sociometry*, Vol. 6, No. 3, 1943.

————. *Training in Community Relations*. New York: Harper & Brothers; 1949.

————, and FRENCH, JOHN R. P. "Research and Training," *The Group*, Vol. 10, No. 2 (January, 1948).

————, and WHITE, RALPH K. "The 'Social Climate' of Children's Groups," in *Child Behavior and Development* (Edited by Barker, Kounin, and Wright). New York: McGraw-Hill Book Company, Inc.; 1943.

LODGE, RUPERT C. *Philosophy of Education*. New York: Harper & Brothers; 1947.

LOOMIS, A. K.; LIDE, EDWIN S.; and JOHNSON, B. LAMAR. "The Program of Studies," *Bulletin*, 1932, No. 17, National Survey of Secondary Education, Monograph No. 19. Washington, D. C.: United States Government Printing Office; 1933.

LOVELASS, HARRY D. *How to Conduct the Study of the Guidance Services of the School.* Circular Series A, No. 51. Illinois Secondary School Curriculum Program Bulletin No. 6. Springfield, Illinois: Office of the State Superintendent of Public Instruction; May, 1949.

LOWELL, A. LAWRENCE. "Inaugural Address, October 6, 1909," *Atlantic Monthly,* Vol. 104 (November, 1909).

LUND, S. E. TORSTEN. *The School-Centered Community.* New York: Anti-Defamation League; 1949.

LYND, ROBERT S. *Knowledge for What?* Princeton: Princeton University Press; 1939.

———, and LYND, HELEN. *Middletown.* New York: Harcourt, Brace & Co., Inc.; 1929.

———, and LYND, HELEN. *Middletown in Transition.* New York: Harcourt, Brace & Co., Inc.; 1937.

MACOMBER, FREEMAN GLENN. *Guiding Child Development in the Elementary School.* New York: American Book Company; 1941.

MALINOWSKI, BRONISLAW. *A Scientific Theory of Culture and Other Essays.* Chapel Hill: The University of North Carolina Press; 1944.

MANN, CARLETON H. "How Schools Use Their Time," *Teachers College Contributions to Education,* No. 333. New York: Bureau of Publications, Teachers College, Columbia University; 1928.

MANNHEIM, KARL. *Diagnosis of Our Time.* London: Kegan Paul, Trench, Trubner & Co.; 1943.

———. *Ideology and Utopia.* New York: Harcourt, Brace & Co., Inc.; 1936.

———. *Man and Society in an Age of Reconstruction.* New York: Harcourt, Brace & Co., Inc.; 1940.

MANSFIELD, HARVEY C. "Government," *American Journal of Sociology,* Vol. XLVII (May, 1942).

MARITAIN, JACQUES. *Christianity and Democracy* (Translated by Doris C. Anson). New York: Charles Scribner's Sons; 1944.

———. *Education at the Crossroads.* New Haven: Yale University Press; 1943.

———. *The Twilight of Civilization* (Translated by Lionel Landry). New York: Sheed & Ward, Inc.; 1943.

MARSHALL, LEON C., and GOETZ, RACHEL MARSHALL. *Curriculum-Making in the Social Studies.* New York: Charles Scribner's Sons; 1936.

MARTIN, EVERETT D. *The Meaning of a Liberal Education.* New York: W. W. Norton & Company, Inc.; 1926.

MATHEWS, C. O. "Grade-Placement of Curriculum Materials in the Social Studies," *Teachers College Contributions to Education,* No. 241. New York: Bureau of Publications, Teachers College, Columbia University; 1926.

MAYHEW, KATHERINE CAMP, and EDWARDS, ANNA CAMP. *The Dewey School: The Laboratory School of the University of Chicago, 1896–1903.* New York: D. Appleton-Century Company, Inc.; 1936.

McCARTHY, DOROTHEA A. *The Language Development of the Pre-School Child.* Minneapolis: University of Minnesota Press; 1930.

McGREGOR, DOUGLAS. "Conditions of Effective Leadership in the Industrial Organization," in *Readings in Social Psychology* (Edited by Newcomb and Hartley). New York: Henry Holt & Co., Inc.; 1947.

———. "The Staff Function in Human Relations," *Journal of Social Issues,* Vol. IV, No. 3 (Summer, 1948), pages 5–22.

McGUCKEN, WILLIAM. "The Philosophy of Catholic Education," in National Society for the Study of Education, *Forty-first Yearbook,* Part I, "Philosophies of Education." Bloomington, Illinois: Public School Publishing Company; 1942.

MEAD, MARGARET. *And Keep Your Powder Dry.* New York: William Morrow & Co., Inc.; 1942.

———. *Coming of Age in Samoa.* New York: William Morrow & Co., Inc.; 1928.

———. *Coöperation and Competition among Primitive Peoples.* New York: McGraw-Hill Book Company, Inc.; 1937.

———. *From the South Seas.* New York: William Morrow & Co., Inc.; 1939.

———. *Growing Up in New Guinea.* New York: William Morrow & Co., Inc.; 1930.

MEARNS, HUGHES. *Creative Youth.* New York: Doubleday & Co., Inc.; 1925.

MEIKLEJOHN, ALEXANDER. *The Liberal College.* Boston: Marshall Jones Company; 1920.

MELLINGER, B. E. "Children's Interests in Pictures," *Teachers College Contributions to Education,* No. 516. New York: Bureau of Publications, Teachers College, Columbia University; 1932.

MELTZER, HYMAN. "Children's Social Concepts," *Teachers College Contributions to Education,* No. 192. New York: Bureau of Publications, Teachers College, Columbia University; 1926.

MERIAM, J. L. *Child Life and the Curriculum.* Yonkers, New York: World Book Company; 1920.

MERRIAM, CHARLES E. *What Is Democracy?* Chicago: University of Chicago Press; 1941.

MERTON, ROBERT K. "Patterns of Influence: A Study of Interpersonal Influence and of Communications Behavior in a Local Community," in *Communications Research, 1948–1949* (Edited by P. F Lazarsfeld and F. N. Stanton). New York: Harper & Brothers; 1949.

MIEL, ALICE. *Changing the Curriculum: A Social Process.* New York: D. Appleton-Century Company, Inc.; 1946.

MILLER, VAN, and SPALDING, WILLARD B. *The Public Administration of American Schools.* Yonkers, New York: World Book Company; 1952.

Mississippi, State of. *A Guide for Curriculum Reorganization in the Secondary School.* Jackson: State Printing Office; 1937.

MOEHLMAN, CONRAD H. *School and Church: The American Way.* New York: Harper & Brothers; 1944.

MONROE, WALTER S. (Editor). *Encyclopedia of Educational Research.* New York: The Macmillan Company; 1941. Revised Edition, 1950.

———, and ENGELHART, MAX. *The Scientific Study of Educational Problems.* New York: The Macmillan Company; 1937.

MOONEY, ROSS L. "Surveying High School Students' Problems by Means of a Problem Check List," Ohio State University, *Educational Research Bulletin,* Vol. XXI, No. 3 (March 18, 1942).

MOORE, ERNEST C. *What Is Education?* Boston: Ginn & Company; 1915.

MOORE, T. V. "The Reasoning Ability of Children in the First Years of School Life," *Studies in Psychology and Psychiatry,* Vol. 2, No. 2. Baltimore: The Williams & Wilkins Company; 1929.

MORE, PAUL ELMER. *On Being Human.* New Shelburne Essays, No. 3. Princeton: Princeton University Press; 1936.

MORRISON, HENRY C. *Basic Principles of Education.* Boston: Houghton Mifflin Company; 1934.

———. *The Curriculum of the Common School.* Chicago: University of Chicago Press; 1940.

———. *The Practice of Teaching in the Secondary School.* Chicago: University of Chicago Press; 1931.

MORRISON, J. CAYCE, and Others. *The Activity Program: A Survey of the Curriculum Experiment with the Activity Program in the Elementary Schools of the City of New York.* Albany: State Education Department; 1941.

MOSSMAN, LOIS COFFEY. *The Activity Concept.* New York: The Macmillan Company; 1939.

MUNTYAN, MILOSH. *Community School Concepts in Relation to Societal Determinants.* Doctor's Dissertation, University of Illinois; 1947.

MURPHY, ARTHUR E. *The Uses of Reason.* New York: The Macmillan Company; 1943.

MURPHY, GARDNER; MURPHY, LOIS; and NEWCOMB, T. M. *Experimental Social Psychology.* New York: Harper & Brothers; 1937.

MURSELL, JAMES L. *Developmental Teaching.* New York: McGraw-Hill Book Company, Inc.; 1949.

MYRDAL, GUNNAR. *An American Dilemma.* New York: Harper & Brothers; 1944.

MYRES, JOHN L. *The Political Ideas of the Greeks.* New York: Methodist Book Concern; 1927.

NASH, ARNOLD S. *The University and the Modern World.* New York: The Macmillan Company; 1943.

National Association of Secondary School Principals and National Council for the Social Studies. *Problems in American Life Series.* (Twenty-two resource units, numbered 1 to 22.) Washington, D. C., 1942–1945.

National Committee on Mathematical Requirements. *The Reorganization of Mathematics in the Secondary School.* Boston: Houghton Mifflin Company; 1927.

National Council of Teachers of Mathematics. *Sixteenth Yearbook,* "Arithmetic in General Education." New York: Teachers College, Columbia University; 1941.

National Education Association, Committee on Social-Economic Goals of America. *Implications of Social-Economic Goals for Education.* Washington, D. C.: National Education Association; 1937.

———. Department of Adult Education. *First National Training Laboratory in Group Development, Group Growth, and Educational Dynamics,* Bulletin

No. 2. Washington, D. C.: National Education Association; 1947.

———. Department of Adult Education. *National Training Laboratory in Group Development, Report of the Second Summer Laboratory Session,* Bulletin No. 3. Washington, D. C.: National Education Association; 1948.

———. Department of Elementary School Principals. *Twenty-fourth Yearbook,* "Community Living and the Elementary School." Washington, D. C.: National Education Association; 1945.

———. *Proceedings and Addresses,* Thirty-eighth Annual Meeting (Chicago, 1899). Washington, D. C.: National Education Association.

———. "Report of Committee on College Entrance Requirements," *Proceedings and Addresses,* Thirty-eighth Annual Meeting (Chicago, 1899).

———. *Report of the Committee of Ten on Secondary School Studies.* Chicago: American Book Company; 1894.

———. *Third Yearbook,* "Research in Constructing the Elementary School Curriculum." Washington, D. C.: National Education Association; 1925.

———. *Fifth Yearbook,* "The Junior High School Curriculum." Washington, D. C.: National Education Association; 1927.

———. *Sixth Yearbook,* "The Development of the High School Curriculum." Washington, D. C.: National Education Association; 1928.

National Nursing Council. *A Thousand Think Together.* New York: National Nursing Council, Inc.; 1948.

National Resources Committee. Report of the Subcommittee on Technology, *Technological Trends and National Policy.* Washington, D. C.: United States Government Printing Office; 1937.

National Society for the Study of Education. *Twenty-ninth Yearbook,* "Report of the Society's Committee on Arithmetic." Bloomington, Illinois:

Public School Publishing Company; 1930.

———. *Thirty-first Yearbook*, Part I, "A Program for Teaching Science." Bloomington, Illinois: Public School Publishing Company; 1932.

———. *Thirty-second Yearbook*, "The Teaching of Geography." Bloomington, Illinois: Public School Publishing Company; 1933.

———. *Thirty-third Yearbook*, Part II, "The Activity Movement." Bloomington, Illinois: Public School Publishing Company; 1939.

———. *Thirty-seventh Yearbook*, Part II, "The Scientific Movement in Education." Bloomington, Illinois: Public School Publishing Company; 1938.

———. *Thirty-eighth Yearbook*, Part I, "Child Development and the Curriculum." Bloomington, Illinois: Public School Publishing Company; 1939.

———. *Forty-first Yearbook*, Part I, "Philosophies of Education." Bloomington, Illinois: Public School Publishing Company; 1942.

———. *Fifty-second Yearbook*, Part I, "Adapting the Secondary School Program to the Needs of Youth." Chicago: University of Chicago Press; 1953.

———. *Fifty-third Yearbook*, Part I, "Citizen Coöperation for Better Public Schools." Chicago: University of Chicago Press; 1954.

NEWCOMB, THEODORE M., and HARTLEY, EUGENE L. (Co-chairman). Committee on the Teaching of Social Psychology of the Society for the Psychological Study of Social Issues, *Readings in Social Psychology*. New York: Henry Holt & Co., Inc.; 1947.

NEWLON, JESSE H. *Education for Democracy in Our Time*. New York: McGraw-Hill Book Company, Inc.; 1939.

———. *Educational Administration as Social Policy*. New York: Charles Scribner's Sons; 1934.

New York State Joint Legislative Committee on Industrial and Labor Conditions. *The American Story of Industrial and Labor Relations*. Albany: Williams Press, Inc.; 1943.

NOREM, C. M. "Transfer of Training Experiments Revalued," *University of Iowa Studies in Education*, VII, No. 6, 1933.

North Central Association of Colleges and Secondary Schools. *Unit Studies in American Problems*. Columbus, Ohio: Charles E. Merrill Company; 1948.

NORTHROP, F. S. C. *The Logic of the Sciences and the Humanities*. New York: The Macmillan Company; 1947.

NORTON, JOHN K., and NORTON, MARY A. *Foundations of Curriculum Building*. Boston: Ginn & Company; 1936.

Ohio State University, The University School. "A Description of Curriculum Experiences." Columbus, Ohio: Mimeographed. Reproduced by permission of the University School, 1952.

OLSEN, EDWARD G. *School and Community Programs*. New York: Prentice-Hall, Inc.; 1949.

———, and Others. *School and Community*. New York: Prentice-Hall, Inc.; 1945.

OLSON, WILLARD C., and DAVIS, S. I. "The Adaptation of Instruction in Reading to the Growth of Children," *Educational Method*, Vol. XX (November, 1940).

ORATA, P. T. *The Theory of Identical Elements*. Columbus: Ohio State University Press; 1928.

PARKER, CECIL, and GOLDEN, WILLIAM. *Group Process in Supervision*. Washington, D. C.: National Education Association; 1948.

PARKER, FRANCIS W. "Syllabus of Lectures and Lessons upon the Philosophy of Education." *The Elementary School Teacher and Course of Study* (*Elementary School Journal*), Vol. 2, No. 1 (July, 1901).

———. *Talks on Pedagogics*. New York: The John Day Company, Inc.; 1937.

PELL, ORLIE A. H. *Value-Theory and Criticism*. Privately published, 1930.

PERSON, H. S. "The Call for Leadership," *Bulletin of the Taylor Society* (now *Advanced Management*), Vol. XVIII (June, 1933).

PETERS, CHARLES C. *Foundations of Educational Sociology.* New York: The Macmillan Company; 1924.

PIAGET, JEAN. *Judgment and Reasoning in the Child.* New York: Harcourt, Brace & Co., Inc.; 1928.

——. *The Language and Thought of the Child.* New York: Harcourt, Brace & Co., Inc.; 1932.

——. *The Moral Judgment of the Child.* New York: Harcourt, Brace & Co., Inc.; 1932.

PIGORS, PAUL. *Leadership or Domination.* Boston: Houghton Mifflin Company; 1935.

PISTOR, FREDERICK A. "Evaluating Newer-Type Practices by the Observational Method," in *Sixteenth Yearbook* of the Department of Elementary-School Principals, National Education Association. Washington, D. C.: National Education Association; 1937.

——. "How Time Concepts Are Acquired by Children," *Educational Method,* Vol. XX (November, 1940).

PLANT, J. S. *Personality and the Cultural Pattern.* New York: The Commonwealth Fund, Division of Publications; 1937.

PLATO. *The Republic.* (Modern Student Library Edition.) New York: Charles Scribner's Sons; 1928.

PRESCOTT, D. A. *Emotion and the Educative Process.* Washington, D. C.: American Council on Education; 1938.

President's Research Committee on Social Trends. *Recent Social Trends in the United States.* New York: McGraw-Hill Book Company, Inc.; 1933.

Progressive Education, Vol. 26, No. 7 (May, 1949), "Educational Change and Social Engineering."

Progressive Education Association, Committee on Social and Economic Problems. *A Call to the Teachers of the Nation.* New York: The John Day Company, Inc.; 1933.

——. *Thirty Schools Tell Their Story.* New York: Harper & Brothers; 1943.

RANDALL, JOHN HERMAN, JR. *Our Changing Civilization: How Science and Technology Are Reconstructing Modern Life.* New York: Frederick A. Stokes Company; 1929.

RAUP, BRUCE; BENNE, KENNETH D.; AXTELLE, GEORGE; and SMITH, B. OTHANEL. *The Improvement of Practical Intelligence.* New York: Harper & Brothers; 1950.

Recent Social Trends in the United States. See President's Research Committee on Social Trends.

REDDEN, J. D., and RYAN, F. A. *A Catholic Philosophy of Education.* Milwaukee: The Bruce Publishing Company; 1942.

REINOELD, C. M. "Time Allotment of School Subjects and Length of School Days," *Elementary Principal,* Vol. XXIII, No. 5 (June, 1944).

ROBERTS, HOLLAND D. "Reading for Personal and Social Action," *Elementary English Review,* Vol. 19 (April, 1942).

ROBINSON, JAMES HARVEY. *The Humanizing of Knowledge.* New York: Doubleday, Doran & Co., Inc.; 1924.

ROETHLISBERGER, F. J. *Management and Morale.* Cambridge, Massachusetts: Harvard University Press; 1941.

——, and DICKSON, W. J. *Management and the Worker.* Cambridge, Massachusetts: Harvard University Press; 1939.

RUDMAN, HERBERT C. *Interrelations among Various Aspects of Children's Interests and Informational Needs and Expectations of Teachers, Parents and Librarians.* Doctor's Dissertation, University of Illinois, 1954.

RUGG, EARLE. *Curriculum Studies in the Social Sciences and Citizenship.* Greeley, Colorado: Colorado State Teachers College; 1928.

RUGG, HAROLD. *American Life and the School Curriculum.* Boston: Ginn & Company; 1936.

————. *Culture and Education in America.* New York: Harcourt, Brace & Co., Inc.; 1931.

———— (Editor). "Democracy and the Curriculum," *Third Yearbook* of the *John Dewey Society.* New York: D. Appleton-Century Company, Inc.; 1939.

————. *Foundations for American Education.* Yonkers, New York: World Book Company; 1947.

———— (Editor). *Readings in the Foundations of Education.* New York: Bureau of Publications, Teachers College, Columbia University; 1941.

————. *That Men May Understand.* New York: Doubleday & Company, Inc.; 1941.

————. *Man and His Changing Society.* (14 volumes published 1921–1937.) Boston: Ginn & Company.

————, and SHUMAKER, ANN. *The Child-Centered School.* Yonkers, New York: World Book Company; 1928.

————, and WITHERS, WILLIAM. *Social Foundations of American Education.* New York: Prentice-Hall, Inc.; 1955.

Rural Life Studies, Nos. 1–6. *Culture of a Contemporary Rural Community.* United States Department of Agriculture, Bureau of Agricultural Economics. Washington, D. C.: United States Government Printing Office; 1943.

SANDERS, WILLIAM J. "Spiritual Values and Education," in John Dewey Society, *Seventh Yearbook,* "The Public Schools and Spiritual Values." New York: Harper & Brothers; 1944.

SANDIFORD, P. "Transfer of Training," in *Encyclopedia of Educational Research* (First Edition). New York: The Macmillan Company; 1941.

Santa Barbara (California) City Schools. *Developmental Curriculum,* Bulletin No. 1, Revision No. 1, November, 1941.

Santa Barbara County (California). *Santa Barbara County Curriculum*

Guide for Teachers in Elementary Schools. Santa Barbara, California: Schauer Printing Company; 1942.

————. *Santa Barbara County Curriculum Guide for Teachers in Secondary Schools.* Santa Barbara, California: Schauer Printing Company; 1941.

SAYLOR, J. GALEN. "Factors Associated with Participation in Coöperative Programs of Curriculum Development," *Teachers College Contributions to Education.* No. 829. New York: Bureau of Publications, Teachers College, Columbia University; 1941.

————, and ALEXANDER, WILLIAM M. *Curriculum Planning.* New York: Rinehart & Company; 1954.

SCHLESINGER, ARTHUR M., JR. *The Age of Jackson.* Boston: Little, Brown & Co., 1945.

SCOTT, EMMETT J., and STOWE, LYMAN BEECHER. *Booker T. Washington.* New York: Doubleday, Page & Co.; 1916.

SHEATS, PAUL H. *Education and the Quest for a Middle Way.* New York: The Macmillan Company; 1938.

SHEED, F. J. "Education for the Realization of God's Purposes," *The Social Frontier,* Vol. I, No. 4, January, 1935.

SHORES, J. HARLAN. *A Critical Review of the Research on Elementary School Curriculum Organization, 1890–1949.* Urbana, Illinois: College of Education, Bureau of Research and Service, University of Illinois; 1949.

————. "Reading Interests and Informational Needs of Children in Grades Four to Eight," *Elementary English,* Vol. 30 (December, 1954).

SLEIGHT, W. G. "Memory and Formal Training," *British Journal of Psychology,* 1911, 4, pages 386–457.

SLESINGER, ZALMEN. *Education and the Class Struggle.* New York: Covici Friede, Inc.; 1937.

SMITH, B. OTHANEL. "Historical Background and Social Perspective," *Educational Forum,* Vol. 7 (March, 1943), pages 217–228.

SMITH, B. OTHANEL. "Is History a Pre-requisite to the Study of Social Problems?" *Social Studies,* Vol. 29, No. 5 (May, 1938).

———. "The Normative Unit," *Teachers College Record,* Vol. 46, No. 4 (January, 1945), pages 219–228.

———. "Science of Education," Monroe, Walter J. (Editor). *Encyclopedia of Educational Research.* Revised Edition, 1950.

SMITH, DORA V. "Growth in Language Power as Related to Child Development," in *Forty-third Yearbook* of the National Society for the Study of Education. Bloomington, Illinois: Public School Publishing Company; 1944.

SMITH, NILA BANTON. *Readiness for Reading and Related Language Arts.* Bulletin of the National Conference on Research in English. Chicago: The National Council of Teachers of English, 1950.

SOROKIN, PITIRIM A. *The Crisis of Our Age.* New York: American Book Company; 1945.

SOULE, GEORGE. *The Strength of Nations.* New York: The Macmillan Company; 1942.

South Dakota Department of Education. *Social Studies Course of Studies for Primary Grades;* Course of Study Bulletin No. 4. Pierre, South Dakota: State Printing Office; 1932.

SPEARS, HAROLD. *The Emerging High School Curriculum and Its Direction.* New York: American Book Company; 1940.

SPENCER, HERBERT. *Education: Intellectual, Moral, and Physical.* New York: D. Appleton & Company; 1860.

Staff of Division I, Teachers College, Columbia University. *Readings in the Foundations of Education.* (Harold Rugg, Editor.) New York: Bureau of Publications, Teachers College, Columbia University; 1941.

STANLEY, WILLIAM O. *Education and Social Integration.* New York: Bureau of Publications, Teachers College, Columbia University; 1953.

STANLEY, WILLIAM O. "Free Enterprise in America," *Frontiers of Democracy,* Vol. 10, No. 81 (December 15, 1943).

———; SMITH, B. OTHANEL; BENNE, KENNETH D.; and ANDERSON, ARCHIBALD W. *Social Foundations of Education.* New York: Dryden Press; 1956.

STENDLER, CELIA BURNS. *Children of Brasstown.* Urbana: Bureau of Research and Service, College of Education, University of Illinois; 1949.

STEWART, FRANK A. "A Sociometric Study of Influence in Southtown," *Sociometry,* Vol. X, No. 1 (February, 1947), pages 11–31.

———. "A Study of Influence in Southtown," *Sociometry,* Vol. X, No. 3 (August, 1947), pages 273–386.

STOREN, HELEN F. *Laymen Help Plan the Curriculum.* Washington, D. C.: Association for Supervision and Curriculum Development, National Education Association; 1946.

STOUT, JOHN E. "The Development of High School Curricula in the North Central States from 1860 to 1918," *Supplementary Educational Monographs,* Vol. III, No. 3. Chicago: University of Chicago Press; 1921.

STRATEMEYER, FLORENCE B.; FORKNER, HAMDEN L.; McKIM, MARGARET G.; and Others. *Developing a Curriculum for Modern Living.* New York: Bureau of Publications, Teachers College, Columbia University; 1947.

STRANG, RUTH. *Subject Matter in Health Education.* New York: Bureau of Publications, Teachers College, Columbia University; 1927.

SUMNER, WILLIAM GRAHAM. *Folkways.* Boston: Ginn & Company; 1906.

SYMONDS, PERCIVAL M. *Education and the Psychology of Thinking.* New York: McGraw-Hill Book Company, Inc.; 1936.

"Tale of Three Conferences, A." *Adult Education Bulletin,* Vol. XII, No. 3 (February, 1948), pages 67–96.

TEAR, DANIEL AMBROSE. *The Logical Basis of Educational Theory from the Standpoint of Instrumental Logic.* Chicago: University of Chicago Press; 1908.

Temporary National Economic Committee. *Economic Power and Political Pressure. Investigation of Concentration of Economic Power,* Monograph No. 26. Washington, D. C.: United States Government Printing Office; 1941.

————. *Trade Association Survey. Investigation of Concentration of Economic Power,* Monograph No. 18. Washington, D. C.: United States Government Printing Office; 1941.

THAYER, V. T. *American Education under Fire.* New York: Harper & Brothers; 1944.

————; ZACHRY, CAROLINE B.; and KOTINSKY, RUTH. *Reorganizing Secondary Education.* New York: D. Appleton-Century Company, Inc.; 1939.

THELEN, HERBERT A. "Engineering Research in Curriculum Building," *Journal of Educational Research,* Vol. 41, No. 8 (April, 1948), pages 577–596.

THOMAS, LAWRENCE G. *The Occupational Structure and Education.* Englewood Cliffs, New Jersey: Prentice-Hall, Inc.; 1956.

THORNDIKE, EDWARD L. "Mental Discipline in High School Studies," *Journal of Educational Psychology,* 15, 1924, pages 1–22, 83–98.

————, and WOODWORTH, R. S. "The Influence of Improvement in One Mental Function upon the Efficiency of Other Functions," *Psychological Review,* 8, 1901.

THUCYDIDES. *The Peloponnesian War.* New York: Harper & Brothers; 1933.

"Time Use in the Junior High School Program," *Bulletin of the National Association of Secondary School Principals,* Vol. 29, No. 130 (April, 1945).

TOCQUEVILLE, ALEXIS DE. *Democracy in America.* New York: Alfred A. Knopf, Inc.; 1945.

TURNER, C. E. "Description of the Malden, Massachusetts, Experiment in Health Education," *Fourth Yearbook,* Department of Superintendence, National Education Association. Washington, D. C.: National Education Association; 1926.

TWISS, G. R. *A Textbook in the Principles of Science Teaching.* New York: The Macmillan Company; 1917.

TYLER, I. KEITH. "Spelling as a Secondary Learning," *Teachers College Contributions to Education,* No. 781. New York: Bureau of Publications, Teachers College, Columbia University; 1939.

"University Elementary School, The General Outline of Scheme of Work." University of Chicago Press. *University Record,* Vol. 3, No. 40 (December 30, 1898).

Urban Government. See National Resources Committee.

URMSON, J. O. "On Grading" in Flew, Antony G. N. (Editor). *Logic and Language* (Second Series). New York: Philosophical Library; 1953.

VAN DOREN, MARK. *Liberal Education.* New York: Henry Holt & Co., Inc.; 1943.

VAN DYKE, GEORGE E. "Trends in the Development of the High School Offering," I and II, *School Review,* Vol. 39 (November, 1931), pages 657–664; (December, 1931), pages 737–747.

VAN TIL, WILLIAM. *Economic Roads for American Democracy.* New York: McGraw-Hill Book Company, Inc.; 1947.

VEBLEN, THORSTEIN, *The Theory of the Leisure Class.* New York: The Macmillan Company; 1899.

Virginia State Board of Education. *Course of Study for Virginia Elementary Schools.* Richmond: State Printing Office; 1933.

————. *Tentative Course of Study for the Core Curriculum of Virginia Secondary Schools.* Richmond: State Printing Office; 1933.

WARE, CAROLINE F., and MEANS, GARDINER C. *The Modern Economy in Action.* New York: Harcourt, Brace & Co., Inc.; 1936.

WARNER, W. LLOYD, and LUNT, PAUL S. *The Social Life of a Modern Community,* Yankee City Series, Vol. I. New Haven: Yale University Press; 1941.

WARNER, W. LLOYD; HAVIGHURST, ROBERT J.; and LOEB, MARTIN B. *Who Shall Be Educated? The Challenge of Unequal Opportunity.* New York: Harper & Brothers; 1944.

WASHINGTON, BOOKER T. *Up from Slavery.* New York: Doubleday, Page & Co.; 1901.

WATSON, GOODWIN (Editor). "Civilian Morale," *Second Yearbook of the Society for the Psychological Study of Social Issues.* Boston: Houghton Mifflin Company; 1942

WEST, JAMES. *Plainville, U. S. A.* New York: Columbia University Press; 1945.

WHITE, EMERSON E. "Isolation and Unification as Bases of Courses of Study," *Second Yearbook of the National Herbart Society for the Scientific Study of Teaching.* Bloomington, Illinois: Pantograph Printing and Stationery Company; 1896.

WHITEHEAD, ALFRED NORTH. *The Aims of Education and Other Essays.* New York: The Macmillan Company; 1929.

WILSON, GUY M. "A Survey of the Social and Business Usage of Arithmetic," *Teachers College Contributions to Education,* No. 100. New York: Bureau of Publications, Teachers College, Columbia University; 1919.

———. *What Arithmetic Shall We Teach?* Boston: Houghton Mifflin Company; 1926.

WILSON, HOWARD E. *The Fusion of Social Studies in Junior High Schools.* Cambridge, Massachusetts: Harvard University Press; 1933.

Wisconsin Coöperative Educational Planning Program, Problems Approach Committee (Camilla M. Low, Chairman). *Guides to Curriculum Building:*

The Junior High School Level. Madison, Wisconsin: State Printing Office; 1949.

Wisconsin State Department of Education. *Guides to Curriculum Building,* Vol. 1, Kindergarten Level. Madison, Wisconsin: State Printing Office, Bulletin No. 12; October, 1947.

———. *Guide to Curriculum Building: The Junior High School Level.* Bulletin No. 8, January, 1950.

WISSLER, CLARK. *Man and Culture.* New York: Thomas Y. Crowell Company; 1923.

WOLFE, THOMAS. *You Can't Go Home Again.* New York: Harper & Brothers; 1940.

WOODWORTH, ROBERT S. *Experimental Psychology.* New York: Henry Holt & Co., Inc.; 1938.

WOOTTON, BARBARA. *Freedom under Planning.* Chapel Hill: University of North Carolina Press; 1945.

WORMSER, MARGOT HOAS. "The Northtown Self-Survey: A Case Study," *The Journal of Social Issues,* Vol. V, No. 2, 1949.

WRIGHT, GRACE S. *Core Curriculum Development, Problems and Practices.* Bulletin 1952, No. 5. Washington, D. C.: Federal Security Agency, Office of Education; 1952.

WRIGHTSTONE, J. WAYNE. *Appraisal of Experimental High School Practices.* New York: Bureau of Publications, Teachers College, Columbia University; 1936.

———.*Appraisal of Newer Elementary School Practices.* New York: Bureau of Publications, Teachers College, Columbia University; 1938.

YOUNG, KIMBALL. *Social Psychology.* New York: F. S. Crofts & Co.; 1930.

ZANDER, ALVIN, and LIPPITT, RONALD. "Reality Practice as Educational Method," *Sociometry,* Vol. 7, No. 2, 1944.

ZNANIECKI, FLORJAN. *The Social Role of the Man of Knowledge.* New York: Columbia University Press; 1940.